Software Engineering for Game Developers

John P. Flynt

with Omar Salem

THOMSON

COURSE TECHNOLOGY™

Professional ■ Trade ■ Reference

ISBN: 1-59200-155-6
Library of Congress Catalog Card Number: 2004106451
Printed in the United States of America
04 05 06 07 08 BH 10 9 8 7 6 5 4 3 2 1

THOMSON
COURSE TECHNOLOGY
Professional ■ Trade ■ Reference

Thomson Course Technology PTR, a division of
Thomson Course Technology
25 Thomson Place
Boston, MA 02210
http://www.courseptr.com

SVP, Thomson Course Technology PTR:
Andy Shafran

Publisher:
Stacy L. Hiquet

Senior Marketing Manager:
Sarah O'Donnell

Marketing Manager:
Heather Hurley

Manager of Editorial Services:
Heather Talbot

Senior Acquisitions Editor:
Emi Smith

Senior Editor:
Mark Garvey

Associate Marketing Manager:
Kristin Eisenzopf

Series Editor:
André LaMothe

Marketing Coordinator:
Jordan Casey

Project/Copy Editor:
Karen A. Gill

Technical Reviewer:
John Hollis

PTR Editorial Services Coordinator:
Elizabeth Furbish

Interior Layout Tech:
Susan Honeywell

Cover Designer:
Mike Tanamachi

CD-ROM Producer:
Brandon Penticuff

Indexer:
Sharon Shock

Proofreader:
Kim Benbow

This book is dedicated to its readers.

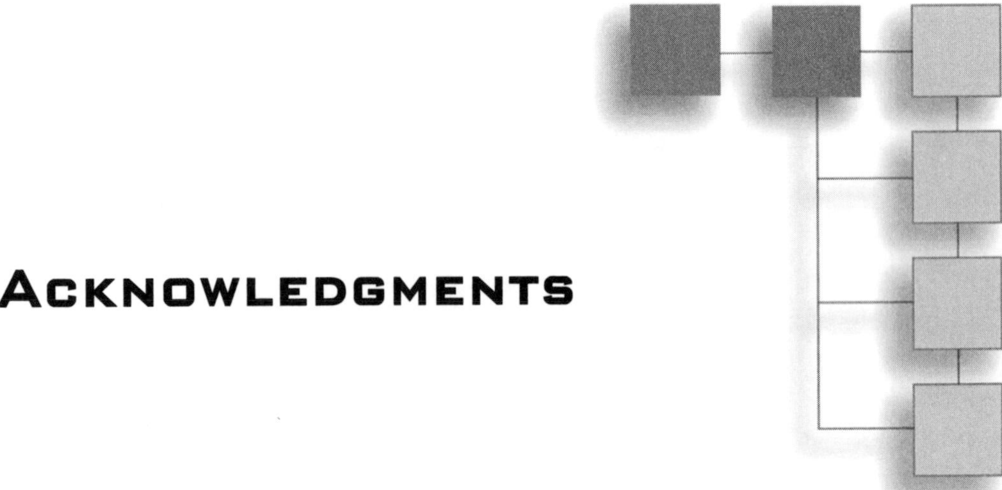

Acknowledgments

Ben Vinson was the lead programmer for *Ankh.* He exerted an enormous effort, and the game simply would not exist had he not been willing to make the effort he did. Ben was instrumental in the software design and saw to development of the game from beginning to end. He was by far the central and greatest contributor.

John Rose was the game designer for *Ankh.* John authored the game design document. He also composed the music, wrote the user's guide, created the installation package, and was helpful in documenting CVS. He was at the center of the effort. (Thanks to Jayme Catalano for keeping track of John.)

Carlos Villar worked as a development and maintenance programmer on *Ankh.* His work on the design, sound, and AI was a strong contribution to the project's success.

Paul Whitehead was the central figure in creation of the art for *Ankh.* He showed amazing drive as he developed the meshes and textures for the game. The game just would not have happened had he not been a part of the team.

Adrian Flynt developed the character art to accompany Paul's work.

Ben Schulz contributed voice talent.

John Hollis was the book's technical reader. John brought to this effort a perspective connected with the larger world of software engineering. John provided an essential element in the development of the content.

Charlie Allbee offered important suggestions concerning audience needs.

Rob Johnson made suggestions about how to structure the text.

Iraj Eftekhari, Deb Mahon, and Tony Caggiano offered encouragement.

Amy Flynt checked the math.

Marcia Flynt helped with contracts and accounting. The book would not have been written without her support.

Many people at Thomson, Premier, and Course Technology did their usual magic.

Karen Gill edited the text.

André LaMothe provided the example of how to write books about developing games.

Emi Smith guided the effort from its conception.

Stacy Hiquet made everything possible.

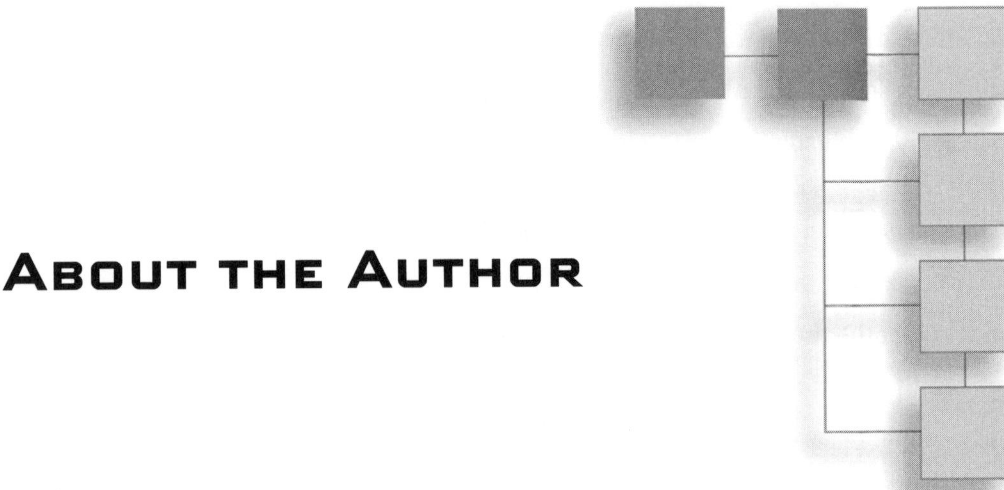

About the Author

John P. Flynt, Ph.D., is a software developer who has worked extensively as a software engineering process specialist. He is president of The ewowe Corporation (http://www.ewowe.com), which specializes in interactive educational software and related products and services. His experience with game development began when he programmed a game for education. He has taught game development and has worked with colleges and universities to create game programs. His educational background includes degrees from the University of Chicago and the University of Colorado. Along with his wife, Marcia, and his children, Amy and Adrian, John lives in the foothills north of Boulder, Colorado.

Omar Salem lives in Denver, Colorado. Prior to becoming a game development teacher, he was a member of the technical staff at Bell Labs/Lucent Technologies/Avaya, where he worked for nearly 20 years. His emphasis is on both development and quality assurance software engineering. He holds BS and MS degrees in computer science and mathematics. To date, Omar has seen 17 large-scale software systems to completion, and all products he has worked on have been successfully deployed.

About the Series Editor

André LaMothe, CEO of Xtreme Games LLC and the creator of the XGameStation, has been involved in the computing industry for more than 27 years. He wrote his first game for the TRS-80 and has been hooked ever since! His experience includes 2D/3D graphics, AI research at NASA, compiler design, robotics, virtual reality, and telecommunications. His books are top sellers in the game programming genre, and his experience is echoed in the Thomson Course Technology PTR *Game Development* books. You can contact André at ceo@nurve.net and http://www.xgamestation.com.

Letter from the Series Editor for Software Engineering for Game Developers

Software engineering. This is a phrase that almost no one on the planet can actually define. Sure, many people have the title of software engineer, many books are written on the subject, and many people have a whole slew of definitions, but at the end of the day, what is it? Well, I will tell you what it isn't. Software engineering is not about C++, and it's surely not about object-oriented programming. Those are tools, and software engineering is simply engineering. And herein is the problem. Engineers in electronics, mechanics, and other fields have been around forever. They are taught how to think, solve problems, organize their work, test, manufacture, assemble, distribute, and so forth. Programmers are just guys who learned a computer language and then made programs; they are not engineers. Before we even knew what happened, there were millions of programs written without proper engineering. Thus, a few years ago, a new term was coined "software engineering" like it was a new idea! I have been software engineering for 25 years; engineering is engineering. And that's where this book comes in.

This book isn't some theoretical masterpiece that uses Venn diagrams and cost analysis to show you how many hours should be spent on a `for` loop. This is a real book, by a real engineer who happens to apply engineering techniques to software. Therefore, you aren't going to learn about something that is unique to software. These engineering techniques will, of course, use tools of the trade such as C++, object-oriented programming, configuration management, UML diagrams, patterns, process improvement, and so forth.

This book is not going to make you a better programmer; programming is an art form. Instead, this book is going to make you a better software engineer. And, in the real world, companies do not need programmers; they need engineers who are reliable, efficient, and expert.

I am excited about this book and its authors, John Flynt and Omar Salem. They're seasoned professionals who have both academic and professional backgrounds. They have worked in the real world and know what the real world wants. In this book, you aren't going to be inundated by useless information, but given exactly what you need: the tools to organize your programming into proper engineering patterns.

So without further ado, start your first program the proper way. Open your engineering notebook, date and sign it, title the program you are going to design, and you are ready to go!

André LaMothe
Game Development Series Editor, 2004

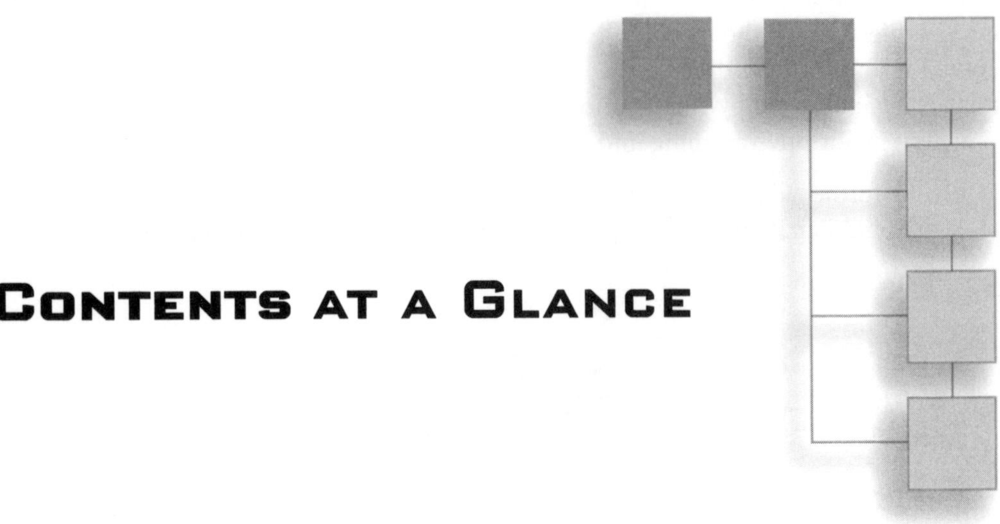

Contents at a Glance

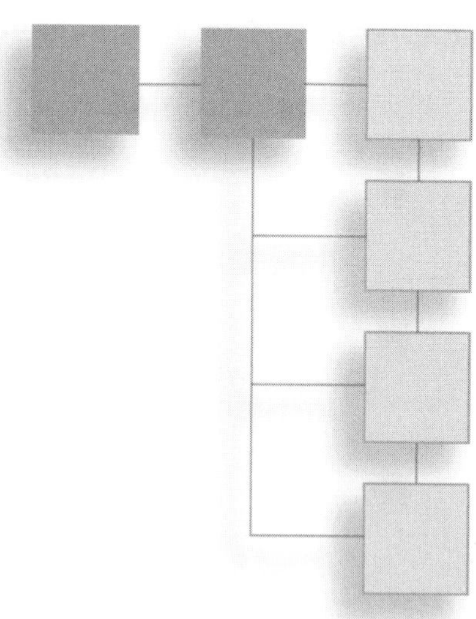

Contents

Introduction

This book is about how a small team of developers can build a computer game using practices that are fostered by software engineering. It takes you through the major phases of the software engineering lifecycle and introduces you to the subjects named in the Software Engineering Body of Knowledge (SWEBOK). The development process that this book documents started from a set of requirements. It guided the team to consistently design and implement a game according to requirements. The team stayed within budget and delivered on time.

The game is called *Ankh Adventure* (or just *Ankh*). (See Figure I.1.) The game provides a 3D graphics engine built with DirectX. Its design incorporates customizable levels and characters. (It features map and character editors.) It provides save and replay options, a particle engine, and MP3 music. The code for the game is extensive enough that you can gain from it a sense of the complexity that characterizes games created by programmers who are working in the game industry. On the other hand, the code is limited enough that you can study it in detail. (The game consists of roughly 30,000 lines of code.)

As you read the book, you will see how the requirements for the game were laid out. The effort started with a game design document. Using the game design document, the team engineered a set of software requirements. To accomplish this, the team employed use cases and other tools of analysis. After that, the team designed the game software. You will be able to follow along through all of this activity. You can see how the team created the configuration management plan from the design. You can see how the team created the test plans by using the requirements and the design. (The artifacts—documents—that resulted from these activities are on the CD.)

Figure I.1
The game stripes start simple and grow in complexity.

In addition, you can see how the team subjected the design to scrutiny to discover opportunities to use software design patterns. With the implementation effort, you can see how the team refactored code to simplify and optimize it. With respect to processes and practices, you can read about how elements of the Capability Maturity Model (CMM) were put to work, how the development team was organized, how reviews were conducted, how templates were used, and how documentation was created.

Specific activities abound. One chapter covers the Unified Modeling Language (UML) in a way that shows that UML is a practical, flexible tool. Another chapter investigates programming using object-oriented programming practices. A chapter on testing explains different approaches to testing and how to develop test plans. A chapter on metrics gives you starter information on how to quantitatively assess games and their development. Also included are chapters on managing the release of a game and planning and executing a revision.

The code for the game is set up so that you can explore it without difficulty. The key to this is that the code is set up in 19 stripes. A *stripe* is another name for a software module. A software module is a collection of classes. Each stripe embodies a set of functionality that is specified in the requirements. The stripes were developed sequentially. Stripe 1, for example, sets up the basic Windows framework of the game. Stripe 2 adds GUI features. By Stripe 4, you can see a character mesh. (See Figure I.2.) By Stripe 9, the game offers characters who are engaged in combat. When you get to Stripe 14, you are in a world of multiple levels and all sorts of features.

Figure I.2
Editors allow you to customize game features.

Whether you are in a classroom or working on your own, one effective way to use the stripes for learning is to study the difference between sequential stripes. Set up your project with the lower of two stripes, and then add the code to develop your code until it resembles the higher of the two stripes. Use the *Design Description* as a guide.

The installation program makes it easy for you to access all the code using Microsoft Visual Studio. Each stripe is set up as a separate project. Just access the folder for the stripe and click on the Ankh.dsw or Ankh.sln file. (An appendix provides you with a little startup help with Visual Studio if you need it.) The appropriate version of DirectX will be installed for you, along with the Boost library and all the assets. Nothing that is already installed on your computer will be disturbed.

The installation program allows you to install stripes selectively. This means that you can adjust the complexity of the game to suit your curiosity. If you want to see just the basic framework for a Windows application, you can install Stripe 1. If you want to see how the characters are set up for combat, you can install Stripe 7. You can look up any of the stripes in the *Ankh Software Design Description*, which is included on the CD. (An appendix provides an excerpt of this document.) Read the use cases at the beginning of each stripe design section to acquire a sense of what the stripe is designed to do. In addition to the use case, the *Description* provides simplified UML diagrams to help you understand how the code in each stripe works.

The installer program attempts to accommodate all your needs. (See Appendix A, "Installation and Setup," for instructions.) You can install only the documentation if you prefer. You can also install an executable for each stripe. Alternatively, you can install a project for each stripe and compile it yourself. If you want to install only the game and the user's guide, that is an option, also. Regardless of what you want, the installation package sets things up for you. Just insert the CD and follow the prompts.

The game has been created using C++, DirectX, Win32 functions, and the Boost library. The game code starts from scratch and uses no MFC classes. Even the dialog boxes are built from scratch. Around 25 percent of the code consists of comments to help you understand how the code works. Object-oriented programming is the best approach to most complex programming tasks, but structured programming can still be useful. (C++ is not a pure object- oriented programming language, and the game does not make a pure application of it.)

Despite extensive discussion of programming, keep in mind that this book is not on how to program using Windows components, C++, or DirectX. Nor is it about how to code a game. It is about software engineering. As a result, this book does not require you to write code. You don't even need to study the game code on the CD. Still, it is hoped that you will thoroughly investigate the code and perhaps begin tweaking it for your own purposes. An enormous effort has been invested in making certain you can do so.

If you want to work with the main executable and perform design work, the game has a variety of character classes. (See Figure I.3.) You can customize characters and add levels.

Figure I.3
Fully implemented, the *Ankh* game provides a challenging subject of study.

You will find that this book is a toolbox. It preaches nothing and advocates no methodologies. This book provides a set of useful tools for software developers in any area, including game software development professionals, game producers and designers, managers, software quality assurance specialists, testers, writers, artists, and those who are involved in education relating to computer science, software engineering, or game development.

Creating a book with a scope as broad as this one necessarily requires that a great deal be omitted. To compensate for the missing details, each chapter provides a list of texts that you can consult to deepen your knowledge of the topics that this book discusses. The books that are referred to represent accounts that practitioners have given of the work they perform. When a reference to a college textbook is included, the textbook is one that the authors have found useful in the industry.

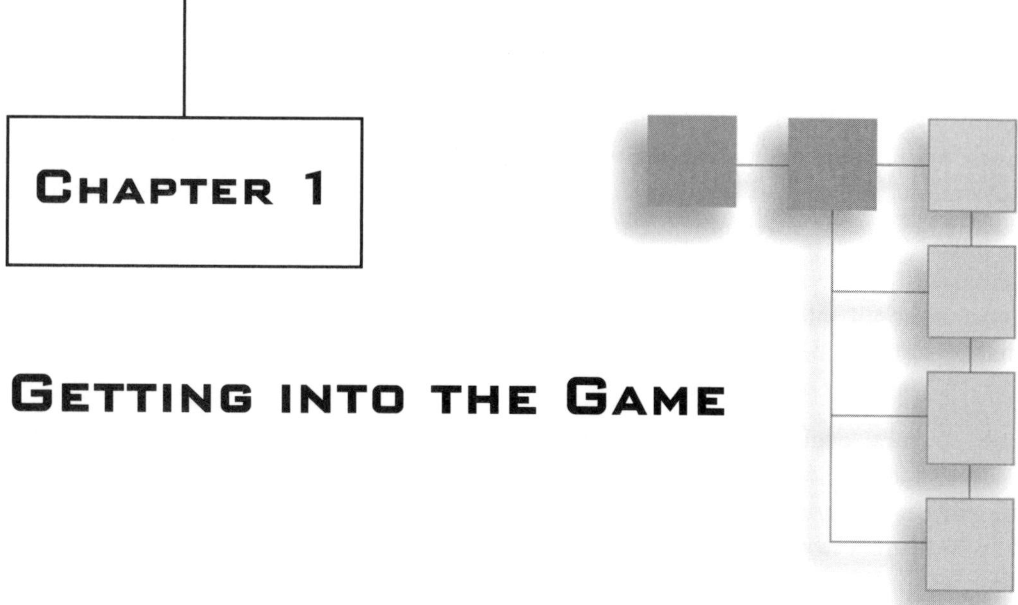

Chapter 1

Getting into the Game

Anyone who develops software for games can benefit from knowledge of software engineering. This book presents software engineering as a toolbox from which developers can select the tools they need. A great deal of latitude characterizes both what tools developers select and how they use them. Acquiring a clear understanding of the tools available to you and how you can apply them enables you to refine your development efforts. Examining these and other themes easily leads to many introductory topics:

- Mixing engineering and art
- Software as a practice
- Software as a professional concern
- Approaches to learning how to design and engineer a product
- The development of *Ankh* and software engineering
- Strategies for making the best use of formalized engineering knowledge
- Learning from skills that you can apply anywhere

Software Engineering and Game Development

If you develop software for games, you can benefit tremendously if you acquire knowledge of software engineering. Software engineering concerns everything that has to do with software development. It can be defined informally as the study and practice of how to improve software development. If you develop games, it is worthwhile to acquire knowledge of software engineering. The following paragraphs explain why.

To start with, consider that game development sustains its own culture, and this culture consists of much more than developing software. Any given game development project involves the efforts of many highly creative individuals who perform a wide variety of work. Among these individuals are those who design games, create graphical assets, compose music, and write dialogues. These are just a few of the many people who might be involved in a game development effort.

It makes little sense to contend that those who do all these things should have any great concerns about software engineering. Software engineering consists of a set of practices that apply to the development of software. Although the software remains fundamental, it forms only part of the picture.

Still, software engineering benefits everyone involved in a game development effort because it allows software developers to identify and apply solid, proven practices to their efforts. Their efforts address the needs of others. Consider, for example, a game designer. This individual works long hours to define precisely the world of the game. This person depends on the software developers to develop the game functionality so that the world of the game can be realized. As the software developers commence their efforts to develop this functionality, they should take care to understand fully what the game designer requires before they begin to develop the software; otherwise, they stand little chance of meeting the designer's expectations.

Software engineering consists of a body of knowledge that guides developers as they develop software. One recommendation that this body of knowledge offers to developers is that they carefully gather and analyze the requirements for the software system they have been asked to build. Another recommendation is that they create a software design that thoroughly addresses the requirements. Among other recommendations is one that developers test the system they develop to ensure that its design and implementation exactly express the requirements.

If software developers follow such recommendations as they work with the game designer, they will appropriately address the needs of the designer. They will make good use of the designer's time, and they will have used established practices and processes. They also will develop a product without redundancy and rework. Using software engineering practices, the software developers will know how to ask the right questions and how to make the best use of the information they gather. Their efforts will make the best use of everyone's time.

Engineering

Software engineering is a formal discipline that is dedicated to enhancing the quality of software development processes and the products that result from them. When a software product possesses quality, it is, among other things, reliable, maintainable, and extensible. A reliable software product is one that performs as specified and lacks defects. A maintainable software product is one that you can fix when it is defective. An extensible product is one that enables you to extend its life by adding functionality.

When a software development process possesses quality, it is, among other things, consciously understood as an engineering process. When it is consciously understood as an engineering process, it is something you view as being open to continuous improvement. In other words, like a software product, you can fix a software development process if it is defective, or you can modify or add to it as part of a continuous effort to improve it.

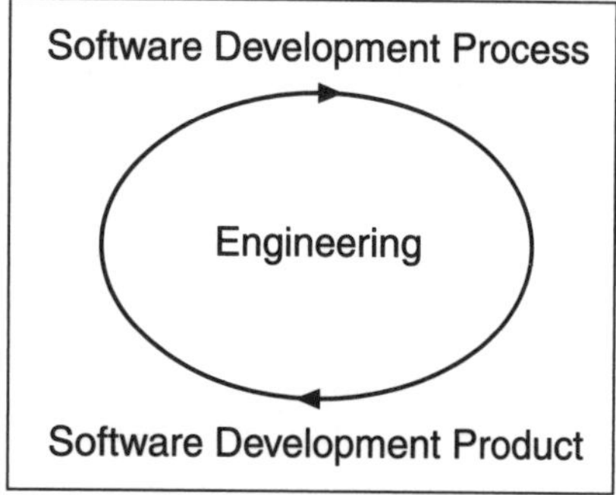

Figure 1.1
Software engineering involves a dynamic of improvement between product and process.

Continuously improving processes lies at the basis of how you continuously improve products. On the other hand, seeking to continuously improve products motivates you to seek new ways to improve processes. Software engineering joins these two activities in a continuous cycle. (See Figure 1.1.)

Cottage Industries and Formalized Disciplines

Chapter 19, "Philosophy of Software Engineering and Game Development," relates ideas about the extent to which market forces have transformed software game development during its first decades of existence. What began as a cottage industry has become an industry that large corporate operations currently dominate. Making games often involves some of the most complex software development efforts to be found anywhere. You cannot undertake such efforts without extensive planning. Furthermore, you cannot sustain such efforts without attention to the processes that support them.

Software engineering is pervasive because developing entertainment software products poses financial risks. Corporations face risks when they hire individuals who do not possess the appropriate professional qualifications. Corporations seek individuals who can perform their work efficiently and effectively. Such efficiency and effectiveness ultimately result from the application of disciplined approaches to work. This discipline results from the application of engineering principles and practices to software development.

Such pronouncements ring of a type of authoritarianism that many programmers and others who are involved in game development find disturbing. Given the romantic images that many of the early game development histories present, the idea that game development has become a realm of engineering expertise rather than heroic drive proves discouraging.

The degree of discouragement depends on how you look at the big picture. The big picture certainly establishes that a few dozen game developers and publishers dominate the industry. It dictates that game development often is characterized by production planning, budgeting negotiations, and large personnel management undertakings. Surviving in this world is difficult. The competition is ruthless, and the odds of success are minimal.

However, outside the inner circle of prevailing corporate interests, many thousands of independent game developers create games that they hope to sell to the mass market. The situation is analogous to some aspects of the music and film industries. Although a few distributors, studios, publishers, and artists occupy the center of the market and speak for most of its revenues, on any day of any year, talented individuals form groups and work together to create new products. Whether they form film production companies, bands, or game development groups, those involved dream of success. They have every right to do so.

The stories that you hear from game developers differ in wonderful ways from the stories that you sometimes hear when you talk to professionals in other areas of the software industry. You often hear how people view software development as a kind of accounting or factory activity governed by marketing and engineering dictates. To an extent, game development has gone in that direction. On the other hand, for those who are interested in becoming involved in game development, dreams of individualized or entrepreneurial success dominate their thinking.

Keep in mind that regardless of how you decide to try to participate in the game industry—as an entrepreneur or as an employed professional—if you proceed with your work in a systematic, disciplined way, you will be able to perform more effectively and stand a strong chance of success. Software engineering provides a set of tools that anyone who is involved in software development can use. Whether the development effort involves a small band of developers or a large corporation matters little.

Repetition and Perfection

Software engineering offers a toolbox that is open to anyone who wants to reach into it. Whether you develop a game on your own or work with a few others, the tools that software engineering offers can help you in the same way that they help a large group of people who are working in a corporate context. The tools provide an immediate, flexible way to formalize your efforts and render them more effective. On the other hand, because you can use the tools of software engineering at will, you are not bound by them to surrender your creativity or proceed with your efforts in a dry, formalized way.

Figure 1.2 provides a rough sketch of Sekhem, the avatar of *Ankh.* This book documents how a team of developers developed *Ankh.* The game begins with a game design document that the game's designer produced. The game design document provides descriptions of the world that Sekhem inhabits and the challenges that he faces. You must transform such information into software requirements. In turn, you transform the requirements into a software design. You then systematically implement the software according to the design path laid down in a software development plan. With the implementation effort guided by the software development plan, the game takes shape. As the game takes shape, you store and manage the files and assets that compose it according to a software configuration plan. To confirm that the game is taking form according to design and in conformity to its requirements, you perform testing on system, integration, and component levels.

Figure 1.2
The game involving Sekhem begins with a game design.

Software engineering releases many potentials. One of the most salient potentials involves freeing yourself, as an individual or a member of a team, from development activities that take place without a strong sense of direction or purpose.

This is mostly what engineering has been about for at least the past 6,000 years. When the builders of the pyramids went to work, they were doing so at the command of a ruling class that wanted them to defy time and achieve immortality by piling up carved blocks in a systematic way. In response to the challenge, nameless engineers over many centuries struggled with the minutiae of metallurgy, geology, rope strengths, labor schedules, heat pressures, pillars, beams, pikes, ramps, and all the rest. The labor went on. In time, the engineers learned to study their failures and successes. They applied planning and discipline to their efforts. Reliability and maintainability entered the picture. Engineering emerged as a discipline of labor.

You can read similar accounts of almost anything that enters into the history of engineering. Among these are galleons, clipper ships, steam ships, railway engines, skyscrapers, telephones, hair pins, bridges, dolls, and pencils. Everything that you can build over time becomes the object of engineering.

To Engineer Is...

Software engineering begins with the notion that it is important to learn from what you do and to apply what you learn incrementally to perfect your capacity to do what you do.

The focus of almost any software engineering activity you care to name involves helping those who perform such activities find ways to gather and retain information about what they do so that they can improve their efforts with each iteration of development.

The scholar of technology, Jacques Ellul, contended that everything is eventually subordinated to *technique.* Technique is a process of refinement that characterizes formalized knowledge. Everyone knows how this works. You do something for the first time, such as bake a cake. The first time is characterized by a lot of extra work. You pursue this path and that. You make mistakes. The counter is strewn with flour and egg yoke. Your efforts result in a sunken, undercooked product.

The next time around, things go a bit more smoothly. You have learned a few things. You fold what you learn into creating a technique for doing what you do. The technique is a procedure, a tried way of doing things. Depending on your personal style of learning, your approaches to technique are more or less regimented. Some people go by numbered lists and measuring spoons. Others work from a tested sense of what comes next and what counts as a teaspoonful of sugar. Whatever the approach, you learn from each iteration. Over time, you eliminate the excess and redundancy of the first try. This is how technique works.

Technique means that you store knowledge about how you do things and then consciously try to use this knowledge to improve how you do things. After a time, you begin to apply technique even to the way that you go about storing knowledge. You refine the information you store to specific categories:

- **Time.** You learn that some ways of doing things take longer than others. There is something painful about doing things that take a long while to complete. Yes, some things you want to last. But compare the experience of sharpening a pencil with a penknife to using an electric pencil sharpener.
- **Energy.** Energy comes in different forms. Some energy is stored up, waiting for use. Water resides in reservoirs. The energy is reserved, ready to generate electricity or run a mill. When the energy is released, you use it either effectively or ineffectively. You learn that when you use stored potentials, it is best to use them effectively. Often, life offers no second chances.
- **Efficiency.** There are hard and easy ways to do things. If you are asked to write a structured essay, you can write a stream-of-consciousness narrative and then take days or weeks to rewrite and refine it into a structured essay. Or you can follow the dictates of your early rhetoric teachers and write an outline. You use the outline to guide and refine your thoughts as you write. With the outline in place, you might still write a stream-of-consciousness narrative, but now the stream is like a river in its course.

- **Reliability.** A bridge builder builds a bridge in soft soil, and after time, the bridge collapses. The builder learns that building a bridge that lasts requires study of the rock beneath the prospective bridge. Reliability involves refining the view you have of the conditions under which you work, the materials with which you work, and the assumptions you make as you work. Such wisdom grows with time.
- **Maintainability.** Imperfection characterizes everything, so even when something is built well, it possesses defects. However, if something is built well, even its defects are accounted for. You can repair a well-built product easily. Consider something as simple as changing a tire on a bicycle. You can anticipate a flat. To improve the maintainability of the bicycle, bicycle designers make it easy for riders or mechanics to change tires.
- **Appropriateness.** Every form of technology is a monstrosity unless it is created in a context of utility. This was the lesson that Mary Shelley might have presented when she wrote *Frankenstein.* It is hard to say, but if you read that story, you find both a technological marvel and the marvel's creator reduced to insanity. Technology that lacks appropriateness generally follows the route of Frankenstein's monster. Examples include leaded gasoline, DDT, weapons that kill with radiation, and automobiles without safety features like seatbelts. You learn to sense when technology is appropriate, and your sense of its appropriateness guides your work as an engineer.

The previous list provides just a few of the possible items. Ultimately, such refinements of the knowledge lead you to develop things in a self-conscious, self-aware way. If you develop things in a self-aware way, technique begins to study itself. This is how engineering works and how software engineering influences game development. Software engineering allows you to improve the way you develop games as you develop them. It allows you to put some distance between you and your work and to assess whether you can introduce improvements in how you do things.

The Path

Consider for a moment the initial efforts involved in developing *Ankh.* The game design document provides information about the game from the perspective of the game designer. The game designer seeks to create a game with a map editor, a character editor, several levels, and a complex world. This set of features allows the avatar, Sekhem, to have a place in which to exist. (See Figure 1.3.)

Figure 1.3
Sekhem enters his world.

Software engineering activities kick into gear as soon as someone decides that providing a world for an avatar involves creating a software program. The first step you take in this direction is to engineer the requirements for the game. When you engineer requirements, you perform your work effectively if you use tools you obtain from the software engineering toolbox. One such tool is the Unified Modeling Language (UML). Another tool is the use case. Chapter 3, "A Tutorial: UML and Object-Oriented Programming," offers an extended discussion of these tools.

Moving from a game design document to an engineering framework for realizing the design calls for an abrupt reckoning with limitations. If engineering is about anything, it is about limitations. To provide safe, reliable products, engineers face the sobering obligation that they must limit every engineered system in scope in one way or another. Every beam that an engineer uses to construct a building can bear only so much weight. Likewise, every algorithm that an engineer uses in the module of a software system can perform poorly if it is implemented improperly. When you determine scope, you establish the general context in which the use and design of every component of the product you are creating can be visualized.

Many things govern scope, and chief among these is complexity. The complexity of a software system results, in part, from the raw number of logical nodes that the software system includes. A logical node is a point at which a decision is made. But software complexity also results from the way that developers design and develop the software. Design affects the efficiency with which the system moves information through its decision points. Development determines the order in which components are created.

If developers do not begin with a clear understanding of the requirements as they work with design and development concerns, the situation that results is analogous to what might happen if builders begin building a tower without first understanding how high it is to reach. (See Figure 1.4.) Up to a point, the construction effort might result in a reasonable structure. But then trouble is likely to begin. For starters, without planning, the builders cannot know how strong the lower walls should be. Even before considerations of this type, the builders would need to reckon with the depth and strength of the foundation.

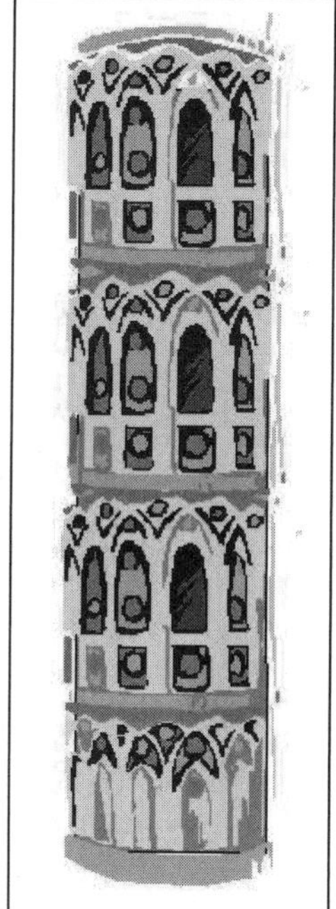

Figure 1.4
Ad hoc development leads to problems.

Reworking the building after several stories have been constructed is not an impossibility, but certain problems result. For example, the cost of the building increases because rework comes to characterize the effort. A change on the top story necessitates returning to lower stories and rebuilding them. Each addition to the structure might require revision of the whole. No one knows, after a time, how much effort any given addition will require. The effort becomes characterized by unpredictability and ad hoc work.

Consider a simple situation in which you create a game that features many characters. If you work steadily forward from the requirements that the designer provides for the game, you can comprehensively profile the character. Given this profile, you can create a design for a general character type. In the world of object-oriented programming, this design is expressed as a data type—a class. The design of the class anticipates repeated instances of the class, and the result is that when it is time to replicate characters in the game, the effort to do so is relatively effortless. A development schedule tells you to create the design after you have created the requirements. The requirements tell you to design the class so that it can accommodate many character instances. (See Figure 1.5.)

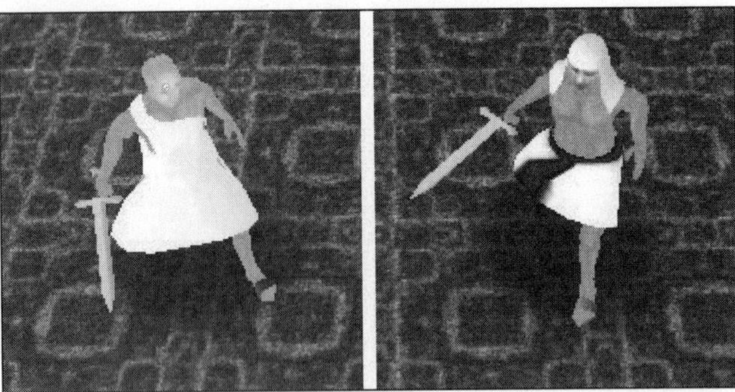

Figure 1.5
Warriors populate the world, and a class accommodates their proliferation.

Integrity

Integrity becomes evident when something can stand on its own and display consistency with itself. When software developers do not engineer games or other software products they develop, the products emerge from rework, inefficiency, and reactionary changes. Such products ultimately lack integrity. One thing that results from lack of integrity is risk.

To achieve integrity and diminish risk, software engineering practices establish that you should consider such issues as scope, architecture, planning, testing, and implementation:

- **Scope.** Requirements establish the scope of a product. They express what the product will provide to its users when it is completed.
- **Architecture.** Architecture tells you how the software that composes the product will be designed physically and logically.
- **Planning.** Scope and design combined allow software developers to plan how they will develop a product.
- **Testing.** Software developers test their work to verify and validate it in the light of requirements and quality objectives, such as performance, reliability, and maintainability.
- **Implementation.** The development of the product, instead of being a point of departure, becomes a manifestation of other activities.

Figure 1.6 illustrates how engineering combines scope, architecture, testing, implementation, and planning to form the basis of the development effort.

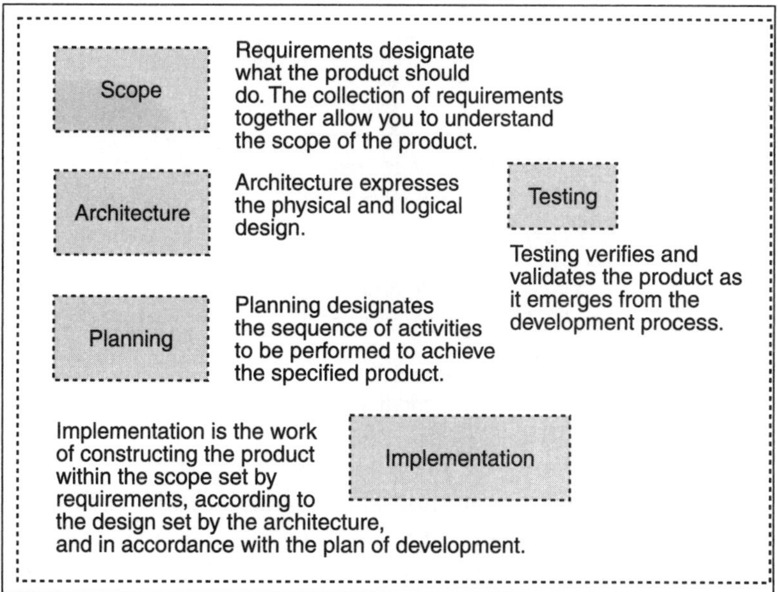

Figure 1.6
Software engineering provides a context for implementation.

Answering Risk with Design

Philosophers contend that nature offers nothing free. Within the environment in which software developers plan software construction efforts, each time they add a module to the emerging system, the module both draws them nearer to the completion of the system and presents the potential to disrupt fatally the development of the system. One particularly hazardous assumption is that because you have created a design, you have created the right design. Risk assessment can control this tendency.

Considerations of risk underlie practically everything that takes place during a development effort guided by engineering practices. At the heart of risk analysis lies the question, "What can go wrong?"

This question possesses importance because it requires that those who are involved in the development effort consider the implications of every action they take. Whenever you add a new component to a game, you make progress toward completing the game. At the same time, everything you add to the game increases its complexity. The more complex the game becomes, the more extensive the implications if you do something wrong.

The issues of design reveal how important it is to assess risk. When you design the software for a game (Chapter 4, "Software Design—Much Ado About Something," discusses design in detail), the decisions you make relatively early in the project about how you intend to architect the software have enormous bearing on the work that follows.

If you create stripes that are too large, for example, you can end up stalling your effort because you need to break a large stripe into smaller ones before you can simplify it enough to be able to complete it. If the stripe is too small, you end up preparing testing material in a manner that is not cost effective. (See Figure 1.7.)

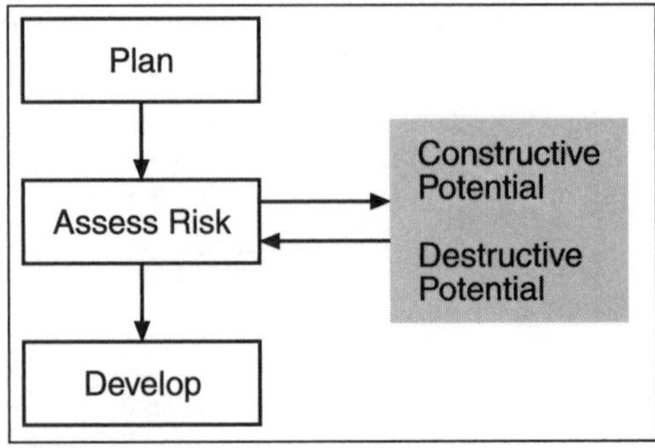

Figure 1.7
Each addition contributes risk.

Developing a world for Sekhem involved anticipating the risks posed whenever features that characterized the world were added to the system. Figure 1.8 illustrates a setting from *Ankh.* This view of the game became possible only after the implementation of thousands of lines of code. The meshes, the tile floor, the AI, the character dialogues, and the lighting each represent the successful completion of a stripe. The design anticipated each stripe, but despite the victory that the completion of each stripe brought, had any one stripe failed to integrate with the whole, the development of the game might have been delayed so seriously through rework that the game could not have been completed on time. (See Figure 1.8.)

Figure 1.8
A complex scene involves increased complexity and risk.

To reduce risk, the team created a design that stipulated that the game should be developed in 14 separate stripes. The team made a strong effort to limit the size of each stripe so that it could redesign a stripe if it proved too difficult to implement. This approach to development, which is based on increments and iterations in the development process, limits the development activity to a selected set of sequenced problems. The functionality that each stripe includes constitutes a subset of the whole. The overall complexity of the system decreases because it is broken into such subsets. (See Figure 1.9.)

Figure 1.9
The design provides an approach to understanding the system. It breaks the whole into a set of problems that you can solve in the best possible sequence.

Game Design and Software Design

It is important to distinguish between game creative design and game software design. Figure 1.10 provides a summary of the differences. The development effort behind *Ankh* began with a set of technical requirements drawn from a game design document. (Chapter 2, "Requirements—Getting the Picture," discusses requirements engineering in detail.) The game design document provides information about the game as an artistic entity. The requirements that are drawn from this document constitute the first step in transforming the vision of the game into a technical specification.

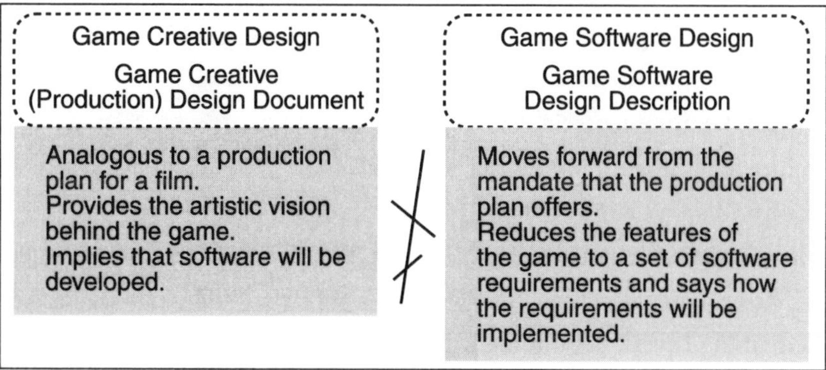

Figure 1.10
Technical and artistic design efforts underlie a game development effort.

Using the software requirements specification, you can create the software design document, which provides information about the game as a software system. (Appendix D, "Software Engineering and Game Design Documentation," provides excerpts from the game design and the software design documents.) When the development team concluded its requirements effort, it had a list of approximately 70 requirements. Most of these were functional requirements—requirements that would necessitate programming. The raw number was not enough to establish fully the scope of the software effort, however. To reach this goal, it was necessary to create the software design specification.

Design and Development

The *Ankh* development effort unfolded as a series of limited objectives that were focused on stripes defined during the software design phase of the project. The design of these stripes involved high-level and low-level activities. At the high level, the team's primary effort focused on determining how to divide the functionality of the system to make implementation possible in the most risk-free manner. The team documented the division of the effort into stripes in the software design description. The description provided the following list of stripes:

Stripe 1—Opening, Requirements 8, 14, 15, 16, 17, 18, 23, 28, 38, 46, 57

Stripe 2.1—GUI Objects, Requirements 18, 52

Stripe 2.2—Floor Tiling, Requirement 43

Stripe 2.3—Mesh Placement, Requirements 13, 43

Stripe 2.4—Save and Load, Requirement 4

Stripe 3.1—Navigate Alexandria, Requirement 13, 14, 15, 16, 17, 36, 61

Stripe 3.2—Sound, Requirements 29, 30, 31, 32, 33

Stripe 4—Character Editor, Requirements 18, 19, 20, 21, 22, 35, 44

Stripe 5—Unit Physics, Requirements 13, 14, 15, 16, 17, 35, 41, 42, 45, 47, 48, 64

Stripe 6—Inventory Items, Requirements 40, 49, 55

Stripe 7—Combat, Requirements 54, 56

Stripe 8—Acquire Skills, Requirements 20, 34, 47, 55, 56

Stripe 9—Acquire Weapon, Requirements 14, 15, 16, 17, 40, 49

Stripe 10—View Statistics, Requirements 14, 15, 16, 17, 18, 19, 20, 21

Stripe 11—AI, Requirements 24, 25, 26, 37

Stripe 12—Remaining Levels, Requirement 27

Stripe 13—Saving and Loading, Requirements 1, 2, 3, 4, 5, 6, 7, 8, 9, 10, 11, 12

Stripe 14—Options, Requirement 39

Stripe 15—Revisions

All of the development activity that took place during the *Ankh* project followed from this list. This list provided, for instance, structural divisions that were replicated in the configuration and testing plans. It also established the basis of the work breakdown structure in the project plan. As for the implementation effort, team members worked wholly within the contexts that the stripes provided. Although members of the team might refer at times to the total size of the game, most of the time, talk centered on the size and characteristics of the current stripe. (See Figure 1.11.)

Figure 1.11
A combat scene and a dialog box represent two stripes.

Each stripe accounted for one or more requirements. To talk about how much of the game had been completed, you counted the number of stripes and the number of requirements. You could say, for example, that 60 percent of the code had been written, but 50 percent of the requirements had been met.

Figure 1.12 shows a UML package diagram. The *Ankh* team used package diagrams to represent stripes that were configured to form the system. Each of the package folders represented a set of classes compiled to provide a given level of functionality to the system. In some instances, one stripe would be heavily dependent on another. In others, the dependencies would not be so direct. Such independence did not necessarily represent irresponsible coupling of classes. (Chapter 7, "P Is for Pattern," discusses class coupling, as does Chapter 6, "Object-Oriented Fantasies and Realities.") Excessive coupling of classes occurs when one class includes objects of another class in a random, messy way. If you create an elegant design, you can plan for dependencies so that you decrease coupling and reduce the risks it introduces.

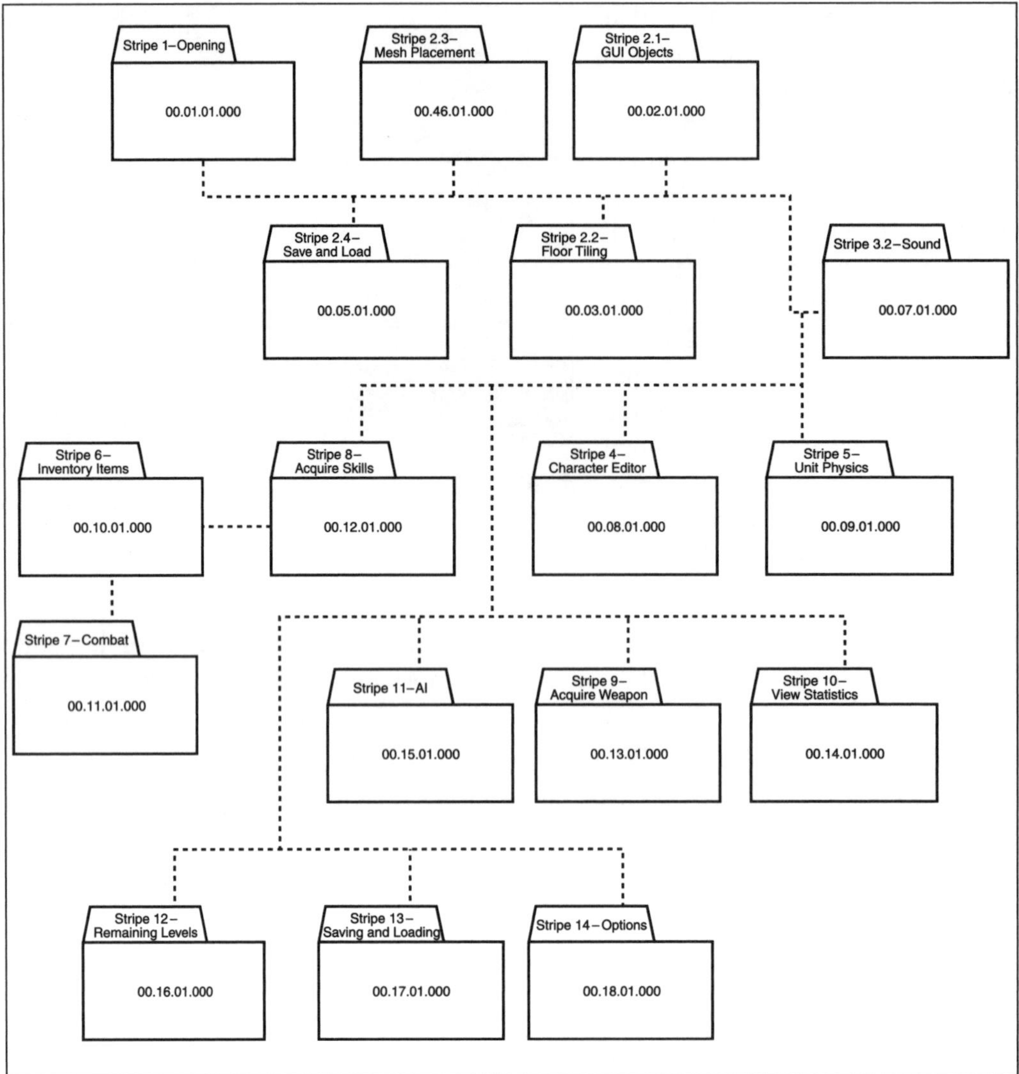

Figure 1.12
The game consists of a set of stripes that encapsulate design features and minimize development risks.

Class Design and Implementation

The *Ankh* software architecture includes approximately 60 C++ classes. In addition to these, the software uses components from the Boost and Microsoft DirectX libraries and a library of global operations. The *Ankh* team used Class-Responsibility-Collaboration (CRC) cards for class design efforts. The team employed them in conjunction with a Task-Object-Remarks (TOR) table to investigate relationships between proposed classes. As the team investigated these relationships, it was able to discern more clearly the essential classes. To track this activity, you can access the requirements specification and the software design description on the CD or consult the appendixes. (Chapter 13, "What People Do—Development Strategies," provides a detailed view of the general approach to development.)

Before each implementation effort, the team had to create low-level stripe specifications. The team used several UML tools, including UML sequence, collaboration, and class diagrams. By exploring the ways that objects communicate with each other, the team could anticipate the difficulties and problems that each stripe posed.

With each cycle of development, stripes tended to increase in size. The sizes of the stripes tended to increase in relation to the responsibilities that the design laid out for them. In this way, the design and the development schedule worked together to confine the growth of the complexity of the game software. In addition, each iteration of the development effort afforded opportunities to assess development risks. (See Chapter 9, "Iterating Design" for the techniques to control the growth of complexity.)

Refactoring and Patterns

The development effort involved using software design patterns as a way to bolster the design and development efforts. You can find extensive discussion of the approach used in Chapter 7; alternatively, class diagrams in the software design description provide a basis on which you can proceed with your own analysis.

As the discussion in many chapters of this book emphasizes, patterns and refactoring provide effective ways to approach incrementally improving software design.

Consider what happens when you program. One approach involves starting out and exploring possible solutions by seeking and solving problems as they emerge. This approach presents drawbacks because it proceeds in a random fashion and lacks a generalized, guiding perspective. A more refined approach involves exerting a strong effort to solve problems conceptually before the implementation effort begins. This approach possesses great merit, because it allows developers to proceed with a generalized view of the system and to make changes in the design without worrying about features that are implemented already.

On the other hand, consider what happens if you rigidly conform to a development model that requires everything to be designed at the start of the project. If you follow this model, the implementation of the design takes place without allowing questions to be asked. Such an approach effectively bars developers from improving the design by applying lessons learned during the development effort.

Software engineering studies indicate that the more time you spend on design, the better. One reason for this is that when you explore problems during implementation, you struggle against the tendency to accept as good enough whatever you happened to have programmed. If the program works, it seems to be good enough. This is often not the case.

But then just because implementation without design poses risks does not mean that development should have no impact on design. Implementation almost always provides valuable insights into the weaknesses of the design. Having no latitude to change design during the implementation effort can force developers into the untenable position of implementing a solution that their efforts have shown to be inferior.

The *Ankh* development effort provided two contexts for design assessment. The first was at the beginning of the project, when the team established the scope and architecture of the product. The context of the second stage of design assessment unfolded during the implementation phase. The team reviewed each stripe in terms of the lessons learned during the development effort. The team could make adjustments to the design prior to the commencement of the implementation effort. (See Figure 1.13.)

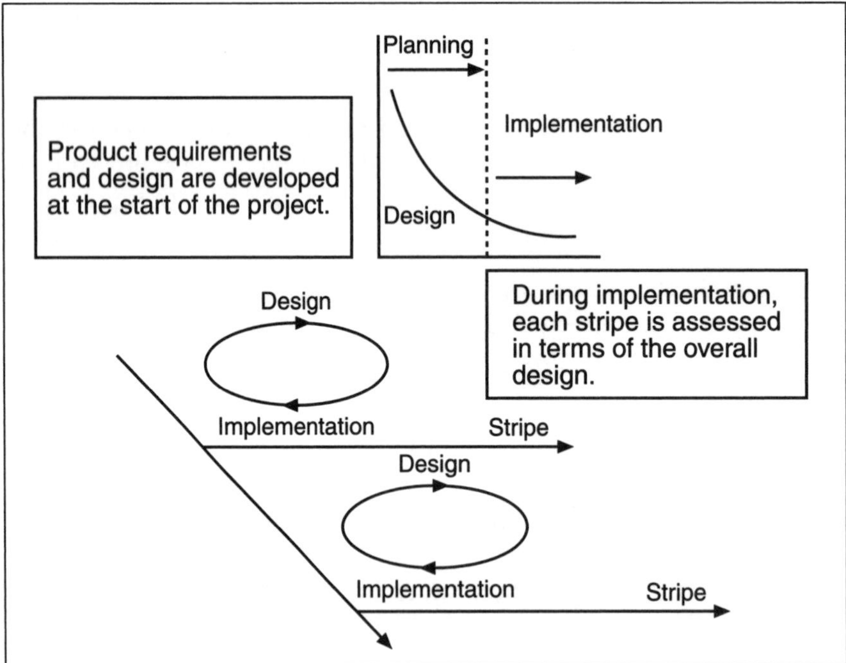

Figure 1.13
Phases of design reduce risk.

One assumption guiding the *Ankh* development effort was that the older (waterfall) models of development did not provide the best approach to game development. Game development requires design flexibility so that the team can incorporate the lessons learned during the development effort into a continuous effort of quality improvement.

Development and Testing

The approach that this book takes to testing involves formalized procedures. To formalize your testing effort, you can use test plans. For the *Ankh* effort, the team developed several test plans. You can find the test plans on the CD in the form of Microsoft Word documents. In one way or another, the test plans use procedures and test criteria that are presented in IEEE standard 829. The development of test plans is discussed in Chapter 11, "Evident Evil—The Art of Testing."

One thing that the testing effort for *Ankh* emphasizes is that you can benefit extensively if you employ use cases. Among other things, use cases provide a ready way to accumulate information in one context and transfer it to another. For example, use cases help you to formulate scenarios with which to understand requirements. At the same time, writing requirements use cases allows you to accumulate information with which to develop scripts for testing efforts.

Behavioral (white-box) testing provides an excellent context in which to establish models for comprehensive test planning. If you establish a development effort based on use cases, your effort begins with use cases that explore requirements. You can then employ these uses cases to develop test cases. This is a patterned approach to testing that you can introduce into any development effort.

Requirements generate the design of the software, and the design generates the general testing divisions. The design divisions are expressed best in use cases for integration testing. Figure 1.14 provides a truncated example of an integration use case, this one for Stripe 14.

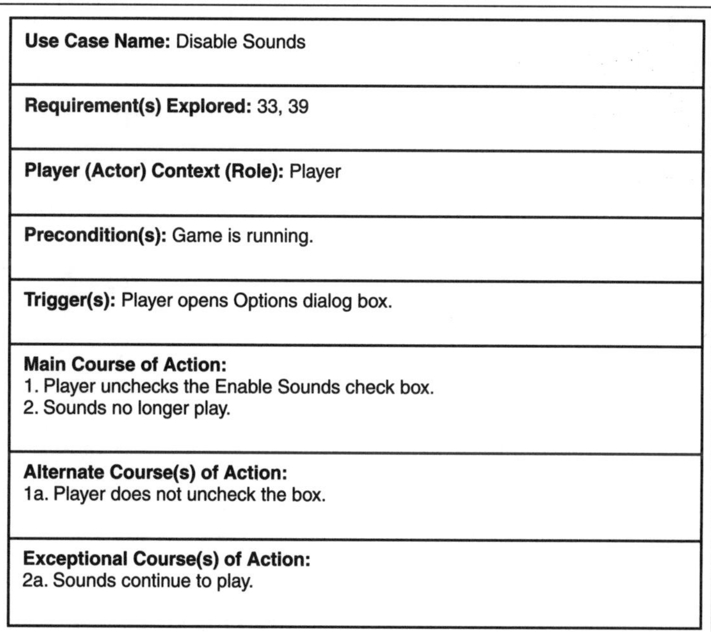

Use Case Name: Disable Sounds

Requirement(s) Explored: 33, 39

Player (Actor) Context (Role): Player

Precondition(s): Game is running.

Trigger(s): Player opens Options dialog box.

Main Course of Action:
1. Player unchecks the Enable Sounds check box.
2. Sounds no longer play.

Alternate Course(s) of Action:
1a. Player does not uncheck the box.

Exceptional Course(s) of Action:
2a. Sounds continue to play.

Figure 1.14
Use cases tie everything together.

Although extensive work is necessary to break the information that a use case provides into tables and scripts that contain specific directions for testing, use cases still can guide the entire game software testing effort. The value of creating use cases for game development efforts becomes especially clear when you consider that with highly integrated team development efforts (efforts in which a high degree of communication occurs between programmers and graphical designers), some of the most original parts of the game arise after the initial design has been completed. During the various passages of implementation, the features that achieve visibility with each new build of the game empower the designers of the game to grasp new potentials for enhancement.

Use cases ensure that potentials for enhancement remain visible to the whole development team throughout the development project. They also prohibit the team from becoming too immersed in details. Likewise, because use cases are developed with specific references to the requirements, they drive the project from start to finish and provide a clear context for regulating things like feature creep and goldplating (activities that can seriously endanger the development effort).

Although they bind the requirements to the design and then the design to test plans, use cases remain a flexible medium for information exchange in all areas of development. Figure 1.15 provides an overview of the relationships that use cases facilitate during the overall development effort.

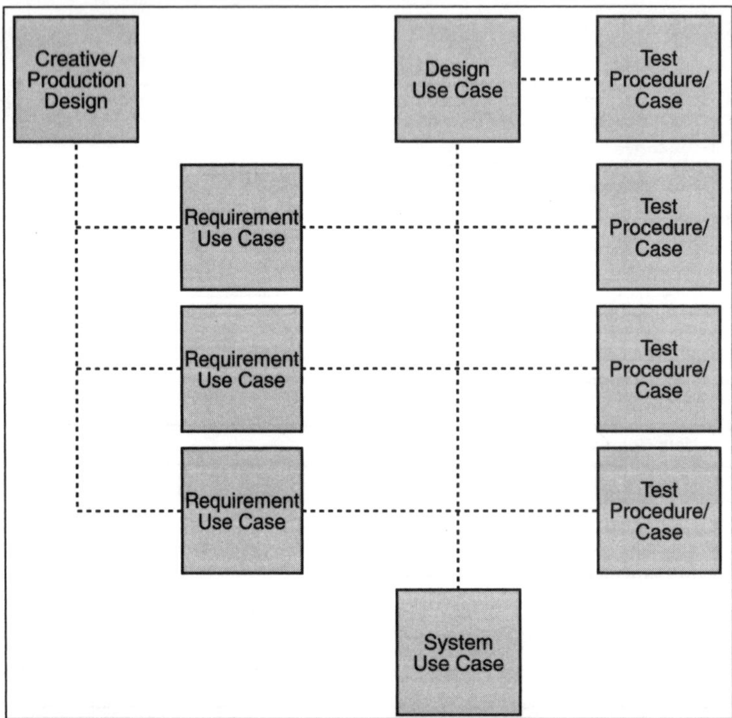

Figure 1.15
Game development efforts that are characterized by highly integrated teams can benefit from use cases.

Code Documentation

An attempt has been made to provide roughly one line of documentation for every four lines of code to help you understand why and how operations and classes have been implemented. The documentation in the code allows you to study the specific aspects of how classes and operations have been implemented. On the other hand, understanding the design and architecture of the code requires a high-level view. Generally, you benefit if you begin with a high-level understanding of a system before you begin examining the code in specific files. That's because the overall flow of design as introduced in this book is from the large to the small.

Learning and Capabilities

Software engineering prescribes no fixed set of procedures or methodologies for creating software. Still, many organizations and individuals present procedures and methodologies as embodying the best approaches to software engineering. As anticipated by the model Jacques Ellul established for technique, there are even organizations and individuals who advocate rejecting or revolting against procedures and methodologies. Regardless of how you might be inclined to view questions concerning methodologies or procedures, the fact remains that software engineering provides you with tools you can use to refine your development practices continuously.

Software engineering can be characterized as a kind of contemporary historical study. People who perform such work shape processes and practices so that they can be improved. In this light, improvement is based on the assumption that you perform a given activity or a set of activities over and over. To the extent that an individual or organization can say that it has documented and can repeat its development activities, it possesses development *capabilities*. The Software Engineering Institute captured this concept and embodied it in the Capability Maturity Model (CMM). Chapter 16, "Process Improvement" discusses this and other maturity models in detail.

Incremented iteration provides the basic approach to developing capabilities. If you recall the general discussion presented previously of how technique involves refining the process of creating something, it becomes clear that developing capabilities through iterations extends the notion of technique.

Formalized development of capabilities involves understating practices, processes, and procedures. Consider the following:

- **Documenting practices.** When you document a process, your actions can be as simple as writing a numbered list. In fact, in most contexts, this is the best beginning. When you write a numbered list to document what you do, consider what happens. First, you establish a benchmark for evaluation. You can ask yourself whether you have forgotten anything. You can evaluate what you have documented and add things you have forgotten. You can elaborate on the items that you have listed, making it possible to explore the specific tasks that each step entails. Add to this that you can copy the list and distribute it to others; this way, others can benefit from what you have recorded and possibly provide valuable insights concerning their own experiences with your practices.

- **Following documented practices and procedures.** A practice differs from a procedure. A procedure is a fixed way to do things. A practice is just a way to do things. It is probably not right to dictate procedures to developers, but at times procedures can prove essential. Consider a situation in which you are working to support your customers. The service manager has put in place procedures for responding to customer complaints. The procedures require you to follow specific guidelines when you meet, acquire information from, and respond to customers. If you follow the procedures, you have a guide to what is essential. You do not need to put your own feelings on the line. You can approach the situation objectively.
- **Collecting data.** Experienced professionals can do at least one thing better than novices. They can estimate how long they will require to perform a given task. They can do this because they have repeatedly gauged their efforts over time and have an empirical basis on which to estimate the effort involved in completing tasks. If you ask experienced programmers how long they think a class with *x* number of operations will require to program, the answers will be based on prior experiences with such work. Collecting data about such experiences can take place in various ways. For an individual developer, the best approach is to use a log. You can automate much of this activity on an organizational level.
- **Review.** Reviews are ways to evaluate practices and procedures formally. If you have made a list of things you do when you perform a given task, you can review this list either on your own or with others. Review allows you to assess the list from different points in time. Note that a difference of time creates a difference of perspective. What applies to differences of time also accounts for the value of group reviews. Group reviews allow you to expose something that you have done on your own to the perspectives that others provide.

Chapter 15, "Team Work," discusses the value of reviews in relation to teamwork. Reviews also relate to documentation, generally, because setting up a review requires that you create a body of information for review. Chapter 18, "Documentation—Learning How to Learn," provides specific information on how to gather and document development activities.

A template provides an especially useful tool for documentation. It furnishes you with a guide that consists of a set of questions that direct your attention to essentials. A template establishes a scope of inquiry or activity. You can use a template to create a context for communicating about specific development efforts. A template does not prescribe how to gather or organize information. Instead, it only suggests.

Maintenance and Revision

A successful software product has a lifetime that extends years or decades beyond its point of release. Software engineering studies indicate that developing a software product accounts for about one-third of its total budget. The maintenance phase of its life accounts for the rest.

The way that you conduct the release process can be instrumental in reducing the expense involved in maintaining a software product. Releasing a software product consists of gathering together the parts of the product that are slated for release, but it also involves evaluating the state of the product as it nears release to ensure that it is ready for distribution. In addition, release management involves preparing the organization for response to the information that the product creates after its release. The most important such information concerns the defects that customers encounter.

As Chapter 17, "Release Planning and Management," discusses, alpha and beta tests can provide solid information on whether a product is ready for general release. Likewise, after a product has been made available for general release, a problem-tracking system can ensure that when customers report defects, developers can respond to the reports in an expeditious, effective way.

Measurement

Chapter 12, "Numbers for Nabobs," discusses the basics of collecting numerical data. Metrics constitute one of the most important aspects of software development because companies increasingly encounter economic pressures that they can address only if they have data that allows them to assess their productivity quantitatively. In addition to the big picture, however, is a small one, the picture that includes the work of the individual developer. Chapter 16 discusses how personalized logs help you collect quantitative data on your own activities. The most likely scenario for such data collection involves tracking the durations and efforts that are involved in given tasks. Among such information is how long it takes you to complete a given task (effort) or how many lines of code you can write in a day (productivity). As pointed out previously, collecting and assessing such information helps you to mature as a developer.

Quantitative information forms the foundation of scientific experimentation. It is the bedrock of positive knowledge. When quantitative data applies to a specific industrial model, it becomes metrics. Key metrics in software engineering are product size, productivity, effort, duration, and reliability. Many other metrics apply, also.

The Industry

As it has evolved, the game software industry, like every other industry, has tended to foster greater specialization. Early on, programmers dominated the game development effort. As the industry has matured, however, programming, although still essential, has become subordinated to production management. In the corporate settings that currently dominate the industry, programmers usually are not the principal developers of games. Instead, they are treated as "resources" hired by producers to implement the software that supports game designs. Game designers create games. Programmers develop the tools with which to create games.

One result is that some programmers have exited the game production side of the industry. Rather than founding game studios, they start software companies that develop software to create games. Among these are companies specializing in engines, algorithms for collision detection, audio production, scripting, testing, and other things. Figure 1.16 summarizes the situation.

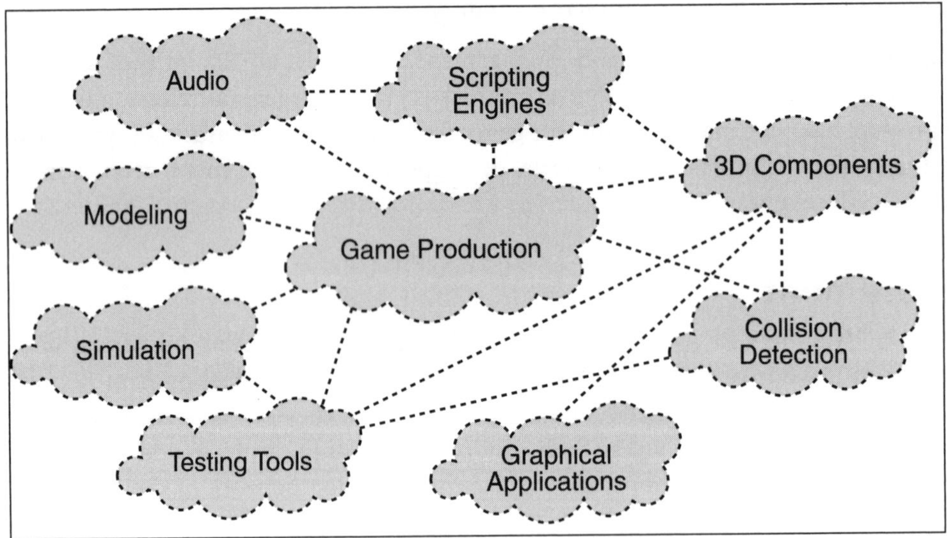

Figure 1.16
Specialized products increasingly characterize the game industry.

Specialization tends to atomize people. On the other hand, a common or core set of skills and practices can counteract the tendencies of specialization. If your interest is in working as a software developer in the game industry, you probably stand the best chance or finding a place if you can extend your skills through generalized software engineering knowledge. One guide to the core knowledge of software engineering is the Software Engineering Body of Knowledge (SWEBOK). As Chapter 19 discusses, although the SWEBOK was developed to facilitate professionalism, it can serve as a ready source of information for those seeking to pursue software development as a craft. It is more or less a list of the bins you can find in a good software development toolbox. Figure 1.17 provides a high-level view of the types of work that the SWEBOK includes.

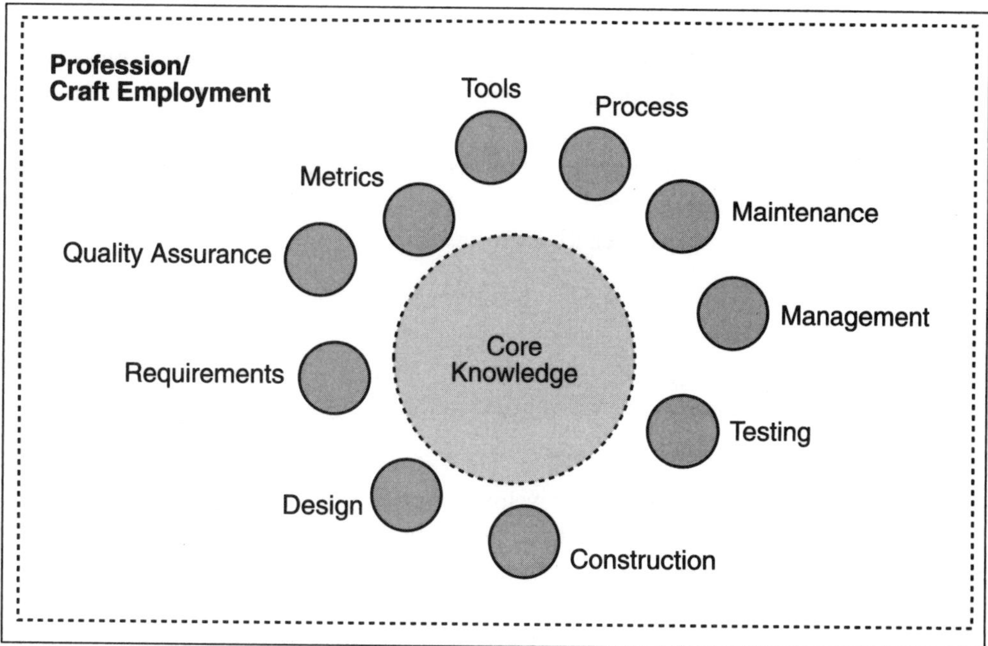

Figure 1.17
Core skills ensure increased success in a competitive industry.

Profession and Craft

This book takes no strict line on whether you should seek certification as a software professional. Generally, you can make a strong argument in either direction. On the one hand, most of the visible game software developers do not possess professional certification as either game developers or software engineers. On the other hand, the type of understanding that one acquires through the study of software engineering might eliminate many of the situations in which developers undermine their own efforts by failing to address elementary engineering issues.

This book provides information on solid development practices. Despite enormous pushes in recent years to shape software engineering into a profession, it remains part profession, part craft. Engineering that is grounded in science tends to be self-critical and oriented toward quantification of knowledge. Engineering that is grounded in craft tends to be oriented toward tradition and best practices. Both perspectives on engineering provide valuable insights.

Large corporations now dominate the game development industry. They are in a position to limit or confine employment specifications and opportunities for game developers to the point that only a highly qualified elite can expect to obtain such jobs.

On the other hand, other forces are at work, forces that are represented in part in the film industry through such efforts as those of Robert Redford and Michael Moore. These efforts are characterized by individuals who are largely self-taught and self-made. Such individuals seek independent roles in which to create products usually spoken for by massive corporate efforts. Their successes serve as inspiration to continue to maintain open, egalitarian access to the body of knowledge and set of practices that given movements seek to make the exclusive property of certified professionals.

Conclusion

This chapter has provided a general perspective from which you can proceed as you read this book. This book discusses software engineering both generally and in relation to the development required for *Ankh.*

Software engineers seek to foster the development of tested and reliable development practices and products. The body of knowledge that constitutes software engineering extends far and wide, but at the core lies the notion that you can gather information about what you do and use it to refine what you do on an iterative, incremental basis. There is no mystery to this, and the approach to developing products does not require an extensive, expensive education that establishes one as a "certified professional." Instead, it requires only a proper attention to science, detail, tradition, and craft. It is a toolbox open to anyone.

Following are a few books that provide more information on the topics touched on in this chapter:

Brooks, Frederick P., Jr. *The Mythical Man-Month.* Boston: Addison-Wesley, 1995.

Demarco, Tom and Timothy Lister. *Peopleware: Productive Projects and Teams.* New York: Dorset House, 1987.

Ellul, Jacques. *The Technological Society.* Trans. John Wilkinson. New York: Random House, 1964.

Humphrey, Watts S. *Introduction to the Personal Software Process.* SEI Series in Software Engineering. Boston: Addison-Wesley, 1997.

Petroski, Henry. *To Engineer Is Human: The Role of Failure in Successful Design.* New York: Random House, 1992.

Pirsig, Robert M. *Zen and the Art of Motorcycle Maintenance.* New York: Bantam Books, 1974.

Shumacher, E. F. *Good Work.* New York: Harper & Row, 1979.

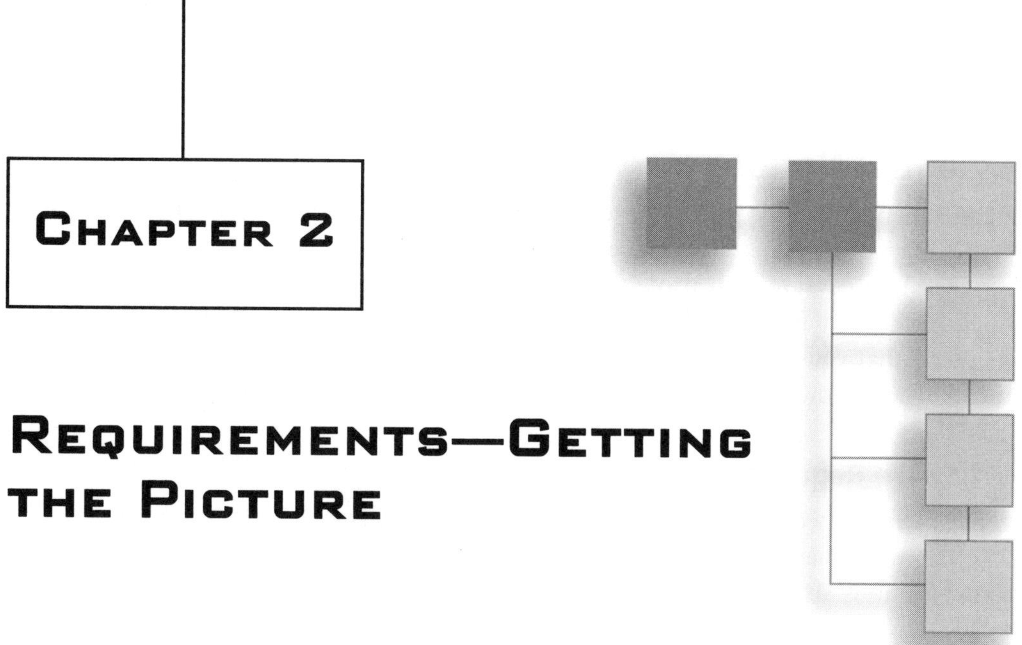

Chapter 2

Requirements—Getting the Picture

This chapter shows you how to start a software engineering project. The chapter is laid out in two parts. The first part gives you a general view of the concepts and tools. The second part, starting with "Engineering Requirements," guides you through specific tasks. At the start of the project, you establish the project scope. When you know the scope, you can determine precisely what you are expected to develop. You designate what you are expected to develop by creating a list of requirements. The requirements list specifically identifies the functionality that lies within the scope you have established. To develop a list of requirements, you use a number of techniques and tools to ensure that your requirements are complete, accurate, verifiable, and worded so that developers can easily understand them. The result of this activity is the contents of a single document, called a *software requirements specification.* Along the way, you also create *use cases* and a *traceability matrix*; these become part of the requirements specification. In addition, you begin work on yet another major document, a *test plan.* A rough sketch of the chapter topics is as follows:

- Identify what counts as a software requirement.
- Establish criteria for making sense of and writing requirements.
- Determine ways to collect or discover requirements.
- Explore how to employ uses cases to refine and analyze requirements.
- Find techniques to confirm that requirements are complete.
- Verify the accuracy of the requirements.
- Trace changes to the requirements.

Essential Notions

Requirements mark the starting place of the lifecycle of any software engineering project. Gathering requirements is the first concerted activity you engage in as a software engineer assigned to a development project. The reason for this is that the software project you intend to develop must first be defined as an engineering problem. You *engineer* requirements so that you can engineer a product. The next few sections explore what requirements are and how engineering processes can ensure that they are properly developed.

What Are Requirements?

A *requirement* is a concisely worded statement that establishes how the software you want to create will behave when it's complete. Sometimes software engineers use *shall* to refer to the relationship that a requirement establishes with the behavior of a proposed system. In other words, after you have implemented a requirement, the system *shall* behave in accordance to the conditions that the requirement establishes.

note

Shall might sound a little medieval these days, but engineers still use it. It serves as a kind of order or promise that the developers will construct the system as described.

During the software development effort, you implement two types of requirements. One type is known as a *functional* requirement. A functional requirement addresses the operations that the system performs. The other type of requirement is known as a *nonfunctional* requirement. The behavior of the system does not usually manifest a nonfunctional requirement. Instead, a nonfunctional requirement applies to the standards or qualities of performance that *constrain* the design or operations of the system. For example, if someone says that the splash screen shall be appealing to the user, the requirement falls under the nonfunctional heading. On the other hand, if someone says that the system shall provide a splash screen, then the requirement falls under the functional heading.

Whether they are functional or nonfunctional, a somewhat overworked point about requirements is that you should not express them in the language of *implementation*. Implementation is the activity of building the software. Requirements specify the objectives of implementation (what), not the implementation itself (how). When you address the functionality of the system without reference to implementation, you address the system from an *external* or *user-oriented* perspective.

To provide an example of the language of implementation, suppose that you say, "The user shall click a dialog button to open a new window." The problem is that "dialog" and "window" echo the language of implementation. Instead, you should say something along the lines of "After the user selects the next level option, the next level appears." Granted, this sounds vague, but this second formulation avoids making the requirement into a premature design decision. The second formulation restricts the wording so that you hear only about what the system does. Determining how this will happen comes later.

Where Do Requirements Originate?

As a software engineer, you might find that you do not create the idea of the game you build. Instead, you build the software that provides the functionality that supports the idea. As an engineer, you translate *features* into *functionality.* To discover what you are to support, you begin the requirements engineering effort.

When you engineer requirements, you spend a great deal of time—sometimes weeks or months—*eliciting* information about the software system you intend to build. In a setting in which games result from business, design, and marketing plans, the game is likely to be something you find described in documents that others create. The people who create these documents are game designers. In other settings, the source of the requirements information is much less formal. For example, you might talk with others and create an idea with them about a game. Regardless of the setting, at the beginning of the engineering effort, you elicit specific functional and nonfunctional requirements. To repeat the point made earlier, these requirements concern not *how* you implement the functionality of the software but rather *what* the software does from a user's perspective.

Eliciting requirements is painful at first. Even if you work from a formal game design document, you must still analyze the document to discover the system features you must support. To accomplish this task, you require information from others. A short list of the resources for this information might be as follows:

- Users of the game you want to create
- Your previous experiences with game development
- Marketing, graphics design, and other experts involved with the effort
- Games that might be modified (mods) to create the game you want to develop
- Designers of the game you want to create
- The programmers who will create the new system

Other resources exist, but the primary idea here is that when you engineer anything, first you figure out what to build, then you figure out how to build it, and finally, you build it. If something is complex and serves many people, then it stands to reason that you are going to need help. You are not likely to find any one person from whom you can elicit all the information you need to collect. The next few sections visit some of the sources of information mentioned in the previous list. Figure 2.1 provides a summary view of the discussion.

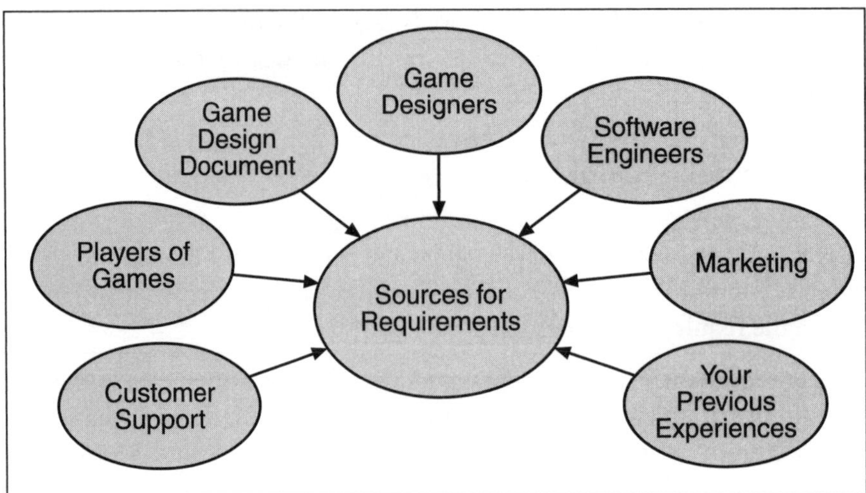

Figure 2.1
Requirements information originates in many places.

Users or Players

The first information resource named in the previous list is the *user*. The user of a game is the *player*. Game designers ask many questions about players because designers target specific player markets. As an engineer involved in a requirements engineering effort, your concern about players might have a different objective, but you should still consider the player important. Because players have a good sense of how a game should feel and perform, they have important information to offer you as you develop requirements. If you develop your software using *prototypes*, players can work as *testers*. From testers, you can audit the *playability* of the game. Players provide you with an important nontechnical basis of information.

Previous Experiences

Your understanding as a software developer of how you have built a game provides an enormously valuable starting place for requirements engineering. If you know how to build a game, you can begin to make candidate statements for requirements modeled on requirements statements you have made in the past. The requirements you generate in this way must address the current system, but knowing key features in previous efforts helps you more quickly locate them in the current effort.

caution

When you use knowledge from the past on a new system, you can begin to *prematurely design* the new system. You begin to implement the features of the system before you fully identify them. To avoid premature design, use previous knowledge only to determine what is needed, not how you will implement what is needed.

Mods

Games that are developed from existing games are called *mods* (for *modified* games). If you use a mod as a template for your new game effort, you can save months of work. However, mods can also create major risks. One risk is to assume that the mod does not possess faults that might end up *costing* you development time rather than *saving* you development time. It could be that the mod has major design flaws or was released without thorough testing. Because such risks inevitably accompany legacy software, if you assume you can take something for granted, you might be inviting disaster. The best policy is to be cautious. When you work with a mod, break away from the tendency to think that you can assume that the mod represents the best possible way to do things. If you use a mod, do not start by accepting every feature of the mod without criticism. Begin your requirements effort as a blank slate. Until you have critically assessed the risks, do not bring anything forward from the mod.

note

An old saying in engineering circles is that engineering innovations are not revolutions; they are evolutions.

Designers and Design Documents

Designers are not necessarily programmers. They are often artists who specialize in *game design.* They sometimes work in a marketing or creative group wholly separate from the engineering group. As an engineer, your first exposure to designers' work might be through a *game design document.* (Appendix D, "Software Engineering and Game Design Documentation," provides a sample game design document.) Such documents, along with their authors, inform you about the audience that the game addresses, the genre and rules of the game, and how the game should look and feel as the user plays it. The game design document lays out the stories, levels, characters, rules, musical themes, and a multitude of other things that go into a game. These are all candidate *features* of the game. From these features, you derive the functional and nonfunctional requirements of the system. Requirements *support* features.

Who Gathers Requirements?

A person who gathers requirements is a *requirements analyst.* A requirements analyst is someone who knows how to work with the documents, processes, and techniques that are involved in the activities encompassed by *requirements engineering* (which is also called *requirements analysis*). Requirements analysts work in several capacities (identifying business processes or data schemes, for example), so if you want to be precise about your language, you refer to someone who is involved with software as a *software requirements analyst.* This person's work involves eliciting, analyzing, specifying, verifying, and managing the functional and nonfunctional requirements of the software system.

Because the activities of requirements analysis extend throughout the lifecycle of the software product, the work of the requirements analyst becomes fairly involved. Consider the following list:

- Obtaining from executives the scope of the game
- Interviewing customers
- Guiding developers through the refinement of requirements
- Analyzing requirements to discover basic system properties
- Maintaining documents that list and elaborate requirements
- Managing how requirements are changed during the development process

This chapter deals with all of these activities.

Why Do You Need Requirements?

Engineering involves stating a problem and solving it. Requirements are how you state a problem. What happens if you state no requirements? Well, then you are not in a position to perform engineering. This might sound a bit arrogant, so let's try another approach. Take the case of the classical hacker. A hacker is something like a performance artist. He performs and then figures out afterward what the performance was about. This is, in fact, what makes the performance worthwhile. Along the same lines, the difference between hacking a game and engineering a game is that the hacker first codes and then discovers after the fact the product or resulting game. The game is a kind of controlled accident. The engineer, on the other hand, specifically plans the game *before* code is written.

Other justifications exist for requirements. Table 2.1 shows you some of the standard arguments.

Table 2.1 Reasons for Requirements

Reason	Explanation
Solving the problem	You must specify the problem you want to solve.
Planning	Unless you specify all the behavior that the system needs to support, you cannot determine how much time you require to create the system.
Testing	Unless you create a list of the things a system is supposed to do, when you finish your development effort, you will have no way to responsibly test whether the system actually does what it is supposed to do.

Reason	Explanation
Extension	If you want to add to a system after it has been released, you will find your work difficult to accomplish unless you know what it does and how you can add to what it does.
Cost	Studies indicate that when products are well specified, they can be developed much less expensively than otherwise.
Maintainability	When products are specified, they can be fixed much more readily than when they are not specified.
Maturity	A software development organization cannot meet the Capability Maturity Model (CMM) standards for organizational maturity without putting in place procedures for engineering requirements.

What Results from Requirements?

When you engage in a requirements gathering (*engineering*) process, your main deliverable is a *software requirements specification.* This topic will be discussed in this section and in the sections that follow, but it will not hurt at this point to repeat that five general activities of requirements engineering are often named in software engineering literature. These are as follows: *elicitation*, *analysis*, *specification*, *verification*, and *management.* You create and use different tools, documents, and processes as you perform these activities. The sections that follow name some of these. Figure 2.2 shows you some of the common requirements tools.

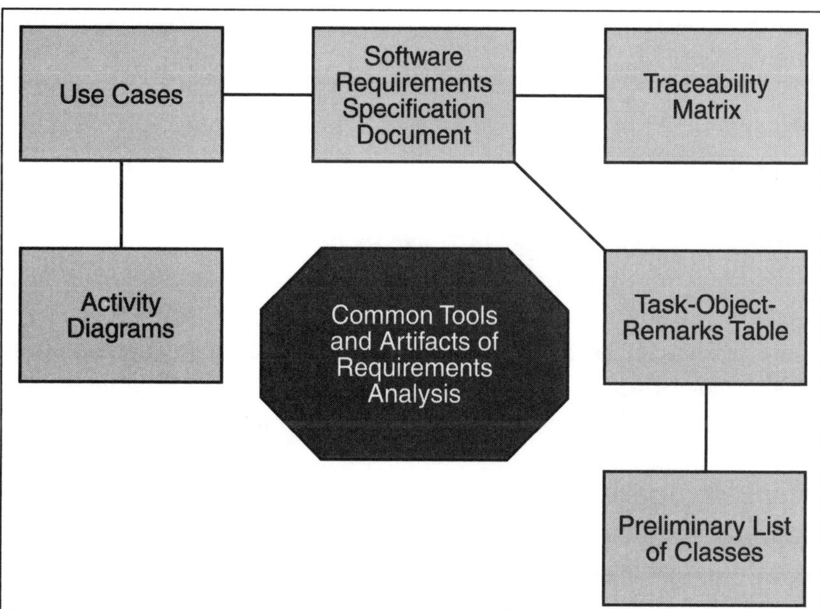

Figure 2.2
Common tools aid in the requirements engineering effort.

Use Cases

You employ use cases in most areas of requirements engineering to help you understand how events occur, how things depend on each other, and whether you have left things out. Use cases involve use case *diagrams* and use case *narratives* and *scenarios.* Chapter 3, "A Tutorial: UML and Object-Oriented Programming," presents a discussion of the Unified Modeling Language (UML) and use case diagrams. This chapter examines employing use cases in the development of a set of requirements for *Ankh,* the game discussed in the course of this book.

A use case is basically something that you write, but the appeal of diagrams is enormous. You can use both diagrams and narratives. You're encouraged to use diagrams as tools of analysis and comprehension (in fact, try using SmartDraw as a kind of surrogate CASE tool for diagramming use cases), but at the same time, it is important to emphasize that in practice, a use case is a document rather than a diagram. When this book suggests, for example, that you create an appendix to your software requirements specification for use cases, it is encouraging you to include text versions of use cases rather than diagrams.

The terms *narrative* and *scenario* designate what might be referred to as *informal* and *formal* versions of use cases. A narrative is just what you would probably expect: a paragraph that tells a short story about how the user interacts with the system. Scenario designates a narrative that has been broken into a *numbered sequence of events.*

Conventions differ. This book presents a set of suggestions. The books mentioned at the end of the chapter provide excellent sources for a deeper, more disciplined, and scientific understanding of how to develop use cases.

Activity Diagrams

The UML provides a tool called an *activity diagram,* which is a flow chart that allows you to show, among other things, how events you have named in use cases can be ordered and traced. (Chapter 3 provides a review of the UML activity diagram.) When you find that the events that make up a use case are difficult to order, activity diagrams can help. Activity diagrams enable you to unravel complex or concurrent event flows so that you can place them in use case scenarios. In addition, activity diagrams are analysis tools, so they provide a ready means of moving into design activities that involve sequence diagrams. (See Chapter 4, "Software Design—Much Ado About Something.")

Software Requirements Specification

This book uses both *use case–driven* requirements development and a more traditional approach based on the drafting of a list of requirements formally stated in a requirements specification. Some analysts consider this approach redundant. It isn't. One reason to both list requirements and present them as use cases is that it makes little sense to start from scratch when developing a game. A list allows developers a ready avenue for starting out the requirements. Use cases can then be used to expand, explore, and verify requirements in the list. Another reason is that the use case–driven approach usually leads from user *needs* to what is referred to as the user *interface*. With games, the opposite is the case. The software engineer involved in creating a game usually knows a great deal about what the game will look like; the question is how to provide a system that achieves what is given.

The Institute of Electrical and Electronics Engineers (IEEE, usually pronounced *I-triple-E*) provides a document template (see Appendix D) that shows you how to organize the information you gather as you specify the requirements for the software system you want to develop. Begin with this template, which is for a *Software Requirements Specification* (SRS).

The SRS feeds into other documents: the *project plan* and the *design document*. The project plan, among other things, lists all the tasks that developers must perform to complete the product. The design document shows how the functionality detailed in the SRS is to be implemented. Unless the SRS is complete, the design specification ends up requiring a great deal of rework.

TOR Chart

A Task-Object-Remarks (TOR) chart allows you to list tentative objects that address the functionality the requirements stipulate. If you make use of the TOR chart from early on in your requirements effort, you will have at hand a good tool for identifying the tasks that your requirements imply and the objects you might name in association with the tasks. For now, this book uses *class* and *object* interchangeably. Chapter 3 explores the differences. A class is a static model used to create objects. You can use a TOR chart to collect names you might later assign to classes.

Traceability Matrix

After you have engineered requirements for a software system (a game), you must maintain and track the requirements. A useful tool for this work is the traceability matrix. To create a traceability matrix, you can use an Excel spreadsheet, a table in a Word document, or a tool such as SmartDraw. The resulting matrix allows you to track and confirm changes to your requirements. You can also use the matrix to trace test cases you develop to verify or validate requirements. A final use for this matrix is to record the priorities and statuses of requirements.

Avoiding Difficulties with Requirements

Before delving into the labor of engineering a set of requirements, it is wise to spend a bit of time reviewing things you should and should not do as you work with requirements. Engineering requirements alone are not enough. You must use care not to create incomplete, spotty, redundant, or inaccurate requirements. Whether you work with requirements statements or use cases, you seek to find the essential behavior of the system and to specify this behavior in nontechnical, clearly stated terms.

Establish the Scope of the Project

One of the major reasons that a software project fails is that those involved in the project neglect to establish a clear project *scope*. What is scope? It is the boundary of the engineering effort. It designates the set of functionality you want to include in the system. With respect to the effort of requirements exploration, scope is where you stop. If you decide to develop a single-player Role-Playing Game (RPG), your knowledge of the scope of the project allows you to determine that you will not invest your time in developing multiple-player or Internet capabilities. Figure 2.3 summarizes the main points.

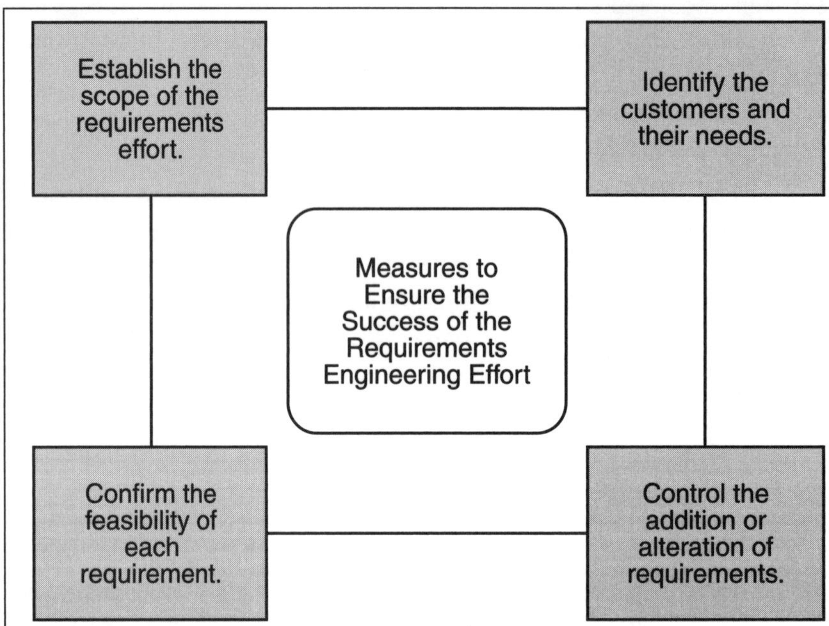

Figure 2.3
Taking a few precautions prevents requirements rework.

Scope Statements

Where do you find information that allows you to establish the scope of the requirements effort? The game design document provides the most readily available source of this information. In the game design document for *Ankh*, for instance, the section of the document that summarizes the game provides most of the information needed to determine the functional features the game software includes.

If you do not possess a game design document, you can establish the scope of the product by creating what is sometimes known as a *scope statement.* Any number of names exists for such a document, but its general intention is to establish the following:

- What the project is intended to do
- What group of people the project should serve
- How long the project should require to build

If you do not begin your engineering effort from a scope statement, then it is likely that your engineering effort will cost more and will take longer to complete. Further, to repeat a point made earlier, your project is also more likely to fail.

Outer and Inner Scope Boundaries

Scope has two types of boundary. The boundaries stem from the fact that any given system or subsystem has *extensive* and *intensive* features. System features can be viewed as such things as the ability to show variable camera angles or support world motion. Such features give the game general qualities that do not vary much from game to game because the technology and design concepts behind such features are common throughout the industry. Such features provide an *outer* scope.

On the other hand, scope can have an *inner* scope. At a given level, for example, an enormous number of player options can be made available. These can be so arcane or cryptic that it is almost impossible that any other game will have them.

To help control the growth of outer and inner scope, you have two ready resources. Both are available in most game design documents. (See Appendix D.) The first resource is the *game overview,* which provides a guide to the extensive features of the game. If no such narrative is available, you can write your own. This can be a general use case *narrative* that describes the features and objectives of the game. Artifacts that capture this narrative are *system context use cases* and *system context diagrams.*

The second resource allows you to obtain an inner scope view of a game. For this, you can draw upon a *sixty-seconds-of-play scenario,* which you usually find in the game design document. There might be a multitude of such narratives, depending on how the game designers who are associated with your project do things. The play scenario establishes the level of complexity you must capture as you develop your requirements. If no such narrative exists, then it is a good idea to compose the scenario yourself. Artifacts that are good for capturing the sixty-seconds-of-play scenario are *use case narratives, use case scenarios, use case diagrams,* and *activity diagrams.*

Identify Your Customers

A customer is sometimes called a *stakeholder*, but here, to keep things simple, the term customer is used. From an organizational perspective, you can describe a customer in many ways. Most commonly, a customer is the *end user* of the game—the player. Many other customers can be found as well. Game designers and people who specialize in developing graphics are customers. People who create music, sound effects, character dialogues, and voice recordings are also customers. All of these people expect what you develop to give life to what they have contributed. Each such specialist is a customer of the requirements effort.

Consider again the customer who is the player of the game. Upon deeper analysis, you will find that the player has many *roles*. Use cases allow you to explore these roles. These roles have different objectives or goals. For example, a player might be someone seeking to set up a session of play. At another time, the player might be someone wanting to know a cumulative score. At yet another time, a player might be someone wanting to learn the game. Each is a different role, and considering these different roles is important to the requirements effort.

When requirements fail to capture functionality that comprehensively addresses the needs of all customers, they are said to be *incomplete*. Generally, the design document for the game provides sections for the features of concern to all the key customers (or stakeholders), but as you elicit software requirements, it is easy to overlook features. To avoid incomplete requirements, develop use cases to ensure you have achieved completeness.

Feasibility

The *feasibility* of a requirement rests on whether the development group possesses the technical and budgetary capabilities to implement the functionality that the requirement stipulates. Technical capabilities stem from the expertise of the developers. Budgetary capabilities depend on a number of factors not discussed here, but one general way of putting it is to say that even if the expertise exists to develop the solution, the money to pay for the development might not. To determine whether a system meets technical and budgetary constraints, managers must possess a clear statement of requirements.

When requirements are clearly stated, development managers can more readily assess the three major feasibility (also called *risk*) factors that every project faces:

- **The number of features.** If you want to create a game with lots of features, then you might be willing to take as much time and to spend as much money as is needed to add the features. Still, even if you have plenty of time and money, you must consider the maximum number of features you can realistically expect to implement and test.

- **The amount of money.** If money is a factor, then you obviously need to limit the number of features. Each feature adds to the expense of the project, and in addition to construction alone, you must pay for quality assurance (testing). If you release a system that has been inadequately tested, the consequences can be painful.
- **The quality of the product.** If you want to produce a product that has the maximum degree of quality, then cost and feature count might not be high on your priority list. It remains, however, that you will have more time and money to spend on the quality of each feature if you limit the number of features.

Features, cost, and quality are feasibility factors that you can understand if you know the scope of the system. Figure 2.4 shows the basic relationship among these three factors.

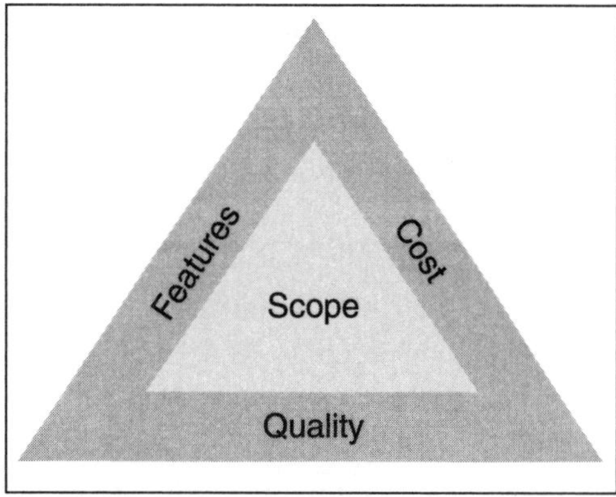

Figure 2.4
Requirements feasibility involves cost, number, and quality.

Uncontrolled Growth

Many software development efforts fail because software developers do not adhere to the requirements specifications as they develop the software. Two major risks in this respect are *feature creep* and *goldplating*. One especially troublesome outcome of feature creep and goldplating is that the testing effort becomes more difficult because the test team might not have test cases or scenarios for the added features. Such untested features might be the cause of problems when the product is deployed. The following sections describe these two types of risk in greater detail.

Avoid Feature Creep

Feature creep occurs when developers, customers, or managers add features to a project even though the scope of the project has already been set. This happens in two general ways. One form occurs when you begin to engineer the requirements list. You can discover features that you add because you think they make the product more interesting. For example, if the game design document lists what you consider a rather bland set of character options, you might decide to add extra options to make the basic list more interesting. Other people might add still more options. In this way, you extend the *specified* features of the game beyond what the designers asked for.

The other form of creep occurs after development begins. Although the specification might state clearly the requirements you are to implement, you extend the requirements as you work when you find something that seems to enhance the game. You add unspecified functionality. Although the functionality specified in the requirements remains the same, the implemented functionality grows. New features result from unspecified work on the product, but the specified product is not more complete.

Avoid Goldplating

Goldplating occurs when developers develop the technology they want to develop rather than the product the requirements specify. Goldplating undermines the development effort because while developers make the game interesting from a technical perspective, they drive the implementation costs of the game sky high. Developers might even fail to implement the features that the requirements specify. Goldplating begins when a programmer finds an interesting innovation on one or another path of implementation that begins with a requirement. Rather than seeking only to implement the requirement, the programmer becomes obsessed with exploring the implementation process itself in something akin to a sophisticated hacking experiment.

What Makes a Good Requirements Specification?

During the requirements engineering phase of the development effort, you create a set of requirements and prepare the way for the design effort. The first sign that you have not successfully completed the requirements is that the design effort becomes bogged down in *rework.* Rework requires that those involved in the design effort eliminate flaws in work performed earlier in the project. What makes a good requirements specification? The answer is that after the design effort begins, you find that you can work steadily from the requirements without having to correct or update them.

Most authorities state that if a set of requirements possesses eight basic qualities, then the success of the development project that follows from them is likely to succeed. Figure 2.5 provides a high-level view of these qualities. The following sections present a bit more detail.

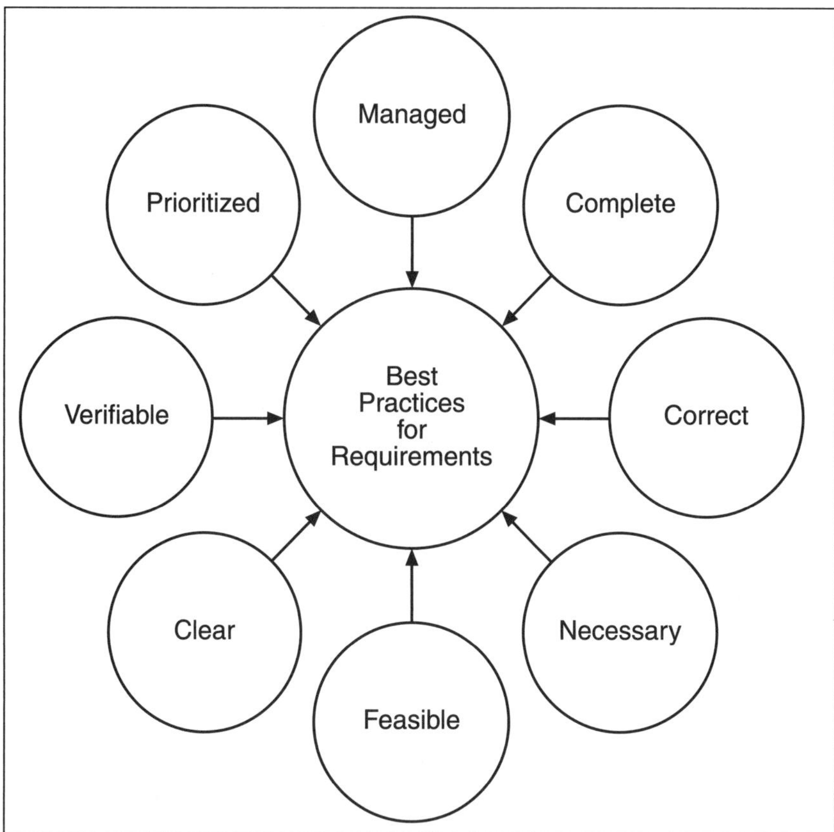

Figure 2.5
Seek quality in requirements engineering.

Make Requirements Complete

To be complete, a set of requirements establishes the scope of the project and states the functionality that must be implemented to reach this scope. Nothing is left out. To achieve this goal, you should explore requirements so that you can see how they relate to each other. The most ready means of exploring requirements is to employ use case scenarios. The goal is to find gaps. Stating a set of requirements without exploring them using use cases might result in gaps, and gaps are costly.

Make Requirements Correct

Correctness has to do with whether the requirement provides the developer with the information needed to implement the stated feature. For this reason, as you elicit requirements, it is important to use different models and views of the product you want to build to ensure that you arrive at the appropriate level of precision for the requirement. Making a list of what you think will need to be implemented does not do the job. Instead, it is a good idea to reduce the complexity of the product and sort out what needs to be implemented. You can't think of everything at once. You must analyze, decompose, and explore the features of the product before you can come to understand how to build it. A requirement is correct when the resulting system behavior supports the feature that the requirement addresses. An incorrect requirement leads to system behavior that does not support the feature that the requirement addresses. Add to this the fact that the cost of a system increases if a problem with a requirement is discovered after a feature has been implemented, for then it might be necessary to do everything over.

Necessary Requirements Only

As you will see when this book explores the narrative analysis approach to requirements, almost any phase of requirements elicitation begins with a set of *provisional* statements. What makes these statements provisional is that some of them will be eliminated. If you do not eliminate redundancies during the requirements engineering phase of your project, you end up dealing with them once again at the design phase. The number of problems then increases. In the requirements phase, everything is open to debate and is fairly easily changed. In contrast, during the design phase, the complexity of the product increases. If you have begun design work for an inessential feature, after a time you are bound to discover your mistake. If you have developed a number of design features that need to be reworked when you decide to remove the redundant feature, you might easily fall behind schedule. When unnecessary requirements are not questioned during the requirements analysis phase, they cause unnecessary complexity during the design and construction phases.

The more you explore the relationships among objects, the more you discover how functionality can be duplicated. When you have made such discoveries, you *refine* or *eliminate* requirements. The process is *iterative* and *incremental.* In other words, you write a requirement as a tentative statement. You explore the requirement using different tools, such as use cases and activity diagrams. Tools help you understand the requirement so that you can rewrite it with greater precision.

Consider the Feasibility of a Requirement

Earlier, feasibility was discussed in the context of the scope of a game. When you include a requirement in a requirements specification, your inclusion brings with it an associated *risk.* The risk goes in the two directions mentioned in the discussion of scope: project feasibility and technical feasibility. Project feasibility has to do with whether you have the time and money needed to implement the feature. Technical feasibility concerns whether the technology you are working with makes it possible to implement the feature. (Chapter 8, "Risk Analysis," investigates risk analysis in detail.)

Generally, each requirement should be subjected to the following question: Can this be implemented? In other words, do you have the time, technology, and testing capabilities necessary to ensure that the feature is implemented *responsibly* and *robustly*? If not, then you might want to remove the feature from the list. Risk has much to do with how you prioritize requirements.

Requirement Priorities

Even if you have fully developed a list of requirements, you are not finished yet. You must evaluate the list to discover, first, which requirements are on the *critical path*. In other words, which requirements support features that are absolutely necessary if the game is to be delivered? Next, you must decide what constitutes a *desired* but unessential feature. Such requirements support features of the game that make it more interesting or marketable than it might be otherwise but are not necessary for it to be released. Still other requirements can be regarded as *secondary*. Secondary requirements support features that can be implemented either as an upgrade or during a subsequent release.

Secondary features possess value because they provide momentum for future development efforts. They can also be the basis of a scheduled product upgrade. If you plan accordingly, you can reuse requirements to implement secondary features during a subsequent release. You are able to begin where you left off.

Eliminate Ambiguity

Ambiguity has to do with whether a single requirement is stated clearly or whether two (or more) requirements can be distinguished. Consider the following two statements:

> *The player shall be able to exit the game at any time.*
>
> *The player shall be able to choose to exit the game at any time.*

Are these statements the same? What are they asking for? It is not the job of the developer to either have to guess or to state the obvious. If a question remains to be asked, it is the responsibility of those who elicit the requirements to ask the question.

Verify and Validate Requirements

All requirements should be validated and verified. These activities involve using use cases and other tools to make the requirements visible in the behavior of the product. This behavior is what the customer expects. Even if a requirement does not strike you as something that can be shown to exist or to work properly, it is possible to set up *test scenarios* in which, either directly or by inference, it can be shown that a given requirement meets the needs of the customer.

note

Verification in general means confirming that the system possesses a feature or requirement. Validation tries to ascertain that a feature correctly provides what the user expects or needs.

Manage Requirements for Change

Requirements must be placed under change control. (See Chapter 10, "Control Freaks and Configuration Management," for a detailed discussion of change control.) As you proceed with your development effort, requirements might change. You track the changes in the SRS by noting how you have changed requirements. In addition, you can use a *requirements matrix.* The matrix allows you to track the status of each requirement. It allows you to see the use cases and test cases that are related to each requirement. It also allows you to trace each requirement to design features (which Chapter 4 deals with).

More extensive issues related to managing requirements are covered in the discussion of software configuration management. (See Chapter 10.) A number of techniques for control, storage, and retrieval of documents and source code come into play.

Engineering Requirements

In this section, you begin the work of moving through a requirements engineering process. One theme developed throughout this book is that you develop a software system *iteratively* and *incrementally.* Requirements engineering works like all other activities involved in software engineering.

Iterative Increments

When you engineer requirements, you face a number of problems. The best approach to solving these problems is to regard requirements engineering as both *incremental* and *iterative.*

In the requirements engineering phase of a project, you visit a requirement many times. For example, you start with a statement culled from a discussion of the game design document. You formulate the requirement and make it a tentative part of the SRS. Days later, you might revisit the requirement and analyze it using a use case. When you examine the requirement through the use case, you might find that its first formulation was limited or defective. You reshape the requirement to accord with the new understanding that your analysis reveals.

In this way, you develop the requirement both iteratively and incrementally. Visited at different stages of the requirements effort, the requirement is examined iteratively. Examined and changed in the light of a growing body of knowledge, the requirement is reformulated incrementally. You engage in the two activities together to gradually refine the requirement.

Cycles of Requirements Development

The development of a set of requirements proceeds incrementally and iteratively. The approach that this text proposes involves four increments—which can be called *phases*— and any number of iterations. The four phases are open to adaptation and are not offered as a methodology. (See Chapter 16, "Process Improvement.") The phases reflect a model used by many companies and presented in many requirements engineering texts. Table 2.2 presents the phases with brief descriptions. Figure 2.6 indicates how they might be viewed as a process flow.

Table 2.2 Requirements Engineering Phases

Phase	Description
Elicitation	Gather information about the requirements from the game design document and other sources. Use information drawn from a game that provides components that are to be brought into the current effort. Create a first draft of the software requirements specification.
Exploration	Create a candidate list of use cases. Create an initial list of requirements. The first use case to be created should be the game context use case. The next case should be the sixty-second scenario. Update the SRS.
Analysis	Develop use cases based on the candidate list. Start with the list of requirements and test for completeness and validity. Add use cases and requirements. Generate a test case for each use case.
Refinement	Prioritize the requirements you generate. Create a requirements matrix. Refine requirements language. Refine test cases. Update the SRS.

The elicitation phase begins with the layout of the SRS, the review of the game narrative, and the incorporation of concepts or elements from a mod. The IEEE SRS template is good to use because it provides a convenient way to centralize the activity of the requirements engineering effort. Use cases can be appended to the requirements document. A matrix can be also be appended, and through the matrix, requirements and uses cases can be traced to the test plan.

Next comes the exploration phase, which involves developing candidate use cases and requirements. Using a task-object-remarks table, you can find relationships among objects, requirements, and use cases that help you eliminate unnecessary requirements and prioritize those that remain.

During the analysis phase, you seek to develop the details of requirements and to discover gaps that your initial pass through the candidate lists might have left open. This phase allows you to develop use cases that are detailed enough to show you how to test requirements. As you prepare test material, you can also establish criteria to use to validate requirements.

In the refinement phase, you determine the priorities and dependencies of your use cases and requirements. You baseline the requirements and use cases for inclusion in the software requirements specification, and you place the information you possess in a requirements traceability matrix.

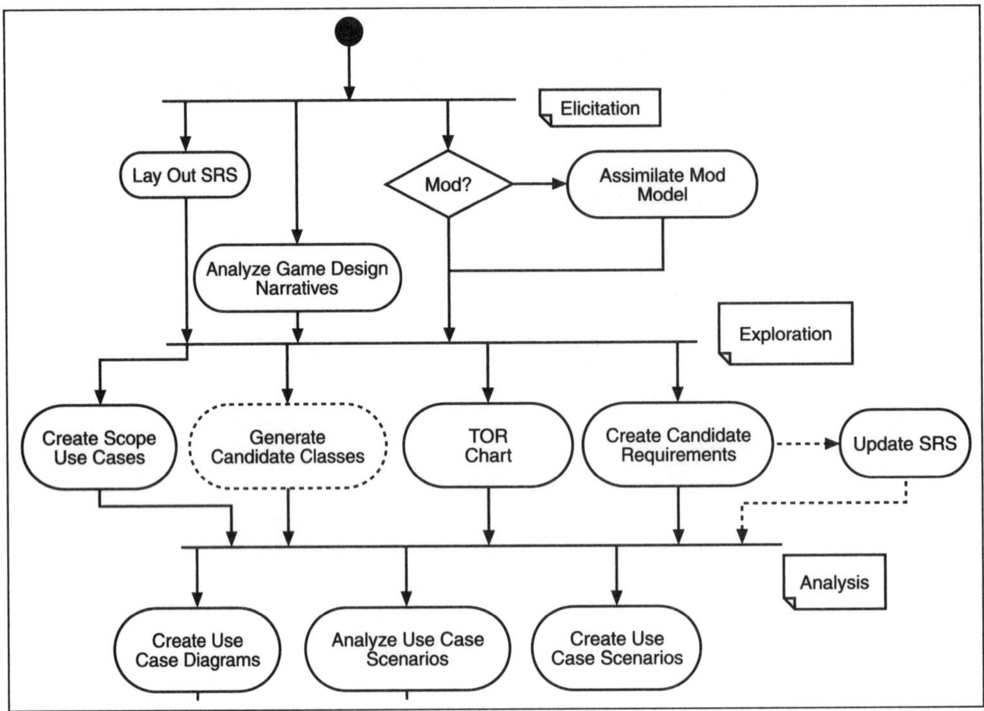

Figure 2.6
Requirements engineering iterates through different types of activity.

Eliciting Requirements

Figure 2.7 provides an overview of the activities that are involved in eliciting requirements.

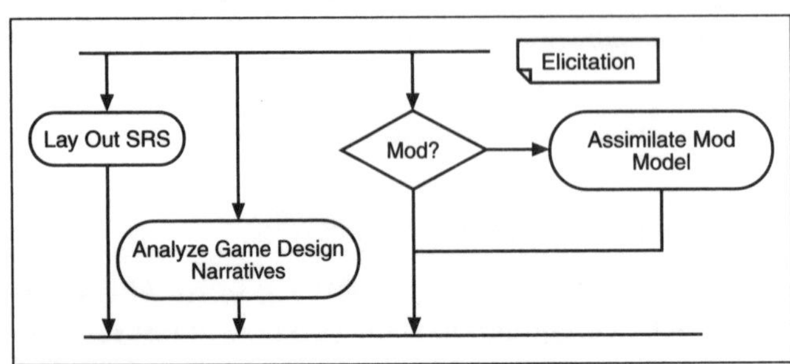

Figure 2.7
Explore requirements using different approaches.

When you elicit requirements, your main tasks are to lay out the requirements document and to begin bringing forward any components from previous games that you think you want to use. Further, you analyze the game design document to discover the scope of the game.

The Requirements Specification Document

The most essential artifact involved in the requirements engineering effort is the SRS. This, together with use cases, is usually the primary *deliverable* of the requirements analysis phase of the software engineering effort. Although it is the end product, it is also a document that you first draft at the start of the requirements phase. As you work through the requirements engineering process, you rewrite this document and use it as the central focus of your development effort.

This section examines the SRS document in detail. (Appendix D provides a sample SRS.) It begins with an overview of the steps used to develop an SRS. These steps are based on the process put in place for development of *Ankh.*

The SRS Template

The first phase of activity shown in Figure 2.7 involves laying out the SRS. To lay out the SRS, you begin with a template, preferably one that you base on the *IEEE Standard 830.* Reasons to use the IEEE template are that it provides the most universally acknowledged template for software requirements specification, and is also open to modification. The description that the IEEE provides of the template continues for several pages, and one thing that you discover as you read it is that the IEEE allows you to use it as you deem necessary. Generally, the main requirement is that you preserve the general form. The template provides the following structure of information:

Table of contents

Introduction

1.1 Purpose

1.2 Scope

1.3 Definitions, acronyms, and abbreviations

1.4 References

1.5 Overview

Overall description

2.1 Product perspective

2.2 Product functions

- 2.3 User characteristics
- 2.4 Constraints
- 2.5 Assumptions and dependencies

Specific requirements

- 3.1 External interface requirements
  - 3.1.1 User interfaces
  - 3.1.2 Hardware interfaces
  - 3.1.3 Software interfaces
  - 3.1.4 Communications interfaces
- 3.2 Functional requirements
  - 3.2.1 Subsystem A name
    - 3.2.1.1 Requirement statement—
    - 3.2.1.2 Requirement statement—
  - 3.2.2 Subsystem B name
    - 3.2.21.2 Requirement statement—
    - 3.2.21.2 Requirement statement—
- 3.3 Performance requirements
  - 3.2.1 Standards
  - 3.2.1 Hardware limitations
- 3.4 Design constraints
  - 3.2.1 Availability
  - 3.2.1 Security
  - 3.2.1 Maintainability
- 3.6 Other requirements

Appendixes

Index

Table 2.3 reviews the sections of the SRS. You can find an example of the SRS for *Ankh* in Appendix D. Generally, every project should customize the template to eliminate parts that are not needed. Ignore parts of the template that have no applicability to your development style.

Table 2.3 Topics of the SRS Specifically Described

Section	Description*
Table of contents	If you set up your document as a FrameMaker, Word, or WordPerfect document, this will be taken care of automatically.
Introduction purpose	State why the product is to be created. In other words, the product furthers a given product line, seeks to explore a given type of technology, provides a given service, or exploits a given market sector.
Scope	State the general constraints that apply to the system. For example, the game is an RPG for a standalone personal computer with a single-user interface.
Definitions, acronyms, and abbreviations	Provide a heading and a brief introductory sentence; then make a definition list of every technical term, abbreviation, or acronym you use in your document. Add to this as you go. It is a good idea to put the terms in bold and to alphabetize them.
References	At a bare minimum, list references to the design document, the test plan, the project plan, and the game design document. What is a reference? Basically, it is the document name, the document number, and the document date. The date might not be relevant, but you should always seek to identify documents that are current with the requirements. You can supplement the references with hyperlinks.
Overview	This can consist of a narrative, a context diagram, or other elements. You can use this section in a number of ways. For example, if you use a context diagram, you can show general subsystems. Provide a general system view of the product that anticipates the details you offer in section 3, "Specific requirements." Make reference to section 3.
Overall description	A document division heading that the IEEE provides. Use it if you need it.
Product perspective	In this section, you explain, for example, that the game is based on a game design document. (In this case, it's the game design document for *Ankh*). You explain the genre of the game—an RPG for standalone personal computer users, for example. If the game is a mod, you identify and explain the extent to which its components or conceptual framework originates with the mod. You also briefly explain how the game works. For example, a single player guides a character through seven levels of combat to seek a final goal. From this section, the reader gains a sense of the derivation, intent, and interactive goals of the product.

(continued on next page)

Table 2.3 Topics of the SRS Specifically Described (continued)

Section	Description*
Product functions	Break the system into its general subsystems, if possible. The subsystems contain classes. The classes provide services, such as Graphical User Interface (GUI) interactivity, Artificial Intelligence (AI), and file save capabilities. Generally, then, you report that the system has anywhere from a few to, say, a dozen basic types of functionality, and you label these types of functionality in anticipation of your high-level system diagram.
User characteristics	Profile the player of the game. For example, the game is designed for players in their teens or older. The levels of complexity range from rank beginner to advanced. If you think that players of a given game will like this one, then draw the comparison here. If you have access to a marketing document or a game design document, then you can draw on it to fill out this section.
Constraints	State what you know about the limitations that apply to the game. For example, it is a single-player game that *cannot* be extended to multiplayer or Internet use. The game should not be expected to run satisfactorily on computers with less than a given performance rating or, on the other hand, will run best on computers that meet specific performance ratings.
Assumptions and dependencies	Explain, for instance, that development of the system depends on the use of DirectX and Win32 functions. Explain, for example, that you are using a given installation package.
Specific requirements	A document division heading that the IEEE provides. Use it if you need it.
External interface requirements	A document division heading that the IEEE provides. Use it if you need it.
User interfaces	User interfaces include interactions (for a PC game) with the keyboard, a mouse, or a joy stick (to name a few). User interfaces also include screens or menus. You can point to an appendix for examples of interfaces. Another approach is to provide a reference to the game design document, where screen shots or mockups might be available.
Hardware interfaces	State whether you need a modem, a joy stick, or anything else to play the game. Identify the standard, if any, that applies to the device. If the system uses stereo sound, say so here. If it plays movies, say that, also.
Software interfaces	State whether the game depends on other software and state the dependency specifically. For instance, the game requires Windows XP.

Section	Description*
Communications interfaces	State here if the game requires a modem or other devices. You can also specify minimum transfer rates.
Functional requirements	A document division heading that the IEEE provides. Use it if you need it.
Subsystem name	Break up requirements according to the subsystem or component to which they apply. You might have to wait a while before you can accomplish this task. It is usually not possible until you have created a high-level design context diagram. When you do this, create abbreviations or codes for each subsystem and prefix them to the requirements number.
Requirement statement	Use statements that specify the requirements. You might want to vary this approach, however. As shown in the SRS in Appendix D, state each requirement and number it. Do not try to list, for example, classes or objects. Provide use cases and other artifacts to supplement requirements statements. Hundreds of requirements statements might appear under a given subsystem. For this reason, you'll find that the IEEE form of specification inevitably becomes disproportionately large in section 3, where the functional requirements appear.
Performance requirements	State the constraints that apply to your game. Performance relates to the performance of the software. If you have set specific requirements for how fast levels should take to appear, then you can state them here.
Standards	If you are developing the game for export or introduction into a specific market, then state the specific standards with which the game must comply.
Hardware limitations	State the hardware limitations that apply to your game. State at least the minimum system requirements. This includes the performance of the machine, the graphics card, and Internet capabilities.
Design constraints	A document division heading that the IEEE provides. Use it if you need it.
Availability	Availability for a standalone computer that runs on a PC is a fairly straightforward proposition, so you need to say only that the game is available to the system user at all times. On the other hand, if the game has Internet dependencies and load or operational factors limit the time the user can access the network, then you can state such limitations here.
Security	State whether the system includes security measures, such as passwords, and whether the system presents security risks.

(continued on next page)

Table 2.3 Topics of the SRS Specifically Described (continued)

Section	Description*
Maintainability	State whether and how the system can be modified—upgraded or fixed.
Other requirements	If anything outside the previous exhaustive litany occurs to you, put it here.
Appendixes	You can include appendixes for use cases and a requirements matrix.
Index	This is optional unless you have a technical writer around who is an expert at generating indexes. Word, WordPerfect, and FrameMaker make it easy for you to create an index even if you are not a technical writer.

*The template here is based on the version of the IEEE template developed by Hans van Vliet, *Software Engineering Principles and Practices*, Second Edition (New York: John Wiley & Sons, 2000), pp. 224–231.

Using the SRS Template

The way you set up your requirements document depends on the development style you adopt. It's good to use the template as a starting point. Section 3 is the most important part of the template, and as mentioned before, this section is used to list requirements statements. An appendix is then used to state corresponding use cases for many of the requirements listed in section 3. Examine the SRS in Appendix D for an example of how to create the primary document.

Using the Design Document for the Game

The documentation for your project depends on how your organization or group sets up your game development project. (See Chapter 18, "Documentation—Learning How to Learn," for more discussion on this topic.) Generally, before the engineering effort begins, the game designers finalize the *game design document.* The game design document is not an engineering document. Do not confuse it with the SRS. For a sample of a game design document, turn to Appendix D or see the documents on the CD.

It is assumed that you have a description of the game from which you can extract much of the basic information about the game. This information begins with two narratives. One tells about the game in a general way. This is the game summary. The other tells about what it is like to play the game. This is a sixty-seconds-of-play sequence. Until you have these two items in place, you have no way to establish the scope of the requirements effort. When you cannot establish the scope, as mentioned before, you cannot know when you have finished your task.

The Game Summary

The game summary is usually a part of the game design document. It might begin the document. Its length varies from a few paragraphs to many pages. It describes the game as a product: theme, objective of play, audience, number of levels (if applicable), type, number of players, strategic points, and so on. From the game summary, you derive a clear concept of what you will have to do, generally, to create the game.

As an example of a game summary, consider a paragraph from the game design document for *Ankh* drafted by designer John Rose:

> Ankh *follows the quest for vengeance undertaken by Sekhem, an Egyptian warrior determined to destroy those who defeated and killed his father. The game focuses on the battles fought by Sekhem and his party of rebel warriors on their journey to the Egyptian capital of Thebes. These conflicts escalate from skirmishes to bloody clashes as the band of adventurers cross the desert sands of ancient Egypt. Along the way, additional characters join the band and new enemies attempt to stop Sekhem's advance. Interaction involves tactical control of the small army during* Ankh*'s many mêlées, including strategic maneuvers, hand-to-hand combat, and spell casting.*
>
> *The player is faced with winning battle after glorious battle, driving Sekhem toward his final confrontation with Uheset, the bloodthirsty Queen of Egypt. Conflicts take place in real time, stressing the tactical and chaotic aspect of warfare. Each level possesses its own ambiance and strategy, from the barren plains of Thebes to the lush splendor of the Dashur gardens.*
>
> *The graphics of* Ankh *illustrate the varied and stylish architecture and landscapes of ancient Egypt. The game's music varies from haunting chants to blood-quickening battle drums. All aspects of the game's art and sound immerse the player in the primal rage of ancient warfare.*

What you derive from this passage begins with looking closely at the nouns. Note that you see such terms as *battle, player, Sekhem, additional characters, enemies, journey, tactical control, strategic maneuvers, chants, drums, music,* and *sound.* Working with this list, you can begin to identify the general scope of the game. For example, the game has a player, not players, and it has a single main character, Sekhem. Additional characters are identified as enemies. There is a journey, which implies the existence of several scenes in which different battles take place. In every battle, players scheme and maneuver to achieve victory. Note likewise that the game offers chants, sounds, and music. And it is evident that there is a winning battle.

The pattern of the game might be stated explicitly. You might recognize this as an RPG or a strategy game. You might also begin to think of many features of games you have already developed that help you understand from the start how this game might be laid out. For example, you might envision real-time or turn-based actions. Such notions possess great value, but at this point, it remains important to resist talking about how you intend to implement the game. The main goal is to derive an idea of what the general scope of the game is. The outer scope should already be falling into place.

The Play Narrative

If the general game description helps you establish the outer scope, the sixty-seconds-of-play narrative helps you establish the inner scope. This narrative is a part of most game design documents, but it might be disguised in one way or another. For instance, you might have to extract it from the game description. Wherever you find it, you will be able to recognize it because it describes what it is like to play the game. Add to this that what it describes has a specific beginning, middle, and end (which Aristotle said any real story needs to have before it can be called a real story). If you have to create a sixty-seconds-of-play narrative for yourself, find someone who knows the game design and work with this person to envision a set of specific gameplay events.

As an example of a sixty-seconds-of-play narrative, consider a passage from the game design document for *Ankh* authored by programmers Ben Vinson and Carlos Villar:

> *When the sequence begins, the narrator reads the back story as the text of the story scrolls from the top to the bottom of the screen. General theme drawings appear in the background of the text. At the conclusion of back story display, the scrolling words and screen fade and the level-one world appears. This is Alexandria. Sehkem walks in from the edge of the map. As he walks, four guards appear ahead of him, blocking the way. The guards declare, "Give up your money!" At this point, the screen dims and the objective of the challenge appears. The screen shows words in the foreground. The message is, "Defeat all enemies." Music starts playing. The reader can hear the words read. The screen lasts two seconds before it begins to fade. Within five seconds, the screen has disappeared and the player again sees Sekhem. The guards approach. They bear short spears and shields. The guards jab with spears. Sekhem must engage each of the guards and kill him. If Sehkem does nothing, he is killed. (If you click on a guard, the character attacks that guard. If you click the right button, Sehkem moves or attacks. If you click the left button, you select.) Chases and attacks follow. A sound accompanies each slash of Sekhem's sword. Sekhem kills all the guards. When each guard is killed, a quiet death cry is heard. When the last guard is dead, the current level fades. The game auto-saves every twenty seconds.*

From the sixty-seconds-of-play narrative, you can begin to establish a fairly precise definition of the inner scope of the game. You can identify specific actions. For example, the main character appears in a setting and faces several enemies. Each enemy approaches, and the player must manipulate the character and kill the enemy. Music plays in the background, and before the battle begins, a narrative appears to tell the player the story leading to the scene. You also learn that to conduct battle, the player clicks the mouse, repositioning the cursor to move the character.

Using Mod Requirements

The title of this section might be a bit difficult to understand. It does not mean that you should go off to a file cabinet or some remote directory on your disk and retrieve a document in which you have made requirements for some components of a game you now want to use as the basis of a new game. On the other hand, you can reuse old games. With respect to the requirements effort, what you have done before can benefit you now because it provides you with a knowledge pattern. To use old components effectively, a few precautions are necessary:

- **Do not cut and paste.** This is not elicitation. It is cutting and pasting. Always start a new SRS and write it without cutting and pasting. Use the old document (if you have one) as a kind of template or reference.
- **Start with the view you have of the new game.** Carry this view back to the old game, somewhat as you might carry a flashlight into a dark place. What your new game allows you to see is legitimate.
- **View critically each notion you gain from a legacy specification.** Evaluate the worth of the old specification using ideas you derive from the context of your new game.

The requirements you will find most useful in a legacy game are those that pertain to the specification of outer-scope game engine features and outer-scope game genre features. For example, *Ankh* is a limited role-playing game with some strategy and action features. The game design document says that it will have a dialogue form of interaction. You know, then, that you will be bringing classes forward from a legacy game that has this same feature. You will not modify the requirements for this feature to any great extent because you don't need to. The strength of the game does not lie in the features of an existing game but rather in features added to the inner scope of the new game.

Preliminaries of Use Case Exploration

Use cases make it possible for you to successfully engineer requirements. Although this book prescribes no fixed method, it can offer a few points concerning how your effort can benefit from using use cases. The first point is that use cases should be regarded as tools or means, not as ends. If you employ use cases as tools, you use them whenever you require a convenient way to explore a problematic aspect of the system you are developing. You can also make use cases a formal part of your SRS, replacing the traditional statements with scenarios of use. Alternatively, you can adopt the approach provided here, one of listing the requirements in section 3 of the SRS and then including an appendix in which you provide use cases to supplement the stated requirements. Whatever approach you adopt, creating use cases allows you a convenient way to formally explore requirements.

A Narrative Template for Use Cases

A narrative use case is best described as a paragraph relating events that have a beginning, a middle, and an end. The beginning is sometimes called the *trigger*. The end is sometimes called the *goal* or *objective*. You can develop a template for a narrative use case as a document with headers, a table, or even a spreadsheet. (You can use SmartDraw—see Appendix D.) The narrative form of a use case should be characteristic of the initial iterations of your requirements-engineering effort, when you seek to establish the outer scope and play context of the game. Figure 2.8 provides a basic template for a narrative use case. The template has been filled in for demonstration purposes.

Use Case Name: Player Starts Game
Requirement(s) Explored: 1
Player (Actor) Context (Role): Player
Precondition(s): Game is installed and ready to play.
Trigger(s): Player selects game-start action.
Main Course of Action: The player selects the game-start action. The system requests that the player select a profile. The player selects a profile and the system loads it. After the system loads the profile, the system displays a message to the player that tells him that the play can begin. The player acknowledges the message that the system has displayed and begins playing.
Alternate Course(s) of Action: The player does not select a profile. The system chooses a default profile.The player does not start the game. The system asks the player if he wants to save his profile. If the player says yes, the system saves the profile.
Exceptional Course(s) of Action: The system crashes when the game begins.

Figure 2.8
Use narrative use cases for preliminary exploration.

A Scenario Template for Use Cases

A use case that includes a numbered scenario serves best for exploring functional requirements. The major difference between a narrative use case and a scenario use case is that the scenario divides the narrative into a numbered list and seeks to explore the actions involved in greater detail. Because this form of use case allows you to track exceptional and alternate courses of action, it is especially suited for tracing the level of detail that is necessary for the full exploration of functional requirements. Figure 2.9 shows a use case template for a numbered scenario.

Use Case Name: Player Starts Game
Requirement(s) Explored: 1
Player (Actor) Context (Role): Player
Precondition(s): Game is installed and ready to play.
Trigger(s): Player selects game-start action.
Main Course of Action: 1. The player selects the game-start action. 2. The system requests that the player select a profile. 3. The player selects a profile. 4. The system loads the profile. 5. The system displays a message to the player that tells him that play can begin. 6. The player acknowledges the message. 7. The player begins playing.
Alternate Course(s) of Action: 3a. The player does not select a profile. 3b. The system chooses a default profile. 6a. The player chooses to exit the game before playing. 6b. The system asks the player if he wants to save his profile. 6b1. If the player responds yes, the system saves the profile. 6b2. If the player responds no, the system exits without saving the profile. 6c. The system saves the profile. 6c1. The player chooses not to save the profile. 6d. The system exits.
Exceptional Course(s) of Action: 6a. The system crashes when the game begins. 6b. The player turns off the computer.

Figure 2.9
Employer scenario use case for requirements analysis and exploration.

Practices and Explanations

In Figures 2.8 and 2.9, the *main course of action* is the course of action that usually occurs. The *alternate courses of action* are those that diverge from the central course of action but do not represent failures of the game. The *exceptional courses of action* provide information that proves useful during test scenarios. You can relate use cases to each other through generalization or specialization (include) relationships and composition (extend) relationships. Use cases usually document less than 15 steps. If they become longer, you might want to reduce their scope and create more specific use cases. One use case can use one or more other use cases. If you want to indicate a connection, just name the use case in the step and underline it for emphasis.

Approaches to Using Use Cases

To expand a bit on the way that the use case templates featured in Figures 2.8 and 2.9 might be used, note that you have options. If you do not know what requirement to state, you can begin by imaging a *context of.* You can then relate the sequence of actions you think might unfold in this context as a use case. The use case helps you identify how the system must function if it is to support the sequence of actions.

You can follow inductive or deductive approaches to requirements discovery and refinement. The use case can serve as an inductive approach to requirements discovery if you collect details and from the details discover a requirement. You can also follow a deductive approach. In this instance, you might begin with a requirements statement and then write the use case as a way of seeing whether the requirement fits into a context of use the system provides. If it does, then you confirm the need for the requirement.

One of the central purposes of requirements exploration and refinement is *to teach yourself what it is that you want to build.* You must *learn about* the product. If completing use cases seems tedious, remember that every time a use case allows you to alter the wording of a requirement (if you use the approach offered here) or to spot a detail you did not at first recognize, it has done its job. The purpose of a use case is to force you to expand and refine your understanding of the system.

Exploration

Requirements exploration begins with trying to name the features that you must support. Your starting places are the narratives you have of the game, the many details about the game that the game specification document includes, and specifications from any legacy game that you want to use as the basis of the new game. Other sources of information might be at hand, of course. For example, you might turn to an expert user of the type of game you want to develop, or you might bring in notions that are wholly new and untried. During exploration, you are doing precisely what the word implies: You are looking around, investigating, prodding, trying to see in every candidate requirement whether you have found something you want to make a part of your game. Figure 2.10 illustrates some of your primary exploration tasks.

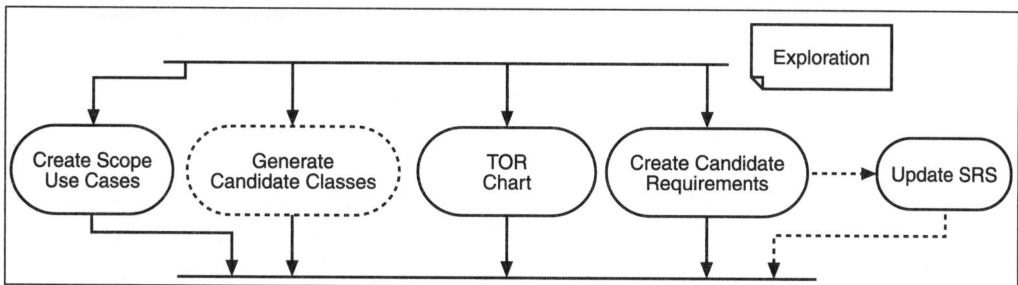

Figure 2.10
Exploration involves use cases and candidate requirements.

Using Use Case Diagrams and Scenarios

One of the first use cases to develop for a game is called the *context use case.* This use case more or less reflects the activity you find in the game summary portion of the game design document, but it excludes as much detail as possible. The goal of the context use case (represented here with a diagram) is to show the outer scope of the game. Other use cases can then be created to explore the inner scope of the game.

Figure 2.11 shows the context use case developed from a combination of the details provided in the game design document and the summary narrative given earlier. As you can see, the use case diagram conveniently summarizes the major occasions of player interaction with the game. It shows the start and end of the game. It also shows that the player can quit the game and restart it.

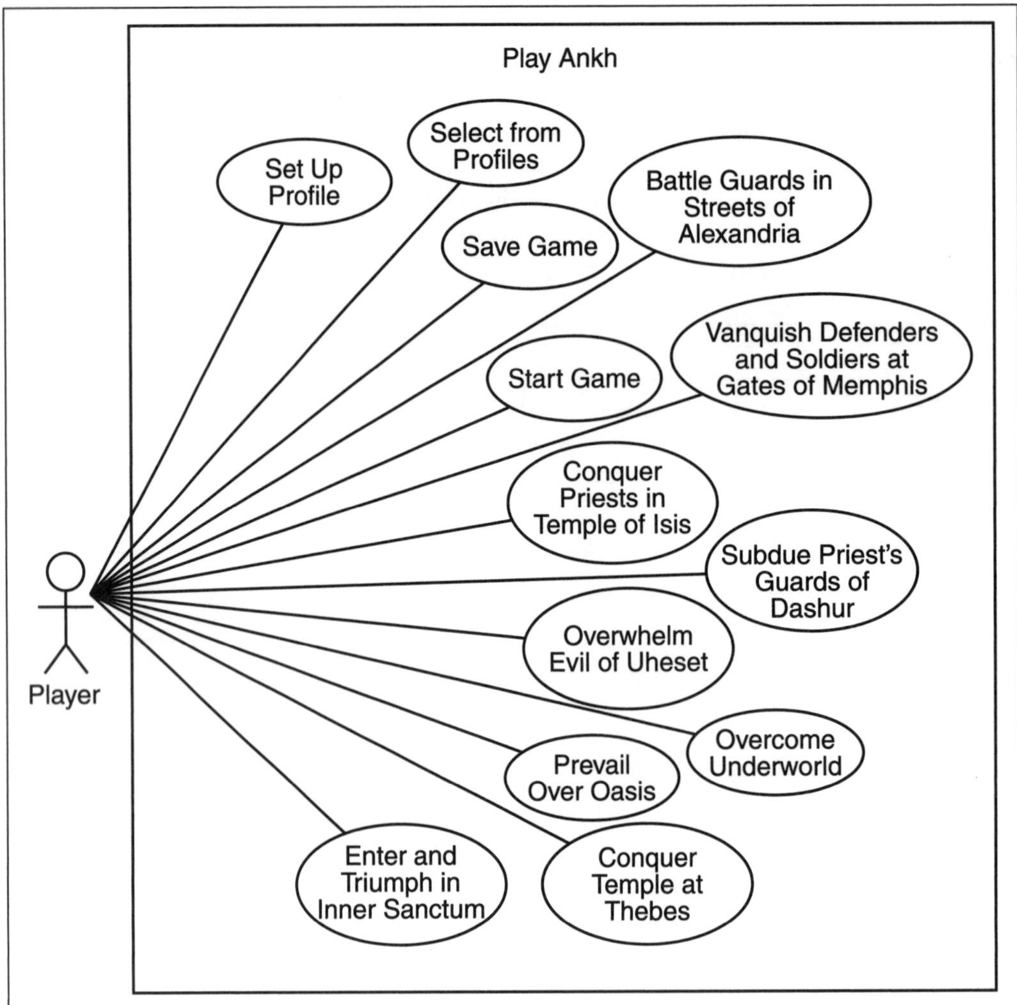

Figure 2.11
A use case context diagram helps scope the game.

The Sixty-Seconds-of-Play Use Case Diagram

Whereas you can establish the outer scope of the game with the game context use case diagram, you can establish the inner scope by creating a use case for the sixty-seconds-of-play narrative. Figure 2.12 shows one use case of several that you can create to capture the events given by sixty seconds of play. Note that even though the use case is selective and still fairly general in its detail, it still begins at a much more in-depth level than the game context diagram. You can unfold a dozen such use cases from the context diagram with relative ease.

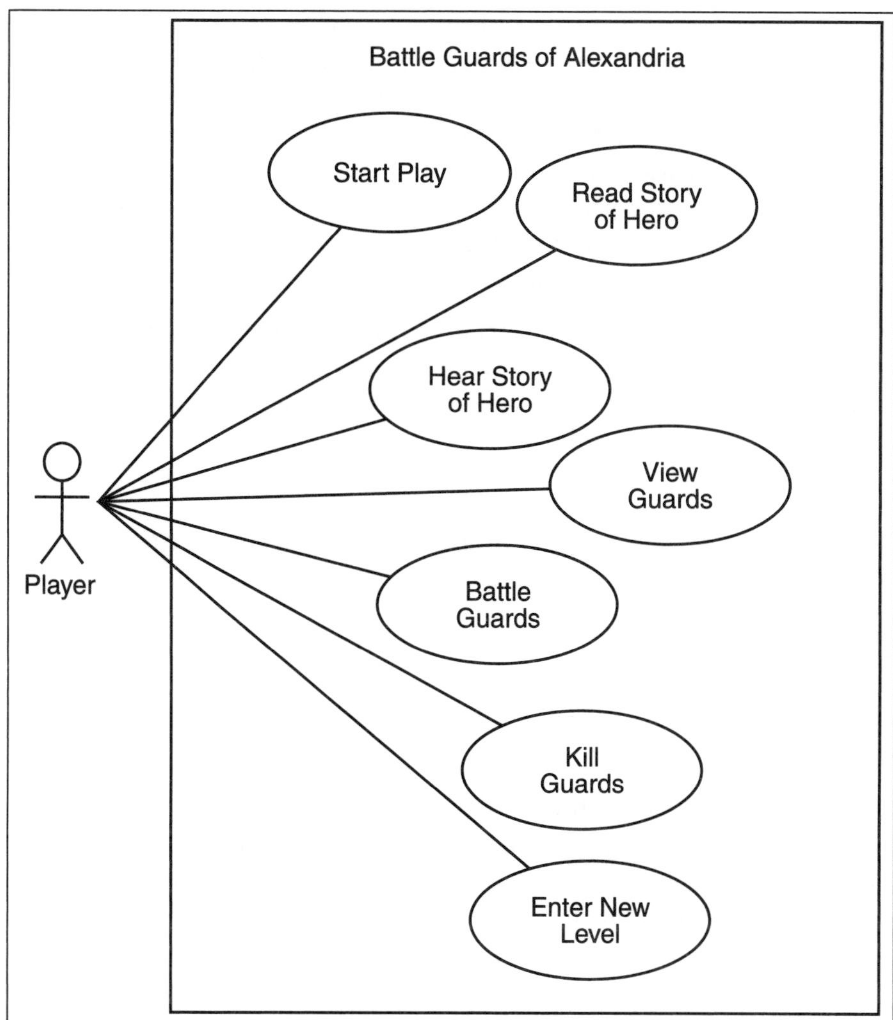

Figure 2.12
A use case diagram summarizes sixty seconds of play.

Making a Starting Specification List

From the start of your project, develop both use cases and a requirements list. Generally, developers either list requirements or use cases. It's best if you do both. You can begin listing your requirements in section 3 of the SRS, and you can record use cases in an appendix of the SRS. You can also maintain this as a separate document that you fold into the SRS as an appendix later on.

You can begin making requirements statements by making statements about what the system should do. Obviously, you can interview people. You can read the game design document over and over again. You can play the game you want to modify. Whatever you do, you formulate statements about what the game should do. You then begin a process of refining these statements. You must test to see whether the statements make sense and are complete. Use cases enable you to expand basic statements because they force you to place the basic statement in contexts of use. The context of use shows you whether the statement is valid or whether it implies that other things need to happen for it to occur.

When you begin to create sentences for your requirements document, word them in the active voice, use the verb "shall," and try to make them pertain to only one feature at a time. Try to use only two subjects—*player (user)* or *system (software)*. Avoid wording that conveys assumptions about implementation.

Here are a few requirements that might be generated from the previous use cases:

> *<Req_1> The software shall have the capability to save the game state from a menu.*
>
> *<Req_2> The software shall have the capability to return to a saved state by loading a file.*
>
> *<Req_3> The software shall have the capability to associate user profiles with saved game files.*

Notice how making a statement about the functionality of the system is a combination of analysis and guessing. The point is that you have to begin somewhere. If you write your statement as a requirement, you are suddenly in the position to begin refining the statement. The important thing is to *formally make the statement.*

After you make the statement, the hard part is over. Then refinement begins. You can make refinement easier if you take a little care up front about how you make your statements. There are a few problems with the statements presented earlier. For example, in requirement 1, the expression "from a menu" assumes implementation details. Likewise, "loading a file" in requirement 2 designates only a capability and yet calls for using a file. Requirement 2 also implies using a file. You can express the requirements more actively if you explicitly mention the player. Here are slightly reworded versions of the three statements given earlier:

> *<Req_1> The player shall have the capability to save the game state.*
>
> *<Req_2>The software shall have the capability to return to a saved state by loading saved information about the state.*
>
> *<Req_3> The software shall have the capability to associate user profiles with saved game information.*

These three candidate requirements are tentative. They are a first go at something that requires much work to refine. The next step for each requirement might be to create a use case to test the statement in a context of use. You begin with the narratives, find statements that summarize what you think the system should do, generate use cases to test the statements, and at last arrive at a full set of statements to describe the functionality that you observe. At first, the process is slow and painful, but as you fall into a pattern of work, you pick up speed.

Finding Potential Class Names

From the start, the assumption is that you are using object-oriented programming techniques. For this reason, you will be using classes to encapsulate the behavior your requirements specify. You should try to name classes during the requirements exploration phase. This chapter provides a few ways to do this. Classes are generic names you apply to the services you want to create. The sooner you can begin thinking about general ways to name collections of functionality, the better. On the other hand, it is important to keep in mind that the purpose of requirements exploration is to explore requirements, not to start the design effort. (See Chapter 4 for detailed discussions of design.)

Two approaches to discovering candidate classes are as follows:

- Analyze narratives for nouns that might qualify as class names.
- Search candidate requirements for prospective classes. In this case, it is assumed that you might be bringing legacy material into play.

You have already glimpsed what is involved in picking through a narrative to find nouns. After you have created a list of nouns, you can proceed to analyze the list to discover whether the nouns can be generalized. For example, if you find nouns such as *priest, guard, minstrel, dancer,* and *merchant,* you can probably arrive without too much trouble on a summary noun, such as *character.* You are then in a position to imagine contexts in which a character can be used. This helps you with both your requirement statement and a tentative name for a class.

In the approach shown here, both the requirements statement and the narrative analysis approach are used to find candidate classes. You can begin naming classes fairly early in the game. When you generate class names from requirements statements, the best approach is to use a TOR chart to explore the initial usefulness of the names.

Using a TOR Chart

A TOR chart provides an immediate way to explore the validity of a candidate requirement. Figure 2.13 illustrates a TOR chart for two of the previous requirements. The concepts behind a TOR chart are pretty simple. In the left column, you can write the requirement in full or substitute the number with which you designate the requirement. In the

Task column, state the requirement as a task. In other words, anticipate the basic function that the requirement seems to call for. What do you need to accomplish?

The next column might seem a little odd. As has been noted, it's good to push ahead with object-oriented thinking as early as possible. For this reason, there is a tentative Objects column. You can use this column as an opportunity to try to name the collection of functionality that you think will answer your requirement. In Figure 2.13, for example, the requirement to save the game might be met with an object called SaveGame. This need not be anything definite at this point, but you can still take a first shot at creating a name.

You can go even further. In the Remarks column, you can say what you think the tentatively named object might accomplish relative to the task you have named.

When you create the TOR chart, everything is flexible. Even if you feel as though you are making up names and classes, you are still moving in the right direction.

Requirements(s)	Task(s)	Object(s)	Remarks
1	Saving game	GameState	1. Initialize game state 2. Save changes
		Replay	1. Use game state 2. Play slower 3. Return to main menu
		Action	1. Track character interactions 2. Track map interactions 3. Receive action updates
2	Restore game settings	GameState	1. Load game state data 2. Apply instant changes

Figure 2.13
A TOR chart allows you to tentatively name requirements and candidate classes.

Analysis

Analysis is sometimes used to designate the entire process of requirements engineering. Here, analysis is used to designate the activity of subjecting candidate requirements to fairly intensive procedures that reveal weaknesses, redundancies, and gaps. The primary artifacts of this phase of activity are use case diagrams, use case scenarios, and activity diagrams. If you have begun work on a TOR chart, it might also be a deliverable of this phase. The emphasis, however, should be on perfecting the requirements though use cases and activity diagrams. Figure 2.14 reviews activities of analysis.

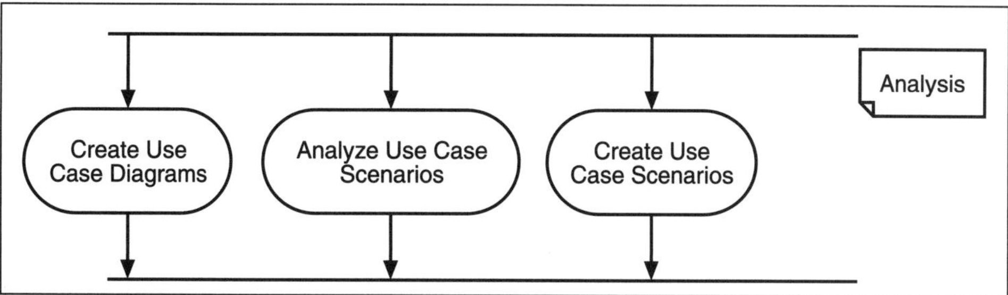

Figure 2.14
Analysis refines requirements and explores relations.

Using Use Cases to Analyze Actions

You analyze a requirement after you have initially formulated it based on the information you have elicited during the first phase of requirements engineering. Analysis of a requirement involves searching the wording of the requirement to see whether it contains the information the developers require to construct the feature that the requirement specifies. Analysis also involves examining whether the requirement depends on other requirements or should be broken down into further requirements.

One approach to analyzing a requirement is to place it in the context of play. You can then break down the context of play into a sequence of actions, and with the sequence of actions, you can generate a use case. At times, you might find that the context of play has a number of alternative paths. One path occurs most often. Analysts refer to this central path as the *basic course of events* or *happy* path. Analysts refer to other paths as *alternate* and *exceptional* paths. An alternate path is one that differs from the basic course of events but presents no problems. An exceptional path is a path in which a problem occurs. Exceptional paths are essential in the development of *test cases.*

To proceed with the analysis, you start with a use case scenario and work through the sequence of events that the scenario captures. As you go, your goal is to discover in what ways the requirement might imply dependencies, represent redundancies, inadequately cover the actions present, or fail to make sense. If the requirement does not cover the action, others should. If others do not, you have found a gap. Consider the scenario illustrated in Figure 2.15.

Use Case Name: Track Player Play
Requirement(s) Explored: 1, 2
Player (Actor) Context (Role): Player playing
Precondition(s): Game started.
Trigger(s): Timer issues message.
Main Course of Action: 1. The player plays the game. 2. The game tracks each action the player performs. 3. The player stops the action. 4. The player requests a replay of the action. 5. The system replays the action. 6. The action replay ends. 7. The player resumes play.
Alternate Course(s) of Action:
Exceptional Course(s) of Action:

Figure 2.15
A use case scenario traces a sequence of events.

In this case, you are analyzing requirements that specify features that allow the user to save the state of the game and play it back (listed above as requirements 1 and 2). The scenario allows you to view each requirement in a context of use. The scenario traces a series of events from beginning to end. When you trace the series of events, you are seeking both to confirm the need of the requirement and to see whether it covers the actions listed. Does the requirement need to be reworded to cover the actions in the scenario? What other requirements are necessary? Are the other requirements specified? Is a requirement missing? Does the requirement still make sense now that you have placed it in a scenario in which it has been conceptually tested?

Although most people prefer to write scenarios, some people use diagrams to start things out. Diagrams allow you to capture actions you think might belong to the scenario without having to figure out from the start exactly when they occur. Figure 2.16 shows a use case diagram with these events.

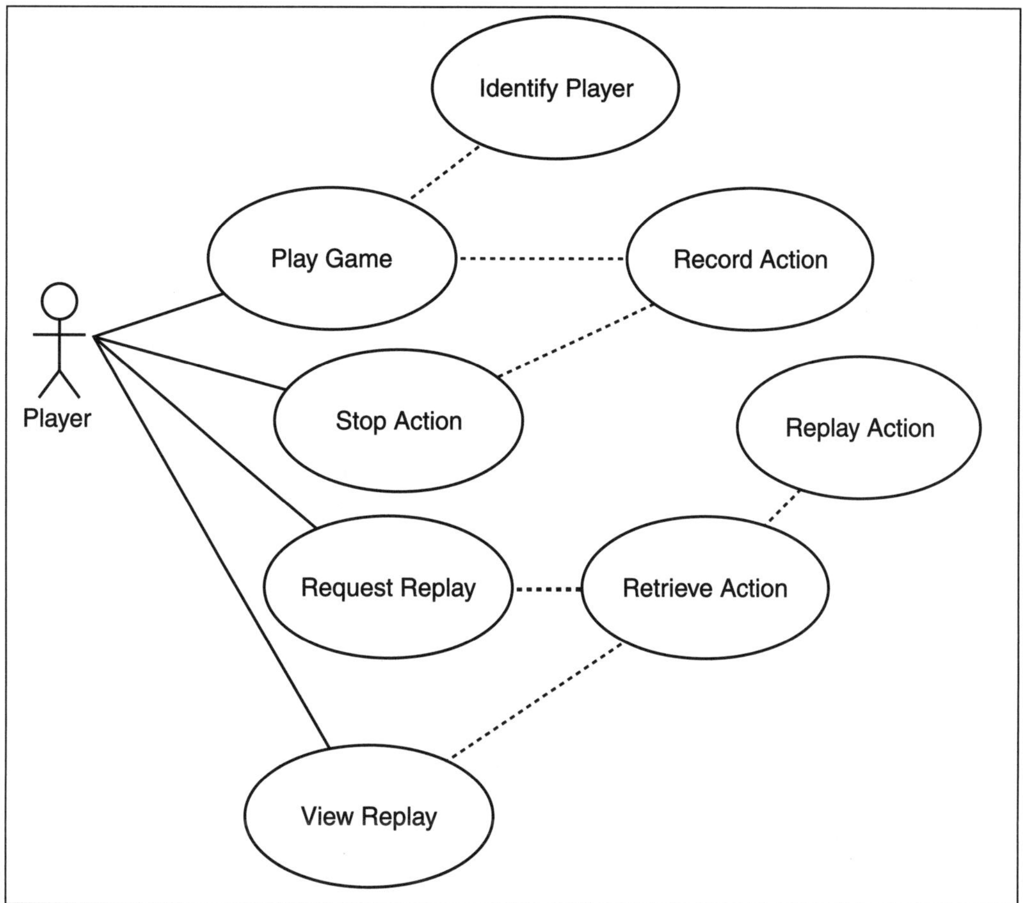

Figure 2.16
Use a use case diagram to explore relations.

Let's consider again the wording of one of the requirements:

> *The player shall be able to replay game actions.*

Using the scenario in Figure 2.15 and the diagram in Figure 2.16, you can extract several angles of functionality from the wording of the requirement. A few are as follows:

- The player interacts with the view of the game.
- The player plays the game according to the player's profile.
- The system records the player's play.
- The system allows information about actions to be stored.
- The system coordinates activities involved in stopping, starting, and replaying the action.

As it develops a requirement, the development team does not attempt to name the specific interface features that support the requirement. Rather, the point of the analysis is to investigate what type of behavior must be supported and to examine whether the named requirement does, indeed, have a context of use and accounts for this use without having to be reworded. It also allows you to see whether it's necessary to add requirements. Likewise, if you were to find that two requirements generate the same scenario, then you might want to eliminate one of the requirements.

Activity Diagrams

If you cannot understand how a sequence of events unfolds, you can use an activity diagram to supplement a use case. The activity diagram allows you to view how action flows from one event to another. The activity diagram is especially useful if you want to capture simultaneous actions—something that a regular flow chart does not allow you to do. (Chapter 3 provides a detailed discussion of action diagrams.) Figure 2.17 shows how the events represented in the use case shown in Figure 2.16 can be illustrated with an action diagram. As simple as it is, the diagram forces you to specifically identify the order of the actions that make up the scenario.

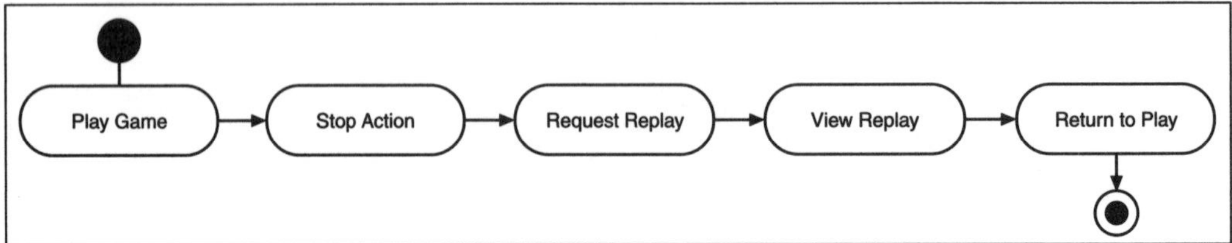

Figure 2.17
You can use an activity diagram to analyze the flow of use case events.

Refinement, Verification, and Validation

Refinement involves tuning the requirements list so that dependencies and priorities become visible. Likewise, refinement is closely associated with verifying and validating requirements. At this point, you can also put in place some formal measures for baselining requirements. A requirements matrix is a handy tool for keeping track of most of the information that emerges during the refinement phase.

When you *verify* requirements, you check to make certain that you are building the system in the right way. When you *validate* requirements, you check to make certain the requirements specification thoroughly addresses the requirements that the customers have presented. If you view the game as a problem statement, validation ensures that you have comprehensively addressed the scope of the problem you have decided to solve. Figure 2.18 illustrates the refinement phase.

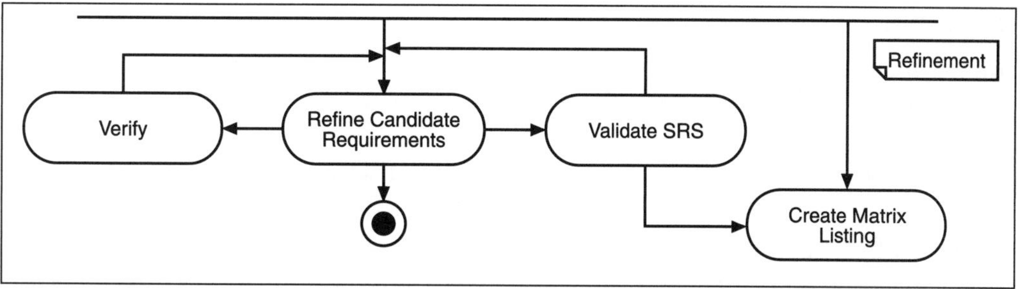

Figure 2.18
Refinement involves verification and validation.

It is good engineering practice to validate and verify requirements before proceeding to the next phase of system development, which is system design. When you have developed the requirements to the point that you think they represent a complete and accurate description of the problem, you establish your first *baseline* for the SRS. A baseline is a controlled version of the document. After establishing the first baseline, you update the requirements document only through formal measures, such as group reviews or individual change requests.

Given the baseline of the SRS, you can develop a *test plan*. The test plan is a separate document that has its own set of priorities and complexities. This book examines test plans in Chapter 11, "Evident Evil—The Art of Testing." (You can also see the example documents on the CD.) In the test plan, you show how you will test the functionality you have specified in the SRS. Two key components of a test plan are test cases and a requirements matrix. The test case documents how you intend to verify and validate requirements. The requirements matrix ensures that you can trace the work you perform as you implement and test the functionality that your requirements specify.

Using Use Cases for Tests

At this point, there is no need to extensively discuss test cases for requirements, for Chapter 11 discusses testing in detail. However, you should develop at least one test case for each requirement listed in the SRS. The exceptional and alternate paths discussed earlier in this chapter are important parts of test scenarios. Although the basis for the test case can be the basic course of events given in the use case you develop to analyze the requirements, you must develop at least one exceptional course of events for each basic course of events.

Each requirement you list in the SRS should have a reference to a test case. To accomplish this, include a requirements matrix as an appendix to the SRS.

Using a Requirements Matrix

You can append a requirements matrix to the SRS. A requirements matrix is a tabular representation of the requirements you name in the SRS. Figure 2.19 illustrates a sample requirements matrix. Notice how the matrix ties together most of the artifacts created during the requirements engineering phase of the software development process. (See Appendix D or the CD for a complete example.) You see the requirements number, so you can trace information to the SRS. On the other hand, you see a test case number, so you can trace information to the test plan. If you have an appendix in the SRS that shows use cases, the matrix provides use case references. On the other hand, the list of classes points to the TOR chart. You can expand the matrix if you want to include other information. Two additional columns might list the names of code files and design stripes. (See Chapter 4.) Also, if you hyperlink the cells of the matrix, you can more easily access named items.

Req No.	Stat	Title	Use Case Ref	Test Case Ref	Dep	Priority	Class Ref
1	0%	Start Game	SG01	SGT01		1	CPlayer CAction CFileMgr CWorld

Figure 2.19
Include a requirements matrix in an SRS appendix.

Refining Specification Dependencies

Notice the columns in Figure 2.19. One column is titled Stat (for Status). A second column is titled Priority. These two column titles affect refining specifications. Although the status of a requirement has more to do with managing the project than with refining the requirement for implementation, it remains important to include discussion of it at this point to prepare for future development efforts. The status of a requirement is the extent to which the functionality that it specifies has been constructed.

When you consider status, you also need to consider what priority the requirement has during the construction phase of development. Generally, there are three ways to rate or set the priority for a requirement. Table 2.4 describes these rankings. As shown in the table, these rankings can be coded as numbers. For example, Essential is coded as priority 1.

One fairly heavy factor in determining the priority of a requirement is whether other requirements depend on it. If a first requirement depends on a second, then the construction of the functionality for second must be completed before the first can be completed.

Table 2.4 Priorities for Requirements

Priority	Description
Essential	This type of requirement is considered a part of the critical path of the product. If it is not completed, nothing else can be completed.
Desired	This type of requirement is not considered a part of the critical path. Often, such a requirement is associated with nonfunctional features. If the requirement is not a nonfunctional feature, it has no dependencies and could be dropped without creating difficulties.
Secondary	This type of requirement is something that you discover has no bearing on the critical path of the project and does not add much that is important to the product. It is so inessential, in fact, that you try to implement it only if you have time to spare after all essential and desired functionality are implemented.

Anticipating and Managing Change

Requirements change during the development process. Changes present challenges if you are not ready for them. To control changes, you can use the following tools and strategies:

- **Change procedures.** Put in place a set of rules to follow every time you change the wording of the requirements document.
- **Review.** At regular intervals, review suggestions for changes. Make no changes to the baselined document unless you have reviewed the changes. (Chapter 15, "Team Work," provides discussion of how to do reviews.)
- **Documentation control.** Place the requirements in the same control system you use for your code.
- **Updating the matrix.** Continue to update the matrix so that you can easily move from the requirements specification to other documents.

The sections that follow review some approaches to these activities. Chapter 10 discusses these topics in the context of software configuration management.

Change Procedures and Reviews

You can easily establish procedures for change with a single document containing a numbered list. You tell the members of the team what to do when they want to make changes. In addition, it is appropriate to designate a change control coordinator. This is someone who has responsibility for knowing document ownership, numbering conventions, review schedules, and procedures for submitting requests for change.

Reviews are the most convenient way for a small team to exercise change control procedures. Generally, each artifact in a requirements effort is assigned to a given individual. The person responsible for the artifact develops it in accordance with the findings of a team. At scheduled intervals, the team reviews the work and approves the changes that have accumulated since the previous review. The coordinator can keep a running tally of who owns what and when reviews take place.

Document Control

The SRS is the most important document in the requirements analysis effort. It contains the primary list of requirements and, in an appendix, the use cases involved in the requirements analysis effort. Other artifacts also result from the requirements analysis effort. These include the requirements matrix and the game design document.

Document control is best accomplished using some type of software that is designed to control changes. A source control application can be used for document control. Chapter 10 provides greater detail on source control issues.

Because requirements engineering is a process of discovery, number your requirements and do not allow the numbers to be changed. Number requirements by using a numbering system that makes each requirement clearly identifiable and unique. Add a subsystem identifier as a prefix to the number. You can also number use cases. Number use cases with a naming convention that is similar to what you use for your requirements. If you create a requirements matrix and place it in an appendix of the SRS, you will have a convenient way to trace the development activity relating to each requirement.

Conclusion

Requirements allow you to capture the scope of your development project. When you develop a game, you approach the game as a problem. You define the problem through requirements engineering. Requirements engineering allows you to precisely define the scope of your development effort, but it also allows you to know specifically what functionality you must implement to support the features that make up your game. During the requirements engineering phase of the product lifecycle, you can establish the criteria you will use to test the functionality of your game. The work you perform during the requirements engineering phase of the project can be captured in several artifacts. Among these are the software requirements specification (SRS), the use case, and the TOR chart.

For further reading on requirements engineering, you might find the following resources useful:

Cockburn, Alistair. *Writing Effective Use Cases.* Boston: Addison-Wesley, 2001.

Dulak, Daryl and Eamonn Guiney. *Use Cases: Requirements in Context.* New York: ACM Press, 2000.

Wiegers, Karl E. *Software Requirements*, Second Edition. Redmond, Washington: Microsoft Press, 2003.

The work you perform during the requirements phase lays the groundwork for the design phase of the software engineering effort. During the design effort, you begin the work of trying to solve the problem you have scoped out during the requirements engineering effort. If the work you have performed during the requirements effort has been done well, you can begin design work with minimal rework.

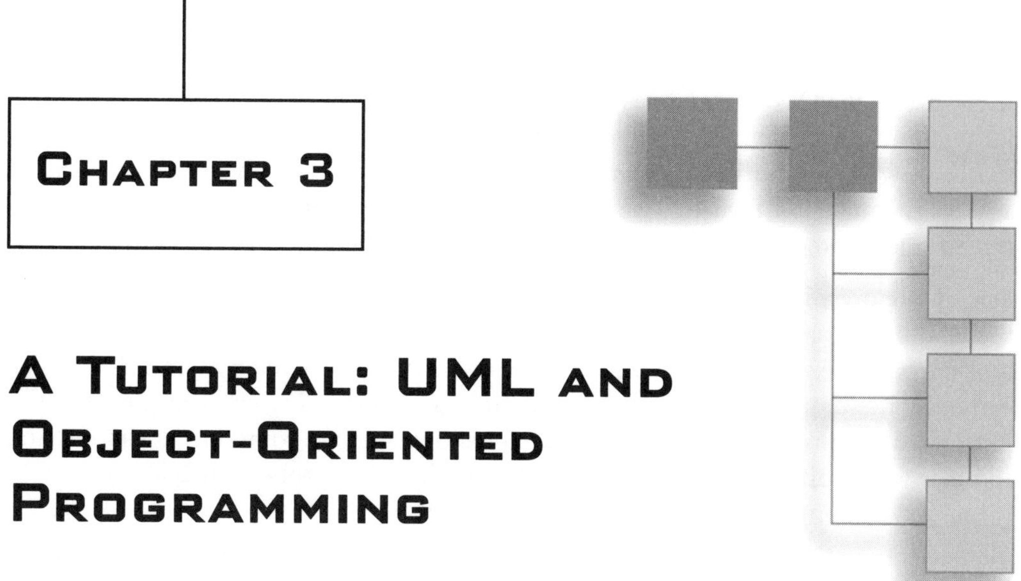

Chapter 3

A Tutorial: UML and Object-Oriented Programming

Almost all successful software systems are built from models. A model is a simple representation of something complex. A model makes it possible for those who want to build a system to visualize the system. It's a way to specify what the system is to do and to guide the construction of the system. A model creates a common language, or a common way of understanding. If you put a model in place, your project can move forward with force and momentum that are otherwise beyond your reach.

The Unified Modeling Language (UML) provides a set of elements that allow you to model software systems. This chapter covers some of these elements, which are examined on three levels: *diagrams*, *modeling elements*, and *views*. In addition, this chapter covers several concepts that are associated with object-oriented design, which is important in the use of the UML.

Even with such a limited set of topics, this chapter has a lot to explain, such as the following:

- Origins of the UML
- Why and when to use the UML
- Elements and relations
- Object-oriented concepts
- Diagrams considered basic to the UML

UML History

The UML "unified" what amounts to dozens of modeling languages that software designers, engineers, and analysts had developed independently during the middle and late decades of the twentieth century. The unification culminated in the work of the Object Management Group (OMG), which in 1997 adopted the UML as a standard (Version 1.1). In 2003, the OMG approved Version 2.0.

If you access the OMG UML site on the Internet (http://www.uml.org), you can obtain most of the information you need to take your study of the UML far beyond the scope of this book. (Also see the list of books at the end of this chapter.) On the other hand, almost any understanding of the language is likely to provide you with the ability to communicate with far more people than you would otherwise when talking about software.

Even if one organization governs the UML's development, it is important to realize that the UML is not associated with any one tool or methodology. Many software modeling tools incorporate its elements. Likewise, it is important to remember that the UML is an extremely useful medium for communication in situations in which you want to draw informal diagrams to illustrate ideas you have about software components and systems. In other words, although it is a good idea to use the UML properly, it is also a flexible, completely customizable medium of communication.

The UML is a general-purpose modeling language. To fulfill its purpose, the UML offers a set of *diagrams*, *views*, and *modeling elements* that help you do the following:

- Gather requirements
- Analyze the requirements you have gathered
- Design software using your requirements
- Document the software you have developed
- Develop test cases
- Plan product releases
- Discuss and conceptualize software

A UML Diagram and Its Elements

This chapter covers nine UML diagrams. To begin, look at Figure 3.1, which illustrates a common UML diagram—a class diagram.

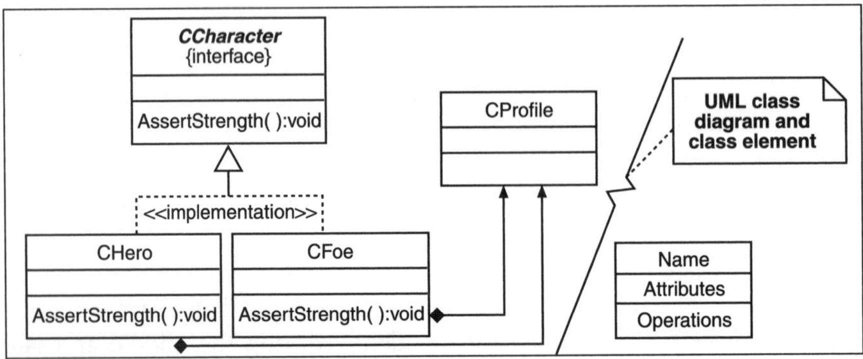

Figure 3.1
A UML diagram explores relationships among classes.

It is not important now to go into the meaning of the elements represented in Figure 3.1. Note, however, the following general notions, which Table 3.1 explains in detail.

- The rectangles that are divided into three parts are examples of *elements* that represent classes. Each class element provides the class name, class attributes, and class operations.
- The lines with the open arrows, closed arrows, and diamonds are examples of elements that represent *relationships.*
- The bold italic of ***CCharacter*** illustrates an *adornment.*
- The numbers on the lines illustrate *multiplicity* (which you might know as cardinality).
- The curly braces enclosing "interface" show the use of a *property.*
- The actual *diagram* is a *class diagram.*
- The box with the folded upper-right corner is a *note.*
- The diagram provides a *logical, static view* of a system of classes.

If this is your first exposure to the UML, these terms might seem a bit alien. Don't be discouraged. The elements that make up the language are few in number and easy to identify. You'll learn more about them in the discussion that follows.

Why Bother with Symbols?

Why bother learning about a set of symbols for communicating about software? The first part of the answer goes back to the notion of modeling things. Almost every successful software system has been modeled. A model is an abstraction of a real system. The UML offers you what amounts to a simple set of tools for modeling. Central among these tools are the diagrams, which are also known as *artifacts.* The artifacts provide you with a ready way to quickly *describe* the system you are working on.

Description is the second big factor. It's a key issue, in fact, when it comes to software design and testing. To view how this is so, consider what it would be like to verbally describe the software system represented in Figure 3.1. The description might go something like this:

> *From a logical point of view, the class system consists of four classes:* `CCharacter`, `CProfile`, `CHero`, *and* `CFoe`. `CHero` *and* `CFoe` *have an attribute or data member that is an instance of the class* `CProfile`. *The relationship is one of composition—strong association.* `CCharacter` *is an abstract class that is used as an interface, and its interface consists of one operation—* `AssertStrength()`*—which is overridden in the two implementations of* `CCharacter`*:* `CHero` *and* `CFoe`. *The return value of* `AssertStrength()` *is* `void`.

Somewhere deep down, you know that this is really talking about a computer program—lines of code. If the computer program exists, you might set aside all this discussion and illustration and instead refer to the code. If implemented in C++, the code might appear as something along the following lines:

```
//declaration CProfile

class CProfile
{
//…
};
//declaration CCharacter as abstract class--interface
class CCharacter
{
protected:
        CProfile *m_pProfile;
public:
     //pure virtual operation
     virtual void AssertStrength() = 0;
};
class CHero: public CCharacter
{
public:
     //overridden version of operation from parent class
     void AssertStrength();
};
class CFoe: public CCharacter
{
public:
     //overridden version of operation from parent class
     void AssertStrength();
};
//implementation…
CFoe::CFoe()
{
     //aggregated instance of CProfile
     m_pProfile = new CProfile();
}
//implementation…
void CFoe::AssertStrength(){/*..*/}
//implementation…
CHero::CHero()
{
     //aggregated instance of CProfile
     m_pProfile = new CProfile();
}
//implementation…
void CHero::AssertStrength(){/*..*/}
```

If you are not yet completely comfortable with the syntax of C++, don't worry. The previous code sample fairly accurately implements both the diagram and the description, but the implementation is not what is important—not here, anyway. What *is* important is the sheer bulk of space and amount of time required to represent and communicate the idea when only the code is at hand to illustrate the idea. Consider what happens if the system includes 30–100 classes, each containing hundreds or thousands of lines of code.

The fact of the matter is that the program cannot be its own model. To model a program, you need something other than the program, and to model something effectively, you need a set of modeling conventions that everyone can agree on to mean the same thing and that everyone uses in roughly the same way. Explaining and showing the implementation are good, but being able to draw diagrams is better.

As an experiment, try returning periodically to this part of the book. Look at the diagram, read the prose passage, and read the code. Yes, perhaps the UML is vague at this point, but almost anyone who conducts such an experiment after a little exposure to the UML reports that the diagram presents the same picture as the prose and the code, but it requires only a fragment of the time. Add to this that the diagram ends up being able to communicate the purpose and flow of the activity in the system with much more clarity than either the prose or the pseudocode.

note

Chapter 10, "Control Freaks and Configuration Management," provides a discussion of naming conventions. When we show the code for a diagramed class, we add a *C* to the name of a class. An example is `CMesh`. The *C* stands for class. The letter *m* and the underscore indicate that the variable is a member of the class. An example is `m_intXCord`.

Starter Terms

The most effective way to become familiar with UML is to use it. Toward this end, we can briefly list some of the main terms and topics of this chapter. Look at Table 3.1. These terms refer to general UML features. We'll build on these features from this point forward.

Table 3.1 UML Starter Terms

General Term	Description
Relations	Represented by solid or dashed lines that might be capped with an open arrow, a closed arrow, or a diamond. They indicate ways that system entities communicate with each other.

(continued on next page)

Table 3.1 UML Starter Terms (continued)

General Term	Description
Elements	Generally, elements fall into three groups: symbols, lines, and labels. Symbols stand for such things as class rectangles and object rectangles. They also represent other things, such as actors and use cases in use case diagrams. Lines stand for associations, links, dependencies, and transitions in state transition diagrams. Finally, labels stand for such items as names and roles.
Diagrams	The nine diagrams discussed in this chapter. Diagrams offer ways to illustrate systems or parts of systems. The diagrams we examine are as follows: class, object, state, sequence, collaboration, activity, component, and deployment.
Views	Ways to look at software systems or system components. They are as follows: component, logical, deployment, use case, and concurrency.
Note	A rectangle with its upper-right corner folded over.
Adornments	Special ways of enhancing the meanings of relations, elements, and diagrams. Examples are underlined words, bolded lettering, and characters that indicate scope, such as +, -, and #.
Extensions	Ways you can customize the UML for your own purposes. One of the most important extensions is called a *stereotype*. You can assign a specific name to almost anything that the UML offers if you use a *stereotype*, which you create using *guillements* (angled brackets, pronounced *Gill-EH-ma*). Example: *<<special characterization>>*.
Properties	Ways to define anything you represent in a UML diagram. To do this, you enclose your definition in curly braces. Example: *{abstract}*.
Multiplicity	A way to show the cardinality of things. The figure that follows shows a many-to-one relationship between the two boxes. Read the star as "many."

UML Diagrams

As was mentioned before, the UML offers several diagrams that you can use as a modeling framework for your software. Examine Table 3.2 for a summary.

Table 3.2 UML Diagram Inventory

Diagram Name	Description
Use Case	A use case diagram depicts the system from the perspective of the system user (also called an *actor*). It shows how the user uses the system to derive some type of beneficial service from it. This diagram can contain one or more *use cases*. Some use cases *extend* others, whereas others *include* others. Some *generalize* or *specialize* others.
Activity	An activity diagram provides an excellent way to explore use cases. It resembles a flow chart and has things in common with state chart diagrams.
Class	A class diagram consists of elements that depict classes and the relationships among classes. Some classes *generalize or specialize* other classes. Other classes *are composed of* objects of other classes. The relationships among classes can be described as *association*, *aggregation*, or *composition*. A class diagram provides a static view of a system.
Object	An object diagram consists of elements that depict objects and the relationships among objects. Like a class diagram, a generic object diagram might represent a system statically or dynamically.
State Chart	Suppose that you want to see how a single object changes—how its *state* changes. Say that it starts with a given value set to 0 and, after a time, the value grows to 1,000. If you want to see how this happens, you investigate the *transitions* in its state.
Sequence	Like a collaboration diagram, a sequence diagram is an *interaction* diagram. Objects in a given system communicate with each other through messages. The sequence diagram shows the sequence in which the messages occur. It allows you to trace the flow of the system activity. In a sequence diagram, a timeline shows the lifetime of each of the objects in the system. Messages connect the timelines.
Collaboration	Like a sequence diagram, a collaboration diagram is an *interaction* diagram. A collaboration diagram shows *how* objects communicate with each other rather than the *sequence* in which they communicate with each other. It provides a way to investigate the logic of the system and the roles of the objects that the system uses.
Component	This diagram allows you to depict the way the architectural components of the system have been grouped. Other terms for components are frameworks, modules, and patterns. Along with the deployment diagram, this provides an implementation view of the system.
Package	Used in a design document, this diagram can show collections of classes. We use it to show the stripes of *Ankh*. Package diagrams can also depict modules, patterns, or frameworks.
Deployment	If you need to show how you are going to install the different parts of a game, you can use a deployment diagram. Assume, for example, that you have a distributed game—one part goes on the client machine, and the other part goes on the server. Along with the component diagram, this provides an implementation view of the system.

note

A class diagram depicts only classes. It does not show the instances of the classes. Such a diagram is *static*. When the instances of the class (in other words, objects) come into existence or go out of existence doesn't matter. What matters are the *relations* between the classes without respect to time. When an object diagram shows only classes, it is static. On the other hand, other diagrams show changes through time. Among these are state chart, sequence, and collaboration diagrams. When a diagram shows changes over time or changes in state, it is *dynamic*.

The sections that follow go into detail in the discussion of each of the diagrams that Table 3.2 lists. For now, you might want to flip ahead and glance at the diagrams. In fact, you should review Table 3.2 several times.

The diagrams are tools. Whether you derive benefit from the UML depends on whether you can use the tools it offers. Grand conceptualizations about how and why you should use the tools are secondary.

Know Tools by Use, Not Definition

Keep in mind that the UML is an extremely flexible standard. For this reason, think of the diagrams as tools that allow you to perform different types of work. To review a bit:

- Use a use case diagram to gather and explore requirements for purposes of design or testing.
- Use an activity diagram to explore the scenarios of use cases.
- Use a class diagram to identify classes and see how classes relate to each other.
- Use an object diagram to see how one object communicates with another.
- Use a state chart diagram to explore how the attributes of an object change.
- Use a sequence diagram to fully explore a use case by tracing the order in which objects send messages to themselves or each other.
- Use a collaboration diagram to view the logic of the system and the way that objects send messages to each other.
- Use a component diagram to explore whether and how subsystems exist within your game product.
- Use a deployment diagram to figure out how to set up the installation package for your game.

Together with the discussion of the diagrams comes a flood of new terms. One thing you can take for granted—the UML goes on and on. This chapter covers a fair degree of detail, but keep in mind that full documentation of the UML requires, at a minimum, many more pages than are available here. The end of this chapter provides a few good reference works.

Use Case Diagrams

A use case diagram allows you to show how someone might use a system. Such a diagram is especially helpful during the early stages of a project, when you are trying to develop or analyze requirements and figure out test criteria for the requirements. Because it is concerned with what people do, a view of the system created with use case modeling is sometimes referred to as a *functional view* of a system. (For specifics on developing functional requirements, see Chapter 2, "Requirements—Getting the Picture.") In other words, you analyze the system in terms of what it is expected to do.

Modeling with use cases involves *use case diagrams.* However, before getting involved in a discussion of creating diagrams, it is important to talk first about use cases specifically. A use case is a description of a sequence of actions that a system performs. On the other hand, a use case is not a description of just any sequence of actions. It is a description of a sequence of actions that produces a result. The result is not just any result, though. The result has to be something that someone who uses the systems finds beneficial. The requirements often specify the result.

note

Keep in mind that a *use case* is not the same thing as a *use case diagram.* Although the two often are referred to as use cases, a use case is primarily something written. A use case diagram is something that illustrates a use case. Use case diagrams are tools you can employ to develop use cases. See Chapter 2 for more discussion on writing use cases.

A use case diagram graphically depicts how the system user experiences or interacts with one or more use cases. Because more than one system user might participate in any given use case, a use case diagram might also feature several system users. Likewise, a use case diagram usually depicts several use cases—sometimes dozens. To familiarize yourself with the basics of a use case diagram, look at Figure 3.2.

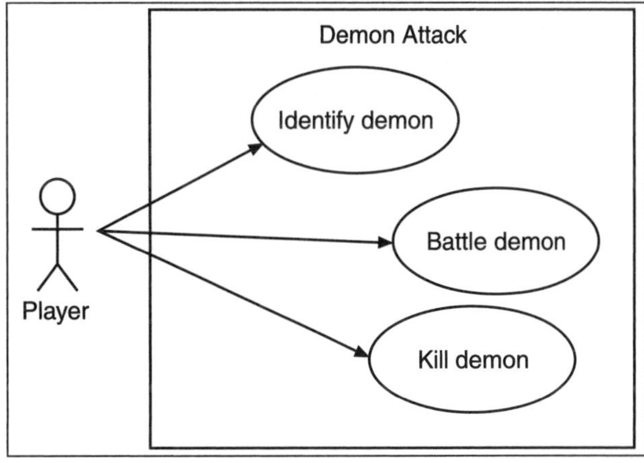

Figure 3.2
An actor interacts with three use cases.

As Figure 3.2 shows, you employ only a few modeling elements, as follows:

- **A stick figure, which represents the user of the system (player).** The stick figure is generically called an *actor*. Any number of actors can participate in a system. Although actors are usually people, they can also be external factors (such as time, alarms, and so on) or other systems.
- **Ellipses, which represent the use cases.** Each use case represented in the use case diagram is named. Generally, the names should begin with a verb ("*Identify* Demon").
- **Lines with open arrows, which represent relationships between the actor and the use cases.** Such lines might also relate use cases to each other.
- **A use case diagram name, which appears inside the box.** Practices concerning use case diagram names differ. You obviously don't need to name a use case diagram if you are experimenting, although it does help.
- **A bounding box, which represents the boundary of the system.** (This is sometimes considered unnecessary.)

In Figure 3.2, a stereotype beneath the actor identifies the actor as a game player (<<Player>>). The actor is not part of the system other than as a user, so you depict the actor outside the bounding box. Next comes the use cases—the ellipses. Each use case has a name, as does the use case diagram. You can have just a few use cases, as in Figure 3.2, or you can have many of them. You can also have many actors gathered around just one use case. Everything is flexible.

The lines, as you see, are topped with open arrows that point to the use cases. Sometimes you see the lines point the other way, at the actor—if the user receives information from the system. In many cases, designers do not use arrows. One rule is that unless you can think of a specific input the actor provides to the system, the line requires no arrow.

Use Cases Tell Stories

A use case is a description of a sequence of actions that the system performs for a user and that results in something the user finds valuable. A use case diagram shows how an actor interacts with use cases. It also shows how use cases interact with each other. Given this start, the language tends to become loosely employed. Sometimes analysts refer to all the activity in a given use case diagram as a use case. This is okay. Generally, what counts as a use case or a system of use cases depends on your level of specificity or generality. How much have you broken things down?

A good way to establish what you mean is to think of the use case diagram as a scenario, a script, or a story. Imagine, for example, the startup session of your game. The start screen comes into view. You are playing a role-playing game. You view the roles (characters) available to you. You select the role you like most. Then you start the game. Look at Figure 3.3 to see how a use case diagram depicts this scenario.

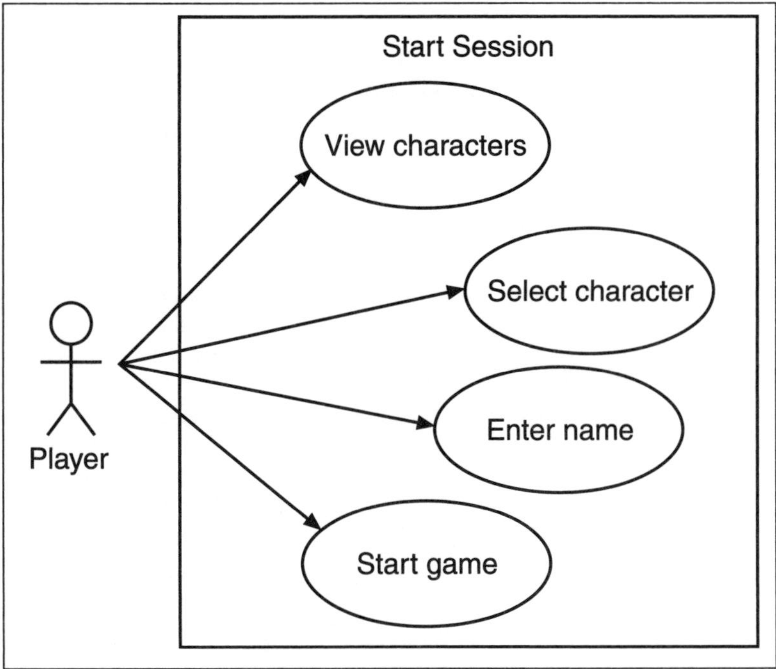

Figure 3.3
A use case diagram tells the story of the start of a game.

Here are a few points to review:

- The set of use cases in the use case diagram represents a bounded sequence or set of activities. This set of activities is a view of the system, an arbitrarily selected path through the possible paths that are available to the system user.
- The use case diagram has a name—a title—that appears inside the system box. The name unifies the action of the diagram.
- A use case diagram depicts a *scenario* of system use. A scenario is a selected path of system use.

What If?

What if? This seems like a simple enough question, and it is. However, at the same time, this question identifies one of the leading roles that use cases have come to play in systems analysis, requirements gathering, and testing. Look at Table 3.3.

Table 3.3 Use Case Diagram Roles

Question Asked	Use Cases Provide...
What if there's one path?	A way to visualize a set of interactions with the system on the part of a single user of the system.
What if there are many paths?	A way to visualize two or more sets of interactions that two or more users in different roles have with the system.
What if roles are unclear?	A way to visualize alternative paths through the same general sequence of actions. This becomes the basis of test scenarios. Use cases have extraordinary value as ways to work out test routines. Here, the important thing to ask is, "What if it does not work?"
What if there is redundancy?	A way to see if you have duplicated actions when you have laid out requirements. When you are able to see the essential actions involved in the user's interaction with the system, you can easily spot when you have had the user do things either needlessly or in duplicate.
What if requirements are unclear?	A way to explore requirements—filling in the details you have forgotten. When you analyze requirements, you can use case diagrams to discover whether you are missing requirements.
What if tests don't seem obvious?	A way to work out test scenarios for any given requirement.

The scenario that a use case diagram depicts might be one among many. As an example of how this is so, suppose that you change just one use in a given scenario. In Figure 3.3, the player selects a role and *starts* the game. In Figure 3.4, the player selects a role but decides to *exit* the game.

Here, then, is an alternative path through the set of actions that comprises the startup use cases. The use case diagrams depict the two scenarios. The two scenarios show how the same set of actions leads to different results.

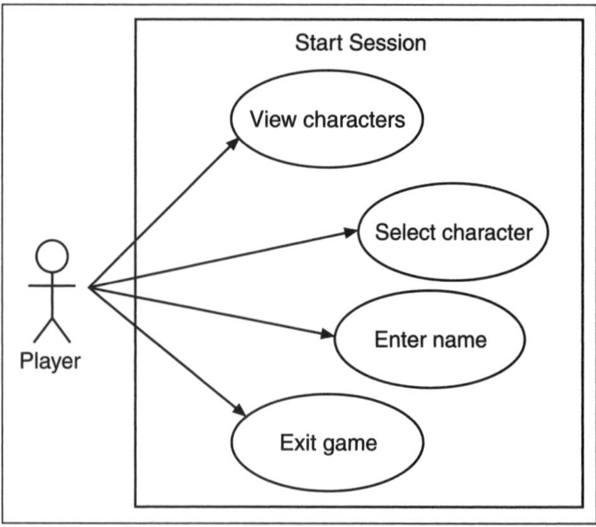

Figure 3.4
A use case diagram depicts one scenario among many.

Use cases and use case diagrams represent events that occur in sequence and can be traced from a start point to a stop point. There are different paths. The fact that you can explore different paths enables you to both eliminate redundant details and fill in details that have been omitted as you have developed a set of requirements.

note

Use case diagrams depict *scenarios*. However, one use case can be broken down into other use cases, so a single use case can represent a scenario. One of the best ways to examine any scenario is to employ an activity diagram. You will learn more about activity diagrams later in this chapter.

Different Use Cases

Use cases relate to each other in different ways. Note the following list:

- One use case can *extend* another use case. In other words, a use case can take what another use case offers and add to it.
- One use case can be said to *include* the actions of another use case. When a use case does this, it includes a complete use case in its own set of actions.
- One use case can inherit the properties of another. In this case, one use case specializes the actions of another case. This is called *generalization.*
- Use cases can be *grouped* together to offer a packaged set of activities.

Making an Extension

When you first lay out a use case or use case diagram, you try to think of a complete activity. This activity can be simple, such as when you select a character from a set of characters in a role-playing game. It can also be involved, such as when you are well into the game (think of *Diablo*) and need to buy the right armor for your character. You might create the following use case narrative:

> *Select Armor. The character goes to the armory and talks with the armory master about acquiring armor. Armor stands in rows, and the character selects the armor he can afford.*

The use case is named Select Armor. Figure 3.5 depicts the use case and the player's interaction with it.

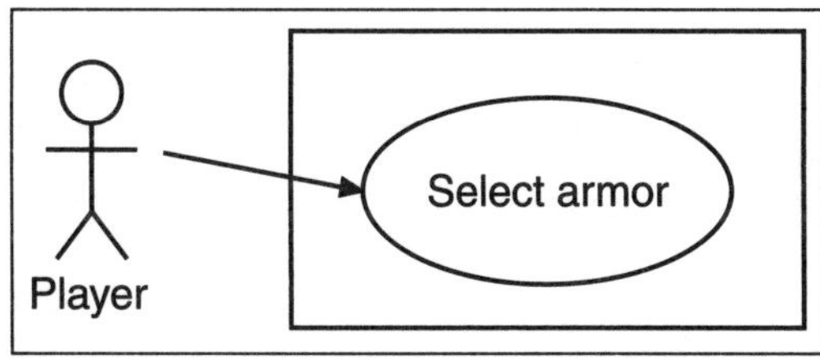

Figure 3.5
The player interacts with the Select Armor use case.

Suppose that you discover something else is possible: You can both buy and trade armor.

> *Select Armor with Trade. The character goes to the armory and talks with the armory master about acquiring armor by trading old armor for new. The character wears armor to be traded, and armor stands in rows and can be selected. The character selects new armor that the armor master values as equivalent to the armor traded.*

This second use case *extends* the action of the first. It is the same, but it also has a new twist: the trade. Figure 3.6 depicts how one use case *extends* another.

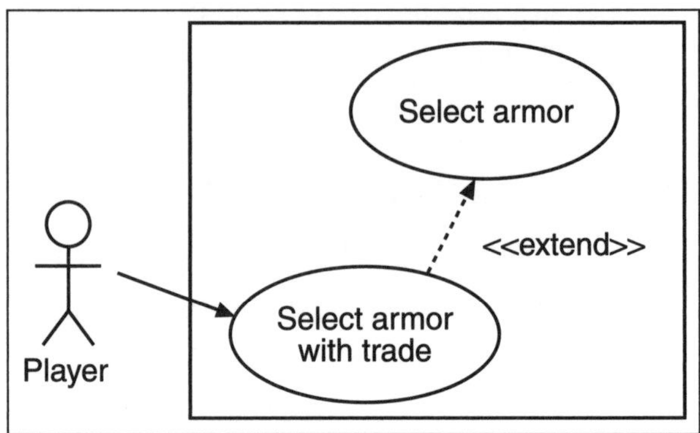

Figure 3.6
One use case extends another.

Figure 3.6 displays a dashed line capped by an arrow. The use case that the arrow points to (Select Armor) is complete. The use case pointed from (Select Armor with Trade) adds features to the Select Armor use case, extending it. The stereotype *(<<extend>>)* tells you explicitly what is going on. When one use case extends another, it adds features to it while leaving it intact. What is extended here is that the transaction now includes using armor in addition to money.

Including

An alternative use case for acquiring armor arises if you consider what it is to acquire armor generally. Suppose that a use case is concerned with bargaining. Acquisition might involve paying any named price. However, suppose that you can also ask if a price can be lowered or offer a lower price than the named price. You can view the bargaining use case as a separate, independent action, but you can also include it in the activity of acquiring armor if an occasion for bargaining arises. Figure 3.7 shows an include relationship.

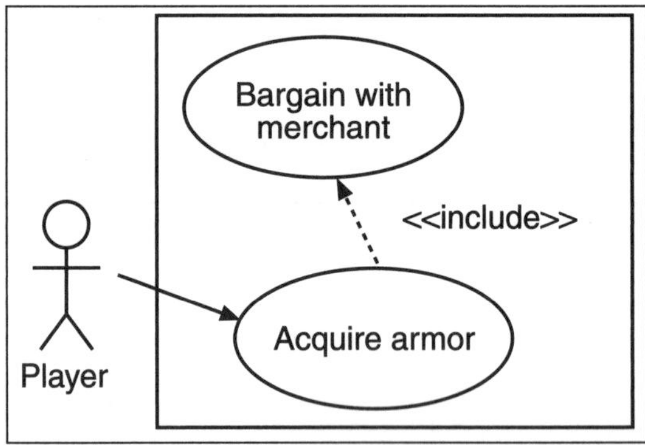

Figure 3.7
Acquiring armor can include bargaining.

Generalization and Specialization

If you want to reuse use case properties, you can use class generalization. *Generalization* is often referred to as *inheritance*. Suppose that you begin with a use case that allows the player to renew the character's life.

> *Renew Life. The player selects the healing box and the renewal option. The player is renewed.*

This use case provides a sequence of actions that restores the character's health. Suppose, however, that the player of a game might use a number of approaches to renewing the character's health. All involve the same actions, but slight differences mark each.

> *Renew Life with Potion. Player opens healing box and selects potion. Player drinks potion, and he is renewed.*
>
> *Renew Life with Charm. Player selects healing box and healing option. Player confirms charm, and he is renewed.*

Figure 3.8 illustrates generalization among use cases.

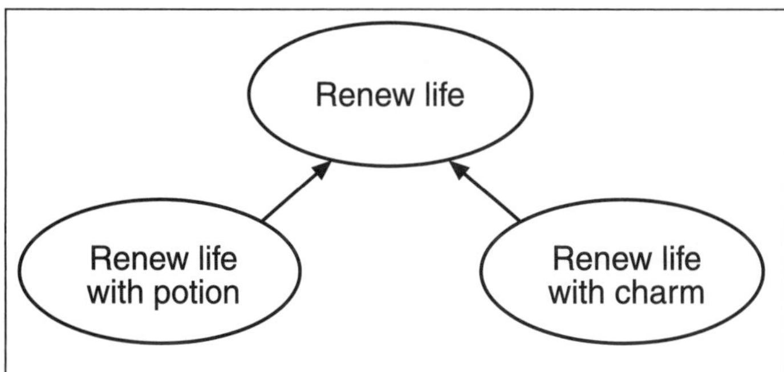

Figure 3.8
Generalization allows two use cases to be derived from another.

note

If you create a use case that embodies all the basic properties of a number of other use cases, you create a *generalized* use case. If you take a generalized use case and adapt it to some special situation, you *specialize* a use case. Such language is derived from object-oriented programming.

Activity Diagrams

An activity diagram possesses great potential as a way to investigate how a use case works. In broader terms, activity diagrams illustrate *workflows*. This section discusses the activity diagram as a way of expanding on the meaning of use cases. Keep in mind, however, that you can use activity diagrams in almost any situation in which you want to investigate how control of flow passes through a system.

Figure 3.9 reviews the use case offered before in Figure 3.4. You can work with the use case in this section to show at least one application of an activity diagram.

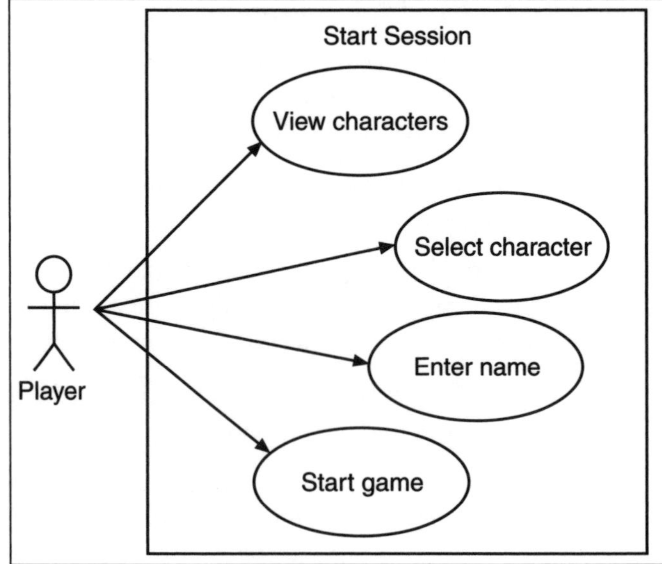

Figure 3.9
To establish a starting point, you might examine a use case story that unfolds something along the following lines:

> *Start Session. The user views the characters that can be selected for the game role. The user selects the character. After the selection is confirmed, the user is asked to enter a player name. The player enters a name, and the game begins.*

This story gives you a good idea of what the use case is about, but if you want to fully explore it for requirements for design purposes, you might need to know just how the scenario under study might unfold. As discussed before, there might be more than one scenario. Suppose that you want to quickly grasp the different paths through the use case.

Note the following features of the activity diagram depicted in Figure 3.10:

- The filled circle designates the start of the flow (the start state).
- The circle with the dot in it represents the end of the flow (the end state).
- Solid lines with open arrows represent transitions or the flow of activity.
- The rounded rectangles are activities.
- Dark bars can be used to show synchronous flows.
- A *synchronous* flow stipulates that either of the actions in the flow might occur first, but both actions must be completed before the flow can continue.

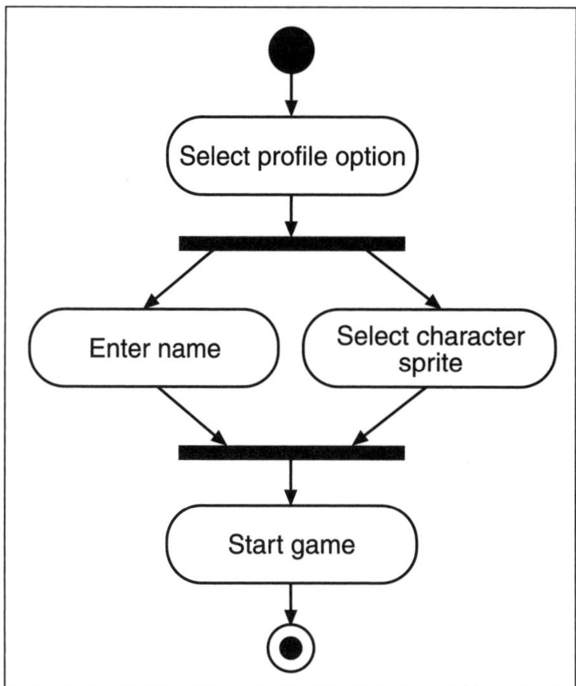

Figure 3.10
An activity diagram illustrates the flow of activity.

note

Developing a sequence or collaboration diagram further extends the process of investigating a use case. Before you can accomplish this, however, you must derive classes from use cases. *Class-Responsibility-Collaboration* (CRC) cards provide a ready tool for deriving classes from use case and activity diagrams. Chapter 4, "Software Design—Much Ado About Something," examines the use of CRC cards in relation to activity diagrams and use cases.

Class Diagrams

If you want to model what a system contains and how the components in a system are related, you can use a class diagram. A class diagram is a tool for *static* modeling. In other words, it does not show you how the system changes. Rather, it allows you to see the components that make up the system, and it allows you to know whether they communicate with or depend on each other and how they relate to each other.

Classes are an essential aspect of object-oriented programming. Before discussing class diagrams, then, it's good to review a few concepts that are central to understanding classes and object-oriented programming. Even if this material is not new, you might want to give it a quick reading to ensure that the terms are fresh for the discussion that follows.

note

No fixed law says that the UML must be used only with object-oriented programming models. Still, the people who created the UML assumed that software should be designed using object-oriented techniques. For this reason, an understanding of objects and classes is important in most discussions of the UML. In recent times, patterns have increased in their importance, which means that knowledge of classes and objects alone no longer suffices for understanding all aspects of the UML. Chapter 7, "P Is for Pattern," discusses patterns in more detail.

Class and Object Basics

Central to object-oriented programming is an understanding of classes and objects. Here are a few beginning points:

- Software engineers design and develop software in components.
- When software engineers develop software in components, they make subsystems that they can reuse in different ways toward different ends.
- Object-oriented programming is one approach to building components.
- At the basis of object-oriented programming is the *object.*
- An object is a set of data together with the mechanisms needed to operate on the data.
- To create an object, a model of the object is created, which is called a *class.* A class is an *abstract* (or programmer-created) data type.
- A class defines the *state* and *behavior* of all the objects that can be created using the class.
- The state of an object is anything that characterizes the object: how large, how small, what color, and so on. The *attributes* of a class define its state.
- The behavior of an object is what the object does. For example, an airplane flies, lands, and taxies. The *operations* of an object make possible the behavior of the object. Because the operations allow only a limited number of changes to be made in the object, they are said to be an *abstraction* of the possible behavior.
- Every class has a name, and its name is its *identity.*
- The operations of a class are called the *interface* of the class.

Figure 3.11 allows you to glimpse some of this language in a friendlier way. You use a class to create objects. An object is an entity that stores information about itself. It also contains ways to change the information it stores about itself. The information is called its state (attributes). The ways of changing things are referred to as its behavior (operations).

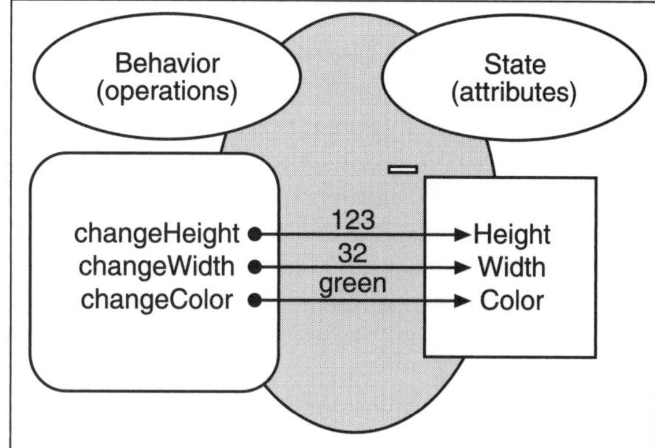

Figure 3.11
Attributes and operations define the state and behavior or classes and objects.

Class Diagrams in Practice

Class diagrams illustrate classes and static relationships. To understand how this is so, contrast a class with a use case. A use case is a sequence of actions. A class is a set of attributes and behaviors. Here's a simple way of looking at it:

- A use case (or an activity diagram) allows you to see a sequence of actions unfold.
- A class diagram allows you to see the things through which actions unfold.

A class embodies state and behavior, as discussed earlier. Another way to express this is to say that a class *encapsulates* state and behavior. The state comprises the attributes. The encapsulation is made possible by the syntax of the programming language and the conceptualization of the class.

Information hiding also applies to classes. A class should not allow users to have direct access to its data—its attributes. The attributes should be *private.* If users want to access or change the state of an object, they should use special operations called *accessors* and *mutators.* These operations should be *public.* The interface is the public view of what the class encapsulates.

A term of great importance when discussing classes is *cohesion.* A class is a set of attributes and behaviors that address a specific type of activity—a specific need. All the operations and attributes of the class should be focused on the same set of needs—or services. Perhaps you have a class called `CMesh`. A `CMesh` is a simple character in a game. The responsibilities of `CMesh` are to move and appear. Table 3.4 profiles the `CMesh` class.

Table 3.4 CMesh Properties

CMesh Attributes	CMesh Behaviors
The mesh has a position characterized by three dimensions: x, y, z	The mesh can be created. The mesh can be destroyed.
The mesh has a size characterized by magnitudes in the range 0 to 10, with 5 as normal.	The mesh moves. The mesh can be visible or invisible.
The mesh is associated with a named mesh file.	The mesh can be resized.
The mesh has visibility status.	The mesh file for the mesh can be changed.

Table 3.4 shows characteristics of a *highly cohesive* class. Notice that the class concerns a narrow set of activities that are focused on the provision of one basic service—in this case, the appearance and movement of the object instantiated from the class. The class does not concern itself with such things as landscape or texture.

Diagramming a Class

Table 3.4 provides a set of items that can be recast using the UML symbol for a class. Figure 3.12 shows the result.

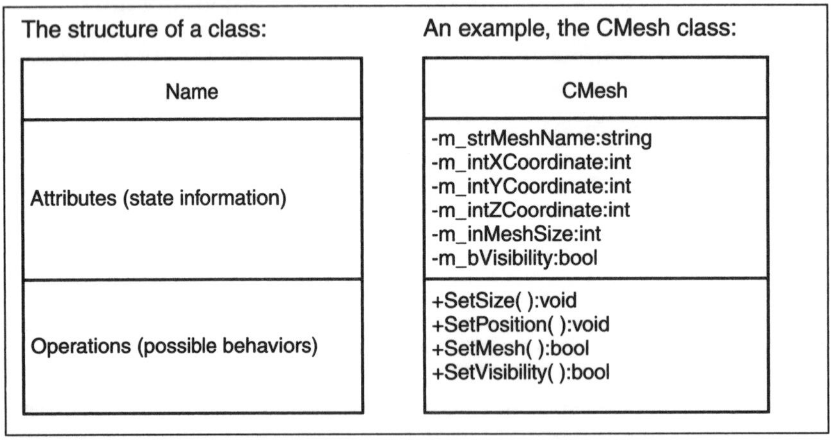

Figure 3.12
The UML represents a class using a rectangle divided for class name, class attributes, and class operations.

Figure 3.12 depicts how the UML graphically represents a class. The representation shows that classes have a name, attributes, and operations. Note the following features:

- The name appears in the first or top division of the rectangle, the attributes appear in the second division, and the operations appear in the bottom division. This is the most common representation of a class. Note that in some cases, the number of divisions can be increased so that properties can be listed. Generally, however, the order is name, attributes, and operations.
- The plus and minus (+, –) signs tell you about the scope of an attribute or operation. The plus means *public*. The minus means *private*. A third such sign, the pound sign (#), indicates *protected*.
- The word following the colon tells you the type of the attribute or the return type of the operation.

The following code declares and implements the UML `CMesh` class representation featured in Figure 3.12. If you are new to C++, don't worry about the specifics:

```
//Declaration...
#include "stdafx.h"

//Declaration...
class CMesh
{
private:
   string m_strMeshName;
   int m_intXCoordinate,
       m_intYCoordinate,
       m_intZCoordinate;
   bool m_bVisibility;
public:
    CMesh(int x, int y, int z,
            string meshName,
            bool visibility);
      void SetSize(int size);
      void SetPosition(int x, int y , int z);
      bool SetMesh(string name);
      bool SetVisibility(bool status);
};

//implementation ...
CMesh::CMesh(int x, int y, int z,
                         string meshName,
                         bool visibility):
                              m_intXCoordinate(x),
                              m_intYCoordinate(y),
                              m_intZCoordinate(z),
                              m_strMeshName(meshName),
                              m_bVisibility(visibility)
{
      /*...*/
}
```

```
void CMesh::SetSize(int size)
{
      /*...*/
}

void CMesh::SetPosition(int x, int y , int z)
{
      /*...*/
}
bool CMesh::SetMesh(string name)
{
      /*...*/
      return true;
}
bool CMesh::SetVisibility(bool status)
{
      /*...*/
      return true;
}
```

Class Relations and Class Diagrams

A class diagram statically represents a software system or subsystem. Table 3.5 lists a few features of class diagrams. Chapter 6, "Object-Oriented Fantasies and Realities," provides extended discussions of these and other concepts.

Table 3.5 Features of Class Diagrams

Term	Description
Service provider	When a class performs a task for an object of another class, the class is called a *service provider.*
Client	When one class receives information from an object of another class, the receiving object is a *client.*
Generalization	One class can be designed so that it becomes a pattern for other classes. The class that serves as a pattern for other classes is a *generalized* class.
Specialization	A number of classes can be derived from the same parent class but modified in ways that make them unique. The child classes are said to be *specializations* of the parent class.
Inheritance	*Generalization* and *specialization* are instances of what is usually referred to as inheritance. The UML term for inheritance is *generalization.*
Attribute	State of a class. Information that defines an essential aspect of the object the class creates.
Operation	Behavior of a class. An activity that changes or communicates information about the state of the class. Operations are often referred to as member functions or methods.

Term	Description
Class interface	The interface is the set of operations (methods) that allows an object to communicate with other objects.
Instance	Another name for an object. An object is an instance of a class. A class can create many objects, and a class can have many instances.
Concrete class	A class that can be used to create an object. It has no abstract operations.
Abstract class	A class that contains at least one abstract operation. An instance of the class cannot be created.
Abstract operation	An operation that must be overridden or implemented in a specialized class. In C++, an abstract operation (member function) is identified with the keyword *virtual.*
Virtual operation	An operation (or member function) that is defined in a base class and that you can override (or redefine) in a derived class. Unlike an abstract operation, the defined operation does not have to be defined in the derived class.
Pure virtual class	Also called an interface class. This class consists wholly of abstract functions and is used purely as a pattern for deriving classes.
Association	One class has an instance of another class. The instance need not be an attribute. The relationship can be general.
Aggregation	One class has an instance of another class. The instance is an attribute, but the attribute might or might not be used.
Composition	One class has an instance of another class, the instance is an attribute, and the attribute is always used.

Class diagrams depict relationships between classes. Two primary relationships describe most of the activity that a class diagram depicts: *generalization* and *association.* Note the following:

- An "is a" relationship characterizes generalization. In other words, one class *is* a version of another.
- A "has a" relationship characterizes association. One class *has* an instance of another class.

These two relationships are illustrated in Figure 3.13. The Weapon class "has a" `Grip`. The Weapon class "has a" `Blade`. On the other hand, `Axe` "is a" `Weapon`, as is `Sword`.

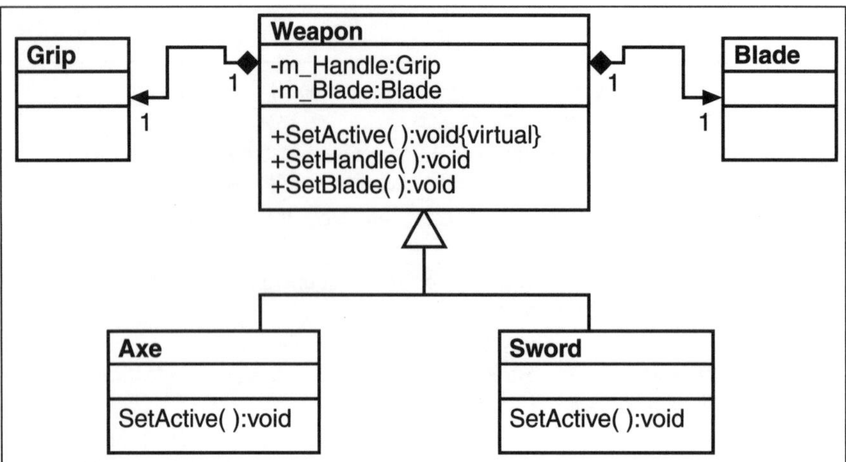

Figure 3.13
Generalization and association in a class diagram.

Note the following features of Figure 3.13:

- The diamonds illustrate composition, which is a special version of association. The diamond shows that the class it touches "has an" instance of the class that its line points to.
- The diamonds touch against the class, `Weapon`, which has instances of `Handle` and `Blade`.
- The closed arrow indicates *inheritance.* It points to the generalized class. The specialized classes (`Axe` and `Sword`) inherit features from the generalized class (`Weapon`).
- The `Sword` class has two *concrete operations.* The two derived classes (`Axe` and `Sword`) automatically inherit these operations. In other words, they become part of `Axe` and `Sword`. The operations are reused in this way.
- The generalized class has one *abstract operation,* which the word "virtual" identifies. When a class has an abstract operation, the classes that are derived from it must make their own versions of the abstract operation. This is why the operation appears in all three classes. This is also how *polymorphism* is implemented.
- Because it contains an abstract operation, `Weapon` cannot be instantiated. For the functionality embodied in this class to be used, other classes must be derived from the class. The derived classes, given that they override any abstract operations they inherit, are concrete classes. In other words, you can create instances of them.

The sections that follow discuss these terms in detail.

Generalization

Generalization is usually defined as a relationship in which one class (a derived or child class) is able to reuse the attributes and operations of another class (a base or parent class). The more common term for generalization is *inheritance*. Generalization also encompasses a relationship in which one class can *implement* another. The UML provides a ready means of illustrating such activities.

Class diagrams show three primary types of generalization that result from the three types of class involved in generalization. Table 3.6 provides a review of terms and their definitions.

Table 3.6 Class Types and Generalization

Type of Class	Description
Concrete	This class contains no operations that a derived class cannot inherit and use without further ado. You can declare an instance of a concrete class.
Abstract	This class contains at least one abstract function. (In C++, this is referred to as a pure *virtual* function.) An abstract operation is one that another class must implement or define. You cannot declare an instance of an abstract class.
Interface	This class contains only abstract operations. It serves as a pattern, forcing its user to implement all the operations that it lists. You cannot declare an instance of an interface.

Concrete Classes

Figure 3.14 illustrates a concrete class, `Weapon`, in a generalization relationship with two concrete derived classes: `Axe` and `Sword`.

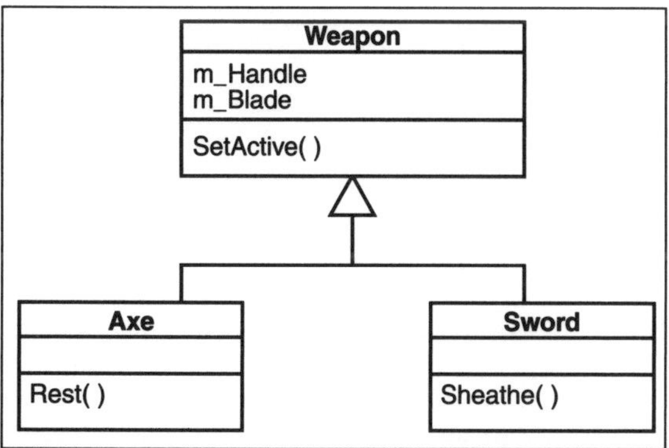

Figure 3.14
Concrete classes are inherited without qualifications.

The Weapon class has two attributes: m_Handle and m_Blade. It has one operation—SetActive()—which two derived classes—Axe and Sword—can access. A public operation within a concrete class, SetActive() automatically becomes accessible in any class that is derived from Weapon.

Axe and Sword *extend* Weapon because each offers an operation in addition to the one inherited from Weapon. When a class is concrete, you can declare an instance of it. In this class diagram, then, you can declare an instance of Weapon. You can also declare instances of Axe and Sword.

Concrete and Abstract Operations

When one class establishes features that are common to several other classes, the class is a *generalization* of other classes. Class designers who create generalized classes have a choice to make. The choice involves whether they want to force those who use the class to specialize specific operations listed in the generalized class. Figure 3.15 illustrates the decisions the class designer makes when evaluating operations that are defined in a generalized class.

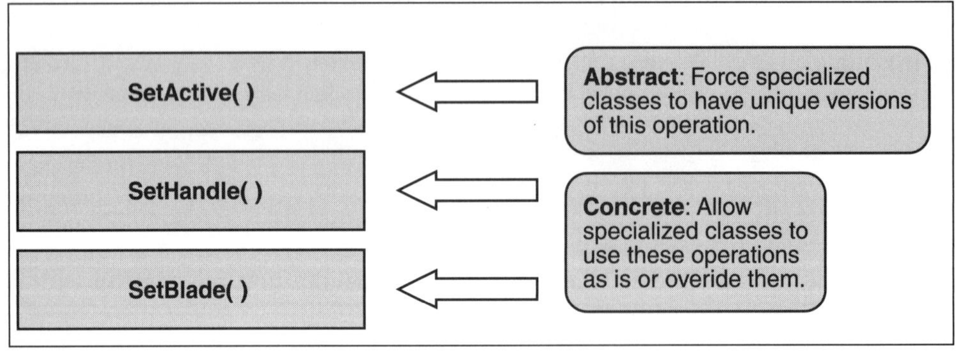

Figure 3.15
Designers make choices about abstract and concrete operations.

Abstract Classes

An abstract class has at least one abstract operation. When a class has an abstract operation, you cannot declare an instance of it. In Figure 3.14, the three concrete classes allow you to declare instances of all three classes. In Figure 3.16, the situation differs, as explained next.

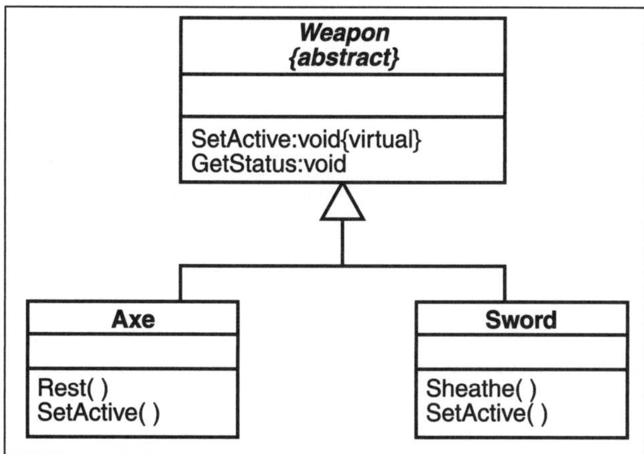

Figure 3.16
Abstract operation creates abstract classes.

In Figure 3.16, the `Weapon` class has a single abstract operation—`SetActive()`—so it is an abstract class. You cannot create an instance of this class. To make use of its operations, you must first specialize the abstract class. To accomplish this, in each of the derived classes (`Axe` and `Sword`), you must implement `SetActive()`. Create a nonvirtual (or nonabstract) operation of the same name, parameters, and return type.

In addition to the `SetActive()` operation, notice in Figure 3.16 that the abstract class includes another operation: `GetStatus()`. This operation is concrete. You do not need to override it in the derived class. Given that each class has an implemented version of `SetActive()`, `Axe` or `Sword` objects can make immediate use of `GetStatus()`.

Interfaces and Polymorphic Activities

You can also use an abstract base class in at least two other ways. One way is to set up a type that imposes a pattern across a set of subclasses. In Figure 3.16, all those classes that are added to the game to define weapons must have a `SetActive()` operation. If many different weapons are stored in a container of the type `Weapon`, it remains necessary to call only one operation to set all the weapons to an active mode.

In addition to forcing a pattern on a set of classes, you can use an abstract class as a parameter type that will accommodate all the derived types of data. Note how the following C++ operation uses `Weapon` as a parameter type.

```
class CCombat
{
//...
public:
```

```
        ArmCharacter(Weapon& wpn)
        {
           wpn.SetActive();
        }
};
```

The `ArmCharacter()` operation calls `SetActive()` for any subclass of `Weapon`, and for this reason, objects of the types `Axe` and `Sword` can be passed to it. This is an example of *polymorphism.*

Interfaces

An interface is a class that has only abstract operations. Figure 3.17 provides one way to represent an interface class. In C++, such a class has pure virtual functions and is said to be a purely virtual class. An interface forces all the derived classes to implement the functions that are named in the interface. An interface provides a ready means to make it possible to achieve polymorphism in operation parameters. You can also use an interface to specialize operations from a parent class.

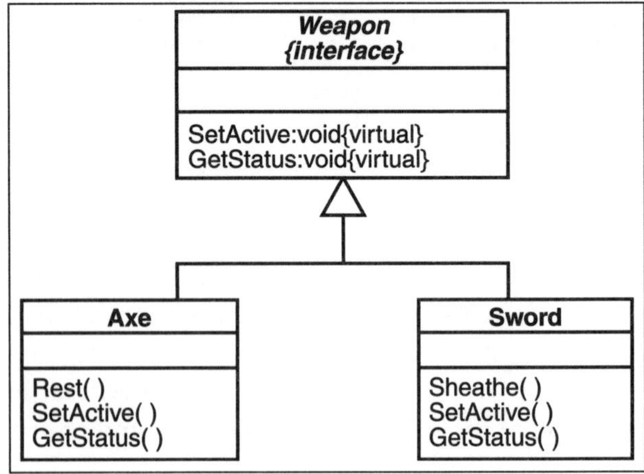

Figure 3.17
A pure virtual (interface) class requires operations to be implemented.

Associations

Classes and their objects relate to each other in several ways. Whereas generalization is reserved for classes, another relationship, *association,* is used to characterize relationships between both classes and objects.

Further, you can represent objects both *statically* and *dynamically.* You represent objects statically in what is known as a generic *object diagram.* On the other hand, you can also represent object relationships dynamically, in what are known as *interaction diagrams.*

To make good use of both class and object diagrams, you need to understand associations. When applied to objects, associations are called *links.*

You use associations to show relationships between objects. Association differs from generalization in a few significant ways:

- Generalization implies that the derived class is a version of the base class. One class "is" another class.

- Objects (or classes) that are related through association are not generalized or specialized versions of each other.
- Associations apply to both objects and classes. Inheritance is a static structural relationship, so it only involves classes.
- Whether an object or a class, when two things are associated with one another, a *dependency* exists between the two.

Both class and object diagrams use lines from one class to another to show that one class depends on another. You can adorn the line in different ways to convey information about the dependency. Figure 3.18 shows a rudimentary association.

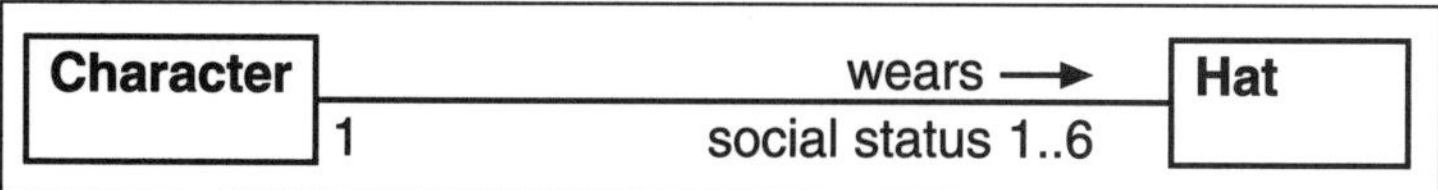

Figure 3.18
An association has a direction and a role.

Note the following features of the association shown in Figure 3.18.

- "Wears" is the name of the association. It allows you to understand what a `Character` object does with a `Hat` object.
- The small arrow to the right of "wears" indicates the direction of the action, so you can read, "A character wears a hat."
- "Social status" is the role that the `Hat` object plays. When you create role names, anticipate the name you intend to use as an attribute name. The `Hat` object is likely to become an attribute in the `Character` class, and `m_SocialStatus` could be the attribute name.
- Only class names identify the objects. Note that the division of the rectangle into name, attribute, and operation regions is eliminated to make things easier to draw. This condensation of features characterizes many class diagrams.
- The numbers at the ends of the relationship (the line) indicate the multiplicity or cardinality of the objects. One character can have from one to six hats.

Visibility and Multiplicity

Visibility refers to what objects can see. An open arrow at the end of the relationship establishes which object is visible. Figure 3.19 shows a pair of classes. You can read the arrow as "can see." In this case, the `Sky` object can see the `Cloud` object. Although how this is so depends on how we develop the classes, one approach is for the `Sky` class to contain an object of the `Cloud` class. When you create a `Sky` object, then, you might also create some

Cloud objects in it, and with the creation of the Cloud object, the Sky object depends on the Cloud object. On the other hand, the Cloud object does not know that the Sky object exists and has no dependency on it.

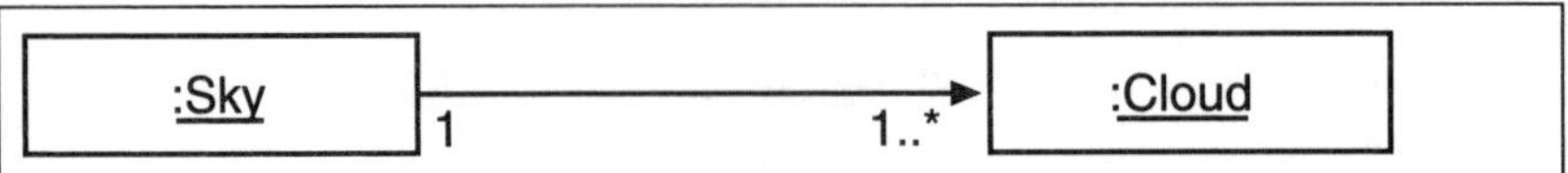

Figure 3.19
Association shows visibility and multiplicity.

Multiplicity is another term for cardinality, which designates the ratio of objects of one class to those of another. Figure 3.19 shows a multiplicity in which for one Sky object, one or more objects of the Cloud class might occur.

Symmetry, Asymmetry, and Coupling

When the arrow points in only one direction, the association is *asymmetrical.* When the arrows adorn both ends of the relationship, the association is *symmetrical.* Generally, designers favor the use of asymmetrical relationships and discourage the use of symmetrical relationships. The reason for this is that if classes are mutually dependent, they are more tightly *coupled.* If classes are more tightly coupled, it becomes difficult to reuse them. Reuse is one of the primary goals of object-oriented design efforts.

note

> One authority wrote, "Coupling is the degree to which elements of the design are connected to each other. For class diagrams, it is essentially a measure of how much a class or object knows about the world around it." (See Charles Richter, *Designing Flexible Object-Oriented Systems with UML* [Indianapolis: Macmillan, 1999], p. 58).

Qualified Associations

If you develop a class that contains a lookup list of objects of another class, you are likely to make use of *qualified association.* Such an association allows you to indicate that you base the relationship between the objects of the two classes on a *key.* Figure 3.20 illustrates a qualified association in which an attribute of the Star class serves as the lookup key in the Sky class. Each Star object has a unique lookup key.

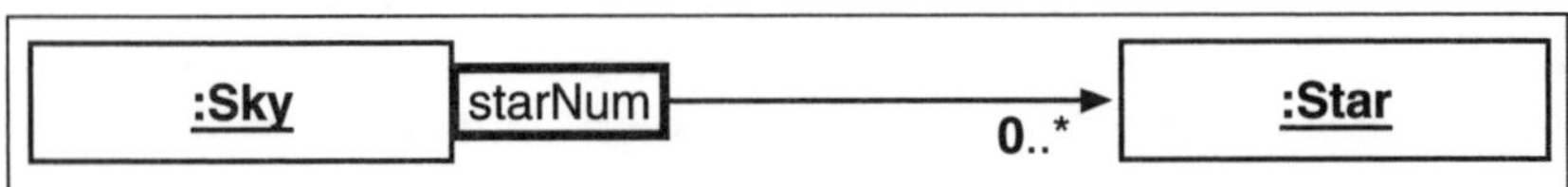

Figure 3.20
One class accesses another class object using a key.

Recursive Associations and Association Classes

Two more terms relevant to associations offer themselves for consideration. When a class has a relationship with itself, the relationship is *recursive.* (Another term for this is *reflexive.*) To save space, this chapter does not illustrate this type of association.

A class that is created solely to allow two other classes to communicate with each other and that lasts only as long as the communication is valid is an *association class.*

Figure 3.21 illustrates an association class. Notice that the name of the class must be the same as the name of the association. The vertical dotted line descending from the association between the `Dock` object and the `Ship` object is called a *dependency* line. The operations that are associated with the "is moored to" class might provide the number of the dock or the time the ship has been moored. By convention, the name of the association and the name of the association class are the same.

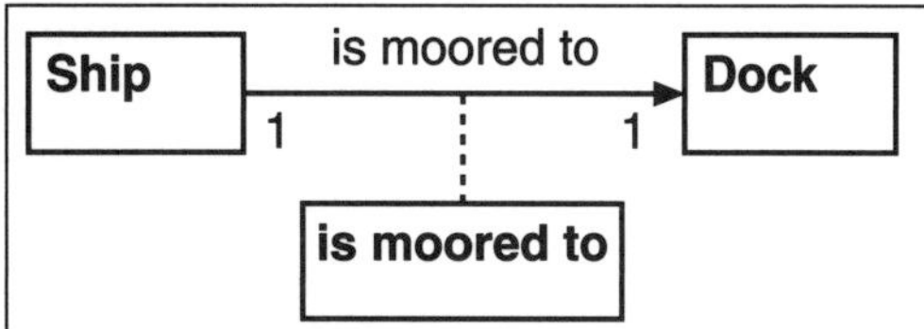

Figure 3.21
An association class shows a complex relationship between two classes.

Aggregation and Composition

Association has two closely related variants: *aggregation* and *composition.* These two types of association provide a way to identify different whole-part relationships that exist between one class and the instances of other classes that it includes as attributes.

Both aggregation and composition imply that one object has an object of another class as an attribute. Note the following points:

- When the composing object must always be a part of the composed object, from its beginning to its end, the relationship is a *composition association.* A filled diamond indicates composition.
- When the composing object might or might not be a part of the composed object but is still given as a reference in the attribute list, the relationship is an *aggregation association.* A hollow diamond indicates aggregation. Figure 3.22 shows an example of composition and aggregation.

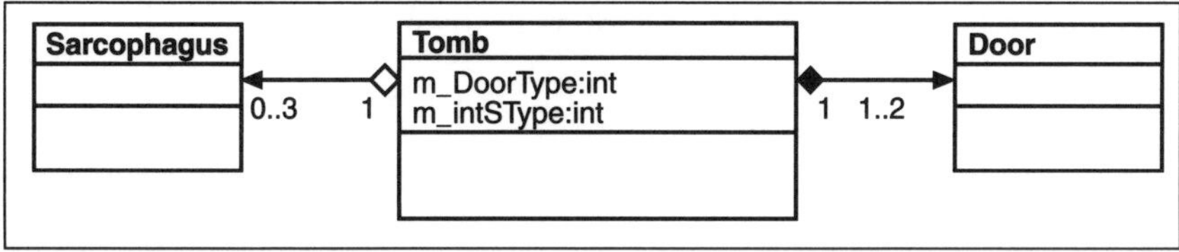

Figure 3.22
Aggregation and composition.

In Figure 3.22, Sarcophagus is in an *aggregated* relationship with Tomb because at times a Tomb object might lack a Sarcophagus. A tomb might be empty. Thus, a Tomb object can be instantiated without a Sarcophagus object.

On the other hand, every Tomb must have a Door, and in Figure 3.22, this relationship is mandated with the use of a *composition* association.

Different Types of Association

To grasp the general dimensions of association, aggregation, and composition, examine Figure 3.23. First, note the way Lightning is in many-to-one relationships with the Axe and Sword classes.

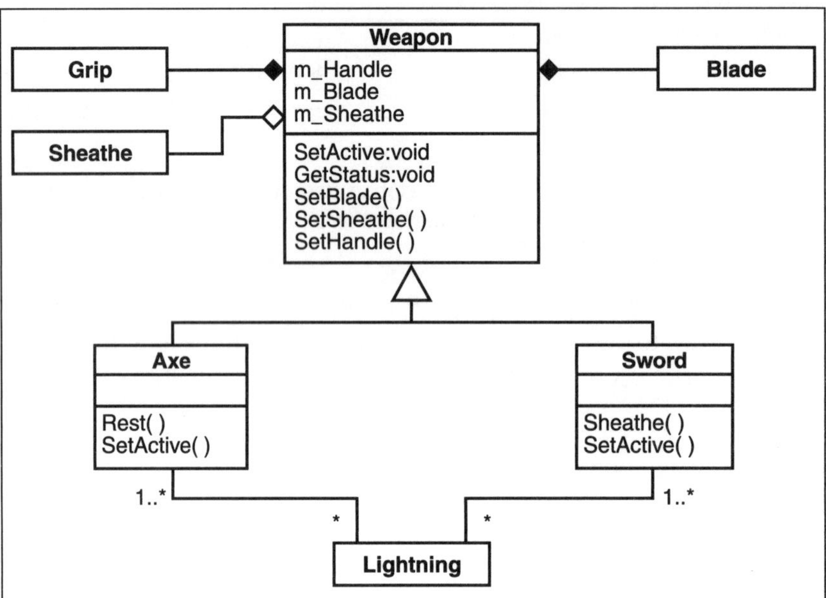

Figure 3.23
The Lightning class is associated with Axe and Sword.

Figure 3.23 shows an aggregation of the Sheath and Weapon classes. Not all weapons have sheathes. The relationship between the Weapon and the Grip and Blade classes is one of composition. Every Weapon must have a Blade and a Grip, start to finish.

Lightning is associated with Axe and Sword. To see how this is so, assume the following use case description.

Weapon Strike. The player battles with Demons. If the Demon is of max power, the weapon creates a flash of lightning every fifth contact with the Demon. The lightning shoots from the weapon.

The question to ask is this: Does the player always manage to strike a `Demon` five times? The answer here is no. It might be the case that the player never strikes a `Demon` five times. `Lightning` is not an attribute of `Weapon`. Rather, it is an object that is created by a given operation of `Weapon`. For this reason, the relationship between the classes that specialize `Weapon` and `Lightning` is a simple association.

Object Diagrams

If you want to model the way objects in a system interact through messages, you use a dynamic diagram. You can use dynamic diagrams to examine relationships among objects. Dynamic diagrams are sometimes referred to as *object diagrams.* An object represents an instance of a class. Object diagrams offer little that you do not use in class diagrams. The following list details a few of the more important differences between class diagrams and object diagrams:

- Rather than show classes, object diagrams represent the objects that classes generate.
- Whereas a class diagram is static, an object diagram is often dynamic. In other words, an object diagram shows how a particular object sends a message to another specific object.
- Object diagrams feature the relationships that are familiar from class diagrams, but in object diagrams, the relationships between objects are referred to as *links* rather than associations. Still, designers commonly refer to the relationships shown in object diagrams as associations. The terms are interchangeable.
- A few adornments not glimpsed in class diagrams appear in object diagrams. These adornments usually involve how objects are named and how objects send and receive messages.

Figure 3.24 shows a class diagram (top) and two object diagrams (bottom).

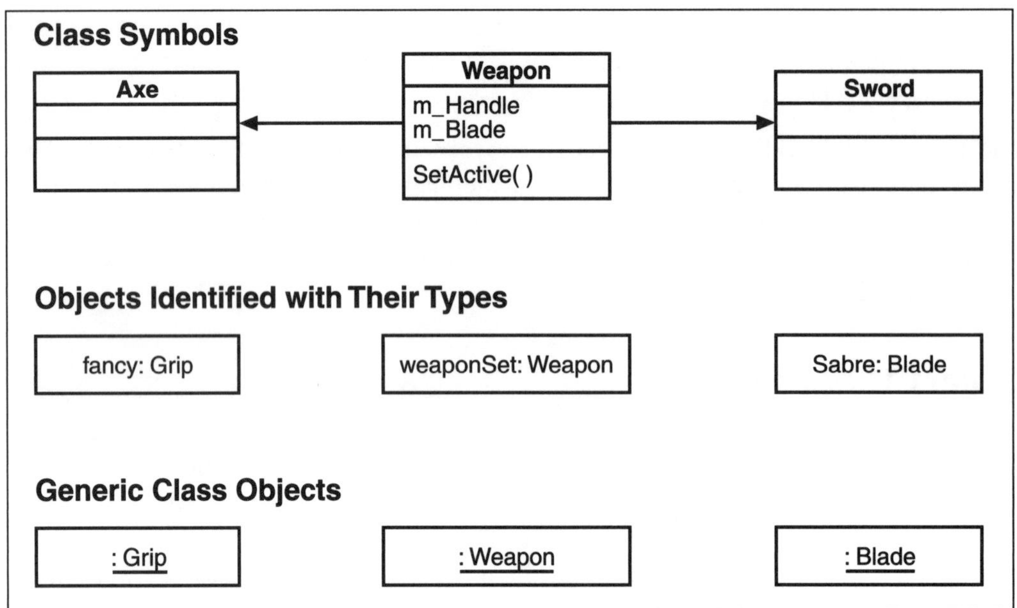

Figure 3.24
Diagrams can represent classes or objects.

Notice the following features of Figure 3.24:

- The first row shows three associated class elements. The names of the classes at the top of Figure 3.24 are not underlined.
- In contrast, in the second row, the names of the objects are underlined. Likewise, the object names consist of compounded parts. The object name comes first (`fancy`), followed by a colon, and the name of the class comes last (`Grip`). The convention reveals that the object is a named instance of the class (`fancy:Grip`).
- The third row illustrates another approach to naming objects: A colon is prefixed to the class name, and the name is underlined. This shows that the object is a generic instance of the class.
- Designers commonly illustrate object relationships both ways. No hard rule dictates when and where a given approach is used.

About Objects

An object represents an instance of a class, and an instance of a class at some point comes into existence and at another point goes out of existence. This is called the *lifetime* of the object. When you diagram how an object changes during its lifetime, your diagram is *dynamic*. Object diagrams are often dynamic.

Objects also actively send *messages* to each other through their operations. (C ++ programmers call operations *member functions*.)

Objects are featured in three important UML diagrams. You've already glimpsed the first in the investigation of class diagrams. This is the generic static *object diagram*. Object diagrams are convenient media for showing the dependencies and multiplicities of objects.

The two other types of diagrams are known as *interaction diagrams*. The first of these is called a *sequence diagram*. Sequence diagrams show the lifetimes of objects and the sequences in which they communicate with each other. The other type of diagram is called a *collaboration diagram*. Collaboration diagrams show how objects communicate with each other.

Links, Dynamic Modeling, and Messages

The relationships between objects are called *links*. For all practical purposes, links and associations are synonymous. Links reveal how messages pass from one object to another. When a model shows how different messages pass between different objects at varying times, the model is called *dynamic*.

Objects communicate with each other via messages. A message is sent whenever an operation executes. Note how messages are related to the following details of an object:

- An instance of a class has to exist. An instance of a class is an object.
- The class defines the operations that are available to the object, and these operations are known as the class interface. All objects of a given class have access to the interface of the class.
- Operations allow objects to send messages.
- The object that initiates the message is the *sender* of the message.
- The object to which the message is sent is the *receiver* of the message.
- To show a message, you use a line tipped by an arrow—which can be referred to as an association or link. The arrow points from the sender to the receiver.

Message Types

When a system processes messages, it passes along *control* of the program from one object to another. An object that has control of the flow is *active*. When an object is active and sends a message, different things can happen. You can classify messages according to what happens. Table 3.7 shows you the messages and how they are classified. In this case, a given object sends a message to another.

Table 3.7 Messages and Their Types

Message	Description
Simple messages	The object can send a message to another object; by sending the message, the object relinquishes control of the flow. No further messages are sent.
Synchronous messages	The object can send a message and momentarily relinquish control. When it does this, it puts itself in a kind of suspended state of activity while the receiver of the message takes control and does something. When the receiver finishes whatever it is doing, it passes a message back to the first object. When this happens, the first object regains control.
Asynchronous messages	The object can send a message to another object and expect no message in return. In addition to expecting no return message, it also retains control of the flow and can send still more messages.
Return message	This is not so much a message as an acknowledgement. If an object is, say, waiting for a reply to a message it has sent, the message it receives to terminate its suspension (or to allow it to continue on with its activity) is called a *return*. Most software designers do not consider this a message, but it can still be traced in an object diagram. In fact, it might be important to do so.

Message Arrows

Now that you know the types of messages, it's good for you to learn the ways to represent these messages. Figure 3.25 illustrates the four arrow elements that the UML provides to indicate messages. Review Table 3.7 if you need help with the terms.

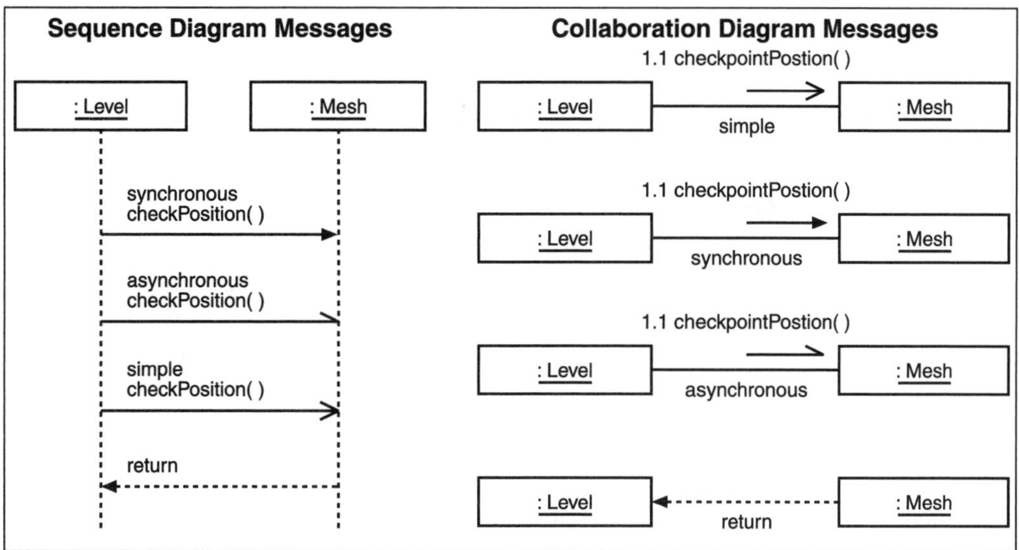

Figure 3.25
Messages fall into four general categories.

Message Parameters

Message parameters form an essential part of interaction diagrams, especially collaboration diagrams. A full discussion of the syntax of messages is beyond the scope of this chapter, but this section will examine a few basics. Figure 3.26 illustrates the basic syntax of a message.

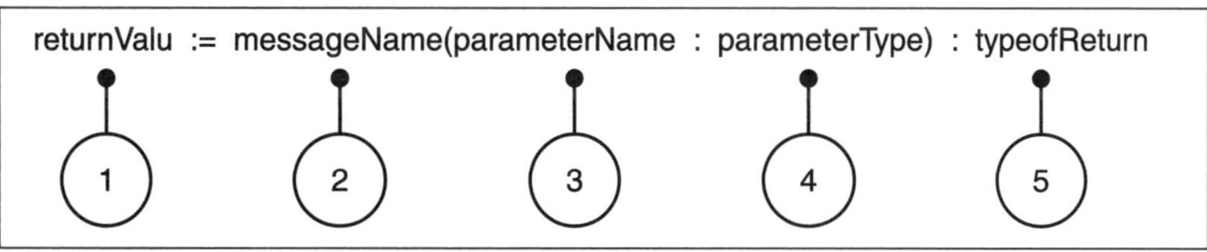

Figure 3.26
The message syntax allows you to show parameters and return values.

In most instances, you need only show the message named followed by open and close parentheses. The following list discusses the syntax shown in Figure 3.26.

- The value returned by the operation that conveys the message.
- The name of the message. In most cases, you will use only the message name followed by open and close parentheses (for example, `startAction()`).

- The value or values that the message conveys.
- The data type of the message parameter.
- The data type of the return value of the message.

Sequence Diagrams

A dynamic object diagram, the sequence diagram allows you to trace the flow of the messages from object to object. To make the flow easy to comprehend, the sequence diagram depicts behavior of an object along two axes: vertical and horizontal. The vertical axis shows the lifeline of each object. The horizontal axis allows you to see how messages pass between objects.

Objects and Lifelines

To create a sequence diagram, you can align the objects of the system or subsystem you want to investigate across the top of the diagram. Then you can draw *lifelines* downward for each object. You can establish nodes on each lifeline that allow you to indicate when one object communicates with another object. Figure 3.27 illustrates a sequence diagram.

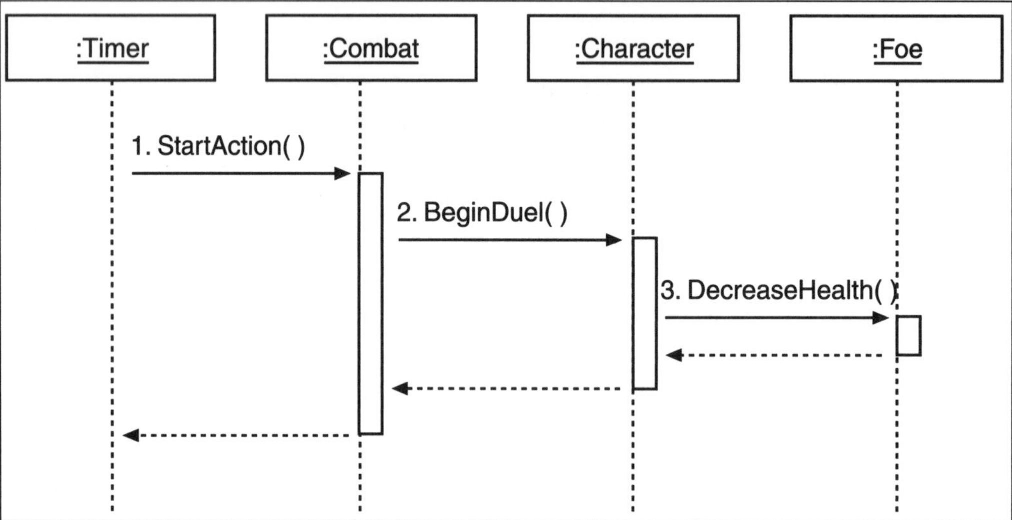

Figure 3.27
Vertical and horizontal axes trace lifelines and message paths.

Four objects stretch across the top of the sequence diagram of Figure 3.27. Note the following features of the diagram:

- The objects appear across the top. Notice here that class names preceded by colons indicate that the objects are generic. Objects do not have to be across the top. They can be located anywhere it is convenient or appropriate to show them being constructed or destructed.
- The vertical boxes are called *activations.* They indicate when an operation is active. They're included here for purposes of illustration, but because all the messages are depicted as synchronous, it might be imagined that they are waiting for return values and remain active.
- The lines going from left to right indicate synchronous messages. Such messages pass control and usually expect some type of return message.
- A dashed arrow depicts return values.
- In all the instances shown here, the messages are in sequence: The timer issues a start time, the AI device tells the character to strike, and the character strikes the foe. When the foe is struck, he returns a value, as does the character and the AI device. When the timer receives the return, it quits.
- You can identify messages in different ways. The notation can be elaborate. To keep it simple, you can use the message or the name of the operations that issue the messages.

How to Read Messages

To make sense of the way the messages work in Figure 3.27, consider the following points:

- The class `Combat` has an operation called `StartAction()`. The message sent from the `Timer` object to the `Combat` object is sent through `StartAction()`.
- The class `Character` has an action called `StrikeEnemy()`. The message that `Combat` sends to the `Character` object is sent through the `StrikeEnemy()` operation.
- The class `Foe` has an operation called `DecreaseHealth()`. The message that `Character` sends to `Foe` is sent through `DecreaseHealth()`.
- In each case, you can replace the operation names with message names, such as *start*, *strike*, and *diminish.*

Collaboration Diagrams

Both sequence diagrams and collaboration diagrams are interaction diagrams. Further, a sequence diagram can be converted into a collaboration diagram and vice versa. If a sequence diagram helps you understand the order in which objects interact with each other, collaboration diagrams allow you to investigate the specific messages and how they contribute to the logic of the system. Figure 3.28 shows a collaboration diagram.

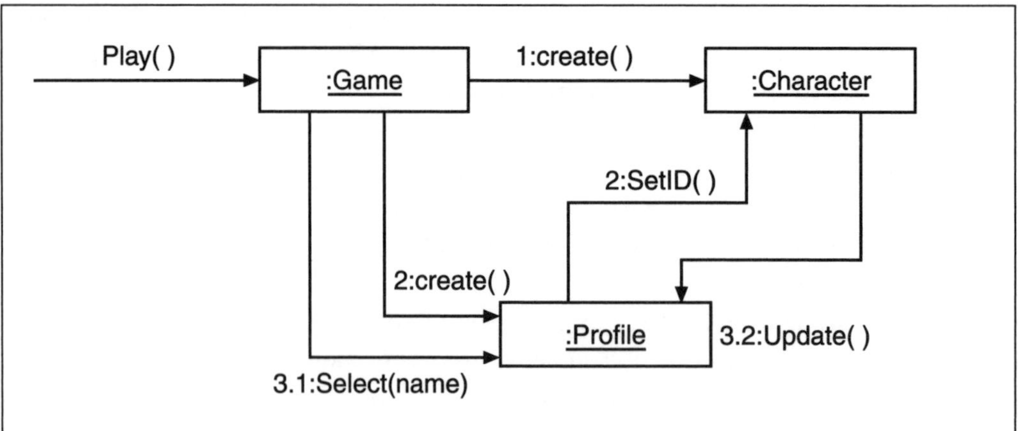

Figure 3.28
Collaboration diagrams aid with understanding how objects form into components through the messages they send to each other.

Figure 3.28 shows a few salient features of collaboration diagrams, as follows:

- Military numbering (1.1, 1.1.1, and so on) shows the path that messages follow as the system completes a given task.
- Objects bear specific or generic names, and the names are underlined.
- Side arrows reveal the direction of the actions of links.
- Labels identify links. Usually, you can add several pieces of information to the label.

State Chart Diagrams

A *state chart diagram* is also called a *state transition diagram.* Such a diagram allows you to investigate how the state of an object changes. Whereas an activity diagram is a convenient tool for examining use cases, a state transition diagram allows you to go into an object at one moment in its life and see how its state changes as you move to another moment in its life.

The most basic use of a state transition diagram is to illustrate an *event.* An event is a bounded happening. You begin at one state, make a transition, and end at another state. This is called an event. The specific items under investigation are the attributes of the object. You examine the values stored in the attributes at one point, you consider the messages or changes the object goes through (the operations that make these changes), and you finish by viewing the changed state of the attributes. Again, this is an event.

Why does an object change? It changes because it receives messages that tell it to change. It receives messages when it interacts with other objects. Messages are sent to an object by *invoking* its operations. The object changes when its state (its attributes) changes in response to information it receives from other objects. When the object changes, the change is an *event.*

Events, States, and Transitions

Three terms describe what happens in a state chart diagram:

- An object starts in a given state.
- The object receives a message. The message need not always come from another object (although it will most of the time). A message might come from the hardware system. The object might send a message to itself.
- In response to the message, the attributes of an object change. The object goes through a *transition.* This transition is said to be an *event.*

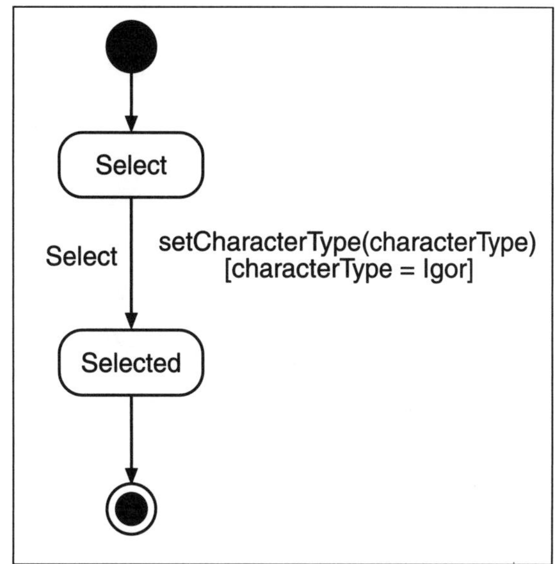

Figure 3.29
State charts show objects in different states.

Figure 3.29 shows a state chart diagram.

Note the following features of Figure 3.29:

- The rounded rectangles represent states.
- The arrows mark transitions.
- The filled dot is called the initial state.
- The circle with the dot inside is called the end state.
- In Figure 3.29, at the Start state, the character attribute has a default type of "character."
- The Selected state shows the changed state of the object.

```
setCharacterType(characterType) [characterType = Igor]
```

- This message specification tells you the action that must take place for the object to change.
- The arrow indicates the direction of the transition.

More on State Transitions

In addition to showing single transitions, state transitions can show composites. A composite consists of a set of states and transitions that can be viewed as a single event. Figure 3.30 shows a composite state diagram. The large rounded rectangle surrounds two states, showing a composite event. The composite event has a name—given in the top of the composite rectangle.

In Figure 3.30, note that the composite diagram shows two states and one transition inside the composite box—which is titled "Exiting." The composite state deals with a set of states that involve the same changes. Although these changes are not shown here, the "selected" action might apply, say, to a setting that says that the state of the game is to be saved. If selected, then the state is saved to a file for future startup activity.

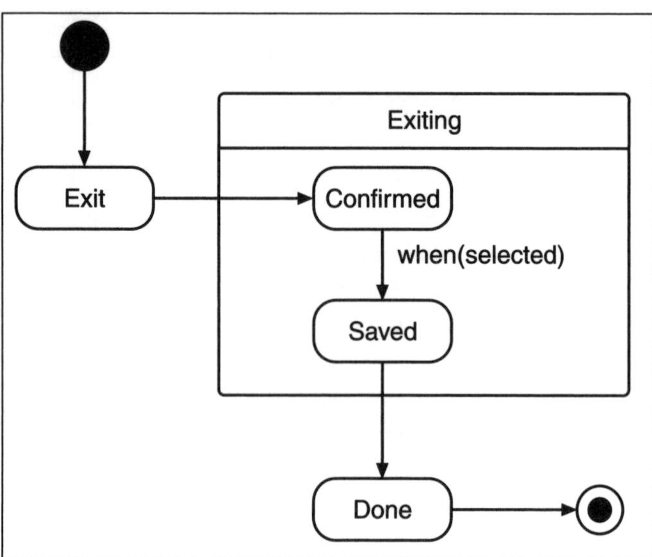

Figure 3.30
Composite states show substates.

Component Diagrams

As you develop your game, you usually develop components that take care of sound, animation, data storage, and other tasks. You might develop these as separate executables. In all such instances, it is a good idea to organize these components so that they are grouped according to the services they provide. A component diagram provides you with the ability to show the groupings of these libraries and resources.

note

A component is sometimes called a *subsystem.* A component is also sometimes called a *module.* A component is occasionally a unit of execution—a set of files compiled into a single dynamic link library. In other cases, a component is a collection of "resource" files.

The organization of the components of a system has both logical and physical implications, but the governing factor in component diagrams is how they are grouped in the system architecture. Figure 3.31 illustrates a component diagram.

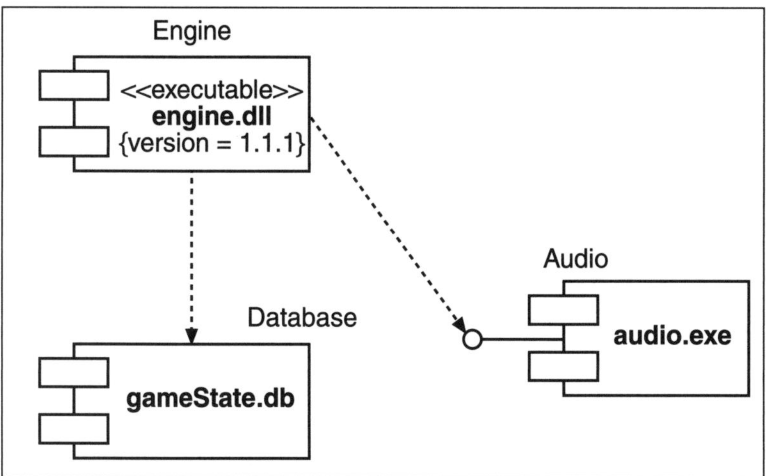

Figure 3.31
Component diagrams depict larger component groups.

Note the following features of the component diagram depicted in Figure 3.31:

- The tabbed rectangles represent components. A component can be a separate executable, replaceable entity. It can also represent collections of files. In this case, the engine for the game, the music player, and the database engine have been set up so that they can be separately installed or updated.
- A stereotype is used with the Engine component. You can use stereotypes and other notation to describe the component.
- Tagged values or properties can provide supplemental information. Here, a property for *version* allows the version number of the engine to be identified.
- The stemmed line extending from the Audio component represents an interface, which is a common feature with components.
- The broken lines with the open arrows indicate dependencies. In other words, the engine uses Audio and Database components.
- A name for each component should appear somewhere near the component. The name is a logical name rather than the name of a file or executable that the component contains.

Package Diagrams

Package diagrams closely resemble component diagrams. They offer a way to group together elements (such as classes) when you create design documentation. The relationships that apply to object and class diagrams also apply to package diagrams. A folder indicates a package. Dashed lines show dependencies. Packages usually contain groups of classes that provide a common service. Figure 3.32 illustrates a package diagram.

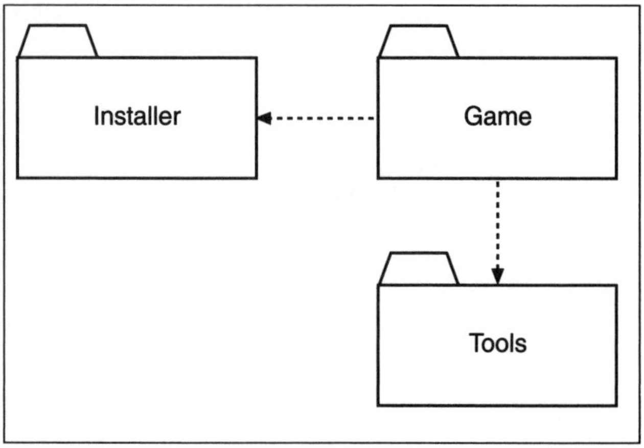

Figure 3.32
Use package diagrams to group elements during the design phase.

Deployment Diagrams

A deployment diagram provides information on the physical location of different components or packages. It differs from a component diagram because it identifies the physical (hardware) locations. Figure 3.33 shows a deployment diagram.

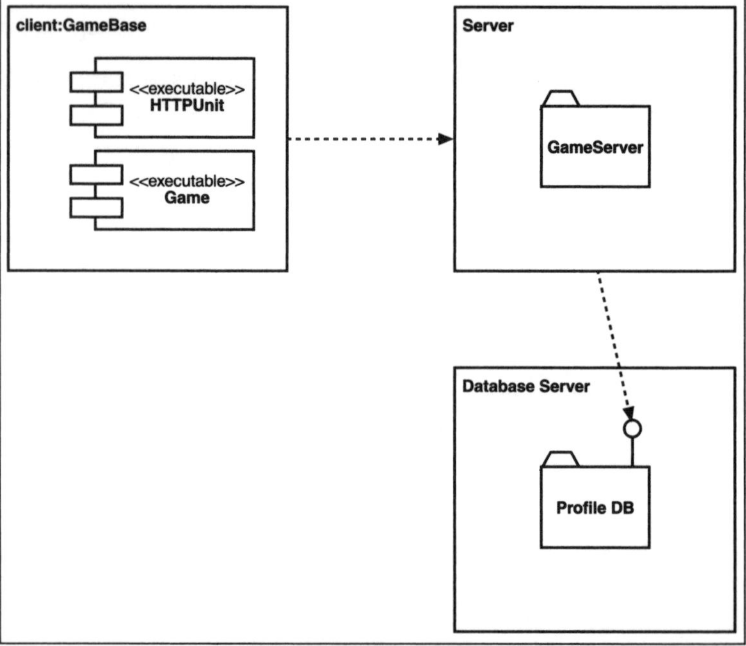

Figure 3.33
Deployment diagrams identify physical system locations.

Note the following features of Figure 3.33:

- The boxes are nodes. A node can be a server or any other physical device on which the system software is installed.
- The tabbed folders are *packages.*
- Packages appear within the nodes, but other elements might appear, also. Examples might be serialized classes that are written to a given server. In this case, you might see a class or object diagram in a node.
- The line with the circle represents an interface. The database package is accessed through its interface.
- Each node is named. The names are arbitrarily assigned but should indicate the type or identity of the hardware designated as a node.
- The dashed lines with open arrows represent dependencies. The client package requires a connection to the server node, and the server node requires a connection to the database node.

Conclusion

UML offers an extensive set of conventions, and acquiring full knowledge of these conventions requires extensive study. However, you can put the knowledge you have gained in this chapter right to work if you use UML notation the next time you plan a program. Use the notation! If you work informally, expanding on an idea or explaining something to someone else, you really cannot go wrong. As long as the notation helps you in your work, it is doing its job. Refine your knowledge as you go.

If you want to investigate the subject more extensively, check out the following books:

Ambler, Scott W. *The Elements of UML Style.* New York: Cambridge University Press, 2003.

Bennett, Simon, John Kelton, and Ken Lunn. *Schaum's Outline of UML.* New York: McGraw-Hill, 2001.

Booch, Grady, Ivar Jacobson, and James Rumbaugh. *The Unified Modeling Language User Guide.* Reading, Massachusetts: Addison-Wesley, 1998.

Booch, Jacobson, and Rumbaugh take you to the source. They unified the things that became the UML. Reading their book allows you to gain a sense of the spirit of the language.

Computer-Aided Software Engineering (CASE) tools incorporate the syntax of the UML. These tools are available widely as both commercial products and freeware. Appendix A, "Installation and Setup," introduces you to SmartDraw. SmartDraw is not a full-fledged CASE tool, but it allows you to manually create UML diagrams. It is also an excellent tool for working with all aspects of game development. (A demonstration copy of SmartDraw is on the CD.)

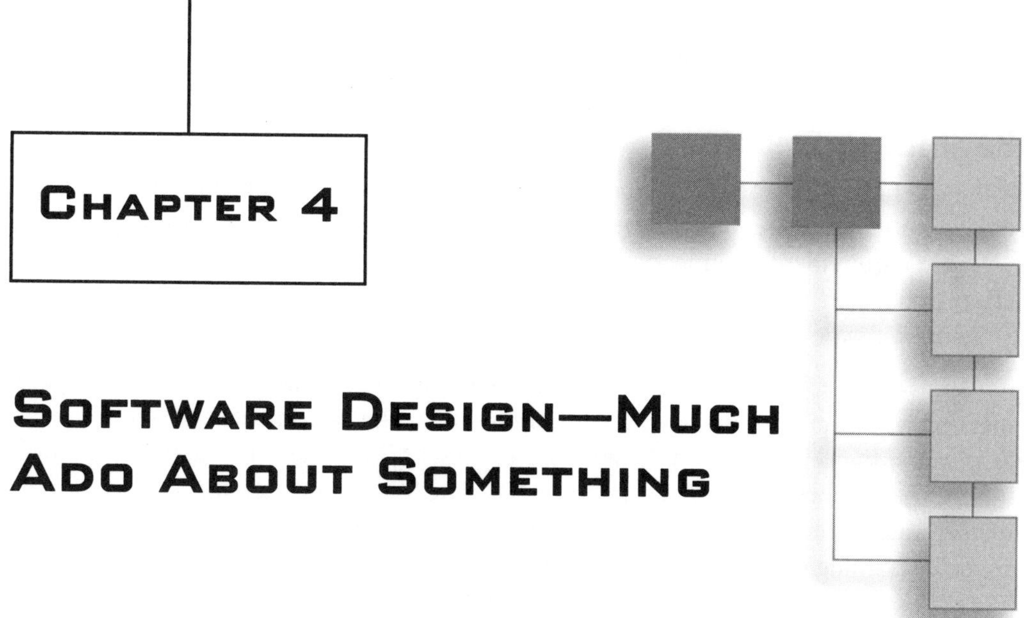

Chapter 4

Software Design—Much Ado About Something

When you design software, you begin with a collection of information you have gathered during the requirements phase of the development lifecycle. This information allows you to define a multitude of software entities that express the functionality that the requirements specify. In addition to creating a group of functional entities, however, you also organize the entities so that they can work together. The software design effort involves understanding what counts as a good software system and then using a select set of tools to discover and depict such a system. In this chapter, you will do things in two parts toward these ends. First, you'll learn the guiding concepts of design. Later, you'll delve into the nitty-gritty of the design effort with *Ankh*. Many factors come into play. Among the topics covered in this chapter are the following:

- Why do design at all?
- The elements of design, including reducing complexity and focusing on responsibilities
- The principles of design, which involve—among other things—abstraction, cohesion, and coupling
- Design patterns, which are also carried into another chapter
- The developing of design using stripes
- The use of design tools, such as interaction diagrams, class diagrams, Class-Responsibility-Collaboration (CRC) cards, and component diagrams
- One approach to creating a design and the contents of a software design description

Beginning Design

After you finish the work of engineering a set of software requirements, you can begin work on the software design. Design work differs from requirements engineering. Software requirements engineering involves discovering *what* functionality you need to create to support the features of your game. Software design involves planning *how* to build the software system according to the requirements.

As discussed in Chapter 2, "Requirements—Getting the Picture," you capture requirements in a *Software Requirements Specification* (SRS). This document states requirements as a list and then elaborates on them with use cases. This chapter introduces another document: the *Software Design Description* (SDD). The SDD shows developers how to build the software system. It does so by taking the information provided in the requirements and transforming it into diagrams and other design artifacts that show developers how to build the software that addresses the needs that the requirements express.

Why Design?

Software engineers design software systems for a variety of reasons. One of the most important reasons is that the complexity of a system tends to increase drastically as you add elements to it. One way to approach the need to reduce the complexity of software systems is to consider Figure 4.1.

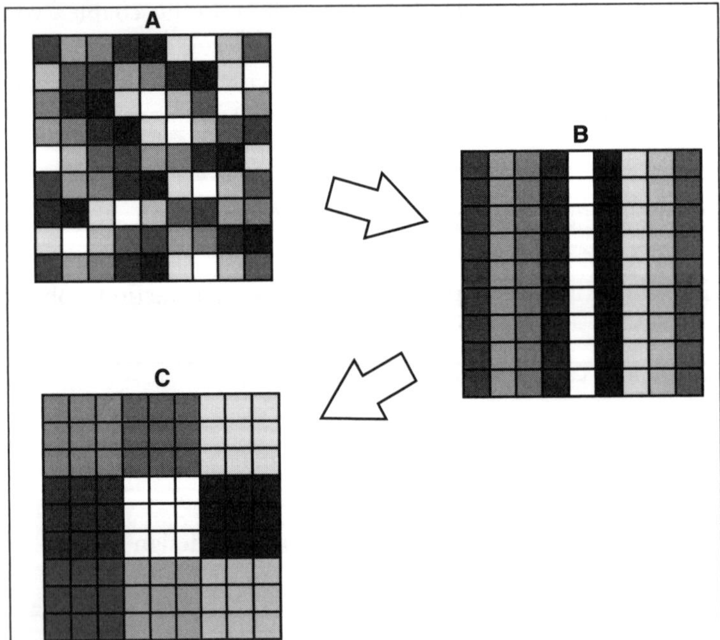

Figure 4.1
Complexity characterizes any random system.

Figure 4.1 (A) shows a set of differently shaded squares arranged in a random manner. If you think of the squares as software components, such as classes, you can arrive fairly easily at a sense of what a design effort might accomplish. Notice in set A how difficult it is to see how many different shades of squares there are. Suppose that someone told you to uniformly change the shades of the squares. Set A would make this task fairly difficult because you would have to work individually with all the squares. The squares have no order. Because no order in the arrangement of the squares exists, the squares are said to be part of a *complex system.*

What can you do with this set of squares? One thing you can do is reduce the complexity by organizing the squares according to their relationships. What relationships? You might name shades of gray first.

Note the following results of analysis:

- Eighty-one squares form the pattern of squares.
- If you group the squares according to their colors, you find nine color groupings.
- The squares occur in sets of nine, so you can create nine sets of nine.
- You can further reduce the complexity by making the groupings symmetrical (putting them in 3×3 matrices).

Figure 4.1 (B) shows the colors regrouped into columns. The analogous situation in software is when, for example, functions of a given type are organized into specific, well-focused classes or classes are, in turn, organized into components that provide specific types of service. Notice how the reorganization reduces the complexity of the design. It is now much easier to see how the squares can be grouped into nine components. Figure 4.1 (C) shows the squares reorganized so that the groups are more *symmetrical.* Figure 4.2 elaborates on the effects of the design effort.

Software design involves examining the elements of a system to find ways to group the elements according to the relationships that pertain between them. Ultimately, this activity involves seeking certain design objectives. To identify the elements and their relationships, you can use *design rules.* Design rules begin with objects and messages. When you reorganize the elements and refine their relationships, you apply *design principles.* Design principles help you identify collaborations of objects. You can move to a higher level of organization when you consider the different possibilities for how to arrange the collaborative elements so that they achieve the best results. For example, notice that the squares went from being in columns to being in matrices. At this level, you apply *design patterns.* At a still higher level, you consider what is known as the *architectural style* of the system. Figure 4.3 illustrates a hierarchy of these concepts of design.

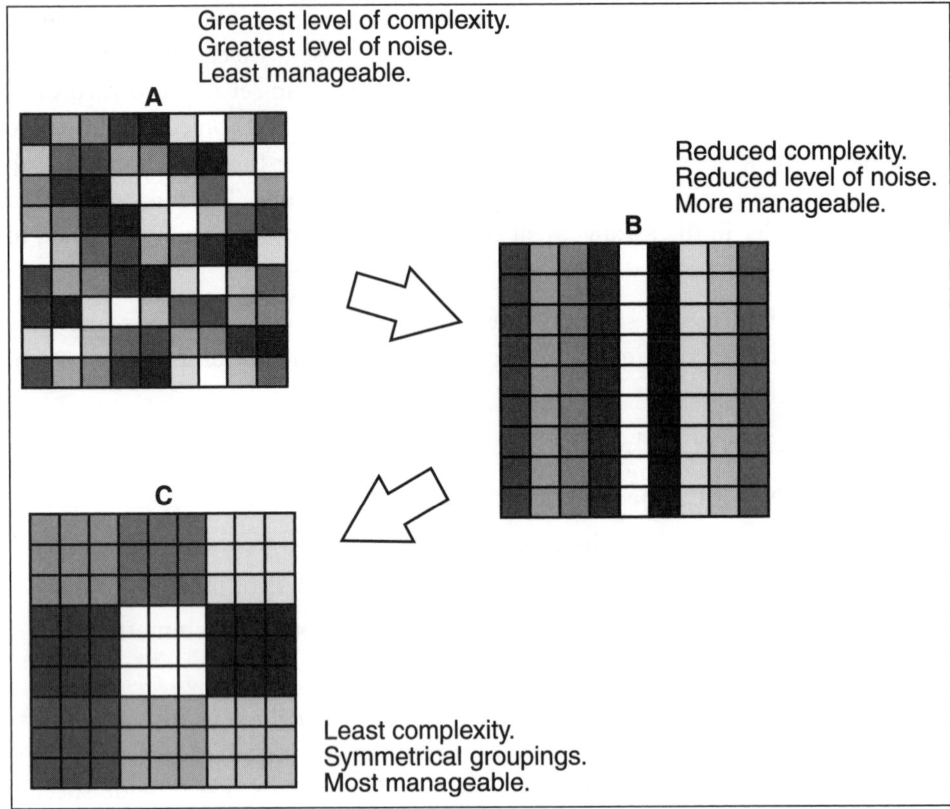

Figure 4.2
Design reorganization reduces the complexity of the system.

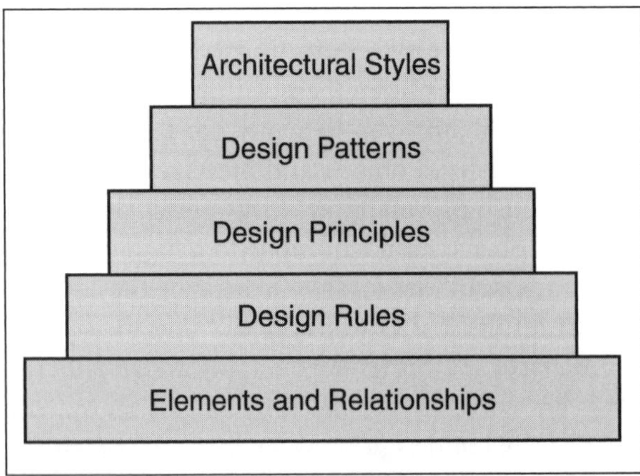

Figure 4.3
Design involves moving from the least to the most encompassing views of the system.

Architecture and Design

In its labor of reducing the complexity of software systems, software design draws upon a collection of practical tools that you use to analyze and refine a system into interacting objects. At the same time, it also draws upon high-level conceptualizations of software systems. *Architecture* provides you with a set of conceptualizations of what a system should be when completed. The architectural vision of the system marks both the beginning and the end of the design journey. It marks the beginning because it provides a set of assumptions that guide the design activity. It marks the end because it calls for a general view of the system as an architectural creation. Figure 4.4 summarizes the perspective.

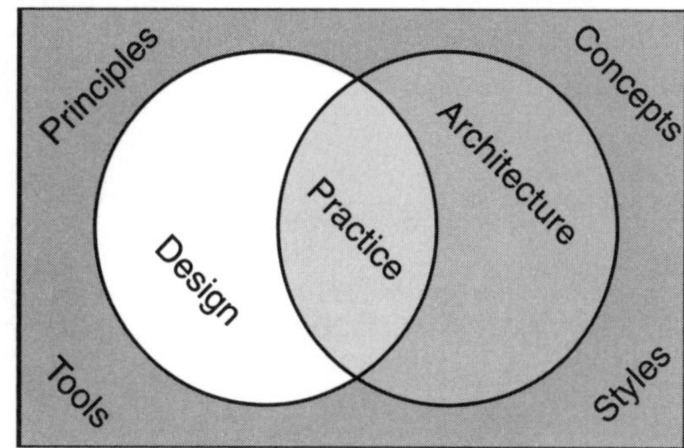

Figure 4.4
Design and architecture meet in practice.

In contrast to architecture, *design* concentrates on details and seeks to organize the elements within a system to produce a system that fulfills the specifications given in the requirements. Architecture and design are sometimes regarded as the same thing. This is not a particularly beneficial way of looking at things. At some moments, you assess a task from an architectural perspective. At other moments, you immerse yourself in details and concentrate on specific features of design. As you move forward in this chapter, it's important to remember the distinction between practical component refinement and overall system style.

Rules for Identifying Design Elements

The approach to design used in the *Ankh* development effort involved *rules.* Ways of defining design elements that formed the groundwork of the design effort were designated as rules. These were not rules in the sense of laws that spell out right and wrong behavior for system designers. Rather, these rules consisted of assumptions that helped designers understand the content of what they were dealing with. The rules fall under five general headings: *state machines, functions, relationships, collaborations,* and *responsibilities.* When you seek to design a system, you can first identify items that fall under such rules. Using the rules as guides, you can then design the system. Figure 4.5 offers a summary view of ways to identify elements.

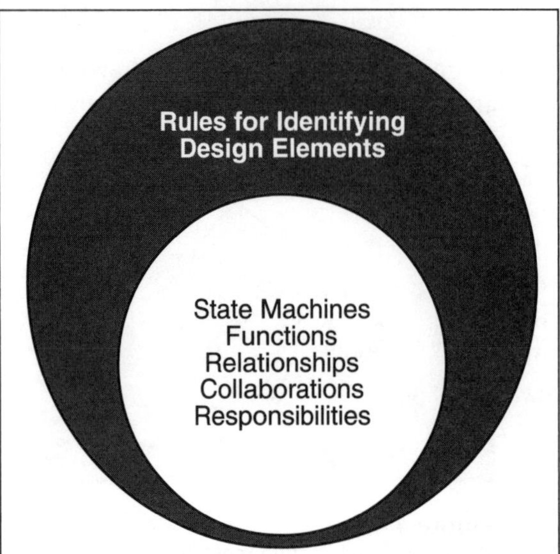

Figure 4.5
Find ways to identify the fundamental elements of design.

State Machines

The generic state machine is one of the first basic elements of design. Generally, a state machine is an entity that is capable of storing information and making decisions based on that information. An object is often identified as a state machine because its attributes store information and its operations respond to input using the stored information.

The point is to establish that a software system can contain entities that store information and are capable of reacting in an indirect fashion to the system around them. When entities behave in this way, they are called state machines or, more simply, objects.

Functions

Another element of design is the function—or operation. In contrast to state machines, operations might not store information. Instead, they might immediately process the information and return a result. Such entities are not state machines; they are usually identified as functions. Functions can be collected together into libraries. The libraries can provide a set of services. An example is the C math library.

Relationships

Whenever one element (whether it's an operation, a class, a state machine, or a component) communicates with another, a relationship is established between the two elements. A relationship can be considered asynchronous when one entity communicates with another without needing to receive information in return. A relationship can be characterized as synchronous when it expects a response or an acknowledgement. The outcome of the relationship between two elements is that messages that the relationships transfer allow the states of elements to change. An element's state is characterized by the information it contains. The message might cause a state change.

Collaborations

When you collaborate with someone to do something, you join with that person to accomplish certain goals. Both functions and state machines can collaborate. From an object-oriented perspective, a collaboration involves division of labor and specialization, so that a group of objects provides the system with a type of service that transcends the service provided by any one object within the collaboration.

Responsibilities

Responsibilities in a software system begin with the requirements specification. Ultimately, with every line of code, you should seek to implement the functionality that the requirements specify. What does not trace back to the requirements deserves questioning. System designers often use role names to illustrate the responsibilities of particular elements. Class and function names convey their responsibilities. Likewise, component names reveal the collective responsibilities of the elements that the component groups together.

Principles of Design

Principles differ from rules on a number of levels. Principles of design guide you as you refine the relationships you develop within and between the classes or components that make up your software system. Principles of design help you know how to reshape the system through incremental refinements. You use these principles to help you determine how to merge, divide, eliminate, and generally refine the elements of your system. Rules, in contrast, relate to the simple identification of visible elements or component groupings of the system. Figure 4.6 offers a summary view of a few common principles of design.

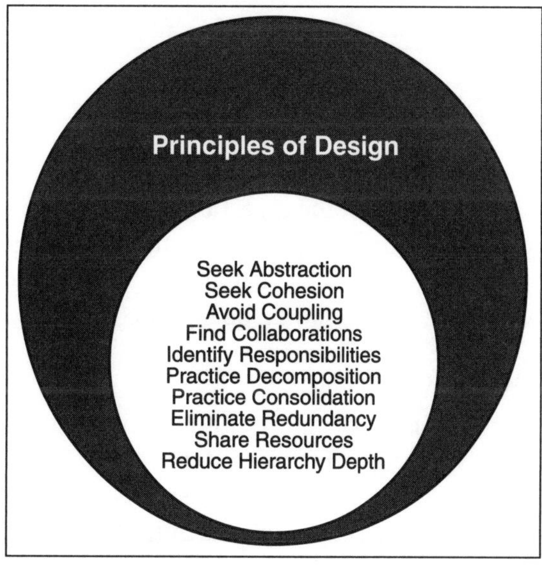

Principles of Design
Seek Abstraction
Seek Cohesion
Avoid Coupling
Find Collaborations
Identify Responsibilities
Practice Decomposition
Practice Consolidation
Eliminate Redundancy
Share Resources
Reduce Hierarchy Depth

Figure 4.6
Establish principles of design.

Seek Abstraction and Encapsulation

Because objects in the real world are complex, people form abstractions to capture their essence. For example, you might employ abstractions to create characters in a game. You create these characters using classes. The characters are less complex than real people because the classes with which they are created allow them to behave in only a limited number of ways and to have a limited number of states. This activity of limiting the characters to behaving and existing in limited ways is a key to understanding encapsulation.

Encapsulation combines attributes (which are the things that hold the state of a object) and operations (which are the things that change the behavior of an object) into a single entity—a class. You use the class to create objects. Each object performs according to the behaviors and attributes that the class encapsulates. It is in this way that a class encapsulates the attributes and behaviors of the characters in a game.

The user of the class should be concerned only with receiving the services that the class provides. Services are provided to an interface. An interface consists of the public operations of a class. The interface simplifies the use of what might be thousands of lines of code; the only thing the user of the interface sees is the operation through which the service is obtained.

You can also apply abstraction and encapsulation to larger design contexts. For example, in the use of components and frameworks, you can package a software component consisting of many classes so that it, too, offers a simple interface. Frameworks abstract the work of large groups of classes so that programmers can easily develop specific types of applications. (C# Forms, MFC, and Java Swing are examples.)

Seek Cohesion

Cohesion describes how well the operations in a class address one specific theme. The theme is usually spoken of as the *responsibility* of the class. Every operation within a class should address some aspect of the responsibility that is assigned to the class. If a class is concerned, for example, with Artificial Intelligence (AI), then it probably has no business providing operations that deal with sizing dialog boxes or regulating audio output. Generally, classes should be highly cohesive.

Avoid Coupling

Coupling is a principle of design because it, like cohesion, can apply to every element in the system. *Coupling* refers to the extent to which elements depend on each other, but it goes a step beyond. Every element in a system, to some degree, depends on other elements in the system. On the other hand, when elements depend on each other too much, their dependencies require that when one part of the system must be changed, many other parts of the system might have to be changed as well. Tight coupling reduces the flexibility of the system. Two major problems result from tight coupling. One problem has already been mentioned: For every one change, many others must be made. The other problem is that if any one part of the system fails, many others will fail, also. Such a system is said to possess a high degree of instability.

Practice Decomposition

Decomposition is a way to achieve both coupling and cohesion. To decompose an entity is to break it into pieces. You break a complex set of system functionality into subsystems to reduce its complexity. Decomposition reveals whether subgroupings exist. You can simplify complexity by breaking noncohesive classes into cohesive classes.

Practice Consolidation

Although approaches to programming differ from individual to individual, programmers commonly solve problems by first decomposing problems into tasks. Each task can then become the subject of a separate function. This type of work can characterize the development of a class. For example, when you design the interface for a class, it is important to see whether operations are redundant. Do you require two function calls when one would do?

Eliminate Redundancy

Each class in a program should address a single responsibility, and no two classes should focus on the same one. Consider a situation in which you have two classes that provide similar services. An example might be classes that create sliders. You develop two classes, one for vertical sliders and the other for horizontal sliders. Clearly, the objects you create with these classes resemble each other closely, with the difference only that objects of the classes adjust for vertical or horizontal positions. Is it worthwhile having two classes? You can eliminate such redundancy by creating one class that allows you to instantiate sliders horizontally or vertically, depending on the setting, say, of one attribute or the value provided to one operation within the class.

Share Resources

You can view resources in several ways. Resource sharing in this context is referred to as relating to a given type of service (or activities that address a given responsibility). The elements that provide a given type of service can be grouped into one class or component. Other components can then draw upon this one class or component for the services it offers. Sharing of resources reduces complexity and supports software reuse. One of the prime means of sharing resources is to create hierarchies and employ inheritance to specialize operations. Another approach is through composition, which involves creating an instance of one class inside another.

Reduce Hierarchy Depth

This principle arose in response to the tendency that inexperienced designers have of creating deep hierarchies. The drawback of using deep hierarchies is that system performance declines when classes become large. Large classes result when a class lower down in a hierarchy inherits an enormous amount of functionality from classes higher up. Each class absorbs memory. Experienced designers seek to reduce the depth of hierarchies to a minimum. Reduced depth provides less coupling and better performance. Rather than seeking extensive hierarchies, designers should seek to accomplish as much as possible through aggregation.

Patterns

Patterns extend principles. Patterns have become so important in recent years that they have permanently altered the basic practices of object-oriented programming. They have added to the principles of object-oriented design the notion that certain solutions to design problems can be applied across any number of instances of application development. Chapter 7, "P Is for Pattern," is dedicated to patterns.

For now, it is enough to observe that a pattern provides a way to understand how to design components. Although one pattern, the Singleton, provides a model for one class, it is generally the case that patterns apply to groups of elements. In other words, they structure components, or subsystems. Patterns can also extend beyond components, becoming models for collections of other components. And patterns can be said, likewise, to apply to entire frameworks and applications.

Here are a few patterns, which are discussed in more detail later:

- **Controller.** Controller patterns find a wide application in the *Ankh* design because the user repeatedly interacts with the system through a variety of objects. Rather than embed event-processing capabilities in interface features, you can use controllers. A Controller pattern allows a dialog box or window to pass events to the system. Such objects should not contain operations that communicate directly with the system.
- **Singleton.** A Singleton is a pattern that can be implemented to control the number of times a class is instantiated. A Singleton can contain a special `create()` function that ensures only a single instance of the class is ever created. The basic game instance can be implemented using a Singleton pattern.
- **Expert.** The Expert patterns solve a problem that often arises when a body of information derived from several sources is needed to respond to a given event. The Expert pattern allows one class to capture this information in one place so that other classes can use it. The alternative is to repeatedly embed expert capabilities in

a number of classes whose responsibilities involve performing activities that have a much wider applicability than the focus of information that the Expert pattern possesses.

- **Bridge.** A Bridge pattern is a way that a *proxy* can be set up. This pattern is often used to eliminate deep hierarchies, which can cause major problems with performance. You can implement a Bridge pattern when, say, one class has a number of specializations based on what might amount to one attribute change. Perhaps you have a `CCharacter` class. You might derive two classes based on whether `CCharacter` is animated or static. This would create the beginning of a hierarchy that might become bulky. Suppose, for instance, that you added audio capabilities later on. To overcome the problem, you might create an abstract class called `CMode`. Two classes named `CAnimateMode` and `CStaticMode` could be derived using `CMode`. `CCharacter` would require only a reference or pointer to `CMode`. It could then acquire the capabilities needed through the Bridge.

Styles

Chapter 19, "Philosophy of Software Engineering and Game Development," uses *style* to refer to the management practices that characterize a game development organization. The parallel with architectural style is intentional. Architectural style defines the comprehensive software design vision that either guides or emerges from the design effort. In some instances, the effort might begin with a dictated style. A larger organization, for example, might have subcontracted the organization for which you work to produce a game of a given description. The architectural style might be dictated to you through the game design and an exacting list of constraints that expressly document how you are to build the game.

On the other hand, you might be involved in an organization that is evolving its own game engine. The way you design the engine might be based on the best architectural information you can find, but you might decide to take specific risks and design components with a completely new approach. You reveal your architectural style in the design that you create.

You can study architectural styles the same way that you study the architectural styles of buildings, and within the game industry, such a trend is well underway. This kind of study is beyond the scope of the current discussion; however, consideration of a few generic styles would be beneficial.

Extensible Design Style

An extensible framework seeks to make a standard set of products fairly easy to produce. It also allows the functionality of the products to be gradually extended through repeated development efforts. Components are added or enhanced within the same basic frame work. If you were to examine the games produced by a company that maintains an extensible game framework, you might find that the characters interact in the same ways from game to game. You might find the AI predictable. In addition, you might note similarities in the way layers are managed. You might find functionality that is clearly built upon the older functionality. Such continuity (to put it politely) occurs because all the games are developed with the same underlying software. This is the framework.

Distributed Design Style

A distributed architecture means that the user interface will be designed on a client-server model. Tiers can be added for processing and database interactions. Components are likely to be packaged as modules (in other words, packaged as separate executables that run on separate machines). Such an architectural style makes the development of the game from the start a top-down, sophisticated undertaking.

Componential Design Style

Many books on "game design" blithely tell software developers to go out and buy things like game engines or Computer-Aided Software Engineering (CASE) tools. The value of this approach to game development is based on the extraordinarily successful history of component-based software in other industries. Unlike extensible design styles, componential design styles allow companies to assemble products from off-the-shelf, well-tested software. Componential design strategies emerge most often in organizations that have no strong desire to enter directly into core game development. Their preference might be to place emphasis on publication, market research, and game design. They then buy the component software that allows them to quickly give shape to the product.

Free-Form Style

Free-form architecture might be where the greatest potential for creativity lies. Generally, free-form styles of architecture use bottom-up design approaches and try to find patterns in what is discovered during the design effort. The creation of *Ankh* falls into this category. This approach seeks empirical information about the design and development process. The *Ankh* effort begins with an atomized set of classes and analyzes them for features that have bearing on design decisions.

Designing for Quality

As a final discussion leading up the actual work of designing a software system, it's necessary to take a short excursion into the realm of quality issues. Quality might seem to be an illusive thing, but in software engineering efforts, quality almost always has a strong impact on the lifetime cost of a software system.

The sections that follow provide a short and traditional list of the elements of quality. Such organizations as the International Standards Organization (ISO) have established a set of quality standards and the ways that metrics can be collected for them. In the context of this chapter, it is acceptable to offer general statements about a few of the ISO and other standards of quality. Figure 4.7 summarizes some of the quality issues.

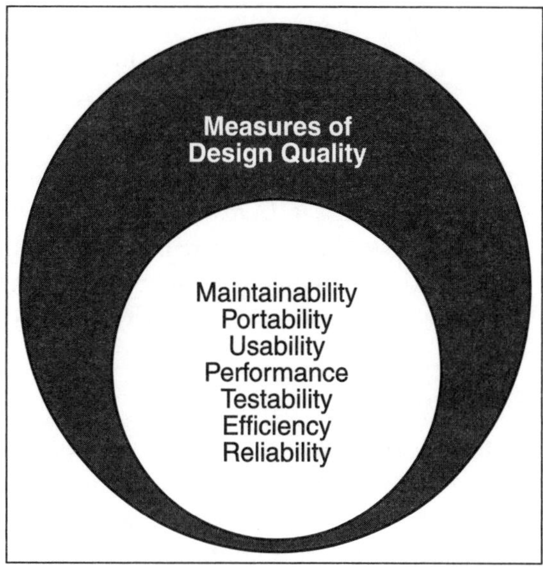

Figure 4.7
Quality design reduces software lifetime development costs.

Maintainability

Maintenance programming characterizes any successful software product. You might relish the idea of participating in one of those organic, experiential adventurers in which you and a small group of colleagues create the next best-selling game, but the reality is that around 70 percent of the work in the game industry involves maintenance programming. In other words, you will be fixing bugs and extending or enhancing a product that already exists. What many people forget about maintenance programming is that a complete software development cycle characterizes it. In other words, to extend a product, you must perform requirements engineering, design, implementation, testing, and release operations.

Software that is maintainable makes success easier than it would be otherwise. When designers design for maintainability, they seek to create software that will be easy to repair and extend. They design with the idea that what they are designing is a beginning as much as it is an end. Chapter 17, "Release Planning and Management," discusses software maintenance.

Portability

Porting software involves moving it from one operating environment to another. A prime example of portability is a game that developers first develop for a personal computer and then later port to a game console. What makes porting easy? What reduces the cost and time needed to port the software? The techniques are fairly standard for those who perform such work regularly. Among other things, calls to the operating system should be collected into specific components. The components can then work to mediate between the rest of the game and the operating system on which the game runs. The discussion in Chapter 5, "Old Is Good—The Library Approach," concerns some aspects of portability.

Usability

Software has several modes of use. Players use a game. But then programmers later in the lifecycle of the game use the classes or components that the original developers create. Usability in the software engineering context takes both realms into consideration, but in this book, the focus centers on how to design the software system so that programmers can extend or reuse it. *Usable software* is software that provides interfaces that are straightforward to use. Usable software is documented so that it can be readily understood. Many issues relating to usability might be addressed. One is primary development practices (see Chapter 13, "What People Do—Development Strategies").

Performance

Many C++ programmers who are involved in an initial experimentation with game development have the experience of watching a game slow down and eventually grind to a halt. Memory leaks are a performance issue. Likewise, programmers who develop deep class hierarchies and store a multitude of the heavy objects in a gigantic vector or queue also know about declining performance. Animation might be sluggish. Information transfer takes time, and the more information there is, the more time that's required. Software *tuning* provides one of the most challenging and technically difficult areas of game development (see Chapter 6, "Object-Oriented Fantasies and Realities").

Testability

Componential isolation of functionality facilitates testability. In other words, effective testing of a software system occurs because the testing engineers can test areas of the system in isolation from each other. Assume that a system consists of 100 components. If test engineers can test individual components in isolation from others, they have a much better chance than otherwise of determining whether the component has performance problems. Testability also involves specifying software so that test engineers know what to test for. Testing involves a wide range of criteria, and unless designers initially design the software for testability, testing engineers find their work extremely difficult. Chapter 11, "Evident Evil—The Art of Testing," addresses some of the central issues of testing.

Efficiency

Efficiency has to do with both the size of the program and the rate at which it performs. Size is related to things like algorithm performance. A given algorithm can be evaluated in terms of the time it takes to complete its work. Added to the raw performance of the algorithm, however, is the complexity of the implementation relative to the task performed. A component that is tangled or mired with complexity might not be the most efficient implementation of a solution even if its performance is as good or better than another, less complex solution. Efficiency involves studying several variables. Chapters 9, "Iterating

Design," and Chapter 12, "Numbers for Nabobs," discuss metrics and other criteria used in evaluating software efficiency.

Reliability

Reliability is a measure of failure rates. In other words, if you run a program a million times, what percentage of the time will it fail? The resulting data is sometimes labeled as the *meantime to failure.* Testers assume from the first that the system will fail.

At the beginning of the test cycle, the software fails often, but as bugs are removed, the failure rate declines to the point where it is rare. It is only when failure is rare that the software is ready to ship. Only then is the *failure rate* said to be acceptable.

note

Chapter 11 covers testing in detail. For an interesting discussion of reliability and failure in traditional engineering terms, you might want to examine Henry Petroski's *To Engineer Is Human: The Role of Failure in Successful Design.* (New York: Vintage, 1992). An experienced engineer, Petroski notes an interesting contradiction in engineering history. "While engineers can learn from structural mistakes what not to do, they do not necessarily learn from successes how to do anything but repeat the success without change" (99). One outcome of this observation in software design is that if a system is forced to fail, you can learn a great deal about how to improve reliability.

Finding Elements and Relationships

This section works toward understanding the preliminaries of design. Some authorities place the activity of describing elements and relationships in a software system as *analysis.* Whatever it is called, it involves taking into consideration the information that has resulted from the requirements engineering phase. Your efforts in Chapter 2, which concerned requirements engineering, resulted in three things:

- **The requirements list.** The list provided a convenient way to track requirements during the requirements engineering phase. The requirements list helped reduce the amount of information so you could understand the scope of the system.
- **The use cases.** The use cases allowed you to understand the context of the requirements and to have at hand a ready way to solidify your understanding of the requirements list. Some experts say that only the use cases are necessary; others contend that the requirements list is necessary and the use cases are throwaway work. Actually, both are necessary. You will return to use cases as you begin your design effort.

- **The Task-Object-Remarks (TOR) chart.** This was a working table intended to provide a ready way to store information about objects and their responsibilities and relationships. Joined with CRC cards, the TOR chart becomes a starting point for your design work.

The work of design requires that you examine the information these artifacts provide and determine whether you can see ways to organize it so that you can create a software system that solves the problems the requirements present. Figure 4.8 illustrates how you can use the information from the requirements phase, together with a set of design tools, to gain an initial view of the primary elements and relationships of a software design.

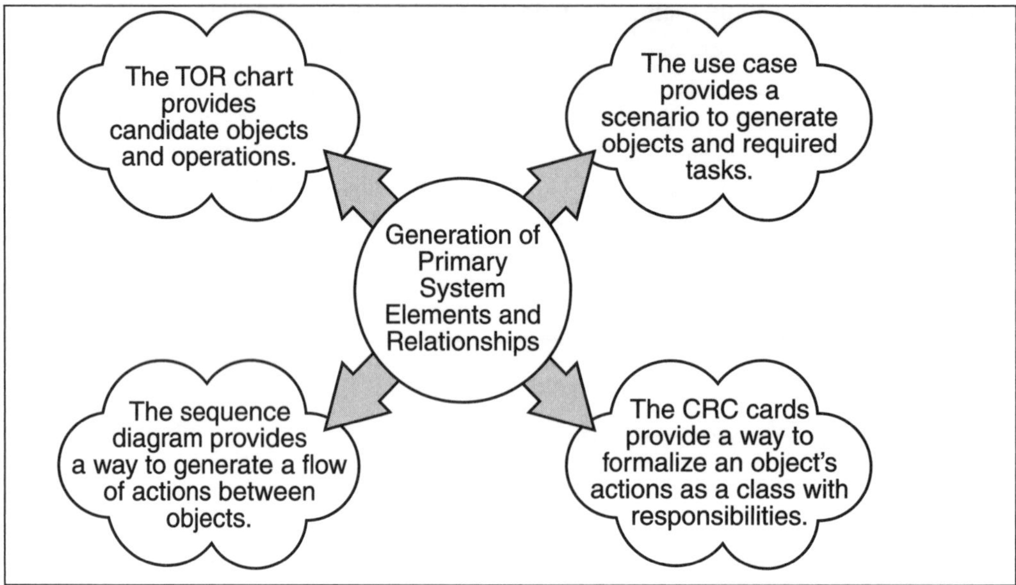

Figure 4.8
Basic design tools allow you to generate objects and their relationships.

Figure 4.8 summarizes activities you perform as you work from requirements to a candidate class list. You start with use cases and a requirements list. From there, you proceed to use CRC cards (described in the next section) to explore collaborations and responsibilities. CRC cards document classes, but at the same time, the content of the CRC card closely corresponds to the object and task listed in the TOR chart. For this reason, the TOR chart is an intermediary step between the requirements statement and the CRC card. The end result of the analysis phase should be a list of candidate classes you can begin putting together through your design effort. Figure 4.9 shows the flow of activity from requirements through a candidate class list.

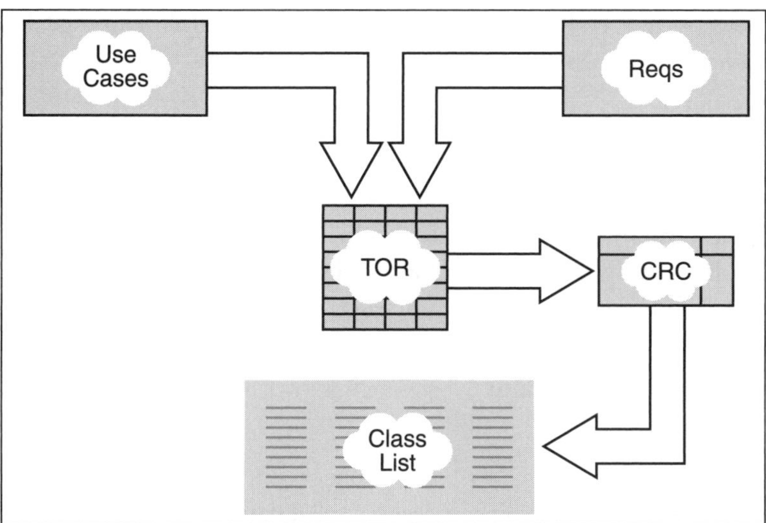

Figure 4.9
Design tools provide a way to move from requirements to candidate

CRC Cards

CRC cards provide a convenient way to explore how classes (or objects of classes) relate to each other. Each class has at least one *responsibility* to provide some type of service to the system. Each class, likewise, *collaborates* with other classes when it delivers services. The classes to which it delivers services are its *clients*. If a class delivers services, it is a *server*.

One way that classes relate to each other is through the services they provide to each other. The collection of services that one class offers to others is through an *interface*. The interface consists of the public operations that a class contains. A CRC card helps you begin to establish what operations it should contain. It does this by offering you the chance to ask why one class communicates with another. Each class is a collection of services. Each collection of services in some way corresponds to the functionality the requirements specify. Figure 4.10 illustrates the layout of a CRC card.

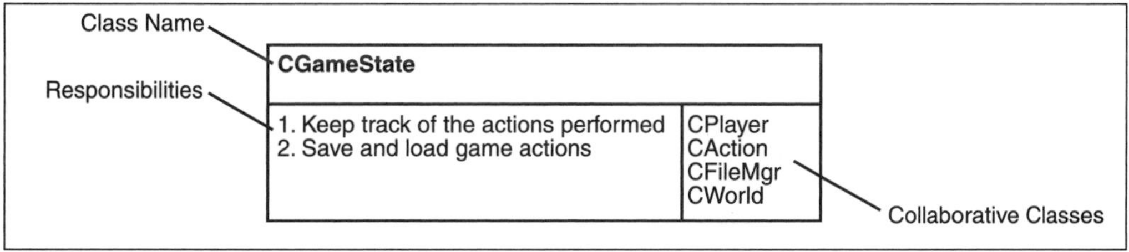

Figure 4.10
CRC cards explore relationships between classes.

The next section discusses using a TOR chart to augment your effort of developing CRC cards. Following are a few procedural steps:

- Use the TOR chart and its task listing to establish the name of a class.
- Use your use cases and requirements to derive the names of objects. Search for tasks that must be completed in light of the requirements.
- Determine what you think this class should do. It must have at least one responsibility. It should not have more than three or four. If this class has multiple responsibilities, these responsibilities should be closely related.
- Discover whether your class seems to require information from another class. If it does, then list this class as a collaborator.

Using the TOR Chart

If you focus on the tasks in the TOR chart, you can derive a candidate list of responsibilities for the classes you name in the CRC cards. A class might have several responsibilities. You can also focus on the object name and decide whether it is a suitable beginning for a class name. To determine the list of collaborative classes, explore the remarks section of the TOR chart together with the dependencies you observed in your use cases. Figure 4.11 illustrates the first few listings from the TOR chart. See Appendix D, "Software Engineering and Game Design Documentation," (or the CD) for the complete chart.

Starting from the TOR chart created during the requirements phase, you can use the CRC cards to generate a tentative list of 41 classes. Even though these classes are preliminary, they serve as a starting point for working through the use cases to identify the final elements and relationships that define the system. Figure 4.12 shows a candidate list of classes. The classes named at this point will be iteratively examined as you move into the next stage of activity, which involves creating stripes of functionality that bring your preliminary class lists under intense scrutiny.

<Req>	Task	Object(s)	Remarks
Req_1	Save game	GameState	1. Initial game state 2. Save changes
		Replay	1. Uses GameState 2. Plays slower 3. Returns to main menu
		Action	1. Track character interactions 2. Track interaction with maps 3. Receive action, update
Req_2	Restore game state	GameState	1. GS→Load(Populate GS) 2. Apply instant changes
Req_64	Game clock	Clock	1. Start and stop 2. Reset 3. Vary speed
Req_3	Associate profile with saved game	Player	1. Get the saved directory 2. Generate directory
Req_4	Allow choosing of file names	Dialogue SaveDialogue FileMgmt OpenDialogue	1. Bring up a list of files 2. Delete game 3. List games 4. Browse directory 5. Confirm overwrite 6. Overwrite game 7. Enter new game

Figure 4.11
A TOR chart provides a list of candidate objects and operations.

1. CAction	11. CFileMgr	22. CLog	32. CSkill
2. CActor	12. CGame	23. CMesh	33. CSlider
3. CAI	13. CGameState	24. CMouse	34. CSound
4. CButton	14. CGraphics	25. CMusic	35. CSoundMgr
5. CCamera	15. CGUI	26. CPanel	36. CSprite
6. CCheckBox	16. CGUIMgr	27. CParticle	37. CState
7. CClock	17. CImageMgr	28. CPicture	38. CStateMachine
8. CDialog	18. CInventory	29. CPlayer	39. CTextBox
9. CEmitter	19. CItem	30. CProfile	40. CWindow
10. CEntity	20. CKeyBoard	31. CProp	41. CWorld
	21. CLabel		

Figure 4.12
The TOR chart provides a list of candidate classes.

Generating Operations

Use case scenarios provide statements that indicate how objects interact through messages. When you work with a use case, you can isolate terms that help you identify objects. One approach is to fall back on the preliminary class list to grab the names of classes that might serve as "collectors" of the actions observed in the use case scenarios. The procedure is fairly rudimentary.

1. Select a requirement you want to begin incorporating into the design.
2. Select the appropriate or corresponding use case(s).
3. Carefully work through the scenario. If you spot a noun that fits one of the classes you have identified on a preliminary basis, bring this forward to become a generalized object in a sequence diagram.
4. Assign actions to objects.
5. Move through the use case until you have assigned all actions in the use case to operations you place in the sequence diagram and assign, tentatively, to objects.

If you return to a scenario dealt with in Chapter 2, you can examine the events that start a game. Figure 4.13 illustrates a use case scenario that was introduced in Chapter 2.

Moving to a Sequence Diagram

If you work from the scenario in Figure 4.13, you can generate a tentative sequence diagram. The sequence diagram attempts to translate the actions in the use case into a conceptual view of objects and relationships. Generally, the names of the messages between the objects don't need to be precise at this point. The purpose is largely to test whether it is possible to envision a sequential flow of activity. The sequence diagram allows you to

Use Case Name: Player Starts Game
Requirement(s) Explored: 1
Player (Actor) Context (Role): Player
Precondition(s): Game is installed and ready to play.
Trigger(s): Player selects game-start action.
Main Course of Action: 1. The player selects the game-start action. 2. The system requests that the player select a profile. 3. The player selects a profile. 4. The system loads the profile. 5. The system displays a message to the player that tells him that the play can begin. 6. The player acknowledges the message that the system has displayed and begins playing.
Alternate Course(s) of Action: 3a. The player does not select a profile. 3b. The system chooses a default profile. 6a. The player chooses to exit the game before playing. 6b. The system asks the player if he wants to save his profile. 6b1. If the player responds yes, the system saves the profile. 6b2. If the player responds no, the system exits without saving the profile.
Exceptional Course(s) of Action: 6a. The system crashes. 6b. The player turns off the computer.

Figure 4.13
Start with a use case to investigate a scenario.

take a set of classes and generate objects from them. Then you explore the sequence of messages that pass between the objects. Figure 4.14 provides a sequence diagram for the scenario in the startup use case.

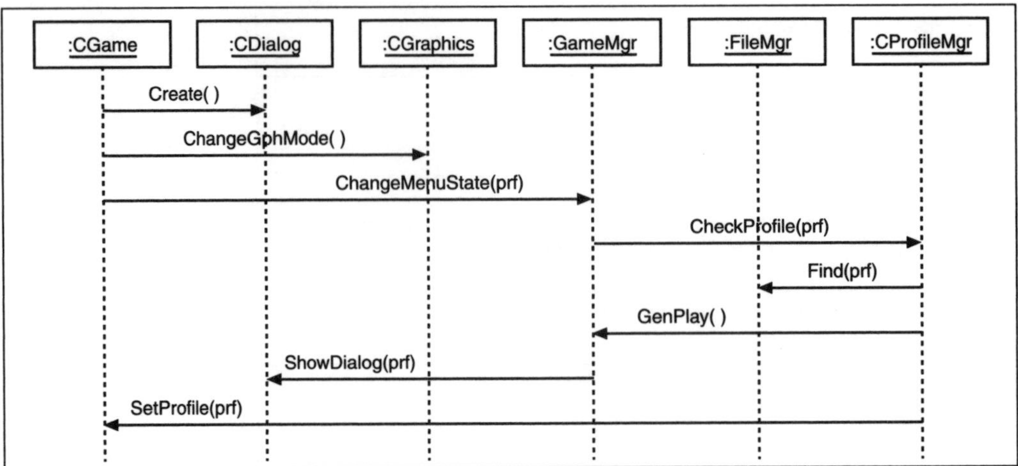

Figure 4.14
A sequence diagram translates the use case scenario into object interactions.

Reframing Operations with a Collaboration Diagram

The collaboration diagram is an interaction diagram, like the sequence diagram. It shows how objects interact. In many ways, the collaboration diagram is simply an alternative view of the information you see in the sequence diagram. On the other hand, it differs tremendously from the sequence diagram because it offers a way to view a set of interactions between objects as a software *component.* Figure 4.15 illustrates the sequence diagram shown in Figure 4.14 recast as a collaboration diagram.

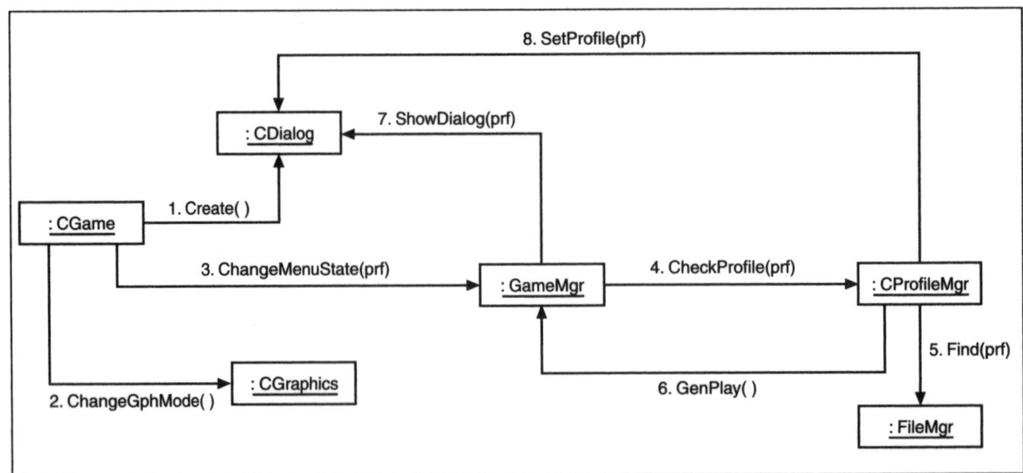

Figure 4.15
A collaboration diagram recasts a sequence diagram to emphasize the operations that relate the objects.

In the current context, as pointed out earlier, a *component* is a set of objects that interact to provide an identifiable service to the overall system. One of the major differences between a sequence diagram and a collaboration diagram is that a sequence diagram shows you the *flow* of activity modeled on a scenario. The collaboration diagram, in contrast, makes it easier to view the collection of relationships between objects as composing a component. Figure 4.16 contrasts sequence and collaboration diagrams.

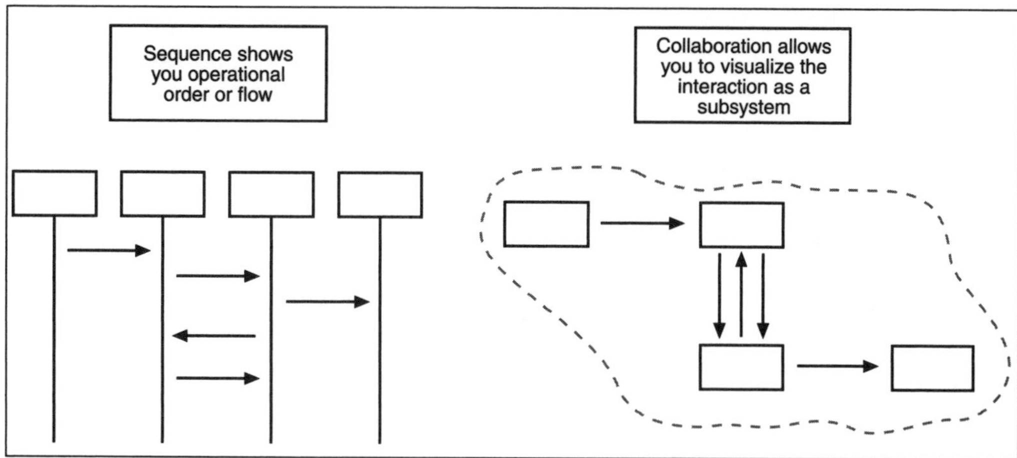

Figure 4.16
Sequence and collaboration diagrams provide different views of the system design.

Low-Level Design Tools

Low-level design activity immediately precedes or accompanies implementation. One goal of low-level design is to refine class and operation names and descriptions into implementation terms. Conceptualizations diminish and class designs become prevalent. To facilitate the gathering of this information, the specific nature of each operation in a class needs to be known. This is the work of the operation specification.

Class Diagrams

Before discussing operations specifications, it's good to review a few notions about classes and class diagrams. Toward this end, the first notion introduced is that a class is a static entity. In other words, a class is a pattern for objects of a given type. Because a class is a pattern, it incorporates attributes and operations that might not be fully visible in the behavior of any one object instantiated using the pattern. To discover the operations in a class, you might have to explore the class in a number of contexts. To accomplish this, you can refine the operations in classes using collaboration diagrams in conjunction with CRC cards and use cases. Note the following:

- Use cases set different contexts of use for a class.
- Different contexts of use require that different operations come to life.
- You can use interaction diagrams to explore contexts of use. The use case can be translated first into a scenario and then into a sequence or collaboration diagram.
- As different operations come to life, you can refine the class. A combination of contexts of use reveals that the class has a range of operations that exploration of no one context of use can expose.
- To ensure that each operation is fully explored, you can write an operation specification. You can supplement this with an activity or state transition diagram to reveal precisely how the operation changes the object that hosts it or calls it. Such a diagram is often called a low-level design tool because it might be the last thing a programmer does before beginning to write the code for the class.

Given full exploration of operations, it becomes possible to know both the attributes and operations of a given class. Figure 4.17 provides a summary view of the activities that allow you to analyze and design a class.

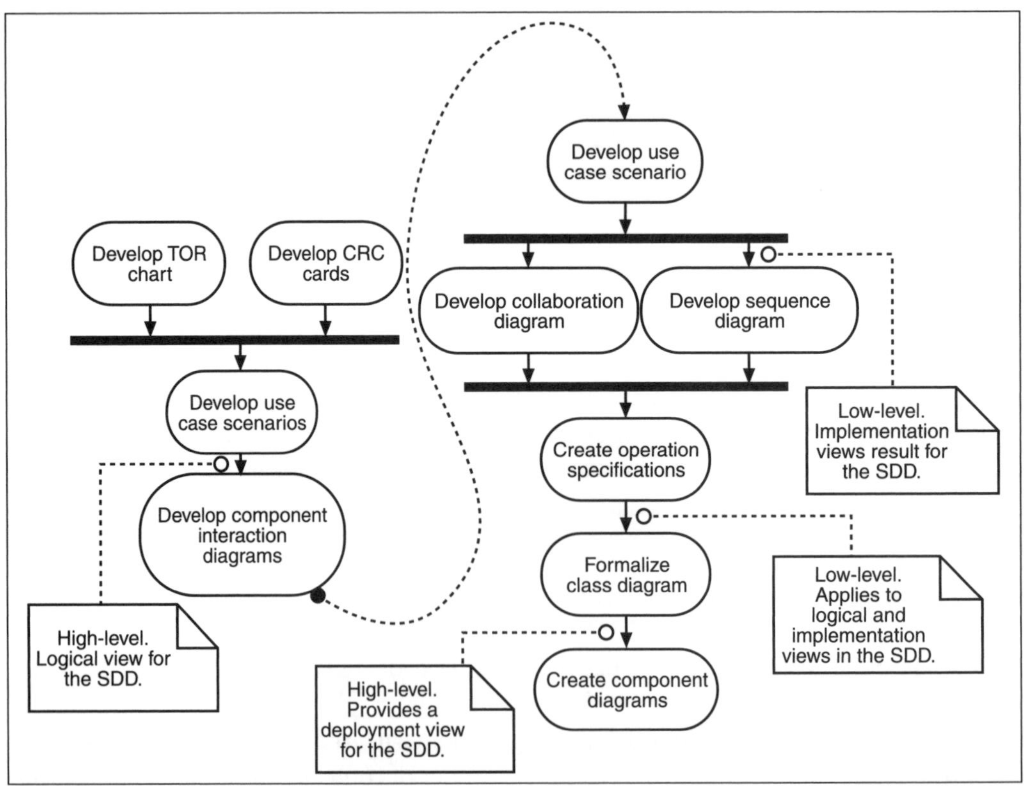

Figure 4.17
SDD artifacts emerge from the design development effort.

Operation Specifications

An operation specification has its parallels in CRC cards and use cases. It is a formal medium for structuring the activity that's involved in developing a software component. As with CRC cards and use cases, creating a template in Microsoft Word or SmartDraw provides a convenient means of documenting your work. Figure 4.18 shows a blank operation specification.

Name
Responsibilities
Class
References (use case, req)
Notes
Returns
Preconditions
Postconditions

Figure 4.18
An operation specification refines the operations. (For more information, see the reference for Craig Larmon at the end of this chapter.)

You can create an operation specification from an interaction diagram. Generally, it is a good idea to create an operation specification after you have worked through most of the high-level activities, such as creating sequence, collaboration, and class diagrams. The following points might be useful when you work with an operation specification:

- When you name a function or method (in UML, an operation), just copy the operation call (message) from the class, interaction, or collaboration diagram into the specification template. Chapter 3, "A Tutorial: UML and Object-Oriented Programming," provides a review of the syntax of messages.

- You derive an operation's *responsibility* from observing what the operation does in the interaction diagram. The language does not have to be formal or even very precise.
- A *precondition* is what must be true for the operation to work.
- A *postcondition* is what is changed after the operation is completed. According to Larmon, postconditions usually fall into three categories: something is deleted or created, an attribute is changed, or an association is created or broken (Larmon, 149).

Component/Package Diagrams

A final way of examining a class is to place it into a context with other classes. This is the opposite of examining the internals of a class. Instead, you put it into a *package* or *component* diagram and see how it works with other classes that compose a single subsystem. Chapter 3 provides a review of component or package diagrams. When you examine the software design description for *Anhk* (later in this chapter), you will have a chance to see how the classes derived from the first stripe design effort are grouped into a component diagram.

Presenting the System Design

The tools of design allow you to depict the design of the software system in different ways. Being able to look at the system in different ways allows you to analyze and refine your system to an extent that would not be possible without such tools. In addition to simplifying your design effort, the tools of design allow you to meet the recommendations that the Institute of Electrical and Electronics Engineers (IEEE) has set for how a software system is to be portrayed in the software description. The IEEE standard dealing with such descriptions is IEEE 1471. The standard calls upon software engineers to portray the systems they create from different viewpoints, but it does not specify which viewpoints should be used. Generally, the viewpoints address different stakeholders in the software product. Viewpoints meet the needs of users of the system, such as

- Developers of the system
- System users
- Those who purchase or take ownership of the system
- Those who have responsibility for maintaining or extending the system

In an object-oriented design effort, among the options for depicting the system are use cases, interaction diagrams, package or component diagrams, and class diagrams. Use cases define the system scope and its use scenarios. Interaction diagrams depict the behavior of the system. Class diagrams depict static views of the system. Package diagrams provide a componential view. If you use these views of a system, you can satisfy the guidelines that the IEEE has established for design description.

The SDD Template

You can use the IEEE's SDD template as a starting point for organizing the views you create during your design effort. The best approach is to shape the document so that it gives expression to the design and development styles your group or organization finds most comprehensible. If you have specific stakeholders whose interests you must address, you can fashion your document to accommodate their needs. You might want to include both technical and nontechnical views, for example, and you might add use cases along with diagrams. Here is a modified version of the IEEE SDD outline:

1. Introduction
   - 1.1 Purpose
   - 1.2 Scope
   - 1.3 Definitions and Acronyms
2. References
3. Conceptual View
   - 3.1 Use Case
   - 3.2 Diagram...
4. Behavioral View
   - 4.1 Object Diagram 1
   - 4.2 Object Diagram 2...
5. Logical View
   - 6.1 Class Diagram 1
   - 6.2 Class Diagram 2...
7. Component View
   - 7.1 Diagram 1
   - 7.2 Diagram 2...
8. Deployment View

How to Set Up the SDD

Appendix D (and the CD) provides an example of the SDD for *Ankh*. The way you set up the SDD depends on your developmental and architectural styles. One approach involves dividing the description into sections that mirror what are referred to as *stripes*. A stripe is one iterative implementation of a game. It is characterized as a design entity that represents a functional subset of the game. Stripes characterize the development effort. A number of justifications exist for following this approach:

- If you divide the architecture according to the ways you iteratively and incrementally implement it, then the document serves as a guide to both the overall architecture of the game and the way the game is implemented.
- In addition to allowing you to inspect the design from different use perspectives, components that are based on stripes enable you to break the description of different classes into manageable and understandable wholes. Every feature, in other words, can be described from the point of view of the responsibility it fulfills; therefore, empty itemizing is not likely to be a problem.
- When the design effort uses stripes, you incrementally move toward a comprehensive grasp of the entire system. At the same time, you discover both functionality and features that might be redundant. If you use stripes, you start from what is simple and move toward what is complex. The arrangement of the SDD can progress in the same way, making the document easier to comprehend. This can prove especially valuable to developers who might inherit the system during future mod or maintenance efforts.

Even if you do not decide to divide your document according to incremental stripes, it still stands that the IEEE recommends division into different views. The following sections provide descriptions of these views. Later on, you'll see the process used for developing the information that fits into these views. The views that are common to most interpretations to the UML are logical, component, implementation, use case, and deployment. Figure 4.19 provides a summary of the SDD views.

Introducing an SDD

The SDD template shown previously begins with an introduction that includes paragraphs on *purpose*, *scope*, and *definitions of terms and acronyms.* In the purpose section, you tell the reader what you think the SDD offers. You are talking about the purpose of the document, not the game. For the scope, help the reader understand the scope of the document. Scope relates to the information that the reader can expect to obtain from the document. In the glossary and definition section, you should list any terms that apply specifically to the game software or its design. Generally, be on the lookout for terms that people ask about during the design effort.

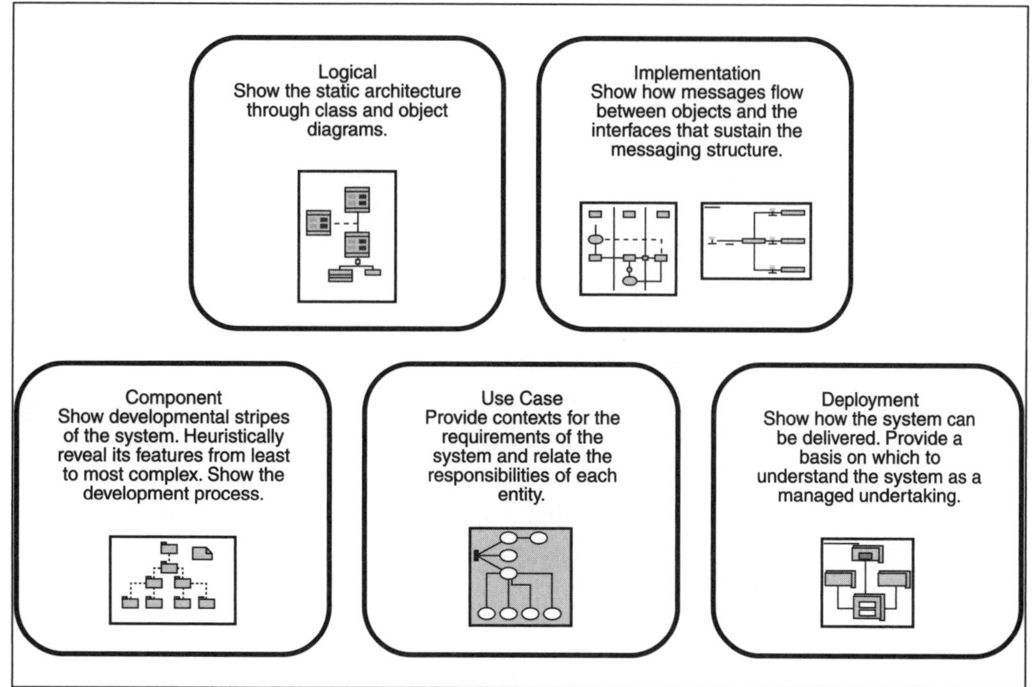

Figure 4.19
Design views address different stakeholder priorities.

You can also add supplemental information to the introductory section. In the SDD for *Ankh*, a section refers the reader to the requirements and other documents that contribute to the design effort. If you set up the SDD early on with hyperlinked references to other documents, your design work can proceed much more smoothly than otherwise because you will not have to search through directories for the relevant resource material.

Conceptual or Use Case View

This view of the system ensures that nontechnical readers of the design description can benefit from reading the design description. On the other hand, all stakeholders can benefit from the use case view. Among those who might be named are play testers, software testers, customers, game designers, software designers, graphics developers, and software developers. In addition, a use case can provide a way to establish the scope of a given component, module, or stripe. Generally, a use case view (in the form of a narrative or scenario) should accompany each stripe description.

Behavioral or Implementation View

The implementation views in the *Ankh SDD* reflect the architecture developed using stripes. Implementation views can be depicted using class diagrams, object diagrams, activity diagrams, state diagrams, sequence diagrams, and collaboration diagrams. Generally, any description of the system that aids in the implementation effort is suitable to include under the implementation heading.

Logical View

The logical views that are most useful are static object diagrams and class diagrams. Class diagrams can work on both high and low levels. Generally, you should create a static object view of each component. For the design effort for *Ankh*, this involved creating a class diagram for each stripe. A stripe is the functionality that represents a set of use cases or requirements that have been selected for a given design iteration. The approach used for *Ankh* involved designing the entire system using stripes and beginning the first iteration of implementation after all the named requirements had been accounted for. The number of logical or static object views provided depends on how many stripes you need to fully design and implement the system.

Component View

Package diagrams show the collections of classes that fall under each stripe. This is a component view. The fact that different stripes might use the same classes is not an issue. Stripes collect the functionality of the system in different ways. Stripe 2.1, GUI Objects, differs from Stripe 2.3, Floor Tiling, which provides the basic framework for layers. Both stripes use a common set of classes. Both use different facets of the interfaces that the classes offer, however, and this is where redundancy can be justified. Describing different facets of use under more than one component view makes it easier for readers to understand relationships between components.

Deployment View

To show how your system is deployed, use a component diagram or a deployment diagram. Chapter 3 discusses these two types of diagrams. This chapter doesn't show how to create such diagrams because it focuses on design. In Chapter 17, however, you will find detailed coverage of release management. Generally, the deployment view can also, in part, reflect the stripes in which the product has been developed. One component, for example, can contain all the functionality of several stripes, but at the same time, subsystems that address different groups of functionality (game, Internet, tools, and so on) can represent both different stripes and different component and deployment groupings.

Designing the System in Stripes

The *Ankh* development effort involved an approach that was iterative and incremental. At the center of this process is the notion of a system *stripe.* A stripe embodies a subset of the functionality described in the requirements document. Generally, the first stripe consists of only the most general system features, such as the framework of the game. With each successive stripe, the features addressed become more refined. The level of detail and complexity grows with each stripe, but because the detail and complexity are *layered,* at no point does complexity become overwhelming.

Increments and Iteration in Stripes

Notions about stripes can be derived in part from an approach to development known as *prototyping.* Prototyping involves quickly and cheaply developing part of a system for purposes of inspection, risk analysis, or customer understanding. Because developers develop prototypes to be thrown away, prototypes usually lack all but the most rudimentary quality measures. They are literally thrown together. The problem with prototypes begins precisely at this point. Although prototypes are thrown together to allow developers and customers to visualize concepts, they can end up as part of the end product. This is like having an unbaked brick at the base of a tall tower. The results prove dismal to recount.

The approach to stripes used in the *Ankh* effort calls for designing all stripes before beginning software construction. Using this approach, each stripe opens the design process to a degree of creativity that is not possible if too much emphasis is placed on the whole system.

The game software industry abounds with stories about how game software developers discover relatively late in the development process the one feature that makes a game a success. Development is not a linear process. On the other hand, things like feature creep and goldplating regularly derail game development efforts. The compromise is to make room for a game design to be extended at regular, controlled intervals. If someone discovers a valuable feature, it becomes possible to assess risks and schedule the inclusion of the feature even though it might not have been a part of the original requirements set.

Figure 4.20 illustrates some of the features of stripe-based development. The general outlines of this approach might be familiar to someone who has had some experience with the Rational Unified Process or the Agile Process. The basic description of the iterative approach to development goes back, however, more than 20 years, to the spiral development models introduced during the 1980s.

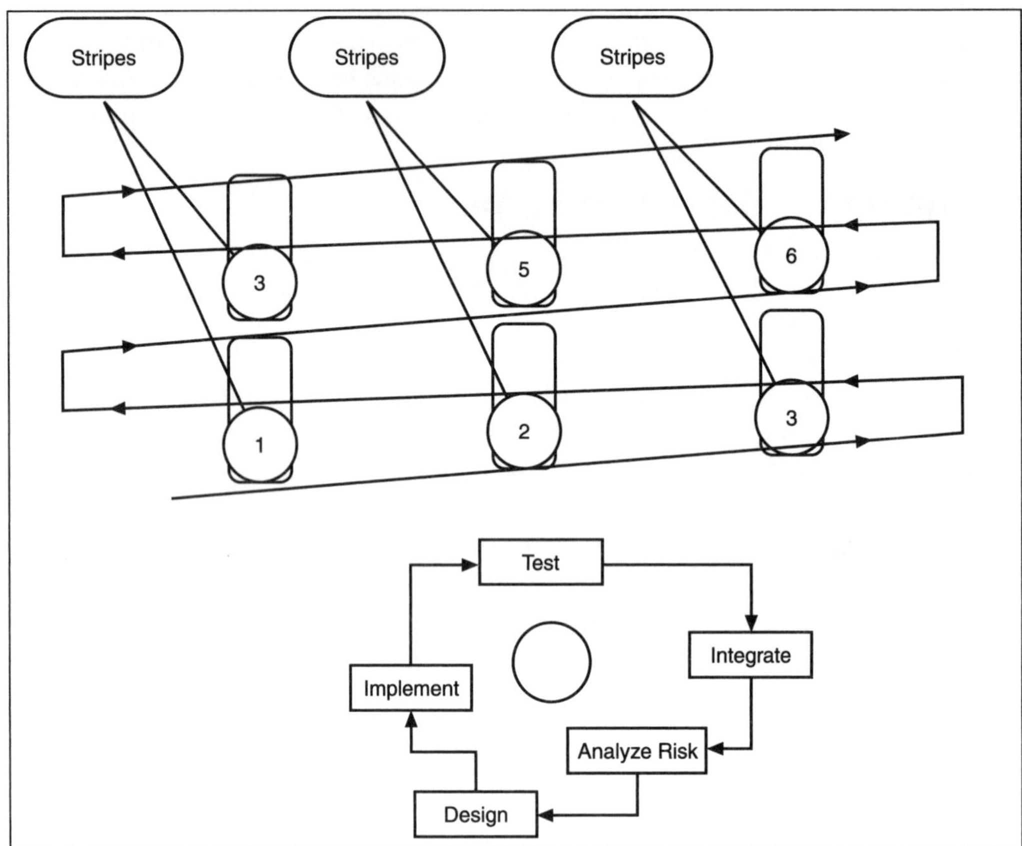

Figure 4.20
The striped-based approach to development involves incremental and iterative implementation efforts. First the whole of the system is designed, but it is divided into components that address stripes.

Team Efforts at Designing System Stripes

The stripe approach to development assumes that you complete a set of requirements and develop a design for the *whole* system prior to starting implementation work on the first stripe. After you have made at least one pass over all the requirements and generated a rough initial design of the system, you start implementation work on the first stripe.

note

If you want to begin implementation on a stripe right after you have designed it, just remember that hidden dependencies lurk within any incomplete design. If you implement too early, you might have to perform extensive rework.

Your work on the first stripe involves selecting and refining the requirements and developing a design for the stripe. As Figure 4.20 shows, after you complete a first iteration of design work on the first stripe, you then start work on the second. For each stripe, you select a set of requirements that you believe cover the stripe, you select a group of CRC cards for the classes you think cover the requirements, and using what you consider to be the appropriate use case(s), you then begin to generate a design. Start by creating a basic object diagram with a tool like SmartDraw. If you can project the diagram onto a screen for the team to view and discuss, you will find that the work goes much better than if you try to use paper. Have copies of all your basic documents on a laptop so that they can be projected on a screen. Then you can grab information quickly for display whenever anyone needs it.

To refer again to Figure 4.20, for example, you first move through the requirements and high-level design of all the stripes before you return to stripe 1 and begin work. At that point, you begin development. You work through risk analysis, design, implementation, test, and integration (or deployment), and your work results in an incremental phase of the game. When you have completed this release, you then move to the next, incrementing and iterating until you reach the full scope of the game and can account for all requirements. (*Ankh* consisted of 19 stripes.)

To determine stripes, begin with your use cases and decide what comes first for you. You should try to implement first either the general framework of the system or features of the system that you feel present especially high risks. High-risk features can be implemented in test harnesses and later folded into the game framework. If you begin with a framework (as was the case with the *Ankh* development effort), you might view your work as moving from greater to less risk. Another approach might involve establishing the framework first but then undertaking to develop risky features. Figure 4.21 shows the basic steps of the *Ankh* design effort.

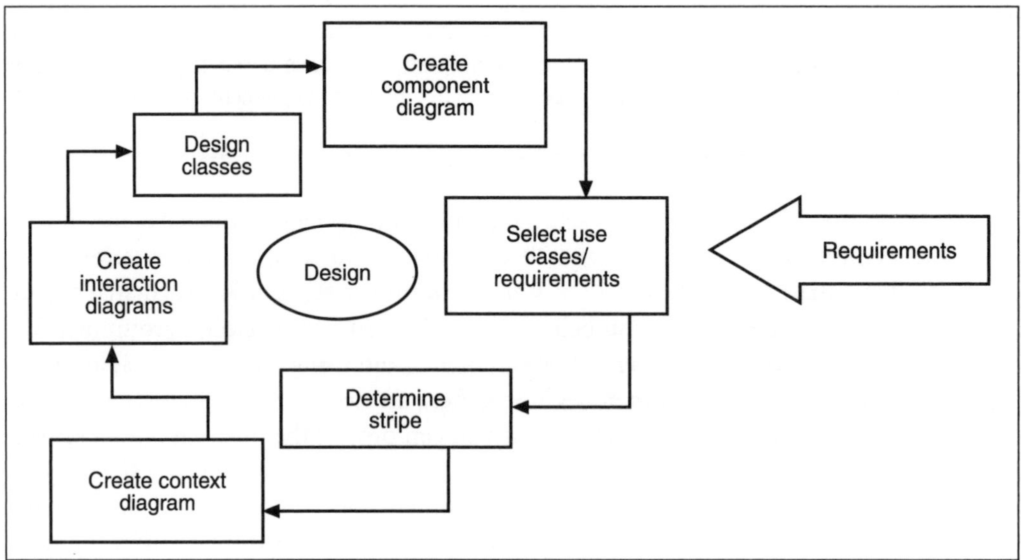

Figure 4.21
Iterate through strip designs until you have a set of components that address the complete scope of the game.

A First Stripe from *Ankh*

Following is the five-step process to generate the content of the software design description:

1. Select requirements and use cases for the stripe and create a unifying design use case.
2. Create a context diagram for the design use case.
3. Create sequence and collaboration diagrams to explore the scenario of the design use case.
4. Create a class diagram to provide a logical view of the stripe.
5. Create a context diagram to show the stripe in relation to other stripes.

Excerpts from resulting software design description are available for your inspection in Appendix D. (The entire document is on the CD.) You might want to open this document as you read this portion of the text.

Figure 4.22 illustrates the four activities that are involved in creating the design document.

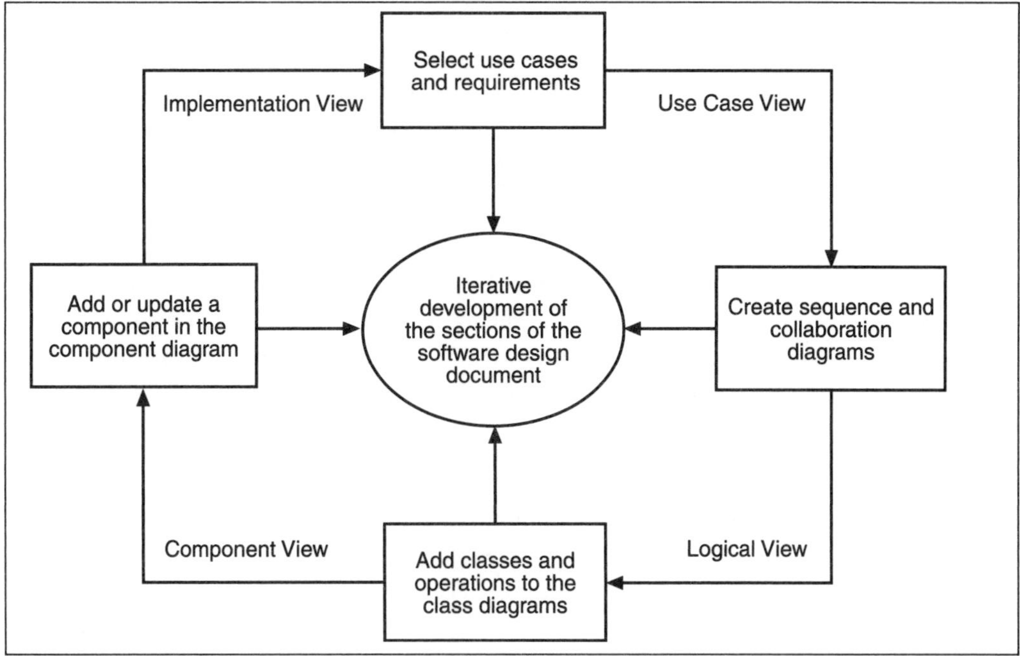

Figure 4.22
Class or logical diagrams grow from other work.

Beginning a Stripe

To begin a stripe, the *Ankh* development team started with the following documents, which were all open for display on a large screen using a projection device attached to a laptop computer:

- The CRC cards in tabular form in a Word document with a hyperlinked table of contents for quick access.
- The game design document, which was kept at hand as a way of having direct information about the game in case the team needed to expand a bit on a given use case or, for that matter, settle a dispute by generating a new use case.
- The *Ankh Software Requirements Specification* set to section 3 so that the team could quickly view all the requirements statements.
- A new project open in SmartDraw, with the UML tool pallet open for creation of class, object, and interaction diagrams.

note

In the first section of the SDD, references to all the associated documents are provided. This makes it much more convenient to develop the SDD. Project the documents onto a screen. Work as a team and move from document to document as team members pursue ideas. In Windows, you can use the Alt+Tab option to go from document to document as needed.

At first, the team debated about what portion of the game to develop first. The team decided it wanted to start with a rudimentary implementation of the framework. Members talked about the splash screen and the menu. They drew a rough system context diagram for these two areas of interest and found that they provided good material for a first stripe. The team then decided to set up a use case for the design effort.

The Use Case for the First Stripe

The use case the team developed for the design of the first stripe is included in Appendix D. The title of the use case is Select Exit at the Game's Start. Note that this use case does not constitute a modification or addition to the requirements list. This use case is for the design effort alone.

> *Use Case: Select Exit at the Game's Start*
>
> *This use case is triggered by the closing of the splash screen. The system shows the basic game window. The system displays the main play options for the game. The player views the options: New Game, Load Game, Continue, Change Profile, Options, Exit. The player chooses one option: Exit. The system acknowledges the choice. The system requests the user to confirm the choice. The user confirms the choice. The system exits. This use case ends when the system exists.*

Starting with a Context

After generating an initial use case for the stripe, the team searched the requirements list to find those requirements that corresponded to the design use case. The team searched through the TOR chart, the CRC cards, the requirements statements, and the use cases time and time again. Team members were careful to continually review assumptions about responsibilities even though these responsibilities were established in the CRC cards. At last, the team arrived at a definitive list of the requirements the first stripe would cover. The requirements involved in the stripe are as follows:

- Req 8 (Software shall have a main menu that will have a load replay option.)
- Req 16 (Software shall support a custom mouse pointer.)
- Req 18 (Software shall support panels, menus, buttons, sliders, text boxes, and pictures.)

- Req 38 (Software shall support a main menu with these entries: New Game, Continue, Change Profile, Options, Exit, Editor, and Load Game.)
- Req 46 (Software shall load in no more than 20 seconds and display a progress bar or some other indicator that loading is in progress.)
- Req 14 (Software shall run only in full-screen mode.)
- Req 15 (Software shall support Alt+Tab key combinations.)
- Req 17 (Software shall support alpha channels.)

The list of requirements addressed was not easy to discover. A good deal of debate took place. The team also spotted some weaknesses. Because the team had all the documents open, however, it was easy to go back and forth between the documents and spot irregularities. The team updated things as it went. Turning on the Track Changes capability of Word gave more cautious team members a sense of security; they were not comfortable with changing anything on-the-fly.

Discovering a Component

To show you how the team worked with the problem of developing views of the first stripe, it is possible to present some "in progress" diagrams. The value of showing the lack of perfection is to reveal the extent to which the design process can be viewed as experimental or *heuristic.* In other words, one thing you can gain from design work is knowledge of the system to be built.

note

If you have explored different approaches to development, you might be familiar with the Agile Process approach to design. According to this perspective, requirements and design should be an active, living process mingled with the implementation effort. The approach used for the *Ankh* effort differs from the Agile Process. Still, this chapter includes references to texts on the Agile Process.

The *Ankh* team's approach was to have the whole team work on the design effort. The team developed the SDD as it went, building its content on a projected screen. The team also set all the diagrams in SmartDraw projects. From there, it was easy to transfer them to the SDD. A team member refined the work afterward. Following a final review, the diagrams could be folded into the design document. (See Appendix D or the CD.)

The team used a context diagram to supplement the use case for the first stripe. This practice was not used very often in subsequent stripes. Dashed relationship lines were used to maintain a sense that the diagram shows tentative relationships. The object at the base of the arrow might contain a reference to the object pointed to. Figure 4.23 shows the Stripe 1 context diagram.

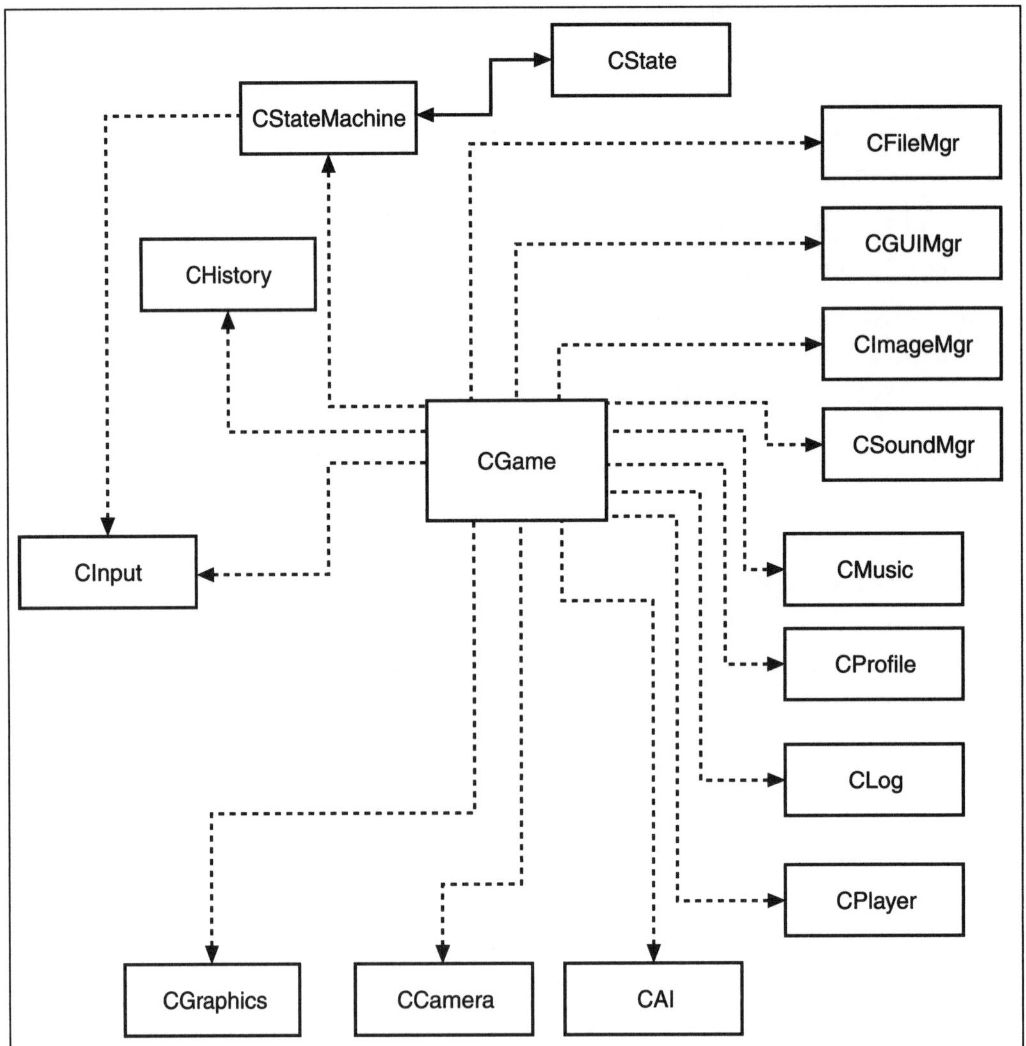

Figure 4.23
The Stripe 1 context diagram for *Ankh* seeks only to show tentative relationships.

Moving to a Scenario

The next step involves looking closely at the design use case and recasting it slightly so that it becomes the basis of a sequence diagram. To create the sequence diagram, the team looked closely at each candidate object. (All objects are addressed at this point as generic objects, so the class names are preceded by a colon.) The team started out by including some unneeded classes in the sequence. For example, it had a `CGraphics` class, and after going back and forth over how this might fit into the initial scenario, it decided to drop it. Figure 4.24 illustrates an early iteration of a sequence diagram for the first stripe.

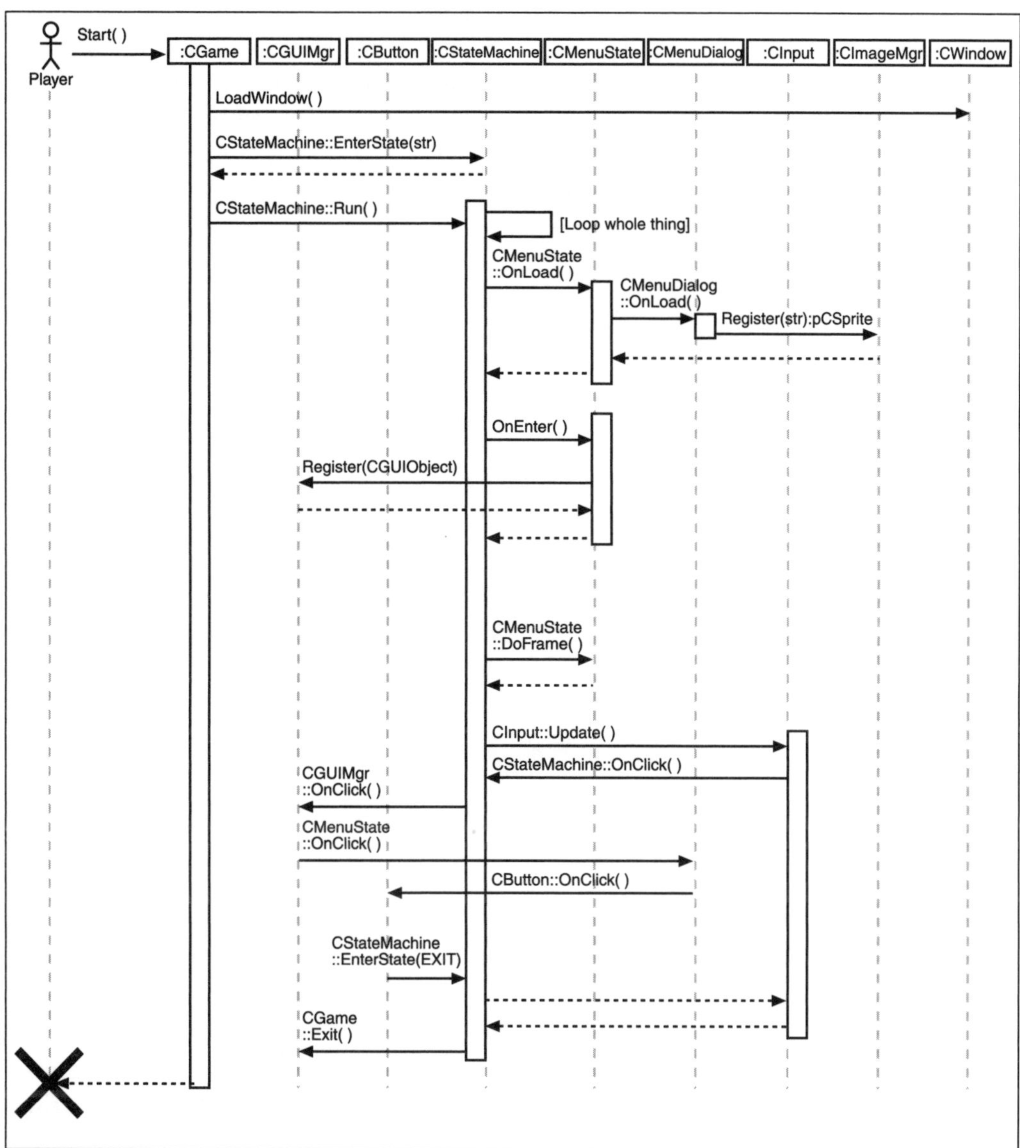

Figure 4.24
Use CRC cards and use case scenarios to create sequence diagrams.

Stripe Collaboration Diagram

The collaboration diagram for the first stripe allows the team to refine the names of the operations and arrive at a clearer visual representation of the operations that each class contains. When you move from a sequence diagram to a collaboration diagram, if you are not using a CASE tool, you might need several iterations before you refine the operations to the point that the flow of activity for the stripe becomes evident. With a CASE tool, you might tend to overlook the value that the difference of the two diagrams provides. Generally, improving a design involves changing the design and seeing the difference that the change makes. In this way, you incrementally view and improve the design. Figure 4.25 shows the collaboration diagram.

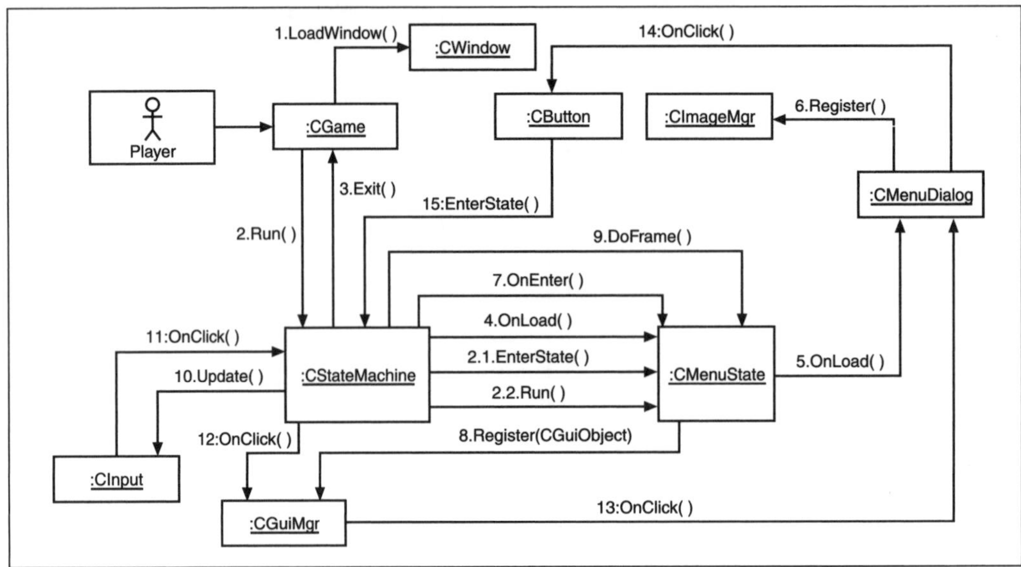

Figure 4.25
The collaboration diagram helps refine the flow of messaging.

As you refine your collaboration diagrams, you might find it beneficial to use operation specifications, which were discussed earlier in this chapter. Although operation specifications are often considered part of the implementation phase, they can be useful during design as a way to explore the conditions that preceded or follow a given message (or function or method call).

Refining Operations and Generating Classes

A class diagram is a static view of the classes that occur in a given component of the system. Class diagrams appear in the section of the SDD that's dedicated to the logical view of the component. Because the static representation of a class incorporates information from a number of components (called stripes), the cycle of development for the class diagrams is slower than the cycle of development for the interaction (sequence and collaboration) diagrams. Any given stripe is likely to make use of only a limited number of the operations of the classes it uses.

Given participation in multiple stripes, each class is likely to possess more operations than are used by any one stripe. For this reason, you are not likely to complete any particular class diagram until you have completed the design of all the stripes of the game. On the other hand, you can begin work on a class diagram as soon as you start the first stripe. With each iteration, you add information to your class and component views. Class diagrams grow with each iteration of the design effort. By the time you reach the final stripe, you can fairly safely conclude that any classes in your proposed class list that have not been included in one or another interaction diagram are not needed.

Figure 4.26 provides an early, preliminary view of a starter class diagram for the first stripe. Note that it was possible, at this point, to fill in only a limited number of operations. With each new stripe, however, the team had a chance to revisit the class, refining its definition as it went. Generally, a rudimentary diagram is enough to get you started. Iteration fills in the details.

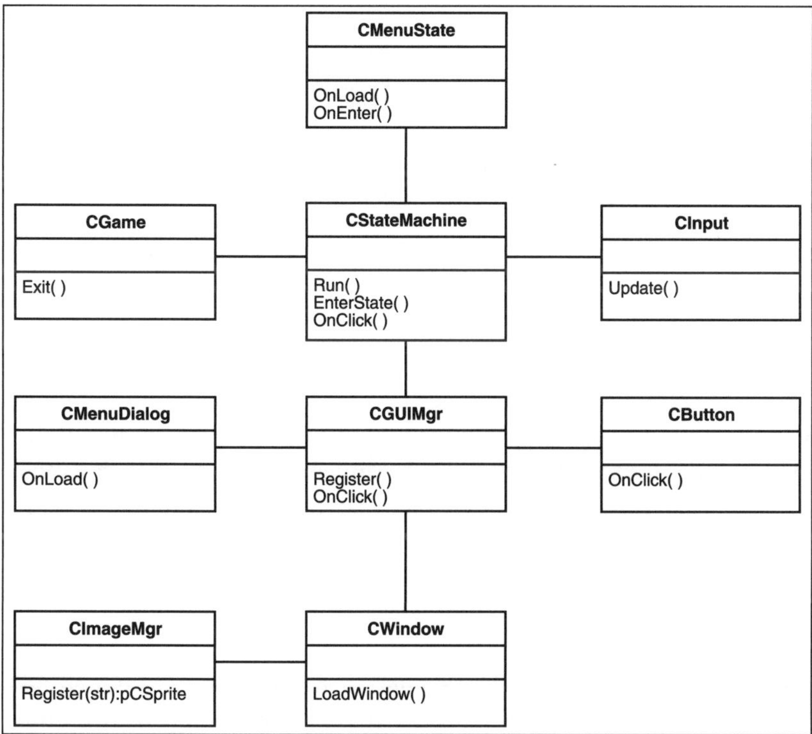

Figure 4.26
Class diagrams receive refinement with each design iteration.

Creating the Component Diagram

The final section of the SDD for this stripe is the component diagram. A group of classes developed during a stripe can be referred to as a component. To illustrate the component, the UML package diagram can be used. The package (file folder) element shows that classes for this stripe are grouped into a single unit. Figure 4.27 illustrates the Start Game component.

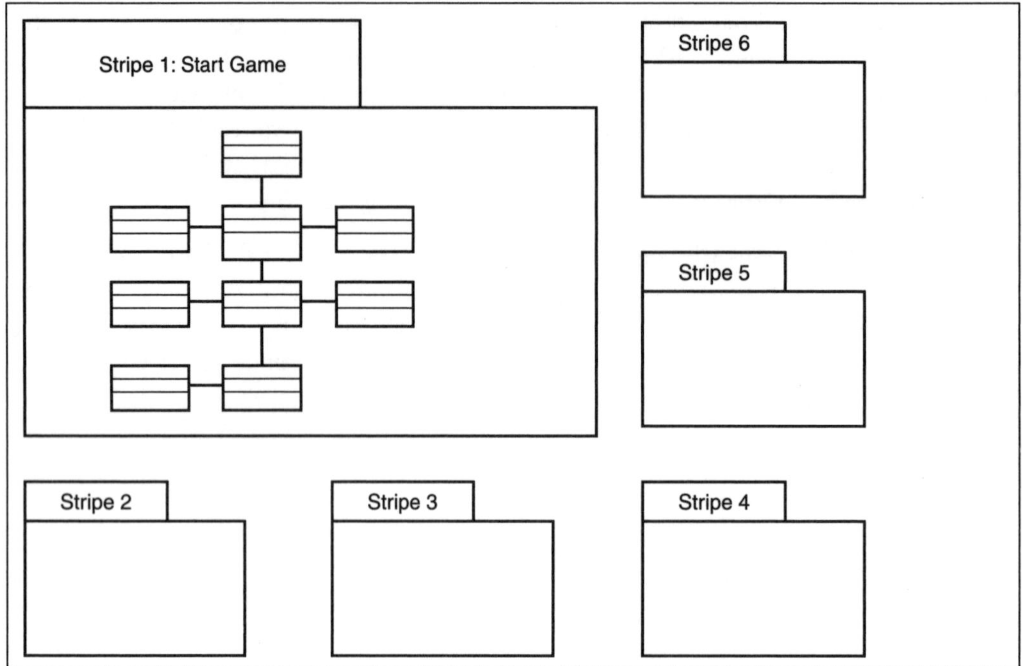

Figure 4.27
The component view provides a starting point for design validation.

Notice in Figure 4.27 that empty packages have been included to depict other components. The other components serve as placeholders at this point. In subsequent iterations, packages can be added to the first stripe to show the dependencies and relationships that characterize each successive stripe. In this way, the design can be iterated and the work on stripes shown.

Verification

In this chapter, the discussions of verification and validation are restricted to a few simple observations that are revisited in Chapters 6, "Object-Oriented Fantasies and Realities," and 7, "P Is for Pattern." The first observation is that the primary way to verify the quality of a design is to see what happens when alternative design schemes are used. For the

Ankh development effort, this involved building the product using a series of stripes. Before each implementation effort, the design of each stripe was inspected.

The design views offer a collective view of the system. They represent one architectural interpretation. But the fact is that many architectural styles might be applied to the system. It is possible to show the appropriateness of a given architecture if you critically assess the way classes are grouped. An excellent approach to this is to begin examining the initial design groupings using patterns.

Conclusion

This chapter discussed the design process. The aim was to show you *one approach* to design: the one used in the development effort for *Ankh*. This design was based partly on some industry-standard approaches. It is not contended that you should use this one approach. Rather, the approach is suggested. When you develop your own approach, you can consider the style of your organization and move forward from there.

Most companies have something resembling a design effort in place. Some tend to merge requirements analysis with design; others keep the two separate. The most mature organizations continuously seek to improve the performance of their software by scrutinizing the assumptions their designers and developers have made about the architecture. Each design effort provides the opportunity to improve on the architectural style. One of the most important results for software engineers is, of course, the game engine, and many of these are now available for purchase by organizations that do not want to develop their own. Groups that want to continue to occupy dynamic leadership positions in the market, however, must have in place a design process that draws upon the skills of those who are most directly involved in the engineering effort to develop state-of-the-art software. The process offered here provides a possible inroad to such an effort.

Hundreds of texts have been published over the years on software design. The list that follows provides you with nonacademic views:

Albin, Stephan T. *The Art of Software Architecture: Design Methods and Techniques.* Indianapolis, Indiana: Wiley Publishing, 2003.

Larmon, Craig. *Applying UML and Patterns: An Introduction to Object-Oriented Analysis and Design.* Upper Saddle River, New Jersey: Prentice Hall PTR, 1998.

Martin, Robert C. *Agile Software Development: Principles, Patterns, and Practices.* Upper Saddle River, New Jersey: Pearson Education, Inc., 2003.

Richter, Charles. *Designing Flexible Object-Oriented Systems with UML.* Indianapolis, Indiana: Macmillan Technical Publishing, 1999.

Witt, Bernard I., F. Terry Baker, and Everett W. Merritt. *Software Architecture and Design: Principles, Models, and Methods.* New York: Van Nostrand Reinhold, 1994.

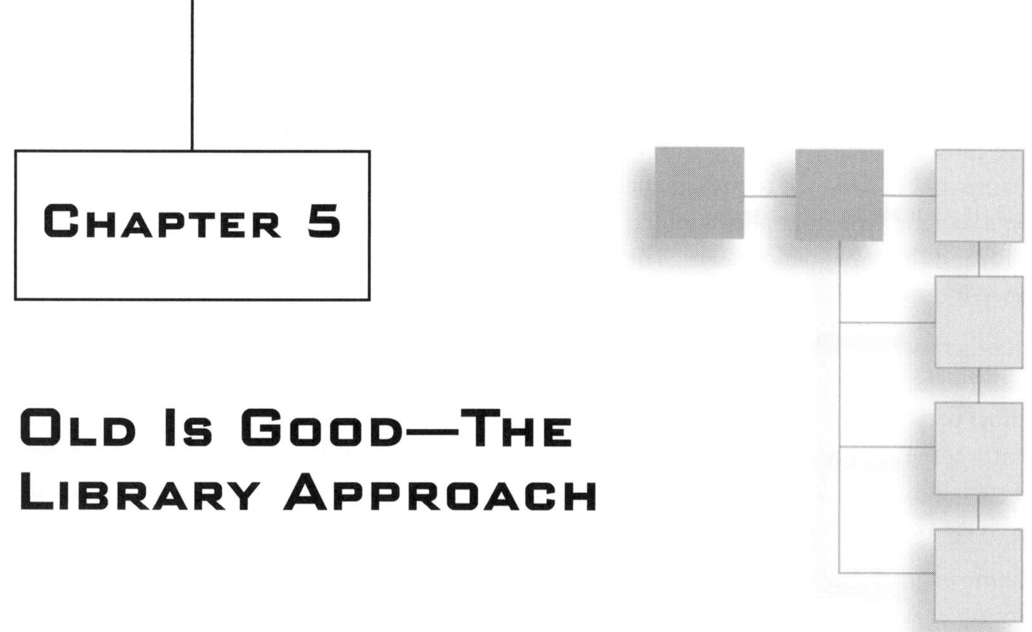

Chapter 5

Old Is Good—The Library Approach

A library is a collection of resources. The description of the resources can vary enormously, depending on the type of project you undertake. From the perspective of software engineering, a library can consist of such things as code snippets, operations, classes, data structures, algorithms, frameworks, patterns, precompiled components, documents, or just about anything that might be used repeatedly during multiple development efforts. The key term, then, is *reuse*. A library serves as a vehicle of software reuse. The question then arises as to what makes something related to software reusable.

Although answering this question is the purpose of this chapter, the topic proves to be much more extensive than this book can cover comprehensively. Still, it is worth trying at least to isolate a few basic ideas. Toward this end, this chapter first identifies the pathways of reuse. It then delves into how software can be made suitable for reuse. Following are among the points touched on along the way:

- Why developers find reusing software worthwhile
- The general ways in which software can be developed specifically for reuse
- How software can be wrong for reuse
- How software that is wrong for reuse can he changed so that it becomes appropriate for reuse
- What prevents software developers from more frequently or profitably reusing software

Libraries and Reuse in General

A software library consists of a body of code that developers can reuse. Reuse results from both planned and unplanned development efforts. On the planned side of reuse, one of the most common types of library is called an *application framework*. An application framework is designed to provide developers with a set of code that enables them to develop a specific type of application. Examples of such efforts are the MFC library, the Win32 API, and the Java Swing classes. These application frameworks allow developers to develop Windows applications.

In other instances, libraries do not result from a planned development effort. Instead, they result from the efforts of developers to save and perfect code for reuse. Because no design effort precedes the development of such libraries, the code simply accumulates over time until, somewhat ironically, it might become a resource for planned development efforts. If such libraries are preserved and refined, documentation can be added, and the code can be reviewed and rewritten to be useful in more general, robust ways.

Game engines fall into both the accidental and the planned categories. If you are a programmer who has been working for several years, it is likely that you have a large store of code you work from whenever you begin a new project. The code you offer does not necessarily represent a complete product, but it does offer parts of a game.

Games that have met with success can also become a source of reusable code. Several game development organizations have made their game code available on the web. In most cases, programmers who are not developing for commercial gain can in this way have access to compete game architectures. In some cases, even if commercial gain forms part of the picture, the code is still available without cost.

Among the Internet sites that might prove useful as general information resources for game code are the following:

- **thefreecountry.com (http://www.thefreecountry.com).** A general resource site for programmers, webmasters, and developers who are involved with security issues.
- **flipcode (http://www.flipcode.com).** Game development news and resources. Good links for DirectX resources and tutorials.
- **Digital Games Research Association (http://www.digra.org).** Necessary to register first, but you can then download resources and tutorials.
- **Game Development Search Engine (http://www.gdse.com).** Provides numerous links to code libraries and tutorials.
- **GameDev.net (http://www.gamedev.net).** Provides multiple links to code sources, tutorials, articles, and other resources.
- **CPP-home.com (http://www.cpp-home.com).** Provides a large store of tutorials and accompanying source samples. Strong on Win32 and C/C++.
- **Game Tutorials (http://www.gametutorials.com).** Immediate links to a wide variety of code libraries for nearly anything related to basic game development. Offers tutorials.

- **Game Foundry. Source Forge (http://gaming.foundries.sourceforge.net).** Provides direct access to a multitude of open source games. The available material overwhelms you at first, but after a time, you can begin to identify specific targets.

This list presents just a few among hundreds of sites where you can obtain resources for C++, DirectX, OpenGL, and a variety of other tools for game development. These resources together constitute an enormous Internet library. Your best bet is to assemble a personalized list of sites you find most useful.

Open C++ Libraries

The Standard Template Library (STL) and Boost offer two of the richest free libraries available to C++ programmers. The STL has been a standard part of C++ since its formalization by the ISO in 1998. Use of the library has become a core element for most programmers working with C++.

The Boost library offers a large collection of highly respected resources for C++ development. Unlike the STL, the Boost library is not standardized. Still, it is well-maintained and provides valuable resources. Among its offerings are a string class that combines capabilities of the STL and MFC string classes and a variety of hash containers. (The STL does not provide a hash class.)

The following short list provides the names of Internet sites that offer information on the STL and Boost:

- **Standard Template Library Programmer's Guide (http://www.sgi.com/tech/stl/index.html).** A guide to the STL sponsored by Silicon Graphics, Inc.
- **ACM Crossroads Student Magazine Introduction to the STL (http://www.acm.org/crossroads/xrds2-3/ovp.html).** A quick overview of key components of the STL.
- **Boost (http://www.boost.org/).** With a few exceptions, the Boost libraries are compatible with the C++ STL. In fact, the Boost organization provides a center to which developers who are developing classes or other resources that might someday be included in the STL can lodge their material for peer review.

Game Engine Libraries

The Internet offers access to thousands of game engines at any given moment. Two general approaches to use characterize most of these. On the one hand, you can download the code, without cost or obligation, and begin hacking at it for learning purposes. On the other hand, you can acquire the code through a license. One type of license is proprietary. Another type is open source. Generally, whether proprietary or open source, the licenses tend to be either free or of minimal cost if you develop a game for personal learning purposes. When you enter the market, however, the conditions and fees stiffen.

If you acquire an engine according to open source provisions, you pay nothing to use it. On an open source basis, the license you agree to when you download the source stipulates requirements along the following lines:

- If you modify the code, you agree to release your modifications to the engine and any of its accompanying tools for use by others.
- You are usually asked to retain a disclaimer in the code or display a logo in a prominent place within the game.
- If a logo, disclaimer, or license statement forms part of the open source agreement, the agreement requests that you refrain from modifying or deleting it.

If you want to use the software without these requirements, you can purchase a license. Prices for licenses vary enormously. Some sell for a few thousand dollars (U.S.), whereas others run much higher.

Among the features that might serve to recommend a game engine are the following:

- **Demo applications.** You should be able to acquire a few demonstration applications with the engine when you download it. Generally, with respect to the demonstration applications, you should be free to do whatever you want with them.
- **Companies that use it.** You should be able to obtain a list of companies that develop products using the engine. A list of customers or users usually appears on the engine site. It is not always the case that a good engine will have many users, but if no one uses the engine, you should be suspicious.
- **Documentation.** Before you decide to invest your time and effort in trying to make use of an existing body of code, spend some time studying its documentation. If you cannot make sense of the documentation, consider going elsewhere.
- **A user group.** A user group or forum is likely to exist for any engine that has received general recognition on an open basis. The *Quake* engines, for example, are everywhere, and many developers on many different sites provide each other with mutual support concerning use and abuse. For commercial engineers, of course, the engine vendor formalizes support and markets it as part of the product.

Profiled Engines

Sifting through the large number of sites that provide game code and engines proves a tiresome task. Still, the time you spend searching can yield worthwhile results. Although most of the resources are probably not useful as the basis of a commercial undertaking, for students and hobbyists, the resources can be genuine assets. Among the sites that possess strong potential for students, hobbyists, and even professionals are the following, all of which feature C/C++ engines that support DirectX or OpenGL on either a Windows or a UNIX/Linux platform.

- **QuakeII.NET.** QuakeII.NET requires Microsoft Visual Studio .NET 2003. This version of Microsoft's 2003 compiler is roughly 98 percent compliant with the ISO standard for C++ compilers. The engine was ported to this platform to demonstrate its compliance. If you have this version of the compiler, you have an excellent version of this fairly robust engine (http://www.vertigosoftware.com/Quake2.htm).
- **Sierra (SCI) Studio.** The SCI Studio was used to create games such as *King Quest*, *Space Quest*, and *Quest for Glory*. You can use this engine on Windows 2000 and XP. In addition, the site provides documentation, tutorials, and scripting tools. You can obtain a demo game, also (http://www.bripro.com/scistudio).
- **Heretic and Hexen.** Raven Software and its affiliate id Software allow you to obtain the source code for *Heretic* and *Hexen* for free if you are not developing for profit (http://www2.ravensoft.com/source).
- **Quake III Arena, Quake III Team Arena, Quake II, Quake.** This is the combined source code for *Quake III Arena* and *Quake III: Team Arena.* It contains project files and related game source code. The code is for Win32 (http://www.idsoftware.com/business/techdownloads).
- **Crystal Space free 3D Engine.** Crystal Space is an open source 3D engine written in C++. Among its features are colored lighting, mirrors, 3D sprites, alpha transparency, true six degrees of freedom, procedural textures, radiosity, particle systems, halos, 16-bit and 32-bit display support, Direct3D support, font support, and hierarchical transformations (http://crystal.sourceforge.net).
- **ClanLib Game SDK.** This development kit handles sound, display, input, networking, files, and threading and is developed for Linux and Windows. It handles 2D display, sound and input support (keyboard, mouse, joysticks), and network support. For 3D support, it uses OpenGL (http://www.clanlib.org).
- **Pathlib.** Pathlib is a C library for finding optimal paths for objects in a map, timing objects and their movements, detecting collisions, and resolving deadlocks (http://pw2.baf.cz/pathlib/pathlib.html).
- **ColDet 3D Free 3D Collision Detection Library.** ColDet is a free 3D collision detection library. Versions are available for use with Microsoft Visual C++ (http://photoneffect.com/coldet).
- **id Software's Wolfenstein.** This is the 3D engine that underlay id Software's *Wolfenstein* (ftp://ftp.idsoftware.com/idstuff/source/wolfsrc.zip).

Criteria for Reuse

Thus far, this chapter has looked at libraries that already exist, but another perspective remains to be developed. This perspective involves the libraries you might develop on your own as either an isolated developer or as a member of a team of developers. When you consider the topic of what code you or your team might want to reserve for reuse, a fairly large number of questions arise. As you answer these questions, you discover many subtle points about why code resource libraries succeed or fail.

A key feature of reuse is that the code you write should conform to the criteria established for standardized libraries. Such criteria relate to every field of software engineering, and it is impossible to cover them all in a single chapter. However, following are some addressable notions:

- Requirements analysis enables developers to develop classes that address exceptional situations or can be extended readily into anticipated uses.
- Design allows classes to be structured with minimum dependencies.
- Documentation provides users with clear explanations and examples of use.
- Testing shows ways in which classes can be optimized or deoptimized.
- Configuration provides information on how a program can be structured so that components can be removed or updated.

Aside from specific software engineering topics, the general observation can be made that well-crafted code almost always readily qualifies for reuse.

What Qualifies for Reusable

Whether or not code is designed to be reusable, the fact of its reuse can be explained fairly readily. The reasons are ultimately numerous, of course, but here are four starting points:

- **Available.** First, code is reused because it is available. In other words, when a programmer has a problem to solve and knows of the existence of code that solves the problem, he is likely to find the code and try to make it work in the new context. At the heart of this type of reuse is knowledge of the code and the ability to find and adapt it.
- **Correct.** A second quality that makes code reusable is that it has been shown to be correct. Code that repeatedly provides a simple service, such as a reliable sorting algorithm, becomes a solid resource that can be identified and used according to the function it performs. No change in the code is needed. Rather, the programmer simply uses it as is. As long as a given problem must be solved, the code that reliably embodies the algorithm that solves the problem has a place in the development effort.
- **Current.** The third quality of reuse fits with the second. Programmers reuse code when they find that it fits in with their current development effort. They likewise reject code that does not. In this respect, for example, code for a sound library that

caters only to 8-bit sound files might not be regarded as a strong candidate for reuse on a 32-bit platform that incorporates MPEG sound.

- **Immediate.** The final quality of reuse is that developers can use the library immediately without having to modify the code it provides. This is the great virtue of the services in the Boost and STL libraries. Programmers can import and use these libraries with relative ease in both Windows and UNIX efforts. This is possible because both libraries have been developed using standard C++ and have been thoroughly tested. Generally, unless programmers seek to optimize them, such libraries require no change or adaptation in a standard C++ development setting.

The Problems of Creating Reusable Code

Not all code qualifies as reusable. When you consider whether to copy code to or from a library, you benefit if you ask a few questions. Among these questions are the following:

- **It is worth it?** This might seem a strange question to ask, but failing to ask it can lead to dire results. The simplest context for understanding this question arises with a piece of code that addresses an uncomplicated but nevertheless specific task and can be written in, say, anywhere from a few minutes to a few hours. In such cases, it might be best to rewrite the code rather than trying to find a library component that serves the same purpose.
- **Does the effort required to refine code for reuse yield a profitable return?** This question involves a bit of cost-benefit analysis. When you fashion code for reuse, the code you fashion usually requires more documentation and testing than other code. The reason for this is that you want to make the code so that many people can use it in many contexts. To provide for such use, you must test the code in the contexts in which you think it might be used. This effort consumes time. It becomes necessary, then, to consider whether the code ever will, in reality, receive use in multiple contexts. If you are unable to name at least a few of these contexts, refining the code and placing it in a library might not be worth the effort.
- **Can the code be maintained?** This is a question that people need to ask about almost any software, but it has special bearing on code that is designed for reuse, because such code stands alone as its own product, apart from any deliverable it might be made part of. Do you have time to maintain a library in addition to developing the application in which you initially use the components of the library?
- **Can you find it after you make it a part of the library?** When you create reusable operations, you must be able to identify them later on if you are to make use of them. For this reason, you face the problem of how to design the library so that its interface is easy to understand and so that the documentation that the library includes clearly addresses its services and contexts of use.

- **Is the library legal?** Issues of legality can arise if the library you are developing or want to develop includes components from libraries that you have purchased. If the purchased libraries are of a proprietary or open source form that stipulates they cannot be made a part of another library, your efforts at constructing a library could be legally hazardous. If you cannot develop a library that is free of dependencies on other libraries (besides the STL or Boost), you might want to reconsider your efforts.
- **Does the code have a large number of contexts of use?** If the code you develop cannot be used in a number of different ways, toward a variety of different solutions, it is probably not worth trying to shape into a library. If you maintain a library of snippets, you might find that in specific situations you remember that a piece of code you once wrote can be brought forward and refashioned to address a similar problem. Cutting and pasting a bit of old code into a new context differs from identifying a generalized pattern or context of use and then writing code so that it addresses such use.
- **Can you write code so that it can be reused in ways that you might not anticipate?** In some ways, this is the hardest question, and it defines a characteristic of the best libraries. Code written to anticipate changing use scenarios is both robust and extensible. The mechanisms of extensibility include abstraction, generalization, and pattern-oriented design.
- **Can you say where the code cannot be used?** This is sometimes as important as asking where the code can be applied. Another way to view this issue is to consider the limitations of the component or class you have designed. Trying to design a class for too many purposes is as inadvisable as designing it for too specialized a purpose.

Taking a Class Approach

Chapter 4, "Software Design—Much Ado About Something," and Chapter 6, "Object-Oriented Fantasies and Realities," discuss in detail some of the issues of object-oriented design. This section touches on a few specifics regarding classes as vehicles for reusable code.

Programming a game with C++ often involves using an object-oriented approach to application development. A game written in C++ that uses object-oriented development strategies is likely to draw together functions into classes. The actions of the game take place through interactions between the objects. In contrast, a game that is written in C might employ a set of libraries that draw together functions and defined values. The actions of the game take place through function calls involving the manipulation of the data that is established to define different states of the game.

Arriving at a conclusive argument for using classes over function libraries is not as easy as it might appear to be, but in the end, the general practice is to design a game as a set of classes. Generally, the software industry has gravitated toward object-oriented programs because such programs contain and control complexity better than do structured programs and function libraries. A class gathers into one place the data that describe the state of the object and the operations (or functions) that control the behavior of the data. Further, classes allow a programmer to modularize the development of the game, so that a change to one part of a game does not impact many other parts of the game.

Using Standard Class Forms

Programmers can more readily use code when they do not have to spend a great deal of time figuring out how to use it. This notion applies to the collection of operations that form the interface of a class or set of classes. If the interfaces for the classes in a library do not conform to a standard model that implicitly identifies the services provided, the user must study the interface of each class in isolation to determine what services it provides. If the difference from class to class proves extensive, the user might not be able to trust even the most generalized notions about class design. Frustration results.

Consistency

Consistency in class construction begins with the way that a class designer designs a class interface. Chapter 6 deals with this topic in more specific detail, but it is important to mention here that applying similar names to similar operations is a good idea. As an example, consider the meaning of the following operations:

```
//mutator...
void SetPos(const POINT& vecPos);
//accessor...
POINT GetPos()const;
```

You can determine fairly easily the meaning of these operations. If you call the `GetPos()` operation, the operation returns a reference to a `POINT`. In other words, if you want to know the values of the current coordinate, you can obtain them from the returned vector. On the other hand, if you call the `SetPos()` operation, you can set the values of the current position by passing a reference to a `POINT` object. The balance of "set" and "get" allows the operation users to understand easily how the operation works. Likewise, the use of a single data type makes using the operation symmetrical and easy.

In contrast, consider the inconvenience that might be occasioned with the following variation:

```
//mutator...
void SetPos(POINT vecPos);
//accessor...
int GetPos()const;
```

In this case, you still see two operations, but the second operation, the *accessor*, suddenly becomes a mystery. You have no way to understand what the single integer value means in relation to the two operations. It might be that some type of look-up strategy is implied, but whatever this is cannot be known without investigations.

Consistency in class design implies using standard approaches to things like accessing and mutating (changing) class data. "Getting" or "setting" the state of the class implies getting or setting the state of the class according to easy-to-understand patterns of use.

Nice Versus Practical Classes

Although you should seek to limit classes so that they provide the services you need, you still can establish what is generally referred to as a "nice" class. Such a class is akin to a standard approach to creating classes. Keep in mind that a nice class is developed in a specific setting and conveys a sense of formalism. It provides a set of services that a given development team might establish as standard. The following list itemizes some possible services:

- Copy construction
- Object destruction
- Assignment
- Boolean operations
- Accessor and mutator operations
- Inequality operations

A class that provides such services possesses a *standard interface.* Note that, among other features, a standard interface provides an explicit constructor. Likewise, it provides operators that are overridden for assignment and comparison activities. And it offers a destructor. As shown in the earlier examination of the accessor and mutator operations, classes that are designed using a standard interface promote understanding and ease of use.

Having defended the notion that standard interfaces facilitate understanding and use, you can also defend the opposite. Situations arise in which it is inadvisable to implement a standard interface. In the following code sample, the definition of the interface has been limited because it makes little sense to fully implement the services that a nice class should provide. Instead, the interface is defined according to practical considerations. In the `CEntity` class, one such consideration is whether the user of the class will ever require an accessor or a copy constructor. Such uses are unlikely, so an option is to declare the copy constructor as private.

```
#ifndef _CENTITY_HEADER_INCLUDED
#define _CENTITY_HEADER_INCLUDED
#include "game.h"
class CEntity
```

```
{
public:
        // constructor
        CEntity(CStdString strName);
        // destructor.
        virtual ~CEntity();
        // Draws the entity
        virtual void Draw();
        // Get and Set methods ////////////////////////////////////////
        virtual void SetMesh(CMesh *pMesh)
                    {m_pMesh = pMesh;}
        virtual void SetPos(D3DXVECTOR3 vecPos)
                    {m_vecPos=vecPos;BuildWorldMatrix();}
        virtual void SetRot(D3DXVECTOR3 vecRot)
                    {m_vecRot=vecRot;BuildWorldMatrix();}
        virtual void SetScale(D3DXVECTOR3 vecScale)
                    {m_vecScale = vecScale;BuildWorldMatrix();}
        ///////////////////////////////////////////////////////////////
protected:
        CStdString m_strName;
        // Pointer to the mesh for this entity
        class CMesh *m_pMesh;
        // The position, rotation, and scaling vectors
        D3DXVECTOR3 m_vecPos,m_vecRot,m_vecScale;
        // A matrix in which to store all our info so we don't have to
        // generate it every time
        D3DXMATRIX m_matWorld;
        // Builds the world matrix according to the 3 vectors (pos,rot,scale)
        virtual void BuildWorldMatrix();
};
#endif _CENTITY_HEADER_INCLUDED
```

Before you implement a standard interface for a class, consider whether you anticipate that you will use the class in unanticipated ways. If you were to create a generic `CEntity` class for a game engine that you anticipated distributing widely, for example, providing a fully implemented standard interface might be mandated. But in the context of use developed here, the time investment that the standard interface requires lacks justification.

Class Implementation

In the declaration of `CEntity` shown earlier, inline versions of mutator operations were created. Here, for example, is the inline version of `SetMesh()`:

```
virtual void SetMesh(CMesh *pMesh)
            {m_pMesh = pMesh;}
```

When you both declare and define an operation in the declaration of a class, your activities implicitly *inline* the operation. When you inline an operation, you request the compiler to create the object code for the operation every time the operation is called. The alternative is for the compiler to create the object code for the operation once and store a lookup to this code in a table. The compiler can create the object code only once and then reference this code when it encounters subsequent calls to the operation. In this way, the compiler reduces the amount of object code that a program requires.

Compiler manufacturers often optimize inlining, so the compiler decides for itself whether to create object code inline. In some instances, you can still force inlining. Specifically, unless your compiler manufacturer has stipulated otherwise, using the keyword `inline` can force inline generation of object code.

With or without optimized compilers, however, a couple of reuse points arise. It makes little sense to write an enormously large operation inline. If you write large operation definitions in the declaration of a class, users of your code might find it difficult to discover what constitutes the class interface. To discover the basic services that the interface provides, the code user must pick through possibly hundreds of lines of implementation code. Such picking can be exhausting and irritating.

Why, then, is it good to implement some operations inline in the `CEntity` class? The answer is that if an operation involves only a `return` statement, it might make much more sense than otherwise to maintain the operation in one place in the program. Ease of maintenance justifies inlining. On the other hand, in most cases you will want to declare and implement your operations separately. This chapter provides separate declaration and implementation of the constructor and two other operations in the `CEntity` class. The implementations of these operations are in separate files, apart from their declarations.

note

You can inline code without cluttering your class declaration if you place inline operations in the header file after the class declaration. When you do this, mark the inlined operations in the declaration with an inline comment, `//inline`. This way, you still achieve the speed that an inline operation offers, but the interface is much easier to read. Here is an example of what this looks like for `SetMesh()`:

```
};//This is the end of the class declaration
       inline void CEntity::SetMesh(CMesh *pMesh)
                   {m_pMesh = pMesh;}
```

Advice is courtesy of John Hollis.

One other point arises. Keep in mind that unless your complier possesses optimizing capabilities, which most modern compilers do, inlining can possibly result in an enormous amount of object code even if the operation declared inline possesses only a few lines of code. Consider the `BuildWorldMatrix()` operation in the code sample that follows. This operation consists of only a few lines of code, but each line calls another operation.

If operations call other operations on an inline basis, a potentially vast amount of object code might result, for each called operation might be generated inline. For this reason, when one operation calls other operations, it should not be defined inline.

```
#include "../game.h"
////////////////////////////////////////////////////////////
// CEntity::CEntity()
// Creates an entity object
////////////////////////////////////////////////////////////
CEntity::CEntity(CStdString strName)
{
        // Set up some default parameters
        m_vecPos = D3DXVECTOR3(0,0,0);
        m_vecRot = D3DXVECTOR3(0,0,0);
        m_vecScale = D3DXVECTOR3(1,1,1);
        m_pMesh = NULL;
        m_strName = strName;
        // Build the default world matrix
        BuildWorldMatrix();
}
////////////////////////////////////////////////////////////
// CEntity::~CEntity()
//Destroys an entity object
////////////////////////////////////////////////////////////
CEntity::~CEntity(){}
////////////////////////////////////////////////////////////
// CEntity::BuildWorldMatrix()
// Builds the world matrix to be used during drawing
////////////////////////////////////////////////////////////
void CEntity::BuildWorldMatrix()
{
        D3DXMATRIX matPos,matRot,matScale;
        D3DXMatrixTranslation(&matPos,m_vecPos.x,m_vecPos.y,m_vecPos.z);
        D3DXMatrixRotationY(&matRot,m_vecRot.y);
        D3DXMatrixScaling(&matScale,m_vecScale.x,m_vecScale.y,m_vecScale.z);
        D3DXMatrixMultiply(&m_matWorld,&matScale,&matRot);
        D3DXMatrixMultiply(&m_matWorld,&m_matWorld,&matPos);
}
////////////////////////////////////////////////////////////
// CEntity::Draw()
// Draws the object
////////////////////////////////////////////////////////////
void CEntity::Draw()
{
        // Set up the world matrix
        Graphics->GetDevice()->SetTransform( D3DTS_WORLD, &m_matWorld );
        // Draw the actual mesh
        m_pMesh->Draw();
}
```

Making Code Efficient

The efficiency of your code depends in most cases on how many redundancies it contains. A redundancy is anything that is performed more than once. When you write code efficiently, you reduce the number of redundancies.

Redundant code occurs on many occasions. One occasion occurs when you declare instances of objects in settings in which such declaration is not needed. Another occasion of needless redundancy is when you allow your program to create multiple copies of an object. The passages that follow examine these two situations.

Needless Declaration

Needless declaration occurs in many contexts. One of the more frequent problems arises when you develop an algorithm through trial and error and along the way create many instances of different types of data but do not in the end clean things up so that the redundancies are eliminated. Consider the following bit of code:

```
int CStateMachine::GetIndex(CStdString strName)
{
    CStdString tempstrName = strName;
    bool flag = false;
    int index = 0;
    // Find the state
    for(int i=0;i<NUM_STATES;i++)
    {
        if(m_pStates[i]->GetName() == tempstrName)
        {
            flag = true;
            index = i;
        }
     }
    if(flag)
    {
        return index;
    }
    else
    {
    // utter failure
    return(-1);
    {
}
```

In this situation, an object of the `CStdString` type was declared and assigned to a local string for testing purposes. Then a flag was declared to register whether the `CStdString` value was found within an array. In an attempt to observe structured programming principles (one point of entrance, one point of exit), a flag was declared and an integer data type was used to store the results of the operation. Likewise, a `for` loop was used to iterate through the array.

The previous sample creates a number of redundant declarations. Consider, likewise, the number of selection statements. The CStdString instance, the flag, and the integer for storing the index value are all in part justified, but at the same time, if the code can be made more efficient, you need to consider whether such declarations are justified. Generally, they are not. Nothing is gained, for example, by replicating the CStdString instance. Likewise, the selection statements are questionable. Rather than iterating through the whole array, you can simply return the index as soon as you find it. And even if you violate strict structural programming principles by doing so, you can exit the loop with a return value.

Consider another version of the operation:

```
int CStateMachine::GetIndex(CStdString strName)
{
    // Find the state
    for(int i=0;i<NUM_STATES;i++)
    {
        if(m_pStates[i]->GetName() == strName)
            return(i);
    }
    // utter failure
    return(-1);
}
```

This version of the operation eliminates much of the redundancy. It still poses a few problems with copying (covered next), but the form it assumes here possesses much greater simplicity and is more efficient.

Needless Copying

Returning to the code in the CEntity, consider the declarations of the operations in the class as presented earlier:

```
D3DXVECTOR3 GetPos(){return m_vecPos;}
D3DXVECTOR3 GetLookAt(){return m_vecLookAt;}
D3DXVECTOR3 GetUp(){return m_vecUp;}
void SetPos(D3DXVECTOR3 vecPos){m_vecPos = vecPos;}
void SetLookAt(D3DXVECTOR3 vecLookAt){m_vecLookAt = vecLookAt;}
void SetUp(D3DXVECTOR3 vecUp){m_vecUp = vecUp;}
```

These declarations are all sound enough as given. The accessor functions return instances of the items requested, and the mutators change values as requested. Redundancy plagues the activity, however. For starters, consider how the arguments are passed to the mutators (SetPos(), SetLookAt(), and SetUp on a copy basis. Copying objects can require an enormous expenditure of effort on the part of the operating system, and the result is a decline in the performance of the program.

You can solve the problem fairly easily by using references. When you designate the parameters as references, no copying takes place. To round out your modifications, you can assign `const` to the parameters. This key word protects the object from change. In this case, when you prevent the `D3DXVECTOR3` from being copied, you restrict what could be a fairly significant drain on resources.

```
void SetPos(const D3DXVECTOR3 &vecPos){m_vecPos = vecPos;}
void SetLookAt(const D3DXVECTOR3 &vecLookAt){m_vecLookAt = vecLookAt;}
void SetUp(const D3DXVECTOR3 &vecUp){m_vecUp = vecUp;}
```

When you pass large objects to operations, you can increase the amount of memory usage if you do not attend to the dangers of unintended copying. There are several points at which passing arguments to an operation can invoke copying:

- If you pass an object to a function and do not use a reference or a pointer, the object might be copied.
- If you declare a local instance of the object for purposes of assigning the values of attributes for temporary purposes, the object can be constructed redundantly during the assignment operation.
- If you return the results of the operation as something other than as a reference or a pointer, again, you can invoke a constructor.
- If you pass the results of the operation to a new instance of the object, you can again invoke the constructor.

Generally, the fewer the copy operations, the better. Using references provides perhaps the easiest approach to eliminating needless copying. Using pointers is also an option.

Reference Counting

In C++, one of the biggest problems that developers face is a memory leak. Memory leaks often occur when a program loses track of how many objects of a given type it has created. Reference counting provides a simple mechanism for making objects easier to track. Although it is not suggested that everyone should use this approach to eliminating the problem, this section does describe the approach and show you how to implement it.

To create a class that can track the number of instances in which it has been instantiated, you can create a constructor that counts each time it is called. For *Ankh*, a situation that merited reference counting arose with image files. It was necessary to ensure that multiple copies of the same image files were not loaded into memory. Video memory is a scarce resource that should be conserved whenever possible.

To implement the reference-counting code, the `CImage` and `CImageMgr` classes were changed. Following are the steps that were used:

- An integer variable, m_iRefCount, was added to the CImage class. This variable tracked the number of objects currently using the image.
- The operations AddReference() and RemoveReference() were added to the CImage class to change the reference count from the image manager as objects requested access to the image.
- When the image manager's Get() operation was called, the reference count was increased. Another function, DoneWithImage(), allowed an object to inform the image manager that it was done using an image and could decrease its reference count.
- If an image's reference count dropped to zero, the CImage object was destroyed and the memory was freed.

Here is the code for CImageMgr::DoneWithImage():

```
void CImageMgr::DoneWithImage(CStdString strName)
{
      CImage *imgFound = NULL;
      for(unsigned int i=0;i<m_vecImages.size();i++)
      {
            // Look for the image with the matching name
            if(m_vecImages[i]->GetName() == strName)
            {
                  imgFound = m_vecImages[i];
                  break;
            }
      }

      // The image couldn't be found...
      if(!imgFound)
      {
              Log->Add("CImageMgr::DoneWithImage()
                    Tried to unload %s, and it does not exist...",
                    strName.c_str());
                    return;
      }
      // Remove a reference to the image (it will unload
      // itself if it needs to)
      imgFound->RemoveReference();
}
```

When the CImageMgr object is destroyed, it loops through the remaining images and unloads them. Because all objects are supposed to destroy themselves before the managers, there should be no images left to destroy at this point. If any are found, they are added to the log file. The data in the log file can determine where the leak has occurred. The code is as follows:

```
void CImage::Unload()
{
     // Only unload if we are currently loaded
     if(m_bLoaded)
     {
               // Release the texture
               if(m_pTexture) m_pTexture->Release();
               m_pTexture = NULL;
               // Add a warning if someone is still holding on to us
               if(m_iRefCount>0)
               {
               Log->
               Add("CImage::Unload()> %s unloaded with\
                   iRefCount=%d (There are objects still\
                   holding onto this image!)",
                   m_strName.c_str(), m_iRefCount);
                   }
                   // Reset reference count back to 0, set unloaded
                   m_iRefCount = 0;
                   m_bLoaded = false;
        }
    }
```

Keep in mind that you can use different approaches to initiating counts. One approach is when you construct an object. Another approach is to invoke the `AddReference()` operation. Also, note that copies will point to the same count set, so the reference count increases with copying. Likewise, note that the `RemoveReference()` operation deletes the primary object when the count reaches zero.

Exceptions and Errors

An error is a problem in the program that a tester can detect or create through testing. The most obvious type of error is a syntax error. The compiler catches syntax errors. Omit a semicolon or a brace, for example, and the compiler is likely to object. On the other hand, errors can also occur in the logic of the program. If you find that the program distorts your mesh, for example, you must go back through the code to find the point at which the program logic fails and the mesh becomes distorted. Such an error is usually referred to as an *internal error*. Testing can eliminate most such errors. If the code is shipped with glaring errors, it usually means that the product has not been tested and debugged sufficiently.

Another type of error is an *external error*. You can view such an error as an exception caused by circumstances that are external to the code. Consider a situation in which your game runs on a computer that resides on a yacht. The owner of the yacht sails out to sea, into a storm. Seeking refuge from the storm, the owner of the yacht battens down the hatches and huddles below decks, where he starts playing your game to pass the time until the weather clears. But then lightning strikes the mast, and electrical static is generated. Your game crashes. This is an external error or an exception.

Why did the exception occur? Strange things can happen with static electrical fields. The static electricity from the storm might have affected the CPU in such a way that an integer was turned into a float or vice versa. The program crashed as a result. It might be that no program could resist the electrical static that the storm generated, but a program can possess a way to handle exceptions. A program that handles all exceptions without crashing is said to be *exception free.*

Handling an exception involves either correcting the exception or shutting down gracefully. In some instances, shutting down is the best alternative. With most Windows office applications, shutting down is a reasonable option, especially if the state of your document can be saved before the application closes. With a heart monitor in a hospital, in contrast, shutting down is not an option. If the software detects an exception, it should have the ability to recover. If it cannot recover, it should generate an alarm.

To respond to an exception, a program must have a mechanism that can detect the exception and then either retry or terminate the execution of the program in response to the exception. This is the basis of `try` and `catch` blocks.

Try and Catch

`Try` blocks offer a place in which you can station code that might generate exceptions. `Try` blocks replace an older technique for handling exceptions. This approach involved putting code in repeated selection blocks. Each selection block could write an error message upon failure. Although in many ways this older approach was reliable, the code tended to clutter up a program. The reduction of such clutter was one of the reasons that `try` and `catch` blocks were added to C++.

C++ provides a `try-catch` mechanism for exception handling. This mechanism includes three primary features, as follows:

- A `try` part, which encloses the code you want to monitor.
- A `throw` part, which enables you to deliver information about an exception when it occurs.
- A `catch` part, which catches the information you have thrown from the `try` part.

C++ offers a number of approaches to using the `try-catch` mechanism. One of the most straightforward is to first create a class that you can use to identify exceptions. You can then use the constructor from this class with a `throw` statement. You can throw an anonymous instance of the class. The `catch` block can then catch the anonymous instance of the exception class. The `catch` block catches the exception because you place a parameter in the argument list of the `catch` block that is of the exception type. When the `catch` block catches the exception, code in the `catch` block can identify the exception and respond to it appropriately.

Declaring Exception Classes

To illustrate how to write code that can handle exceptions, this section begins by creating a fairly lightweight hierarchy of classes that handle exceptions. To create this hierarchy, consider that exceptions fall into two general categories. Some are fatal, whereas others are not. A fatal error requires you to gracefully close things down. A nonfatal error leaves two options: gracefully closing things down, or logging the error, issuing a warning, and going on with the game.

In *Ankh*, an abstract exception class was created from which to derive classes that addressed the two main types of exceptions. The abstract class, `CException`, established the basic model for all exceptions that the game might throw and provided a general data type that could be used in all `catch` blocks. Every `catch` block could catch objects derived from `CException`. The member operations included a default constructor, a constructor in which to embed a message about the exception, and operations that could record and obtain data about the exception. Each exception could be identified with a number and a message associated with the exception. The code is as follows:

```
class CException{
protected:
     // Description of the exception
     CStdString m_strDesc;
     // The file in which the exception occurred
     CStdString m_strFile;
     // Which line number
     int m_iLine;
public:
     // Default constructor
     CException(){}
     // Creates an exception
     CException(CStdString strDesc,CStdString strFile,int iLine);
     CStdString GetDesc() const {return m_strDesc;}
     CStdString GetFile() const {return m_strFile;}
     int GetLine() const {return m_iLine;}

     // Returns the full description of the exception
     CStdString GetFullDesc() const;
};
```

Defining Exception Classes

note

The STL offers a class called `exception` that provides an excellent approach to handling errors. This class provides an operation, `what()`, that you can use to report the error being thrown. A set of four runtime and three logic error classes are derived from `std::exception`. Several basic exceptions can be processed: `bad_alloc`, `length_error`, `out_of_range`, `runtime_error`, `bad_cast`, and `overflow_error`. See the reference to Cameron Hughes and Tracey Hughes at the end of this chapter for more information.

Given the creation of the abstract base class for exceptions, the team then proceeded to create two derived classes. The two derived classes address the two types of exception handling routines developed for the game. One logs the exception and goes on. The other logs the exception and closes the game. When the program logs an exception, the result is what the team labeled a warning exception. When an exception results in the close of the game, the exception becomes a fatal exception. The code for the exceptions reads as follows:

```
// Used for fatal exceptions. When a fatal exception is thrown,
// we must terminate the game.
class CFatalException : public CException{
public:
      // Creates an exception
      CFatalException(CStdString strDesc,CStdString strFile,int iLine);
};

// Used for warnings
class CWarning : public CException{
      CWarning(CStdString strDesc,CStdString strFile,int iLine);
};

--------Implementation-----------
/////////////////////////////////////////////////////////
// CException::CException                              //
// Creates an exception                                //
/////////////////////////////////////////////////////////
CException::CException(CStdString strDesc,CStdString strFile,int iLine)
{
      // Store the description of the exception
      m_strDesc = strDesc;

      // Get the relative path to the file (this is so that if the user
      // has the source code installed, we can drop the source straight
      // into the Exception message box to help debug)
      int idxAnkhSource = strFile.find("ankhsource\\src\\");
      m_strFile = strFile.Right(strFile.length() -
      idxAnkhSource - strlen("AnkhSource\\src\\"));
      m_strFile.Format("..\\%s",m_strFile.c_str());
      m_strFile = FullPath(m_strFile);
      // Store the line number
      m_iLine = iLine;
}
/////////////////////////////////////////////////////////
// CException::GetFullDesc                             //
// Returns a full description (with source code) of   //
// the exception that was thrown                       //
/////////////////////////////////////////////////////////
CStdString CException::GetFullDesc()
{
```

```
    CStdString strFullDesc;
    // If we can, read in the source file where the exception occurred
    // and put this information in the description as well
    char buf[256];
    CStdString strSource;
    std::ifstream fsSource(m_strFile);
    // We found the source file! Grab the source code from around
    // the line where we threw the exception and add it to the
    // description
    if(fsSource.is_open())
    {
        for(int iLine = 0;iLine<m_iLine;iLine++)
        {
            fsSource.getline(buf,256);
            if(iLine>=m_iLine-8)
            strSource.Format("%s\n%s",strSource.c_str(),buf);
        }
    }
    strFullDesc.Format("%s\n(%s:%d)\n\nSource:\n%s",
           m_strDesc.c_str(),m_strFile.c_str(),m_iLine,strSource.c_str());
    return(strFullDesc);
}
//////////////////////////////////////////////////////
// CFatalException::CFatalException                 //
// Creates a fatal exception (thrown when the game   //
// must be terminated                                 //
//////////////////////////////////////////////////////
CFatalException::CFatalException(CStdString strDesc,
                                 CStdString strFile,int iLine)
{
    // Store the description of the exception
    m_strDesc = strDesc;
    // Get the relative path to the file (this is so that if the user
    // has the source code installed, we can drop the source straight
    // into the Exception message box to help debug)
    int idxAnkhSource = strFile.find("ankhsource\\src\\");
    m_strFile = strFile.Right(strFile.length() -
               idxAnkhSource - strlen("AnkhSource\\src\\"));
    m_strFile.Format("..\\src\\%s",m_strFile.c_str());
    m_strFile = FullPath(m_strFile);

    // Store the line number
    m_iLine = iLine;
    // Add the information to the log
    Log->Add("FATAL EXCEPTION: %s",GetFullDesc().c_str());
}
```

Throwing Exceptions

Given the implementation of concrete exception classes, it is possible to equip the program to throw clearly identified exception objects at any location where it is reasonable to insert a `try` block. One such location is in the `WinMain()` operation. To accomplish this, the programmer surrounds the game code with a `try` block and catches the possible exceptions. The result is that either the code exits the game or the activity is logged.

When the `try` block throws a fatal exception, due to the forms of overloaded constructors that have been created, it is possible to furnish a description of the exception as an argument to the constructor. It is also possible to identify the source file in which the error occurred and the line number of the code that was executed last. The exception class automatically checks for the existence of this source file and, if it finds it, adds the block of code directly into the description of the exception. This description appears in a dialog box that displays when the program throws the exception. Although this feature is probably not something you want to ship with a game, it proves useful for debugging. The `try` and `catch` blocks for the exception handling routine in the `WinMain()` operation are as follows:

```
int APIENTRY WinMain(…)
{
// Our CGame object
CGame *pGame;
try{
     // Set up our global instance pointer
     g_hInstance = hInstance;
     // Initialize the game object, and have it run
     pGame = new CGame();
     pGame->Run();
     // Now simply delete the game object. We're done
     delete(pGame);
       }catch(CFatalException exFatal){
     // Shut down the game by deleting the game object
     delete(pGame);
     // Show a message box with information about the exception
     MessageBox( NULL,exFatal.GetFullDesc(),
                 "FATAL ERROR",MB_OK);
     return 0;
     }catch (CWarning exWarning){
     // Just log the warning
     Log->Add("WARNING: %s",exWarning.GetFullDesc().c_str());
       }
}
```

To throw a fatal exception, you can create a helper operation. Used in the `CImage` class, the program throws a `FatalExcepion` object if it fails to find an image file. The code is as follows:

```
bool CImage::LoadFromFile(CStdString strFname)
{
     // The image info structure holds width, height, formats, and so on
     D3DXIMAGE_INFO info;

     // Try to load the texture
     if(FAILED(D3DXCreateTextureFromFileEx(…)
     {
          throw FatalException(__FILE__,__LINE__,
               "CImage::LoadFromFile ->
               Failed to load %s!",strFname.c_str());
          return(false);
     }
}
```

Compatibility and Maintainability

When a body of code is compatible with another body of code, its potential for reuse increases. Compatibility has to do with how well operations, classes, or modules interact. If you add a module to a program and find that the addition of the module requires that you change either your original code or the code in the added module, the two sets of code are not readily compatible. Compatibility means that the two bodies of code can be used together without rework.

Along other lines, maintainability bears heavily on reuse. When a body of code is readily maintainable, it can be changed with relative ease. One effective way to reduce the work involved in changing code is to reduce the number of times you have to make the same change. You usually have to repeatedly make the same change if the code contains many passages that have been cut and pasted from some previous body of code. Remember that if you copy a defective piece of code to several places in your program, to correct the defect, you must visit each place where you have copied the code.

Reducing Redundancy

You improve the maintainability of your code if you decrease the number of times a maintenance programmer must change parts of the code to make a single change in one area of logic that the code offers. If you develop code through frequent copy-and-paste operations, you might find, in the end, that maintenance of your code becomes difficult. To solve this problem, you can take precautions to properly modify code as you copy and paste it or to reduce the number of times you copy and paste.

As an example of how copy-and-paste practices lead to problems, consider the duties you contract when you copy and paste. Usually, you copy the code in one block. The change usually involves altering the names of local variables to correspond to the new context of use. After the code is in place, if you find a way to improve the original block, you also need to change the code in the copied block. Likewise, you face a similar obligation if you spot an error in the original block. Add to this another problem. Each time you change the context of a block of code, you face the need to change the documentation.

Clearly, such repeated tasks reduce ease of maintenance and increase chances that errors will occur. Among the chief problems are that the documentation and variable names remain unchanged and that an improvement to one block might not be made to another, resulting in code that lacks symmetry.

Eliminating duplicate blocks of code begins with not creating them in the first place. Short of this, however, when duplicated blocks do exist, you still have the option of finding such blocks and merging them. To accomplish this, you can first isolate the duplicated functionality in a distinct operation. You can then call this operation in place of the duplicated blocks. To illustrate this situation, consider an early stage of the first stripe of *Ankh*. In the early stripe, a programmer created two sliders: horizontal and vertical. The approach used to create the sliders was to copy and paste a block of old code into two distinct functions. A situation of dual maintenance responsibilities resulted. The following bit of code illustrates the situation:

```
// CSlider update method. This is for a horizontal slider…
void CSlider::Update()
{
      int iMouseX=Input->GetMouseX();

      // Call parent update
      CGuiObject::Update();
            //Change the Slider's location to the mouseX if pressed
      if (m_bPressed)
      {
                  if (((iMouseX + (m_sprSlider->GetWidth() / 2))
                        <= m_iRight) && ((iMouseX -
                        (m_sprSlider->GetWidth() / 2)) >= m_iLeft))
                  m_iSliderPos = iMouseX;
      }

}
```

As you can see, the `CSlider::Update()` operation takes care of vertical motions. Creation of this code involved solving only one problem: vertical sliding. After solving the first problem, it's necessary to turn to the second problem: implementing a horizontal slider. At start is to copy and paste code to create an `Update()` operation for another object that provides horizontal motion. Most of the code is identical.

```
void CScrollBar::Update()
{
      int iMouseY=Input->GetMouseY();
      // Call parent update
```

```
    CGuiObject::Update();
    //Change the Scrollbar location to the mouseY if pressed
    if (m_bPressed)
    {
            if (((iMouseY - (m_sprScroller->GetHeight() / 2))
            >= m_iTop) && ((iMouseY +
            (m_sprScroller->GetHeight() / 2)) <= m_iBottom))
            m_iScrollPos = iMouseY;
    }

}
```

The problem here is that much of the code is, indeed, the same. The question becomes whether it is worthwhile to have one slider object for both horizontal and vertical motions and to needlessly proliferate objects (`CSlider`, `CScrollbar`). To overcome this problem, you can merge the different blocks into a single `CSlider` class and implement a single operation:

```
void CSlider::Update()

{
    // Get mouse x and y
    int iMouseX=Input->GetMouseX();
    int iMouseY=Input->GetMouseY();
    // Call parent update
    CGuiObject::Update();
    // Make sure we're in bounds
    if(m_iStyle == HORIZONTAL)
    {
        if(m_iSliderPos > m_iRight - m_sprSlider->GetWidth()/2)
            m_iSliderPos = m_iRight - m_sprSlider->GetWidth()/2;
        if(m_iSliderPos < m_iLeft + m_sprSlider->GetWidth()/2)
            m_iSliderPos = m_iRight - m_sprSlider->GetWidth()/2;
    }
    else if(m_iStyle == VERTICAL)
    {
        if(m_iSliderPos > m_iBottom - m_sprSlider->GetHeight()/2)
            m_iSliderPos = m_iTop + m_sprSlider->GetHeight()/2;
        if(m_iSliderPos < m_iTop + m_sprSlider->GetHeight()/2)
            m_iSliderPos = m_iTop + m_sprSlider->GetHeight()/2;
    }
    //Change the Slider location to the mouseX if pressed
    if (m_bPressed)
    {
        if (((iMouseX + (m_sprSlider->GetWidth() / 2))
            <= m_iRight) &&
                ((iMouseX - (m_sprSlider->GetWidth() / 2))
                >= m_iLeft) && m_iStyle == HORIZONTAL)
            m_iSliderPos = iMouseX;
        else if(((iMouseY - (m_sprSlider->GetHeight() / 2))
                >= m_iTop) &&
```

```
                ((iMouseY + (m_sprSlider->GetHeight() / 2))
                        <= m_iBottom) && m_iStyle == VERTICAL)
                m_iSliderPos = iMouseY;
        }
}
```

This new block of code might appear more involved than the two original blocks code, but the advantages in terms of maintenance are significant. The functionally now exists in one location. Add to this that if you want to refactor the code, you can more readily do so with code that you have placed in one location. (See Chapter 6 for a discussion of refactoring.)

The Danger of Early Optimization

If eliminating duplicated code blocks can decrease the number of times you have to make a given change, refraining from early optimization can ease the difficulty of making a change. Optimization involves, among other things, concentrating algorithms into brief, often cryptic lines that are extremely difficult to decipher. Most programmers tend to optimize after they work out the basic logic of an operation.

Optimization can cause problems, however. When you optimize a body of code, you almost always make it more difficult to understand and change. Because code written early in a project is likely to be changed as the project progresses, optimizing code early in a project makes little sense. But it is also the case that even during later stages of development, optimization might be a problem. That is because it is almost impossible to know when a given body of code will require no more changes.

One remedy to premature optimization is to eschew it. Unless performance issues force you to do so, it is best to strive first for ease of maintenance rather than optimization.

Using Shallow Hierarchies

Avoid deep class hierarchies. As is discussed in greater detail in Chapter 6, each level in a hierarchy adds weight to the classes in the hierarchy. If a user of your library instantiates a given object of a given class, the penalty should not be that the resulting program suddenly slows down in an unexpected way or absorbs an enormous store of memory. To eliminate such problems, change aggregation to generalization. Poor design efforts can easily allow frequently instantiated objects to be defined within deep hierarchies.

Installation and Ease of Use

You can create utility classes that facilitate operations in other classes. Such operations (or classes) can be fairly lightweight and easy to port along with the classes they support. As the team developed *Ankh*, it tended to park utility operations in a file called `utils.cpp`. These utility operations were retained as global functions to make them easier to use.

Using a namespace, such as *Ankh*, could help make them easier to integrate with other utilities in the future by avoiding function name collisions. Among the operations in the utility category are those that provide a means of locating resources. Usually, resources reside in either the same directory as the executable or in specified directories. For example, when you execute the program from the IDE and try to load data\something.`png`, the compiler might seek a path relative to the project file instead of the executable and thus cause an error. To remedy this situation, you can develop two utility functions: `GetAddPath()` and `FullFileName()`. They provide the full path to the correct location. The code is as follows:

```
//////////////////////////////////////////////////////////////////////
// GetAppPath()                                                     //
// Returns the current path that the game is running in             //
// Best used when loading/creating files to make sure we are        //
// looking in the correct place                                     //
//////////////////////////////////////////////////////////////////////
CStdString GetAppPath()
{
     // Start out as nothing
     static CStdString strPath = "";

     // If it's our first time, do the actual name lookup
     if(strPath == "")
     {
          // Get the file name of our app
          char buf[MAX_PATH];
          memset(buf,0,MAX_PATH);
          GetModuleFileName(NULL,buf,MAX_PATH);
          // Starting from the last character,
          // move back until we find a '\'
          for(int i=strlen(buf)-1;i>0;i--)
          {
               if(buf[i] == '\\') break;
          }
          // Insert a null char, and then put the result in strPath
          buf[i+1] = '\0';
          strPath.Format("%s",buf);
     }
     return(strPath);
}

//////////////////////////////////////////////////////////////////////
// FullFileName(CStdString strFile)                                 //
// Takes the relative path given in strFile, and appends on the     //
// full path to the executable. This makes it safe to start the     //
// app from any location. (The game will still be able to find its //
// data files.)                                                     //
//////////////////////////////////////////////////////////////////////
```

```
CStdString FullFileName(CStdString strFile)
{
     CStdString strFullPath;
     // Remove backslash at beginning if we need to
     if(strFile[0] == '\\')
     {
          strFile = strFile.Right(strFile.length()-1);
     }

     // If the full path is already in there,
     // return the original string
     if(strFile.Find(GetAppPath())>0)
     {
          return(strFile);
     }
     // Otherwise, append the app path to the file name
     strFullPath.Format("%s%s",GetAppPath().c_str(),strFile.c_str());
     return(strFullPath);
}
```

You can craft operations that are similar to `GetAddPath()` and `FullFileName()` and place them in a utility file or in a class that is designed as a repository for utility operations. The drawback of creating a class is that even if you want only one function, you must instantiate an instance of the class, which means that you might invoke a heavy construction cost if the class has a lot of baggage. On the other hand, using functions from a file library is not terribly elegant in object-oriented parlance. Static operations in a class are another alternative, because they are part of a class but don't require an instance. Still, if the operation library proves easier to use and renders a program that performs more efficiently, maintaining a function library makes sense.

The Boost and STL Libraries

As mentioned earlier in this chapter, commercial and freeware libraries offer standard data structures, algorithms, and other items useful in game development. Among those available for C++ are the STL and Boost libraries.

Even with the availability of the STL and Boost libraries, developers still like to develop code from scratch. If you want to craft your own container class, you are certainly free to do so, but every day you invest in perfecting your container is a day you lose toward developing your game. Add to this that the product that results from your labor is more than likely to be inferior to the product available through Boost or the STL. If dozens or even hundreds of world-class programmers work on a given library for tens of thousands of hours, what results is more than likely going to be more robust and efficient than what a lone individual can complete during a few days of dedicated programming.

The discussion goes on, even with respect to those who use the STL and Boost libraries. Advanced programmers enhance the STL and Boost classes in a variety of ways, but except for fairly infrequent occasions, it is unlikely that redeveloping STL or Boost capabilities will render a better product. This is especially true if someone whose primary business is developing a game, not optimizing string classes or data structures, undertakes the development effort.

Using the STL

You can use the STL in several contexts. To focus on one of many uses, consider the `CGuiMgr` class of the *Ankh* code, which uses an STL vector. The `CGuiMgr` class tracks all of the GUI objects under its management. The number of objects that `CGuiMgr` manages tends to be indeterminate and varying. At the same time, the class should be able to iterate through the objects it manages fairly quickly and access them randomly. Given such requirements, an STL vector was the best type of container for the job.

Implementing a vector from scratch always remains an option, but the STL makes such implementation unnecessary. The vector type needs to be of the `CGuiObject` class. Creating the constructor for `CGuiObject` involves only providing the data type to the template constructor. The code is as follows:

```
class CGuiMgr{
[el}
//Our list of GUI objects
std::vector<CGuiObject *> m_guiObjects;
}
```

To add a GUI object, you can simply call `Register()`, which registers the instance of `CGuiObject` with the manager:

```
void CGuiMgr::Register(CGuiObject *guiObj)
{
     // Make sure we don't already have this one registered
     if(GetIndex(guiObj->GetName())<0)
     {
          m_guiObjects.push_back(guiObj);
     }
     else
     {
                Log->Add("CGuiMgr::Register() - >\
                Tried to register %s but it was already \
                registered!",guiObj->GetName().c_str());
     }
}
```

To remove an instance of `CGuiObject` from the vector, you can use one of the operations that the vector class provides. In this instance, the program uses the `erase()` operation. In this code segment, a `for` loop that is predicated on an iterator controls the action. The iterator is a special kind of pointer furnished by the STL library. It works in conjunction with the `begin()` and `end()` operations of the vector class. Using the iterator, `i`, you can traverse the vector. It is possible to dereference the iterator and in turn call the `GetName()` function of the `CGuiObject` class. An alternative, not used here, is the `find()` function, which is implemented in the STL as an operation in the vector class. The code is as follows:

```
// Removes the GuiObject from the GUI manager's control
void CGuiMgr::Unregister(CStdString strName)
{
      std::vector<CGuiObject *>::iterator i;
      // Find the object
      for(i=m_guiObjects.begin();i<m_guiObjects.end();i++)
      {
            // We found a match; erase it from the vector
            if((*i)->GetName() == strName)
            {
                  m_guiObjects.erase(i,i);
                  return;
            }
      }
}
```

Using Boost

For game developers who are using C++, the Boost library offers capabilities that can be considered to be a superset of the STL library. Among the classes that the library offers are those that help with writing GUI code in a Win32 setting. As a part of the *Ankh* development effort, the code included `OnClicked()` and `OnKeyPress()` functions (among others) to handle events. The effort that is required to implement handles from scratch is extensive. Boost provides an elegant alternative.

As an example of how the Boost library provides a solution, consider the `CImageButton` class. To implement a handler for this class, the program included a function pointer to the `CGuiObject` class for the `OnClicked`, `OnMouseDown`, and `OnMouseUp` events. The Boost library features a class called `boost::function`, which allows you to add function pointers. To set up a basic function pointer, you use `boost::function`*X* where *X* is the number of arguments to be passed into the function. You then list the types of the arguments. As you list the types, start with the return type. In the instances shown here, the return type is `void`:

```
boost::function0<void> OnClicked;
boost::function3<void,int,int,int> OnMouseDown;
boost::function3<void,int,int,int> OnMouseUp;
```

Following the definition of the function pointers for the `OnClicked()`, `OnMouseDown()`, and `OnMouseUp()` operations, the program links the operations to those invoked when a given event occurs. Consider, for example, an OK button. The OK button needs to be linked to an `OnClicked()` operation. To link the button and the action that follows for its use, you can use the `boost::bind()` operation. As the following code example shows, in the `CMenuState` class, the `boost::bind()` operation links the `OnClicked()` event that is associated with the Exit button to the `butExit_OnClicked()` operation. You can call the `boost::bind()` operation at any time, but it makes the most sense to do so when the button is created.

```
void CMenuState::OnEnter()
{
...
// Set up some event handlers
    buttons[EXIT]->OnClicked =
    boost::bind(&CMenuState::butExit_OnClicked,this);
}
```

The STL allows you to create function pointers, and the operations in the Boost libraries in some ways anticipate them. The difference is that although the *Ankh* team did not abandon the STL, it found a library that both complements and extends it.

Documentation and Deployment

Documenting your code is an essential aspect of reuse. It is impossible in the space available in this chapter to treat this topic comprehensively, but a few points of value might be presented. (See the texts listed at the end of this chapter for a more comprehensive treatment.)

Watch for Cut-and-Paste Code

A frequent problem with comments is that they are pasted into a program along with a reused segment of code without being updated to reflect the new context in which the code is used. The frequency of such occurrences is fairly amazing. It is often easy to ignore the comments while working through the changes to the code.

A solution to the problem is to eliminate as many of the starting comments as possible so that you force yourself to write new comments. If you use this approach and do not write new comments, you at least spare the user of your code the problem of trying to understand the code by reading comments that discuss a context that is not applicable to the current use of the code.

Do Not Address Obvious Things

When you address implementation, explain operations or algorithms that are not obvious. Granted, after working for hours to solve a problem, it is sometimes tempting to write a testimonial to the effort, but the fact remains that the user of the operation might have little use for such information. Generally, you should address what the function returns. In other cases, as mentioned earlier, you should address aspects of the operation that represent complex algorithms. Consider the following operation:

```
//Wraps the STL map find function and returns
//a string version of the key,
//regardless of the value stored
bool GetKey(string keyName);
```

Implementation details clutter up the documentation provided with the operation. In the end, the user receives little information about how to use the operation. This should be rewritten, perhaps along the following lines:

```
//Returns true if the provided string is found
bool GetKey(string keyName);
```

State the Common Use First

When documenting an operation that might be used in a number of contexts, programmers tend to gravitate toward creative uses. As interesting as such interpretations of the function might be, the best approach is to document the most common, straightforward activity. Consider the following bit of documentation:

```
//If used in conjunction with the ResetWorld() function,
//can facilitate the update operations
MAP& SetMap(int mapID);
```

The problem with the above is that the reader really doesn't learn anything about what the `SetMap()` operation does. An alternative is to provide simple terms of use:

```
//Returns current map according to ID
//CLayer::GetID() returns the current map ID
MAP& SetMap(int mapID);
```

Show How to Do Things

When you write documentation, avoid providing comments on how *not* to do things. Consider what it would be like if a swimming coach first taught swimmers how not to swim. Negative admonition usually results after a newly implemented function burns an unwary programmer. Consider the following:

```
//Don't use MAP objects that you have not tested for existence!
MAP& AddMap(const MAP& A, const MAP& B);
```

The comment is worthy of considering, no doubt; however, the reader has no idea, except from inference, what the operation does when it is used correctly. This is what the reader needs to know. An alternative might be along the following lines:

```
//Returns new instance of map that combines
//common coordinates from the two MAP parameters
MAP AddMap(const MAP& A, const MAP& B);
```

Avoid Preaching

If you find that you have written as many lines of documentation as you have of code just to guide yourself through the intricacies of the operation, you probably need to rethink things. You should probably consider whether you are adding anything helpful to your program. Generally, anything beyond a brief explanation of use probably belongs in an accompanying user's manual. Consider the following epistle:

```
//When you use this operation, you can cut down
//on how long it takes you
//to get up and running. You know it is bad to put
//fixed paths into a program. This
//function makes it unnecessary to do so.
//But the thing is that you must use it!
bool CImage::LoadFromFile(CStdString strFname)
```

Although such comments sometimes make for interesting reading, they seldom contribute to the ability of the user to use the code in an expedient way. When programming *Ankh*, the team determined that for each 100 lines of code, 30 sufficed for comments. Some experts contend that many, many more lines are needed, up to several for each line of code.

Self-Documenting Code

Here the object of discussion is the documentation you write as a programmer. This is in contrast to the automated documentation approaches that are available with C++, Java, and C#. (You can generate HTML documentation with C++ by using the utility class provided with the Microsoft IDE.) With Java and C#, you can generate XML or HTML comments into convenient user-oriented documents.

In contrast, you can manually create self-documenting code if you attend to how you name operations and parameters. Generally, consider the following practices:

- Operation names should consist of at least two words.
- The first word should be a verb.
- The second word should be the object of the verb.
- The two words should be combined by capitalizing the second word. Whether you capitalize the first word is up to you.

A second concern is how you name the parameters of operations. Parameters names should help with the identification and use of the operation. Using a single letter is inconsiderate. Using generic terms is also inconsiderate. Consider the following operation:

```
HRESULT DoRectangle(IDirect3DSurface9* sa,
                    IDirect3DSurface9* sb,
                    int n1, int n2, int n3, int n4, int n5);
```

The problem with this operation is that the reader does not receive the slightest hint from its name or its parameter names what it does.

If the purpose of the operation is to copy one surface onto another, the name of the operation merits being changed to something along the lines of `CopySurfaceToSurface()`. If the integer values represent anything but arbitrary numbers, then what the numbers represent merit being identified with parameter names.

```
CopySurfaceToSurface(IDirect3DSurface9*  SourceSuface,
                     IDirect3DSurface9*  DestinationSurface,
                     int NumberOfRects, int DestinationRow,
                     int DestinationCol, int NumOfCols, int NumOfRows);
```

The user gains from the second version of the operation a fairly clear idea of what the operation is about and what values it uses to accomplish its work. To clear up the last few details, you can add a line of documentation.

Conclusion

Libraries of code can be created from collections of usable snippets. Libraries can also be the result of long, concerted, and well-designed efforts. An example of the first type of library might be the collection of code that you accumulate over the years as you work on different projects. Snippets are short bodies of code that accomplish specific tasks but that can be adapted fairly readily to different contexts.

Designed libraries take an entirely different turn. They are designed to accommodate a wide variety of uses in different contexts. They seldom require adaptation. Fully designed libraries are tested like any other software product. They are tuned and optimized. Users of designed libraries are presented with an interface that attempts to hide details of implementation from them.

Well-crafted code is often readily suitable for reuse, but even then, if it is to become a part of a planned library, it usually requires reworking. Reworking extends to both writing the code so that it is easy to use and maintain and providing good documentation. This chapter moved from identifying a few standard sources of reusable code (game engines and formalized function and container libraries) to a few of the practices that you can use to tune code for reuse. The goal has been to suggest a few of the many things you can do to enhance your code through the use of libraries or, on the other hand, to tune your code so that it might better qualify for reusability.

Among the books that provide good information on libraries and how to craft or rewrite code for reuse are the following:

Cargill, Tom. *C++ Programming Style.* Reading, Massachusetts: Addison-Wesley Publishing Company, 1992.

Carroll, Martin D. and Margaret A. Ellis. *Designing and Coding Reusable C++.* Reading, Massachusetts: Addison-Wesley Publishing Company, 1995.

Hawkins, Brian, *Preventative Programming Techniques: Avoid and Correct Common Mistakes.* Hingham, Massachusetts: Charles River Media, 2003.

Hughes, Cameron and Tracey Hughes. *Mastering the Standard C++ Classes: An Essential Reference.* New York: John Wiley & Sons, 1999.

Llopis, Noel. *C++ for Game Programmers.* Hingham, Massachusetts: Charles River Media, 2003.

McConnell, Steve. *Code Complete: A Practical Handbook of Software Construction.* Redmond, Washington: Microsoft Press, 1993.

Meyers, Scott. *Effective C++: 50 Specific Ways to Improve Your Programs and Designs.* Boston: Addison-Wesley, 1998.

Misfeldt, Trevor, Gregory Bumgardner, and Andrew Gray. *The Elements of C++ Style.* New York: Cambridge University Press, 2004.

Sutter, Herb. *Exceptional C++: 47 Engineering Puzzles, Programming Problems, and Solutions.* Boston: Addison-Wesley, 2000.

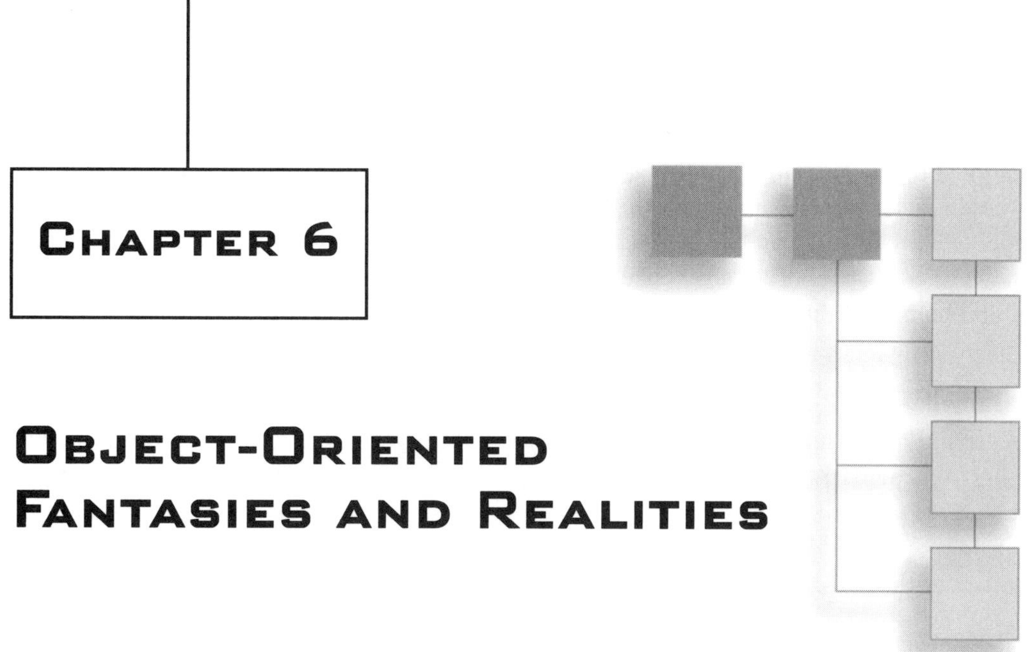

Chapter 6

Object-Oriented Fantasies and Realities

Creating object-oriented programs was once considered something on the order of a revolution. The revolution is now over, however. Languages such as C++, Java, and C# have been developed as object-oriented languages, as have Visual Basic and even Perl, and object-oriented programs characterize every field of programming. With the capacity of chips to store more code, object-oriented programming now prevails even in the world of device drivers, where procedural code was once considered superior because it required less memory. The object-oriented paradigm dominates the programming world because it provides a powerful approach to combating complexity. As the average program grows in size, so does the need to control complexity. Object-oriented programs provide one of the most effective means of accomplishing this.

The discussion of object-oriented programming provided here accepts the superiority of the object-oriented paradigm for game development. On the other hand, object-oriented programming is not the only thing that can be used in game development efforts. The discussion goes in a number of directions. Among the topics covered are the following:

- Conceptualizing object orientation
- Abstraction as a way of limiting the world
- Encapsulation as a vehicle of defending a limited world
- Strategies for developing classes and systems of classes
- Conventions for object-oriented development

Class Beginnings

You likely have heard of object-oriented programming, and if you have developed code for a game, you probably have done so using object-oriented code. For that reason, it is assumed that you know a few things about object-oriented programming. Maybe you are even an accomplished object-oriented programmer. But even if you can create object-oriented programs, you might become somewhat nervous when a software engineer shows up and starts using terms like *interface*, *client*, or *services* when talking about classes and objects. If this is so, this chapter provides some useful information.

The Concept of Class

In general programming terms, *class* is a keyword that you use to create customized data types. Another term for a customized data type is *abstract data type*. When you use a class, you create *instances* of the data type that the class defines. An instance of a class data type is said to be an *object*. A class is a static entity that is evoked again and again to create objects of the class. An object is a dynamic entity that you can create, change, and destroy.

The data type is a model of something. The class data type models objects in two ways. In one way, it stores information about the object it models. The information about the object it models is said to be the *state* of the class object. A class also allows the information that the object stores about itself to be changed. The capacity of the object to change the information it stores is said to be its *behavior*.

The operations of a class mediate its behavior. In this book, the term *operation* appears in place of *member function*, *property*, and *method*. This term is derived from the UML. At times, however, you might see *member function* in deference to C++ programmers.

The state of an object is captured in its attributes. Again, derived from usage that the UML has fostered, *attribute* makes it possible to avoid confusion arising from such terms as *data member* and *property*.

Scope

The syntax of a C++ class begins with the use of the keyword `class`, the name of the class, and opening and closing braces to designate the scope of the class. A semicolon terminates the declaration. Following is an example:

```
class CStateMachine
{
};
```

The braces define the *scope* of the class. The scope of the class is by default *private*, which means that anything declared or defined inside the braces cannot be accessed outside the class. Usually, the attributes of a class are placed in a private scope. In contrast to private scope is *public* scope. In C++, use of the keyword `public` class makes everything following it accessible outside the class. Following is an example:

```
class CStateMachine
{
public:          //keyword for public scope
     void DoFrame();   //operation can be reached outside the class
private:               //keyword for private scope
     CStdString m_strNextState; //attribute cannot be reached
};
```

In this example, `CStateMachine()` contains an operation called `DoFrame()` and an attribute called `m_strNextState`. `DoFrame()` is public because it follows the keyword `public`, and `m_strNextState` is private because it follows the keyword `private`. A third keyword, `protected`, allows derived classes to access attributes or operations that follow it. This topic is discussed at greater length later in this chapter.

Construction

When you create an object using a class in C++, you do so using a *constructor*. You use a constructor to create an *instance* of a class. Creating an instance of a class differs from simply declaring an identifier that is reserved for the class. When you construct an object, you allocate memory for it. A constructor is a function that has the same name as the class. It has no return type. In addition to a constructor, C++ classes can have *destructors*. A destructor is a function that has the same name as the class. Its purpose is to remove the instance of the class from memory. A destructor has no return type. It is preceded with a tilde (~). Following are some examples:

```
class CStateMachine
{
public:          //keyword for public scope
     CStateMachine();  //constructor
     ~CStateMachine(); //destructor
     void DoFrame();   //operation
private:               //keyword for private scope
     CStdString m_strNextState; //attribute
};
```

Interface

The list of all public operations that a class provides is said to be its *interface*. The interface provides a set of *services*. Note the code sample that follows:

```
class CStateMachine
{
public:
     CStateMachine();
     ~CStateMachine();
     void EnterState(CStdString strName);       //interface operations
     void HandleGUIEvent(CStdString strObjectName,
                    CStdString strAction,
                    CStdString strParams);
     void DoFrame();
```

```
     SetCurrentState(CState * state);  //mutator operation
     const CState* GetCurrentState()const;    //accessor operation
private:
     int GetIndex(CStdString strName);  //utility operation
     class CState *m_pStates[NUM_STATES];
     class CState *m_pCurrentState;
     CStdString m_strNextState;
};
```

The previous interface consists of seven operations, and each operation provides a service. Besides the constructor and destructor, operations include `EnterState()`, `HandleGUIEvent()`, and `DoFrame()`. Each of these operations provides a fairly complicated service. Two other operations provide services of a less complicated type. One is called `GetCurrentState()`, which is an *accessor* operation. It accesses a value that defines the state of the class object. Another is called `SetCurrentState()`, which is a *mutator* operation. A mutator changes a value that defines the state of the class object.

At the bottom, after the `private` keyword, is one more operation, `GetIndex()`. This operation is said to be a *utility* operation. It cannot be used outside the class.

You create the class attributes using abstract data types. The first two are of the type `CState`. Two instances of `CState` are created through *forward declarations.* The forward declaration tells the compiler to wait until it finds the definition of the class that is forward declared. In this way, you can avoid difficulties that arise when the game has a complex header structure and might not have reached the files that contain the declarations of the data types used. The last element's type, `CStdString`, is from the Boost library.

```
class CState; // forward declaration

class CStateMachine
{
public:
     CStateMachine();
     ~CStateMachine();
     void EnterState(CStdString strName);
     void HandleGUIEvent(CStdString strObjectName,
                   CStdString strAction,
                   CStdString strParams);
     SetCurrentState(CState *state);  //mutator operation
     CState* GetCurrentState()const;    //accessor operation
     void DoFrame();
private:
     int GetIndex(CStdString strName);
     class CState *m_pStates[NUM_STATES];  //uses the forward declaration
     class CState *m_pCurrentState;    //uses the forward declaration
     CStdString m_strNextState;
};
```

Abstraction

One of the key concepts in object-oriented programming is *abstraction.* When you abstract something, you remove it from an immediate context and place it in a more generalized context. When you create classes, you are concerned with two basic types of abstraction. One type of abstraction has to do with the things that allow you to recognize an object. The other type of abstraction has to do with how you determine that changes can be made to an object. These two forms of abstraction are usually referred to as the state and the behavior of an object.

Abstract States

Consider, for example, how you might picture a tree. Outside your window, a burly spruce might stand. You perhaps have a ready picture of a spruce when you close your eyes. The spruce features silvery, light-green needles and reddish-brown bark. Not far away is a cottonwood tree. This cottonwood tree possesses grayish bark and broad leaves of a light green color. A third tree might be a willow, with whitish bark and narrow leaves that are dusty gray-green in color. The immediacy of each context makes necessary the use of adjectives for distinctions. The more the adjectives come into play, however, the more the common characteristics of the trees tend to stand out. With respect to the trees mentioned here, two features receive repeated mention. These are bark and leaves.

A third feature might be the cones or nuts that the trees shed. At least for the trees mentioned, you can tell them apart based on their needles or leaves and their bark. An abstraction of this situation arises when you create a class for describing trees. The class takes the following form:

```
class CTree
{
      string barkDescription;
      string leafDescription;
};
```

The class begins with a simple description of the states of the trees mentioned. Using `barkDescription` and `leafDescription`, you can briefly distinguish the objects you create with the `CTree` class. You create two attributes. Because you have a way of describing a tree that you can apply to all of the trees mentioned thus far, the descriptions have been removed from the immediate contexts of the individual trees and placed in an abstract context. When something is abstract, it is applicable across many instances of the thing it has been created to describe.

Abstract Behavior

The work of abstraction continues when you consider the behavior of trees. A forester or botanist would probably be able to name an immense number of ways in which trees change from day to day or season to season. The attributes for CTree focus on a few distinctive features. One of these is the tree's growth: height. With the addition of this attribute, you can consider whether the height of the tree changes from time to time. If it does, you can create an abstraction of the change in the form of an operation. In this case, the operation can be called SetHeight():

```
class CTree
{
      string barkDescription;
      string leafDescription;
      float height;
      void SetHeight(fload height);
};
```

Each of the trees considered has a multitude of qualities. Specific instances of trees have been abstracted to arrive at a generalized version of a tree. Attributes abstract the state of trees. Operations abstract their behavior.

Encapsulation

Abstraction is a conceptual undertaking. Encapsulation is a capability of C++ that makes abstraction possible. You have already seen the beginnings of encapsulation in the previous discussion of scope. When you limit how and when information stored within an object can be accessed, you have the beginnings of encapsulation. A class encapsulates state and behavior.

```
class CTree
{
private:
       string barkDescription;
       string leafDescription;
       float treeHeight;
   public:
       void SetHeight(fload height);
};
```

With the addition of the scope keywords, you reinforce the way that the class encapsulates state and behavior. The scope of the class prevents the information that the class stores from being generally available. The use of the scope keywords refines this further. You cannot access the information stored in the attributes directly outside the class. You can only access information about the height of the tree. The accessor operation SetHeight() makes this possible.

Encapsulation in this way serves as a means for refining abstraction. A class is abstract because a programmer has arbitrarily determined that only a limited number of a potentially vast number of features of a given entity is relative to the program being written. On the other hand, features of the language—such as braces, keywords, and scope—allow the abstraction to be achieved through encapsulation. An object encapsulates state and behavior. Abstraction is the means by which the state and behavior of a class are derived from the many specific instances of things that the class is said to represent.

Cohesion

A class represents an abstraction of some object in the real world. Often, however, a class emerges from an odd collection of attributes and behaviors and seems to lack a central focus. Consider the following class:

```
class CThing
{
     string bookName;
     string monthName;
     string address;
     public:
     void SetBookName(string bn){bookName = bn;}
     void SetMonthName(string mn){monthName = mn;}
     void SetAddress(string ad){address = ad;}
     int AddNums(int a, int b){return a + b;}
     void AddColor(COLOR& color);
};
```

This class tends to create questions in a number of ways. First, it is not evident what this class might be used for. Because the name designates no specific object, it is unclear why this odd collection of data exists. In addition, if you inspect the interface, you find that a group of accessor operations precedes an operation that adds two integers. An operation that adds color occurs last.

The problem with the class as a whole is that it is not *cohesive*. When a class is cohesive, it has a central, clearly evident line of business, and its interface provides services that address this line of business. Achieving cohesion within a class involves shaping it so that its operations bear on the business or entity it abstracts. Consider the following class:

```
class CArithmetic
{
int numA, numB;
public:
       void Add(int a, int b);
       void Subtract(int first, int second);
       void Divide(int first, int second);
       void Multiply(int a, int b);
};
```

As simple as it is, `CArithmetic` possesses superior qualities over `CThing` because `CArithmetic` offers a centralized, focused set of services. It is cohesive because it clearly addresses one idea in both its name and in the work its operations perform.

Given this starting place, when class designers find a class that contains operations that address several lines of business, their remedy involves creating separate classes and then moving operations around until each of the resulting classes addresses one line of business.

Responsibilities

When you create a tightly cohesive class, you achieve a much praised design goal, but you also face a few liabilities. Generally, cohesion of a class can be defined in terms of its responsibilities. If the responsibilities focus on one line of business, all is well. But consider a situation in which something is missing. The following class illustrates a few problems:

```
class CSale
{
      float saleSub;
      float saleTotal;
      vector<float>items;
      float tax;
      void AddItem(float item);
      void SetTax(float tax);
      void SubTotal();
};
```

The problem here is that operations are missing. For example, although the class clearly focuses on the business of allowing the user to process a sale, services relating to calculating the total and the tax are missing. The problem here, then, is that although the responsibilities of the class are cohesive, they are not completely fulfilled. Effective class design in this instance reduces to examining the process fully to ensure that the class comprehensively encapsulates the attributes and operations that address its responsibilities.

Coupling

Abstract classes work in conjunction with each other to give expression to complex activities. When you model complex activities, it often becomes necessary to create a large number of classes. Assume here that you set about modeling a bank account. You think for a while and then create three classes, as follows:

```
class CName
{
      private:
      string firstName;
      string lastName;
      string middleI;
};
class CAccount
{
      private:
      CName accountHolder;
```

```
     string accountNumber;
};
class CCustomer
{
     private:
     CName customerName;
     string customerNumber;
     CAccount(CName cust);
};
```

The CAccount class contains an attribute of the CName type, and the CCustomer class contains attributes of the CAccount and CName types. The result of this set of relationships is that if you want to use the CAccount, you must also use the CCustomer and CName classes. The classes are *tightly coupled.*

Tight coupling creates a problem because it requires that when you want to perform what seems to be a simple operation involving, for instance, the setting of the attributes of a single object created with an abstract data type, you must learn all sorts of things about other abstract data types. For example, CCustomer involves you with CAccount and CName. To use CCustomer, then, you must also use CAccount and CName. The classes are coupled.

Decoupling

Creating tightly coupled classes is possible if you give consideration to what is called *data coupling.* All programming languages offer default data types, and users of the language will readily understand these data types. For C++, the STL provides the string class. If you change the classes presented earlier so that they communicate with each other using STL string parameters, you alter the situation so that the classes can still effectively communicate and yet are not tightly cohesive. Consider the following code, altered from the first version:

```
class CName
{
     string firstName;
     string lastName;
     string middleI;
     string GetFullName(){return firstName+middleI+lastName;}
};
class CCustomer
{
     string customerName;
     string customerNumber;
     string GetCustomerNumber;
};
class CAccount
{
     string accountNumber;
```

```
    string accountHolder;
    SetAccountHolder(string fullname);
};
```

The altered set of classes communicates using STL strings. The capacity to communicate through strings arises with the use of accessor operations that return strings rather than abstract objects.

Inheritance

If you ever need to remember the quintessential aspects of object-oriented programming with C++, tattoo the letters *P-I-E* on your forearm. *P* is for polymorphism, *I* is for inheritance, and *E* is for encapsulation. Now the discussion will turn to inheritance, which comes in two forms. One form of inheritance begins with a collection of similar or associated classes and tries to discover whether a common or *generalized* version of the classes might be created. This is *generalization*. The other form of inheritance begins with a single class that stands as a common model or template and queries whether this can be used to provide a common pattern for a large number of *specialized* classes that might be derived from it. This approach is called *specialization*.

As you might suspect, generalization and specialization imply that you are investigating a group of classes from two vantage points. It is likely, for example, when you seek to generalize a set of classes, that you are either engaged in a design effort that will lead to an implementation effort or that you are engaged in a remedial effort to try to bring order to a group of classes that seem to offer similar operations that might best be merged into a common parent entity. Reworking a set of classes tends to be a much more demanding task than designing and then implementing a set of classes. However, in either case, given a proper regard for principles of design (see Chapter 4, "Software Design—Much Ado About Something," for a review), you can tremendously improve the performance, testability, and maintainability of your game code through such efforts.

Generalization

Generalization is analogous to induction. Induction involves collecting items until you have enough of them to begin sorting them according to common features. That, at least, is one way to put the matter. As an example, imagine that you collect marbles for many months. At some point, you decide to begin examining your collection. As you examine the marbles, you find similarities and differences. On the basis of such discoveries, you begin to arrive at conclusions about how many species of marbles exist, what purposes marbles can be used for, and so on.

In the design effort for *Ankh*, it did not take long to conclude that buttons, drop-down list, sliders, and other visible features of the game could be grouped according to common features. Some of these features could be anticipated in an abstract generalized class, CGUIObect. (For more information on abstract classes, see the section "Abstract Classes" later in this chapter.) Figure 6.1 illustrates the resulting class hierarchy.

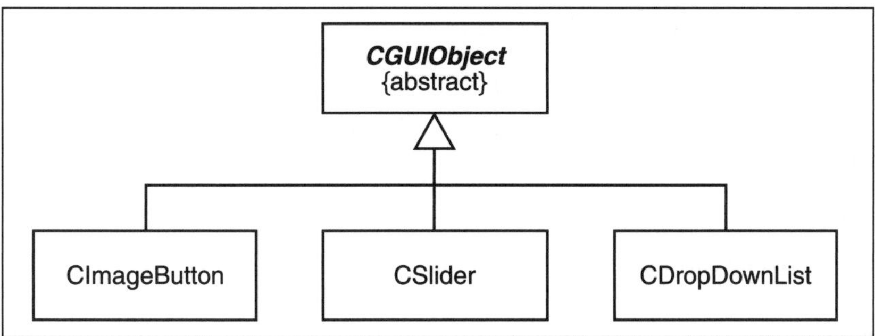

Figure 6.1
An abstract class collects features that several GUI items embody.

In the generalized approach to creating a hierarchy, it was easy to name several GUI items. After a time, creation of an abstract class, CGUIObject, that could be used as a pattern for the GUI items became evident. Reasons for generalization might be summarized along the following lines:

- Two or more classes have common attributes.
- You see occasions in which the design of your game might benefit from being able to make use of polymorphism with respect to a group of classes.
- Two or more classes have common interface features.
- Two or more classes might not initially have the same attributes or interfaces, but with a little rework, you can redefine them so that they possess common attributes and interface features.

Specialization

Specialization involves finding a class that might be heavily laden with attributes and operations that address different sets of responsibility. Generally, a class should have a central responsibility or at least a core set of closely aligned responsibilities. If you see one class undertaking several lines of business, you probably have a candidate for specialization. To specialize a group of classes, you begin by investigating the ways in which the class you initially inspect concentrates on too many responsibilities. An iterative design activity in *Ankh* involved a struggle with a catch-all class that was used to manage graphical features. This was the class CEntity. After some discussion, it was decided that CEntity should be defined as an abstract class and then followed by three derived classes: CActor, CProp, and CItem. Figure 6.2 illustrates the resulting hierarchy.

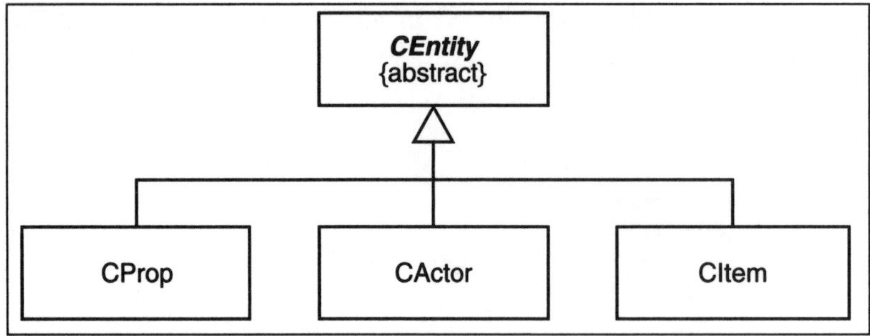

Figure 6.2
`CEntity` specialized into three implementations.

The process involved examining a single class and deciding that it contained enough responsibilities to justify specialization. The criteria for such a decision are along the following lines:

- Each of the specialized classes contains at least one unique attribute.
- The classes you specialize differ in ways other than a single value they assign to an attribute in the generalized class.
- All of the specialized classes have some features that can be defined in the generalized class.
- Each of the specialized classes contains at least one unique operation.

Before leaving this topic, consider the second point in greater detail. Needless specialization occurs when developers create derived classes that do nothing more than assign a different value to an attribute that the generalized class names. Figure 6.3 illustrates an instance of needless specialization. Notice that the classes that implement the abstract class do nothing more than assign a unique value to a common attribute.

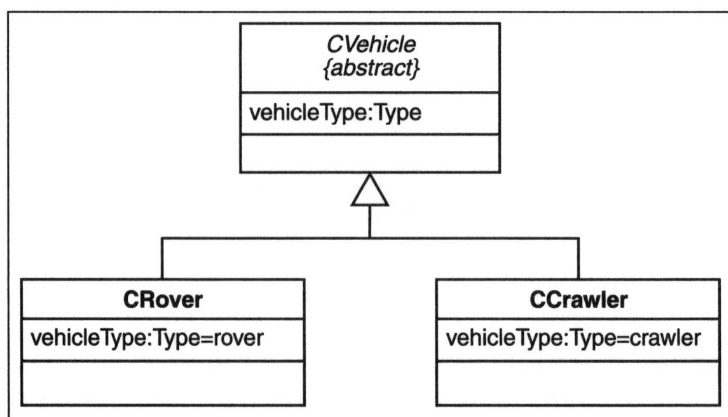

Figure 6.3
Needless association occurs when specialized classes do nothing more than assign a unique value to a common attribute.

Associations

The UML designates aggregation and composition as variations of association. As pointed out in Chapter 3, "A Tutorial: UML and Object-Oriented Programming," distinguishing the three notions of how classes relate to each other involves remembering three basic notions:

- **Association.** Assume that one class contains an operation in which one of the parameters is another class type. The two classes are in this way in association with each other.
- **Aggregation.** Assume that one class contains a pointer of the type of a second class. The pointer might or might not be assigned an object, depending on different behaviors of the class that contains the pointer. In this respect, then, you can view the object that the pointer points to as impermanent.
- **Composition.** Assume that one class contains attributes of another class type. The attributes are initialized upon construction of the class object. Under no conditions are the attributes not initialized.

These distinctions might not cover all situations and might be defective in some respects, but they provide you with a starting point from which it might be possible to make sense of a distinction that the authors of the UML seemed to labor over rather extensively.

For convenience, the term *aggregation* is used to refer generally to situations in which one class in some way contains an object of another class. If it is necessary to concentrate on specific details, the terms will be used with greater precision.

Aggregation or Hierarchy?

Is creating aggregations better than creating hierarchies? In the design of *Ankh*, aggregation was preferable to hierarchies. Given the extent to which inheritance occupies a central place in the world of object-oriented programming, this preference might seem somewhat arbitrary.

Inheritance tends to create performance and maintenance issues. The performance issues arise because deep hierarchies can require that when the constructor for a derived class is invoked, the constructor for the base classes is invoked also. The result can be heavy resource use. Maintenance issues arise because a derived class has dependencies on the parent class. If a derived class depends on values set in the base class, then if the derived class requires different value types, you must make changes to both the derived class and the parent class. Such performance and maintenance issues comprise what is known as *inheritance coupling*.

Aggregation

Sometimes aggregation is a reasonable alternative to inheritance. The situation encountered on *Ankh* involved two classes. One class, called `CImage`, loaded an image. The other class, called `CImageMgr`, managed the image after it was loaded. From one perspective, it made sense to create a base class that included management and loading capabilities and a derived class that specialized the loading capabilities for ease of use. But then inheritance brought with it a situation in which any change in the specifications of image would have required changes to two classes. Creating an association solved the problem. A container of the `CImage` type was set in the `CImageMgr` class, which left both classes with greater independence. To anticipate the need for an alternative image type, the option of creating an abstract image class was left open. The abstract image class could be implemented through distinct versions of `CImage`. Figure 6.4 illustrates the situation.

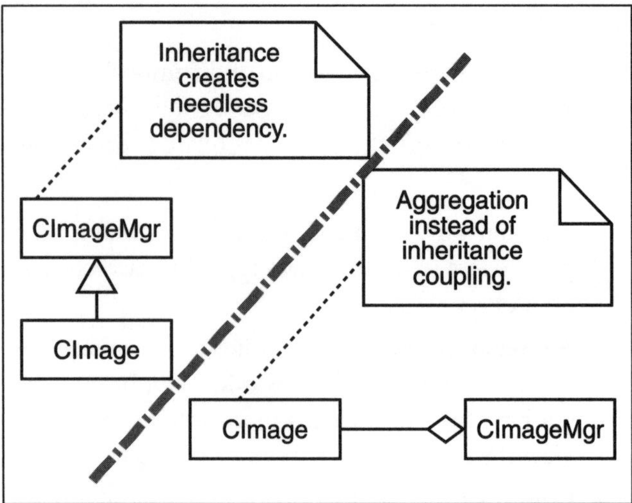

Figure 6.4
Aggregation created a dependency structure less characterized by class coupling.

Composition

Composition can reduce the complexity and depth of hierarchies. As Figure 6.5 illustrates, although a shallow hierarchy was maintained, composition relationships were created between `CMenuState` and the other classes. The composition relationships occur low in the hierarchy, thus reducing the overall coupling of the system in the event, for example, that other classes are to be derived from `CState`. Composition proves to be more flexible than inheritance because it allows complex relationships to be isolated.

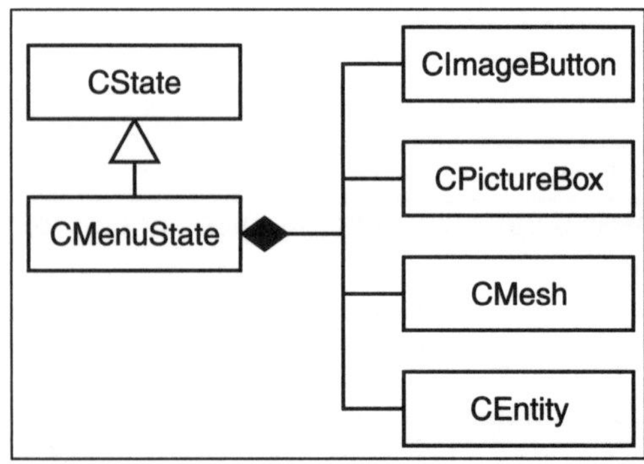

Figure 6.5
Composition can be used to isolate complexity.

Abstract Classes

An abstract class is a class that contains at least one abstract operation. In C++, an abstract operation is known as a *virtual* operation (or function). A virtual operation offers only a signature line. To define the virtual operation, you derive a class from the class that contains the virtual operation and then define the operation in the derived class.

C++ offers two basic types of virtual operations. One is called a *pure virtual operation* and can be recognized by the terminating null expression (=0). The other might best be called an *abstract operation.* It can include a definition of the function. Consider the following code sample:

```
class CTop
{
      static int number;
public:
      virtual void SetVal(string v)=0;
      virtual string GetVal()=0;
      int GetNumber(){return number++;}
      virtual ~CTop(){}
};
int CTop::number = 0;

class CNextA:public CTop
{
private:
     string value;
public:
      void SetVal(string v){value=v;}
      string GetVal(){return value;}
      ~CNextA(){}
};

class CNextB:public CTop
{
private:
      string value;
public:
      void SetVal(string v){value=v;}
      string GetVal(){return value+value;}
      ~CNextB(){}
};
```

CTop is an abstract class that contains two pure virtual operations and one concrete function. The destructor of CTop is set as virtual so that the inheriting classes can perform cleanup with their own destructors. The static integer in CTop enables counting of all the objects created with the two derived classes.

Unless you override the `SetVal()` and `GetVal()` operations, the inheriting classes remain abstract. It is not necessary to override the `GetNumber()` operation. Table 6.1 provides some summary information that applies to pure virtual, virtual, and concrete operations.

Table 6.1 Practices of Design

Topic	Discussion
Public inheritance	For the most part, although C++ provides for *private* and *protected* inheritance, what you are usually seeking is *public* inheritance. Public inheritance makes the derived class an instance of the base class. Private inheritance basically cuts the derived class off from the base class, so the features of the base class are implemented wholly in terms that the derived class provides.
Redefinition of operations	If you intend to provide operations in a base class that are to be redefined in a derived class, force the redefinition by making the base class operations pure virtual.
Pure virtual operations	A pure virtual operation is declared as purely virtual. It has no implementation.
Virtual operations	A virtual operation can be defined, and this definition is inherited by default. A virtual function does not need to be declared in the inheriting class if the base class definition will suffice.
Concrete operations	Concrete operations are inherited and should not be declared in the derived class. If you declare them, you usually overload them by changing their parameter list.
Public and virtual	When you use public inheritance, you should declare as virtual as many of the base class operations as possible. This helps establish that you want the derived class to specialize the base class.

Polymorphism

Working from the `CTop`, `CNextA`, and `CNextB` classes given earlier, you can create an STL vector to store instances of the two derived classes. The vector created here is of type `CTop`. Because `CTop` serves as a pattern for the derived classes, storage of the derived objects in the vector container provides an example of polymorphism.

```
//CTop data type allows the operation to receive
//data from all the derived classes
void ChangeValue(CTop* val);
int main()
{
      const int SIZE = 10;
      vector<CTop*>list;
      for(int count = 0; count < SIZE; count++)
      {
            list.insert(list.end(), new CNextA);
            list.insert(list.end(), new CNextB);
```

```
}
for(count = 0; count < list.size();)
{
     list[count++]->SetVal("A");
     if(count < SIZE/2)  //polymorphic passing of list items
     {
          ChangeValue(list[count++]);
     }
     list[count++]->SetVal("B");
}
for(count = 0; count < list.size(); count++)
{
     cout << "\n" << list[count]->GetVal();
     cout << "\t" << list[count]->GetNumber();
}
for(count = 0; count < list.size(); count++)
{
     delete list [count];
}
/code left out
void ChangeValue(CTop* val)
{
     val->SetVal("UU");
}
```

You can pass both `CNextA` and `CNextB` to the `ChangeValue()` function because the parameter of this function is defined as `CTop`. The displayed values show that polymorphism allows the values to be changed regardless of the subtype of the class:

```
A     0     UUUU  1     B     2     AA    3     UU    4
BB    5     A     6     BB    7     A     8     BB    9
A     10    BB    11    A     12    BB    13    A     14
BB    15    A     16    BB    17    A     18    BB    19
```

Coupling Problems with Collections of Classes

Maintenance problems and complexity can arise during the development of a game if no one takes time on a regular, iterative basis to examine the relationships between classes and to develop policies for controlling or reducing coupling and other forms of dependency. Complexity grows randomly during the development effort if programmers regard classes as an open set of resources that can be extended without risk through inheritance. Complexity also grows if programmers do not use restraint in the ways they aggregate classes. Each new derivation or aggregation creates added weight to a given hierarchy.

In light of the dangers that complexity presents, now is a good time to extend a few points about coupling touched on earlier. The list presented next by no means exhausts the topic, but it at least establishes a few possible constraints.

- **Identities.** An identity can arise between two classes, A and B, if class A contains an instance of class B and class B contains an instance of class A. Several reliable avenues exist for avoiding identity relationships between classes. Chapter 7, "P Is for Pattern," explores a few of these avenues. For now, however, note that most identities can be resolved between two classes by reworking the associations so that only one class contains an instance of the other.
- **Representation.** As mentioned earlier, it is sometimes considered good practice to include accessor and mutator operations in your classes. The reason for this is not purely formalistic. Accessors and mutators provide a ready way to prevent one class from directly accessing data from another class. Direct access of data violates the general principle of data hiding, which is a particular application of encapsulation. One class should, as a general rule, interact with another class through a service interface. If you design the interfaces of the classes you implement so that the data that the interface supplies serves the needs of many classes, you eliminate the primary way that representation couples classes.
- **Inversion.** Inversion occurs when a given class establishes relationships with the subclasses of another class. In most such situations, the way this happens involves the creation of a pointer. The class that develops the dependency does so through a pointer to the subclasses of another class. The problem with this is that a situation can easily arise in which the client class requires a second pointer. If the second pointer is to another subclass in the same hierarchy as the first, the complexity of the client class increases because it now holds two distinct pointer types. The solution to this problem is to try to implement pointers as high in a hierarchy as is possible. Polymorphism allows the pointer to the generalized class to accommodate references to many subclass instances.
- **Inheritance.** This type of dependency has already been discussed. One thing to keep in mind is the extent to which hierarchies create complexities that are related to construction and destruction of objects. Hierarchies require sensitivity to the need, for example, of virtual destructors. They require attention to the drawbacks of initializations of attributes that might be needlessly invoked among base and derived classes.
- **Multiple inheritance.** Multiple inheritance involves the use of more than one base class to create a derived class. C++ allows multiple inheritance. The hazards of this form of inheritance cannot be overly stressed. Generally, it is best to avoid multiple inheritance.

Points on Class Design and Implementation

Previous sections have dealt with a variety of notions that are central to object-oriented programming. At this point, it becomes appropriate to concentrate on some of the issues that arise with the implementation of classes. It is impossible to list in any brief form the many issues that arise with the implementation of classes in C++. It is possible, however, to pursue lines of thought that have proven fairly pervasive over time.

Information Hiding

Discussion of encapsulation brings with it a concept that is often viewed as synonymous with encapsulation but is more a product of policy than anything specifically implied by scope. The concept is that of *information hiding*. When you hide information, your goal is to reduce the complexity of the relations between classes by ensuring that one class knows as little as possible about the information that another class contains.

The primary means by which information hiding can be achieved are the interface of the class and the use of the `private` keyword to deny class users access to any part of a class that the interface exposes. The importance of this approach to class design and implementation arises from its bearing on what is sometimes called *common coupling*.

Common coupling occurs when programmers develop classes in what might be regarded as an extremely immature way. As an example, consider the situation that arises with the following section of code:

```
void CD3DFont::Unload()
{
      if(m_pFont)m_pFont->Release();
      m_pFont = NULL;
      m_iHeight = 0;
      Log->Add("Font destroyed: %s",m_strName.c_str());
      m_strName = "";
      CImage::Unload();    //direct call to a function
                           //from another class
}
```

In the previous code sample, a call is made to a function from another class. The implication here is that the call can be made on a static basis. `CImage::Unload()` performs some mysterious work that is invoked at this point with no explanation.

The principle of information hiding stipulates that one class communicates with another through fairly formalized relationships. Among other things, if a client class accesses information from a service class, the client class should use an operation that the interface of the service class provides. To accomplish this, the client class must contain an instance of the service class, and it must call information from the service class as much as possible through the portals that are provided by the parameters of its own interface operations.

In the previous code sample, the use of the external function is especially offensive given its position inside the `CD3DFont::Unload()` function. The situation could be improved, however, if the `CD3DFont::Unload()` either contained an associated instance of the service class or received information from the service class through a parameter argument.

Generally, the principle of information hiding stipulates that the operations inside a class should be self-contained. This policy extends in two directions. In one direction, it pertains to the attributes of the class. The attributes should be private, and accessor functions should regulate how client classes derive information about the attributes. On the other hand, information about the insides of the operations of the functions should also be private. If information enters the scope of the class, it should do so through attributes that are included in the definition of the class or parameter, set in the interface operation.

Refactoring

The Agile methodology is currently one of the most pervasive approaches to software development. Methodologies tend to come and go, but they usually gain popularity because they provide excellent insights into how to develop software. This is certainly true of the Agile methodology.

The Agile methodology views software development as iterative and test-driven, and a key element in its success is its advocacy of a practice known as refactoring. According to Martin Fowler, the originator of the practice, *refactoring* involves changing software so that the behavior of the software remains the same while the internal structure of the software is improved. (See the reference to Martin Fowler at the end of this chapter.)

The success of the Agile approach depends on the ability of developers to create software to which new behavior can be added without needing to change the existing code. For this reason, refactoring plays a central role. Refactoring encourages developers to incorporate the quality of extensibility into the software they create. In this context, extensibility captures the notion that a body of code can be extended without being changed.

Modularity

Ultimately, object-oriented programming might be said to begin with the idea that software can be developed in a modular form. Modularity involves controlling complexity through encapsulation and abstraction, as noted earlier. But modularity also involves creating software so that it is, from the start, extensible. The key to extensibility in many ways lies in abstraction. Abstraction ensures that a given module can be viewed as providing a service that other modules can use. To make use of the service that the module provides, the client modules should have to do nothing more than call to the interface that the service module provides. Figure 6.6 illustrates the way modules (also called *components* or *packages*) might be depicted in a UML diagram.

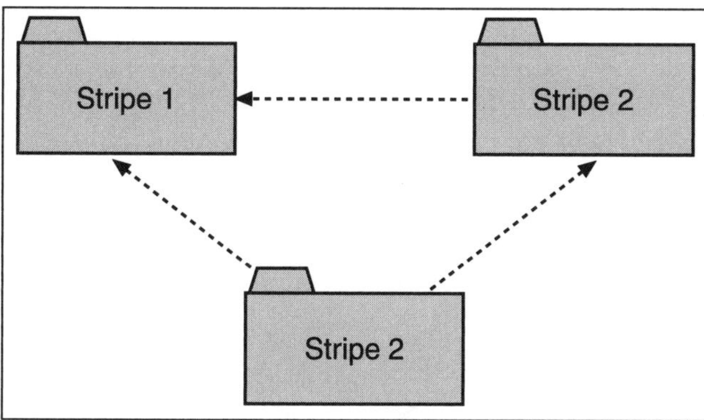

Figure 6.6
Component or Package architectures, which are based on the modular approach to development that object-oriented programming fosters, lay the groundwork for extensibility.

You can view a module as a class or set of classes. You can refer to it as a package or a component. Whatever its name, a module provides a limited, defined set of services that contribute to a software system and can be accessed readily as developers add new behavior to the system.

With iterative and incremental approaches to software development, modularity is crucial; otherwise, the development activity erodes into a reactive, unstable process. At any given stage of development, the modules that comprise the system must bear and accommodate the addition of new behavior to the system. As the discussion of design in Chapter 4 shows, the approach to development for *Ankh* depended on the creation of robust stripes (components or modules) to which other stripes could be added during the development process. Figure 6.7 illustrates the cycle of activity that characterized the development effort. Each iteration began with an investigation of requirements for the next stripe of development.

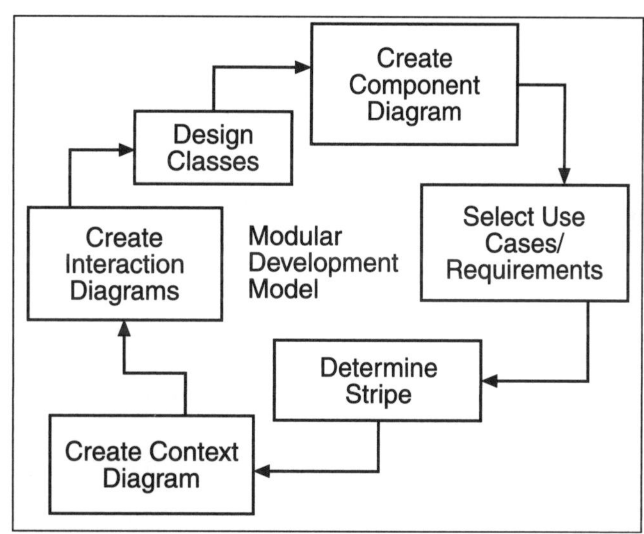

Figure 6.7
The development effort for *Ankh* was based on modular development.

Modular development is ideal for game software development efforts. Flexibility facilitates the discovery of features that often provide the most appealing aspects of games. If an iterative, modular approach defines the development process, regular openings are created for the investigation of how the requirements of the game might be extended to incorporate newly discovered innovations. On the other hand, the effort cannot succeed if the modules that comprise the existing system are not stable and extensible. Figure 6.8 illustrates the chain of iterations.

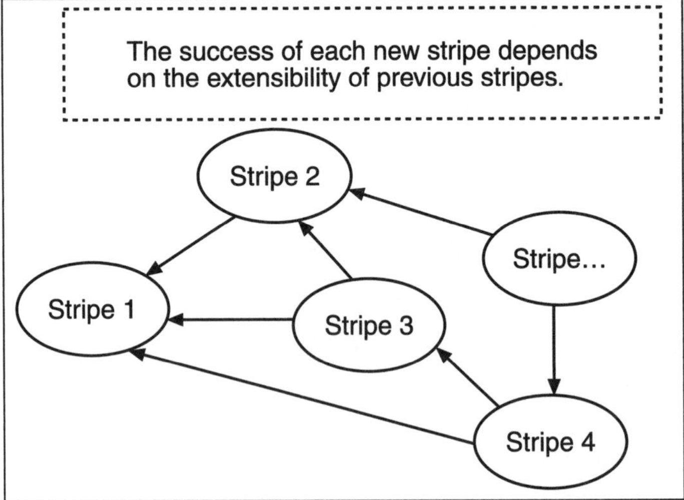

Figure 6.8
The *Ankh* development effort was based on the stability and extensibility of the stripes from which each new iteration began.

What Destroys Modularity?

Chapter 4 explored reasons that design and requirements efforts fail. Besides those, you can add a number that specifically addresses object-oriented paradigms and the goal of extensibility. The ideas offered here are derived from the Agile methodology. (See the references at the end of this chapter.) Table 6.2 summarizes some of the properties of software that tend to reduce extensibility.

Table 6.2 Terms Applied to Extensibility

Problem	Description
Rigidity	When you cannot change software without difficulty, it is rigid. Tightly coupled classes that lack clearly defined responsibilities characterize rigid code. Any change tends to cascade, for example, into the need to effect many changes. Because each change represents a point at which the system resists change, it is clear how rigidity develops. Rigidity is resistance to change.
Fragility	When you cannot change software without it being broken, it is fragile. Complex, two-way dependencies often characterize systems that are fragile. For example, if you have two objects that mutually depend on each other, changing one is likely to break the other. Were the direction of dependency one-directional, this would be less likely to happen.

Problem	Description
Immobility	When software lacks sequential flow, it tends to be immobile. One example of this is when a number of global or static variables tend to nail a body of code into place, so that moving a variable to a local setting requires a fairly involved effort to determine just how and in what ways the information it works with depends on external processes.
Software viscosity	When developers develop software without following a general design, they tend to solve problems in random ways. For this reason, among others, reading and understanding the code becomes extremely difficult. The resulting code is akin to an anthology that collects the works of vastly different writers. The reading can be slow and painful.
Environmental viscosity	When changing code becomes painful, developers might neglect to implement changes according to design. One especially common cause of this is slow compilation time. Lack of things like forward declarations and other include-reducing measures can lead to cumbersome link and build activities. When developers face painfully long builds, they try to minimize the ways in which they change code. The result is that they often put design principles aside.
Needless complexity	When developers stray from the targeted requirements, they might begin writing something akin to a work of anticipatory fiction, anticipating features that no one has planned and that ultimately will never be added to the product. Any unused feature of the software, such as needlessly normalized classes, tends to add to the bulk of the software and, ultimately, to the features that require testing and maintenance.
Needless repetition	Copying and pasting and premature optimization can increase redundancy. In addition to needlessly repeated blocks of code, copying and pasting can result in things like unchanged and thus completely meaningless comments. Variable names can become completely estranged from their original contexts.
Opacity	When code is difficult to understand, it takes more time to change. At the same time, developers habitually seek to optimize code. If code optimization is performed relatively late in a development effort, the harm might be minimal. On the other hand, premature optimization can lead to an absurd situation in which developers need to rewrite code that was written earlier in a project so that they can understand it clearly enough to change it. If it is assumed that code should always be written so that it can be changed easily, the assumption that a development process can reach a point at which it is okay to optimize code into a cryptic essence clearly deserves to be challenged.

General Remedies

The problems that Table 6.3 presents are restatements of problems that software engineers have long identified. Such problems destroy modularity because they disrupt the continuity of the development effort as a planned undertaking. They work counter to the goals that object-oriented techniques of development establish because they challenge development as an undertaking that design guides and requirements constrain. And they lead, in the end, to a tendency to revert to code-and-test tactics that are characteristic of inveterate hackers.

Object-oriented programming promotes a philosophy of development that combats the ills that Table 6.3 details. At the basis of this philosophy rests the disposition to begin every task by focusing on an entity that can be clearly identified in terms of a set of responsibilities. The virtue of this disposition is that right from the start, developers are encouraged to decompose systems into coherent, clearly defined collections of behavior.

Using Refactoring

Refactoring offers a set of powerful analytic tools that augment the basic work of object-oriented programming. Refactoring offers powerful tools of analysis because it is iterative and at the same time characterized by a well-tested set of principles and practices. Among the principles are the following:

- **Promote single responsibility.** Each class should focus on a single responsibility.
- **Promote extensibility.** According to this principle, each class should be developed so that if it is either extended or used as the basis of extension, it does not need to be changed extensively to accommodate the extension.
- **Promote the Liskov Substitution Principle.** In other words, when you specialize a base class, the specialized class should still implement the base class. If the specialized class does not fully implement the base class, so that recasting becomes necessary, something is probably wrong.
- **Resist dependency inversion.** Instead of aggregations at the low level, aggregations should be limited to the base class. And, if possible, the base class should be abstract.
- **Resist interface segregation.** One class should not contain operations that clearly belong in another class.

Practices of Refactoring

Refactoring involves changing code so that it is easier to maintain. As Fowler and others who have written extensively on refactoring contend, no definitive set of principles can be said to determine when you should refactor. One term that appears often in the literature is "smell." If you come across a segment of code that you find falls under the metaphor of "smelling bad," it is probably time for refactoring. Although this chapter later provides a detailed representation of the items that Fowler lists, consider the following situations for starters:

- **Classes, operations, or parts of operations might be difficult to understand.** You have programmed to solve a problem, and solving the problem, rather than preparing the program for future changes or readability, has been your central preoccupation. Now that the primary problem has been solved, you can look again at the code and change it so that the solution you have implemented can be understood more easily.

- **You have written a program that contains duplicated logic.** In this case, you might have found it easy to do something several times rather than making use of single operations or classes that encapsulate the logic in a clear, precise way.
- **You are examining code that you wrote in the past and find it difficult to know how and where to add additional functionality.** You wrote a program that implements its logic correctly, but now you must add functionality to it. Before you begin adding more functionality, you can benefit by taking time to simplify the code to make it easier to work with.
- **You have been given a body of code and are expected to understand it.** You find the code you are working with complex and difficult to understand, and you do not know how to test it. By refactoring the code, you can prepare the way for much more efficient programming in the future.

As this list indicates, no specific objective needs to mark the beginning of a refactoring effort. The main emphasis is that as you move forward in a development project, you can use refactoring to continuously simplify and clarify your code.

Specific Ills and Remedies

This chapter does not afford enough space to demonstrate how you refactor code, but it can point out a few general notions. One of the first is that refactoring is iterative and incremental. It usually proceeds in small, well-tested steps. As you go, you constantly seek to expose new opportunities for reducing complexity and making the code you are working with easier to understand.

Do not confuse refactoring with efforts to optimize code. At times, refactoring can optimize code, but optimizing code often moves in precisely the opposite direction of refactoring. Likewise, do not confuse refactoring with an effort to reduce the number of code lines. Fewer code lines can be a result, but overall, little reduction in the lines of code is likely to result, and in some cases, the number of code lines might increase.

Refactoring often begins with examining the names of attributes and the names of operations. It easily involves elimination of redundancies and long, clustered sets of logic. Refactoring can easily extend to examining hierarchies and component collections of classes to establish whether a pattern might be substituted for an ad hoc body of code. Table 6.3 provides a summary of some of the occasions for refactoring that Fowler and others have named. To supplement the first table, Table 6.4 provides a list of the refactoring techniques that Fowler and others have named.

note

Method and *operation*, along with *member function*, designate the same thing. Fowler, following Java conventions, uses *method* rather than *member function* (for C++ programmers) or *operation* (for UML users). Likewise, he uses *field* to refer either to variables that are local to an operation or to data members (C++) or attributes (UML). This book preserves Fowler's names for the techniques of refactoring but uses *operation* to refer to methods and attributes to refer to class data members.

Table 6.3 Occasions for Refactoring

What Prompts Refactoring	Description
Duplicate code	The same code appears several places. Possible remedies: pull up method, extract method extract class, form template method.
Long operations	Methods in the class are too long and complex. Possible remedies: extract method, replace temp with query, replace method with method object, decompose conditional.
Large classes	A class contains so many operations that they can be subgrouped. Alternatively, a class contains numerous attributes. Possible remedies: extract class, extract subclass, extract interface, replace data value with object.
Long parameter lists	A constructor or an operation contains multiple parameters, many of which might not be needed. Possible remedies: replace parameter with method, introduce parameter object, preserve whole object.
Divergent change	A given class has been changed in several ways, each of which represents a different interpretation of the class. Possible remedies: extract class.
Shotgun surgery	This applies to a set of classes. It might be, when you go to make a single change, that you have to touch several classes before you can make the change work. Possible remedies: move method, move field, inline class.
Feature envy	A given method in class A makes more use of class B than it does of class A. Possible remedies: move method, move field, extract method.
Data clumps	A set of data appears often, in different classes or within a given class, clustered together into some temporary set of values. Possible remedies: extract class, introduce parameter object, preserve whole object.
Primitive obsession	A set of primitives that clearly represents a record or some other object is repeatedly used in a class or set of classes. Possible remedies: replace data value with object, extract class, introduce parameter object, replace array with object, replace type code with class, replace type code with subclasses, replace type code with state/strategy.
Switch statements	Switch statements are used repeatedly throughout a program to redirect activity through the same basic set of operations. Possible remedies: replace conditional with polymorphism, replace type code with subclasses, replace parameter with explicit methods, introduce null object.
Parallel inheritance hierarchies	You have begun two or more lines of descent from a single base or set of base classes. Each line of descent tends to carry the same group of operations. Possible remedies: move method, move field.

What Prompts Refactoring	Description
Lazy classes	A derived class adds nothing to the hierarchy. Possible remedies: inline class, collapse hierarchy.
Speculative generality	One or more operations have been added to a class in anticipation of a use of the class that does not yet exist. Possible remedies: collapse hierarchy, inline class, remove parameter, rename method.
Temporary fields	Temporary fields are used within operations that prove difficult to understand. Possible remedies: extract class, introduce null object.
Message chains	One object requires an object from another class, which requires an object from yet another class. Possible remedies: hide delegate.
Middle man	Class A communicates with class C. Class B conveys most of the communications between A and C and yet contributes little or nothing to the conversations. Possible remedies: remove middle man, inline method, replace delegation with inheritance.
Inappropriate intimacy	When the class directly accesses information in another class. Possible remedies: move method, move field, change bidirectional association to unidirectional, replace inheritance with delegation, hide delegate.
Alternative classes with different interfaces	Two classes might have methods that do the same thing but have different names. The fact that they do the same thing but are named differently proves confusing. Possible remedies: remove method, move method.
Incomplete library class	If you use a library that features classes that contain operations that are in what you consider the wrong classes, the situation can become confusing. Also, you might expect a given library class to have an operation that it does not, so you feel the need to place such an operation in the class. Possible remedies: introduce foreign method, introduce local extension.
Data class	A class is simply a set of data. It has not been developed so that it encapsulates the behavior of the data. Possible remedies: move method, encapsulate field, encapsulate collection.
Refused bequest	A specialized class requires little of the interface that the base class offers. Possible remedies: replace inheritance with delegation.
Comments	After you have refactored your code, you find that many comments are cosmetic or unneeded. Possible remedies: extract method, introduce assertion.

Source: Martin Fowler, Kent Beck, John Bryant, William Opkyke, and Don Roberts. *Refactoring: Improving the Design of Existing Code* (Addison-Wesley: Boston, 1999).

As mentioned, Table 6.4 provides a summary of the refactoring techniques listed by Fowler and others. The list provided here is but a partial representation of the full list, but it indicates the richness of approaches to cleaning up code refactoring offers. See the texts listed at the end of this chapter for a more comprehensive treatment of the subject.

Table 6.4 Refactoring Techniques

Technique	Description
Change bidirectional association to unidirectional	If you have a two-way relationship between classes, and it is clear that one of the classes no longer needs the services provided by the other, you can eliminate the superfluous association.
Collapse hierarchy	If you have created a subclass, but the subclass has few or no distinct attributes or functions, you can eliminate or at least merge the subclass features back into the base class and eliminate the subclass.
Decompose conditional	If you have a complex `if-then-else` statement, decompose it into operations.
Encapsulate collection	An operation returns a collection. Because this can be a costly operation, you can improve the situation if you provide only read-only views of the container contents. You can also provide accessor operations for adding and removing items.
Encapsulate field	Abide by object-oriented design principles and make attributes private to the class. Provide accessor and mutator operations.
Extract class	One class contains operations that perform work that two classes should perform. Create two classes and separate the operations accordingly.
Extract interface	You can create an interface class if you find that two or more classes share a common set of operations.
Extract method	If one or more code fragments can be placed in a single operation, create a single operation with a name that identifies its purpose.
Extract subclass	If two classes share the same features, it makes sense to create a common base case. (Using language that was introduced earlier, you can generalize the two classes into a common base class, which you will probably want to make abstract.)
Form template method	If you find that you have created the same methods in two or more specialized classes in a hierarchy, you can move the methods up the hierarchy.
Hide delegate	If class A needs to know about the state of class B, you can create a middle class that enables you to obtain the information you need without closely coupling A and B.
Inline class	You have a class that apparently has no real purpose. Move its operations inside another class and delete it.
Inline method	One function calls another, and the operation called adds nothing. You can put the called operation into the body of its caller.
Inline temp	You have a temp value to which you assign the value that the operation returns. Take out the temp and use the operation.
Introduce assertion	If you need to ascertain the state of the program, create an assertion operation that returns the state.

Technique	Description
Introduce foreign method	A relationship exists between classes A and B. A needs B to have an additional operation, but B cannot be changed. You can add an instance B to A and use this to create an additional operation that provides the needed operation.
Introduce local extension	If you have a class that you cannot modify but you need to add an additional operation, create a derived class and add the operation there.
Introduce null object	If you have a situation in which you check for a null value, you can create a class that acts as a null value.
Introduce parameter object	If you have a group of parameters that you should treat as a single object, create a class to hold them.
Move field	If you have a field within a given class that is used more by an external class than by the one of which it is a member, move it to the external class.
Move method	You have an operation that is used more by another class than the class of which it is a member. Move it to the other class.
Preserve whole object	If you sometimes retrieve several values from an object using several different calls, you can send the whole object instead.
Pull up method	If you have a hierarchy in which several subclasses contain the same operation, move the operation higher up in the hierarchy.
Remove middleman	Picture three classes: `CDoctor`, `CReceptionist`, and `CPatient`. The `CDoctor` in this case goes through the `CReceptionist` to do everything, and the `CReceptionist` does nothing other than deal with `CPatients`. The `CReceptionist` can be removed, so that the `CDoctor` communicates, say, with both the `CPatient` and `CReceptionist` directly.
Rename method	If the name of an operation does not clearly indicate the purpose of the operation, change the name.
Replace array with object	An attribute of a given class is becoming rather complex to deal with. You can turn the attribute into a class and then use an instance of the class in place of the old attribute.
Replace data value with object	If the attribute of a class becomes complex enough to require supplemental data or even its own operations, create a separate class to model this attribute and use an object of the new class as the attribute.
Replace delegation with inheritance	If you find that you are using several of the operations of an object used as an attribute, you should probably consider deriving your class from the class used to create the attribute.
Replace inheritance with delegation	If you have a subclass that makes little use of the features of a base class, eliminate the subclass relationship and replace it with one in which you create an instance of the needed class in the base class.

(continued on next page)

Table 6.4 Refactoring Techniques (continued)

Technique	Description
Replace method with method object	If a class contains an inordinately complex method, take the method out and make it into its own class.
Replace parameter with explicit methods	If you have a single operation that contains a selection statement that invokes significantly different actions, break the selection statement into separate operations.
Replace parameter with method	If you have an object that passes the result of an invoked operation, eliminate the parameter and just use the invoked operation alone.
Replace temp with query	If you have created a temporary variable in which you store the result of some combination of values and that you use in two or more situations, replace the temporary value with a query operation.
Replace type code with subclasses	If a type conveys numeric codes that do not change its behavior, you can replace the numbers with a new class.

Source: Martin Fowler, Kent Beck, John Bryant, William Opkyke, and Don Roberts. *Refactoring: Improving the Design of Existing Code* (Addison-Wesley: Boston, 1999). See Table 6.3 for a list of various opportunities of use.

Conclusion

At this point in time, most everyone who is involved in the development of a game engine is going to use object-oriented programming. Among the key concepts of object-oriented programming are abstraction, encapsulation, polymorphism, and generalization (also known as *inheritance*). It is important to realize that abstraction lies at the basis of most design efforts. Abstracting the features of a game into a set of objects is one of the main tasks involved in developing a game engine. This chapter explored the principles and practices of programming that object-oriented programming fosters.

Use of component architectures helps eliminate some of the complexity that systems of classes pose. Components (also called *modules*) offer a way in which groups of classes can be viewed as providing a central service or set of services to a software system. Developing software systems incrementally and iteratively using a component architecture based on collections of classes offers a good way to realize the benefits of software engineering based on object orientation.

In some ways, for every solution that object-oriented programming provides, a set of problems also emerges. Avoiding things like closely coupled classes that lack focused responsibilities requires a great deal of work. One of the most effective approaches to eliminating the problems that arise through object-oriented programming is to use refactoring.

Drawing from Martin Fowler, Kent Beck, and others, this chapter offered a summary of techniques for refactoring. Refactoring involves incremental, iterative development that is integrated thoroughly with testing. The objective of refactoring is not so much to achieve the implementation of a specific set of design principles as it is to free code from such things as complexity, lack of clarity, difficulty of extension, and needless comments.

The following books provide deeper insight into the topics covered in this chapter:

Braude, Eric. *Software Design: From Programming to Architecture.* Hoboken, New Jersey: John Wiley & Sons, 2004.

Coplien, James O. *Advanced C++ Programming Styles and Idioms.* Reading, Massachusetts: Addison-Wesley, 1992.

Fowler, Martin, Kent Beck, John Bryant, William Opkyke, and Don Roberts. *Refactoring: Improving the Design of Existing Code.* Addison-Wesley: Boston, 1999.

Lippman, Stanley B. *Inside the C++ Object Model.* Reading, Massachusetts: Addison-Wesley, 1996.

Martin, Robert C. *Agile Software Development: Principles, Patterns, and Practices.* Upper Saddle River, New Jersey: Prentice Hall, 2003.

Meyers, Scott. *Effective C++: 50 Specific Ways to Improve Your Programs and Designs.* Boston: Addison-Wesley, 1998.

Meyers, Scott. *More Effective C++: 35 New Ways to Improve Your Programs and Designs.* Boston: Addison-Wesley, 1998.

Richter, Charles. *Designing Flexible Object-Oriented Systems with UML.* Indianapolis: Macmillan Technical Publishing, 1999.

Sutter, Herb. *Exceptional C++: 47 Engineering Puzzles, Programming Problems, and Solutions.* Boston: Addison-Wesley, 2000.

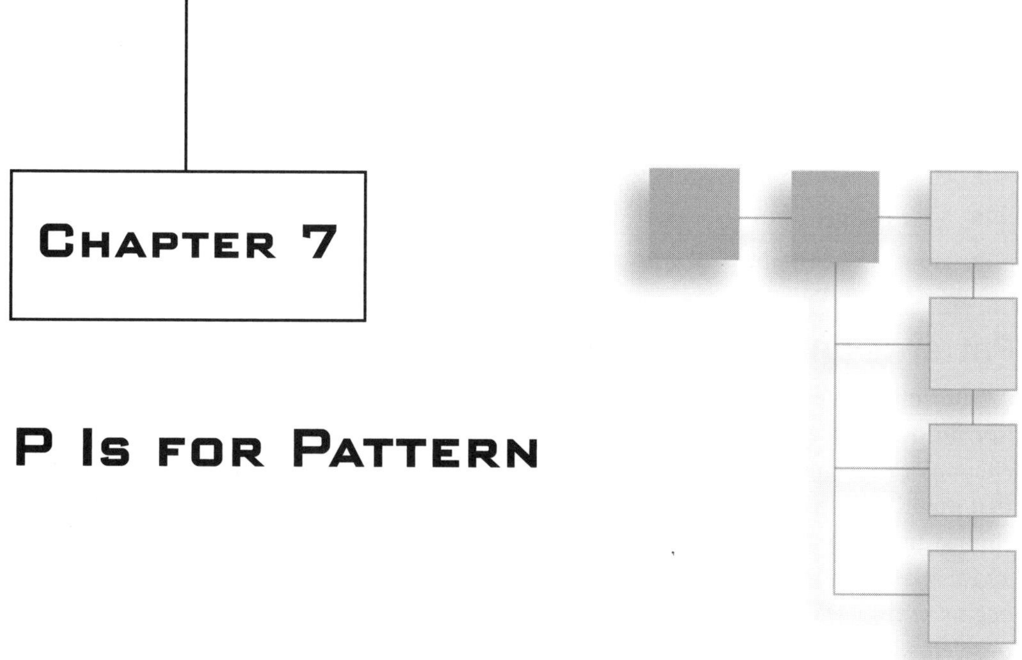

Chapter 7

P Is for Pattern

Patterns provide a set of ideas about how to solve problems that arise as you program a game. Most patterns show you how to work with a collection of classes. Likewise, most of the articles and books on patterns illustrate patterns using UML diagrams. Given this situation, before you try to understand how patterns work, it is a good idea to familiarize yourself with the topics covered in Chapters 3, "A Tutorial: UML and Object-Oriented Programming," and 5, "Old Is Good—The Library Approach." On the other hand, you don't need to put off studying patterns until you have learned UML or object-oriented programming techniques. In fact, the tendency in recent times has been to study all three together.

When you use patterns, the work you perform as you move from problem to solution takes place in a context that includes much more than creating the interfaces to classes. Instead, your work involves finding the pattern that most appropriately solves the problem you face and then applying your programming skills to elegantly constructing a set of classes that gives expression to the pattern. Given this beginning, you can then use the techniques of refactoring to tune your program. (See Chapter 6, "Object-Oriented Fantasies and Realities.")

If you use patterns and refactoring in combination with object-oriented programming, you end up with programs that are easier to understand and maintain. Although the use of patterns obligates you to learn yet another layer of programming skills, the result justifies the extra effort. This chapter covers the following topics, among others:

- Where patterns originated
- Patterns in the context of object-oriented programming and game design
- Why patterns improve the quality of your game

- How to identify a software design pattern
- Nine patterns from the Gang of Four and other sources
- How to document your own pattern

Patterns and Their Contexts

A pattern provides a way to solve a design problem, but a pattern is not simply the solution to a design problem. Instead, a pattern describes a context in which you might encounter a given type of design problem, and it helps you identify an approach to design that might address the design problem. A pattern describes the problem to be solved, the context in which the problem occurs, and a strategy you can use to solve the problem. To arrive at an understanding of what programming based on patterns is about, this chapter begins with a short historical narrative of other approaches to solving programming problems.

The History of Patterns

The history of patterns begins in the realms of psychology, anthropology, and architecture. In the history of psychology, you might have heard of Carl Jung, who introduced the term *archetype.* An archetype is a symbol or collection of symbols that tells you about the state of your mind. Another use of patterns emerged with what became known as Gestalt psychology. Here, again, psychologists used patterns as the starting point of therapy. In the realm of anthropology, you might be familiar with the work of Ruth Benedict, who wrote an influential book called *Patterns of Culture.* By studying patterns in relation to ceremonies or rituals, Ruth Benedict contended, it is possible to understand why people do what they do. And in the realm of architecture, the name Christopher Alexander possesses great significance. He contended that architects should use patterns to shape the space people live in.

The notion that programmers can enhance their programming practices if they use patterns achieved widespread recognition in the mid-1990s. A key element in this recognition was the publication of a text by Eric Gamma, Richard Helm, Ralph Johnson, and John Vlissides titled *Design Patterns: Elements of Reusable Object-Oriented Software.* (See the reference at the end of this chapter.) The emergence of programming based on patterns represents what might be viewed as the culmination of several phases of programming history. Figure 7.1 summarizes these phases. Understanding how these phases lead progressively toward patterns helps reveal the value of pattern-based programming strategies.

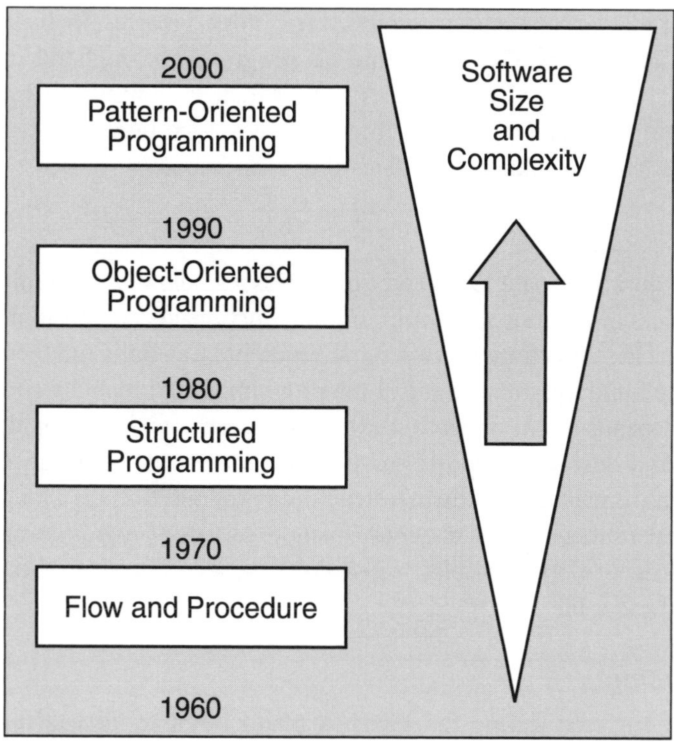

Figure 7.1
Objects and patterns result from increased software complexity size.

Flow Charts

From early on until well into the 1970s, the flow chart as the plan of a program was central to programming. Programming using this model often assumed that a program consists of a fairly deterministic course of events. The events occur one after the other, from the beginning to the end of a program. Because a continuous flow of logic characterized a well-designed procedural program, programmers considered the use of the go-to statement a serious problem. Extensive use of such statements could render the logic of a program indecipherable. Programmers adopted flow charts as tools to eliminate go-to statements and ensure the smooth flow of program logic.

Historically, charting programs worked well because the programs were relatively short by current standards. Programs were short because computer hardware could not easily accommodate large bodies of code. Other physical limitations intervened, also. Programmers often wrote code by hand and then transferred it to punch cards or entered it for batch processing using Teletype terminals and tape drives. Such work was slow and painful. For an engrossing account of how such limitations affected game developers, read

Brad King and John Borland's *Dungeons and Dreamers.* One story involves Richard Garriott's early programming adventures. Garriott wrote his programs in longhand in notebooks even before he was sure he had a computer with which to compile them. Needless to say, given such requirements, precision of intent characterized flow-oriented programs. (See the reference to King and Borland at the end of this chapter.)

Structured Programming

Structured programming arose during the late 1970s and early 1980s and allowed programmers to establish the best practices of functional decomposition. Functional decomposition involves, among other things, placing the actions that a program uses into functions and then pulling together the functions to build the overall logic of the program. The readability and logical success of the program depends on the design of the functions, each of which should, among other things, have one and only one purpose: provide only one avenue of entrance (the parameter list), and have only one point of return. A structured program features a long list of functions and no code that a function does not encapsulate. Structured programming advocates often discouraged the use of global variables. When global values occurred, the best practice was to place them in a header file.

Object-Oriented Programming

Object-oriented programming surfaced during the 1980s. A major point of interest for game developers is Bjarne Stroustrup, who released C++ in 1983. Stroustrup used notions that he derived from studies of Algol (short for Algorithmic Language) and Simula.

Historians say that Simula (invented in Norway in the 1960s) was the first object-oriented language. Simula embodied many of the best features of object-oriented programming, but programmers did not use it widely. Limited demand accounts for the limited use. When Simula first appeared, programs generally failed to achieve the size and complexity that were necessary to encourage programmers to break from the paradigms of logical flow and functional decomposition.

Unlike Simula, C++ enjoyed wide recognition right from the start. Its popularity lay in part in the way it extended C. C++ allowed C programmers to transition easily to an object-oriented language. Authorities also explain that the average size of computer programs, augmented by increased hardware processing powers, required a new paradigm for controlling complexity. By extending C and providing for encapsulation, inheritance, and polymorphism, C++ emerged easily as the leading object-oriented language.

The framework forms what you might consider one of the key results of object-oriented programming. A framework consists of a collection of classes with which a programmer can create a standard software application. Examples of frameworks are the Microsoft Win32 API (a procedural C API, not an object-oriented one) and MFC. Such frameworks provide components that allow programmers to develop Windows applications. The framework provides roughly 80 percent of the code that the end product might contain. The work of the programmer involves creating the functionality that the framework delivers to the application user. Accounting programs exemplify framework-based software.

Patterns

During the 1990s, with the standardization of C++, the emergence of Java, the widespread use of SmallTalk, and the general prevalence of object-oriented programming, component engineering became prevalent. A component often consists of a collection of classes that perform a specific service within a software system. Patterns provide a convenient way to understand components. A component resembles an architectural feature, such as a sheltering roof or a farmhouse kitchen (to use two examples drawn form Christopher Alexander). A pattern enables programmers to commence programming tasks with a component view of their work.

Patterns and Objects

Chapter 6 discusses both object-oriented programming and refactoring. The points covered are along the following lines:

- Object-oriented programming allows programmers to capture the state and behavior of a real-world object.
- Polymorphism, inheritance, and encapsulation form key elements of object-oriented programming.
- In addition to inheritance (also known as *specialization* or *generalization*), association, aggregation, and composition form important facets of object-oriented programming.
- Refactoring furnishes a rich variety of techniques for eliminating inelegant programming practices and shaping programs so that others can understand and maintain them.

To this list, you can now add the work of patterns. Like procedural and structure programming, object-oriented programming, combined with refactoring, provides what theorists call a *design paradigm.* A design paradigm is a general way of understanding how to develop programs. Patterns extend the object-oriented paradigm. Patterns provide descriptions of commonly encountered design problems that programmers can address using standard solutions. Figure 7.2 summarizes the dynamic that exists among object-oriented programming, refactoring, and patterns.

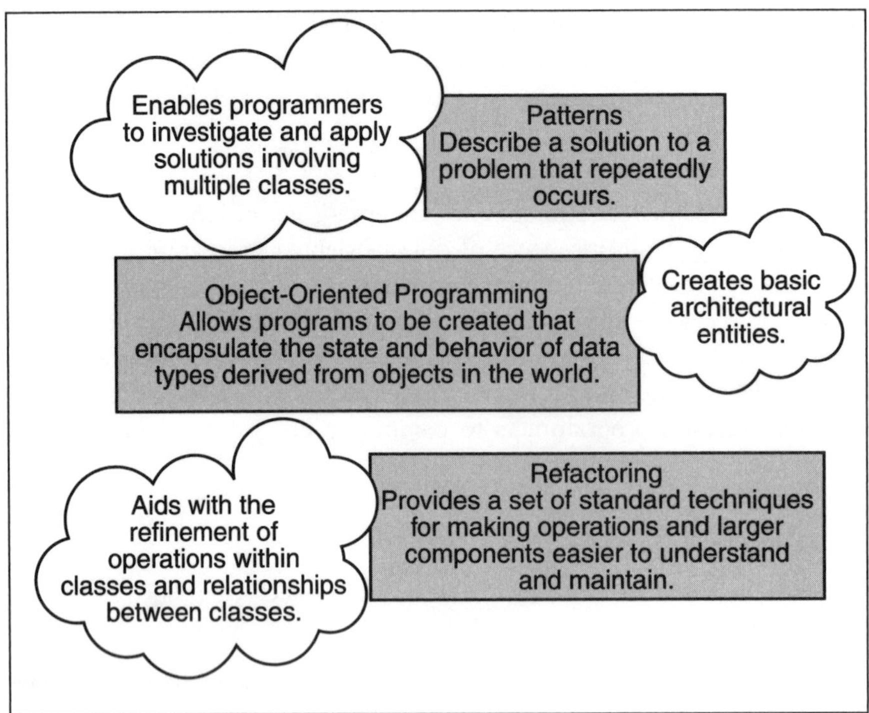

Figure 7.2
Object-oriented programming, refactoring, and patterns complement each other.

Pattern Origins

If you want to display a fair degree of sophistication about patterns, read *The Timeless Way of Building* (*TWB*) that the architect Christopher Alexander wrote several decades ago. (See the full reference at the end of this chapter.) This book provides a meditative, philosophical view of how a great architect understood and solved the problems he typically faced when designing living space. It is a fundamental document in the history of software engineering because it establishes a technique for solving problems that can be applied to any number of software engineering contexts. Consider the following passage:

> *There is a definable sequence of activities [that] are at the heart of all acts of building, and it is possible to specify precisely under what conditions these activities will generate a building [that] is alive. All that can be made so explicit that anyone can do it (TWB, 10).*
>
> . . .

> *Although the process is precise and can be defined in exact scientific terms, finally it becomes valuable, not so much because it shows us things [that] we don't know, but instead, because it shows us what we know already, only daren't admit because it seems so childish and so primitive (TWB, 13).*
>
> . . .
>
> *To make the pattern really useful, we must define the exact range of contexts where the stated problem occurs and where this particular solution to the problem is appropriate (TWB, 253).*

As you might surmise from the preceding passages, a strong parallel exists between architectural conception and software design. Alexander contends in so many words that architectural knowledge consists of a set of solutions embedded in contexts of understanding. These solutions answer innumerable problems that builders over the centuries have discovered as they have explored different living spaces. Many of the solutions resonate with simplicity, yet people have consumed lifetimes discovering them. Add to this one other characteristic. In many instances, the greatest difficulty that builders face begins with the preservation of the solutions they have discovered. For someone to understand a solution fully, the builder cannot divorce it from the context in which it was discovered.

The discovery of patterns, then, for builders and software engineers alike, begins in three places. First, they must preserve the context of the problem. Second, they must describe the problem. Finally, they must document the problem.

In many cases, programmers use UML diagrams to document patterns explicitly. As Alexander wrote of building architecture, "If you think you have a pattern, you must be able to draw a diagram of it" (*TWB*, 267). Such a statement might sound demanding, but it remains that UML and other diagram-based approaches to documentation increase the efficiency of the software development effort.

GoF

Design Patterns: Elements of Reusable Object-Oriented Software, mentioned earlier in this chapter as the classic work on software patterns, was authored by Eric Gamma, Richard Helm, Ralph Johnson, and John Vlissides. This group of software engineers has become known as the Gang of Four (GoF). The appellation has become the basis of a convention that software engineers use when they document patterns. Pattern developers provide a reference to the GoF. This activity is covered in greater detail later in this chapter.

One point that the GoF emphasizes is the centrality of pattern discovery. Practices such as those fostered by refactoring and iterative and incremental design and development enable you to explore problems in a way that creates opportunities for defining and using patterns. Given this orientation, the implication from the first is that the GoF provides a living document on patterns rather than a statement of law. When you describe the problem in the context in which it occurred and join this with a description of the solution, you have a candidate design pattern. You can refer the pattern to a passage in the GoF, but you are not obligated to find justification for your pattern in the GoF.

Kinds of Patterns

As Figure 7.3 illustrates, design patterns come in many shapes and forms. The GoF initially provided only three groupings of patterns, all based on purpose. They categorized the purposes of patterns as *creational*, *structural*, and *behavioral*. To this basic division, the Gang of Four added a supplemental distinction: *scope*. Scope allows designers to indicate whether a pattern, regardless of category, applies primarily to classes or the object instances of classes. Accordingly, creational patterns relate to creation of objects, structural patterns concern how classes and objects can be composed, and behavioral patterns emphasize how classes or objects interact and how responsibility is distributed among them.

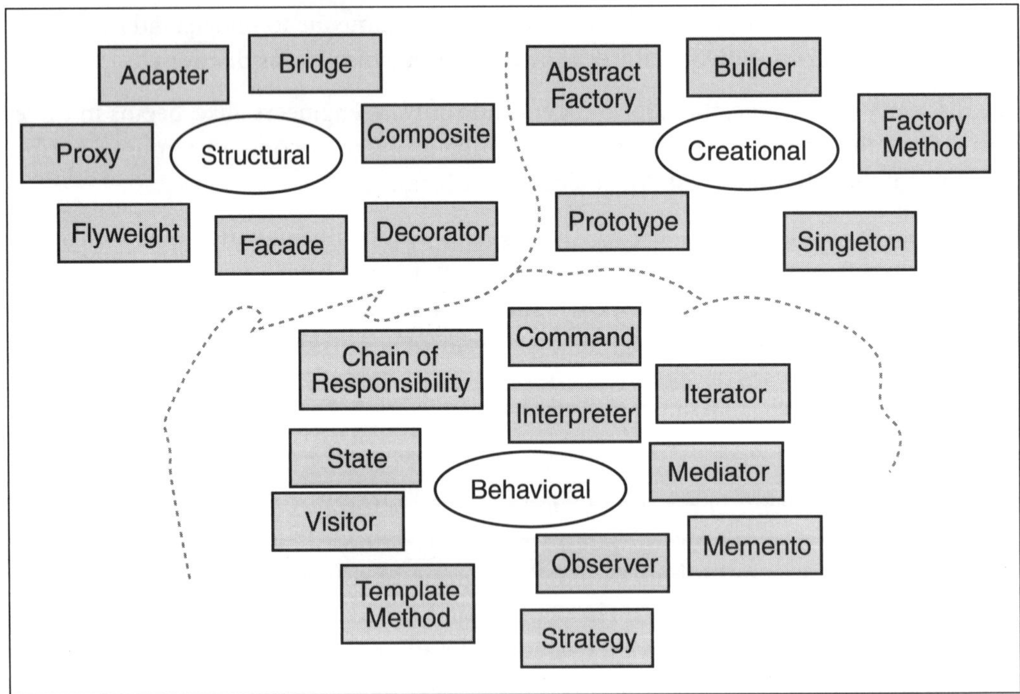

Figure 7.3
The GoF groups patterns into three categories.

As time has passed, software engineers have tried to find new language for identifying pattern categories. Some say that you can sort patterns into *architectural, design*, and *idiomatic* bins. This set of categories parallels the earlier division. Architectural patterns concern how software engineers can construct entire software systems. Design patterns encompass the patterns that the GoF proposed. In other words, design patterns involve the creation of classes and objects. Idiomatic patterns concern approaches to design that are specific to given programming languages.

A third way of viewing patterns divides them into *conceptual, design*, and *programming* categories. According to this version, a conceptual pattern describes anything that relates to how a developer might design an application. A design pattern, remaining true to the GoF notion, covers anything pertaining to collections of classes and objects. Programming patterns, once again, relate to uses of programming languages.

A Short List of Patterns

The primary list of patterns that software engineers use in the design and development of software products has remained stable. The primary list consists of the patterns presented by the GoF. At the same time, developers have created many other patterns. Table 7.1 summarizes the patterns that the GoF present. The sections that follow investigate some of these patterns in detail. Also included is a unique pattern based on the code in *Ankh*.

Table 7.1 Patterns and Descriptions

Pattern	Description
Abstract Factory	You need to create several class instances that are derived from the same abstract class. To accomplish this, you create a single class that manufactures the objects you need.
Adapter	You have a class that requires a given interface. You cannot change this class. On the other hand, a class is at hand that provides the services you require, but the interface is not quite right. To remedy the situation, you create a class that holds a reference to the class that provides the services and adapts the interface for use by the class that requires the services.
Bridge	You have one class that is a specialization of another. You would like to make it so that you have more flexibility than what the specialization provides, so you limit or eliminate the way that the specialization works by delegating responsibility outside your primary hierarchy to classes in which you encapsulate the qualities you seek. In this way, rather than creating a heavy, deep hierarchy, you bridge over to what you need. Aggregation and composition replace inheritance.
Builder	You want to be able to create objects of a given class with a fair degree of flexibility. To reach this goal, you create a class with several operations that are capable of either building or acquiring complex features.

(continued on next page)

Table 7.1 Patterns and Descriptions (continued)

Pattern	Description
Chain of Responsibility	An object from one class passes a request to an object from another class, which in turn passes a request to an object from yet another class. The chain can go on. You normalize and control this process by developing handlers for the chained events.
Command	You must convey a message complex enough to merit the creation of a class that encapsulates the attributes and operation that comprise the message. To accomplish this, you create an abstract object from which you can derive such a command object when needed.
Composite	You have a set of objects that you group together to create what you want to treat as a single component. To accomplish this, you create one class that serves as an abstraction of the composite class. You can implement the abstract class to serve as a composite class.
Decorator	You have one class that offers a given set of functionality. You want to enhance this functionality without changing the class. To accomplish this, you create a second class that enhances the functionality of the first. The second class is a decorator class.
Factory Method	You want to have a user class create varying instances of a service class. To accomplish this task, you create one class that is able to express the primary set of needs that defines the user class. You create other classes that anticipate the services that the service class is to offer. Then, within the user class, you create a factory operation that can determine the required instances of the service classes.
Façade	You have a collection of classes that provide multiple involved but essential operations that you would like to access in a friendly, familiar way. To reach this goal, you define a single class that provides a fresh new interface that has the capabilities you want to access from the collected objects.
Flyweight	You have several specific items that share a common set of features. Rather than repeating these features, you create one class that allows the objects to share the feature set.
Interpreter	You have developed a hierarchy of classes that models a set of rules. You can use an interpreter to evaluate the rules.
Iterator	You have one class that contains in some way a set of objects. You want to be able to visit these objects in a specific sequence to convey messages to them. To accomplish this, you employ an iterator pattern. The iterator pattern accesses one element at a time and tracks the position of each element relative to the next.
Mediator	If you have a set of objects and want to have in place a single class that encapsulates the way any given client objects might interact with objects in the set, you can mediate the relationships between the client and the other objects by using an object from a class that is designed as a mediator.
Memento	You want to capture the behavior of a given class and store it for later retrieval. To accomplish this, you create a class that stores the information you want to retrieve. In this instance, the information is protected.

Pattern	Description
Proxy	You do not want to instantiate an object of an especially heavy nature unless you are sure that the state of your game mandates its instantiation. To solve this problem, you create a proxy class. The proxy class is a stand-in class for the heavy class. The proxy class might have the look and feel of the heavy class, but it serves only as a stand-in until either it or the game knows that it is time to load the heavy class.
Observer	You want to use one class to process events that another class presents. To make it possible for objects of a first class to notify objects of a second class, you can follow two courses of action. First, you can create a container of the second, observed objects in the first class. Second, you can equip the second class with an interface that allows its objects to be updated readily.
Prototype	You want to be able to create instances of classes that you cannot name or do not care to name when you build your system. Imagine, for instance, a type of object created from graphical primitives according to the state of your game at a given moment. To meet this need, you create a prototype pattern. The prototype pattern includes an abstract class that offers an interface that is common to all the possible concrete instances. The prototype pattern also incorporates a creator class that uses the abstract class to shape specific instances of prototyped classes.
Singleton	If you need to know that only a single instance of an object can be created, you can create a singleton class. Generally, a singleton class offers operations that other classes can access to obtain unique services.
State	You have a set of states that you want to audit. You can distribute information about the set of states across classes that are designed for this purpose.
Strategy	You have one class that needs to be configured to accord with differing occasions of use. Rather than creating multiple versions of this class, you create a separate class that manages the features of your class so that you do not need to change it. The second class provides a strategy for the first class that allows it to meet the requirements of its contexts of use.
Template Method	You have a class or collection of classes that provides a set of elementary operations that you have to adapt in small ways every time you want to use them to effect a slightly altered version of what they do as a group. To avoid the necessity of writing slightly varied routines repeatedly to accomplish slightly varied tasks, you create a class that brings these elementary operations into one group that you can control with a single, facile call. The class that gathers and orchestrates the features is called a template method class.
Visitor	You have one class that needs to communicate with a number of classes that it contains, say, as compounded objects. To make this possible, in each of the compounded classes, you create an operation that allows the compounding object to visit it. The compounding object then has an operation that can traverse through the compounded objects and convey a message through the visitor operation.

How to Document Patterns

Approaches to documenting patterns differ. Generally, it is a good idea to use the pattern template that is considered appropriate in the setting in which you work. At some companies, for instance, a patterns collection group might create a template for patterns. Most such templates originate with the headings that the GoF uses. The headings of the GoF template are as follows:

- Intent
- Also Known As
- Motivation
- Applicability
- Structure
- Participants
- Collaborations
- Consequences
- Implementation
- Sample Code
- Known Uses
- Related Patterns

As useful as these headings are in guiding the documentation of patterns, many pattern developers elect to follow a shorter course. This chapter follows the shorter course and uses the following headings:

- Name
- Intent
- Problem
- Solution
- Participants and Collaborators
- Consequences
- Implementation
- GoF Reference

The next few sections offer descriptions of the items in the shorter list. Figure 7.4 provides a summary of some of the elements of a pattern description.

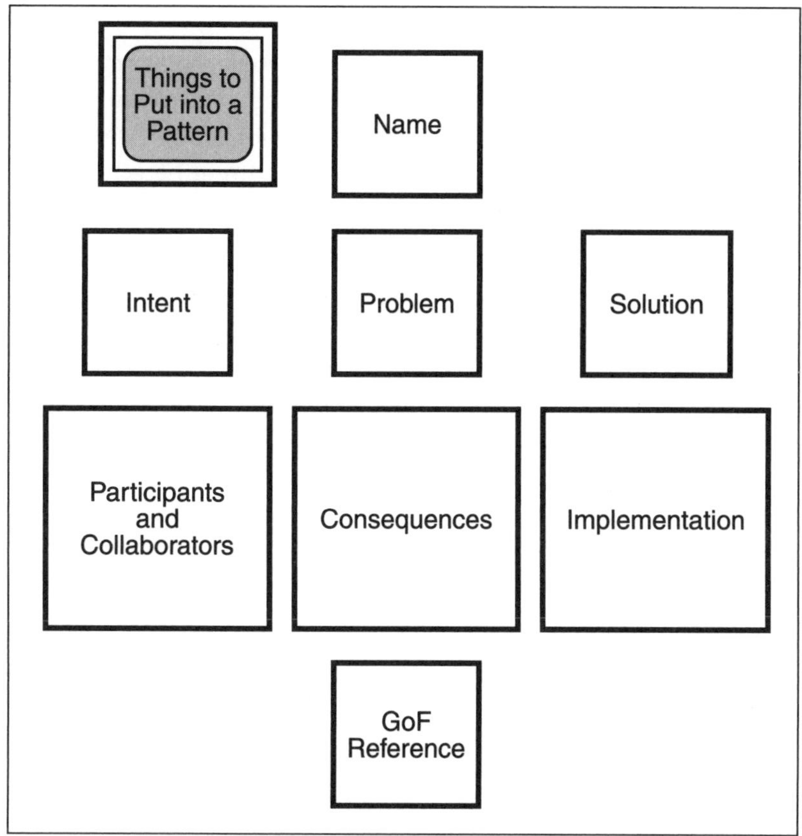

Figure 7.4
Develop patterns according to current models.

Name

Each pattern possesses a unique name. As with the name of a class, the name of a pattern should serve as a mnemonic for the solution that the pattern implements. As you can see from the patterns that Table 7.1 lists, the names that the GoF created emphasize the solution rather than the problem. Usually, pattern names consist of a single word or a phrase consisting of no more than three words. The names are brief because the pattern from the start concerns an abstract entity, and longer names tend to restrict abstraction.

Note that in many instances a given pattern goes by several names. This happens because developers discover the same pattern in different contexts, document their findings, and only after publication find that someone else has identified the same pattern. Cross-references provide a convenient way for pattern developers to identify duplicates. The literature provides a convention of writing "Also Known As" when several names for the same pattern have arisen.

Intent

As the GoF list implies, the intent is what motivates you to document the pattern. Your intention relates to the context in which you are working and what you want to achieve with the pattern. The intent you establish might and perhaps should be more than only the solution to a specific problem; therefore, most designers work toward a generalized scope. The reason for this is that a pattern that people can use in many contexts throughout a system is likely to be more successful than one that cannot.

Intent also encompasses the principle(s) of design you seek to concretize through your pattern. In this respect, you must view a pattern as both a practical solution to a problem and evidence that a given type of problem can be solved according to a given principle of design. Statements of intention that resonate practical and theoretical concerns tend to be more convincing than those that are restricted to practical concerns. If a pattern proposes only a theoretical agenda, it is not properly a pattern.

Problem

The problem statement includes a description of the context. Pattern developers sometimes refer to "forces" and "constraints" when specifying the information that a problem statement ideally includes. A force can be anything that has bearing on the problem, the context of the problem, or the solution to the problem. Although the discussion of a given force probably should be restricted to what helps the user of the pattern understand and apply the pattern, a larger number of factors help identify a problem. Among just a few forces that come to bear on a problem are whether the problem affects performance, program maintenance, program extensibility, and testing.

Forces also work as constraints. Following the lead of two pattern experts, James Coplien and Brad Appleton, stating a problem involves recognizing the minimal criteria for pattern validity. Among these are the following:

- **Concrete.** It does not help to state the problem as an abstract principle. If you have no context of implementation and no specific remedy to provide, you do not yet have a pattern.
- **Supported by evidence.** When you document a pattern, you should do so on the basis of empirical evidence of its efficacy. If you base the validity of the pattern only on conjectures about how it might help its user, you fall short of providing a useful product.
- **Useful.** A pattern that documents an obvious solution is not likely to prove very useful to anyone. Generally, a pattern gives expression to a principle of software design. The pattern can help developers bridge a difficult gap between an abstraction and a practical way to implement code according to the abstraction.

- **Generality of application.** Patterns should not be simple snapshots of the components of a system. It is not enough, for example, to capture the way a set of classes provides a service to your system and then to designate these classes as a pattern. A pattern has to do with the design of systems in general and needs to show how someone can achieve a given principle of design in many contexts.
- **Grace.** Patterns provide a means by which software developers can achieve greater control over and comfort with the software they create. If a pattern lacks grace, it is probably not a very good pattern. In this respect, software engineering and architecture share a concern for engineering aesthetics.

Solution

The solution that a pattern offers should describe how to achieve the solution that the pattern offers. The description can include almost any type of information that you find beneficial. Most texts feature, for example, a UML diagram. Such a diagram can show the abstract form of the pattern and provide a place to discuss alternative approaches to its implementation. Generally, pattern developers discuss the solution that the pattern offers in specific contexts, those that directly answer problem statements. Such an approach ensures that the presentation of the pattern proceeds quickly and efficiently. After all, the presentation of the pattern should allow developers to move directly into the implementation of a patterned solution in the program they are working on. Although theoretical discussion in this respect can result in extra work, it remains important in the statement of the solution to provide information that enables a developer to understand the different contexts in which to implement the solution.

Participants and Collaborators

The notion that one pattern might relate to others should not seem strange. The abstract factory pattern, for example, stands as a relative of the method factory pattern. Explaining one in the light of the other can be helpful. On the other hand, it is also the case that one pattern incorporates another. For example, a pattern might use an iterator pattern in conjunction with a command pattern. If this happens, the description of the primary pattern should include discussion of why and how supplementary patterns are used.

Consequences

When implemented, patterns can have both positive and negative consequences. Every system is cybernetic. In other words, a change in one part of the system is likely to result in some impact on other parts of the system. For this reason, documenting negative results of the implementation of a pattern is as important as documenting what is positive. In some spheres, developers regard neglect of such documentation of dangers as unethical, and their stern attitude is probably justified. If you have not thoroughly tested the implementation of a pattern, it is appropriate to at least state that no adverse consequences have *as yet* been discovered. Generally, however, if a pattern proves successful in a well-documented set of contexts, little reason exists for not publishing it.

Implementation

Most pattern developers show how to use the pattern by providing code samples. In fact, developers are likely to regard with skepticism a presentation of a pattern that lacks an example of implementation. When you provide an example of an implementation, the documentation you place in the code should be refined. Likewise, developers generally refrain from showing implantation details that are not immediately relevant to the operation of the pattern.

GoF Reference

Provide page references to the GoF. Some developers provide chapter references. The problem with the chapter references is that the chapters do not necessarily explore single topics. Ideally, the GoF reference points to a specific GoF pattern, but it might also be the case that the reference points the reader only toward the pattern context.

Applied Patterns

The sections that follow discuss some of the opportunities for implementing patterns for *Ankh*. The explanations provided concern the ways that the patterns were interpreted and implemented rather than the generalized pattern definitions found in texts such as those by the GoF. The patterns that the GoF provide represent inroads to refactoring class relationships. They can guide the perceptions of the designer as he approaches the task of improving the quality of a program. The patterns investigated in this respect are as follows:

- Singleton
- Composite
- Chain of Responsibility
- State
- Strategy
- Observer
- Façade
- Memento
- Command

In addition to applying patterns that the GoF furnished, the team experimented with the derivation of its own pattern, which it named the boss pattern. This chapter provides both a diagram and a sample implementation of this class.

Singleton

A singleton pattern provides a way that you can restrict a class so that only a single instance of it can be created. Within the context of *Ankh*, the CGame class fits into the singleton pattern. The CGame class owns everything; therefore, it provides a context in which it is possible to access all objects. Creating more than one instance of CGame amounts to creating a new game. For this reason, during any given session of play, no more than one instance of the CGame class occurs. Table 7.2 summarizes the features of the singleton pattern.

Table 7.2 Singleton Features

Topic	Feature
Intent	You want to restrict the use of the class to one instance.
Problem	You want to provide a place in which several client objects can communicate readily, and you want to ensure that you can control the number of object instances.
Solution	You have only one instance of the object.
Participants and Collaborators	A single operation creates an instance of the singleton, and one operation controls how the singleton can be accessed.
Consequences	Client objects do not require knowledge of the state of the singleton object because the singleton object contains the instances of the client objects.
Implementation	You can implement a static instance of the singleton class.
GoF Reference	See pages 127–134.

The following code example shows the declaration of the CGame class. The pointers that the class encapsulates become much more manageable as attributes of a singleton class than would be the case, for example, than if you declared them as global instances of their respective classes. A few functions have been added to the class to enable tracking of its state and version.

```
class CGame
{
public:
      CGame();
     ~CGame();
     // The run method is basically like "main." It does everything.
     int Run();
     // Get and set operators ///////////////////////////////
     bool IsRunning(){return m_bRunning;}
     void SetRunning(bool bRunning){m_bRunning = bRunning;}
     ////////////////////////////////////////////////////////
private:
     // Here is the massive list of game classes
     CGraphics *m_pGraphics;
```

```
    CCamera *m_pCamera;
    CAi *m_pAI;
    CPlayer *m_pPlayer[NUM_PLAYERS];
    CLog *m_pLog;
    CProfile *m_pProfile;
    CGuiMgr *m_pGuiMgr;
    CImageMgr *m_pImageMgr;
    CStateMachine *m_pStateMachine;
    CInput *m_pInput;
    CFontMgr *m_pFontMgr;
        // static int m_iCount;
    float m_fVersion;
        // Are you running?
    bool m_bRunning;
};
```

note

The approach that the *Ankh* team took to a singleton differs from standard singleton approaches. One reason for this is that the team considered it important to have global pointers for graphics and sound. Because these point to member variables of `CGame`, they would be destroyed upon exit. Further, it is clear that they are always up to date, because they get set in the constructor of the "singleton" object.

A standard approach would have involved using a private constructor, a static data member (`CGame* m_instance`), and a static public member operation (`CGame* GetInstance()`. Further, a destructor could be used to ensure an instance of the game is destroyed upon program exit.

One of the most significant aspects of this implementation of the singleton class is that the class creates the objects that are required for the creation of the game. The `Run()` operation contains the code that accomplishes this task. Its implementation is as follows:

```
//////////////////////////////////////////////////////////
// CGame::Run()                                         //
//////////////////////////////////////////////////////////
int CGame::Run()
{
    // Set the graphics mode
    m_pGraphics->SetGFXMode(800,600,false);
    m_pInput = new CInput();
    Graphics->SetFont("John Handy LET",24);
    Input->SetPointer("MouseCursor.png");
    StateMachine->EnterState("Menu");
    while(IsRunning())
    {
        MSG msg;
        if (PeekMessage(&msg, 0, 0, 0, PM_REMOVE))
        {
            if (msg.message == WM_QUIT)
                break;
```

```
                TranslateMessage(&msg);
                DispatchMessage(&msg);
            }
            else
            {
                // Do the frame
                StateMachine->DoFrame();
                Sleep(0);
            }
            if (GetAsyncKeyState(VK_ESCAPE))
            {
                PostQuitMessage(0);
            }
        }
        return(0);
}
```

Composite Pattern Features

A composite pattern enables you to treat objects from a set of primitive classes as a single component. To accomplish this, you create one class that serves as an interface for the primitive classes. Both the primitive and the composite classes can implement the interface type. In the design of *Ankh*, the team found an opportunity to assert a composite pattern in the design when it examined the relationship existing among the dialog elements it had created. Because these primitives acquired meaning only when composed into a graphical entity, unifying them with a composite pattern made sense. See Table 7.3.

Table 7.3 CGUIObject Composite Pattern Features

Topic	Feature
Intent	Simplify the presentation of graphical primitives.
Problem	Most of the graphical primitives in the windows tend to be used exclusively in the dialog box, so it makes sense to create a component that treats these primitives as one.
Solution	Create a `CGUIObject` class that pulls the primitives together.
Participants and Collaborators	Among the participants were `CButton`, `CPanel`, `CLabel`, and `CTextBox`, which were generalized as `CModalDialog`, and `CEnvironmentDialog`, and `CInventoryDialog`. These, in turn, were generalized as the `CModalDialog` class.
Consequences	It became much easier to manage the `CGUIObject` objects, which could be placed in a container that accommodated all the basic graphical components that were associated with dialog boxes.
Implementation	Find the graphical user interfaces relative to the dialog box, and generalize them into an abstract class, `CGUIObject`. Then create a container for items of the `CDialogue` class in the `CWindow` or other contexts.
GoF Reference	See pages 163–173.

Figure 7.5 provides a UML representation of the `CGUIObject` composite pattern. The implementation used in *Ankh* remains somewhat limited because the pattern wasn't utilized in its entirety. Full use implies that the composite serves in a recursive role. In other words, the pattern might be used in one of its own subclasses to create a container. Notice, however, that `CModalDialog` generalizes three dialog types. This represents an extension of the pattern.

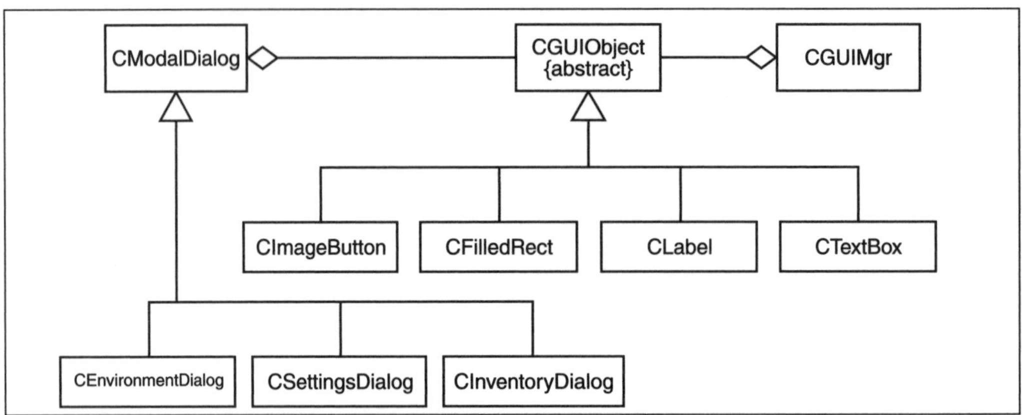

Figure 7.5
The `CGraphic` composite pattern gathers together graphical primitives.

Chain of Responsibility Pattern Features

A chain of responsibility occurs when several objects in succession pass a message that has the same content and intent. The chain of responsibility pattern enables you to simplify your message transfer because, for example, you can create a handler class or appoint an operation with a given name to accomplish the transfer. With the *Ankh* design effort, the team discovered an occasion for a chain of responsibility pattern at work in the component model used in our dialogs. The `OnClick()` operation could be written in each instance to transfer messages along the chain to the appropriate level. Full implementation of this pattern calls for a handler class, but the team decided to develop a common interface. See Table 7.4.

Table 7.4 CDialog Chain of Responsibility

Topic	Feature
Intent	User interface elements tend to communicate messages, one to another, along a chain.
Problem	It is easy to lose track of the flow of the message if the classes involved contain operations that have different names that behave in different ways.
Solution	Standardize the transfer of messages through a common interface feature that focuses on the given responsibility.

Topic	Feature
Participants and Collaborators	Participant classes implement a common handler, `OnClick()`.
Consequences	You can avoid difficulties in handling events because all classes transfer a common message in a common way.
Implementation	You implement a common operation for each of the chained classes.
GoF Reference	See pages 223–233.

Figure 7.6 provides a UML representation of the `CDialog` chain of responsibility pattern.

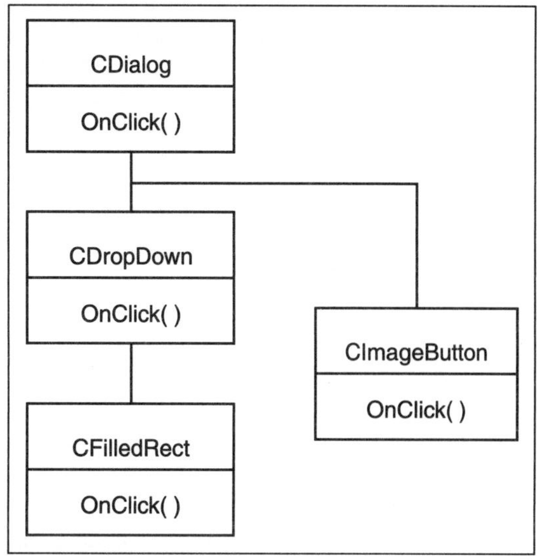

Figure 7.6
A chain of responsibility automates message transfer.

State Pattern Features

When the development team approached the state pattern, it found occasion to use it to manage general game states. The pattern can be valuable if you have a set of states that you want to audit. You can distribute information about the set of states across classes that are designed for this purpose. To audit the different states, you use a separate class to represent each state, all derived from a single abstract class. When you switch between the respective objects from the implemented classes, you can obtain, using the same interface, information about the different states. Among distinct game states are "menu," "game in play," and "map editor." See Table 7.5.

Table 7.5 Game State Pattern

Topic	Feature
Intent	You want to make it as easy as possible to obtain information about the current state of the game.
Problem	You face a problem of wanting to obtain general state information about the game. Obtaining the information requires adding attributes to the game object or creating classes, such as a history class, to store state information.

(continued on next page)

Table 7.5 Game State Pattern (continued)

Topic	Feature
Solution	Create a state class from which you can derive objects that represent the main states of the game.
Participants and Collaborators	`CPlayState`, `CMenuState`, and `CMapEditorState` provide key classes for the game. `CState` is an abstract class.
Consequences	Storage of the state of the game is facilitated. You have only to set up criteria for when to access a given state to update its object.
Implementation	An abstract state class defines an interface that provides information about key elements of the game state. You can derive classes from this for each of the game states and access them as needed.
GoF Reference	See pages 305–313.

Figure 7.7 provides a UML representation of the `CState` state pattern.

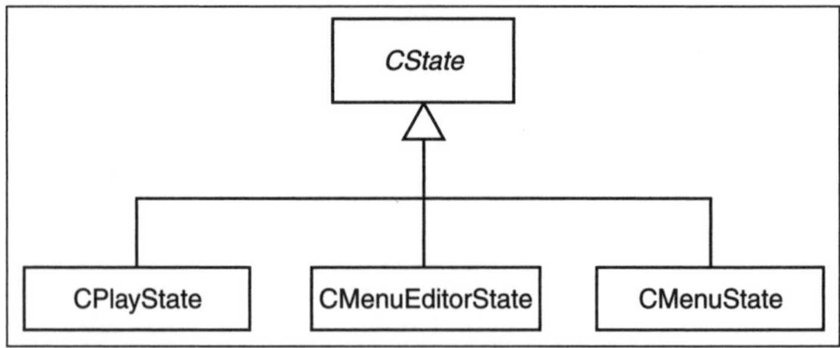

Figure 7.7
You can audit game states by using a state pattern.

Strategy Pattern Features

The strategy pattern allows you to extract a basic type of behavior from a given class and place the behavior into separate classes. The separate classes then embody complex interpretations of the common behavior. An abstract base class provides an interface that is suitable for accessing the complex interpretations, which are embodied in concrete derived classes.

With *Ankh*, one candidate area for this pattern is the *attitude* that the character takes up in different play contexts. Three such attitudes are those for *defensive*, *offensive*, and *magical* play. Although the player might invoke the same set of operations with relation to changing game contexts, the force, health, and other aspects of play change, and these changes represent changes of strategy. Creating an abstract class for strategy and then using derived classes with complex characteristics to provide different behaviors helps simplify the movement between contexts. The client class can then form an association with the strategy class to adopt the appropriate context of play. See Table 7.6.

Table 7.6 Strategy Pattern Features

Topic	Feature
Intent	Simplify changing between complex contexts of game behavior.
Problem	When gameplay moves from one context to another, subtle, complex changes in the overall nature of play take place. If one class takes care of all such concerns, the information that the class must contain becomes extremely complex.
Solution	Abstract the context of play into a strategy class and derive classes that can contain the information needed for changing contexts.
Participants and Collaborators	`CAI` is an abstract class. `CMagicAI`, `COffensiveAI`, and `CDefensiveAI` embody different contexts of play.
Consequences	Using an abstract AI class provides a convenient way to centralize the definition of different AI contexts. Although defensive, magical, and offensive might be the first contexts, you can add others as the game increases in scope and depth. You can first add several levels with themes only vaguely designed. Having in place a strategy pattern makes it easy to negotiate the design issues.
Implementation	Create a `CAI` class. Then derive strategy classes from `CAI` for each leading context of play. For example, `CMagicAI` and `COffensiveAI`, in addition to `CDefensiveAI`, might serve as common interpretations.
GoF Reference	See pages 315–323.

Figure 7.8 provides a UML representation of the `CAI` strategy pattern.

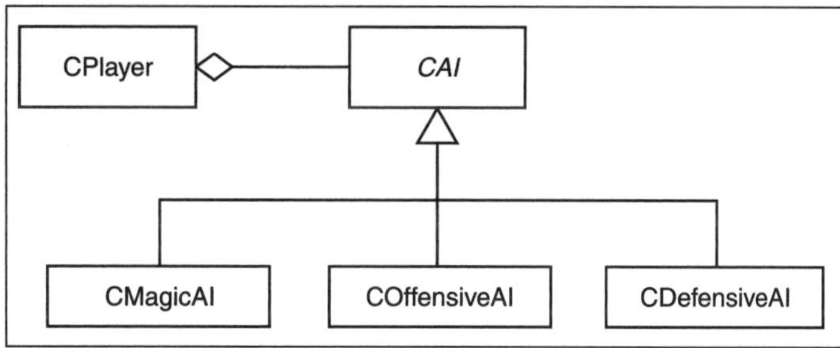

Figure 7.8
The strategy pattern simplifies complex changes of attitude.

Observer Pattern Features

If an object of a first class is the source of events for one or more objects of a second class, you can create a collection of objects of the second class within the first class, along with operations for adding objects of the second class. For the second class, you must define an interface that allows the first class to update all its instances. The outcome of this relationship between the two classes is that the first class observes the second class. The observer pattern characterizes this relationship.

As the team worked with the *Ankh* design, it discovered an occasion for implementation of an observer pattern in the relationships that existed between the `CGuiMgr` class and all the classes derived from the CGUIObject class. By creating a container of the CGUIObject type in the CGUIMgr class, the team allowed the events that the CGUIMgr class processed to be channeled to the objects that were derived from the CGUIObject class. In accordance with the observer pattern, the team made the CGUIObject an abstract class. See Table 7.7.

Table 7.7 Observer

Topic	Feature
Intent	Provide an easy way to notify different objects of generalized type of events.
Problem	Objects regularly require notification of events channeled through another class. You want to avoid having to wrap or otherwise filter objects so that the notifying class can update them. Further, you want to avoid a cumbersome, inefficient hierarchy.
Solution	You can create a container of an abstract type in a first class that channels the events. You can implement an interface for the abstract type that allows the first class to notify the objects of the classes that implement the abstract class.
Participants and Collaborators	CGUIMgr, CGUIObject, and classes that implement CGUIObject, such as CView.
Consequences	The container in CGUIMgr hides the complexity of the event-notification process. The interface that is implemented for the classes derived from CGUIObject allows all objects that are stored in the container in the CGUIMgr to be audited or updated readily.
Implementation	Create a container of objects of the CGUIObject type in the CGUIMgr class. Create an abstract class, CGUIObject. Provide this class with an interface that enables the GGUIMgr to audit or notify objects of its derived classes of events that it processes. Provide the CGUIMgr class with an operation that allows objects of the CGUIObject type to be added to the container. You can add additional operations as needed.
GoF Reference	See pages 293–299.

Figure 7.9 provides a UML representation of the CGUIObject observer pattern.

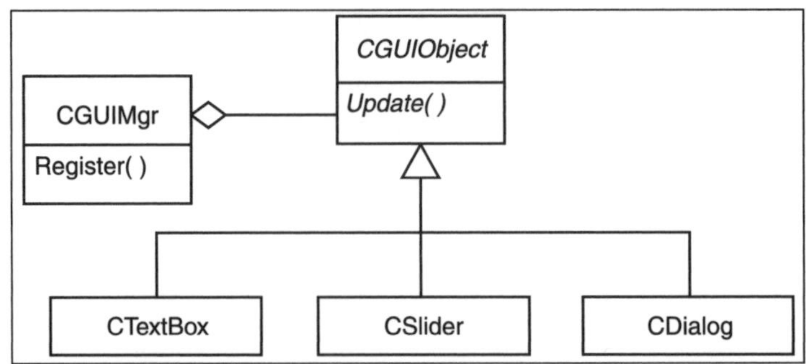

Figure 7.9
With the observer pattern, a container enables a contained object to be notified of events.

Façade Pattern Features

You'll often want to use complex classes or components in a way that hides the complexity of the classes. The key to achieving this goal is to expose a limited set of operations from the assembled classes or components. A façade pattern helps with this situation. A façade class allows you to wrap the interfaces from the complex classes in operations that are friendly and specific to your context of use.

The occasion the team found most promising for the use of the façade pattern emerged when it undertook to make use of the DirectX and Win32 API objects. Having set up the objects for devices, services, and other elements, the team required continuing use of only a narrow range of the total interface features. Further, because the team tended to use constant values to create instances of the DirectX and Win32 API objects, allowing continuing exposure of operations was unwise. For this reason, the team created `CGraphics`, which both facilitated and restricted access to the DirectX and Win32 API objects. See Table 7.8.

Table 7.8 Façade

Topic	Feature
Intent	Simplify access to the interfaces that the DirectX and Win32 API components offer.
Problem	The richness of the DirectX and Win32 API interfaces becomes a liability if access to them is not restricted to a relatively narrow scope. After you initialize the game, for example, you have little need for the vast majority of operations. Accessing such operations can create complexities that are difficult to control. You need a way to capture the operations of these components and restrict them to the context of your game.
Solution	Create a single class that wraps the interfaces that the complex components offer in a convenient, restricted set of operations.
Participants and Collaborators	These are objects that are drawn from the DirectX and Win32 API components. `CGraphics` provides operations that access the DirectX and Win32 API capabilities.
Consequences	`CGraphics` reduces the complexity of the graphical components. Use of the interfaces becomes easier because parameters can be simplified or set with default values.
Implementation	Create a `CGraphics` class that contains instances of the relevant GDI and DirectX objects. Wrap operations from the DirectX and Win32 API objects in `CGraphics` operations that restrict scope and facilitate use.
GoF Reference	See pages 127–134.

Figure 7.10 provides a UML representation of the `CGraphics` façade pattern.

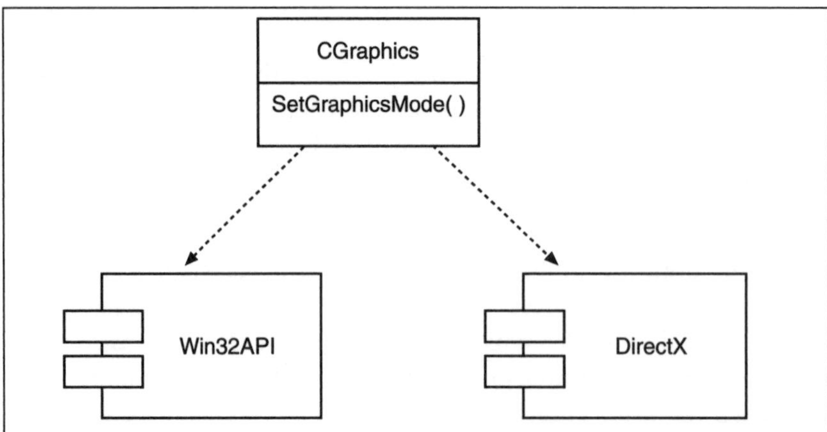

Figure 7.10
A façade pattern refines and customizes access to other interfaces.

Memento Pattern Features

During gameplay activity, actions unfold one after another according to the actions that the player takes in response to the challenges that the game presents. At certain moments, players might want to stop the gameplay and replay recent action sets. Although this is not the exact equivalent of an undo command in a word processing program, it does make use of similar features. For the replay or undo actions to occur, the application must be able to store and retrieve a series of application states that have been recorded in some type of database. When the user issues the undo or replay command, the system must retrieve and apply the stored information. The memento pattern readily facilities this activity. (See Figure 7.11.)

Ankh used the memento pattern when functionality was implemented to support game replay commands. The primary classes for this interaction were `CHistory` and `CWorld`. `CHistory` provides a container of `CWorld` states that can be popped when the player requests a replay of game actions. See Table 7.9.

Table 7.9 Memento

Topic	Feature
Intent	Provide a way that you can store and replay states of the game.
Problem	You need to be able to store the game events and, upon request, replay them. This activity encompasses everything that occurs in the game world during a given sequence of gameplay. You must retrieve all actions if the continuity of the game action is to be saved.

Topic	Feature
Solution	Designate the world as an originator object. Designate another object, which stores states of the originator object, as a memento object. Store the states in a stack that you can pop upon request.
Participants and Collaborators	Examples are `CHistory` and `CWorld`.
Consequences	A container of `CHistory` objects stores successive states of `CWorld`. The system retrieves `CAction` instances from the `CHistory` container when events in the world must be replayed. Because the `CHistory` object stores all the information that the system requires to replay a sequence of play, a container of `CAction` objects streamlines replay actions. It is necessary to refine `CHistory` only to the point that it can access and provide the information that `CWorld` processes during play sequences.
Implementation	Create a `CHistory` object that can record states of `CWorld`. Create a sequential container of `CAction` objects. Refine `CHistory` until it accesses, stores, and provides information that is necessary to address fully any given state of `CWorld`.
GoF Reference	See pages 283–291.

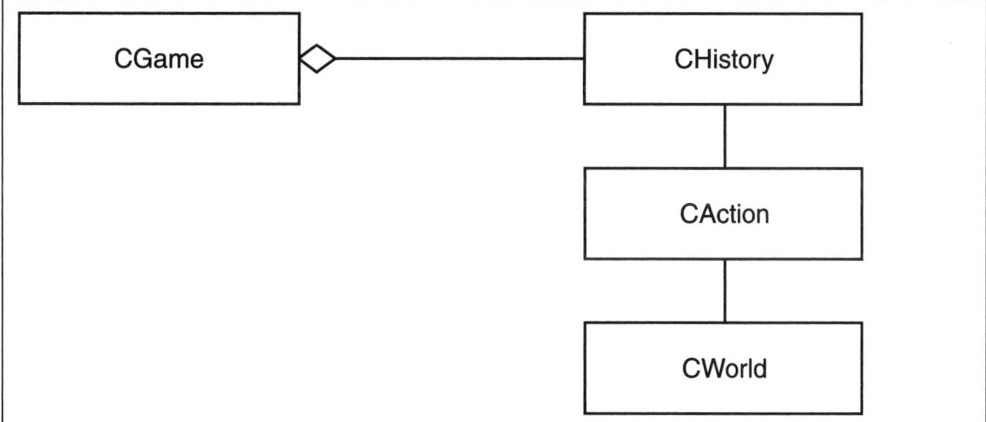

Figure 7.11
A memento pattern facilitates game replay.

Command Pattern

At times, commands you pass from one object to another become complex enough to merit the creation of a separate class that embodies the command. In such cases, the command has both a state and a behavior. Such a situation arises when the command is in some way responsible for tracking instances of itself. A ready example arises when a message you send to a menu disables a menu item. The command should be able to detect when the menu item has been disabled. The command pattern accommodates such transactions.

In the context that *Ankh* provided, an occasion for a command pattern arose in the interactions between the `CEntity` and `CHistory` classes. `CEntity` needed to notify `CHistory` of updates using a complex message, one that needed to be able to track its own history. To accommodate the complexity of the message transfer, a `CAction` class was created. Both `CEntity` and `CHistory` could then interact using `CAction` instances. See Table 7.10.

Table 7.10 Command Pattern Features

Topic	Feature
Intent	Consolidate the complexity of a message transaction to reduce the complexity of the transaction.
Problem	The complexity of the interactions between the `CEntity` and `CHistory` classes was extensive enough that effecting the transaction required storage and manipulation of data that were relative to the message transfer. Both classes needed to be equipped with such capabilities.
Solution	Create a class to embody the message.
Participants and Collaborators	Examples are `CHistory`, `CEntity`, and `CAction`. `CAction` embodies the message.
Consequences	The complexity of the interactions between the classes is reduced because the state and behavior of the message are encapsulated in the `CAction` object.
Implementation	Create a `CAction` class that is capable of containing the information passed between `CHistory` and `CEntity`. Provide an interface that retrieves the information that the interactive classes require.
GoF Reference	See pages 233–242.

Figure 7.12 provides a UML representation of the `CHistory` command pattern.

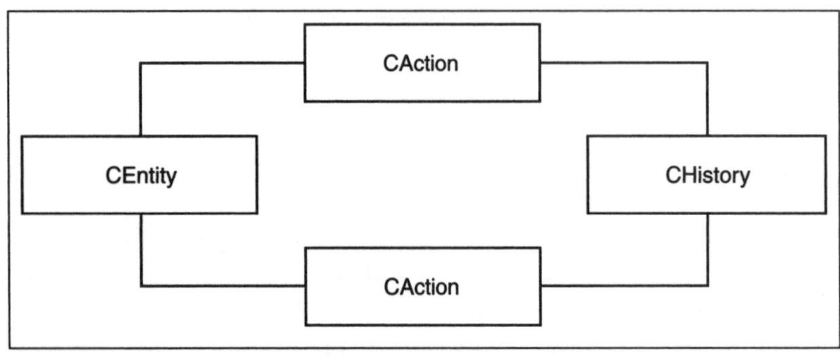

Figure 7.12 Develop patterns according to current models.

Boss Pattern

The patterns that the GoF supplies cover design problems that are common in most application areas. Applying these patterns to contexts that are specific to game development usually involves refactoring game code until it assumes a form amenable to pattern-oriented design strategies. In other cases, rather than refactoring code, you can turn to the patterns and consider whether you can combine or alter them to accommodate an occasion that does not perfectly fit any one pattern but clearly displays features of one or more patterns.

To illustrate this approach, it is possible to offer a custom pattern the team developed to address an occasion in which it wanted to manage resources. The problem the team faced was that it wanted to track resources that were instantiated for the game but, at the same time, given a resource that did not exist, it wanted to have the ability to instantiate the resource upon detecting a need for it. The team wanted to store all instances of resources in one convenient place and have at hand an interface that would allow us to add, retrieve, delete, and detect the existence of any specific resource. The answer to this need arose in the boss pattern. See Table 7.11.

Table 7.11 Boss Pattern Features

Topic	Feature
Intent	Provide a way to easily track the existence of resources. If a resource exists, use it. If a resource does not exist, create an instance of it and place it in a container for detection, access, and deletion.
Problem	During the life of the game, you must load many large images. In some instances, you can load duplicates of an image. In other instances, you face the danger that a resource that the program has added might be added again. Such transactions reduce the efficiency of the game and pose problems of resource allocation and management.
Solution	Create a class that maintains a list of loaded resources. When you try to load a resource that has been loaded already, it returns a pointer to the loaded resource. If the resource has not been loaded, it loads the resource and returns a pointer.
Participants and Collaborators	These include `CResourceMgr` and the resource classes it tracks. In addition, an abstract `CResource` class should be present.
Consequences	`CResourceMgr` maintains a list of objects of the `CResource` class and provides an interface that allows the resources to be tracked, loaded, and unloaded.
Implementation	Create a `CResourceMgr` class. This class provides `Get()` and `Release()` operations. Create a collection of resource objects in this `CResourceMgr`. The resource class should have an interface that provides `AddReference()`, `RemoveReference()`, `IsLoaded()`, and `Unload()`.
GoF Reference	See pages 127–134.

Figure 7.13 provides a UML representation of the `CResourceMgr` boss pattern.

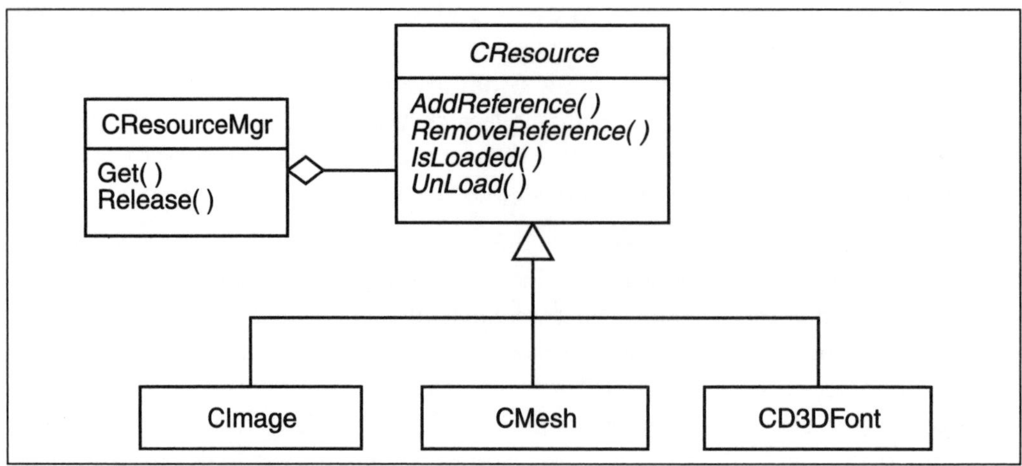

Figure 7.13
The boss pattern provides a way to track resources.

Boss Implementation

The following code sample illustrates the implementation for the boss pattern for the `CImage` class.

```
class CResource
{
public:
      CResource();
      ~CResource();
      // Removes a reference from this resource
      virtual void RemoveReference();
      // Inline members ////////////////////////////////
      virtual void AddReference(){m_iRefCount++;}
      void SetName(const CStdString &strName)
      {
            m_strName = strName;
      }

      void SetFileName(const CStdString &strFname)
      {
            m_strFileName = strFname;
      }
      CStdString GetName(){return m_strName;}
      CStdString GetFileName(){return m_strFileName;}
      bool IsLoaded(){return m_bLoaded;}
      virtual void Unload(){m_bLoaded = false;}
```

```
    virtual bool Load(CStdString strFile)
    {
        m_bLoaded = true;return(true);
    }
    ////////////////////////////////////////////
protected:
    // What is your name?
    CStdString m_strName,m_strFileName;
    // Your reference count
    int m_iRefCount;
    // Are you loaded?
    bool m_bLoaded;
};
//////////////////////////////////////////////
// CResource::RemoveReference()              //
// Removes a reference to this object,       //
//  unloading it if necessary.               //
//////////////////////////////////////////////
void CResource::RemoveReference()
{
    // Decrement reference counter
    m_iRefCount--;
    // If you hit 0, unload the resource to save memory
    if(m_iRefCount==0)
    {
        Unload();
    }
    else if(m_iRefCount<0)
    {
        // Shouldn't really have a negative count
        Log->Add("CResource::RemoveReference() - >
            %s has a negative reference count...",
            m_strName.c_str());
    }
}
class CResourceMgr
{
public:
    // Default constructor
    CResourceMgr();
    // Destructor
    ~CResourceMgr();
    // Gets a resource. If it has not yet been loaded, the manager
    // will load it.
    class CResource *Get(const CStdString &strName);
    // Gets a Font resource
    class CD3DFont *GetFont(const CStdString &strName,
                            int iHeight);
    // Releases a resource, decrements its reference count, and
    void Release(const CStdString &strName);
```

```
private:
     // Your list of resources to manage
     std::vector<class CResource *> m_lstResources;
     // Loads a resource from a file by calling its 'Load' method
     bool Load(const CStdString &strName,
               const CStdString &strFile);
     // Loads an image object
     bool LoadImage(const CStdString &strName,
                    const CStdString &strFile);
     // Loads a font object
     bool LoadFont(const CStdString &strName,int iHeight);
     // Load a mesh resource
     bool LoadMesh(const CStdString &strName,
                    const CStdString &strFile);
};

//////////////////////////////////////////////////
// CResourceMgr::Load(...)                       //
// Loads a resource and adds it into the list  //
//////////////////////////////////////////////////
bool CResourceMgr::Load(const CStdString &strName,
                        const CStdString &strFile)
{
     // Get the extension of the file
     int idxDot = strFile.Find(".",strFile.length()-4);
     CStdString strType =
            strFile.Right(strFile.length() - idxDot - 1).ToLower();

     // Load an image file
     if(strType == "png" || strType == "jpg"
                         || strType == "bmp" || strType == "tga" ||
                            strType == "pcx" || strType == "gif")
     {
          return(LoadImage(strName,strFile));
     }
     else if(strType =="x")
     {
          return(LoadMesh(strName,strFile));
     }
     else
     {
          return(false);
     }
}
/////////////////////////////////////////////////////////////
// CResourceMgr::Get(...)                                  //
// Gets a resource or loads it if it is not loaded        //
/////////////////////////////////////////////////////////////
CResource *CResourceMgr::Get(const CStdString &strName)
{
```

```
    CResource *resFound = NULL;
    for(unsigned int i=0;i<m_lstResources.size();i++)
    {
        // Look for the image with the matching name
        if(m_lstResources[i]->GetName() == strName)
        {
            resFound = m_lstResources[i];
            // Load the image if you need to
            if(!resFound->IsLoaded())
                resFound->Load(resFound->GetFileName());
            resFound->AddReference();
            return(resFound);
        }
    }
    // No resource found... try to load 'strName' and name it.
    // Same as the file name (except without the full path).
    if(!Load(strName,FullPath(strName)))
    {
        Log->Add("CResourceMgr::Get() -> Couldn't find/load %s",
                                        strName.c_str());
        return(NULL);
    }
    // Re-call yourself to get the image you just loaded!
    return(Get(strName));
}
///////////////////CIMAGE////////////////////////
// Holds basic information about an image
class CImage : public CResource
{
public:
    // Default constructor
    CImage();
    // Default destructor
    ~CImage();
    // Loads an image from a file
    bool Load(const CStdString &strFname);
    // Frees memory used by the image and sets loaded to false
    void Unload();
    // Get and set methods ///////////////////////////////////////////
    IDirect3DTexture9 *GetTexture(){return m_pTexture;}
    float GetWidth(){return m_fWidth;}
    float GetHeight(){return m_fHeight;}
    float GetTexCoordX(){return m_fTexCoordX;}
    float GetTexCoordY(){return m_fTexCoordY;}
    /////////////////////////////////////////////////////////////////
private:
    // Holds the Direct3D9 texture for the image
    IDirect3DTexture9 *m_pTexture;
    // Holds direct3d related info
```

```
    D3DSURFACE_DESC m_descTexture;
    // The texture's width
    float m_fWidth;
    // The texture's height
    float m_fHeight;
    // The rightmost x texture coordinate
    float m_fTexCoordX;
    // The bottommost y texture coordinate
    float m_fTexCoordY;
};

///////////////////////////////////////////////////
// CImage::LoadFromFile(CStdString strFname)     //
// Loads the image from the given filename        //
///////////////////////////////////////////////////
bool CImage::Load(const CStdString &strFname)
{
    // The image info structure holds width, height, formats, and so on
    D3DXIMAGE_INFO info;

    // Try to load the texture
    if(FAILED(D3DXCreateTextureFromFileEx(Graphics->GetDevice(),
            strFname,
            0,0,0,0,D3DFMT_UNKNOWN,
            D3DPOOL_MANAGED,D3DX_FILTER_NONE,
            D3DX_FILTER_TRIANGLE,
            D3DCOLOR_XRGB(255,0,255),&info,NULL,&m_pTexture)))
    {
        FatalException(__FILE__,
                __LINE__,
                "CImage::LoadFromFile -> Failed to load
                        %s!",strFname.c_str());
        return(false);
    }
    // Get info from the texture
    D3DSURFACE_DESC desc;
    m_pTexture->GetLevelDesc(0,&desc);
    m_fWidth=(float)info.Width;
    m_fHeight=(float)info.Height;
    // Set up your texture coordinates
    m_fTexCoordX = (float)(m_fWidth/desc.Width);
    m_fTexCoordY = (float)(m_fHeight/desc.Height);
    // Set the file name
    m_strFileName = strFname;

    // You are now loaded
    m_bLoaded = true;
    return(true);
}
```

```
/////////////////////////////////////////////////////////////
// CImage::Unload()                                        //
// Unloads the image and sets the loaded flag to false     //
/////////////////////////////////////////////////////////////
void CImage::Unload()
{
      // Only unload if you are loaded currently
      if(m_bLoaded)
      {
            // Release the texture
            if(m_pTexture) m_pTexture->Release();
            m_pTexture = NULL;

            // Warning if someone is still holding onto you
            if(m_iRefCount>0)
            {
                  Log->Add("CImage::Unload()-> %s unloaded with iRefCount=
                              %d(Object still holding image!)",
                              m_strName.c_str(),m_iRefCount);
            }
            // Reset reference count back to 0, set unloaded
            m_iRefCount = 0;
            m_bLoaded = false;
      }
}
```

Conclusion

Pattern-oriented programming, combined with refactoring, provides an extension of object-oriented programming. As conceived originally, object-oriented programming sought to furnish a set of components that programmers could use without having to modify them. This goal had many virtues, but it fell short in situations in which the provided components did not encompass all the functionality that an occasion of use required. To solve this problem, classes were grouped into larger collections, and with such groupings arose the observation that the groupings occur in patterns that address specific problems. To augment the observation, the practices that the architect Christopher Alexander had embodied in his documentation of architectural patterns were ready at hand. The result was that the Gang of Four, which included Eric Gamma, Richard Helm, Ralph Johnson, and John Vlissides, was at hand to formulate a collection of 23 basic patterns for software engineering.

This chapter investigated some of the fundamentals of patterns. In addition to discussing how to define a pattern, this chapter briefly defined a few of the patterns that Gamma and others have documented in terms of *Ankh*. A unique pattern, the boss pattern, controlled resource counts in *Ankh*.

Using patterns requires that you investigate the existing patterns, their occasions of use, and the possibilities that refactoring affords you as you refine or increment the design of your game. Generally, you can achieve the best results if you begin your design efforts with a ready store of patterns.

To investigate patterns comprehensively, turn to full-length texts on the subject. The text by Gamma and others tends to be the central reference point for advanced programmers who have acquired grounding in patterns. Other texts explain and illustrate patterns for beginners. Because of the general trends that have prevailed in software engineering practices over the past decade, the predominant number of works currently available on patterns addresses Java implementations. However, although some patterns address specific language implementations, the majority does not. Even those that do address specific languages can be altered with little effort to fit another language context.

The following publications provide deeper insight into the topics covered in this chapter:

Appleton, Brad. "Patterns and Software: Essential Concepts and Terminology." http://www.enteract.com/~bradapp/docs/patterns-intro.html

Coplien, James O. "Software Patterns." http://hillside.net/patterns/definition.html

Horstmann, Cay. *Object-Oriented Design & Patterns.* Hoboken, New Jersey: John Wiley & Sons, 2004.

Martin, Robert C. *Agile Software Development: Principles, Patterns, and Practices.* Upper Saddle River, New Jersey: Prentice Hall, 2003.

Richter, Charles. *Designing Flexible Object-Oriented Systems with UML.* Indianapolis: Macmillan Technical Publishing, 1999.

Shalloway, Alan and James R. Trott. *Design Patterns Explained: A New Perspective on Object-Oriented Design.* Indianapolis: Addison-Wesley, 2002.

Vlissides, John. *Pattern Hatching: Design Patterns Applied.* Reading, Massachusetts: Addison-Wesley, 1998.

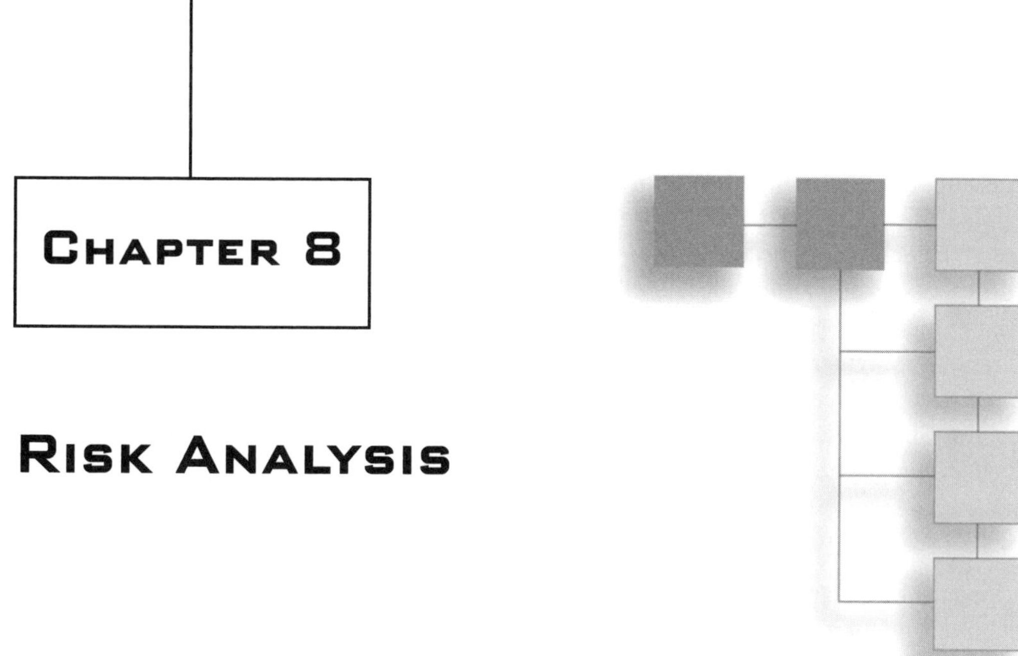

Chapter 8

Risk Analysis

Risk analysis requires that you look at how you develop software and ask yourself whether the way you develop software poses dangers to your project's success. For a game, the dangers range from how members of a development team get along, to whether the organization has budgeted enough time and money for the team to finish the project, to whether the game is worth creating.

This chapter approaches software risk analysis from a traditional perspective but adds to this perspective several considerations that are not found outside the game industry. Among these considerations are those involving the aesthetics and technical innovation involved in game development. An important aspect of software engineering involved with game development is that it must encourage and protect creativity. The reasons for this are legion, but one in particular is that developers often add creative features to a game late in the development effort. Failing to consider the risks of allowing either too little or too much latitude in the development effort is one of the many aspects of risk analysis that this chapter investigates. The topics covered in this chapter include the following:

- Defining risk as a category of software engineering
- Establishing criteria to use for risk analysis
- Analyzing risks so that you can prevent them
- Developing a risk management plan that is suitable for your setting
- Tracking and controlling risk

The Story of Risk

The story of risk involves many stories stretched out across a narrative that includes losses of life, lawsuits, failed products, returned products, failed development efforts, breakups of development teams, breakups of individuals, and as might be expected, bankruptcy. The stories stretch far out into space, too, to things like lost Mars probes (for missions that launched successfully) to rockets exploding just a bit above the launch pad (for those that did not launch successfully). These have been among the most costly losses. The Mars probe disappeared when the two teams that were developing the software used different measurement systems (metric and avoirdupois). The Ariane 5 rocket crashed after a software engineer left a few lines of test code in the launch program that shut off the engine. Stories like this are mortifying for organizations like NASA and the ESP, which have to budget projects years (sometimes decades) in advance and then, sadly, often do not discover the problems until months in to flight. Add to this the billions of dollars (U.S. or EU) required to finance a doomed effort.

Closer to home are the many games that possess irritating errors or that development teams create for game players who do not exist. Many games never reach a market because the teams involved in their development become embroiled in disputes and break up. Others become sidetracked in feature generation, so that money enough to finance them to completion does not exist. Still others reach the market full of errors, thus harming the reputation of the development group responsible for their creation. And still others reach the market with relatively few problems only to fail because no one buys them.

Software engineering risk assessment begins with a mandate to identify, address, and reduce or eliminate problems in the software development effort before they cause the development effort to fail. As Figure 8.1 illustrates, how it goes from this starting point depends on how those involved in the development effort choose to anticipate risk. Three basic avenues characterize the activity that follows:

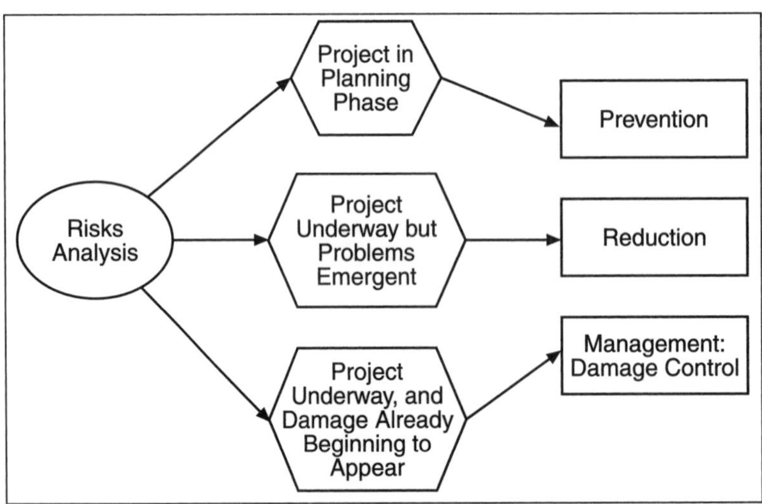

Figure 8.1
Risk analysis involves prevention, reduction, and damage control.

- **Prevention.** In its best form, risk assessment commences and the project starts up. It allows those who are involved in the planning and initiation of the development effort to recognize and either alter or eliminate practices that are destined to cause problems.
- **Reduction.** In a second form, risk assessment can provide wisdom, not about how to eliminate risks (in some situations, risk cannot be eliminated) but how to reduce risk.
- **Damage control.** In a third form, risk assessment provides developers with suggestions or procedures for solving problems after they have erupted in an uncontrolled or unexpected way. In such situations, the objective cannot be to reduce or prevent risks. The objective must be to control the damage.

Applied Risk Analysis

A risk consists of anything that can delay a project, increase its cost, create liabilities for the organization, adversely affect the quality of the software product, or work to the detriment of those involved with the development or use of the software product. Assessing such risks involves having tools at hand with which to identify them, describe them, analyze them, and remedy them. Although the tools of risk analysis might be available and effective, just realizing that a risk exists tends to be the hardest part of risk analysis. When people are deeply committed to or involved in a project, the force of cognitive dissonance tends to prevail. Cognitive dissonance is a term that social psychologists use to describe the tendency of people to deny that something they are doing is in some way responsible for harm that others suffer. A programmer who has just finished working days or weeks on a given program, for example, is not likely to volunteer that the program possesses errors and might be badly designed. The effort that the development requires seems to stand as evidence that the result must be good. Nothing could be further from the truth, however. If risk assessment is to occur, a strong program of risk assessment needs to be in place.

Programmers are not the only ones who have trouble discovering the risks that characterize the work they perform. Generally speaking, everyone who is involved with software development or any type of product development faces risks. Discovering the risks requires a painful, concentrated effort, not of finding faults, but of assessing the product to discover those situations in which its development or use might lead to irregular results. Finding the situations in which irregularities arise begins, generally, with a division of the world into two general playing fields. One of these has to do with external risks. The other has to do with internal risks. Figure 8.2 provides a high-level view of these two divisions of risk.

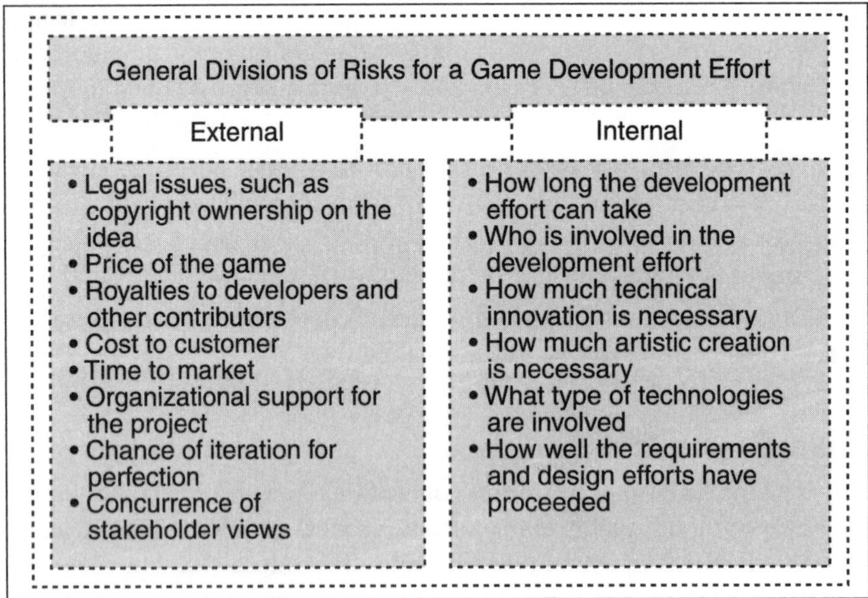

Figure 8.2
Risk assessment deals with external and internal risks.

External Risks

External risks for a software development effort consist of anything that provides for the successful completion of the project. Among these are the following:

- **Financing.** Does enough money exist to fund the development effort? Ultimately, the executive group must find funding for the project. Funding originates from a multitude of sources, but a leading risk in any funding or investment situation arises because investors usually want to audit what the company does with its money.
- **Organizational support.** Does the organization support the development effort? Given adequate funding, the dynamics of the organization come into play. Consider the difference between an organization that trusts its developers to undertake creative, experimental work and an organization that trusts no one and demands that fairly high-level game and software designers plan every activity in advance.
- **Resources.** Where are you working, and what equipment are you using? If you are part of a startup venture, you might be using the back room of a coffee shop or an idle college classroom in which to do some or all of your work. But in other areas, where you are involved in a mature or maturing corporate effort, the amount of money that executives or managers budget for development resources heavily

impacts the efficiency of developers. For example, if your organization purchases a well-supported configuration management system, you might spend less time figuring out how to negotiate glitches in the system than you do when you use freeware. This is not a jab at open source products. However, it is true, generally, that if your company purchases supported tools, you can expect other developers to have responsibility for fixing product bugs in a timely way.

- **Customer support.** Can the market sustain its demand for the game? If no one wants to buy your product, you are probably in trouble. But even before anyone buys your product, you still have customers. Such customers consist of the artists, managers, executives, and others in your organization who are expected to support and defend your development effort. Whether such people support your effort might depend on whether you have periodic demonstrations of the game you are developing.
- **Creative support.** Who is providing game resources? Can you find graphics artists and musicians? Can these people produce the resources you need? A major factor for larger organizations is the amount of money available to purchase the rights to different works of art. The price tags rise with the product's profile. When you reach the point at which the theme of the game reflects a soon-to-be-released movie, the sums involved increase enormously. In any event, stealing even the smallest identifiable sound bite from a creative source poses enormous and unjustified risks.

One important general consideration with respect to external risks involves protecting the development team from knowledge of such risks. Such a priority might appear ironic, but consider the implications if members of the team lie awake at night preoccupied, not with pipeline performance issues, but with next week's venture capitalist visit.

Internal Risks

On the internal side, issues become much more complex. As Figure 8.2 illustrates, the issues that arise often involve the development team. Among the leading concerns are the following:

- **Equipment.** Equipment is just what you would expect. Are the computers that the programmers use powerful enough to reduce compilation time to an acceptable minimum? Are the RAM and graphics cards powerful enough to enable developers to develop without having to battle system limitations? Does the equipment on which developers develop the game correspond in its description to what those who will purchase the game possess?
- **Team members.** How do the members of the team work together? A team can remedy a bad idea for a game or a poor design, but if dispute, distrust, and desertion characterize the effort, the development effort stands little chance of success.

Even with a brutally impersonal corporate effort, in which individuals supposedly mean little, if members of the development team cannot work in complementary ways, management will find that replacing people and rekindling lost inspiration are nearly impossible tasks.

- **Technology.** What kind of technology is being used? Technology refers to things such as shaders and alpha channels, capabilities that seem mundane after a time but at some point in history deeply impressed those who were first introduced to them. New technology poses two general types of problems. The first occurs when new technology *does not* form a part of the project. The second occurs when new technology *does* form a part of the project. In the first situation, risk develops if the game features nothing appealing and represents only a modification of an old game. In the second situation, risk develops if the developers who use the new technology require a great deal of effort and time to perfect their innovations.
- **Creative input.** Is the game creative? No game can succeed if its creative elements lack luster. Three of the main components of any game are its script, its audio tracks, and its graphics. Such elements might seem distant from the immediate concerns of software engineering, but they are not. From the requirements forward, the software engineering effort succeeds only if it comprehensively addresses the needs of all stakeholders. For this reason, attention must be afforded to software developers who are capable of implementing functionality that supports superior dialogue, music, and graphical efforts.
- **Product development duration.** What's the estimated time to market? A key risk characteristic of development schedules involves failure to balance quality, cost, and timeliness. A game that is delivered two months after another company has released a similar game faces diminished chances of success. On the other hand, a game that is released before another and yet possessing serious errors faces as many troubles as one delivered late. And if the development costs exceed the budget that the company has established for the game development effort, executives might decide that the risk of proceeding with the effort exceeds the likelihood that the game will generate the revenues needed to cover its extended development life.

What Promotes Risk Assessment?

This topic concerns the factors that contribute to the ability of an individual, a team, or an organization to understand and respond to risks. If people react fearfully to risk assessment efforts, such efforts might result in more harm than good.

General Attitudes Toward Risk and Risk Management

What happens when people assess the risks that accompany a game development effort? Figure 8.3 provides a summary of some of the general tendencies that promote willingness to engage in risk assessment activities.

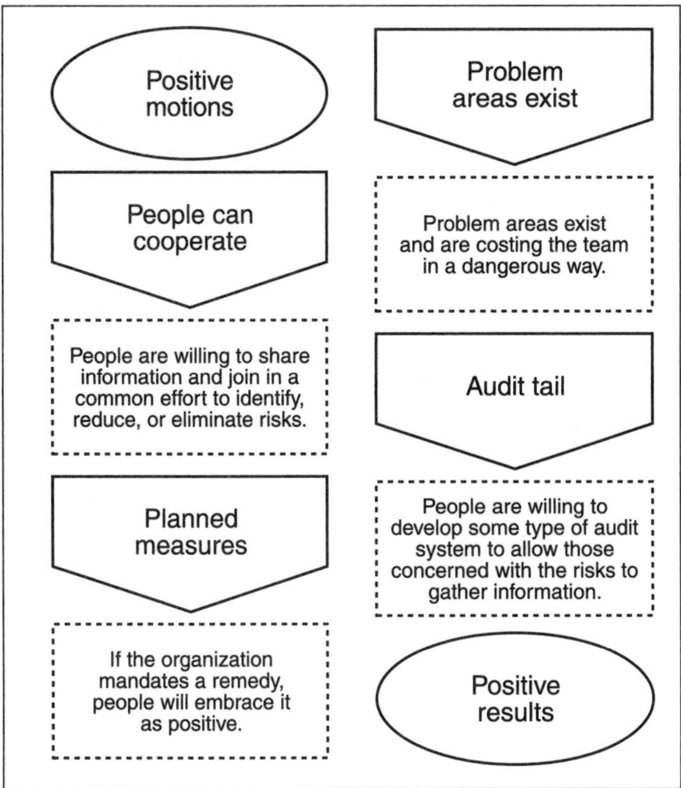

Figure 8.3
If risk assessment meets with positive attitudes on the part of those involved, positive changes result.

Consider that if you accept risk openly, you more willingly take measures to prevent risks from adversely affecting you. On the other hand, if you fear risks because you consider them a challenge to your competence, you either ignore them or try to explain them away. Organizations work the same way. Some development groups behave recklessly, charging into a game development project without thought about what to do if things go wrong. When bad things begin to happen, no one knows how to respond. No one has a contingency plan in place. In the worst of situations, everyone begins blaming everyone else.

Contrast the worst situation with the best. In the best of situations, everyone undertakes the project with enthusiasm, but at the same time, reason prevails. Reason says, among other things, that risks accompany any effort, simple or complex, and that some attention at the start of the project should be given to what to do if things go wrong.

Look again at Figure 8.3. The following list describes some of the ideas:

- **Problem areas.** Whether you work alone or in a group, taking time to discover the problems that characterize your effort remains essential to a productive risk assessment program. Two groups, for example, might begin developing a role-playing game with common themes, the same number of layers, the same world descriptions, and many other common features. The teams might have adequate equipment and expertise. They might be funded sufficiently. And yet one effort might fail whereas the other succeeds. The question to ask focuses on what risk factors one team anticipated and dealt with that the other did not.
- **Receptivity to risk analysis.** Cooperation resides at the root of a group's ability to receive information about risks. If you view information about risks, not as an opportunity to escape danger, but as a criticism, you will tend to turn away from those who openly speak about risk. Some organizations are so pathologically embedded in fragile, unplanned development efforts and games of ego dominion that they cannot stand openness. The same goes for code. People can be afraid of code walkthroughs or reviews and keep their work to themselves. They are this way because they fear criticism. Such fears can lead to major risks, for those who isolate themselves from opportunities to receive information about their work will not have the opportunity to improve it.
- **Auditing.** "Audit" here does not just refer to the kind of formal assessment of performance that might characterize, say, activities that are involved in achieving ISO certification. Instead, audit in this case encompasses self-imposed, self-regulating techniques for acquiring information. Among these are surveys, questionnaires, and reviews. On the other hand, quantitative or formalized information often proves invaluable in identifying risks and deciding how to deal with them, so audit also refers to formalized mechanisms for gathering information. The point here is that if an organization is open to the collection of information, it more likely will be able to negotiate risk factors.
- **Plans for responding to risk.** A risk management plan can be as simple as a suggestion that people avoid walking where water has been spilled. It is strange that people who would issue such warnings easily might also find the notion of implementing a risk management plan threatening. A warning to walk around spilled water can be easily presented in a clear context that leaves no one offended, and procedures can be presented in the same way. Still, written procedures that are issued to a group of programmers for performing different tasks often have the appearance of being punitive. To avoid the danger of this happening, an organization can encourage those who deal with risks to pose their plans in positive language and to reward those who work with the plans through praise or other incentives. If risk management appears to be punitive and remedial, everyone will seek to avoid it.

Things That Foster Awareness

Things that foster awareness of risks come in many forms. Generally, the more that an organization opens itself to communication among its employees, the more ably it deals with risk. Figure 8.4 provides a summary view of some of the group or organization qualities that foster risk awareness.

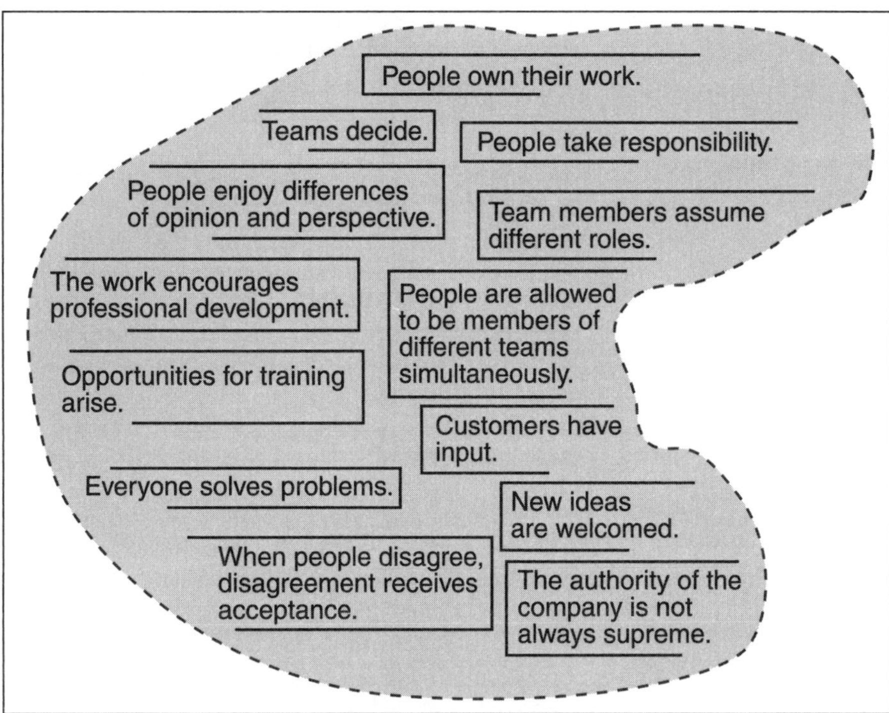
People own their work.
Teams decide.
People take responsibility.
People enjoy differences of opinion and perspective.
Team members assume different roles.
The work encourages professional development.
People are allowed to be members of different teams simultaneously.
Opportunities for training arise.
Customers have input.
Everyone solves problems.
New ideas are welcomed.
When people disagree, disagreement receives acceptance.
The authority of the company is not always supreme.

Figure 8.4
Risk awareness begins with organizational or group awareness.

As Figure 8.4 shows, risk awareness does not begin with suspicion, doubt, distrust, authoritarian security measures, or draconian proceedings that are characteristic of a world supposedly laden with dreadful events. Rather, for software engineering and game development, risk awareness begins with fairly undemanding activities that are open to everyone.

Table 8.1 itemizes some of the key elements of risk awareness. Later, this chapter covers the specific risk management techniques that positive organizational attitudes can foster.

Table 8.1 Risk Awareness

Item	Discussion
People assume responsibility.	Everyone can contribute to the dialogue without necessarily sounding critical.
Team members assume different roles.	If people are not assigned to narrow slots of activity within the group, they are more likely to be aware of how miscommunications might lead to problems.
People own their work.	If people can feel they own their work, they will care more for it.
Teams decide.	If a group of people arrives at an understanding of a risk, it is likely that many facets of the risk will be discussed, and the risk will be known that much better.
People enjoy differences of opinion and perspective.	A consensus does not require conformity. If people disagree on risks and risk-management measures, the differences can still be documented.
The work encourages professional development.	Risk management is not censorship or punishment. If lack of knowledge characterizes a risk, those who lack knowledge deserve to learn.
Opportunities for training arise.	When a team needs training to adjust for a risk, training should be provided.
People are allowed to be members of different teams simultaneously.	Cross-team development tends to be enormously beneficial to both development organizations and individuals within those organizations when it comes to risk assessment. The reason is that risk usually develops in gaps.
Everyone solves problems.	The notion that only a few people are responsible for risk management is extremely hazardous.
If people disagree, disagreement can receive acceptance.	If people express differences of opinion, they tend to try to explore the issues in greater detail to findstrengths and weakness. If such explorations occur in game development contexts, the results are likely to be beneficial, even if consensus is not reached.
Customers have input.	Customers vary from people who play games to artists who want their products represented in the best possible way.
The authority of the company is not always supreme.	This one is a bit tricky. The point here is that when risk analysis takes place, if everyone thinks about the situation in authoritarian terms, it is likely that the first response will be one of trying to escape blame. When information that reduces risk is the goal, no one should feel threatened.
New ideas are welcomed.	Stagnation poses a major risk to any organization that is trying to anticipate risk.

Goals

Even though a set of standard risks can be obtained from any of a dozen good texts on software engineering, the risks that a group or organization discovers depend on the goals it sets for itself. The goals have to do with the business and technical objectives that characterize the culture of the organization. Establishing a common set of goals that all game development groups could adopt is an almost impossible task. Still, here are a few ideas:

- **Reduce lost productivity.** Such a goal is not necessarily one of increasing productivity. Rather, its focus is on reducing waste. Things like rework, sloppy documentation, poor class design, bad use of libraries, and other such things can cause an enormous amount of lost productivity. Lost productivity means that developers have less time to use toward refining and perfecting the selling features of the game.
- **Increase productivity.** Such a goal contrasts with that of decreasing lost productivity, because it addresses the idea of finding cheaper, quicker, and better ways to create a game. Granted, the first implication might be that what results from this is some sort of sordid game factory, but this is not the intent. Rather, just consider the numerous games that fail to get to market. It could be that those who are working on the product are not productive enough to meet the deadlines that the publisher has set for the game.
- **Increase opportunities for aesthetic expression.** This goal implies that when you develop an engine, you make it flexible and extensible and that your efforts toward risk assessment allow you to increase the opportunities that the development project offers those who are trying to introduce innovative art into a game effort.
- **Increase opportunities for technical innovation.** This goal implies that you do not lock yourself into modification of existing game engines but trust your development capabilities enough to try things that are fairly risky. If you know how to manage and control risk, you are in a better position to undertake the type of risk that innovation mandates.
- **Create a safer environment for experimentation.** This goal involves several things. Experimentation cannot occur in an environment that is so beset by unanticipated problems that no one has time to do anything except fight fires. Risk assessment enables developers to understand how much leeway a schedule involves and to gauge whether creativity will lead to a cool new feature or a disruption in the schedule.
- **Reduce the number of errors the game has when it ships.** Risk assessment involves investigating the approaches used to obtain requirements and create designs. Introduce flexibility into the design stage so that iterative design efforts allow adjustments to be made as the development effort goes forward. (This approach also is advocated by the Agile philosophy of software development.)

- **Increase the quality of the product.** Yes, this is a platitude, but it is a good one. Any new feature is a risk, even if it is technically sound. Why this is so involves asking about how a new feature affects the entirety of the game as played. At the same time, quality stems from a multitude of factors that can be dealt with as anticipated risks. Risk assessment involves trying to think of unexpected events that might occur when new features are added.
- **Add to the quality of the development experience.** Risk assessment can make a development effort much easier than it would be otherwise. If people express dissatisfaction with game development work, something really must be wrong. However, if development involves what appears to be uncontrolled chaos, it becomes understandable that expressions of dissatisfaction might, after all, be heard periodically.

This list is far from complete, but the message should still emerge. Unless risk management or risk assessment takes place in a positive context, the danger arises that the undertaking has no goal beyond that of correction. Risk assessment involves more than correction.

Strategies

In addition to setting goals, groups or organizations that engage in risk assessment must arrive at a suitable set of strategies. Because the strategies that emerge depend on the culture of the group or organization, it's not possible to provide a comprehensive list. The list that follows can serve as a starting point, though. It arises from the general notion that most groups or organizations have a fairly common set of risk-assessment tools.

- **Culture and awareness.** The first strategic measure involves attending to the culture of the group or organization. Refer to Table 8.1, where risk awareness is discussed.
- **Responsibilities.** Responsibilities in this context respect those to whom risk assessment tasks are assigned. Generally, regardless of how much a group encourages everyone to be on the lookout for risks, some individual or group of individuals must undertake to formalize and store information about risks and to host meetings and reviews in which strategies can be evolved for addressing risks.
- **Standard ways of talking about risk.** As strange as it might sound, when people do not have a way to talk about risk assessment, the talk can become soured easily. Risk assessment and complaining are different. The difference is that risk assessment involves informed discussion toward definitive ends. Likewise, risk assessment provides a set of tools that people can use to collect information and create remedies.
- **Standards.** Chapter 6, "Object-Oriented Fantasies and Realities," discusses notions of organizational maturity. Standards can provide models for collecting, assessing, and formulating response to risk. Among the examples that might be set forward in this respect are those pertaining to how risk analysts develop questionnaires, conduct reviews, or write reports.

- **Roles.** The SWEBOK provides a category of expertise that corresponds to risk management. Within an organizational framework, risk management can be a highly specialized undertaking. The individual who is involved in such work is a risk management expert, someone with refined skills regarding all phases of risk management.
- **Best practices.** Best practices enable individuals to chart a course of life-long development. One of the chief reasons for staying informed about industry happenings is that technical publications and technical conferences provide ready avenues for information about what works best among communities of software engineers. Risk assessment involves continuously examining current practices to discover how they might be less risky. Risk is reduced when practices that have been evaluated for risk can be tried across a community of practitioners.

The Paradigm

The remaining sections of this chapter concentrate on describing and showing different aspects of a paradigm that represents any of a number of techniques and philosophies of risk management. Putting this flow of activities to work in your own group or organization requires that you shape it to accord with the culture of your organization, because each organizational setting is bound to be unique. Figure 8.5 represents the larger features of the risk management paradigm advocated in this chapter. A classical presentation of this model appears in Robert N. Charette, *Software Engineering Risk Analysis and Management* (New York: Intertext Publications, 1989).

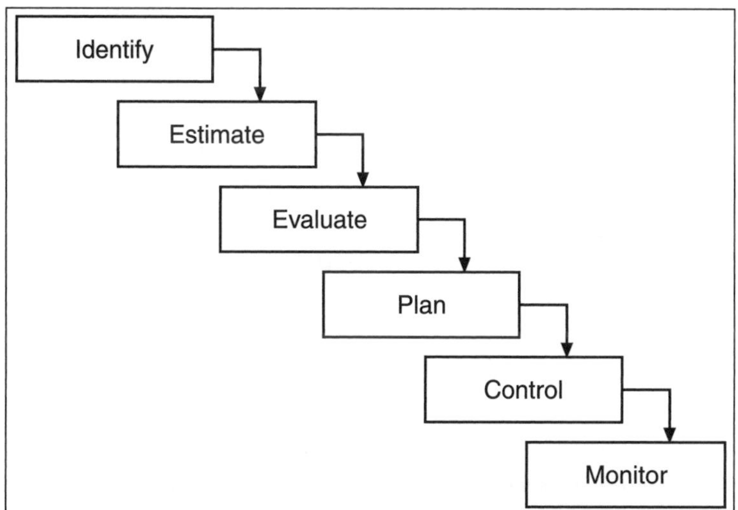

Figure 8.5
General approaches to risk assessment extend across the development lifecycle from gathering information to testing remedies.

Identifying Risks

Risk has to do with chance. Chance plays a part in the development project because no one possesses complete knowledge of all the factors involved in the development project. In other words, uncertainty characterizes the undertaking, and it arises in several ways. Consider the following conditions:

- **No information.** This type of uncertainty is called *descriptive* or *structural* uncertainty. It occurs in several ways. For example, when a project starts, little data exists by which to judge whether anything is going forward according to schedule. In another situation, no data about a given type of project might exist. Consider, in this light, a setting in which you join a team that has developed many games for single players but has now decided to create a massively multiplayer game.
- **Limitations of measurements.** In some situations, any type of quantifiable or even clearly descriptive information about the undertaking proves difficult to find. Problems arise because what you are trying to measure tends to be extremely difficult to reduce to a fixed, measurable form. This type of uncertainty is called *measurement uncertainty*. An example of this type of uncertainty might be whether a game will appeal to its players. How do you measure whether someone will find a game pleasurable to play?
- **Unknown results.** This type of uncertainty can be called *event uncertainty*, and it arises because no one knows the result of a given combination of factors. This type of uncertainty occurs when those who are responsible for risk assessment either cannot or do not sufficiently analyze the source material and do not, therefore, arrive at information that allows anyone to comprehend adequately the scope or severity of consequences. Consider a situation in which you are immersed in a development effort that is on schedule but suddenly discover some trendy feature you feel must be added to a game. Suppose that you proceed without first stopping to establish clear requirements, create a design, or produce a development schedule. You proceed with development. The situation is laden with uncertainty, because you do not know what you are looking for and you do not know what you will find. The result that emerges is little more than accident.

Given this beginning, it is possible to offer a few generalizations about how to begin identifying risks. Risk occurs in situations in which you have no model from which to derive a sense of what works. Risk also occurs when you do not possess a medium by which to estimate or track progress. Finally, risk occurs when you do not properly establish boundaries for what you are trying to accomplish. Three terms sometimes used to summarize these areas of risk are *scope*, *resources*, and *schedule*. These and other central ideas are covered in the passages that follow.

Scope Risk Identification

Most of the technical details of game development fall under scope. Among the things considered are programming languages, graphics, functionality sought, platforms addressed, errors, configuration management issues, requirements and design, testing, component integration, system integration, and installation, to name a few of the more visible. In each of these areas, risk occurs for a multitude of reasons, but the following sections address those that might be considered most common.

Scope Creep

Scope creep, more commonly known as *feature creep*, occurs when requirements fail to constrain the development effort. If requirements change, risk arises, because the development project might suddenly encompass much greater functionality, and increased functionality requires more testing, results in more problems with integration, and might impact every component of the system.

Scope creep arises in various ways. One of the more common ways emerges when programmers randomly decide to add what they consider to be interesting features to the game. The requirements for the game do not call for these added features. The features might be discovered by chance. Adding them requires time and creates the need for additional testing. At the same time, while additional, unspecified features become visible, other features, clearly specified, remain undeveloped.

Another common source of creep arises when developers decide to incorporate an external body of code. Consider, for example, a set of sound components. Ostensibly, it looks as though the components will save an immense amount of development time. They appeal to everyone because they seem to enhance the appeal of the game enormously. But then when the sound components are imported, the work of making them compatible with the main components of the games can prove extraordinarily costly.

A third form of creep occurs when developers, rather than turning to an established library, decide to implement algorithms on their own. A task that is budgeted to involve a fairly brief development effort ends up requiring a large expenditure of time and results in a poorly tested body of custom code. Given this beginning, consider the following items and how they characterize possible occasions of scope creep:

- No one has produced a clear and bounded set of requirements.
- No one has consulted records of past projects to find out how long a task will require to perform.
- No one has performed an estimation of how long the task will require.
- Something has been designated as part of the effort, but no one has checked to see whether it or anything like it has been done before.

- An all-or-nothing solution has been chosen without first testing, in isolation, whether at least a few of the features of the solution offer feasible, effective contributions to the project.
- A large body of code is being folded into the project because a few of its capabilities are beneficial.

In each of these instances, the project grows in scope because either the features or the effort involved in the creation of the features grows as the project is underway. Scope creep removes the possibility that the developers can stabilize the project and test it for completion. It is one of the leading causes of project failure.

Scope Gaps

Gaps reveal that the development team has not given enough attention to the scope of the project. When developers create a scope description and formalize it through a set of requirements, they create risks if they neglect to use tools like use cases to investigate the meaning of the requirements. Further, if the developers do not pursue some type of design effort, they tend to begin work before they have a solid sense of how they are to implement the functionality of the system.

The approach used on *Ankh* proved reliable. (See Chapter 9, "Iterating Design.") This approach involved working in stripes. Each stripe consisted of a collection of functionality that could be implemented as a single logical and physical component. The work on each stripe began with a use case representing a typical and unified set of behavior for the stripe. The obligation was to create a design based on the use case. The design information provided the following artifacts:

- A class diagram for the stripe that includes all classes that contribute objects to the stripe.
- Collaboration and sequence diagrams that trace the messaging involved in the scenario that the use case presents.
- A representation of the stripe in the context of other stripes (or components).

Given this preliminary activity, development on the stripe could proceed. At the same time, the stripe design effort provided the opportunity to review and revise the design prior to beginning the coding. In every instance, some revision was possible, and one of the common results was the discovery of a gap. On the other hand, when this type of requirements-and-design verification activity was not completed, it was usually necessary to rework the stripe. This was particularly the case with the second stripe, when nearly four development weeks were lost. Consider the following items and how they characterize possible occasions of gap creep:

- Development begins without a strong effort to analyze and verify the requirements.

- Features creep into the product, and gaps arise because no thorough investigation has been conducted to determine what is needed to make the planned and unplanned features compatible and complementary.
- Development begins before an effort has been made to design the product.
- Development begins without a design, and an attempt is made after the fact to bring what amounts to an accidental product into compliance with a design.

Scope Dependencies

Scope dependencies include both external and internal factors. An example of an external factor is a library that you purchase from a vendor and decide to use in selective but indispensable parts of your game. Any number of dependencies might exist. You might plan, for instance, that the library will support seven important features. You are progressing nicely, with nearly half of the project completed, when you discover that you can accomplish your goals in only four of the seven targeted instances. The dependencies are then factors in the completion of the game.

Internal dependencies reduce to segments of functionality that must be implemented if others are to be implemented. For *Ankh*, a dependency for the development of levels was the map editor. Without a map editor, there could be no levels. This was so because characters, buildings, and other features were introduced to each level only through the editor. Without the editor, features could not be assigned. The risk that this approach to the game involved was significant, but this risk was mitigated by introducing it early in the project.

Given this beginning, consider the following items and how they characterize possible occasions of dependency creep:

- No one has performed a sanity check on each type of functionality that a library intended for use supposedly provides.
- Parts of the game that will impact many other parts of the game are not scheduled for early development.
- You have decided to use a library, device, or tool that developers anticipate finishing at a certain point during the project.
- Certain components tend to have an enormous number of features, whereas others have very few. In other words, design considerations have not given enough attention to the distribution of risk.
- You have decided that, because something is difficult to figure out, you should wait until late in the project to figure it out. By then, you reason, you will know enough to resolve it.

- You have not considered alternate courses of action for deliverables that lie on the critical path. If one solution does not work, no one has given consideration to whether it is possible to substitute another, less complex solution.

The tasks that are involved in identifying risks to your game development schedule might seem to be the sole responsibility of the project manager, but this is not so. Creation of the schedule often involves contributions from every member of the development team. In many instances, project managers call upon members of the team to provide estimations of the time required to create required functionality. Unless each team member reliably estimates the time required to perform tasks, the project manager cannot formulate a realistic project schedule. Risks other than those entailing estimation also apply to the game development schedule. Among these are the risks that delays and dependencies pose.

Schedule Risks Identification

Estimating how long the performance of a given task will take can become an element of risk if you consider the implications of the profile of risk presented earlier (lack of historic data, means of measurement, and definition of result). Developers often fail to recognize that estimating *how long* something will take to complete involves folding together at least three bits of information, as follows:

- **Effort.** Effort is the raw amount of time you think you will require to complete a task. In the world of effort, the phone never rings, no one ever takes a long lunch, no meetings require your attendance, and snow, rain, or wind never prevent you from putting in a day's work.
- **Duration.** Duration enters when you consider that the phone, after all, does ring, and that all the other things named in the first bullet do enter the picture. Maybe you think of the workday as an eight-hour adventure behind company doors, but in fact, the time available to you to work a programming task is much less than that. If you decide, for example, that the task is a forty-hour effort, you might find that that two weeks, not one, are required to complete it. The duration of the task extends over the total number of days required to expend the effort.
- **Calendar.** Even if you carefully determine the total amount of time you must dedicate each day to meetings, the water cooler, and talk on the telephone, other factors still intervene. One is that you might not be able to work because management has scheduled the team for training, you are not allowed to work weekends, or your vacation has arrived. The duration of a task receives definition through its insertion into a calendar that you and the organization establish as the fundamental context for task completion. Table 8.1 provides a few specific items that commonly enter into estimations.

Table 8.1 Common Estimation Risks

Item	Description
Day	Consider that your workday might allow you a relatively brief time for concerted effort.
Learning curve	Every new task poses the prospect that you will have to acquire new information before you can complete the task.
Tracking	You will probably have to spend time preparing reports on your activities. Tracking your progress is an accompaniment to primary development activity.
Testing	After you complete a task, you might have to incorporate its results into a larger project. Integration and testing time might be required.
Reviews	Scheduling time to meet with others for things like reviews might occasion the need for additional hours.
Complexity	Not every task is equal. If you implement a simple sort routine, you are done in a fraction of a day. If you decide to use a sophisticated sort routine, several days might elapse before you are done.
Requirements	When you are given a task, do you take time to understand precisely what it is that you are supposed to deliver? It might be that understanding the task will require much longer than what it takes to read a requirements document.
Others	If you are working with someone else, have you gauged how much more or less productive the other person might be? Also, consider the number of people you must communicate with.

Resource Risk Identification

Resources pertain to funding, developers hired for the primary development team, and developers hired on contract. The risks that are involved in each of these areas can overshadow all others. That lack of funding might dwarf all other concerns is probably fairly conspicuous, but consider the risks involved in heavy project turnover or faulty contracted services.

Cost

Cost has two sides. On the one hand, cost has to do with securing funding. Securing funding involves a vast collection of activities associated with sales and marketing. As a software engineer, this is not your line of work. On the other hand, as a software engineer, attending to whether your work contributes to excessive cost *is* your line of work. Following are areas of risk relating to cost:

- **Already done.** This involves failure to ask whether a library or other resource is available and does not need to be created.
- **Not yet proven feasible.** This is failure to establish that a given type of functionality has been implemented and will have to be proven to be feasible as the project progresses. Implementation of untried technology is bound to increase the cost of the product.

- **Inadequate support.** This is failure to determine whether you have the support you need before you commit to completing a task.
- **Wishful thinking.** Risk lies with thinking that if a solution does not exist to a given problem, the team will find the solution by the time the problem becomes an issue in the project. For example, assume that you want to do something amazing with a feature effect. No one yet knows how to do it, but you begin with the assumption that because the need for the effect is a month or two off, someone will have figured out by that point in time how to do it. If you set this feature as a central selling point of the game, you might enormously increase the cost of the development effort if you end up having to extend the development effort by weeks or months while developers try to create what has not been created before.

Developers Hired Full Time

The biggest risk relating to developers hired for a project is whether they will leave before the project is completed. People quit for a variety of reasons. At other times, people are fired. Both forms of turnover are costly. Other problems relate to competence. Some people seem to possess skills, but when they're called upon to perform, they can't. Given this start, here are a few ways to itemize risk associated with resources:

- **Emotions.** Find out during the interview process whether someone is going through some type of emotional passage that might lead him to leave the project early.
- **Professional concerns.** If an individual is overly qualified for the position you are putting him in, he is likely to leave unless you provide him with greater responsibility.
- **Team incompatibility.** Have multiple members of the team interview the prospective member to determine whether his personality is compatible with the team.
- **Technical fit.** Inspect or in some other way evaluate the work that an individual has performed to determine whether it reveals a level of sophistication and competence that is suitable for the current undertaking.

But even with these observations, a competent developer still requires some time to learn what a project is about. Learning about a project can require anywhere from a few days to several weeks, depending on the complexity and scope of the software and the people involved. Games tend to fall into general categories, such as tactical and role-playing, and an experienced developer usually requires little time to understand the general layout of such games. Likewise, at this point in the industry's history, it is unlikely that more than 15 percent of the overall functionality of any given game is going to represent technology that is in any way new.

Even if most experienced developers know most of what goes into the engineering of a game, each game offers specific implementations that differ from every other game. If the lead developer asks a developer who is new to the project to fix an error in the code that creates special effects, the new developer might require several days to complete the task, not because he lacks competence, but because, for instance, someone who was responsible for the code previously optimized it and then did not properly comment the optimization. Such concerns lead to a second set of risk categories:

- **Software engineering disposition.** This is failure to establish that people who join the team can produce work that others must be able to maintain.
- **Disposition toward design and requirements.** This is failure to establish that people who join the team can work according to a set of requirements and within the context that a design provides.
- **Scheduled work.** This is failure to establish that the people who join the team can estimate the time required to perform work and can work according to a schedule.
- **Ability to follow up.** This is failure to establish that the people who join the team can look professionally upon the work that others have done. For example, they will not set about trying to fix everything needlessly that they themselves have not done.

Contracts

A final category of risk identification in relation to resources concerns contracts. Contracts involve both people and products. If your game development effort requires something that you cannot do yourself, you might hire a contractor. An example of this might be the acquisition of high-end audio products. The cost of setting up a sound studio can be enormous, because it requires the physical modification of a building so that a room is insulated from outside sounds. To avoid such costs, you can contract companies or individuals who possess such facilities.

As wise as seeking contractors for specific products and services might be, certain problems might still arise. Here are a few:

- **Vague requirements.** You do not clearly state what it is that you want. If your game requires realistic whale sounds, you probably expect legally acquired and edited sounds taken from recordings of whales. It the sounds turn out to be human imitations of whales, you have not received what you requested, regardless of how clever the fabrication might be.
- **No contract.** You do not establish, in writing, what you expect and when you expect it.

- **No background research.** You do not ask for samples of products and services and use these to establish that the contractor provides the type of product you are looking for. Consider, for example, what would happen if the contractor delivers files of the wrong format and explains when challenged that you did not specify the format.
- **No standards.** You fail to examine whether the contracting organization subscribes to an established set of quality assurance standards, such as those that the ISO and the SEI provide.
- **All in one basket.** You do not distribute risk so that alternatives are available if a contractor fails. If you are going to turn everything over to a given individual, that person should have a solidly established record with your organization.

Estimating Risk

You estimate risks to determine how much damage they might do to your project or product. During the investigative phase of risk analysis, you usually arrive at several ways that you can determine how to estimate the extent to which a risk can affect your project. You can now formalize this measurement and begin establishing which risks pose the greatest threats according to the criteria you have developed.

Scope Risk Estimation

You can estimate scope risk by rating risks according to how much they might impact a project. In this light, you can examine scope issues in terms of whether the risks evaluated impact the critical path. The items that go into the critical path of a game development effort involve the essential features of a game.

At this point in time, for example, it is almost impossible to envision a game that does not offer the following features:

- Audio
- 3D animation
- Free of fatal errors
- Scoring capabilities
- Map/character customization capabilities

This list represents nothing more than a beginning, but it still supports the central notion that some features of a game cannot be dropped. Would it be worthwhile, for instance, to deliver a game that has no sound? Who would buy it?

Risk estimation requires that you rank the risks you identify. For example, assume that you cannot negotiate the audio capability. Sound, then, lies in the critical path. But then assume that the requirements state that the sound encompasses both a default sound capability and customized sound capabilities. You can implement the default soundtrack with little risk because you already have at hand a sound library that can fulfill your needs. On the other hand, assume that the requirement is extended so that it states that the sound capability shall accommodate MP3 and several other formats, and that the game player shall be able to configure a jukebox that plays different combinations of selections for each level depending on the health status. You can break this down a bit and in the process set up a basic ranking of risks associated with the audio capabilities of the game:

- **Low risk.** Basic sound with music that your organization owns. Uses standard components from the audio component library developed for a previous game.
- **Medium risk.** Ability to play music using several formats. No customization of the play sequence through selection. The player simply plays his own soundtrack. The functionality is available through a plug-in that can be licensed for minimal cost.
- **High risk.** Customized track-selection and select-to-scene capabilities. Complete customization of sound selection and occasion of play. This entails tracking each level and scene of play in conjunction with storing and selecting from a library of user-loaded soundtracks. It involves combining plug-in modules and customized code.

Estimating risk does not involve trying to solve the problem. Instead, it involves trying to establish different views of the risks that the problem poses.

Schedule Risk Estimation

As an example of an issue that frequently arises in schedule estimation, consider software errors (also known as *bugs* or *defects*). Errors pose a risk to your game because you cannot deliver your game to your customers if it possesses an unacceptable number of errors. If your game crashes frequently, you might end up with legal liabilities from a consumer group, and even if this does not eventuate, it is almost certainly the case that game reviewers will prove unmerciful in their condemnation of the game.

The point in the life of the game development effort at which a risk arises affects how much the risk impacts the cost and schedule of the game development effort. You increase your chances of success if you take this into consideration. An example of how this works arises when you consider the cost of a software error. The longer that a software error requires to fix, the more fixing the error costs. For example, an error that is detected after the product has been delivered usually involves a cost *at least seven times* greater than the cost of an error that is detected during the early stages of the development effort. Figure 8.6 depicts this situation.

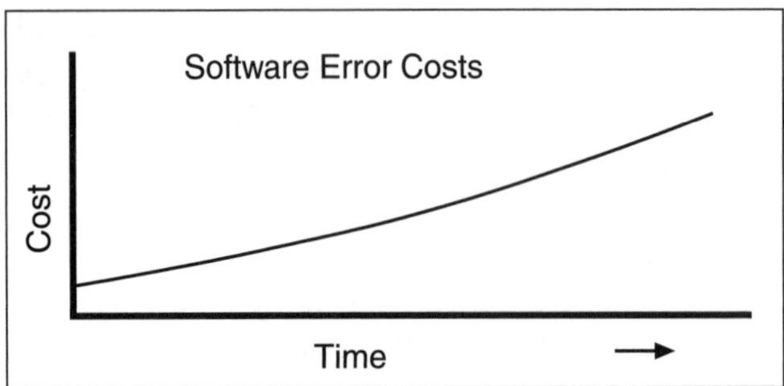

Figure 8.6
Software error costs increase over the life of the software project.

An assessment of the costs of software errors shows that anticipating the cost of fixing errors can be one of the most significant factors in the risk profile of any software product. As Figure 8.7 illustrates, if the number of errors detected in a software product remains constant over time, the effect is that cost increases even as revenues from the product increase. Ultimately, errors either eat up profits or make the product so costly to maintain that it must be taken off the market. This is especially the case after the release of the product, when the cost of defects skyrockets.

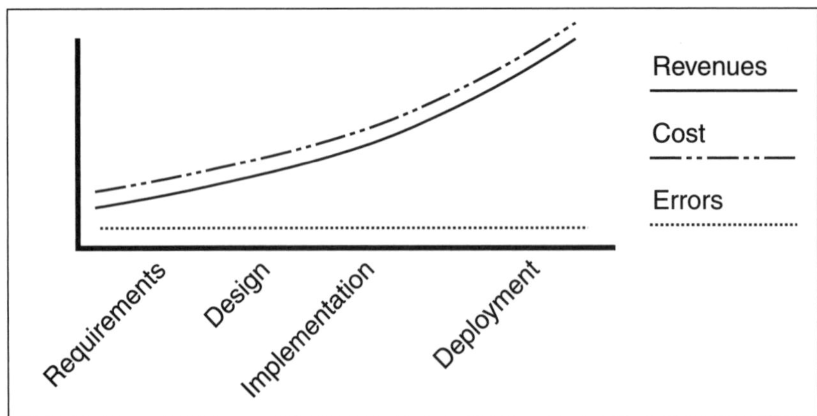

Figure 8.7
Increasing error counts with increasing time presents high risk.

Given this scheme, then, it becomes possible to create a ranking of possible defects based on when they are likely to occur during the development process. Certain errors are likely to occur during the requirements phase. Others are likely to occur during design and implementation. Still others arise at deployment time. It's possible to draw from this discussion the following tentative generalizations:

- **Highest risk.** During the requirements phase, risks are associated with poor requirement definition. Lack of good requirements accounts for up to 80 percent of failed products.
- **High risk.** During the design phase, risks are associated with poor product design. Lack of good design might lead to poor product performance, but development efforts that fail due to lack of poor design number far fewer than those that are characterized by poor requirements and scope statements.
- **Medium risk.** During the implementation phase, risks tend to be associated with scope creep and goldplating. Other risks include poor documentation of code, cutting and pasting, and early optimization.
- **Low risk.** During the deployment phase, risks are associated with final builds of the installation package. Failure to package the product conveniently for installation will occasion rework, but this rework should involve only the installation program.
- **Distributed risk.** Testing takes place in all phases. It's mentioned here as an indication of how a single form of neglect can affect risk in a major way. Testing is the primary way that risk can be assessed during the development process, so neglecting to develop a test plan that covers each point of the requirements invites risk.

Resource Risk Estimation

Estimating risks that are associated with people might seem arbitrary, but every day, project managers who are staffing up for a project try to use solid criteria for judging whether they want to hire a given individual. Here are a few approaches to establishing risk categories for people you want to work with:

- **Team health poses the highest risk.** If the people who make up a development team cannot work together, the game will not happen. Even the presence on the team of an extraordinarily capable individual does not guarantee its success.
- **Individual compatibility poses high risk.** If you cannot establish that an extremely capable candidate programmer has stayed with a project to the end, you should perhaps ask a few more questions.
- **Technical capability poses high risk.** If an individual possesses no technical competence, then regardless of his commitment to the game development effort, he is not likely to contribute much to the success of the effort.
- **Individual emotional stability poses medium risk.** An individual who has superior technical capabilities might become embroiled in emotional difficulties that make it difficult for him to cooperate with others. The factors here are multitudinous.

- **Professional competence poses lower or medium risk.** A degree or the fact that someone has held a job before do not ensure that a software engineer possesses the ability to work competently with a team. Around 40 percent of the people who are currently working in the software industry lack degrees in computer science or software engineering. Likewise, candidates who have extensive resumes might lack evidence of even a single completed project. The point is not that records of degrees or experience prove poor indicators of abilities; rather, generalizations pose risks.

Evaluating Risk

When you evaluate a risk, you determine the general characteristics of your response. Determining a response involves investigating what happens if a risk becomes a reality. In other words, to evaluate a risk, you determine the courses of action you will consider in the event that a problem arises. Again, as with risk estimation, you can rank risk responses. Whether a given risk response scenario fits a given risk depends on a number of factors. One of the chief considerations in this respect is the stage of the development effort during which the problem arises. As mentioned earlier, dealing with risk usually involves considering three general courses of action, and these courses of action present a generalized approach to ordering risk responses:

- **What measures can you take to eliminate the risk?** This is the most preferable avenue. If you can discover a risk response that eliminates a risk, it should be ranked highest. This is the common sense of the issue. On the other hand, preventive measures can sometimes become risks themselves. After all, if you fall into the habit of eliminating anything that is at all risky, it is likely that your game will be completely without interest to game reviewers and prospective buyers.
- **What measures can you take to reduce the risk?** This is the second most preferable approach to risk response. If risk is a part of life, anticipating the risk to the point of knowing what to do when it occurs can do much to reduce the overall damage.
- **What measures can you take to contain the damage after it has occurred?** This is the worst alternative. Here, you assume that the problem occurs. Now you must accept the penalty and simply try to recover.

Evaluating Risks That Are Associated with Scope

The best approach to reducing the risks that are associated with scope is to detect errors early in a game development project. Risk assessment with an emphasis on risk prevention focuses on trying to find ways to put in place proper testing and quality assurance measures as soon as possible. Some development methodologies emphasize creating a test strategy before programmers write code. The Agile approach advocates this practice, as does extreme programming. These approaches possess virtue because they fully incorporate the notion that if you think through a test scenario before you begin programming, your coding effort will begin as a kind of defensive, informed effort and will tend to be more proactive than reactive.

In addition to early testing, requirements analysis has proven effective as a way of reducing the scope of risk. A solid majority of software projects that fail can be traced back to inadequate requirements or requirements to which the development team did not adhere. Poorly developed requirements might force the development team to rework substantial portions of the code. Because testing and the creation of reliable requirements make a significant difference in the cost of the development project, putting in place people who possess these skills early in the development effort proves to be a significant risk-reduction measure.

Evaluating Schedule Risks

You can evaluate risks that are associated with schedules fairly easily if you consider that most errors originate with an incongruity between the task and how the developer estimates it. Among the many approaches used for estimating tasks are the following:

- **Breaking the work down into small units.** This approach involves exploring a task until you find its constituent parts. Generally, the smaller the unit of work estimated, the more accurate the estimate.
- **Delving into historical data to discover how much time completion of the last such task required.** You can examine old project schedules, documentation, logs, or any other record of work to obtain historical data that might help you to estimate the duration of the task before you.
- **Turning to a group.** One example of this is called the Delphi approach. The Delphi approach is a fairly involved process that requires, among other things, obtaining information from a group of experts. Your goal is to establish minimum and maximum estimations of damage and scope that you can use to tune your assumptions about risk.
- **Using a model.** Models abound, and of the most popular is the PERT chart. Dozens of estimation models have been derived from the PERT chart. Using this approach, you assess risk in terms of dependencies. Because a PERT representation of a task reveals simultaneous and sequential actions, it allows you to study different profiles of risk. Figure 8.8 illustrates how a PERT chart can track a series of actions that together comprise a task. Note that the chart forces you to see that it might be possible to drop some activity if a bind develops. To do this, however, you must determine the critical path of the task. In other words, you determine the features you must implement to complete the task.

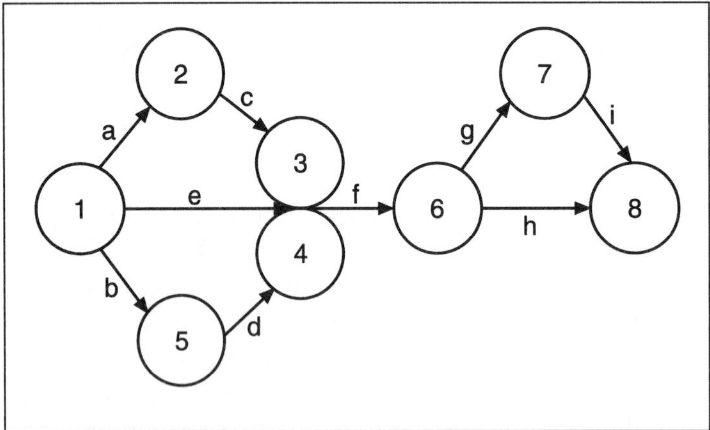

Figure 8.8
Closely analyzed, estimations using tools like a PERT chart allow you to see which features can be dropped in the event of a time crunch.

Evaluating Resource Risks

Evaluating risks that are associated with resources can focus on how people are recruited for a development effort and what measures you can take during the development effort to ensure that everyone on the team communicates effectively.

As an example of how to approach finding the right team members and then finding the right fit for them, consider the following scenarios:

- **Prevention.** During the interview, you ask the prospective candidate to write a program that accomplishes a given task. If the program appears to be written fairly competently, you have clear evidence that the programmer possesses the technical competence needed for the project.
- **Reduction.** You cannot find people who possess the level of expertise you want, but you do find several who seem to be marginally acceptable. You can assign such people to roles that are supervised by a technical lead and develop functionality that does not lie on the game's critical path.
- **Control.** Despite a technical assessment at interview time and being assigned to a role under a lead, someone is still not performing well. Damage control might involve seeking some type of remedial training or terminating the individual as soon as possible. As painful as it is to see someone fired, carrying the weight of someone who accomplishes no productive work can bring the project to a halt.

Planning for Risks

When you plan for risks, you take into consideration the strategic goals you want to establish for your development effort. Strategy is like a battle plan that a general formulates. The strategy establishes the general philosophy of risks. In software engineering circles, the equivalent of the battle plan is the risk control plan. The work of creating a control plan is sometimes called *risk management.*

Figure 8.9 provides a generalized template for a risk management plan.

- Introduction
  - Scope and Purpose
  - Overview
    - Objectives
    - Aversion Policies
  - Organization
    - Management
    - Responsibilities
    - Job Descriptions
  - Aversion Program Description
    - Schedule
    - Major Milestones
    - Budget
- Risk Analysis
  - Identification
    - Survey of Risks
    - Sources of Risks
    - Risk Breakdown
  - Risk Estimation
    - Probability of Risk
    - Consequences of Risk
    - Criteria for Estimation
    - Sources of Estimation Error
  - Evaluation
    - Methods to Use
    - Assumptions and Limitations
    - Risk References
    - Evaluation Results
  - Risk Management
    - Recommendations on Results
    - Aversion Options
    - Aversion Recommendations
    - Control Processes

Figure 8.9
A plan for risk management helps limit the risk management effort to those areas of risk that are most pressing.

Planning and Scope

One of the most common strategies used for scope management involves the creation of a scope statement early in the project, in addition to a set or requirements. A statement of scope establishes the limits of the functionality that the development effort will seek to implement. The statement of scope can serve to establish the product constraints.

Using a scope statement implies that the risk management strategies center on risk prevention and reduction. In contrast to this might be an approach that incorporates a weaker scope statement and a sketchy set of requirements but imposes a stringent demand for continuous employment of use cases to reduce the risk of activities that occur during the development effort. This approach affords much greater freedom to the developers but also assumes that the developers possess a high level of professionalism.

An approach that strategically centers on risk control might advocate negotiating for the most remote possible date of delivery. If you make the assumption, for example, that creativity is more important than anything else, then you need to budget for many delays and rework sessions. You must anticipate unanticipated features and the rework they occasion. The strategy, then, is to accept the rework that creativity might involve. Such a plan is most characteristic of settings that involve research and development efforts.

Planning and Scheduling

Managing schedule risks involves establishing a project plan. But beyond that, you must use the project plan according to a given strategy. Examples of different approaches are as follows:

- If the development effort falls behind schedule, features will be cut.
- If the development effort falls behind schedule, no features will be cut, but measures will be taken to reduce the depth of given features. For instance, all features must conform to those that were already developed in previous efforts.
- If the development effort falls behind schedule and the schedule reveals that, despite reduction of features by 20 percent, the game still will be delivered late, the development effort will be cancelled.

Strategy also calls for general measures that involve shifting risks to different areas of the schedule. Here are a few approaches:

- The team will try to do a first pass of the game as quickly as possible so that it can provide a demonstration session to the investment group. To accomplish this, testing will be deferred. It is more important at this stage to secure funding than it is to produce a product of the highest quality.
- The team will move forward only with highly stable components. It will begin with solid requirements and develop functionality that is robust and componential. The team will not perform rework as it proceeds.

- The team will use a mixed approach based on a triage of the system components. A good basic engine is already in place. The components that the team brings forward will not be tested. Testing will take place only for the components that are developed anew. The team also will perform thorough integration testing.

Planning and Resources

Planning how to manage people who are committed to a development effort usually begins with implicit assumptions. For example, you usually accept a job developing a game with the assumption that you are going to be able to work on the game until it is ready for delivery. This is a safe enough assumption, but planning for resource risks also involves anticipating variations in theme. Consider the following scenarios:

- It is important to find incompatibilities among team members as early as possible. Anyone who is not technically competent or shows an inability to work with others will be removed from the project as soon as possible. Because it's necessary to move in a fairly decisive manner, the team will try to find people who will work on a contract basis to alleviate legal liabilities in the management approach.
- Competence and compatibility issues will be discerned as early in the process as possible so that additional training or team-building sessions can be implemented quickly. This approach focuses on building a team that can be together for a long while and working with people on a fairly extensive basis.
- The schedule is the most important factor. It doesn't matter whether personality conflicts are decreasing the efficiency of the team, but only whether the deliverables are being presented according to schedule. Resolving differences isn't crucial, but enforcing a schedule is.

Controlling Risks

When you control risks, you follow procedures that you establish in your management plan. Following the procedures involves using the criteria and options that your plan presents you to follow through on risk situations. If you have established strict response measures, you will have set criteria along the lines shown in Table 8.3.

Table 8.3 Control Measures

Risk	Response
Sound components exceed budget by 20 percent	Revert to old sound library. Put aside new work.
Delay of mesh components	Shift effort to tuning AI.
Excess of 15 errors per unit of code	Halt new feature implementation and temporarily reassign everyone to testing.
Hiring new people for the project	Verify that everyone has shown a sample of previous work.
Personality conflicts threaten the team	Have everyone complete the self-assessment form and talk with them about their contributions. Review assignments with everyone who scores less than 60 percent.
Possibly unreliable contractors	Do not assign work without contract. Audit progress.

Scope Control

The requirements document is essential in controlling scope. In this respect, continuously verify that functionality is being delivered according to the requirements specification.

Schedule Control

The project plan forms the primary medium through which you can assess risks that are associated with schedule. Given the creation of a good set of requirements, you can use the project plan to establish the schedule by which the functionality that addresses the requirements can be implemented. As the project moves along, you can evaluate estimations against actualities and gain a sense of whether your estimations have a predictable pattern of error. Generally, experts do not advise that you revise your estimation but rather that you leave it as you originally made it and adjust it using a formula that you develop based on your findings.

Resource Control

Take measures at the beginning of a development effort to ensure that a good team is formed. After that, a team member's performance depends on timelines and quality of work. Task dependencies prove essential in being able to monitor the performances of individual team members. If one person does not complete tasks on time and occasions delay for others, you need to take action. Along one line, the individual who is responsible for the delay might be under too much pressure. If that's the case, take measures to distribute his work among others, thus freeing him to concentrate on the problem that might be causing the delay.

Monitoring Risks

When you monitor risks, you engage in an activity that most clearly parallels what has been discussed elsewhere as process improvement. At this phase of risk control, you can assess risk proactively. If your organization develops several games in succession, each game development effort can generate a set of data that you can use to shape a general risk plan for all products that your organization creates.

On the other hand, if the effort is isolated, you can use data collected for the post mortem to assess the project itself, without consideration to other projects. A key aspect of such self-assessment involves examining the budget to see whether it exceeded the plan. Another key aspect of self-assessment is whether the project took longer than was planned. In each area, surveying to what extent select risk factors caused schedule delays serves as a way to confirm the accuracy of risk identifications, estimates, and evaluations.

Scope Monitoring

Monitoring scope risks involves obtaining information that will enable you to anticipate adjustments in the technology you plan to implement and the processes you intend to use for future development efforts. Accumulating data toward these ends involves using a database to store data relating to how well you do in your identification, estimation, and other work with risk. For example, if you track the number of nonspecified features that ended up being a part of the product, you place yourself in a position to assess the extent to which these features might have delayed the deployment of the game. On the other hand, if you detected dangerous delays early on and were in a position to transfer and adjust responsibilities so that the schedule could continue on track, you confirm the validity of specific strategies and tactics.

Schedule Monitoring

Collecting data about a project is helpful in monitoring the schedule. Discovering the features that occasioned the greatest schedule lag can enable you to plan accordingly for the next effort. In this respect, you can associate the greatest risks with those items that caused the greatest delay. At the basis of such estimations is the discrepancy between planned and actual schedule estimations. If risk is correlated directly with how much time was estimated for each task, it becomes possible to adjust the weight of risk for a given task up or down on the basis of whether the task was completed early or late.

Resource Monitoring

Tracking how well people do or whether given contractors deliver on time is at the center of resource monitoring. Assessing the situation involves more than learning who should not be hired or contracted the next time around, however. Among other lessons are the following:

- If someone did not perform well, is it possible to assess whether his performance improved after he was reassigned work or assigned to work with different people?
- If a contractor delivers on time, is it important to note contributing factors? For example, were the requirements stated articulately? It might be, for example, that a good contractor received a difficult, poorly crafted set of requirements and in the end failed to deliver because of the requirements.
- If certain measures such as reviews and walkthroughs tended to improve the performance of the development team, you might be able to establish quantitatively just how much productivity increased as a result of such activities.

Conclusion

This chapter dealt with some of the concerns of risk analysis. It investigated how to identify risks, which involves searching the proposed project for moments of possible stress. It also investigated risk estimation, which requires inspection of identified risks and developing ways to rank them according to how they might affect the project. In addition, this chapter investigated risk evaluation, which involves exploring the impact that risks might have on the project. It also explored risk planning. A leading element in a risk planning effort is a written plan for risk management. The chapter provided a simple template that you can use as the beginning of a risk management plan. Next, the chapter focused on control of risk. Risk control requires acting on the strategies and tactics laid out in the risk management plan. Finally, the chapter turned to risk monitoring, an activity that you can characterize as process improvement.

Generally, risk analysis should be a part of every game development effort, but it is probably best to use some degree of restraint before leaping into a risk analysis effort that requires a full-time commitment from someone on the team. Generally, for smaller development efforts, it is best to make risk management a part of everyone's work. A few additional tasks, dedicated to risk assessment, can enable a team to institute risk-control measures responsibly.

This chapter described only the most general aspects of risk management. Among the many excellent books on risk management are the following:

Charette, Robert N. *Software Engineering Risk Analysis and Management.* New York: Intertext Publications, 1989.

Karolak, Dale Walter. *Software Engineering Risk Management.* Los Alamitos, California: IEEE Computer Society Press, 1996.

Kendrick, Tom. *Identifying and Managing Project Risk.* New York: ANACOM, 2003.

McMannus, John. *Risk Management in Software Development Project. C.* Burlington, Massachusetts: Elsevier Butterworth-Heinemann, 2004.

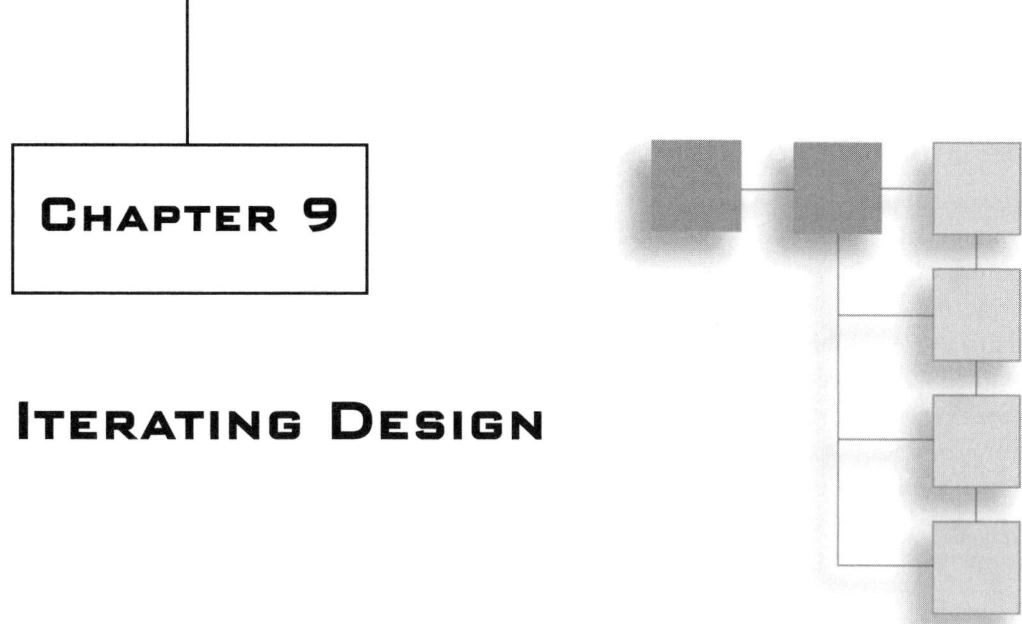

Chapter 9

Iterating Design

This text refers to a collection of classes that provide a specific set of capabilities to a game as a *component.* (See Chapter 4, "Software Design—Much Ado About Something," for a review of design concepts.) For development purposes, a component is a *stripe.* Each stripe, in turn, usually represents several stages of development. A *stage* is an iteration of the development effort involving creation of the functionality embodied in a given component.

This development effort—which moves from state to stripe and eventually to completed game—lies at the basis of iterative design. If you break down your development project into cohesive design pieces and then iteratively develop each piece until you achieve the design goals you have set for your product, you move forward in a steady way toward a robust product. Given this model, this chapter covers the following topics:

- Learning the basics of iterating design
- Selecting the right size components
- Applying principles that are derived from object-oriented programming, refactoring, risk analysis, and patterns to your design effort
- Effectively using the software design document
- Projecting plan considerations with iterative design efforts
- Testing on an iterative basis
- Knowing when to break off an iterative effort
- Knowing when things have gone wrong

Iterative Design Basics

The design of a game consists of the evolving view you have of the operations, classes, and components that embody the functionality that the requirements document for your game presents to you. Because maintaining fairly strict control of the scope of the requirements remains fundamental to the success of a game development effort, restraint should characterize anything that you do when it comes to changing, expanding, or dropping requirements. If restraint in the treatment of requirements characterizes successful game development efforts, however, a different perspective applies to design. Design benefits from continuous exploration. You can afford to show greater flexibility when engaging in design efforts as long as you work within the scope that the requirements establish and have a development plan that enables you to concentrate your efforts on specific game components.

Appendix D, "Software Engineering and Game Design Documentation," contains numerous documents, one of which is the *Ankh Software Design Description.* The *Description* provides a glossary of terms that is useful to review here. Table 9.1 provides a summary of the items that the software design document presents.

Table 9.1 Design Glossary and Definitions

Term	Discussion
Behavioral view	A representation of the system that shows objects created from the classes that are named in the logical view.
Component	A collection of classes that share the same set of responsibilities. One stripe might have dependencies distributed among several components.
Component view	A representation of the system that shows the collections of classes that have common system responsibilities. Component views take two forms: internal and external.
Conceptual view	A representation of the system using either a use case or an object diagram. If the general object diagram is used, the boxes depict class objects.
External Component view	A view of a component shown with all other components active during its lifetime. As stripes are developed, components take on definition; therefore, any given component shown in the documentation of a stripe might not appear in its entirety. However, the component appears in its entirety relative to the specified functionality for the stripe. Likewise, all other components with responsibilities within the stripe are represented in the same way. This representation of the system is intended to show the general features of the system that exist when a given stripe has reached completion.

Term	Discussion
Internal Component view	A view of the component or components that contain the primary functionality of a given stripe. This representation of the system exposes the features of the system that are specific to a given stripe. It does not represent the system as a whole.
Logical view	A representation of the system that shows the classes that compose the system and their static relationships. Included in this view are known attributes and operations of classes.
Stage	A version of a stripe. Stripes might have stages, which are, again, reflected in the build history of the system. The stripe stages do not, however, have bearing on the design. They are implementation measures.
Stripe	A set of functionality embodied in a single component of the system. Stripes represent both logical and physical views of the system. They are logical because they define a specific build status. Each stripe is represented in the configuration scheme of the system. All dependencies for a stripe should be stored with the stripe. The stripes provide a history of the construction of the project.
Use Case view	A proof of concept for the stripe. To create a use case for design, the developer works from the game design document and creates a scenario that captures a representative subset of the functionality that the stripe is intended to implement.
View	A way of looking at the system. Views are conceptual (use case and entity), logical (class), behavioral (sequence and collaboration), and component (internal and system).

Applied Design

As you can see from Table 9.1, iterative design involves a few basic ideas. You can place them in a list fairly readily:

- First, you take time at the beginning of your project to formulate a set of requirements. You do your best at this point to study the game design document thoroughly to discover the functionality you must develop if you are to address the features that the game design document presents. Being careful to fully assess the scope of the game is an essential part of this effort.

- Second, having studied the requirements thoroughly, you try to create a view of how you might implement the functionality. The most facile approach to this goal is to employ an object-oriented perspective and make a list of objects you think might contain the functionality. Try using a Task-Object-Remarks (TOR) chart to achieve this goal. Basically, such a chart allows you to name things you think the software must accomplish to fulfill the requirements. You are free to start with an object, a task, or a responsibility. Where you start makes no difference; the chart allows you to begin collecting ideas about how you intend to implement the functionality of the game.
- Third, you can begin formulating the findings of your TOR chart into a well-defined list of classes, and you can place these in a Class-Responsibility-Collaboration (CRC) list. (See Appendix D for the CRC list for *Ankh.*) The CRC list consists of tables divided into three parts. One part lists the class, another part lists the responsibilities that the class should address, and the third part addresses the classes with which the class communicates. In this way, you reach a point at which you can begin assessing how the classes might be formed into components. A component is an area or portion of the system in which classes are coupled fairly tightly and in which you might recognize after brief study a single set of services or a single general capability.

If you work the CRC list in a systematic way, you can draw a complex diagram in which you illustrate the relationships that pertain between all the classes you have named in your CRC effort. To reduce the complexity of this undertaking, you can break the system into components. Breaking the system into components constitutes an architectural manipulation of the design of the system. That's because when you group classes into components, you have a view of the system that begins to show you what might be called the *specific gravity* of various components. When you begin to sense the pull of certain centers of gravity, you have a way to assess the relative weights and positions of the classes within each component. Likewise, you have a way to question how the interfaces of classes can be designed so that they communicate in an efficient way and achieve other design goals, such as ease of maintenance and low coupling. Figure 9.1 illustrates the flow of activity that is characteristic of a stripe.

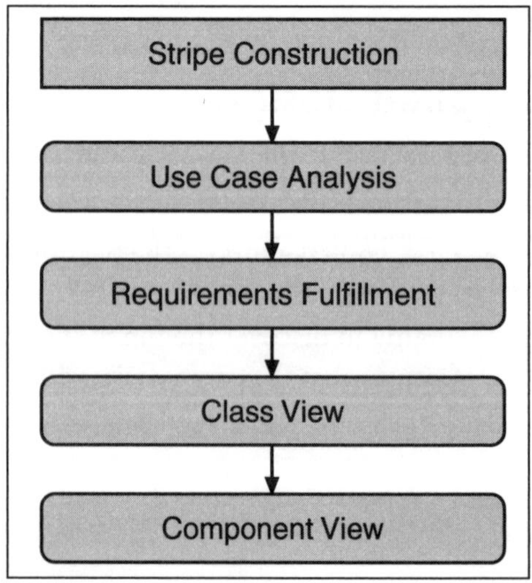

Figure 9.1
Stripes present a flow of activity from requirements to components.

Software Systems and Gravity

When a solar body begins forming, it is probably safe to assume that one particle attracts another because both particles, possessing mass, also possess gravity. As the number of particles comprising the growing solar body increases, the gravity of the solar body increases. After a time, the gravity of the body grows to an immense scale, attracting not only particles but also planets.

More time passes, and then you find that the gravity has grown so great that the particles crush against each other to the point that they begin to generate heat. If the pressure grows great enough, a thermo-nuclear reaction ensues. The explosion tends to push particles out, generating light to the surrounding space. At the same time, gravity continues to exert its influence on the surrounding space. An equilibrium exists.

When you develop a software system, you toy, at least metaphorically, with forces of attraction and repulsion that in some ways bear comparison to the life of a solar body. At first, the system might be extremely tenuous, consisting of little more than a few functions or classes. After a time, the functions or classes form bonds, so that the gravity and complexity of the system grows. Eventually, you have a game that delivers an enormous number of functional capabilities and yet is vast and complex.

Reversing Gravity

Success in software development involves creating a counterforce to the tendency of the system to become vast and tightly coupled. A first approach to this is to create both a vision of the components that comprise the system and a plan by which you can sequentially develop, refine, and integrate components. When working with components, you can put in place a set of practices based on refactoring and the use of patterns. Such practices allow you to investigate and rework operations, classes, and components to achieve the design goals you have set for your development effort.

The software that makes up a game must remain accessible to its developers. If the software is so optimized, coupled, or diffuse in its integration as to be impossible to understand, it is not nearly as maintainable as it could be. Iterative design, above all, provides a way for the density and complexity of software systems to be reduced to reasonable levels.

Conceptualizing Iteration

Iteration begins with determining a context of iteration, and one approach to this is to use the notion of a stripe. A stripe is a selection of functionality you decide you want to implement at a given point in your project. Generally, a stripe should represent a well-defined set of functionality. You should be able to see the results of the completion of each stripe. Its completion should bring you a degree of satisfaction and serve as a platform from which to understand, view, and develop other stripes. Likewise, a stripe should enable you to think creatively about your design, in such a way that if you suddenly realize that you can add a feature that will tremendously enhance the game, you have a basis on which to determine the overall impact that the implementation of the feature will have on your development effort.

You can adjust and scale stripes. Each stripe, as an iteration of design, allows you to perform risk analysis, testing, and design refinement. Each stripe also allows you to create a unified subset of the game. Finally, each stripe enables you to view what you have accomplished and what remains to be completed. Figure 9.2 illustrates the perspectives that a stripe affords.

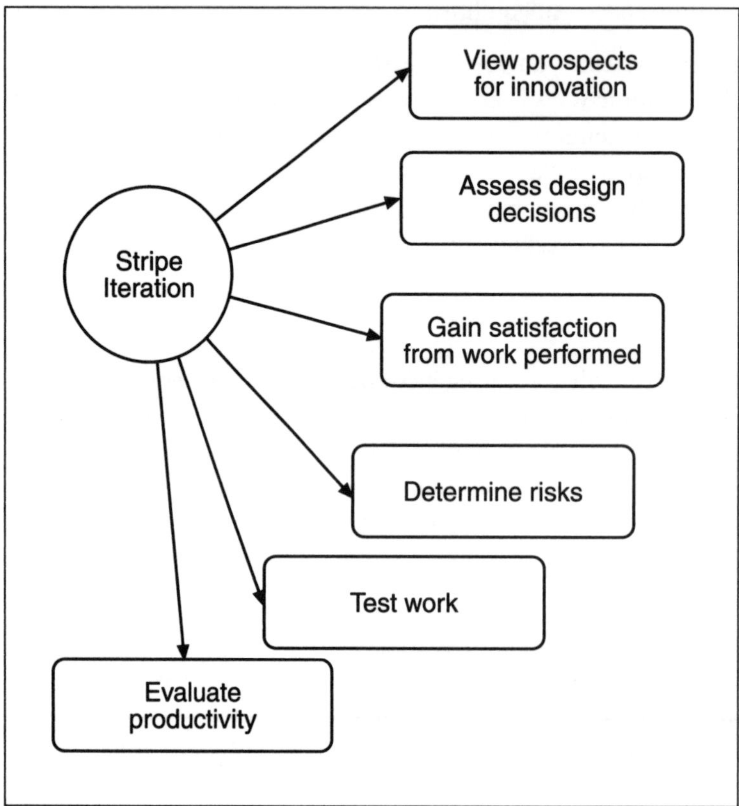

Figure 9.2
Each stripe affords a sense of the project's history and potentials.

Ankh Development Using Stripes

The sections that follow trace several stripes of the development effort for *Ankh.* The code for the stripes is available on the CD. By examining the stripes, you can retrace how *Ankh* was developed. Each stripe is a component or collection of classes that implements the functionality that is documented in a use case. Most stripes also consist of stages, or versions. The use cases and component diagrams in this chapter and the software design document allow you to follow the iterative approach to development that was used. To conserve space, a few stripes have been omitted from this chapter, but you can still go to the CD and the software design document for the full version of the document from which the material in this chapter has been drawn.

Stripe 1—Opening

Each stripe of a game can consist of a set of stages. You can identify a *stage* as almost any set of functionality that you want to establish as a baseline within the context of a stripe. When *Ankh* was developed, the first stage of stripe 1 was nothing more than a proof of concept that the component set up for the game shell provided a framework for achieving a full-screen version of the game and displaying bitmaps and a revolving mesh. Figure 9.3 provides a screen shot of the stripe.

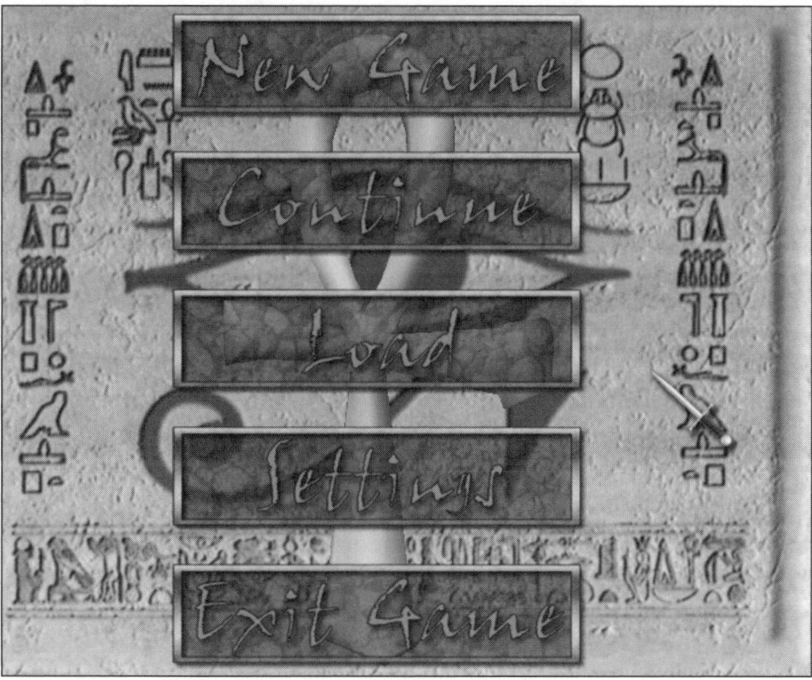

Figure 9.3
The first stage of a stripe offers an opportunity to test concepts.

Use Case Scenario

Every stripe originates with a use case. A use case, as mentioned in Chapter 4, provides a tool for testing one set of functionality within a stripe. Because it serves largely as a proof of concept, a use case does not need to be comprehensive. The use case for a stripe might be one scenario among what might be many hundreds of scenarios. One scenario for each stripe can adequately guide the implementation, because even one use case forces the development to achieve a specified design objective. The result is that the project remains within scope, and the development effort conforms to the schedule. As the game grows in completeness, you can develop numerous test scenarios. For the first stage of the first stripe, it was enough to state that the user can view the full-screen version of the main icon of the game.

Component View

The component view of a stripe illustrates the classes that are involved in the implementation of the stripe. In the software design document, the component view can appear in two ways. In one way, it can represent an internal view of the component. In this view, a class diagram can be summarized so that the viewer views only the most general composition patterns. In the other way, the viewer can view one component among many. Generally, the further a game moves toward completion, the more components appear in relationships with other components. This became the case with *Ankh* when implementation of levels became the chief concern. After designing and implementing the classes that created such components as the map editor, the character editor, and the first level, the team implemented the later levels by doing little more than calling on the services that the interfaces of stable components provided. (For a component view of Stripe 1, see Chapter 4.)

Stripe 2.1—GUI Objects

For the second stripe, the team decided to work first with the development of items that provided for things like dialog boxes and text fields. This approach to development had several advantages. For example, the team felt it could implement the GUI items with little trouble, so by undertaking to implement them first, the team placed itself in a position to pursue several project tuning activities, such as setting up the software configuration management system, establishing the folders and file structure for the classes, and familiarizing itself with naming and documentation conventions. In addition, when it performed what it considered to be simpler, more routine tasks, it could begin gathering project metrics more easily.

Use Slider Use Case

Testing a single GUI object served as a convenient way to demonstrate the functionality that the GUI objects provided. Figure 9.4 illustrates the Use Slider use case.

Use Case Name: Use Slider
Requirement(s) Explored: 18
Player (Actor) Context (Role): Player
Precondition(s): Game is running.
Trigger(s): Player views window with slider.
Main Course of Action: 1. Player opens first window and views slider. 2. Player selects slider with the left mouse button and the cursor. 3. Player moves the slider by holding the left mouse button. 4. Window text displays numerical indicators of slider position, 0 to 100.
Alternate Course(s) of Action: 2a. Right-click brings no change. 3a. Letting up on the mouse releases slider. 3b. Pressing again re-engages the slider. 4a. Move from 0 to 100 and 100 to 0.
Exceptional Course(s) of Action: 1a. Window distorts slider tract. 2a. Slider does not respond.

Figure 9.4
The Use Slider use case focuses on the slider.

GUI Objects Component View

The object component diagram for the Use Slider use case illustrates the classes developed to provide the functionality that the use case stipulates. The component views for the early stripes provide internal views of the system. The GUI classes specialize `CGUIObject`. Figure 9.5 illustrates the GUI Objects component view.

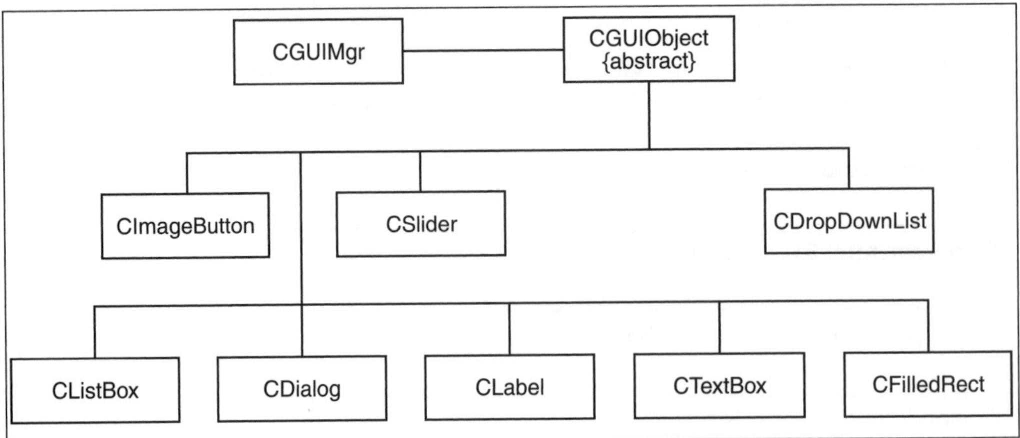

Figure 9.5
A class diagram view provides material for a component view of GUI elements.

Stripe 2.2—Floor Tiling

Initially, the development of GUI objects, floor tiling, mesh placement, and saving and loading entities set with the map editor were included in a single stripe. However, the stripe was far too large. The first indication of the problem was that the team fell behind schedule. After several weeks, everyone realized that the stripe did not involve a single component. Rather, the stripe merged work into a single component that should have been developed in several components. When the team realized what was happening, it iterated the design. It found that its work with the GUI objects could be understood more easily as a single stripe. This opened its view to several other areas of development. One result was work with floor tiling.

Select Tile Use Case View

The use case view of the floor tiling component centers on the simple activity of selecting a tile for the layer. Figure 9.6 illustrates the Select Tile use case.

Use Case Name: Select Tile
Requirement(s) Explored: 43
Player (Actor) Context (Role): Player
Precondition(s): Game is running.
Trigger(s): Player wants to change the layer tiles.
Main Course of Action: 1. Player selects the map editor view from the game menu. 2. Game displays the editor view with tiles. 3. Player inspects the displayed tiles. 4. Player selects a tile. 5. Player closes the map editor. 6. Player views world with the selected tile.
Alternate Course(s) of Action: 2a. Player closes the map editor without new selection. 4a. Player deselects the tile.
Exceptional Course(s) of Action: 2a. Game does not display the editor. 3a. Game does not display tiles. 6. The world does not display the selected tiles.

Figure 9.6
The map editor allows the user to select a tile.

Level Floor Tiling Component View

The component view for the Level Floor Tiling component showed the need for a class that was not anticipated initially: `CTileMap`. This class encapsulates responsibilities for drawing the tile map. Figure 9.7 illustrates the Floor Tiling component view.

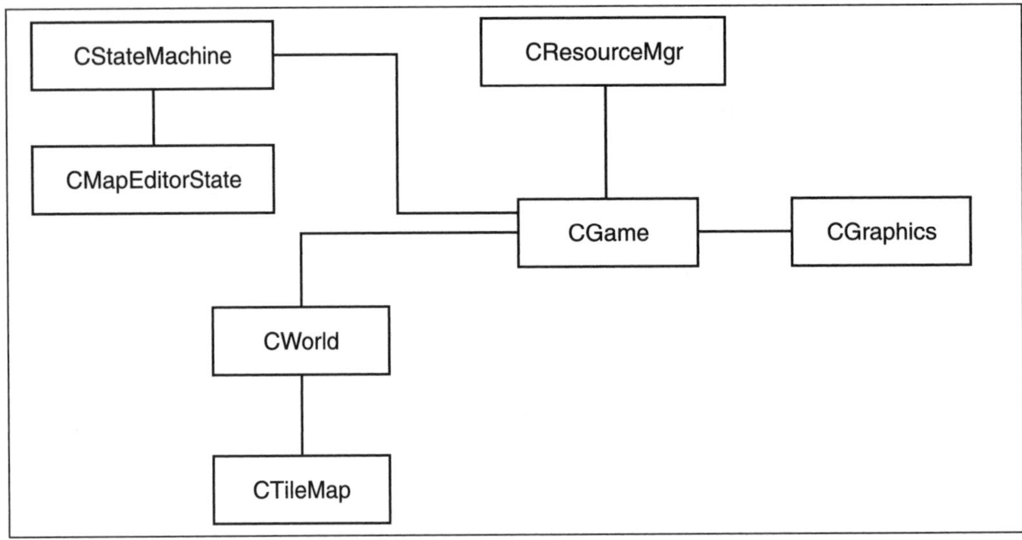

Figure 9.7
The map component for tiles incorporated a new class: `CTileMap`.

Figure 9.8 provides a screen shot of the floor tile for *Ankh*. The menu items are not fully implemented at this point in the game development.

Figure 9.8
Implementation of Stripe 2.2 allows customization of the floor tile.

Stripe 2.3—Mesh Placement

Deciding how to implement functionality for the mesh placement in the map editor extended once again to examining how to break down the work on the stripes to smaller collections of functionality. Mesh placement depends on the existence of the floor; therefore, breaking the floor into separate components simplified the work of moving on to implement the functionality of creating editor capabilities for placing a mesh.

Select a Building Use Case View

The use case view of the Mesh Placement component centers on selecting and placing a mesh for a building. Figure 9.9 illustrates the Select a Building use case.

Use Case Name: Select a Building
Requirement(s) Explored: 43, 13
Player (Actor) Context (Role): Player
Precondition(s): Game is running.
Trigger(s): Player wants to change tiling.
Main Course of Action: 1. Player opens the map editor. 2. Player selects a building from the drop-down box. 3. Player clicks on the map and places the building on the map. 4. Player closes the editor.
Alternate Course(s) of Action: 2a. Player closes the map editor without new selection.
Exceptional Course(s) of Action: 1a. Game does not display the editor. 2a. Game does not display tiles. 3a. The world does not display the building on the map.

Figure 9.9
The map editor allows the player to select a building.

Mesh Placement Component View

The component view for mesh placement involved using only classes that the team anticipated in its initial design. Figure 9.10 illustrates the Mesh Placement component view. To view a screen shot of the implemented component, see Figure 9.31.

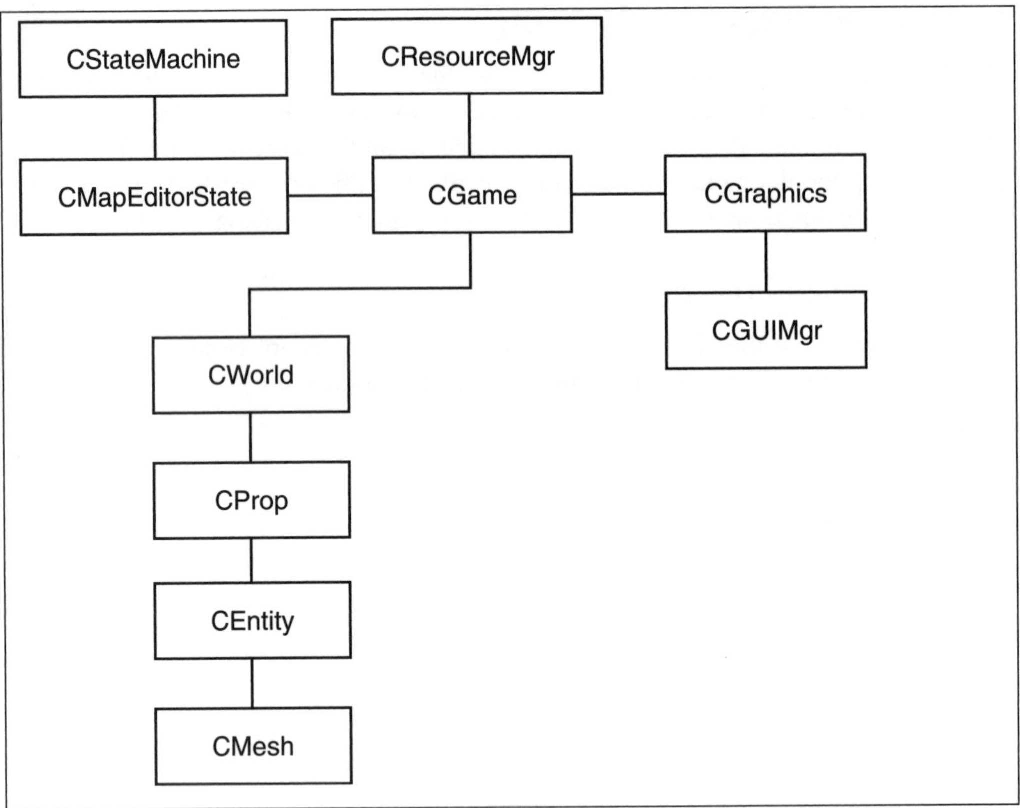

Figure 9.10
Mesh placement involved no unanticipated classes.

Stripe 2.4—Save and Load

The final bit of work on the map editor was to create load and save functionality. The implementation of this functionality involved work that the team anticipated expanding later on, when it would complete the stripe for saving and loading the game replays. For this reason, the team was careful to limit the scope of development activities needed for this stripe. Premature optimization or implementation might have brought rework.

Save a Map Use Case View

The Save a Map use case traces the basic activity of saving and loading. The functionality that the use case encompasses can be extended later to encompass saving a sequence of game states. Figure 9.11 illustrates the Save a Map use case.

Use Case Name: Save a Map
Requirement(s) Explored: 4
Player (Actor) Context (Role): Player
Precondition(s): Game is running.
Trigger(s): Player wants to save a map.
Main Course of Action: 1. Player opens dialog box from map. 2. Player enters the name of the file and saves. 3. Player chooses the Save option. 4. Player reopens the map and views elements as before.
Alternate Course(s) of Action: 2a. Player closes dialog box and continues play.
Exceptional Course(s) of Action: 1a. Game does not display Save option. 2a. Name of file is left out of dialog box.

Figure 9.11
The map editor allows you to save a map.

Save and Load Component View

The component view for the Save a Map use case involved no complexities. The primary concern was to filter information from the `CFileDialog` class. Figure 9.12 illustrates the Save and Load component view.

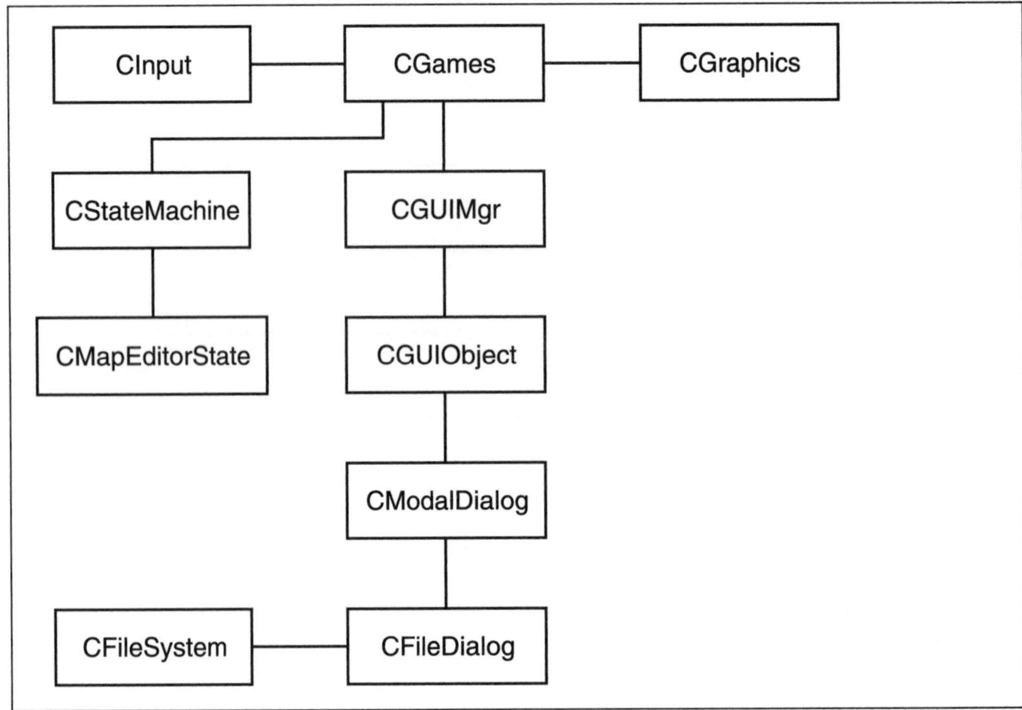

Figure 9.12
The Save a Map component exposed the need for `CFileSystem`.

Stripe 3.1—Navigate Alexandria

The map editor makes possible the positioning of the meshes that make up the city. You then can navigate through the city as a way of testing the camera and other features of the game engine.

Navigate Alexandria Use Case View

The use case for this stripe involves visiting structures placed in the map and viewing them from different angles. Viewing a given structure might involve inspecting a mesh from 360 degrees, moving the camera, or in some other way manipulating the level in ways that might be restricted after you have fully implemented the features of the game. Figure 9.13 illustrates the Navigate Alexandria use case.

Use Case Name: Navigate Alexandria
Requirement(s) Explored: 13, 14, 15, 16, 17, 35, 61
Player (Actor) Context (Role): Player
Precondition(s): Game is running, first level.
Trigger(s): Player to view different parts of the level.
Main Course of Action: 1. Player views level from front. 2. Using the cursor as a guide, player moves through level. 3. Player views obelisks from different perspectives. 4. Player views buildings from different perspectives. 5. Player views statues from different perspectives. 6. Player views columns from different perspectives. 7. Player views trees from different perspectives.
Alternate Course(s) of Action: None.
Exceptional Course(s) of Action: 3–7a. Objects do not reveal different perspectives.

Figure 9.13
The navigation stripe confirms mesh movement.

Navigate Alexandria Component View

The component view for this stripe brings the `CCamera` class into play. For now, you can adjust the camera position and angle arbitrarily to provide full views of all the items on the level. Figure 9.14 illustrates the Navigate Alexandria component view.

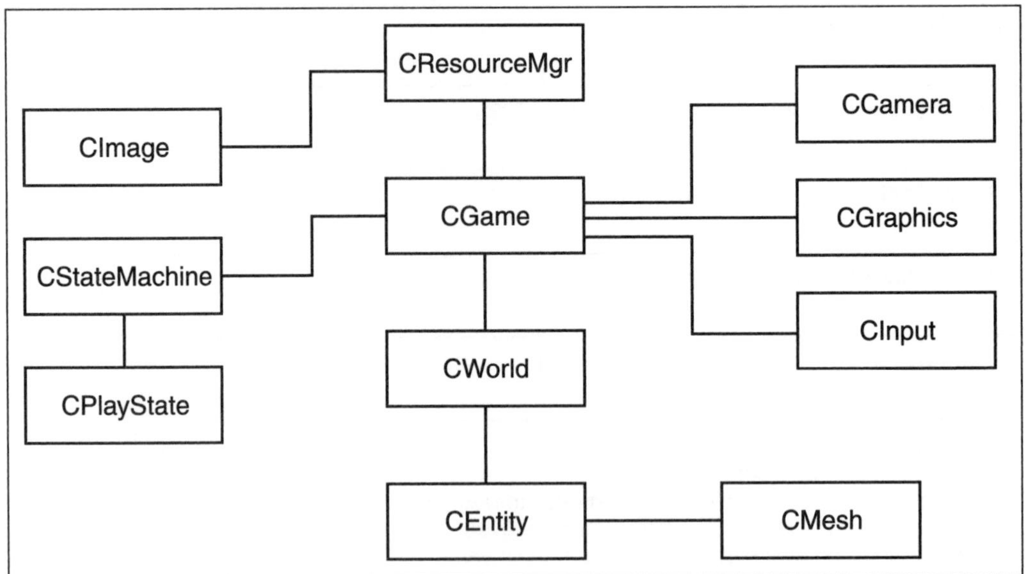

Figure 9.14
Navigating the city allows you to test camera angles.

Stripe 4—Character Editor

The character editor stripe allowed the team to place a character on a level and manipulate the character through the level meshes. No artificial intelligence or combat capabilities were in place, because the primary objective was to simplify and refine the operations involved in character motion. The meshes for this level model a fictional version of Alexandria, Egypt.

Create Character Profile Use Case View

The game provides the ability to build both levels and characters. The character editor, like the map editor, serves as a tool with which to construct the game. Later, players can use the character editor to build custom characters. Figure 9.15 illustrates the Create Character Profile use case.

Use Case Name: Create Character Profile
Requirement(s) Explored: 18, 19, 20, 21, 22, 35, 44
Player (Actor) Context (Role): Player
Precondition(s): Game is running.
Trigger(s): Player wants to customize the character profile.
Main Course of Action: 1. Player opens character editor. 2. Player assigns character attributes. 3. Player selects a mesh for the character. 4. Player saves character for play. 5. Player exits character editor.
Alternate Course(s) of Action: 2a. Player closes dialog box and continues play. 4a. Player exits character editor without saving.
Exceptional Course(s) of Action: 3a. No mesh appears. 4a. Character profile is not saved.

Figure 9.15
You can use the character editor for game development and for custom characters.

Character Editor Component View

Work with the character editor did not lead to creations of additional classes, but it did lead to refinement of existing relationships. Figure 9.16 illustrates the Create Character component view.

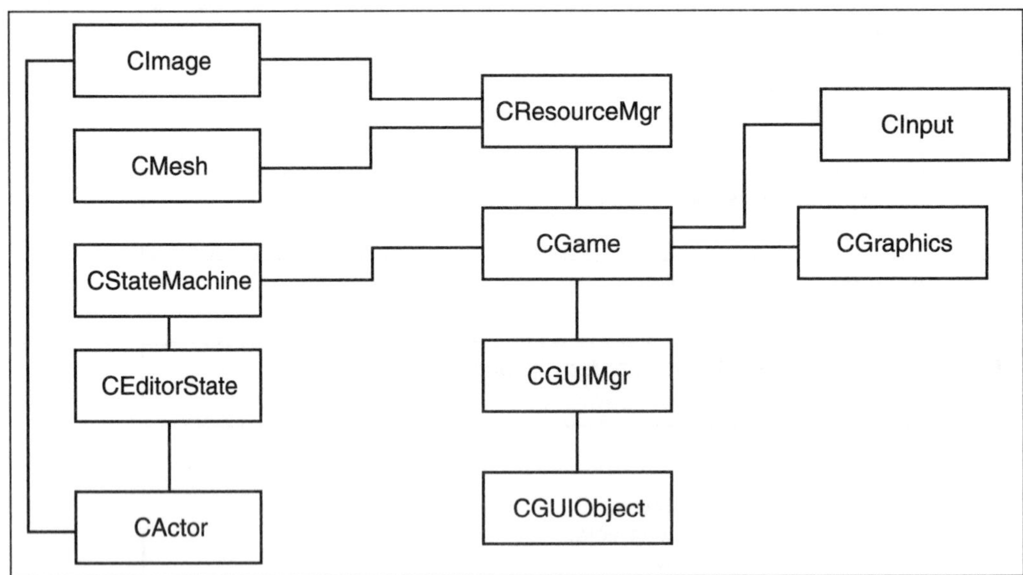

Figure 9.16
This stripe marked the addition of the `CActor` class.

Stripe 5—Unit Physics

Unit physics has to do with the operations limited to moving a given feature in the game, most notably characters. Given that the animated meshes represent human beings, the functionality developed for one human being, Sekhem, proved a solid basis on which to develop the functionality appropriate for priests, guards, and other characters.

Walk Character Use Case View

The Walk Character use case involves moving one character, Sekhem. The use case shows the turn-based design of the game. First, the player selects a character and a distance for the character to move. Then the player moves. Figure 9.17 illustrates the Walk Character use case.

Use Case Name: Walk Character
Requirement(s) Explored: 13, 14, 15, 16, 17, 35, 41, 45, 47, 48
Player (Actor) Context (Role): Player
Precondition(s): Game is running.
Trigger(s): Player wants to move character.
Main Course of Action: 1. Player selects character. 2. Player selects destination. 3. Player moves character. 4. Game moves character the designated distance.
Alternate Course(s) of Action: 2a. Player selects distance several times.
Exceptional Course(s) of Action: 1a. Character cannot be selected. 4a. Character does not move.

Figure 9.17
You can demonstrate unit physics by using a single character.

Unit Physics Component View

Implementing the functionality in the Walk Character use case required working with a substantial set of classes. Again, *Ankh* features humans only as animated characters, so the work put into the unit physics for the use case covered most of the character animation scenarios in the game. Figure 9.18 illustrates the Unit Physics component view.

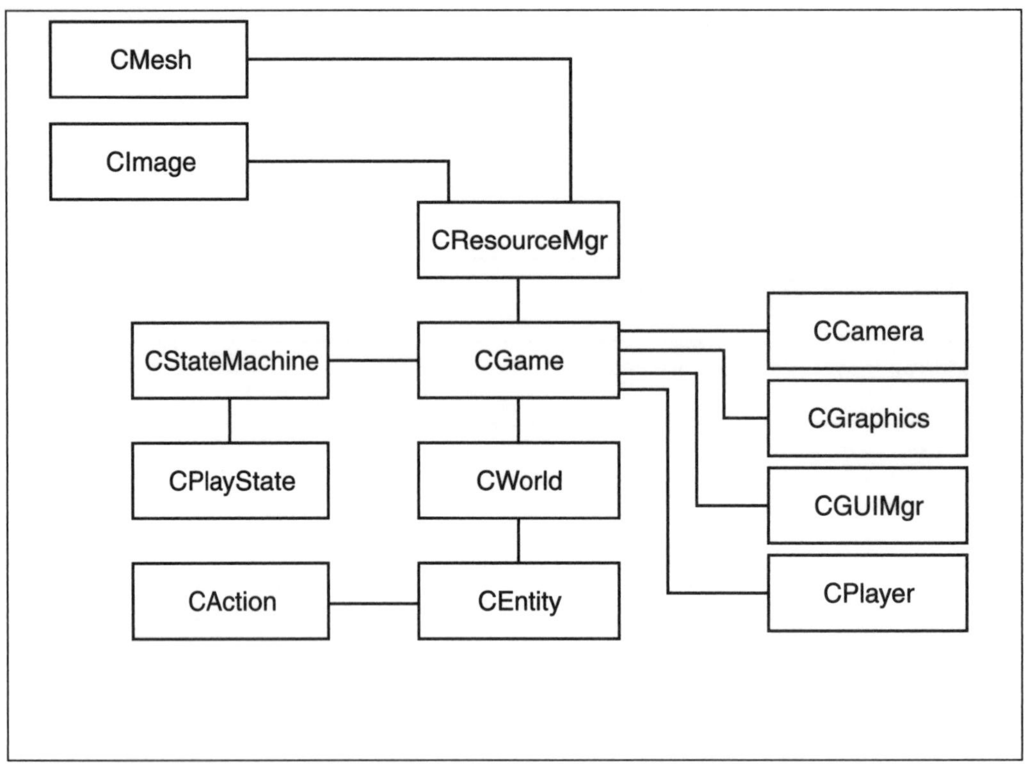

Figure 9.18
Walking the character involves using a large component.

Stripe 6—Inventory Items

Inventory items include weapons, healing charms, magic potions, and other items. The game is designed to allow inventory manipulation in several ways. For example, characters can swap items. In the use case created for inventory item, the scenario assumes a kind of closet to be the source of inventory items.

Select Inventory Items Use Case View

Players can add or drop inventory items. In the use case for this stripe, the team investigated only the acquisition of inventory items from a fixed source, such as a closet or chest. This view of the stripe allowed the team to test only one of many possible scenarios, but it still served, given that the character takes possession of the inventory, to confirm the basic functionality involved in inventory transactions. Figure 9.19 illustrates the Select Inventory Items use case.

Use Case Name: Select Inventory Items
Requirement(s) Explored: 40, 49, 55
Player (Actor) Context (Role): Player
Precondition(s): Game is running.
Trigger(s): Player wants to add to character inventory.
Main Course of Action: 1. Player opens inventory. 2. Game displays inventory items. 3. Player selects inventory items. 4. Game assigns the selected items to the character.
Alternate Course(s) of Action: 3a. Player does not select items.
Exceptional Course(s) of Action: 1a. Game does not display inventory option. 2a. Game assigns no items.

Figure 9.19
Inventory items involve different acquisition scenarios.

Inventory Items Component View

The functionality that is involved in the creation of the component for inventory items uses much of the functionality that was developed for the unit physics stripe. The major addition is the `CAction` class, along with the uses made of `CEntity`. Figure 9.20 illustrates the Inventory Items component view.

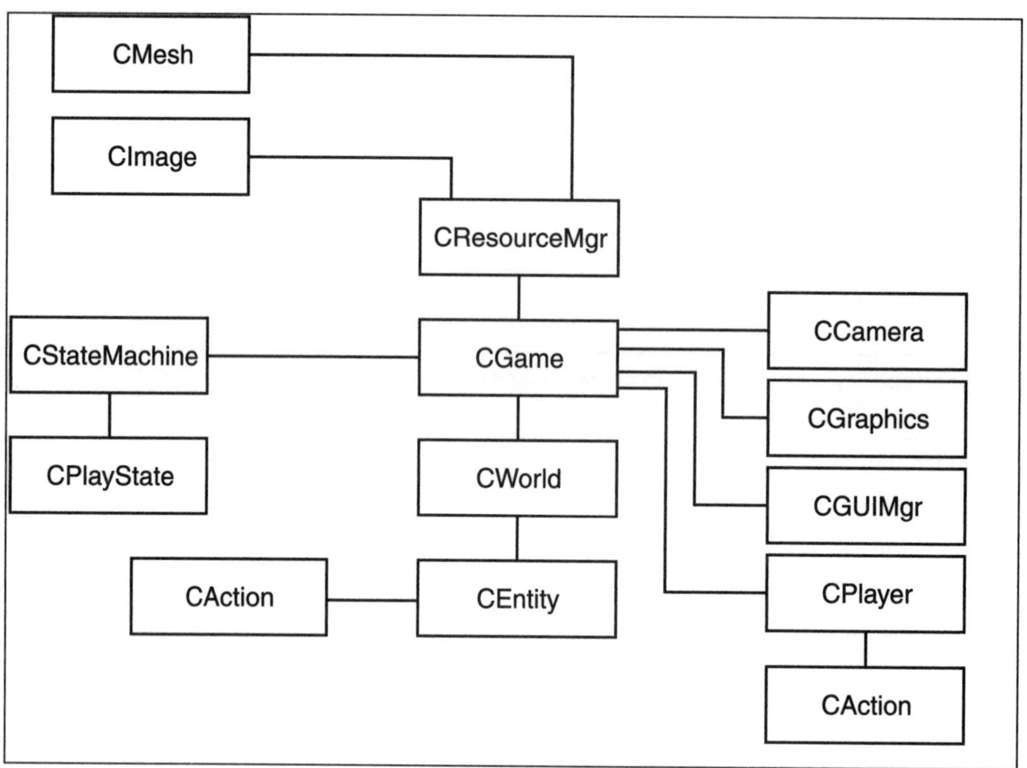

Figure 9.20
The set of classes for the inventory acquisition stripe became extensive.

Stripe 7—Combat

Combat comprises the set of actions that characters perform when they battle each other. Each level offers several battles. In fact, the unifying action theme of the game is battle. The game depicts battles as turns the characters take in striking or warding off blows. Battles also incorporate skills and levels of difficulty.

Battle Guard Use Case View

Although a battle on most levels consists of a situation in which Sekhem finds a cluster of enemies, the use case for this stripe is still suitable because it anticipates the behavior of all enemies, in clusters or alone. In this instance, Sekhem battles a guard. Figure 9.21 illustrates the Battle Guard use case.

Use Case Name: Battle Guard
Requirement(s) Explored: 54, 56
Player (Actor) Context (Role): Player
Precondition(s): Game is running.
Trigger(s): Player positions Sekhem for a battle.
Main Course of Action: 1. Player guides Sekhem into battle setting. 2. Guard approaches with blows. 3. Player guides Sekhem through fight. 4. Player guides Sekhem to slay guard. 5. Guard dies.
Alternate Course(s) of Action: 1a. Player draws back from battle.
Exceptional Course(s) of Action: 1a. Guard does not approach. 2a. Guard freezes.

Figure 9.21
Battles occur with groups of enemies, but a scenario that involves a single combat is still suitable for the stripe.

Battle Guard Component View

One of the main points of effort in this stripe involved implementing the operations of `CAction`. Until this point, `CAction` had not been enhanced for the types of activities that combat requires. Figure 9.22 illustrates the Battle Guard component view.

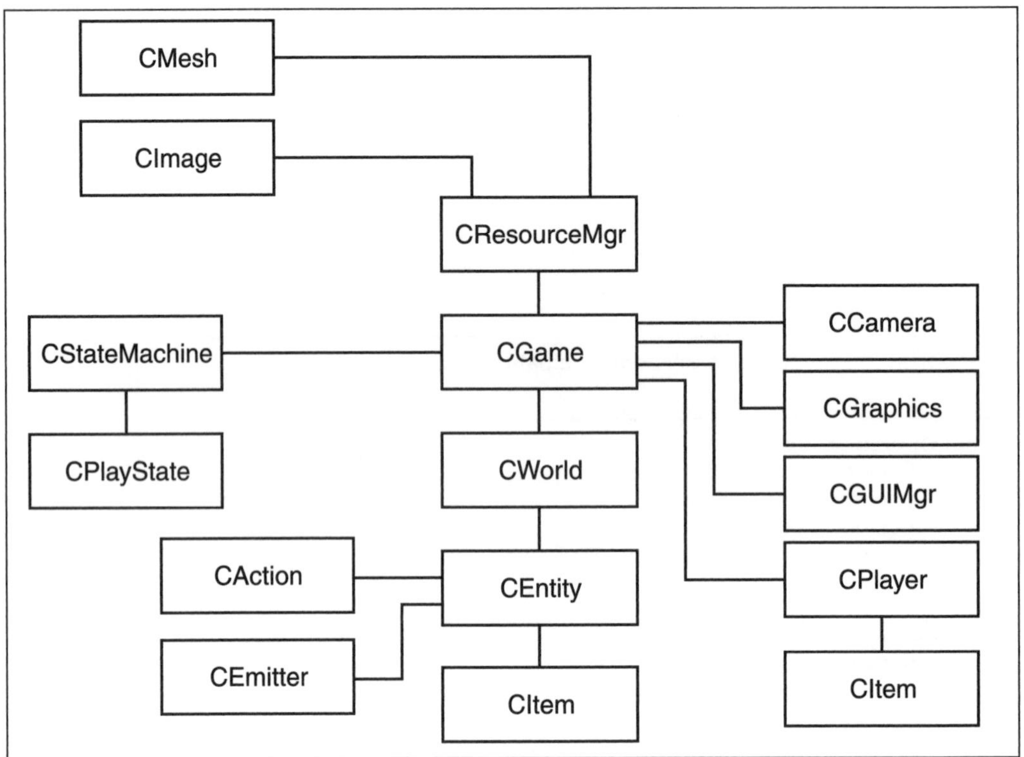

Figure 9.22
Addition of operations to `CAction` was a central concern.

Stripe 8—Acquire Skills

Characters can gain skills throughout the game. Special potions and spells are two forms of skill. In a fully implemented game, the skills can extend to many forms, such as the powers of priests or the resilience of warriors.

Acquire Skills Use Case View

To simplify the acquisition of skills, the design provides a palette and allows the player to select skills and skill attributes from it. To test the design of the skills-acquisition component, a test scenario might stipulate the acquisition of a lone skill. Figure 9.23 illustrates the Acquire Skills use case.

Use Case Name: Acquire Skills
Requirement(s) Explored: 20, 34, 47, 55, 56
Player (Actor) Context (Role): Player
Precondition(s): Game is running.
Trigger(s): Player wants to aquire skills for the character.
Main Course of Action: 1. Player accesses the skills palette. 2. Player selects skills according to budget. 3. Player applies skills to character. 4. Player closes skills palette and resumes play.
Alternate Course(s) of Action: 2a. Player lacks budget 2b. Player closes skills palette without skills selection.
Exceptional Course(s) of Action: 1a. Game does not display skills palette. 2a. Player cannot apply skills to character.

Figure 9.23
Acquiring a single skill demonstrates how the process works.

Acquire Skills Component View

For the implementation of the skills component, the team developed `CPlayState` to provide the state and behavior that skills encompass. At this stage of the game, only limited implementation is needed to serve as a proof of concept. Figure 9.24 illustrates the Acquire Skills component view.

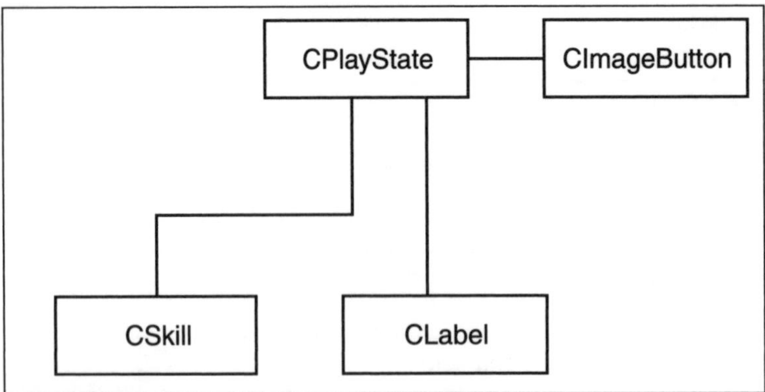

Figure 9.24
`CPlayState` tracks skills.

Stripe 9—Acquire Weapon

Weapons are fairly involved, and setting up the component for acquisition and use of weapons is intricate. Among the weapons that the game provides are broadswords, scimitars, spears, bows, daggers, whips, and axes. Because Sekhem and other characters can change their weapons, the functionality to add and drop weaponry is essential.

Acquire Weapon Use Case View

Even though weapons come in various forms, setting up a use case for the acquisition of just one weapon serves nicely to demonstrate general capabilities. The specific implementation of the weaponry acquisition component calls for a dialog box that might be implemented in any number of ways, but here, the use case assumes that the source is a generic armory. In the initial design, the player can acquire weapons from several sources, including scavenging. Figure 9.25 illustrates the Acquire Weapon use case.

Use Case Name: Acquire Weapon
Requirement(s) Explored: 6, 14, 15, 17, 40, 49
Player (Actor) Context (Role): Player
Precondition(s): Game is running.
Trigger(s): Battle stops and player seeks weapons.
Main Course of Action: 1. Player navigates character to the armory. 2. Game displays weapons. 3. Player chooses a weapon. 4. Player views cost verification. 5. Player applies weapon to character. 6. Player navigates character back into play.
Alternate Course(s) of Action: 3a. Player does not choose weapon. 5a. Player resumes play without applying a weapon.
Exceptional Course(s) of Action: 2a. Game displays no weapons. 4a. Cost cannot be computed. 5a. Player cannot apply weapon to character.

Figure 9.25
An armory serves as a generalized source of weaponry.

Acquire Weapon Component View

A complication of the scenario for acquiring weapons is that you must purchase or in some way restrict them when characters acquire them. Two classes—`CWorldState` and `CShopDialog`—provide the operations necessary to regulate the acquisition of weaponry. Figure 9.26 illustrates the Acquire Weapon component view.

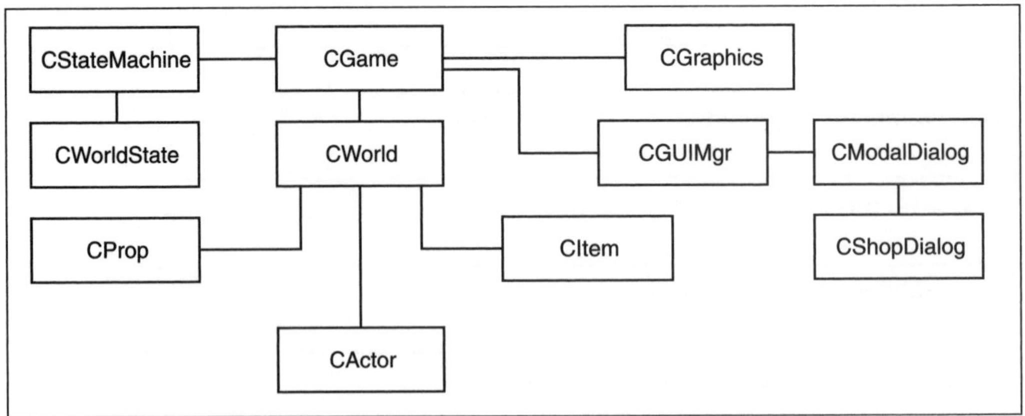

Figure 9.26
Weapons require regulation through a dialog for purchasing.

Stripe 10—View Statistics

Statistics tell you about the health of the characters. The game provides a status card of sorts, which allows you to view most of the statistics that relate to a character simultaneously. Making the changing statistics of the characters easy to view forms an important task of the game interface design.

View Strengths Use Case View

Viewing of strength statistics requires considering whether all statistics are relevant at all times. In this instance, the team developed a use case that calls only for a dialog to display statistics. This implementation required refinement later in the game. Figure 9.27 illustrates the View Strengths use case.

Use Case Name: View Strengths
Requirement(s) Explored: 14, 15, 16, 17, 18, 19, 20, 21
Player (Actor) Context (Role): Player
Precondition(s): Game is running.
Trigger(s): Battle has ended and player wants to view strengths.
Main Course of Action: 1. Player accesses Strength dialog box. 2. Player selects increased strengths for character. 3. Player exits Strength dialog box. 4. Player views adjusted strength statistics.
Alternate Course(s) of Action: 2a. Player does not adjust strengths.
Exceptional Course(s) of Action: 2a. Strengths are not correct. 2b. Strengths do not show. 4a. Game does not show adjusted strengths.

Figure 9.27
A single use case investigates strengths in general.

View Statistics Component View

`CStateDialog` provides an implementation of `CDialog` that is appropriate for the statistics view. The complexity of the level remains minimal and simply expands functionality that was developed previously. Figure 9.28 illustrates the View Statistics component view.

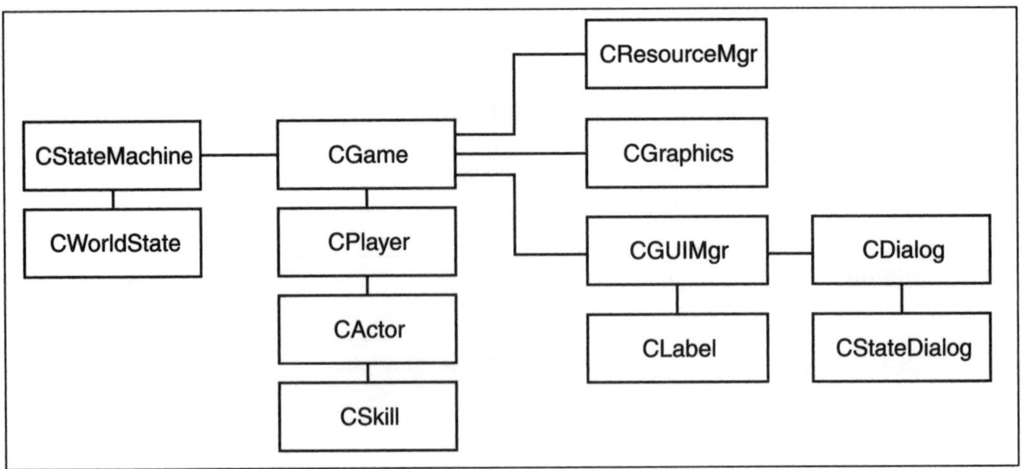

Figure 9.28
`CLevelDialog` provides an interface to the character and game statistics.

Stripe 13—Save Replay

Earlier in the development effort, the team developed the save and load capabilities that are required for customizing characters. At this point, it becomes possible to expand the basic set of functionality to allow implementation of the capabilities associated with saving and storing game events.

Save Replay Use Case View

You can store game events at any point in the game. Because storing the state of the game requires that much of the game to be implemented for storage, this stripe is best implemented last. Figure 9.29 illustrates the Save Replay use case.

Use Case Name: Save Replay
Requirement(s) Explored: 1, 2, 3, 4, 5, 6, 7, 8, 9, 10, 11, 12
Player (Actor) Context (Role): Player
Precondition(s): Game is running.
Trigger(s): Player wants to save a sequence of play.
Main Course of Action: 1. Player selects Save option. 2. Player chooses location and name for the saved file. 3. Player closes Save option. 4. Player resumes play.
Alternate Course(s) of Action: 3a. Player does not save.
Exceptional Course(s) of Action: 1a. Game does not display Save option. 2a. Player leaves out file name.

Figure 9.29
Storing events for replay requires extensive game functionality.

Save Replay Component View

At the heart of the replay component is the `CHistory` class, which tracks and stores game events. The use case assumes that the game captures events on a continuing basis and then retrieves them upon demand. Figure 9.30 illustrates the Save Replay component view.

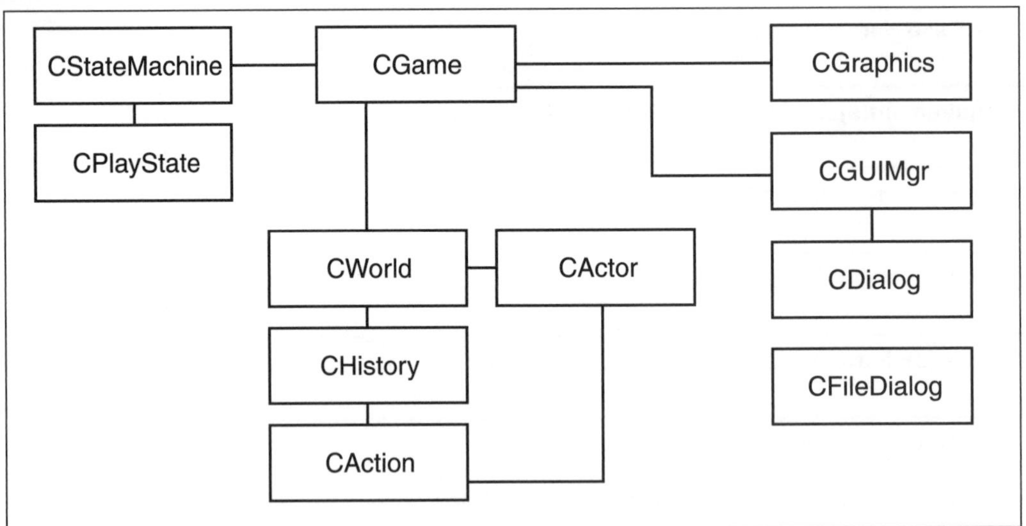

Figure 9.30
Storage of a sequence of events makes use of the `CHistory` class.

Map Editor Resources

The map editor serves both as a tool of development and as a tool that game players can use to customize levels. As mentioned earlier in this chapter, when the team set out to design the map editor, its first plan for development included a stripe that was far too complex to allow for smooth implementation. As a result, it experienced a schedule delay and other difficulties. Among other things, it found itself bogged down in the details surrounding implementation of the dialog boxes.

When the team backed off from the picture a bit and examined the situation for what it was, it found that it had included too much in the stripe. It remedied the situation by considering the components of the map editor. One component was the tile floor. Another was the dialog box capability. Still another was the capacity of load and save. When the team broke these into separate stripes, the complexity of the task diminished, details of implementation became much clearer, and it was possible to proceed with confidence into the development of what became the full functionality of the map editor. Figure 9.31 shows a screen shot of the map editor used to place a mesh. (It was pleasing to everyone to at last make use of Paul Whitehead's meshes, because this opened up many new testing and tuning opportunities.)

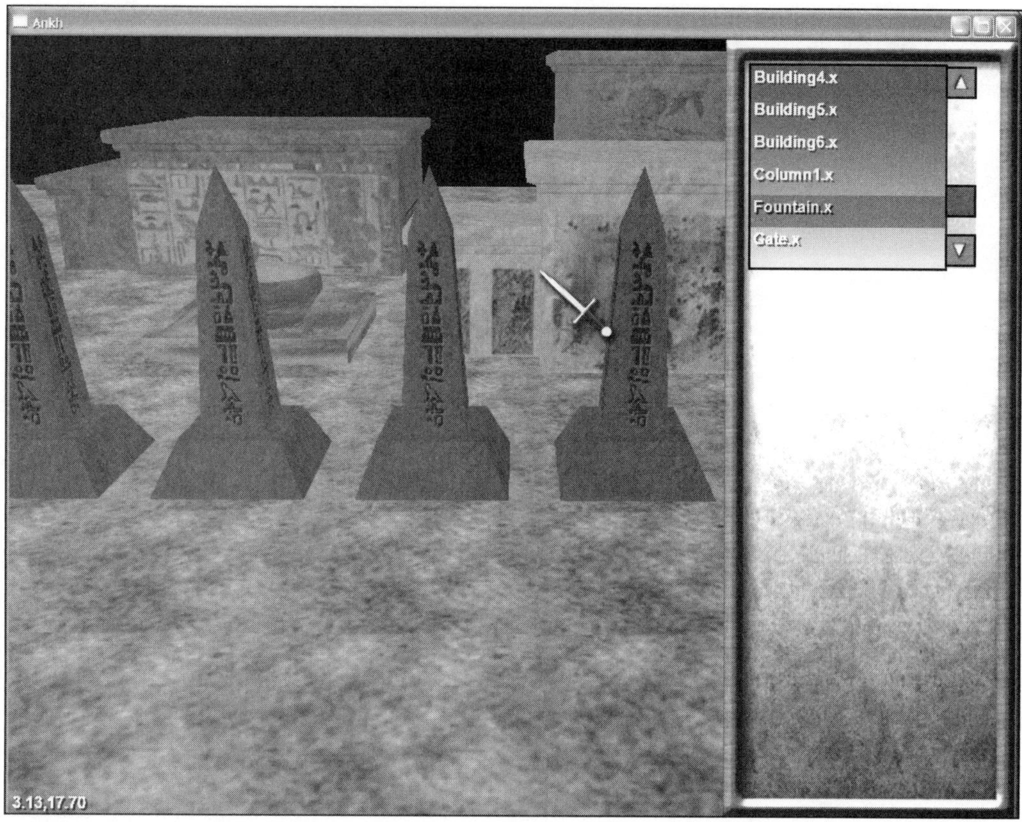

Figure 9.31
Stripes 2.0 through 2.4 implement the map editor.

Construction Using the Map Editor

The map editor as a tool for development is invaluable. The functionality of the map editor tremendously facilitates the construction of layers. Figure 9.32 illustrates the map editor that was used to begin construction of the first level. At this point in development, it is possible to set the camera at a high angle. It is also possible to maintain wide views of the layer area, so objects in the layer can be positioned easily to accord with the game design document specifications. (Some of this functionality was eliminated from the deliverable.) Figure 9.32 illustrates construction of the level as conducted by Ben Vinson.

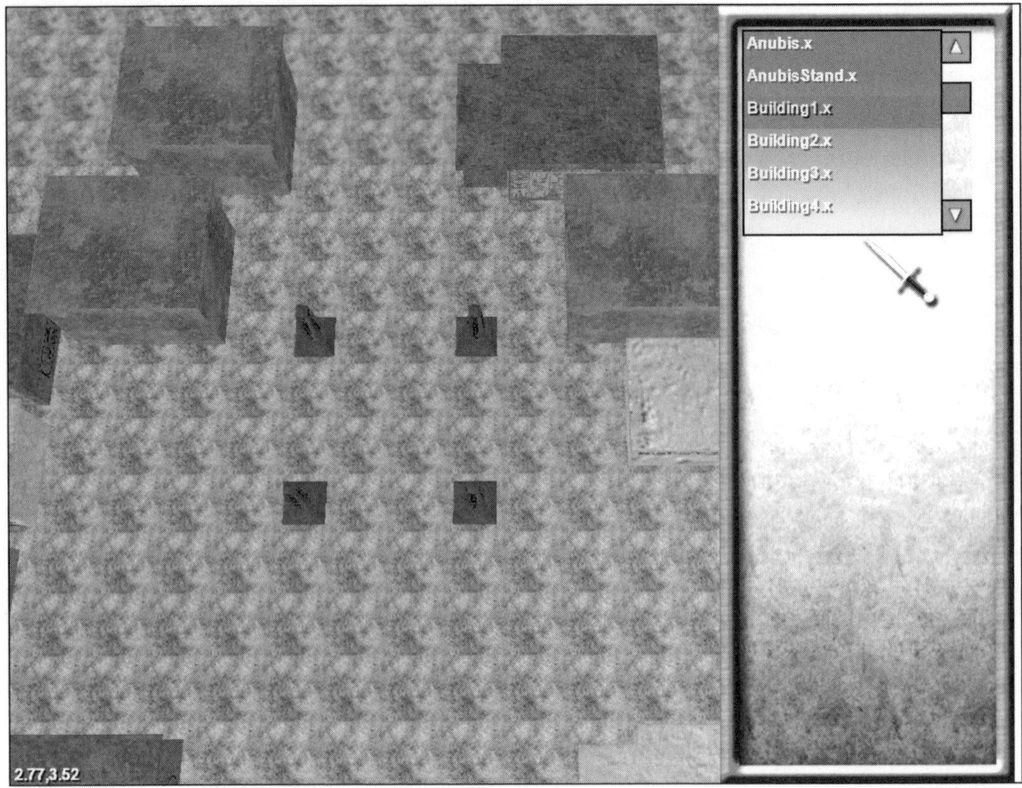

Figure 9.32
Ben Vinson used the map editor to construct the first level.

Game Design Specification

So that you have some perspective, all of the stripes detailed thus far could be developed using only one layer as a base of development. Combining the map editor with a thoroughly detailed design document made the construction of the game levels fairly easy. Figure 9.33 provides a view of the first level from the game design document, as specified by *Ankh* game designer, John Rose. To view the complete game design document for *Ankh*, access the game design documentation directory on the CD.

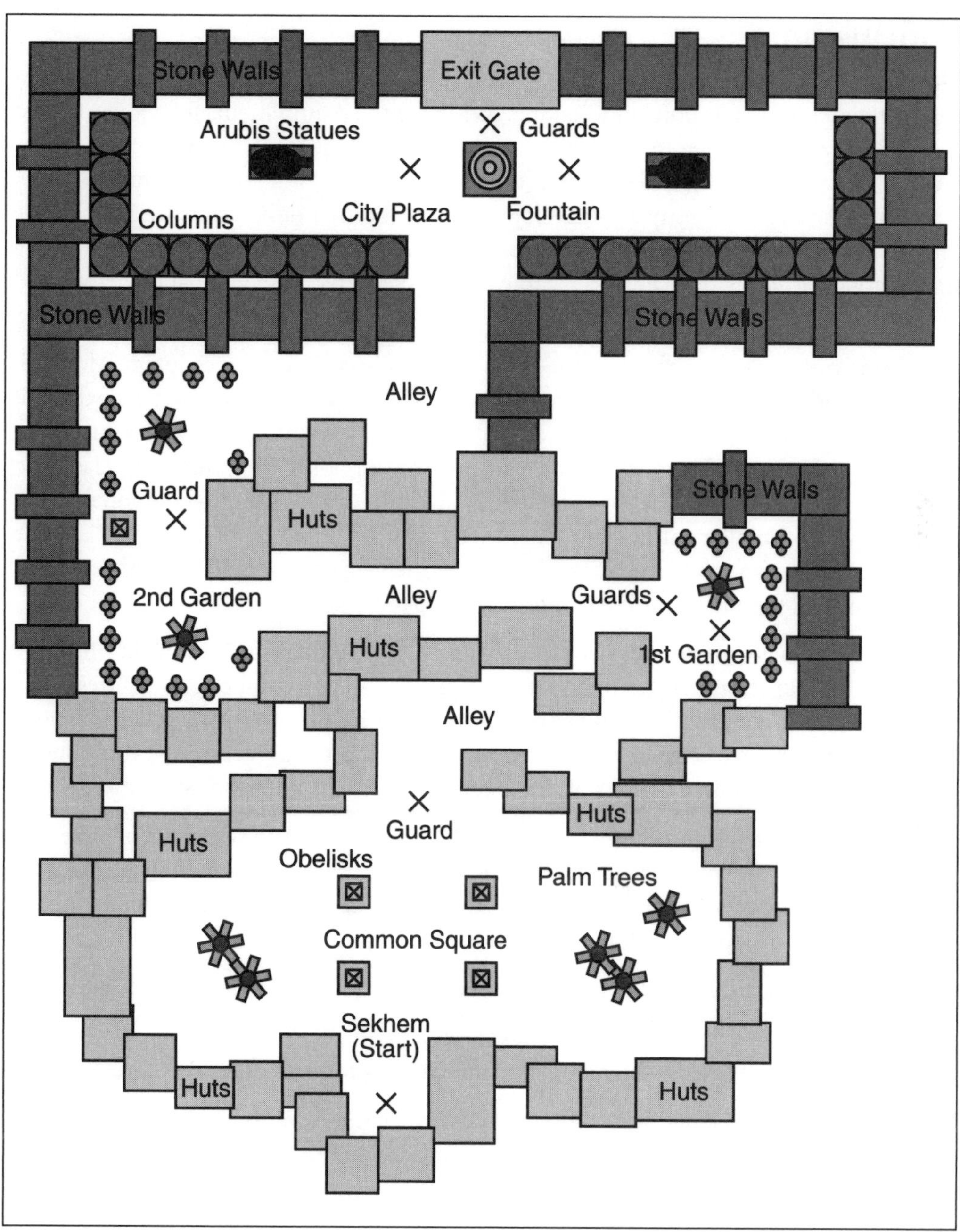

Figure 9.33
John Rose's view of the first level.

Conclusion

This chapter showed movement through the iterative design and implementation of *Ankh*. Design can be a flexible undertaking. As long as the requirements for the game exist in a stable form, the design remains open to alterations as the implementation effort proceeds. The key to successful design iteration lies in establishing stripes of functionality that can be understood easily and developed readily. From a design perspective, a stripe can be depicted as a component, which can be defined as a set of classes that provides a single service or set of services to the game as a whole. A use case view can be employed to verify the design of a stripe.

The theme of this chapter remains the same as it has been in earlier chapters. Although some methodologies of software development allow requirements to be flexible, it remains that a stable set of well-scoped, well-defined requirements underlies successful software development. From this basis, you can develop a set of preliminary classes to address the requirements. Then you can begin to group the classes into components and provide a way of implementing components. Two stripes might involve substantially the same set of classes and the same components, but each stripe represents the implementation of specific refinements of the component's capabilities.

As you proceed with a game development project, realize that you can break one large effort into smaller efforts. If you find that the development of a component requires much more time than anticipated, you might benefit from taking time to consider whether your effort can be redirected so that you attempt to develop limited aspects of the component. You can view these limited aspects of the first component as independent components.

Although no vast literature exits for the approach to iterative design presented here, several current methodologies provide perspectives on design that have proven highly successful for application development. These approaches are also suitable for game development. For further explorations, see the following books:

Braude, Eric. *Software Design: From Programming to Architecture.* Hoboken, New Jersey: John Wiley & Sons, 2004.

Liberty, Jesse. *Clouds to Code.* Birmingham, United Kingdom: WROX Press Ltd, No Date.

Martin, Robert C. *Agile Software Development: Principles, Patterns, and Practices.* Upper Saddle River, New Jersey: Pearson Education, Inc, 2003.

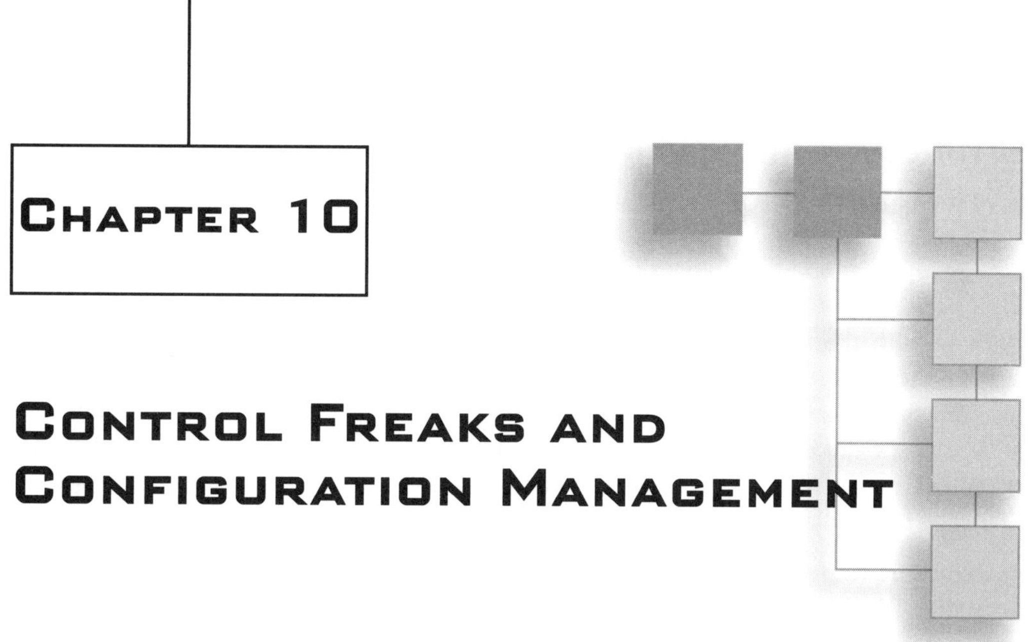

Chapter 10

Control Freaks and Configuration Management

During your game development effort, you are likely to create many thousands of lines of code. In addition, you or those with whom you work will create many assets, such as sound and graphics files. To ensure that you do not lose, overwrite, or accidentally delete such files, you can put in place a Software Configuration Management (SCM) system. An SCM system has both software application and policy divisions. In the software application division, you choose and implement a software application that allows you to track versions of your files. You also select a software application that allows you to create an installation package. In the policy division, you create a software configuration plan. The software configuration plan enables you to document how you want to set up the directories for your development effort. It also allows you to establish conventions for writing code and naming files. Following are some of the topics covered:

- Establishing a culture for configuration activities
- Establishing policies for configuration practices
- Selecting tools for version control and installation
- Analyzing the design document to discover prospective directory structures and file names
- Setting up a build schedule
- Creating baselines using the software design and the project plan
- Arranging for disaster recovery
- Assisting with the creation of the installation package

Software Configuration Management in General

SCM is a requirement that most standards organizations establish as a starting point for organizational maturity. The term "configuration" applies to both the equipment you use for development and the changes in the files that the software system you are developing comprises. As a software configuration manager, you might find yourself during one hour working with the names of all the code and asset files that your game encompasses. During another hour, you might find yourself erasing a drive on a test machine so that you can conduct a test installation. Configuration also applies to identifying the elements of the system and auditing the status of each element in relation to each other element. When you perform this type of work, you ensure that one developer does not repeat or delete the work of another developer.

As a software configuration manager, you are in a position to select tools and set policies that allow the development team to work in an efficient, effective way. Among possible responsibilities, you might help the team develop polices to cover code integration, testing, and the use of private and shared resources. In addition to helping focus on policies, you work extensively with the version control system. Throughout the development process, the team's collective effort forms an increasingly valuable product, and you must take measures to ensure that versions of files and assets are managed continuously so that developers do not work in counterproductive ways by deleting or needlessly rewriting each other's work. In addition to version control, you are concerned with disaster recovery and product security.

As a configuration manager, your job can extend over numerous activities that en-compass responsibilities for designing, developing, testing, and deploying the software in a coherent, coordinated fashion. Figure 10.1 provides a summary view of these activities.

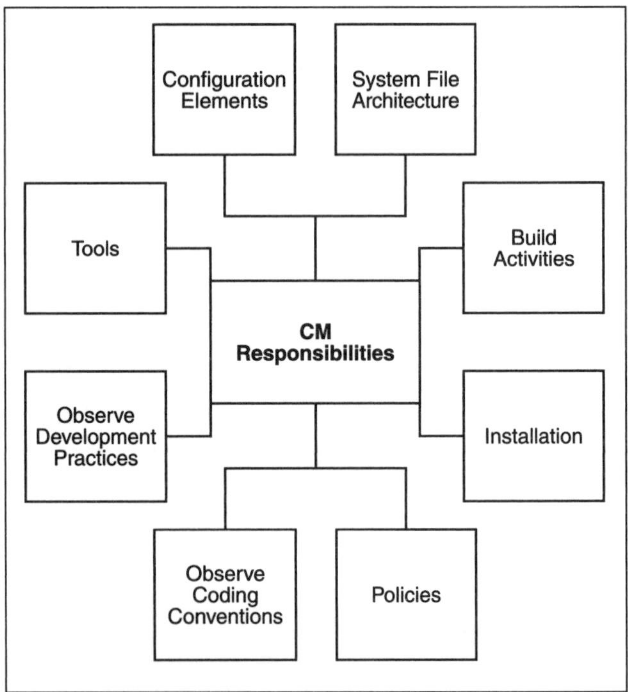

Figure 10.1
Software configuration management involves performing a variety of different activities.

Policies

Software configuration management concerns can be divided into two general areas. One is *policies*; the other is *development activities.* With respect to policies, the configuration manager is the person on the team who creates the culture and policies that guide the team as it maintains its code configuration. Creating a culture involves vocalizing good practices and helping others put good practices to work. Creating policies involves creating documents and programming tools that formally describe and restrict code management activities.

Defining Roles

Practices as policies possess effectiveness if they reflect and reinforce conventions. To establish conventions, you can build awareness among team members of how roles can foster consistent practices. Probably the most common roles encompass development, testing, and configuration management. These three roles are welded together by a common set of practices that serve to ensure that code is not needlessly lost, duplicated, or deleted, that changes are merged, that progress is audited and evaluated, and that the product remains safely stored. Figure 10.2 illustrates the dynamic that emerges. As a software configuration manager, you are likely to find that although your work is distinct and in some ways at odds with the work of testing and development, you are nevertheless central to ensuring that everyone else on team finds it easy to participate in the development effort.

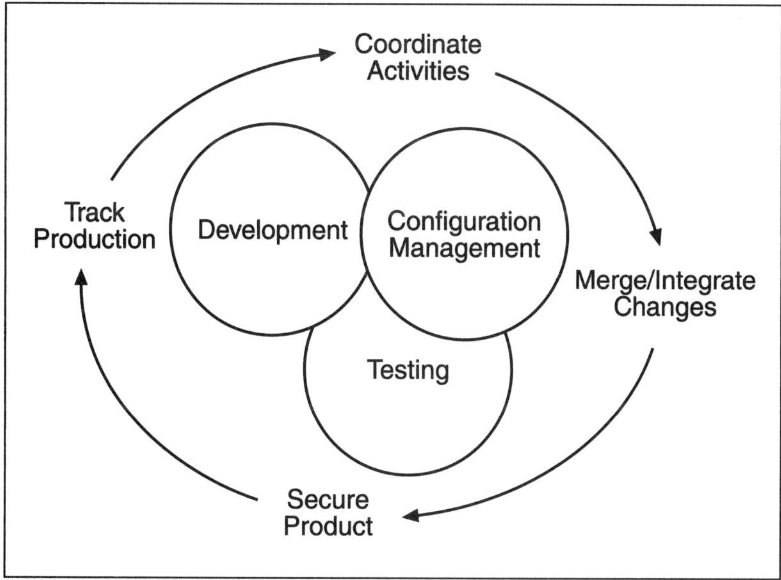

Figure 10.2
Roles emerge and foster a fundamental dynamic of responsibilities.

Change Control Parameters

When you work as a software configuration manager, you are often in the position, especially at the initial stages of a project, of establishing parameters that the rest of the team can accept or challenge as it creates its configuration policies. Although comprehensively naming these parameters requires much more space than is available in this chapter, it is still possible to select from the many possibilities a set that gives you an idea of the issues that often erupt when members of a team begin debating what they find acceptable or unacceptable in the creation of configuration policies.

The following list summarizes a few of the many policy issues that arise during a development effort:

- **Strict change control.** You can configure your version control software so that whenever a developer checks out or checks in code, he must perform a set of mandatory actions. These can include activities such as adding comments to the code, adding comments to a log, or running tests. You also can set up strict requirements on how and whether developers can create branches and how long they can maintain private versions of code before merging or integrating.
- **Flexible change control.** If you work with a development team that consists of individuals who possess a strong degree of professional maturity, you might decide that the best policy involves sticking with a basic configuration management system and leaving it to developers to decide for themselves how to do things. In such settings, you must depend on developers to communicate frequently with each other to resolve conflicts in code and to schedule divisions of labor that allow everyone to work in a concerted manner.
- **Propagating changes.** Assume that you have one module that provides functionality that two other modules require. Assume, further, that you can develop the first module in a rudimentary way so that it provides the functionality that the other two modules require but does so in a slow, cumbersome way. When you approach the problem of how to develop these three modules, you face a problem of propagation of changes. If you hurriedly develop the first module and then immediately launch into work on the second and third modules, you likely will have to return to the first module, make changes to increase efficiency and ease of use, and then change the second and third modules to reflect these changes. It is worthwhile to consider policies relating to this. One approach, for example, might be that you don't change the names of operations (functions). Likewise, if you are to implement improved functionality, you might not change the parameters and return values of the improved operation.
- **Version numbers.** Version numbers can be a problem. Chapter 17, "Release Planning and Management," provides a discussion of numbering formats, but here the focus is on how much detail you want to capture during the development process.

Some numbering systems use a combination of the date and the time to provide a unique version stamp for each build. Others use a simple system that increments the number for each build. Generally, it is important to assess whether your version control software supports the type of numbering template you want to implement. If your system cannot automate the numbering template, it is probably a good idea to consider another template (or possibly another versioning system).

- **Release naming.** In many software development settings, developers use nomenclatures rather than numbers. For example, some development teams name releases after rocks: mica, feldspar, granite, obsidian, and so on. Developers use names rather than numbers when numbers create needless confusion. Imagine, for example, that you plan to release your game at version 1.0, and you have had all the boxes and literature printed up to indicate as much. At the last possible moment, a marketing representative wants to release a special "limited" version. To deal with this situation, using a name rather than a number proves extremely useful.
- **Files between branches.** Many developers adamantly insist that branches should not share files. This is usually an excellent policy. But if your team allows for special cases of branching, it might be more convenient to share files. Imagine a situation in which you decide temporarily to create two branches so that you can explore the options provided by two successive releases of a component library. Except for those files to which you want to apply the questioned library components, you share all files between the two branches. Because this is a temporary, experimental branching operation, sharing is probably a reasonable option.
- **Maintain the current version.** Even if the primary code line is not ultimately harmed, difficulties can be created if developers manage their files irresponsibly. Consider what happens if someone is working on a local drive, fetches files from an earlier version, and replaces current versions with them. An extraordinary amount of work might become necessary before the work that results can be integrated fully with the work of others. Because such things happen, accidentally or intentionally, it is reasonable to restrict permissions in certain ways.
- **Permissions.** Developers should probably be the only people who have full permissions to check in and check out files. If other people have access to the code, harm might result. One obvious area of concern is whether the code is secure. In some instances, state-of-the-art development efforts represent extremely valuable company assets. Although it requires extra work to set up the system so that restrictions govern code and asset file access, the effort might be worth it.
- **Source cleanup.** When developers check in files, they can leave a great deal of test code in them. They also can leave them uncommented. Finally, they can leave them in need of a great deal of tuning. Establishing policies about how much work should be put into cleaning up a file prior to checking it in can result in a substantial improvement in productivity.

Setting Up the System

Generally, a software configuration manager does not work alone to choose the development environment. The choice of a development environment usually rests with the culture of the company, the requirements of the customer, and the preferences of the project manager and the team as a whole. After the development environment has been specified, however, it often remains the responsibility of the configuration manager to help all members of the team maintain the same environment for the duration of the project. Among the responsibilities that fall under this heading are these:

- **Maintaining the same basic equipment configuration.** It is usually considered essential that everyone work with the same compiler. The same goes for any software application used in the development effort. Even the use of two versions of the same compiler can create problems. Battling errors that result from differences that arise from conflicting versions of development equipment wastes development time.
- **Checking on upgrades of the integrated development environment.** It is more than likely that on a project that extends for a month or more, new releases of software used in the development effort will occur. You can deal with such releases in two ways. You can make a decision at the start of the project not to use upgrades or releases that occur after the commencement of the development effort. This is an extreme position, and in some cases might be impossible to honor. The other approach is to carefully evaluate the effects that a new release has on the development effort. You can use branching to offset some of the risks of using newly released software. This topic is discussed later in this chapter.
- **Maintaining licenses for software.** One hazard that any development company faces arises from strictures regarding ownership and uses of software. Even if you are using open source software, sometimes development efforts must proceed with permissions. Likewise, using a pirated copy of a commercial application to develop a commercial product creates enormous liabilities, even if the application plays a minor role in your development effort. To ensure that all members of the team have legally sound working environments, the software configuration manager sometimes ends up as a kind of friendly auditor.

Selection of Tools

Selecting software applications that address version control, installer creation, and trouble tracking involves addressing a list of requirements that are specific to your project. On the other hand, certain requirements are general and tend to extend almost any project. Whether specific or general, the requirements you use to select tools establish what you will be able to do as you proceed with your development effort.

Version Control Applications

It is almost universal that a development team will want to exert tight control over versions of software created during the development effort. A version control system is the primary, if not sole, means to such control. Later sections of this chapter discuss use of version control software fairly extensively. Table 10.1 provides a set of criteria you can use to evaluate a version control application.

Table 10.1 Version Control Tool Evaluation Criteria

Item	Discussion
Operating system	If you are developing in a Windows environment, you need to choose a system that is suitable for Windows. Selecting a recently ported system is probably not a good idea.
Dependencies	If you select a version control system that depends on Oracle, SQL Server, or some other database, you might have to acquire a license or licenses for the database in addition to the licenses for the version control software. If you use a system like Concurrent Versions System (CVS), you can avoid this situation, but then factors that mandate use of a commercial database might dictate a different choice.
Current version	Even if a vendor promises the world, you probably shouldn't invest in a first release. Likewise, use caution in using an untested release. If a stable release exists, use it.
Customization	Software applications that provide you with extensive customization options also tend to be more difficult to use. Consider whether you really need several custom features.
Size	The size of an application can be a major factor. If the application is so large that you need to upgrade everyone's workstation just to install the client, you should consider other options. On the other hand, even the server can be an issue. If the application requires disk and storage capacities that are far outside the requirements of the other software applications used on your project, again, you might want to reconsider.
Cost	Although many small development teams will choose SourceSafe or a flavor of CVS, excellent version control systems are available from companies like IBM (Rational) and Borland. The proprietary version control systems are usually part of a suite of applications, and if your company has a culture and the funds available for such products, they are worth considering.

(continued on next page)

Table 10.1 Version Control Tool Evaluation Criteria (continued)

Item	Discussion
Installation	There are two sides to the installation of a version control system. One side is the server side, which involves setting up permissions, file structures, and backup and restore procedures, among other tasks. The other side is the client, which among other things allows the user to check out and check in files. Installing the server should be quite a bit more involved than installing the clients, but limitations apply. Consider a situation, for example, in which you must first configure an Oracle database before you can install your version control manager. This might be worth doing. However, if it is worth doing, the price in terms of time and money could be substantial.
Branching	If a version control system does not enable you to branch with relative ease, something is wrong. Among the things to look for are whether and how easily you can change the name of branches, whether branch numbers or names can be incremented automatically, whether keywords can be used, and how easy it is to identify and access files of a given label.
Merging	A version control system should reliably track files and notify you when it discovers stale, conflicting, or unstable files. It also should provide you with file histories. As time goes on, version control systems that are capable of automatically resolving severe conflicts might be available. For now, unless you can afford an expensive commercial system, it is best not to put too much confidence in automated merging that involves resolving difficult code conflicts.
Promotion	You will probably want to set up versions as baselines, as the team did with the *Ankh* effort. When you do this, you apply a label to a given version and then branch it according to a level of promotion. See how easily the system you are evaluating handles such tasks.

TortoiseCVS

For the *Ankh* project, the team chose to use TortoiseCVS. TortoiseCVS is an implementation of CVS that runs on Windows. CVS and TortoiseCVS are software that you can acquire through the GNU General Public License. This license basically stipulates that although you can copy and use the software, you cannot change it. Following are some websites that provide information and downloads:

- **TortoiseCVS.** Access http://www.tortoisecvs.org/index.shtml.
- **Concurrent Versions System.** Access https://www.cvshome.org.
- **Free Software Foundation.** Access http://www.gnu.org.

TortoiseCVS is convenient for Windows users because it integrates into Windows Explorer. When you access files under version control management, you access them the same way that you access any other file in Windows Explorer. When you open a file directory, for example, the TortoiseCVS options are available to you as pop-up menu options. Using these options, you can check out, update, commit, and view differences in versions. Figure 10.3 shows a screen capture of folders that have been placed under TortoiseCVS management.

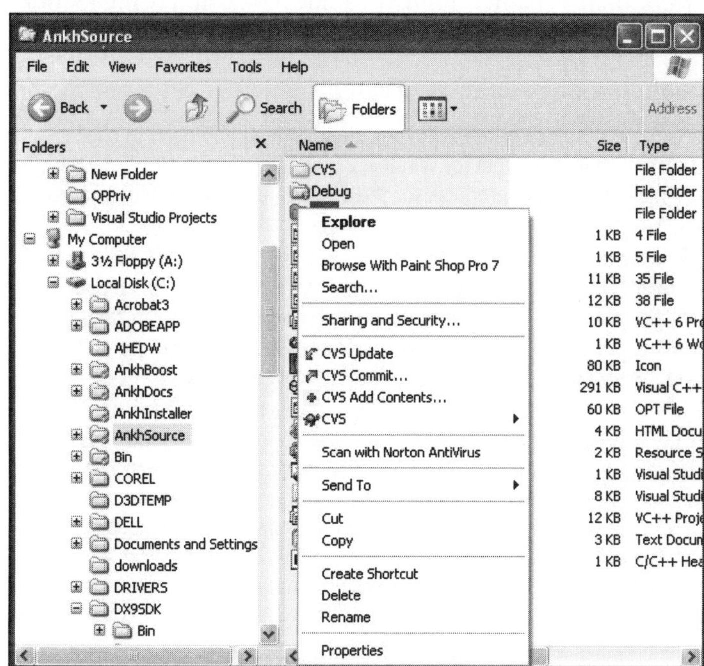

Figure 10.3
Integration with Windows Explorer makes TortoiseCVS easy to use.

Although TortoiseCVS does not manage builds or allow you to enforce change control policies, it does allow you to tag, branch, and merge versions of files. It also allows you to access log information by using such utilities as CVSWeb. TortoiseCVS stores differences between versions of files and then assembles these differences when you request it to do so. Specific uses of TortoiseCVS could easily consume several chapters of this book. To learn how to use TortoiseCVS, go to the sites mentioned previously and read the instructions provided with the application.

Installer Creation Applications

An application for creating installation programs allows you to designate the files and directories you want to have created when your application is installed, and it allows you to designate which material you want placed in the directories. Table 10.2 provides a set of criteria you can use to evaluate applications that create installation programs. You can obtain commercial applications for creating installation programs from Wise and InstallShield. Free of charge, Microsoft offers the Windows Installer (MIS). The *Ankh* development team chose an application from Jordon Russell called Inno Setup (ISTool). Later on, in the "Installation" section, this chapter discusses a sample session using ISTool.

Table 10.2 Installation Creation Tool Evaluation Criteria

Operating system	If you are developing in a Windows environment, you need to choose a system that is suitable for Windows. InstallShield and Wise provide the best commercial products for the creation of installation packages for Windows.
Customization	Of the two most popular commercial installers for Windows, Wise and InstallShield, Wise is said to be the most difficult to use. Difficulty of use generally means that you get a greater variety of customization options. The *Ankh* team selected ISTool because it was free (as is the Windows installer from Microsoft, MSI) and easy to use.
Cost	For the *Ankh* project, the team decided to use ISTool, which is freeware. This application was perfect for *Ankh* because the game was designed to be installed on the Windows operating system and had no complexities that might have justified investment in a commercial product. If you are involved in a project in which you want to customize and automate your installation options using files from a database, you might find that the professional and enterprise options justify the price.
Ease of use	Selecting files and creating directories should be easy. Likewise, you should be able to customize names and set install options for files and directories as you go. These are the basics. For more involved operations, the efforts increase in complexity, as does the price you need to pay.
Scripting capabilities	To add dialogue, download options, and other features to your installation routine, your installer application should provide a convenient scripting option.
MSI support	The ISTool does not use Microsoft Windows Installer (MSI). MSI provides a store of capabilities that allow you to control the installation and removal of your application, but it is generally considered difficult to use. Wise and InstallShied are alternatives to MSI, as is ISTool.

Problem Reporting Applications

You can use a tracking system for problem reports in various ways. During the development phase, you can use such a system to log defect reports. For criteria on applications for reporting problems, see Chapter 17.

Creating an SCM Plan

When establishing policies for software configuration management, it is a good idea to reserve specific planning with respect to directories and files until the design of the software has been baselined. Using the software design, you then can proceed confidently with structuring directories and creating items such as build schedules. In addition to managing the configuration of the software, you can establish coding conventions. Configuration information regulates how the development team names files and directories. Coding standards regulate what goes inside of files, such as how you name classes, operations, and class attributes. Together, a configuration plan and a set of coding conventions allow the team to proceed with a coordinated effort.

Introduction
  Purpose
  Scope
  Definitions
  References
Management
  Organization
  Responsibilities
  Interface Control
  Plan Implementation
SCM Activities
  Identification
  Control
  Status Accounting
  Audits and Reviews
  Release Process
Tools and Techniques
Supplier Control

Figure 10.4
The IEEE standard provides a starter set of categories for an SCM plan.

Using a Template

The IEEE Standard 1042 provides a template for a software development plan. Figure 10.4 provides a summary view of the IEEE template.

As with any template, it is a good idea to review the included headings to see if they offer reasonable guides for gathering and organizing information that is relative to your project. Exclude headings that you find superfluous. Table 10.3 reviews the topics introduced in the template shown in Figure 10.4.

Table 10.3 SCM Template Topics

Topic	Discussion
Introduction	This is the first division of the document. This section provides a way to present the general dimensions of your plan.
Purpose	Point out that the purpose of the plan is to set polices and establish tool customization priorities. Also, indicate that the plan provides a guide to the structure of the directories and modules (or stripes) that embody the design. In addition, specify that the plan establishes a working basis for regulating testing, file merger, integration, and release activities.
Scope	The scope extends to the whole of the game software product. One qualification is that the scope of the software configuration plan cannot be fully specified until the software design specification is completed.

(continued on next page)

Table 10.3 SCM Template Topics (continued)

Topic	Discussion
Definitions	The definition list includes terms that help the reader understand how your game software is designed and used. With the development of *Ankh*, for example, the design of the configuration for the directories and files was predicated on the creation of stripes, so it was worthwhile to include "stripe" in the list of defined terms.
References	Two important references are those to the software requirements specification and the software design specification. The software requirements specification provides a reference for testing. The software design specification provides information you need to set up directories and plan baselines and releases. If you have developed supplemental documents, such as a coding standards document or a release management plan, you can provide references to them under this heading.
Management	This is a major section of the document. It explains how you intend to manage the SCM program that the document specifies.
Organization	You can use this section to explain that the SCM plan applies to the group on a consensus basis and is intended as a guide, not a set of dictates. On the other hand, you can point out that certain stipulations must be observed strictly.
Responsibilities	Roles can be described in this section. Developers have responsibilities to name files and directories according to the conventions that the document provides. Among other things, you can provide suggestions or stipulations about checking out and checking in code.
Interface Control	You can use this section to discuss use of the version control system and the installation creation package. Control issues pertain to permissions and use.
Plan Implementation	The implementation of the plan can appear as a table that shows needed stages of development. The preliminary plan, for example, might establish policies and practices. Then a detailed plan might follow the first baseline of the software design specification.
SCM Activities	This is a major section of the document. It easily can become the largest and most important part of the document, because it provides information about the details of day-to-day operations.
Identification	Under this heading, you can list criteria for how to identify versions. It would be appropriate, for example, to designate your numbering template or to list the pool of terms from which you can draw to designate releases. You can include file-naming conventions, in addition to approaches to using labels and keys.
Control	You can state policies in this section. Issues that are suitable for discussion include policies you intend to assert through strict enforcement or to use as specifications for customization of tools.

Topic	Discussion
Status Accounting	You can name the types of information you want to collect through software configuration management activities. The information for which you can obtain summary reports depends on the tools you use. For example, you can obtain information about incremental versions of files between baselines, identity of system users, problems with stale or conflicting files, and the time required to effect mergers.
Audits and Reviews	You can use this section to address how to review code or the SCM process. An audit might involve identifying the quality assurance measures that a standards organization provides. Review might pertain to the maintenance of the SCM plan.
Release Process	In this section, you can provide a list of key items to be attended to during the release phase of your game software development effort. If the information you want to include in this section proves too extensive, you can create a separate document, a software release plan.
Tools and Techniques	This is a major section of the document. In it, you can name and discuss reasons for buying, leasing, or acquiring through open source whatever applications you decide to make a part of the SCM effort. Obvious candidates are the version control system, the installation creation application, and the problem reporting system.
Supplier Control	This, too, is a major section of the document. If you use vended or acquired software, you should collect information in this section that allows you to document license agreements, contact service and support representatives, and understand release schedules.

Coding Standards

Chapter 13, "What People Do—Development Strategies," discusses the practical use of coding standards. In the current context, the discussion can involve approaches to structuring and presenting coding standards. It is a good idea to provide a reference to this document—if you create it as a separate document—in the software configuration plan. See the item for "References" in Table 10.3.

Reviewing the Plan

It is probably not a good idea to try to create a software configuration management plan in one work session. Rather, you should create the plan over the period extending from the start of the project to the beginning of the software implementation. For most efforts, the implementation of the software begins after the software has been designed. The design enables everyone to understand the architecture of the software. The architecture, in turn, enables the software configuration manager to determine with a fair degree of accuracy just how the directory structure for the software should be laid out. Figure 10.5 illustrates the flow of activity that might characterize the creation of a configuration plan.

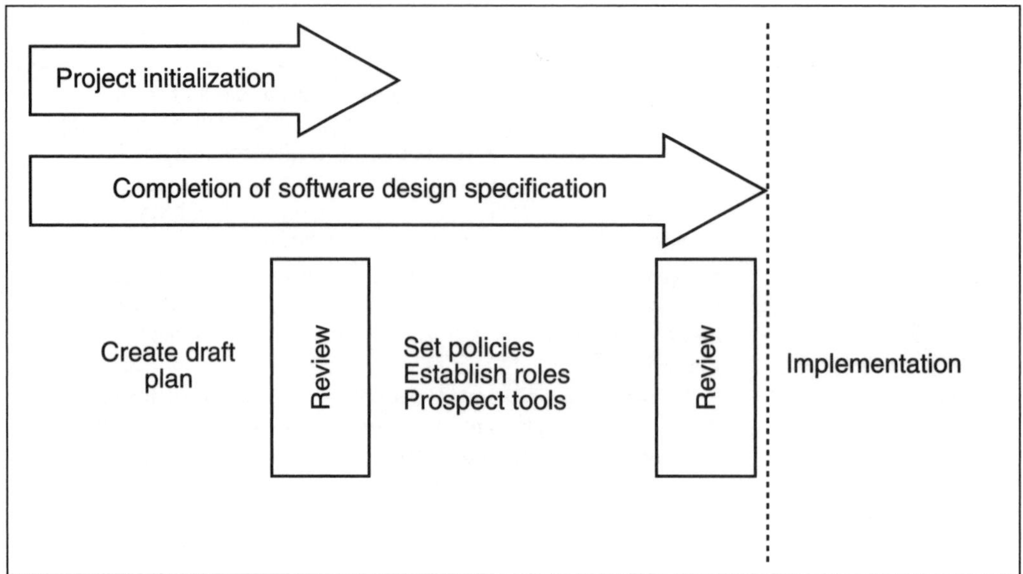

Figure 10.5
Information about design establishes a firm basis for the finalization of the configuration plan.

Development Activities

Especially on smaller teams, configuration management can involve a dual role, one that combines configuration management and development. When this happens, the individual in this role can become frustrated because he has the unenviable task of being responsible for both specific development tasks and maintenance of the software configuration for others. To keep such work in perspective, the best approach is to define specifically the work that constitutes configuration management. If the work is well defined, the person who assumes such responsibilities will be able to know the set of essential tasks and plan accordingly.

Auditing Program States

SCM involves being able to tell how and to what extent files change between work sessions. Such information proves essential to the development effort because developers must be able to know with certainty how their work affects the work of others. If two developers work on the same file, for example, they must be able to determine if their changes represent successive states of the software. If this is the case, it is likely that the developer whose changes are second in succession will be able to merge his work into the files that the first developer modified. The state of a program, then, can be characterized as a point in its development when a given degree of functionality has been developed.

Knowing both the time at which the program has been modified and the changes that have been made in the program allow developers to determine how to judge and guide their efforts in implementing functionality.

Build Activities

If auditing the state of a software system is the first concern of SCM, performing builds is the next. Builds during the development process represent incremental assemblages of the functionality of the system. Probably the best terms to apply to such assemblages are "versions" or "revisions." During the development phase of a game software lifecycle, developers can create hundreds of such versions. In each case, to create a version, developers build and compile the system. As the number of lines of code increases, building and compiling the system can become a drawn-out process. For this reason, developers prefer to restrict builds to encompass only files that have been changed during a given session of work. Working on a file or set of files and building and compiling the system using only changed files allows developers to check their work continuously. But it remains that if the entire system is to be assembled from the work of many people, all the changes must be integrated.

Because comprehensive integrations of newly developed or revised code often require that the build has hours to run, developers write scripts to automate build routines. Developers generally program these to run at night. As the developers build a product, they can generate a log of warnings and errors. Then they can inspect a record of the build to see what problems occurred. They usually perform builds on a daily basis. Policies regulate actions to be taken with respect to different build results. For example, a policy might stipulate that if a given version of a given file creates errors, the programmer must revert to the previous successful version of the file and work forward until he discovers the problem. If this is too draconian, the programmer might not be allowed to proceed with the implementation of further functionality until he eliminates all the problems from the existing build.

Program Files and Components

Given that you have completed the software design specification, you are in an excellent position to plan the directory structure of the product. You can map the directory structure on a tentative basis and then add it to the configuration management plan for revision as the project progresses. In an object-oriented context using C++, you know that most classes will have corresponding header and implementation files. To establish the directory structure, you must examine the software architecture. As shown in Figure 10.6, the *Ankh* team created a table in which prospective files could be organized via functional groupings. Early in the project, you can name the files tentatively on the basis of the classes for which CRC cards have been created.

In addition to setting up directories and creating an initial set of files, early configuration work involves evaluating and planning components—files of classes that are treated as single units. Some components are derived from third-party software libraries. These might be in the form of binary files. Others might be in the form of code that must be compiled but that become separate executables when compiled. Regardless of how the components come into existence, it remains that they have versions, and differences of version present a risk to the stability of the system. For this reason, it makes sense to track the components of the system in much the same way that you track versions of files. Figure 10.6 provides a table created for the *Ankh Configuration Management Plan.*

Boost//.	**Game//.**	**Graphics//.**	**State//.**
convenience.cpp	basic data.txt	CCamera.cpp	CCharacterState.cpp
exception.cpp	CAI.h	CCamera.h	CIntroState.cpp
operations_posix_windows.cpp	CEntity.cpp	CD3DFont.cpp	CMapEditorState.cpp
path_posix_windows.cpp	CEntity.h	CD3DFont.h	CMenuState.cpp
	CException.cpp	CGraphics.cpp	CMenuState.h
	CException.h	CGraphics.h	CPlayState.cpp
CVS//.	CFileSystem.cpp	CImage.cpp	CState.h
Entries	CFileSystem.h	CImage.h	CStateMachine.cpp
Entries.Extra	CGame.cpp	CMesh.cpp	CStateMachine.h
Entries.Extra.Old	CGame.h	CSprite.cpp	
Entries.Old	CLog.h	CSprite.h	
Repository	CPlayer.cpp	CTileMap.cpp	
Root	CPlayer.h	CTileMap.h	
	CProfile.h		**Input//.**
GUI//.	CResource.cpp		CInput.cpp
CGuiMgr.cpp	CResource.h	**Sound//.**	CInput.h
CGuiMgr.h	CResourceMgr.cpp	CSound.cpp	
	CResourceMgr.h	CSound.h	
	CSettings.cpp	CVS	
	CSettings.h		
	CWorld.cpp		
	CWorld.h		

Figure 10.6
A table allows you to examine the ways in which you can group prospective code files.

Controlling Development Domains

Generally, files that are stored on the server constitute the shared domain, whereas files that are stored on the drives of developers constitute private domains. Even with a strong effort to define and implement a coherent directory and file configuration, configuration management efforts can fail if developers allow control of the configuration to migrate from the server to the drives of developers. Notice in Figure 10.7 that the broken lines indicate the files that developers transfer to each other locally. The solid lines indicate files under version control. The number of possible file combinations increases enormously when developers begin combining files in this way.

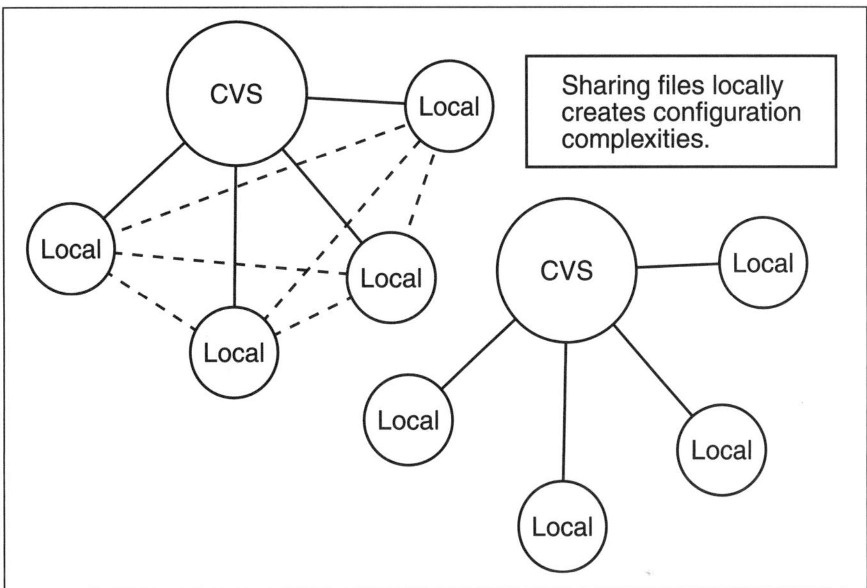

Figure 10.7
Establish protocols for file use to reduce the complexity of versioning.

Figure 10.7 illustrates what happens when developers begin trading files they are working on without using version control. Ultimately, the complexity increases exponentially. You can prevent this sort of thing by setting policies that make the dangers clear to everyone. Even the use of game assets can lead to problems, because all files are subject to change, even if they seem to be finished graphical or audio objects.

Baselined Versions and Releases

You can apply the term *baseline* to any version of your software and the artifacts (documents, diagrams, and so on) that apply to it. A baseline is, as the word implies, a line that you can use as a start, or base, of something else. Because a baseline is the start of something else, when a document or a set of implemented functionality has been baselined, the implication is that a review has taken place. A review is a formal examination, and it results in a conscious assertion by those who engage in it that the item under review meets or does not meet certain standards of quality.

Developers can create a version of a product at any point during the development cycle, and given versions can become baselines in a continuing effort. This is the approach that the team used in the development of *Ankh.* The *Ankh Software Configuration Plan* used the product design presented in the *Ankh Software Design Specification* to establish that the configuration scheme would be structured according to the stripes that the design anticipated.

In Chapter 13, in Figure 13.15, you can see the way that the stripes were configured. In Chapter 17, Figure 17.3 illustrates the stripes alone. The overall development effort is aided by a configuration scheme that makes the development something other than a long process that begins with the creation of files and ends with the final release of the product. Creating versions as baselines allows those on the project to incrementally examine the way that the development activity is proceeding and take measures to improve their effort as they go. Part of this effort involves examining the cohesiveness of the configuration. At each baseline, developers can take measures to clean up files and refactor code to eliminate redundancy and inelegance. Figure 10.8 shows the relationship among reviews, baselines, versions, and stripes. The shaded circles represent points of review.

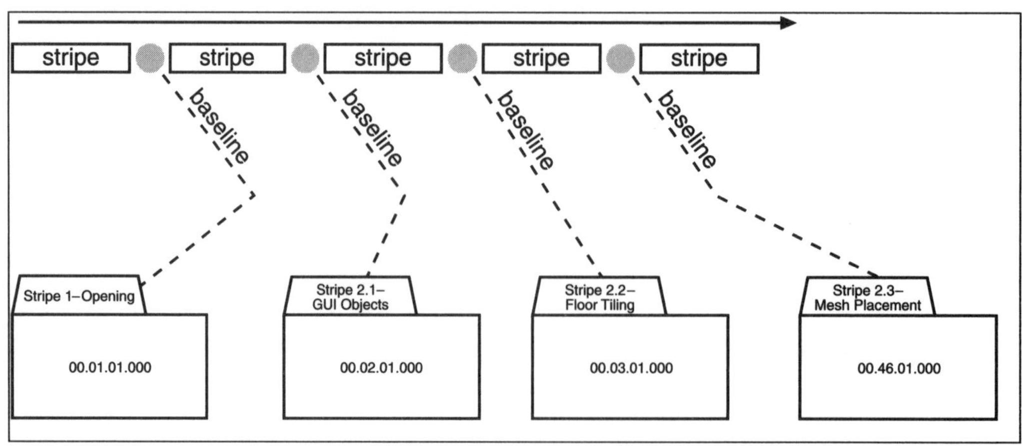

Figure 10.8
Versioning in conjunction with reviews and baselines enables developers to maintain the integrity of the configuration.

Branching Models

The term *branching* receives elaboration throughout the next several sections, but for starters, it applies to how you designate the lines (or branches) of code you are going to develop as you go. You can view a line of code as a set of files you maintain as a distinct development unit through successive builds. At the start of a development effort, it makes sense to think about what you want to allow with respect to branching, for if you do not, you can end up with a project that consists of many parallel efforts that must be merged with each other.

Concepts

Certain vocabulary items that refer to the version control and other configuration activities constantly crop up during any given development effort. For this reason, it is useful to review a few of these terms. Generally, illustrations help tremendously, but as yet, no standard UML diagram exists for showing version control operations.

Code Lines (Trunks), Deltas, and Merging

Figure 10.9 illustrates the most elementary type of version control activity software configuration. The long solid line is the *primary code line* or *trunk*. The primary code line or trunk is the collection of all files and assets that make up the system. In this situation, the developer might be pictured as opening a file, modifying it, and then saving it and trying to compile it. Practically everyone learns how to program using this approach.

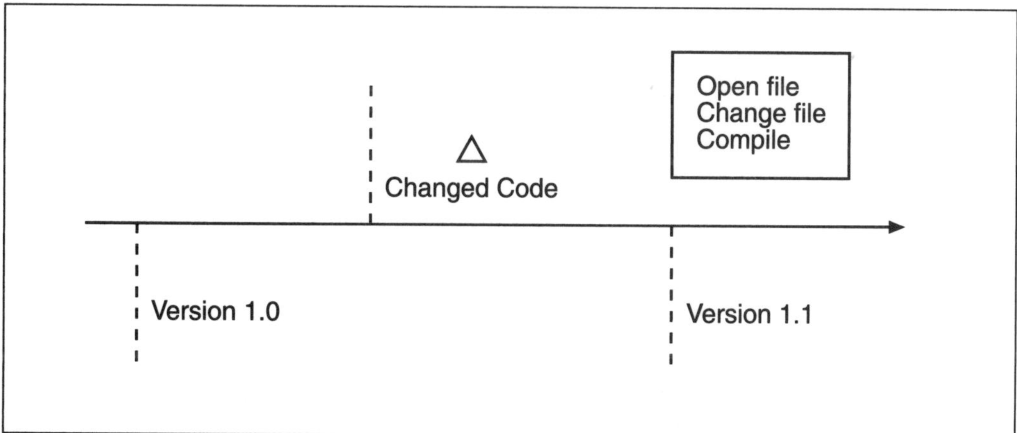

Figure 10.9
Beginner programming patterns involve a single branch of code.

The primary line of code for the beginner programmer migrates to a new state every time the beginner makes a change in the code. Because a backup file is not created, each time a state change occurs in the code, the previous state vanishes. Because the previous state vanishes, the beginning programmer soon discovers one of the first big problems with this way of doing things. Losing the difference (*delta*) between any two successive states means that it is no longer possible to *revert* to a previous state if something goes wrong.

One of the first lessons to arise from this situation is that it is extremely useful to "save off" a version of a file. Figure 10.10 illustrates the situation. Now the programmer has a backup copy of the code at each success stage. As much of a revolution as this approach to development might bring to the efforts of the beginner, one immediate result is that the number of versions of the software tends to equal the number of software sessions during which a change has been made to the code line.

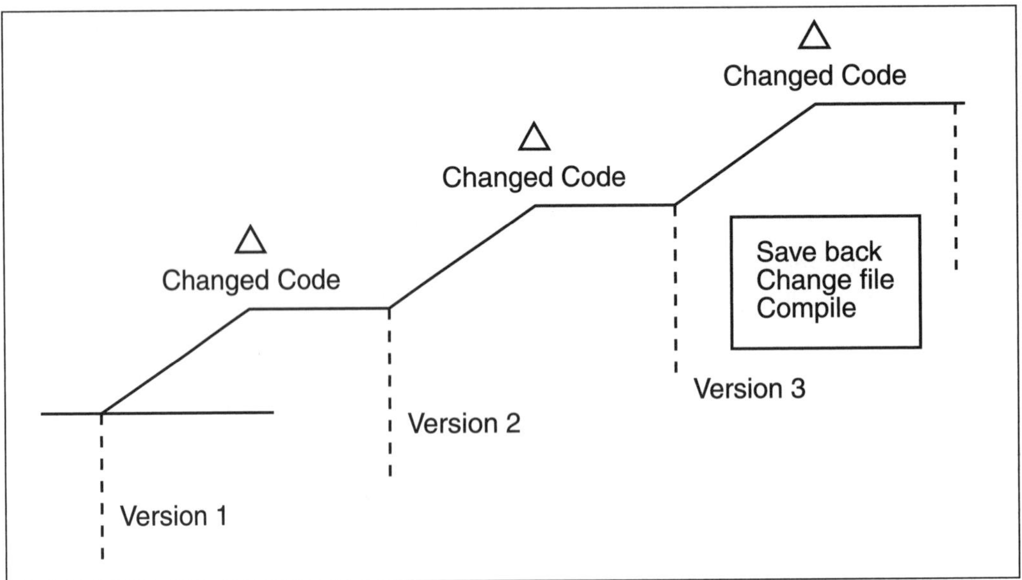

Figure 10.10
Saving to a new version or saving a backup preserves the delta.

Branching and Merging

Although initiating each coding session by saving back a version of the primary line of code has its advantages, the proliferation of archived files becomes a management problem. The question becomes whether there is a way that the trunk can change in a more restricted way. A simplified illustration of one approach to remedying this situation is shown in Figure 10.11. Here, the approach is to create a copy of the main line of the code. When you make a copy in this way, the copy is a branch. The branch is the set of files that make up the system. Then the branch is changed. If the changes prove acceptable, you can merge them back into the main line of code.

This approach allows the programmer to have what might be viewed as a temporary branch of the primary line of code for development purposes. The great advantage to this approach is that it preserves the integrity of a primary line of code while providing a way that development can occur on a provisional basis, away from the primary line of code.

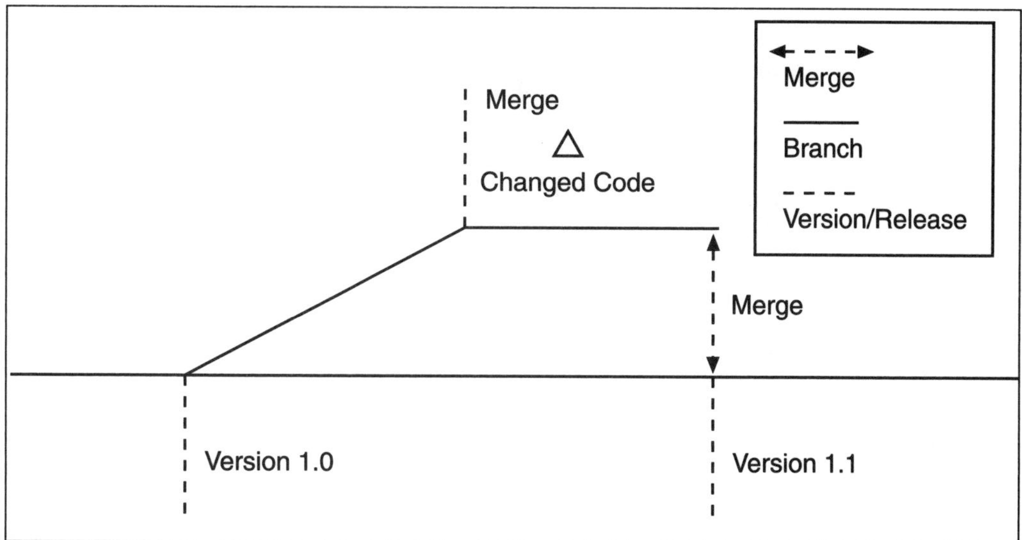

Figure 10.11
Version control begins with the notion that temporary branching can restrict the scope of change.

Trees and Stale and Conflicting Files

The utility of branching becomes a little more evident if you consider the actions of two or more programmers. Consider the situation that Figure 10.12 depicts. In that figure, two developers make changes in the primary line of code. Both start with the code at version 1.0. They obtain branching copies of the primary line of code, work on separate parts of it, and then merge the code back into the primary line of code. Momentarily branching for purposes of development allows both programmers to work simultaneously, make changes to the code, and then merge their changes back into the primary line of code. What makes the merger easy is that both developers start with the same version, and both merge their changes back into the code in sequence.

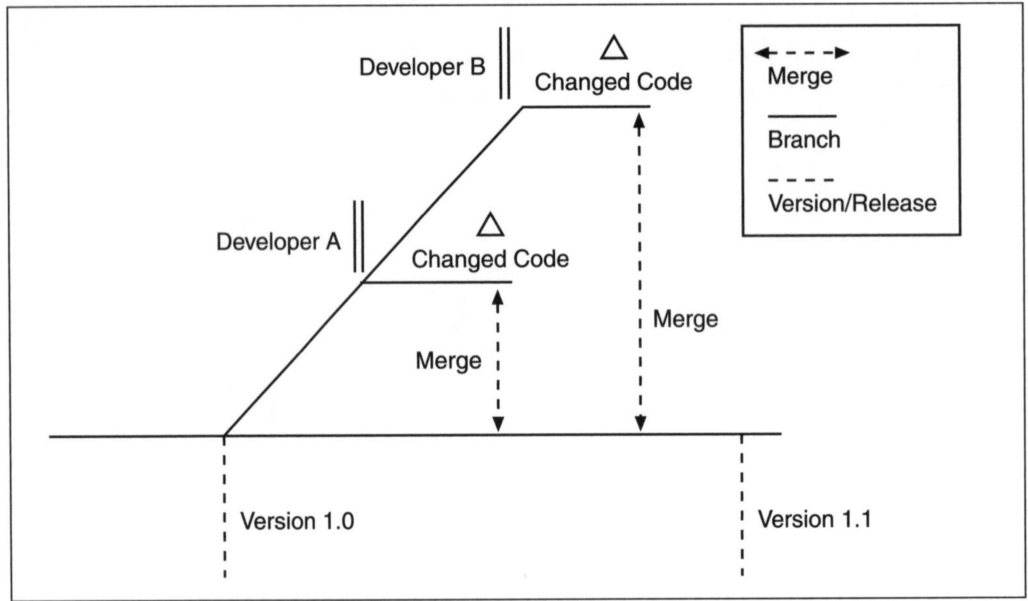

Figure 10.12
Two programmers work simultaneously through temporary branches and then merge their changes back into the primary line of code.

In the situation that Figure 10.12 represents, both developers begin with the same body of code, work on distinct files, and merge their changes in succession. As smooth as this operation seems to be on the surface, when several developers work on a primary line of code, one developer often submits changes that create difficulties for others. In one such situation, code becomes *stale.* Figure 10.13 illustrates what happens. Notice that developer B created a temporary branch of the code and went to work. Then developer A created a temporary branch of the code and likewise went to work. Developer A merged his changes with the primary line of code before developer B finished his work. When developer B tried to merge his code, he found that the main line of code was not the same as what he started with. For some or all of his development effort, then, he has been working with a stale version of the primary line of code.

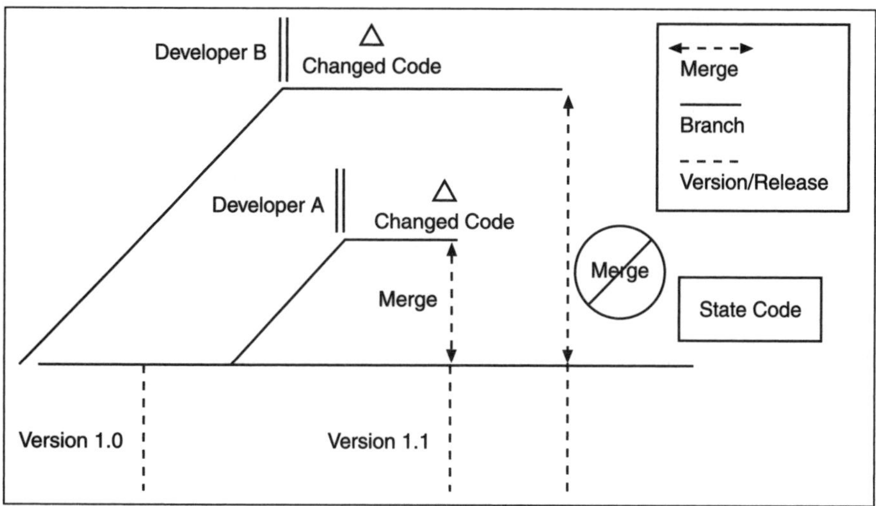

Figure 10.13
Stale code results when a developer begins work with code that has already been rendered out of date.

Yet another situation arises when two developers create temporary branches of the code and change the same lines of code in different ways. Figure 10.14 illustrates the situation. In this instance, developer A and developer B start off in good fashion with the same primary line of code. But then they change the same sections of the branched code, and when they go to merge their changes, they find they have a *conflict*. When this happens, the two developers must meet and decide which set of changes should be retained.

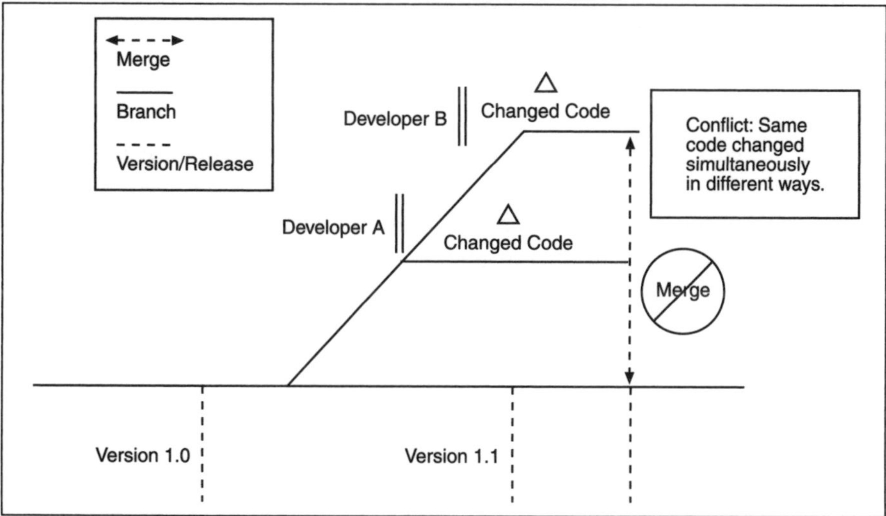

Figure 10.14
A conflict can occur when two developers change the same lines of code.

Tip of the Trunk and Labeling

The discussion so far has intended to drive home the idea that branching is any activity that allows developers to duplicate a primary line of code for development purposes and to isolate deltas. On a day-to-day development basis, a version control application, such as CVS, allows multiple developers to "check out" and "check in" code. The versions of code created in this way represent deltas in the sense that the CVS system creates a database that contains all the changes that occur between files. As these changes accumulate, you can view the latest configuration of the software system as the *tip* of the branch. To provide the information needed to designate what constitutes the tip, you use a version *label*. The label is a list of all the files and all the changes in the files that bring the primary line of code (or branch) to a given state.

Integration and Versions

If you take a given label and merge all the changes to form a primary line of code, you are on your way to integrating the changes fully. For the work on *Ankh*, the development team performed integrations at each baseline. The integration involved creating a clean build of the code that embodied the functionality specified for a given stripe. In each instance, the team tried to make it so that each stripe, as a baseline, represented a clean starting point for the next stripe. Technically, then, if stripe 6 ended up being completely unacceptable, the team could have redone it from scratch by using a different view of the design.

Architecting Branching

In addition to the practical aspects of branching already mentioned, a more abstract level of branching often receives attention. The abstract level of branching has to do with different approaches to how developers design both development builds and product releases.

Parallel Development

The two most generalized approaches to developing builds and product releases involve parallel and serial development. Parallel development allows you to create two or more branches of a software system and then maintain these branches simultaneously. Figure 10.15 illustrates parallel branching architecture.

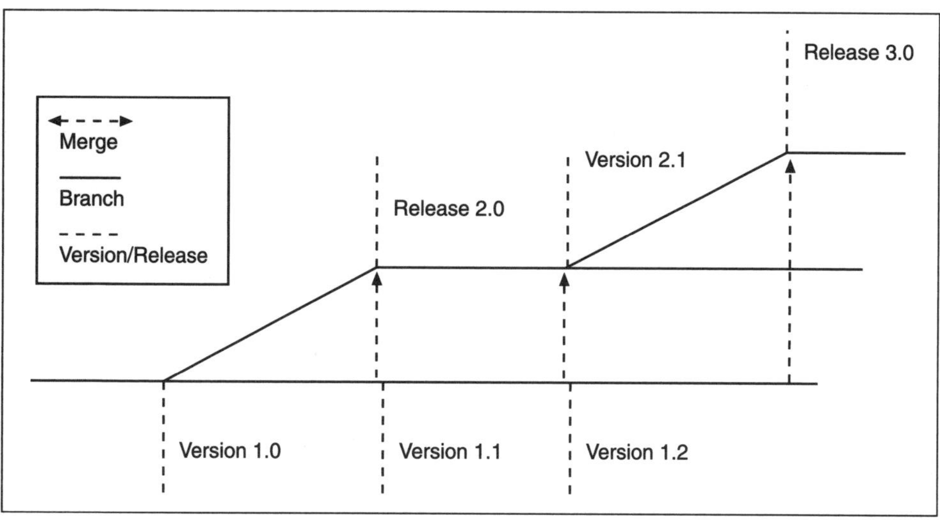

Figure 10.15
Parallel build and release architectures require that, at some point, you must maintain several separate and possibly irreconcilable versions of your software.

The enduring problem that arises with parallel development efforts is that you end up having a set of primary developers and a set of maintenance developers. The primary developers start a new version of the product by grabbing the primary code line at a given point, usually from the most recent release, and then extend it in ways that ultimately prove either difficult or impossible to merge with the previous release.

However, there is some virtue to parallel development efforts. They allow you to extend the profitability of a given body of software even as you develop a new version of it. In Figure 10.15, for example, it is likely that versions 1.1 and 1.2 would be purely maintenance releases. Maintenance releases usually do not involve the development of new functionality. Instead, they represent only the removal of defects.

With version 2.0 in Figure 10.15, notice what happens. The merge line has only one arrow, meaning that the developers merge the changes that have been made in versions of release 1.0 into versions of release 2.0. The merger is in one direction, because if it went both ways, customers of release 1.0 and its versions would receive free of charge the functionality that was sold with release 2.0.

It is also the case, however, especially with release 3.0, that the merging work becomes increasingly complex. Defects are going to be detected in any branch of the software, so the more branches, the more defects. With the increased number of defects comes an increased number of fixes. All the fixes represent changes that must be merged if the entire product is to evolve in a consistent way toward successive releases.

Many developers arrive at the conclusion that development efforts involving multiple dimensions are too costly and too complex. Unless you can afford an expensive version control application, this is true. Even then, a leading factor in any software development setting is the cost of programming labor. The more branches that exist, the higher the cost of maintenance and service.

Serial Development

Parallel development efforts pose problems. Most developers believe that serial development is preferable to parallel development. Figure 10.16 illustrates a serial development effort.

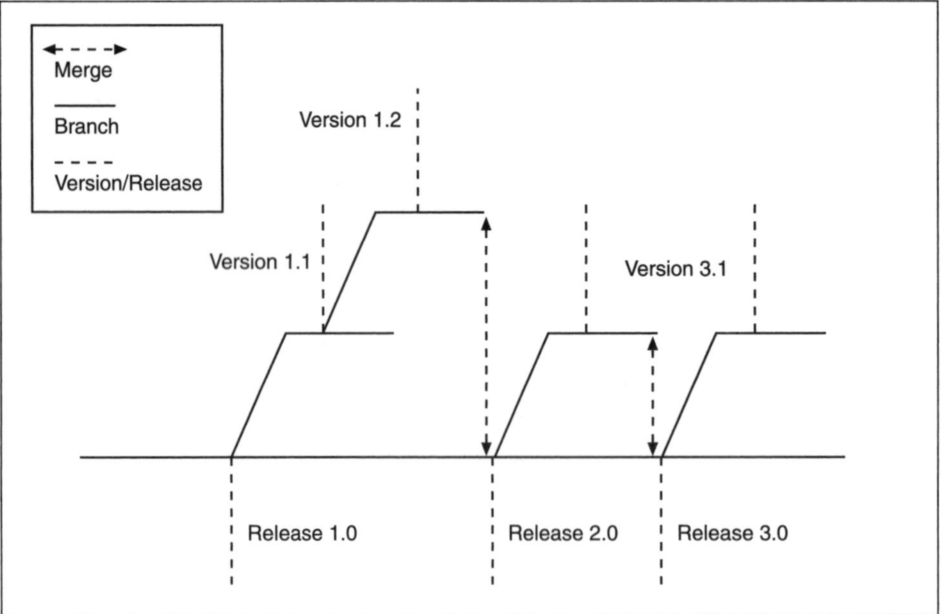

Figure 10.16
Serial development involves the maintenance of one primary line of code.

The advantage of a serial approach to development is that the only branching that occurs is on the temporary level, which means that the software system is branched only while new functionality is being developed. As soon as the new functionality has been tested, it can be integrated into the primary line of code. The functionality of the product continues to grow, but separate maintenance efforts are not sustained.

A serial development effort mandates relatively brief maintenance histories. In Figure 10.11, for example, version 1.1 might represent a maintenance fix, but it also represents an extension of functionality that is folded back into the primary line of code to become part of release 2.0. The extent to which activity on release 1.0 can continue is determined by what developers designate as the functional enhancement of version 2.0. If the versions of release 1.0 begin to encroach on release 2.0, it is time to discontinue support of release 1.0 and begin moving customers to the purchase of an upgrade.

Notice in Figure 10.11 that each new release represents a branch that is folded back into the primary code line. When a development effort proceeds in this way, it is sometimes called *branching to release.* On the other hand, because over the history of the product an effort is made in sustaining a serial form of product extension, the primary code line is said to be *flat*, or *one-dimensional.*

Branching and Version Control Practices

Branching practices encompass what you do from day to day as you work with your code. The most significant such practices have to do with how you check out and check in your code and how you merge it. In addition to these basic practices are those that establish limitations on how long you work on your code between merges and if and to what extent you test your code when you check it in. Establishing practices to define such activities can make an enormous difference in how smoothly day-to-day work proceeds.

The following list discusses practices that are related to branching. It also addresses issues that frequently are encountered in day-to-day development efforts:

- **Local directories.** The directories that developers maintain on their workstations are said to be *local.* When directories are local, they are assumed to be *private.* In other words, one local directory should not be able to access another local directory.
- **Shared directories.** The directories that the CVS or other version control systems make available to developers are *shared.* They are shared in the sense that a developer can access the version control system and obtain the most recent version of the primary line of code at any time. Everyone has access to this shared body of code. However, no one can change it arbitrarily.
- **Revision control.** When software is revised, it can be called a *version* or a *release. Revision control* applies to both versions and releases. Usually, version designates a prerelease development build of a software system. Release, on the other hand, usually applies to the state of the product during beta or general availability (production). It still stands, however, that policies and practices determine how people use the words.
- **Checking out.** When a developer accesses the primary line of code and *copies* its most current version to a local directory, he checks out the code. In reality, however, nothing is checked out in the sense of removing code from the version control system.

- **Checking in.** When a developer copies files from local directories to the version control system, the operation is called *checking in* code. This operation does not replace existing code. The version control system usually tracks only the changes in the code, which it stores in a database. The files in the main line of code are not replaced.
- **Merging.** Changes involve both whole files and parts of files. Merging changes that involve different versions of different files usually requires less of an effort than merging changes that have taken place in a single file.
- **Regression.** This term is used as a noun to designate what happens when someone makes a change in a body of code that reveals a defect in something that has been viewed as stable.
- **Reverting.** If a new version of code reveals severe defects, you might have to *revert* to a previous version. It makes little sense to take such actions when the version you are working with represents generally sound code. Reverting does make sense, however, if the obstacles you face are because of external factors. Perhaps between two versions of your code, you have decided to begin using a new release of a third-party library. Much to your chagrin, you find that the new release is seriously flawed. Rather than pick through the current version and edit it so that it excludes the troublesome components, you might revert to the previous version of your own code and start with a clean slate.
- **Locked files.** If you check files out and want to have exclusive use of them, you can *lock* them. Generally, this is the most common and effective approach to preventing conflicts.
- **Exclusively locked files.** Some version control systems allow for locked and *exclusively locked* files. The distinction is you can share a locked file. One person only can use an exclusively locked file. It would make sense to have locked files shared between two developers if the developers are trying to reconcile a problem. They would want to restrict access to themselves until they finished their work. Someone making a crucial change to a key component might want to have an exclusive lock on a file.
- **Collaborative tools.** A version control system is a collaborative tool, but a version control system also *contains* collaborative tools. An example of a collaborative tool is one that allows two developers to work simultaneously on a single file. The tool might lock individual lines or merge files dynamically.
- **Binaries.** Some software configuration managers refuse to store binaries. Binaries consume a lot of disk space. In addition, if you work in an environment in which you check in or check out code across Internet connections that have slow transfer rates, binaries prolong check-in and check-out operations.

- **Stable release.** Developers usually refer to a version of a product that lacks significant defects as a stable release. Your picture of stability can depend on time and the types of defects that you face. In some cases, a release is considered stable when its rate of defects reaches an acceptable minimum. If this point is reached, the primary criterion for stability is likely to be that the software does not crash but instead shows problems that relate to the finer (benign) aspects of its functionality.
- **Unstable release.** It is probably inappropriate to speak of an *unstable* release, because a primary criterion for release should be stability. Still, an unstable release usually is characterized as one that contains memory leaks, freezes, or crashes. Many developers maintain that there is no reason that an alpha release should be so well tested that it no longer crashes. One reason for an alpha release might be to verify the instability of a proposed release.
- **Modularity.** Modularity relates to parts of a system that can stand on their own. This can happen in any number of situations in which a set of functionality becomes a separate plug-in. Many developers allow a module to be maintained as a separate line of code.
- **Tag.** A tag identifies a label. One label can have more than one tag. A label is a list of files and assets. A tag allows you to identify the label as pertaining to a given build, version, or release.
- **Key.** A key is an abbreviation. Developers often use keys in scripts so that they can package the files for a build more easily.
- **History.** Each file has a history, and each version or release of a system has a history. The history is the cumulative set of changes that have been made from one point in time to another.
- **Status.** Files and systems have different statuses. If you have not merged two files into the primary line of code, the files are not synchronized. Files can be stale, conflicted, or corrupted. The same applies to systems. A label can be incomplete if some of its files are locked exclusively, thus preventing it from being built. Status usually has a bearing one way or another on whether you can or cannot accomplish a build.
- **Comments.** Comments in relation to configuration management usually pertain to a brief statement that developers input when they check in code. The comment summarizes the task that the developer has accomplished.

Promotion

This section is included largely out of respect for tradition. Chapter 17 provides a parallel discussion, but its focus is on releasing a product. This chapter provides a perspective on promotion that focuses on development. Software system promotion involves historically describing the system configuration according to its status and with relation to the project plan.

Development

A game software product begins its life with the development phase. During this phase, builds usually occur at least once each day. The frequency of builds depends on the time the build takes. One common approach is to have automated builds occur each night. A log report is generated from the build, and developers attend to the log report each morning before proceeding with the development of new functionality.

During the development phase, you should make regular backups of the software for disaster recovery purposes. Most standards require that companies store copies of their source code and other assets offsite. Small game companies might not do this regularly, but it makes sense to capture a snapshot of your software on CDs periodically and to store the CDs at a different location. A trusted employee's house is not a bad choice. A deposit box is better.

The most central configuration concerns of the deployment phase are code conflicts, merges, and incrementally developed code. Unit testing tends to be the prevailing type, although integration and system tests can be part of a standard cycle. The team used this approach on *Ankh*, where each stripe went through integration and system testing. This phase ends when developers have implemented all specified functionality.

Configuration concerns are largely those of daily builds and the efforts of developers and testers to implement adequately the functionality stated in the requirements specification. Often, implementation efforts do not take place with attention to the overall, integrated functionality of the system. Through formalized testing, regressions are detected. The goal during this phase is to implement specific functionality rather than test a wholly integrated system. Indeed, because the system remains largely incomplete during this phase of development, testing the whole system is impossible.

Quality Assurance

This phase could also be called *debugging* or *alpha testing*. It marks a phase in the software cycle when you deal with the system as a complete product. The primary activity of this phase is searching for and eliminating defects detected in the wholly integrated functionality of the product.

The work of this phase might involve substantial integration efforts if it's necessary to refactor significant areas of functionality. Refactoring can cause regressions if problems with dependencies are detected. In addition, this phase is complicated because defect reports usually have significant bearing on regulating the actions of developers. As test results are logged, developers must be prepared to put in long hours refining the system as a whole.

Beta

The beta phase of the development cycle marks a point at which you can release the product to customers on a trial basis. The product at this point is likely to be fairly stable. Its functionality is complete. The purpose of the test is to comb the software for defects.

Configuration management continues at this phase as a process of managing the release. Integration is not likely to be a problem. Tasks of this phase consist largely of closely tracking defect reports, fixing defects, testing the fixes, and closing out the reports.

Release

After the product is released, the software configuration manager usually must assemble all the code and assets for the software and store them in a secure place. The need to create a copy for the vault can result directly from business agreements.

The release of the product begins the maintenance phase of the software lifecycle. The branching of the product determines how the development team addresses defect reports. With the release of the software comes the need to begin planning the next release. The team must make decisions about how much effort to put into maintaining the current release. One crucial factor is the extent to which defect reports can be viewed as opportunities to begin developing features of the next release.

Configuration management at this point focuses primarily on either the serial or parallel definition of the software product. If the release strategy involves a parallel effort, the team will maintain the release as a separate branch and create maintenance branches from it. If the development strategy involves a serial effort, the team will make a strong effort to create maintenance branches that merge back into the primary code line for the product.

Management Issues

Three areas of concern for configuration management are those that involve the individual practices of developers, the type of testing that is done prior to the check in of code, and how the team plans for catastrophes. The next few sections discuss the topics encompassed by these areas of concern.

Individual Practices

Configuration management issues relating to workspaces deserve attention. Generally, an individual developer who is part of a team works on one area of code while other team members work on other areas of code. Reviewing the assumptions and rules that define this activity can help promote practices that enable individuals and teams to work more effectively. The following list names a few issues that arise in this respect:

- **Focus development on the primary line of code.** Development activity that does not focus on the primary line of code creates a liability. Stories about schisms destroying projects illustrate the importance of focusing on the primary line of code. Problems usually arise when headstrong developers begin using different approaches to solving problems and develop redundant sets of functionality. Another situation arises when someone is brought in for a few days as a contractor. The contractor comes and goes, and the result is a component that functions perfectly when compiled on the contractor's computer but, lacking integration, is so problem plagued that no one can make it work during the next integration.
- **Use integration and baselines.** The *Ankh* development team decided to use integrations and baselines implicitly to enforce configuration policies. The approach used stripes as occasions for bringing all the development activity into a comprehensive integration that had to be synchronized across the board. Using the project management schedule as a strategic guide and the configuration management plan as a kind of archeological map, you can re-create the development history of the game. Although the *Ankh* team effort possessed many distinctive (or eccentric) characteristics, the advisability of such incremental, iterative approaches to development is acknowledged almost universally.
- **Merge on a frequent and shallow basis.** The more changes you make between builds, the longer it's going to take to resolve difficulties. Obviously, keeping files out for days on end is probably going to create problems. The policies you set are up to your team. One rule is that a work session should involve one task. Of course, tasks can be longer or shorter, but if you analyze your work, you can probably break down longer tasks into shorter ones if the tasks you initially encounter extend over several days or weeks.
- **Do not use the repository in a sloppy way.** In most smaller development settings, you are at liberty to create files as you need them. Generally, however, you should add files that clearly express the architecture that the software design specifies. For example, within this context lies the creation of files for the declaration and implementation of code for each of the classes named in the design. Along the same lines, you can create logical groupings of files on the basis of how classes are grouped architecturally. Adding directories or files that fall outside or distort these boundaries of design leads to increased system complexity. For this reason, take time to review additions before making them.
- **Anticipate dangers of private builds.** Private builds become a problem when developers maintain code on local drives for long periods. The longer you go without merging your code with the main line code, the more merger problems you are likely to encounter. Among the most obvious problems are those associated with stale code. Other problems arise when you access code from library or Internet

sources and create dependencies that have not been integrated fully. Generally, cycling your code through a consistent schedule keeps your configuration synchronized.

- **Be cautious of third-party inclusion.** This and the next point concern problems that arise when you have to deal with libraries that have their own revision histories. Your configuration is made more complex because you suddenly must anticipate a calculus of change that exists between your revision patterns and those of the libraries you have used. To anticipate revisions, you might find that you are doing things like changing the name of the directory that holds your audio components because every month the components receive an update. It would have been easier if you had created a parallel branch in which you tracked the successive releases of the audio library components. Other than using separate branches for third-party libraries, you might also consider that a thorough analysis of risk should precede decisions to include external libraries. One question to ask is whether the candidate for inclusion has a stable revision history and a stable current release.
- **With third-party code, consider separate branches.** Many configuration managers advocate maintaining third-party libraries as separate branches. The reason for this is that any third-party library has its own revision history, and tracking this revision history is made easier if the library is not buried in history of your primary line of code. If you do not take measures to identify the separate history of the library, you will end up at some point picking through files to find out why the next build failed when someone locally downloaded a library file from the Internet. With the *Ankh* project, this type of problem occurred even with the Boost library, which tends to be well documented.
- **Enforce policies.** Policy avoidance and defiance are much less common than the kind of quality slippage that sometimes characterizes work performed under pressure. As a developer, it is easy to use the pressures that usually characterize the last part of a development project to throw aside many quality assurance measures. Although programmers seldom fail to program according to form, they often neglect comments, work on a given checked out version of the code for days on end, or become sloppy about updating local configurations. This type of sloppiness leads to delay. Policies should be nothing more than formal statements of common sense and best practices. If you do not abide by a policy, it should be evident that your actions will result not in administrative punishment but rather in delay or failure of the development effort.
- **Coordinate work.** Although CVS tracks the history of any file and makes it possible to eliminate many conflicts, if you can use the design document and the project plan and coordinate tasks so that dependencies do not create bottlenecks, your project likely will proceed with greater expedience and less frustration.

- **Anticipate releases.** When preparing a release, the configuration manager often cleans up directories and conducts quality assurance audits of files. As a developer, you can help with this effort if you anticipate releases and attend to day-to-day quality assurance activities. One such activity is to eliminate inessential material, be it temporary assets used for testing or code that has been commented out. Along with eliminating inessential material comes providing suitable comments in your code. The configuration management plan can facilitate this effort by providing a checklist of such tasks.
- **Consider the identity and quality of assets.** When you develop locally, you tend to find assets on your own and insert them into your local configuration. When you do such things, consider how you name the file, whether the file represents legally acquired property, and whether its quality is consistent with the overall quality of your team effort. Most of the time, when you use such assets, you do so provisionally, but then weeks later, after you have long forgotten the problem, someone else begins work on the code and finds it confusing. Maybe it takes only 10 minutes to investigate the issue and decide that the Dr. Seuss character was not, after all, a part of the plan. The problem is enlarged if the asset is associated with an obscure bit of functionality. Unless the testing operations are thorough, you can end up with a situation in which a player of your game sends you an e-mail asking whether the Dr. Seuss character was really supposed to be part of the dungeon scene. What is worse is when the e-mail arrives from a lawyer making inquires about your company's legal right to use the Dr. Seuss character. Configuration management can help with this situation, at least ostensibly, by enforcing naming conventions. One simple measure is to ask everyone to name test assets in an identifiable way.

Test Coordination Issues

When developers check in code, they can subject the code they check in to certain kinds of tests. Sometimes such tests are rudimentary. Other times they are complex. Generally, the more involved the tests, the less likely developers will check in their code on a frequent basis. Infrequent checking in of code can result in merger nightmares. In addition to this basic problem, the way that integration is established as a part of the configuration management scheme can have a significant bearing on both testing and development.

Disaster Recovery Issues

Any banking or medical operation that uses software is likely to be required by law to maintain backed up data. The requirements are not quite so stringent with respect to maintaining backed up development files, but the impact on the lives of those involved in the effort can be just as significant. If the hard disk on the server crashes and the files that the system comprises are lost, the price of the system increases by the value of the time needed to reconstruct the lost files. Likewise, the team might require as much time to reconstruct lost software as was taken to create it in the first place. If the development team is supposed to finish work on a software system by a given date, then one automatic implication of lost development files is that the team will no longer be able to deliver the software by the given date. This often leads to the cancellation of the software project.

Automated Builds

One of the basic jobs involved in software configuration management is the creation of scripts that automatically build the software system at regular intervals during the development process. For this reason, this chapter devotes some attention to how you can create a script for automated builds. The procedure provided here is general. References to books that contain greater practical implementation information are listed at the end of this chapter. Among the activities that fall under this heading are these:

- Setting up automatic build and compile routines
- Designing and writing the scripts to accomplish automated builds
- Running the scripts

Installation

Configuration managers sometimes create installation packages. More often, configuration managers work with programmers who are responsible for creating installation packages. At the point of release, the configuration manager often assumes the role of release manager. As is discussed in Chapter 17, release management involves a wide variety of important details. In some cases, the configuration manager, like the developer who is responsible for the installation package, will have a task list that the release manager assigns.

As a developer or a configuration manager, you are responsible for creating an installation package. The *Ankh* development team used ISTool.

ISTool

ISTool is the best current freeware installer for Windows programs. It is easy to obtain, reliable, and easy to use. You can obtain ISTool from jrsoftware.org, and the best starting place is to select the Inno Setup QuickStart Pack from the Web page list of download options. The download is quick, and the installation is clean and immediate. You can begin using it without preliminaries.

The license language is typical and uninvolved:

- Must retain all copyright and notices.
- Binary redistribution must retain copyright notice and Web site addresses.
- The origin of the software must be represented correctly.
- Modified versions must be labeled clearly.

Creating a Project

To use an installation package, you create a project and then select files you want to use. Figure 10.17 shows the main working window of the ISTool with the File List view open.

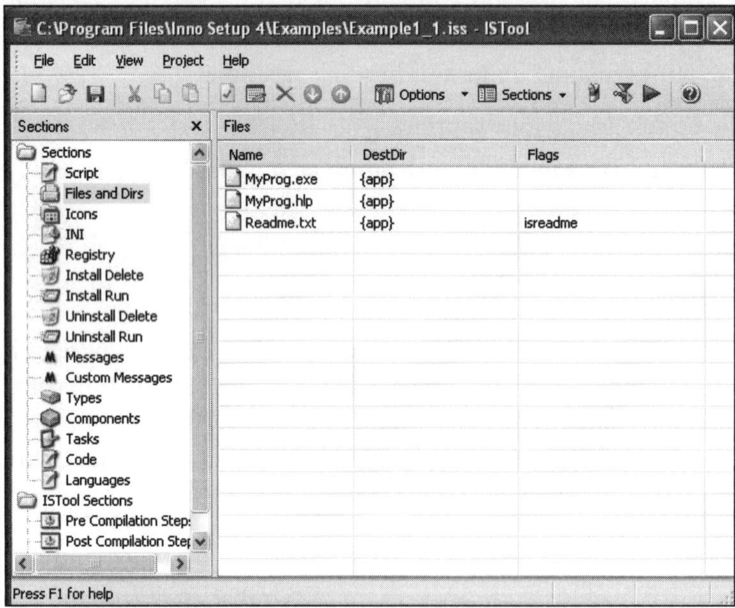

Figure 10.17
A tabular layout provides a summary view of file information.

To add a file to the installation package, you right-click, which opens a file selection window. Using the directory browser, you select the file you want to use. You can then set the destination directory, the destination name, and other information that allows you to customize the installation package.

Adding a Script

A script enables you to designate which prompts the installation operation will evoke and how the user's responses will be processed. Figure 10.18 shows the main working window for ISTool with the Script view open.

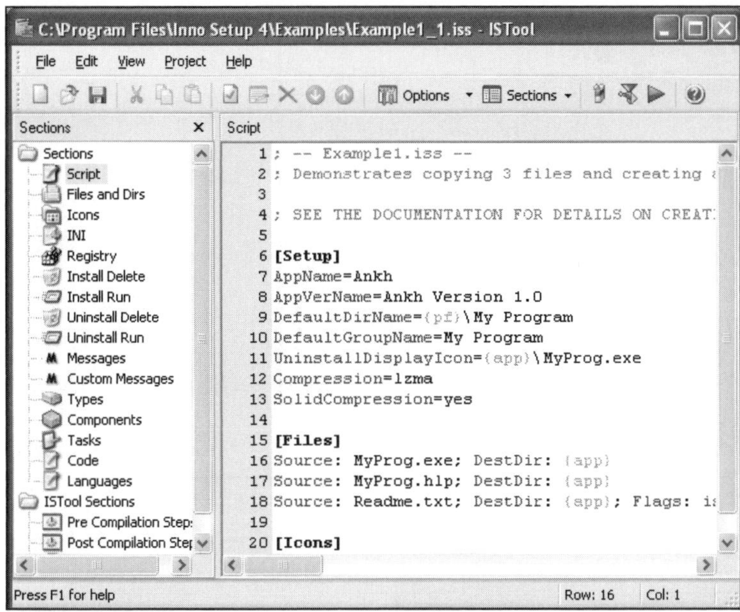

Figure 10.18
The scripting option for most installation packages is essential.

Compiling and Testing

To compile your installer using ISTool, select the compile option from the Project menu. Figure 10.19 indicates the installer options.

After you select Compile Setup, a log window is generated, and you can run a test version of your installer. For the sample project, Figure 10.20 shows the resulting interface.

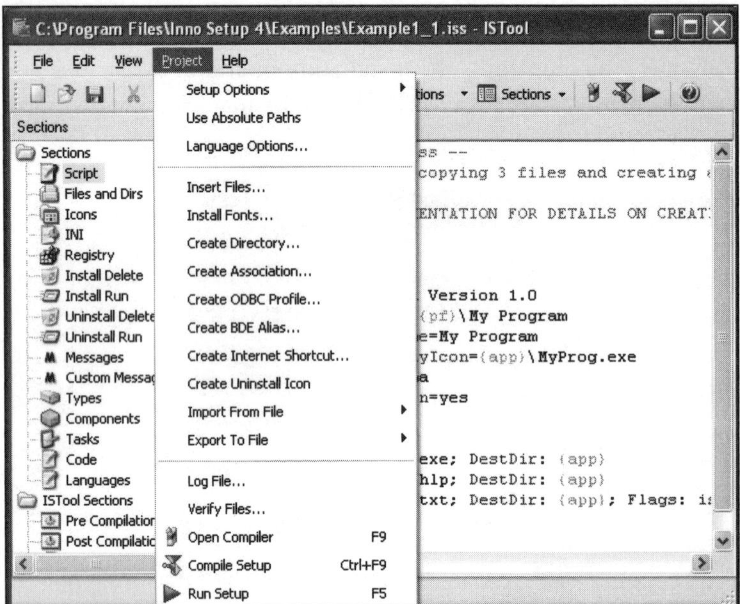

Figure 10.19
ISTool provides you with a rich variety of project options.

Figure 10.20
The installation interface that results leads users through a standard installation session.

Conclusion

SCM encompasses many tasks. At the beginning of the project, the software configuration manager can work to build an SCM plan and encourage everyone to consider such issues as which tools to use for SCM and which policies to set formally and informally. Other early concerns involve coding standards, selection of installation tools, and how the software design specification can be addressed most effectively through the build process.

In addition to setting policies for the group, the software configuration manager can work to encourage everyone on the team to consider good local practices. For example, team members might benefit from a review of the problems that can arise if they do not merge their code on a reasonably frequent basis or when they add files to the configuration that the design of the product does not justify.

The software configuration manager can facilitate the development effort by creating and driving an SCM schedule that builds and integrates the components of the system. As an extension of this activity, the development effort benefits tremendously if baselines of the system are created in accord with the architectural mapping laid out in the software design specification and the production schedule laid out in the project plan.

Creating an installation package for the game can in some cases be the responsibility of the software configuration manager. Even if the release manager has the ultimate responsibility for creating the installation package, the software configuration manager likely will be responsible for selecting and configuring the tools with which the installation package is created.

For further reading on SCM, you might find the following resources useful:

Berczuk, Stephen P. with Brad Appleton. *Software Configuration Management Patterns: Effective Teamwork, Practical Integration.* Boston: Addison-Wesley, 2003.

Cockburn, Alistair. *Agile Software Development.* Boston: Addison-Wesley, 2002.

Compton, Stephen B. *Configuration Management for Software.* Ed. Joan R. Callahan. New York: Van Nostrarand Reinhold, 1994.

Hass, Anne Mette Jonassen. *Configuration Management Principles and Practice.* Boston: Addison-Wesley, 2203.

Kenefick, Sean. *Real World Software Management Configuration*, San Francisco: Apress, 2003.

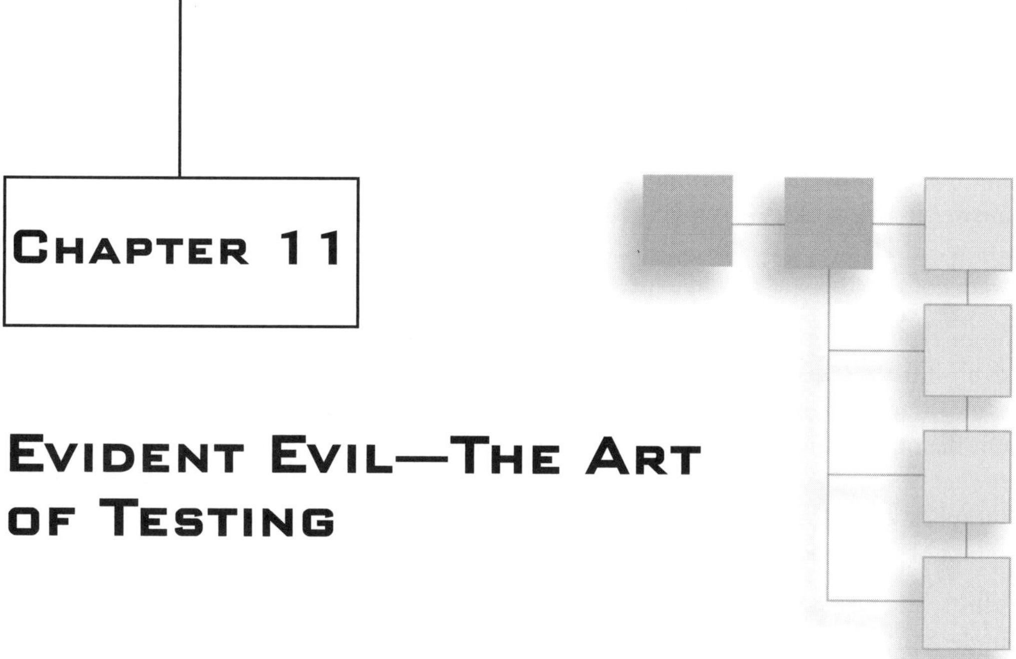

Evident Evil—The Art of Testing

This chapter examines software testing. Software testing constitutes one of the major aspects of software development. It involves investigating software to discover its defects, which come in two general types. One type of defect arises when you have not developed your software according to specification. Another type of defect arises when you have developed software so that you add things to it that the specifications have not anticipated. From one perspective, your game fails to do what you expect it to do. From the other perspective, your game does things that you do not expect or want it to do. To eliminate defects, you subject your game to a variety of tests. Among these tests are those involving components, integration, and the system as a whole. Testing presents an enormous field of practice and study, but the following topics provide a good starting place:

- Identifying what counts as a defect
- Formalizing testing
- Creating documents to guide testing
- The types of domain knowledge that testing involves
- Using test reports and test templates
- Recognizing and guarding against coverage risks
- Efforts and effects of testing
- Different testing roles

Basics of Testing

Software testers explore software to discover whether it contains defects. To understand the implications of this assertion, consider what it means to find a defect. What does it mean to say that you think a program is defective? Perhaps it means that the program does not do what you *expect* it to do. But then what does it mean to expect something? One answer to this is that when you have expectations, you have been told or have intuitively arrived at an understanding that the software should behave in certain ways. When software does not behave as you expect it to, something is wrong. The software is defective.

Some types of misbehavior are obvious. Others are not. You are playing a game, and suddenly it freezes up and you have to reboot your computer manually. You try again and the same thing happens. This counts as a defect that almost anyone can recognize intuitively. On the other hand, you play the game and everything seems to be okay. However, even though you know you have landed a killer blow on Manfred, the Barbarous, his strength inexplicably increases, defying the logic, intent, and objectives that govern every other aspect of the game.

This type of defect might be something you grasp intuitively, but it is more difficult to understand precisely how to address the problem—especially if you are not a veteran game player or a programmer. Some players might try to rationalize the odd behavior. The rationalization might go along the following lines:

"Oh, well, on this level, when Manfred, the Barbarous attacks you, let him beat you to a pulp and *don't* hit him. His power will diminish to nothing, and *he'll* die. If you hit him, he'll become more powerful, and then *you'll* die. On the next level, however, if you do this, Manfred will pulverize you. This is a subtle part of the game known only to the elite players."

If you assume that the programmers specified Manfred's behavior as consistent throughout the game, you can assume that such behavior is not an intended, expected part of the game, not even for elite players. Such behavior is accidental, unexpected, and defective.

The defect that the tester searches for has been inserted into the game through the development effort and represents something that must be eliminated. The defect does not result so much from the requirements or the design (assuming they are consistent) as it does from faulty implementation. Manfred, like all characters, is supposed to inflict damage when he successfully strikes a blow. Like all characters, he is supposed to suffer a loss of health when struck. A software defect makes possible the reversal of this behavior.

As Figure 11.1 illustrates, the software tester works from the software specifications and creates a test case. The test case establishes a way that the tester can work from the specifications to test the behavior of the software within a strictly defined context. Using information derived from the specifications, the tester defines initial and resulting conditions for the test case. If the specifications stipulate that Manfred should lose health when struck, and the tester discovers that Manfred instead gains health when struck, the software fails the test case. When the software fails the test case, the tester forwards a defect report to the maintenance programmer.

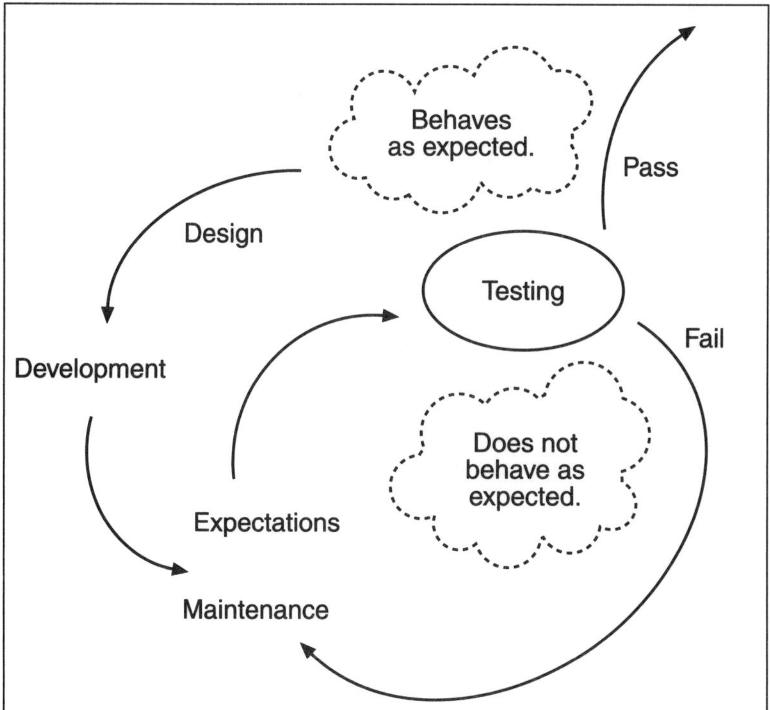

Figure 11.1
A defect is an implanted or created form of misbehavior.

Software testers differ from programmers because they detect defects instead of altering the code to eliminate them. Testers apply formalized test cases to the software, and based on the results of the test cases, they forward reports of defects to programmers. Working with the information that the testers provide, programmers eliminate the defects. Testers then verify that the programmers have eliminated the defects.

Three Concepts

Figure 11.2 illustrates three concepts that are central to testing. Although testing involves many other things, understanding what verification, validation, and exploration entail helps you grasp the basic reasoning that motivates the development of different approaches to testing.

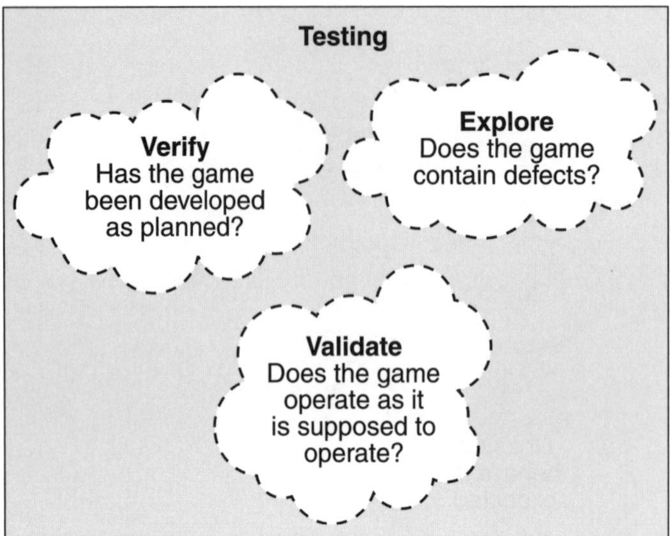

Figure 11.2
You can view testing as verification, validation, and exploration.

Verification

Before developers plan a software product—a game—they specify it in one form or another. In this book, a set of requirements specifies the game. Requirements consist of a set of sentences, a set of use cases, or both. They establish how the game is expected to behave. When you test whether the game satisfies the requirements, you verify that the developers have developed the product in accordance with the requirements.

Validation

Even if developers develop a game so that it ostensibly looks like it satisfies the requirements, it still might not. Consider, for example, a requirement that two numbers shall be added and a correct answer shall result. Suppose that 2 and 4 are added, and the result is "cat." To validate this situation, the tester first must determine the appropriate answers. (In this case, assume that the requirements really mean numbers.) It might be that in a metaphysical dimension beyond the mundane, 2 and 4 really do make "cat." But the tester knows that only numbers are expected. Using this information, the tester designs a validation test. If the numbers result in numbers and if the result is correct according to standard arithmetical reasoning, the implemented software possesses validity.

Requirement: Number added to number shall result in correct answer.

2 + 4 = 6
2 + 4 = cat

?

Exploration

Testing attempts to find defects that the development process has inserted into the software product. Validity and verification offer the most direct ways to discover defects, but testers have other approaches to testing. These tests involve not so much what is supposed to be implemented (which, again, you can determine if you investigate the requirements and the design of the software) but what is *not* supposed to be implemented. When you investigate what is not supposed to be implemented, you enter into an exploratory realm of testing. In some realms of testing, bugs become butterflies.

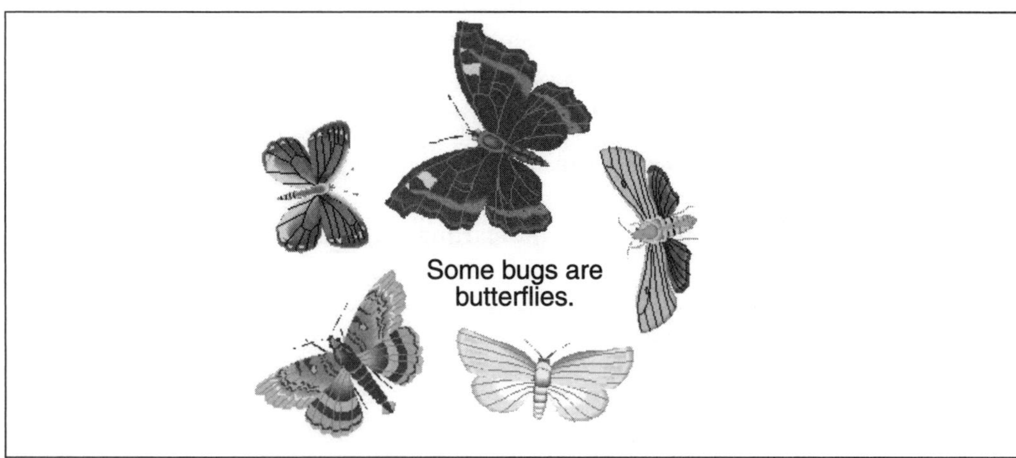
Some bugs are
butterflies.

Bugs become butterflies because exploratory testing involves finding out whether the software still behaves as specified when it is subjected to demands that it behave in ways that are not specified. Testers figure out how to break things. Breaking software involves getting it to behave in ways that are not specified. For example, in *Ankh*, a field in the character designer allows the player to enter an arbitrary name for a character. Normally, players would type a name, such as "Babba," "Rah," or "Slick." But what happens if someone decides to type a series of spaces? Discovering the answer requires exploratory testing. If the system accepts spaces, it might still perform perfectly okay. At a later moment of play, however, the player would see a blank line in the character selection list. When you click the blank line, the character that is named using the spaces appears. Is this how you want the game to behave?

Formalized Testing

The story of how you formalize testing begins with the story of how you test without formalization. When you test without formalization, you conduct what is known as *reactionary*, or find-and-fix, testing. A great deal of programming falls under this heading. A programmer types a few lines of code, tries to compile or build, and observes whether the compiler detects a syntax error.

When a game involves tens or hundreds of thousands of lines of complex code, reactionary programming no longer works. Instead, testing must take place according to an overriding plan. Testers formulate tests that cover the entire scope of the product and investigate as many logical or operational pathways through the product as possible.

Designing tests involves considering phases of development. Software begins with some type of specification. It takes form through design. It is implemented, deployed, and maintained. A type of testing corresponds to each of these phases. For example, you can conduct behavioral, or functional, testing to verify that developers have implemented the requirements. You can conduct integration testing to confirm that the modules or components constructed to satisfy the requirements can be merged together. When you conduct system testing, you can take the system and observe whether it can be installed and operated on different operating systems of computers.

As Figure 11.3 illustrates, you can encapsulate your testing activity in a relatively small number of formal tests. Many more tests with exotic names can supplement these basic forms of testing, but the core tests remain the starting point of almost any comprehensive testing effort.

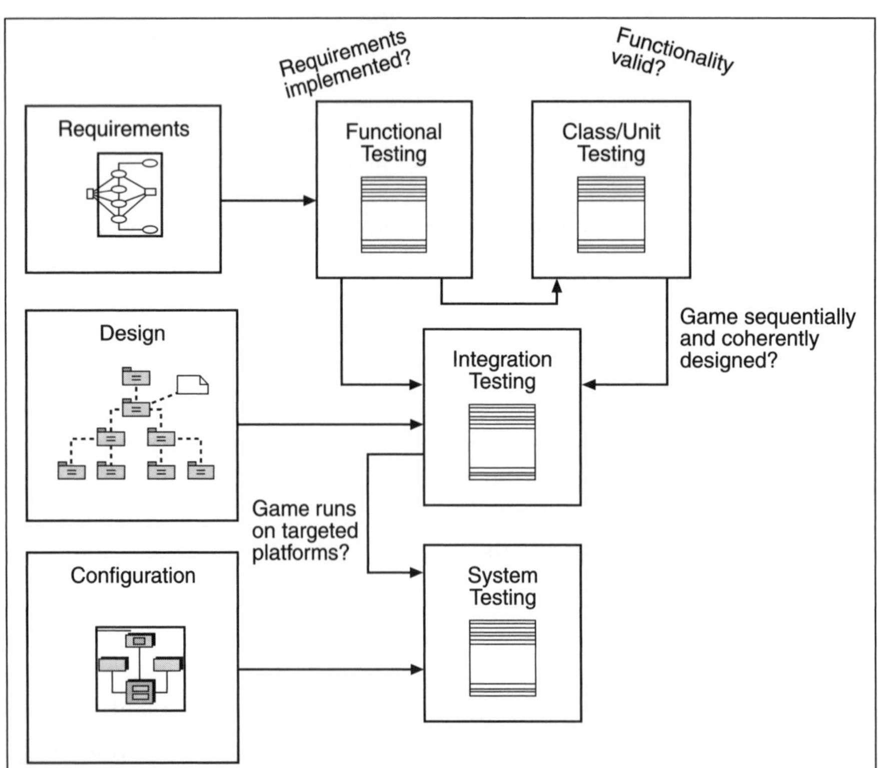

Figure 11.3
Test plans reflect development phases.

Approaches to Analysis

Games differ in at least one respect from other forms of software because they rarely lack some type of preliminary documentation. On the other hand, games resemble most other forms of software because the documentation on which they are based often lacks detail. When you formally test a game software product, you might have to spend a great deal of time analyzing the game software so that you know how to test it.

General Domain

Computer games, generally, constitute a domain of software. This domain comprises game genres, character types, learning scenarios, and a multitude of other items. As a game software tester, you apply knowledge of these items in a number of ways. Among many possibilities, for example, you formulate test scenarios, plan test strategies, and understand how much of the behavior of a game the test plan should cover. Without domain knowledge, it might not be easy to determine how much to test the scope of a game's behavior or what level of detail specific test cases require.

Domain knowledge extends in every direction and excludes nothing related to game development. Figure 11.4 illustrates a few common terms that are associated with game design.

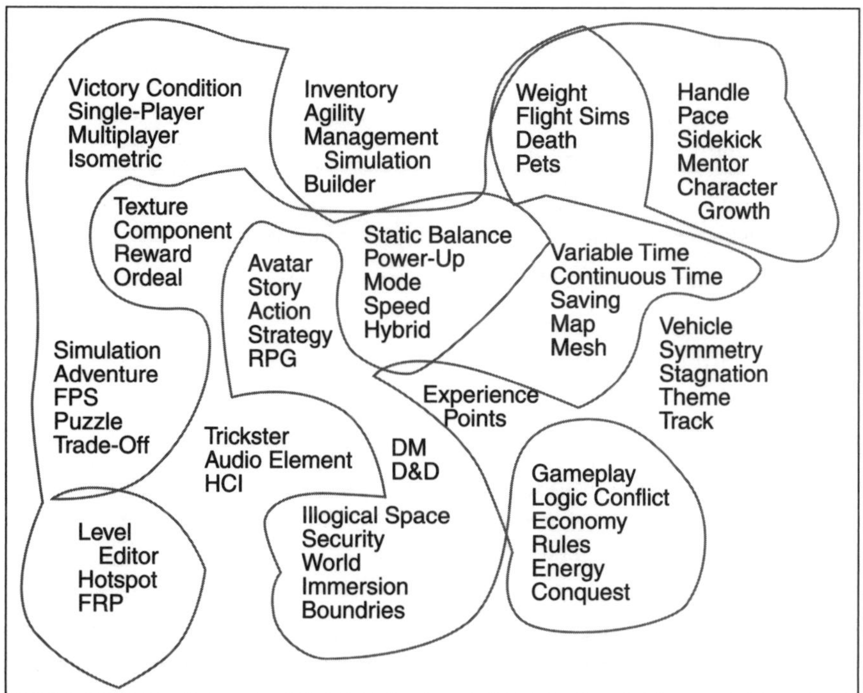

Figure 11.4
Domain knowledge furnishes a context in which to scope the testing effort.

General game development domain knowledge provides you with insights that help with the following tasks, among others:

- Understanding the genre of the game so that you can focus testing to cover the behavior that is most crucial to your game's genre
- Testing requirements specifications
- Estimating the performance standards that your game should achieve in light of benchmarks derived from knowledge of other games
- Profiling the operational characteristics of the game to determine whether they are on par with those of other games
- Being able to communicate readily with both game designers and game software developers during the testing effort

Application

You can consider application knowledge a subset of the more generalized domain of computer game knowledge. When you address application concerns, your attention shifts to a context that relates to the features of the game that express the current or forefront technologies that games embody. In recent history, among these are such items as particles, shadows, wavering motion effects, bump maps, refinements in collision detection, multiplayer voice interactions, databases, and security extensions. In addition to current and forefront technologies, games embody standard game application technologies. Among these are dialog boxes, buttons, sliders, console layouts, help options, and navigation components. Application domain knowledge enables you to test the game more effectively in some of the following ways:

- Designing test cases for verification and validation of requirements
- Understanding what parts of the game represent new techniques and deserve special attention
- Making use of standard testing artifacts to address standard game features

Architectural

Games also comprise architectural components. You can identify these components in numerous ways. From a design perspective, you work with modules. You can test modules for encapsulation, coupling, and complexity. The UML provides tools that you can use to depict architectural features. Among these are class, sequence, and package diagrams. (See Chapter 3, "A Tutorial: UML and Object-Oriented Programming," for discussion of these tools.) Testing that is related to architectural issues can involve both implemented code and design documents. Architectural domain knowledge helps you with some of the following activities:

- Understanding how to structure the integration test plan
- Knowing what test cases you can use from the design documentation as the basis of the integration and system test plans
- Establishing test criteria for test cases involving modules

Detail (Class)

Detailed design encompasses the development of functions and classes. You can consider global functions as utility objects that you can test much as you might test a class object. Classes involve interfaces, operations (which C++ programmers call member functions), attributes (also known as class variables), accessor and mutator operations, and a variety of other features that are specific to programming tasks. Knowledge of the detail domain helps you to conduct structural or white-box testing. Such testing requires that you work with the code. Among the tasks that such detail knowledge helps you perform are the following:

- Creation of test harnesses for classes and functions
- Insertion of static and other functions into classes to audit object states
- Writing standalone programs that you can use to test specific instances of objects
- Working with test tools like those from the Boost C++ testing library

Maintenance

Chapter 17, "Release Planning and Management," discusses testing as it relates to software after release. Just before the release of the game, testers face an intensive effort to guide the game through acceptance testing. Acceptance testing in general software efforts focuses on the customer. This is true to some extent in the game world, too, but it is more accurate to say that acceptance testing in the game world consists of formal measures that testers implement.

As an example of the challenges that you face when you test a game for release, consider a scenario in which your group has targeted Microsoft as a customer. Microsoft has established an extensive list of criteria that games must meet if they are to be included in its game suite. At last count, this list of criteria stretched to more than 100 pages. (For a humorous review of the list, see Mike McShaffry's book, *Game Coding Complete.* A reference appears at the end of this chapter.) Following are some paraphrases of a few of the test conditions for Microsoft:

- The application performs primary functions and remains stable during functionality testing.
- The application does not create temporary folders or place files in the wrong locations.

- The application remains stable when it processes a long file name.
- The application remains stable when it is directed to use unavailable devices.

After a game has been released, its characteristics as a software product change. For one thing, a game's life does not usually include addition of new features and functionality. Perfection of its existing features and functionality defines the focus of the programming and testing efforts exerted toward it. Generally, this phase of a software product's life is anything but trivial. On the average, 60 percent of the expense that is involved in a software product accrues after its release. Domain knowledge of maintenance efforts enables you to augment your efforts in the following ways:

- Understanding how to develop test procedures that address user-oriented issues.
- Working with a trouble tracking system.
- Verifying and validating software fixes on a revolving basis. In other words, you might have to verify first that a bug that a user reports is valid and then, following the efforts of the maintenance programmer, verify that the bug has been fixed.

The "V" Model

You can align testing activities with the software development cycle. One approach to this is the "V" model. The "V" model starts with requirements and moves downward, on the left leg of a "V," through design and detail design. Then it begins upward, on the right of a "V," with implementation of classes, functions, components, and finally the whole system. Figure 11.5 illustrates the flow of activities related to the domains discussed previously.

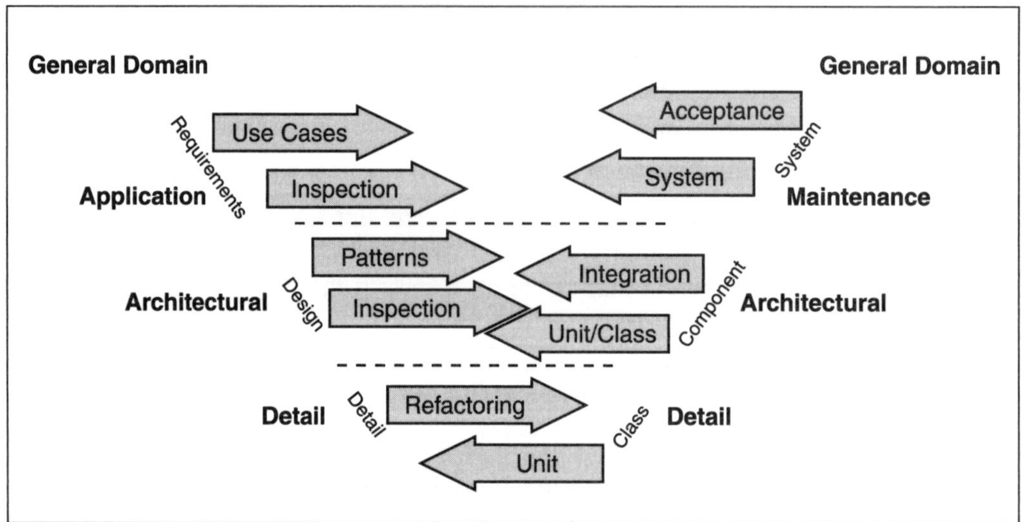

Figure 11.5
You can depict testing activities as a V that emphasizes design on one leg and development on the other.

Ways to Test

Testing involves more than playing the game. Playing the game constitutes a significant chunk of the activity that is involved in testing; however, the tests that you create often focus on implementation rather than on gameplay. Whereas you might view the experience of playing the game as the big picture, working at the software engineering level, you concentrate on an atomized view of the game that encompasses searching for defects in how the behavior has been implemented. For this reason, you might tend to view the game as a system that consists of components, modules, and performance characteristics, not as something you play.

note

Playability and *usability* testing differ from testing that focuses on classes, integration, components, and systems. Playability and usability tests directly address how players of the game interact with the game's visible features. They also address the aesthetic qualities of the game. If you work as a software engineer or software developer, such testing is definitely your concern, but you might be able to accomplish your work much more readily by structuring your test plans so that expert (or other) playability and usability testers are brought into the picture. You might view your job as structuring and supervising such tests. Others follow test cases that you set up for them.

Inspection

Inspection involves examining items that are usually placed in the category of documentation. You use inspection as your primary mode of testing when you have the luxury of beginning your testing work at the beginning of a project. This is a good way to do things, but unfortunately, many development groups do not bother to retain testers until relatively late in the project. Here are some focal points of inspections:

- **Requirements.** Participate in the development of requirements. Test the requirements to discover whether they are redundant, poorly worded, or fail to address the functionality of the game.
- **Use cases.** Assist with the development of use cases for requirements. Determine whether the use cases address requirements adequately. Verify that the trigger and ending conditions have been included. If a use case is excessively long, suggest that it be broken down into two or more use cases. You can begin creating test cases (or test procedures) using the use cases developed for requirements.
- **Design.** Inspect the software design description. If the development team employs UML diagrams, check the diagrams for accuracy and completeness.
- **Configuration.** Inspect the configuration management plan to determine whether the coding conventions, configuration policies, and other such items provide a comprehensive framework for development.

- **Documentation.** Test documents to ensure that they are identified and numbered correctly. If the versioning scheme creates confusion, report the problem.

In each case, you can test documentation and other inspected artifacts using the same tools that you use to inspect code. In other words, create a test procedure and follow it. If the procedure shows a problem, report it.

Unit or Class Testing

The traditional term for testing that involves examining the smallest components of the software product is *unit testing*. Unit testing most commonly identifies the activity of testers as they work along with the implementation effort. Unit testing can involve almost any part of the software product before it is integrated into the complete system. The focus of testing at this level is to examine behavior in isolation, before it is folded in with other behavior and rendered, as a result, complex.

Another term for unit testing is *class testing*. The terms are interchangeable because both relate to the smallest components in the software system. With object-oriented development efforts, the smallest unit is the class. In procedural development efforts, the smallest unit is the function. For the development effort for *Ankh*, almost all of the system consisted of classes. Still, in a few instances, global functions were used. Combining classes and libraries of functions characterizes many C++ development efforts because C++ does not require that programmers use only object-oriented constructions.

note

When you use UML to illustrate global functions, you can name the function as though it were an object and then comment it so that readers can understand its origin.

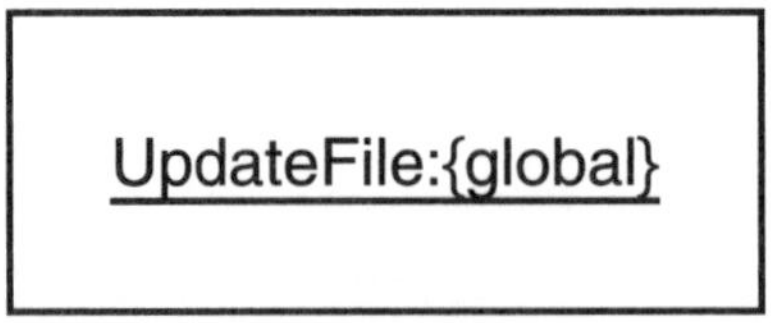

Unit testing involves a large set of tools, some of which are illustrated in this chapter. For now, an important point to emphasize is that unit (or class) testing offers the primary medium through which you can test functional requirements. Note the following:

- **Component test plan.** You can use the component test plan to detail most of the test procedures you intend to execute to verify and validate the implementation of the functionality that the requirements specify. With *Ankh*, the team began its component testing by examining use cases that were included in the *Ankh Software Requirements Specification.* Each use case provided a starting point for the creation of a test procedure for the requirement.

- **Black-box testing.** You can employ black box testing to test the behavior of components. A class object is a component that receives parameter information and returns a result. You can base a test case on these two points of interaction.
- **White-box testing.** State-transition diagrams illustrate the work of white-box testing. Such diagrams allow you to understand how the attributes of objects change as they perform their work. White-box testing offers a powerful analytical tool to evaluate the robustness of components at their most elemental level.

See "Using Templates" later in this chapter for more information about the tools you use to conduct unit or class testing.

Integration

Integration testing involves creating test procedures to detect defects that result when developers assemble the components created at the class level into modules. Interactions among several classes usually characterize the life of a module. When two objects exchange messages, the message that the first (client) object communicates to the second (server) object can cause problems. Among common problems are those involving improper instantiation of server objects. Improper instantiation of the server objects results in failure of the client object. The error you detect, however, might indicate only that the client fails. You must analyze the interactions of the assembled objects to determine the real source of the failure.

Planning integration testing requires that you understand the design of the software system. For this reason, you can most effectively create an integration testing plan after you have completed the software design specification. With the *Ankh* development effort, the team created a design that comprised 14 stripes (or modules). Planning the integration efforts began with developing use cases for each integration event. The use cases established behavioral scenarios that characterized expected system behavior following each integration. (See Figure 11.6.)

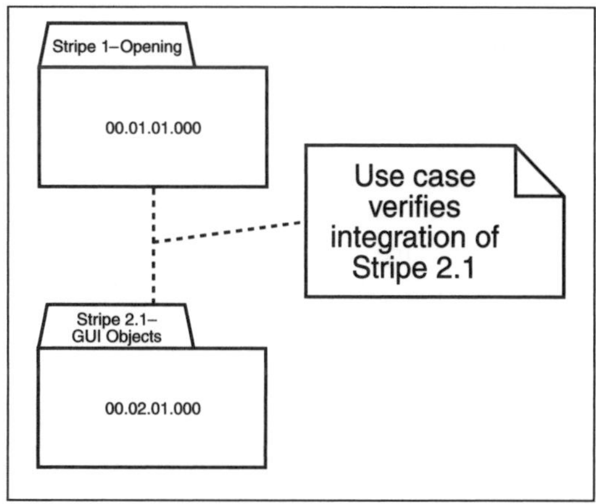

Figure 11.6
Use cases for integration provide conceptual frameworks from which to begin test planning.

Creating use cases to visualize integrations serves as a reliable way to ground a testing effort. Each integration use case provides a conceptual framework in which to understand what functionality should be newly visible as a result of the integrated stripe. You then can work from this understanding to test the specific behaviors that characterize this new situation. Using the collection of 14 integration use cases developed for the *Ankh Software Design Specification*, the *Ankh* development team easily generated the initial set of test procedures that composed the *Ankh Integration Test Plan.*

System

Consider what happens when a player installs a game. The installation succeeds if the player can begin playing the game immediately after the installation concludes. It fails if this is not the case. System testing involves examining the behavior of the software as a complete entity. Its goals consist largely of ensuring that the player knows the game only as an experience that begins and ends with what happens in the game.

The context of system testing encompasses using systems that represent those that you expect your customers to use. It involves assembling the completed software into an isolated entity. To test this entity effectively, you first should remove dependencies. To accomplish this, testers create a system test environment. Such an environment is usually a bare-bones operating system installed on a machine that you consider typical of your customers. In most development settings, the systems testing effort involves several environments that mirror those of anticipated customers.

A system test plan consists of specifications of the targeted operating systems and machines. It also provides test cases that require you to perform installations. On more detailed levels, it can establish criteria for stress tests. A stress test can involve, for instance, seeing what happens if the system on which you install your game has little available RAM. How does the game then perform? Another test involves system failure. If a power outage occurs, for example, how much data does your game lose?

As with component and integration tests, an effective approach to developing system tests involves creating use cases. You can use common installation scenarios or stress conditions as the basis of your use case development effort.

Planning Activities

When you plan test activities, you create test plans that address both different approaches to testing and different aspects of the system being tested. (See Figure 11.7.) You set these two priorities because no one type of testing suffices to test all aspects of the system. Likewise, the best way to test different aspects of the system is by using different approaches to testing. To confirm that the requirements have been met, for example, behavioral (black-box) testing allows you to set up tests based on the use cases in the software requirements specification. To investigate performance and complexity issues, you can use structural (white-box) testing. Test plans allow you to think through the approaches you want to use and establish how you want to analyze the system for testing.

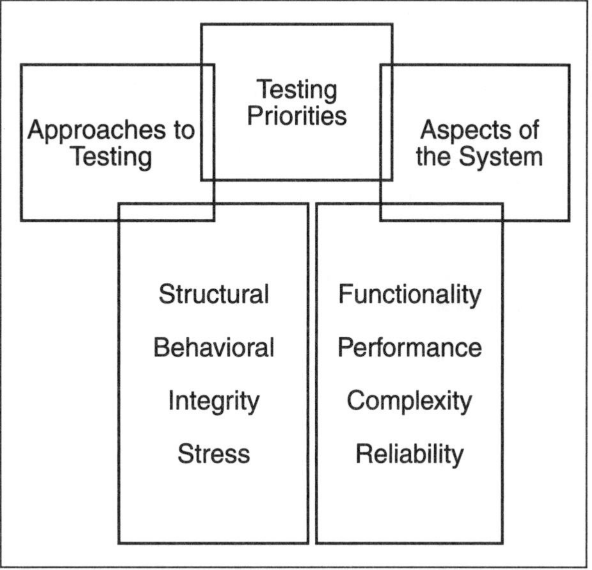

Figure 11.7
Test plans lay the groundwork for approaches to testing and different ways of analyzing the system.

Project Test Plan

You can quickly generate a project test plan if you use a template. IEEE standard 829 provides one of the most common test plan templates. (For information about IEEE standard 829, which provides one of the most common templates, refer to "Using Templates.") The project test plan provides a context in which you can plan the overall testing effort. Among the tasks it can help you complete are the following:

- **Specific plans.** Use the project test plan to determine what test plans you want to write. Figure 11.8 illustrates the plans created for *Ankh.* You might determine that other plans best suit your needs. For example, the *Ankh* development team decided not to create an acceptance test, but such a test would have been mandated had a game publisher been in the picture.
- **Testing targets.** When you work at the project scope, you can consider what aspects of the project possess the greatest importance. If you have developed a game intended to display graphically superior features, you might draft playability and usability plans that require you to subject these features to particularly harsh scrutiny. Any type of testing can be accommodated as long as you take time up front to plan your testing strategy.
- **Testing risks.** The primary risks that any testing effort faces usually encompass resources, schedule limitations, and granularity of testing. For example, if you do not test enough, the quality of the game declines. If you try to test too much, your testing effort almost inevitably fails to reach completion. If you lack testers or testing resources, even if you have planned well, you might fail to test the product adequately.

- **Testing priorities.** Priorities often reflect development cultures. If you work with a group that centers its efforts on performance, your primary testing effort might involve component test plans. Such plans often require construction of test harnesses designed to generate precise data to use for optimization. On the other hand, priorities often arise from scheduling and resource limitations, so you might find that you concentrate on the project test plan so that you can distribute limited efforts as effectively as possible.
- **Scope and intensity of testing.** A general view of the testing effort allows you to plan the degree of coverage you want to achieve. Only by segmenting, analyzing, and defining a specific testing agenda can you determine the scope and intensity of the testing effort.
- **Scheduling.** A project test plan often contains a detailed testing schedule. This almost always occurs when the testing effort resides in a group that works separately from the development group. When the development and testing efforts are merged, however, you can fold the testing activity into the project test plan. For the *Ankh* effort, testing efforts were not separate, so the project test plan referred the reader to the project development plan for information about the testing schedule.

Component/Class Test Plan

The component or class test plan often features test procedures accompanied by tables containing multitudes of test cases. In addition, you might find that this plan includes specifications for test harnesses and automated testing scripts. Such tools allow you to perform intensive structural testing at the component level. A component test plan often comprises the most exacting plan in the suite of plans you develop for a software product. It also can contain both behavior and structural test specifications. Among the tasks that this plan can help you perform are the following:

- **Designation of test cases.** For the *Ankh* development effort, the component test plan named test cases that corresponded fairly directly to the use cases named in the requirements specification. Further, the emphasis of the component test plan was on behavioral testing. Structural testing was reserved for a relatively few instances in which performance issues were estimated to be high risks.
- **Naming and specification of scripts.** Whenever an automated testing script is required, you can provide it as a supplement to a primary test procedure. You can assign each requirement a primary test procedure. The primary test procedure (which also can be referred to as a test case) can provide references to supplementary tables of test cases or separate test procedures.

- **Naming of classes to be tested.** Name the classes and the features of the classes that you want to test. To accomplish this, you identify initial and expected final states of the objects you investigate. To carry out the test, you might have to design a test harness that will set initial values and go from there.
- **Convert requirements use cases to test cases.** The component test plan provides a context by which you can convert use cases drawn from the requirements specification into test procedures (or test cases). The value of starting with use cases is that you work with material that you have already substantially refined, so most of the information you require, if not already provided, is at least clearly outlined.
- **Formalization of test reports.** Document every test so that you can record the result of the execution of the test in a convenient, self-evident fashion. One approach to this is to use a formalized test report. (See "Test Report Templates" later in this chapter.) In other instances, you can embed test cases in tables that allow you to include pass/fail results along with the cases.
- **Summarization of test results.** Summary test reports provide a view of the overall testing effort. Although it is important to establish that no test failed (or to explain why you waived a failed test), it also is important to be able to account for the percent of the overall planned testing activity you completed. You can summarize the percent of overall functionality that you estimate you covered.

Integration Test Plan

The integration test plan should provide a clear roadmap for how you intend to test the system as the developers construct it. As the developers assemble the modules (or stripes) of the system, the integration test plan should indicate how you intend to confirm that the assembly is acceptable. With the *Ankh* testing effort, the team reached this goal by creating test procedures based on the use cases that appeared in the design document. Among the tasks that an integration test plan can help you perform are the following:

- **Set specific criteria for pass/fail of integration.** When you set criteria for integration testing, consider the percent of functionality you want to see covered before you accept integration as successful. For example, you might establish that for each integration, the requirements included in the newly integrated module be tested individually to establish whether anomalies have developed or performance has declined.
- **Determine the depth of regression testing to be performed.** You can set up tables of test cases at this point to establish how much you want to test. If the testing for each integration involves following a scenario based on use cases, you should designate which use cases you want to use. These can become standard models for regression that you can use with each successive integration.

- **Establish the extent to which black-box and white-box testing are to be used.** The integration plan provides a context in which you can set general polices and practices regarding how you want to test integration. For example, you can say that you want to verify functionality only, or you can designate that you test for performance problems that might follow each integration.
- **Convert design use cases into integration test cases.** As with the component test plan, if you draw upon the use cases that you have developed during the design effort, you might find that a substantial portion of your work has already been done.

System Test Plan

You can use the system test plan to assemble the pass/fail criteria you want to assert against the overall system. Among the tasks that this plan can help you perform are the following:

- **Establish items to be installed.** You can draw on the configuration plan to determine which components, assets, and documents should be installed. Testing the installation, then, involves determining whether all the components, assets, and documents have been installed. It also involves determining whether anything other than these items has been installed.
- **Establish targeted environments.** You can designate the machines and systems you have targeted.
- **Performance.** You can designate what, specifically, you consider successful performance on the targeted system. One approach to this is to assign specific time values to tasks you think the system should be able to perform.

Acceptance Test Plan

An acceptance test plan allows you to name procedures and pass/fail criteria that represent the perspective of your customer. Among different approaches to acceptance testing are alpha and beta testing. Beta tests receive the greatest attention because they allow your customers to use your product in a friendly way. Friendliness involves providing feedback that helps you identify and repair lingering defects. Other types of acceptance testing involve exacting or legally stipulated items that you must confirm have been addressed to the satisfaction of the client. In such situations, you might find that you turn your software over to testers who work for your client. They apply a given set of tests to your software and then advise you about the results. Publishers often have a game testing system of this type in place.

Organizing Test Planning Documents

A convenient way to organize documents involves creating a project test plan and then making references to other, specialized test plans in the References section of this document. In this way, you can use a standard template (such as the IEEE 829) to provide coverage of common topics while referring readers to specialized documents for specific testing issues, such as test cases and test reports. Figure 11.8 shows a basic document hierarchy similar to the one that the *Ankh* team used.

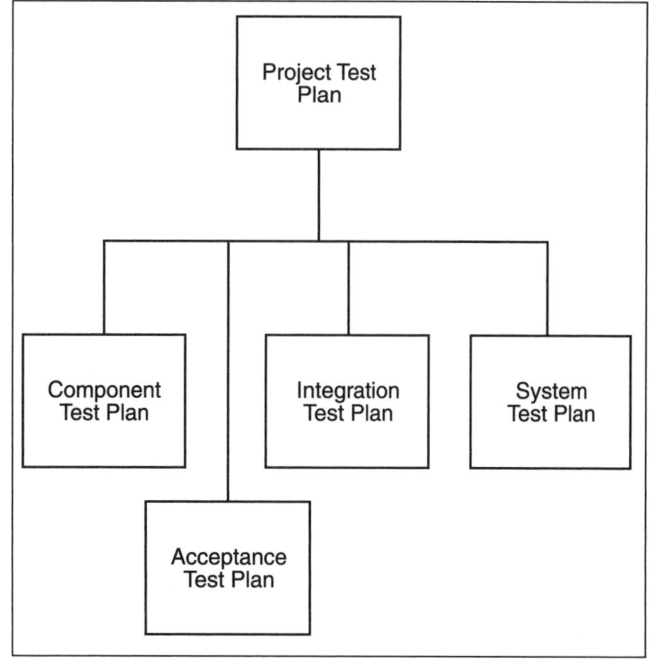

Figure 11.8
A simple document hierarchy directs readers from a project to a test-implementation view of testing activities.

Using Templates

You can group the templates that you use for developing testing artifacts into a simple set:

- **Tables with multiple columns.** Tables provide a convenient way to store the data derived from testing. This proves especially true when you want to document test cases and must provide, in the process, specific itemizations of how you intend to combine input values.
- **Test cases.** As a part of its standard 829 commentary, the IEEE furnishes several extremely useful tabular templates for test cases. These templates provide headings you can implement in a document format, but the tabular form tends to make everything easy to understand.
- **Test reports.** As with the templates for test cases, the IEEE also furnishes sample test reports. Test reports have few sections, but often you must supplement each section with extensive tables of output values.
- **Test document outlines.** Templates for documents help you understand how to organize test cases, test reports, and tables of generated values so that you can readily access them.

IEEE 829

Standard 829 for test plans constitutes one of the best starting places for generalized test plans. Figure 11.9 provides topics from IEEE Standard 829. For a specific listing of the topics and extensive discussion of how to use them, you can consult the IEEE Web site (http://www.ieee.org). The template's superiority lies in its ability to help you focus on the types of testing you want to perform. The *Ankh* team employed the template to create the project test plan. The project test plan presented general policies and definitions. For specific information on testing, the plan referred the reader to other documents. Figure 11.8 illustrates how the primary test plan based on IEEE 829 relates to the other three test plans.

IEEE Standard 829 Test Plan Template

Test Plan Identifier
References
Introduction
Test Items
Software Risk Issues
Features to Be Tested
Features Not to Be Tested
Approach
Item Pass/Fail Criteria
Suspension Criteria and Resumption Requirements
Test Deliverables
Remaining Test Tasks
Environmental Needs
Staffing and Training Needs
Responsibilities
Schedule
Planning Risks and Contingencies
Approvals
Glossary

Figure 11.9
Project test plans can use the IEEE Standard 829 as a starting point.

Among the most important topics are those that relate to how you want to approach the overall test strategy. Thinking these topics through from the start helps you determine how you can anticipate risks involving coverage. Ultimately, every test strategy must dictate that not everything can be tested. You can test only what you have the time and resources to test. Because of this, you must give consideration to how to best compensate for limited testing. The template helps you do just this when it asks you to name things like the features to be tested, the approaches to be taken, the items you intend to designate for testing, and the risks you anticipate.

Table 11.1 discusses the topics that IEEE Standard 829 includes. (The CD includes the test plans developed for the *Ankh* development project. Appendix D, "Software Engineering and Game Design Documentation," provides instructions about how to access the documents.)

Table 11.1 IEEE Standard 829 Topics

Topic	Discussion
Test Plan Identifier	The identifier should allow you to identify both the document type and the version of the document. The identifiers that the *Ankh* team used consisted of abbreviated document titles and a number designating the level of release. The identifiers were as follows: AnkhSWTP1_0.doc (project test plan, first version), AnkhSWCTP1_0.doc (component/class test plan, first version), AnkhSWITP1_0.doc (integration test plan, first version), and AnkhSWSTP1_0.doc (system test plan, first version).
References	The References heading in the project test plan for *Ankh* included the names of the documents that contained specific testing information. This approach to documentation reduced the amount of general information included in the subordinate test plans (the integration, system, and component test plans). Subordinate test plans included a reference to the project test plan. Reducing redundant information decreased maintenance work.
Introduction	The introduction explains the overall test plan. If you want to use a minimum of narrative, you can use a diagram representing documents and their associated purposes.
Test Items	Test items designate identifiable components, classes, operations, logical entities, or other testable entities. Identifying test items allows you to determine the types of test plans and test suites that you want to develop. For example, if you work in an object-oriented context, you name classes, operations, and modules as test items.
Software Risk Issues	Testing risks can go in many directions. Two key elements are how much time you have to test and the scope and complexity of the system you are responsible for testing. See "Assessing Risks," later in this chapter, for more information.
Features to Be Tested	Those who play the game experience the features of the game. Software requirements specify the functionality that supports the features of the software. The features of the game, then, concern how it is played. Use cases provide an excellent way to name and describe features. You group features by placing them in general subheadings. After grouping them, you can assess their importance in relation to the testing effort.
Features Not to Be Tested	Features that you do not intend to test consist of those that your team planned but decided to exclude from the current release. Among these are functionality that might be implemented but left unused, documents, "trusted" components, and nonfunctional requirements. The more formally you test your game, the more you must clearly indicate what you have and have not tested and the extent to which you have covered the features you have tested.

(continued on next page)

Table 11.1 IEEE Standard 829 Topics (continued)

Topic	Discussion
Approach	When you describe your approach, you describe what might be viewed as the terrain of your testing activity. In other words, you might explain that the testing effort encompasses class, module, and system testing, and that module testing is specified in the integration test plan. You might explain that regression testing forms, in your approach, an important element of integration testing. In addition, you might indicate that your approach addresses multiple platforms, strives to generate valuable metrics, and will adhere to a strictly planned (documented) course. See "Ways to Test," earlier in this chapter, for specific information on this topic.
Item Pass/Fail Criteria	Pass and fail criteria apply both to individual tests and the overall test effort. This section allows you to establish policies, such as that the test scenario of every test case must be completed and reported before the test suite containing the test case can be said to be complete. Further, you can say that every test case that a procedure contains must pass before the test procedure can pass. On the other hand, you might designate percentages of acceptable coverage. Generally, a test case does not pass until it has shown that the software flawlessly furnishes the behavior set as the pass criteria for the test case.
Suspension Criteria and Resumption Requirements	This section provides a space in which to list such reasons for suspension. One commonly occurring reason for suspending testing is that a given type of testing no longer generates useful data. For example, if you are testing a given field and have tested boundary conditions and 75 percent of the numbers you could enter into the field, you can suspend testing. Another commonly occurring reason for suspending testing is that you have detected a defect in the software that shows that any results that follow will be unreliable. Until maintenance programmers eliminate the defect, further testing is a waste of time.
Test Deliverables	This section allows you to state specific deliverables, such as test cases, test reports, and test plans. When you complete this section, name items such as logs, tables, summary reports, reviews, and documents that should accompany your test documentation effort.
Remaining Test Tasks	You purposely exclude some test items, and other test items fall outside the scope of your testing effort. Just because such items fall outside the scope of your testing effort does not imply that anyone should assume they should not be tested. For this reason, after you have completed the actions named in the test plan, you describe testing tasks that might still need to be tested.

Topic	Discussion
Environmental Needs	This section names the tools you use for testing. The tools include software and hardware. For example, in most industrial settings, it is considered essential to establish a separate and distinct test environment from the ground up for testing purposes. When you describe environmental needs for testing, you identify everything you need to establish and sustain the testing effort.
Staffing and Training Needs	Staffing and training needs can relate to tools required to perform testing. How this works out depends on the culture of your organization. You can include a schedule that names those who are to perform testing.
Responsibilities	Defining roles facilitates the development effort. You can set policies about how you want the testing effort to proceed. Even if roles are mixed, you can establish ground rules about what responsibilities people have when they work as testers.
Schedule	For the *Ankh* effort, a separate test team was not established. Because of this, the testing schedule was folded into the project plan. When setting up the project plan, the project manager sets up specific testing tasks to be assigned to testers. Many industry experts contend that software products benefit if the managers assign testers and developers to separate groups. There is great virtue to this approach. In a setting in which separate teams exist, the test manager should create a distinct test plan. The testing schedule should provide information about when testing is to begin, what amount of time is to be allotted for testing for each component or stripe, and when testing is to be completed.
Planning Risks and Contingencies	Risks include what happens when you do not have enough time to test everything that you plan to test. Another issue is what to do if you lack people to perform testing. A risk is anything in the testing effort that endangers the completion of the game development effort. If the testing effort can endanger the schedule, you should list it.
Approvals	Name the people who should approve the test plan. This includes the project manager and the test manager, but you can designate many other people, too.
Glossary	Include a glossary of the terms that apply to your project. Even if you think that things like "black-box testing" are clear to everyone, ensure that disagreements or misunderstandings do not occur. Definitions ensure that everyone has a common understanding of basic terms.

Test Case Template

The IEEE defines a test case as a specific action, usually isolated from others, that you take to evaluate the performance characteristics of a software system. The view taken in this book is that the expression "text case" can be used interchangeably with "test procedure." Still, it is important to note that some testers use the expressions to designate different things. Accordingly, a *test case* is said to be a specific action performed to evaluate a specific software property. On the other hand, a *test procedure* is said to consist of a set of test cases. Again, the approach to testing that this book presents merges the two. Many development organizations commonly do the same thing.

To expeditiously formulate a test case (or a test procedure), you can use the IEEE standard 829 template. To accomplish this, you can begin by creating a table for the test case using a word processor (Word, FrameMaker, and so on) or a tool such as SmartDraw. If you use this approach, you expend the greatest effort when you create the first test table. After that, the effort involves copying, pasting, and modifying. If you want to assert a specific set of policies for creating test cases, you can include instructions in the first table you create. Figure 11.10 illustrates one of the templates that the *Ankh* tests used.

Test identifier: Provide the abbreviation for the stripe, an underscore, "ITC," an underscore, and an integer identifying the version of the test procedure of case. Example: S1_ITC_001
Requirements adressed: List the requirements that the stripe addressed.
Prerequisite conditions: List conditions for operation of stripe. This is usually stripes that should already be implemented, libraries, or other such conditions.
Test input: Describe what you do as a tester. Mouse clicks or other user actions. Use a table if necessary.
Expected test results: Start with the results named in the use case.
Criteria for evaluating results: Start with the scenario given in the use case. System responds as prompted and allows user to complete use case actions without defects.
Instructions for conducting procedure: Copy items from the use case.
Features to be tested: Name the features or provide a table or other representation.
Requirements traceability: Name dependencies.
Rationale for decisions: Name any reasoning that qualifies the pass/fail criteria.

Figure 11.10
IEEE standard 829 provides a template that you can use to create test cases.

To use the template effectively, you can create two or more columns instead of just one. If you use several columns, you can more effectively detail the information that you want to use to conduct the tests. Table 11.2 discusses the information that's included in the test plan.

Table 11.2 Test Case Headings*

Heading	Discussion
Test identifier	The unique identifier that you use for test cases varies with the approach that you adopt to testing. For the *Ankh* testing effort, because most of the test cases were general, the team used a simple type of identifier. In more intensive testing environments, this scheme can be extended to accommodate large numbers of test cases or test cases that identify different types of testing scenarios. The numbering scheme for the *Ankh* test effort was as follows: The letter *R* or *S* (for requirement or stripe) and the number of the test case, an underscore, letters designating the type of test (ITC for integration, CTC for classes, STC for system), an underscore, and an integer identifying the version or segment of the test case. *Example: S001_ITC_01.*
Requirements addressed	List the requirements that the test case addresses. This activity extends in two directions. For black-box test cases (also known as functional or behavioral testing), a test case might address only one requirement. For the *Ankh* effort, because each black-box text of the requirements originated with the use case included in the requirements document, it made sense to address only one requirement at a time. For test cases concerning stripes or modules, you should include the requirements that cover the functionality of the stripe or module. For the *Ankh* effort, the integration test plan listed test cases derived from the software design specification. The software design specification included use cases for each stripe. Determining the correctness of system responses with respect to stripes was the central focus of integration testing.
Prerequisite conditions	Prerequisites can be specified in a number of ways. If you are testing classes, for example, the values of attributes when an object of a class is instantiated constitute testable preconditions. The test case can specifically list the values that define the preconditions. On a broader basis, when you are dealing with modules in the integration test plan, you might designate dependencies on other modules. This approach also provides a context in which regression tests can be performed.

(continued on next page)

Table 11.2 Test Case Headings* (continued)

Heading	Discussion
Test input	Detailed test cases require that you provide tables of values you want to use for testing. For the *Ankh* effort, the development team worked at several levels. At the most general level, the team designated input as general as the action. In other cases, the team evaluated operations through stress and similar tests involving specified data. For example, trying letters, numbers, nonletter characters, and blank spaces in the dialog box fields involved creating tables that listed such values.
Expected test results	For the black-box tests of the requirements, the use cases included in the requirements specification made it easy to determine expected results. Having at hand such ready-made scenarios for testing constitutes a major reason for including use cases in the requirements specification. With brief rewording of the scenarios and insertion of specific test data, the use cases almost always completely anticipate the categories of information states in the test case. If you are testing classes, you can define expected test results at specific levels. For example, you can use sequence, collaboration, or state diagrams to determine the values you expect to see when messaging occurs. In basic terms, for example, given that you have created an instance of a class, what value do you expect when you use a given operation with a given set of parameter values?
Criteria for evaluating results	When you evaluate the results of testing, you do so using criteria such as acceptable variations and performance profiles. In other words, you try to provide a generalized context in which you can judge the significance of the results you have obtained through testing. That a given operation returns zero means nothing unless you have established a context in which you can tell whether such a return value properly expresses the conditions set for the operation. In other cases, it is possible to speak fairly broadly. For example, given that a use case from the design specification establishes the context of performance, it might be reasonable to write that evaluation of a stripe cab be based on system responses. The *Ankh* testing scenario designated that the system should perform as prompted and allow the user to successfully complete the action named in the test scenario.

Heading	Discussion
Instructions for conducting procedure	If you create use cases for both requirements and design efforts, you can begin writing instruction sets for test cases by copying the scenario from the use case. If you do not use this approach, then you can formulate a numbered list of steps you intend to follow as you conduct the test. If you are using a test harness, you should provide enough information to allow readers of the test case to repeat the actions you name. It is helpful, for instance, to tell the user of the test case to copy code into the harness (if this is what you do) and how to proceed from there.
Features to be tested	A requirement designates the functionality that is to be implemented to support a feature, so to establish the feature to which a test of a requirement relates involves inspecting the game for specific ways that the implementation of the requirement affects the player's experience of the game. If you employ a use case approach to requirements engineering, the use cases in the requirements specification provide the best starting place for identifying features to be tested.
Requirements traceability	Requirements tend to be mutually dependent, so you should trace dependencies. Requirements often address modules or stripes, so you should trace them to modules and stripes. On the other hand, when given classes embody the functionality a given requirement has designated, then you should trace the class to the requirement.
Rationale for decisions	Most test results fall into four categories, as follows: *pass, fail, deferred,* and *cancelled.* Regardless of the result you reach, it is beneficial to make a statement that helps the reader know how the test case can be used in different ways to accord with different circumstances. As an extreme example, you might set up tests for the numbers 1 through 100. You could say that if you test 0,1, 100, and 101 (boundary conditions), the other tests are not needed.

*See Figure 11.10 for a sample test case.

Test Report Templates

Test report templates provide you with an expeditious way to record test results. Figure 11.11 illustrates a test report template that is suitable for reporting the results of test cases or test procedures. The test report template guides you as you create tables or other artifacts for recording the results of testing. As with test cases and test procedures, the best approach to organize test reports involves using a table.

Test report identifier: Provide the abbreviation for the stripe, an underscore, ITC, an underscore, an integer identifying the version of the test case, an underscore, and the word "Report." Example: S1_ITC_01_Report
Summary: Say how many faults were found and how many revisions were necessary before the stripe passed all tests. Say how the stripe was tested.
Variances: Describe any way that the test case used conditions that differed from those implied by the use case in the software design specification.
Comprehensive assessment: If you have additional documentation, reference it here. Attach it to the document with a reference to this report.
Summary of results: Say what the problems were that caused the failures.
Evaluation: **Pass** ☐ **Fail** ☐ **Deferred** ☐ Say whether the stripe passed or failed. If you have further information, add it.
Summary of activities: For each time, list how much time was required. If not applicable, indicate "n/a." Units: h—hour(s). Do not record in other units. Example: 0.5 for half an hour. **Test design:** **Driver development:** **Execution:** **Stripe revision:**
Approval initials of tester:

Figure 11.11
A test report template guides you through either recording test results or developing tables and other artifacts to record test results.

Effectively developing testing reports requires examining how much information you must record if you are to document the results of testing. For the vast majority of tests involving fields and buttons, you might find that it is best to use a single table to combine test procedures or cases with reports. In other instances, the test reports might require that you document a succession of results that are more easily understood if examined in isolation. In this case, a table similar to the one shown in Figure 11.11 might be best. Table 11.3 discusses the information included in the test report.

Table 11.3 Test Case Headings

Heading	Discussion
Test report identifier	For the *Ankh* effort, the identifier involved the abbreviation for the stripe, an underscore, a three-letter designation of the type of test (ITC, for integration test case, for example), an underscore, an integer identifying the version of the test case, an underscore, and the word "Report." *Example: S1_ITC_001_Report*
Summary	The summary should provide an overview of the test. You can write a summary. To make things easy, you can check boxes for Open, Completed, Failed, or Complete-Passed.
Variances	Variances can describe differences in initial test conditions, procedures, and results. While it is important to conduct consistently repeatable tests, you often need to make allowances for unanticipated aspects of the planned testing routines. Chief among such variations are those that arise due to limitations of time. For example, if you stipulated 100 test cases but due to scheduling limitations decided to test a sample of this, you can note this as a variation.
Comprehensive assessment	You can refer readers to a table of summary values, or you can provide a simple description of the results. The purpose of the report is to provide developers with information about how the system failed (or passed) the test you applied to it. In contrast to the Summary section, this section calls for specific testing data. You can provide, for example, specific data to help with further analysis of the defect.
Summary of results	Say what the problems were that caused the failure. If you set up a table in this section, you can provide metrics on how many times you conducted the test before it rendered a passing result and how much effort you expended to remove the defect.
Evaluation	The easiest approach to this might be to create check boxes.
Summary of activities	As the template featured in Figure 11.11 indicates, important metrics center on duration and effort. The information that you call for when you summarize activities depends on what you or your organization views as important. Key metrics, such as number of testers, duration, and effort, are usually beneficial.
Test design	If you develop a standard set of testing tools, you can create a set of check boxes that enables you to indicate quickly which standard design you applied. See "Tables for Testing" later in this chapter for a list of table types that you can employ to guide test design.
Driver development	If you apply a standard test harness to a multitude of test cases, you can provide a reference to the files that contain the driver. Readers of the report can then view this material to see how it was implemented.

(continued on next page)

Table 11.3 Test Case Headings (continued)

Heading	Discussion
Stripe (module) revision	This topic proved useful in the *Ankh* development effort because the team conducted development and testing in the context of specific stripes. It was important, then, always to trace activities to stripes.
Approval initials of tester	It is important to identify those who are involved in a given test scenario. This information proves useful if the defect is still current and if you are gathering historical data.

Tables for Testing

Tables are one of the most used type of testing artifact. To set up tables for your testing effort, you might find that it is best to take some time at the start of your project to create table templates. To create table templates, you can review your test plans and derive from them the types of tables you will need. Experienced testers often develop an extensive set of table types that address specific testing needs. In her book *Introducing Software Testing,* Louise Tamres provides an extensive review of tables she has developed. (The complete reference appears at the end of this chapter.) Among the tables that Tamres discusses are the following:

- **Decision.** A decision table allows you to organize information along the lines typical of logical tables. Such tables are useful when you have multiple conditions that correspond to multiple actions.
- **Keystroke/mouse action.** This table tracks keystrokes or mouse actions against fields and buttons. Among other tasks, this table provides a convenient way to track the minute test cases that are involved in testing user interfaces.
- **Test procedure summary.** This table enables you to coordinate test procedures when you have a set of test procedures that consist of many test cases or when you have test cases that involve procedures or a set of subordinate test cases.
- **Boundary condition tables.** This table provides a way to ensure that you cover the relatively few values you apply to a test scenario involving boundary conditions.
- **Cross reference.** This can be a general utility table for tracking test procedures and test cases. For example, suppose that you face a set of dependent operations. You might use one dialog box in the GUI to enter values and then, later, access another dialog box to retrieve the values. You might find it necessary to cross reference the results of the two sets of interactions.
- **Test management.** Test management involves tracking the performance of tests and the results. You might want to create a table that summarizes the results of dozens of test procedures.

- **Test cases, procedures, and reports.** With the *Ankh* development effort, the team used tables for test cases, test procedures, and testing reports because these things provided a convenient way to reduce the amount of writing involved in creating testing material.
- **State transition.** You can use tables to track the changes in objects. If you first create a UML state transition diagram when you use such tables, you can readily visualize the attributes that the table contains.
- **Test requirements.** Summarizing requirements in a table ensures that you can track your testing progress.
- **Failed and passed reports.** Summarizing testing reports, generally, makes it easier to gather metrics and present summaries.

note

Companies like IBM (Rational) and Borland manufacture testing tools that automatically generate tables. For cottage industry endeavors, you can create tables using a spreadsheet, such as Excel, Lotus, or Quattro Pro. Use spreadsheets if you anticipate extensive work with metrics or if you want to access data for automated test scripts. If you want things to be easy to use, the table features of word processors, such as Corel WordPerfect, Microsoft Word, or Adobe FrameMaker, are the best. A final option is a general-purpose application, such as SmartDraw.

Limitations of space make it impossible to provide extensive discussion of how to use tables, but a simple scenario can illustrate a few key ideas. (For comprehensive treatment of the topic, see the book by Tamres listed at the end of the chapter.) As an example of how the *Ankh* test effort used a table, consider the dialog box in Figure 11.12.

Figure 11.12
A table helps you control the testing of dialog boxes.

The dialog box shown in Figure 11.12 is the central control dialog box that the player sees during most of the game. To designate an action for a turn, the player clicks one of the buttons. The dialog box features three sliders that indicate health and other points. Testing the dialog box requires the tester to investigate the behavior of each of its features.

To set up a testing table that facilitates this effort, you create a matrix that shows the test cases that guide you as you subject each of the features of the dialog box (such as buttons and fields) to the possible inputs (mouse clicks, keystrokes, scroll actions, and so on).

As Figure 11.13 illustrates, after you have created a table to track the keystrokes and mouse actions against sliders, fields, and buttons, you can easily work through each test case that the table names and record the results.

Cursor Location / Key/Mouse Action	Left Mouse	Right Mouse	Scroller	LM + Key	RM + Key	SRL + Key	Non Act Key	Middle Mouse	g	w	s	a	z	Esc	Expected Result	Exceptional Result	Pass/Fail
Walk button	+	–	–	–	–	–	–	–	+	–	–	–	–	–	Squares appear around character.	None	P
Weapon button	+	–	–	–	–	–	–	–	–	+		–	–	–	Opens Weapon Selection dialog box. See TC D-10.	None	P
Status button	+	–	–	–	–	–	–	–	–	–	+	–	–	–	Opens Status dialog box. Display only.	None	P
Scroll button	+	–	–	–	–	–	–	–				+		–	Shows Inventory dialog box. See TC D-11.	None	P
Sleep button	+	–	–	–	–	–	–	–					+	–	No action.	None	P
HP field	–	–	–	–	–	–	–	–	–	–	–	–	–	–	No action.	None	P
MP field	–	–	–	–	–	–	–	–	–	–	–	–	–	–	No action.	None	P
AP field	–	–	–	–	–	–	–	–	–	–	–	–	–	–	No action.	None	P

Figure 11.13
Track involved test case scenarios using a table.

The table in Figure 11.13 is set up so that the column on the left names buttons and sliders (fields), and the top row identifies actions. The plus and minus signs signify that the tester should try the action, but only those actions that a plus sign marks should elicit a response. The two columns containing result information allow you to know the specified result or, if the specified result does not occur, to note what did happen. If you take an action and the expected result occurs, the test case or procedure passes. P indicates pass.

This table satisfies the basic criteria for setting up a test case. When you use such a table, you should exercise caution to ensure that you distinguish each test case. In this instance, either clicking on the Walk button or pressing the G key results in the action described. (Note that the table should indicate if the Shift key is used with any other keys.) If the test fails for either input, this table requires that you employ the Exceptional Result column to explain how the test failed. Perhaps a better approach would be to set up the keys in the Cursor Location column. This table decreases the number of rows but can introduce some confusion.

Testing Activities

When you perform testing activities, one maxim is that you should test as many things as possible as much as possible. What and how much you test depend to a great extent on how you plan your efforts and what tools you employ. Tools consist of documentation, strategies, and test programs. The following few sections concentrate on strategies and programs that you can create.

Test Cases and Procedures

Test cases and test procedures are documented instances of testing. The IEEE distinguishes between test procedures and test cases, but the practice in this chapter is to use the two expressions interchangeably. The IEEE defines a *test case* as a specific, isolated instance of testing. A *procedure* is defined as a collection of test cases. In practice, however, a procedure can consist of test cases; likewise, a test case can be a procedure. Testers also employ the expressions *test scenario* and *test script* in much the same way that they do test case and test procedure. Context determines meaning.

Although the specific terms that apply to testing might be open to interpretation, a few recommendations drawn from the IEEE should be followed fairly strictly:

- **Identified start state.** Every procedure or test must commence with a clearly defined set of conditions. In other words, when you design a test, you identify the state of the system from which the test is to be initiated.
- **Procedures that can be repeated.** A second stipulation is that you describe the test that you perform so that it can be repeated. To achieve this goal, you can use a script of actions you perform to complete the test. You can supplement your test procedure with data tables and other artifacts. If you find yourself plodding through directories and files to find test scripts, data, result information, and other such items that you have not documented as part of your test scenario, it is unlikely that you have created a test that you or others are likely to be able to repeat. Documenting a test procedure amounts to writing a set of instructions that others should be able to use.
- **Identified end state.** A test determines whether or not the system properly transitions from one state to another. Because transitions constitute primary criteria for a test, as part of your test, you must identify criteria you can use to establish that transitions result in specified changes. Just as you designate the state of the system at the start of the test, you designate the state of the system at the conclusion of the

test. The way you designate the concluding state depends on the type of test you are performing. If you work at a behavioral level of testing, describing what the game does might suffice. On the other hand, if you are working at a structural level, you might need to know the specific values stored in object attributes.

Every test in some way tests a change in the system. You must be able to know, identify, and evaluate these changes.

Converting Use Cases to Test Cases

Converting use cases to test cases constitutes a central activity of testing in object-oriented development efforts. This occurs because the use cases you develop during the requirements and design phase of your development effort can anticipate almost every behavioral scenario of the software product. What results is a substantial body of material from which you can draw most of the information you require to create test plans and develop test procedures or test cases. (Page limitations make it impossible to discuss this important activity in detail in this chapter. For a full description of how to convert a use case to a test case, see the section titled "Use Case Confirmation" in Chapter 14, "Practice, Practice, Practice.")

Using Outlines

An alternative to converting use cases to test procedures is developing test outlines. This approach to testing predates object-oriented programming, but it remains an instrumental part of many testing efforts. One reason for this is that many testers enter the development process only after the product has been substantially completed and the available documentation traces the design of the product in a rudimentary, incomplete way.

When this type of situation arrives, the tester can initiate a testing process based on tracing the activities that the product is supposed to perform. An outline allows you to begin a general level and gradually refine the outlines as you collect more information about the product. As you go, you can begin supplementing the outline with use cases, test cases, testing tables, and other artifacts.

Test Suites

A test suite is a group of test procedures that you package together to investigate what you consider to be an area of behavior that the test procedures commonly address. A test suite, for example, can address a module that provides GUI services. The test cases in the suite investigate classes, operations, assets, and other items that you have determined to support GUI capabilities. Ideally, you can use the tests that you develop for one component in a test suite for others in the suite.

Black-Box Testing

Black-box testing is also called *behavioral* or *functional* testing. To perform black-box testing, you create a test procedure that establishes a set of start conditions for a given scenario of change you expect to take place. To investigate this change, you establish a clearly defined set of results. You then write a procedure that allows you to operate the system so that it goes through the changes you have anticipated. The test succeeds if you can repeatedly perform the same operations, beginning from the same set of conditions, and end up with the same results.

Black-box testing is most frequently applied to verification and validation of requirements. The approach employed for *Ankh* involved converting the use cases from the requirements specification into test procedures. Each use case provided a scenario of use. The scenario of use began with trigger conditions and ended in a given state change. The test procedure formalized this scenario. The testing, then, investigated only the behavior of the system. The way that the system structurally affected the changes that were investigated was left to other types of testing.

White-Box Testing

White-box testing is also known as *structural* testing. It has some of the features of black-box testing (beginning conditions, test scenario, end conditions), but with white-box testing, the granularity of the test activity becomes much finer. The objective involves investigating the specific changes of state that objects undergo as the system transitions from the beginning conditions to the end conditions that your test describes. This type of transition is known as a *state transition.* UML tools provide ways to trace and depict such transitions.

To execute white-box test procedures, you develop several types of artifacts. Among these are main function programs that you employ to instantiate and explore class objects, operations you add to a class so that you can derive information from objects of its type as they go through state transitions, and complex test harnesses that allow you to investigate the interactions of objects from different classes.

You can refer to the code that you write to conduct such tests as test *harnesses.* Harnesses allow you to execute operations in isolation. Because a test harness executes a given body of code in isolation, you can develop it any way you want without fear of corrupting the entire program. Reducing the amount of system interaction limits the complexity of the material you are testing.

Harnesses with Static Class Operations

Some testers use static operations and attributes to report object counts and states. You can use a static attribute as a gauge for the activities of all instances of a given class.

Therefore, if you include static functions in your classes, you can maintain tallies of object counts and the cumulative values of attributes among class objects. In most cases, when you output values, you should output to a log file. The following program shows only the basics:

```
namespace test{
class CThing
{
private:
        string thingName;
        int thingPower;
        int id;
        static int testTotal;
        static int testPower;
        static int testName;

public:

CThing(int power):id(0),thingPower(power)
{
        testTotal++;
        id = testTotal;
        testPower = power;
}

static void ShowAttributes()
{
        cout << "\nTotal - " << testTotal << endl;
        cout << "\Power - " << testPower << endl;
}

~CThing()
{
        cout << "Destructor: " << testTotal << endl;
        testTotal--;
        cout << "Count: " << testTotal;
}
};

int CThing::testTotal = 0;
int CThing::testPower = 0;
} //end test nsp

int main()
{
       using namespace test;
       cout << "\n" << "Harness";
       CThing* t1 = new CThing(0);
       CThing::ShowAttributes();
       CThing* t2 = new CThing(10);
       CThing::ShowAttributes();
```

```
        delete t2;
        getch();
        return 0;
}
```

Class Test Harnesses

To create a class test harness, you can develop a template class as your primary test harness. The advantage of using a template class for a test harness is that you can establish temporary messaging systems that simulate those that occur in the game. To make a class harness system work effectively, you should explore the design of the game to discover whether class hierarchies afford you opportunities to make use of existing code features as you develop your test harness. Using abstract classes in your template definition makes it easier to manipulate complex message exchanges. The following bit of code creates two classes, one of which is a template. The template class enables you to immediately put the tested class to work:

```
/*
------------------------------
The template declaration in this program sets up a class
that can receive generic data types.
The calls are cascaded, as in
ctrObjD.getFirstOfItems().getDataMName();
------------------------------
*/

template <class SDataS>
class CTestContainer
{
private:
        SDataS firstOfItems;

public:
        CTestContainer(SDataS setVal):firstOfItems(setVal)
        {}

        ~CTestContainer(){}
        SDataS GetFirstOfItems()
        {
                return firstOfItems;
        }

        void SetFirstOfItems(SDataS setVal)
        {
                firstOfItems = setVal;
        }
};//end of CTestContainer Class
```

```
class CGameClass
{
private:
      string boxName;
      long boxNumber;

public:
      CGameClass(string bName, long bNum):
                                    boxName(bName),
                                    boxNumber(bNum)
      {}
      ~CGameClass(){}

      string GetDataName()
      {
            return boxName;
      }

      long GetDataNumber()
      {
            return boxNumber;
      }
};//end CGameClass class

int main()
{
CGameClass dMObj("Helper", 45);

/*
The CTestContainer constructor uses the CGameClass type.
Having done this, it is then possible to access
operations associated with the object.
*/

CTestContainer<CGameClass> ctrObjD(dMObj);
cout << ctrObjD.GetFirstOfItems().GetDataName() << "\n";
cout << ctrObjD.GetFirstOfItems().GetDataNumber() << "\n";
cout << "\nEnd of program.";
getch();
return 0;
}
```

Module Testing Harnesses

One of the biggest tasks that you face as a tester involves testing modules—classes that work together to provide an identifiable service to your game. (The *Ankh* development team referred to modules as stripes.) Being able to test modules requires that you have an architectural view of the system that enables you to determine if a set of classes behaves correctly as a service provider.

With the *Ankh* development effort, stripe testing began with the isolation of the classes that composed specific stripes. To develop a module test, the team first had to establish the behavioral scope of the test using a design use case. Then the team was able to use a sequence diagram to scope out how to test specific class interactions for the stripe. (See Figure 11.14.)

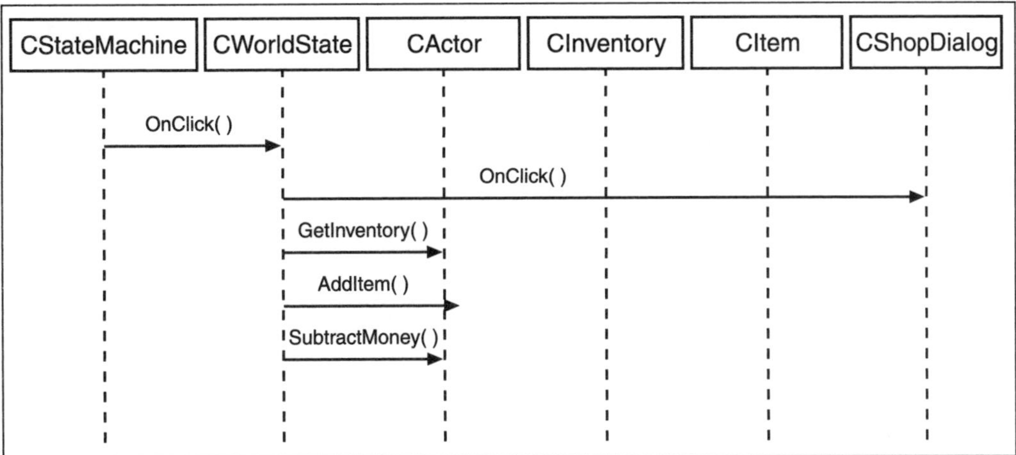

Figure 11.14
A sequence diagram is a starting point for module testing.

Although Figure 11.14 shows only six classes and a set of five message exchanges, it still provides an excellent start for testing. If you start from such a beginning, you can construct a test harness that allows you to create instances of these classes and then proceed from there to specific types of tests. When you develop harnesses for testing modules, your objective is to create a context that resembles the entire system but is simpler. Such test harnesses require planning.

Assessing Risks

Risk assessment is an area of quality assurance, but testing can contribute to risk assessment in important ways. This chapter emphasizes the way that risk assessment can involve determining the extent to which your tests cover the complete scope of the game and provide a suitable level of testing granularity. In the large world of quality assurance, many considerations that go beyond this relatively limited horizon come into consideration. For example, quality assurance efforts endeavor to determine how maintainable software is. In other words, given that something is bound to go wrong at some point, how much effort (cost) will be required to fix the problem?

In the smaller world of test-specific work, two quality assurances that come into play are testability and complexity. *Testability* is the extent to which you can reliably test the software. *Complexity* is sometimes said to be a measure of how many logical paths you can take as you operate a software program. If a program possesses high complexity, you have to expend a greater effort to test it. Given that you have limited testing resources, if the complexity is great and you are to competently test the software, you might have to tell the project manager that the duration of the project must be extended to accommodate the testing effort. (This is likely to meet with objections.)

Coverage

Consider the class diagram that Figure 11.15 illustrates. In this diagram, class A communicates with class B. After it has received a return value from its communication with class B, class A communicates with an abstract object of class C. Depending on the return value communicated to A from B, the abstract object of class C can be instantiated as an object from class D, E, F, or G.

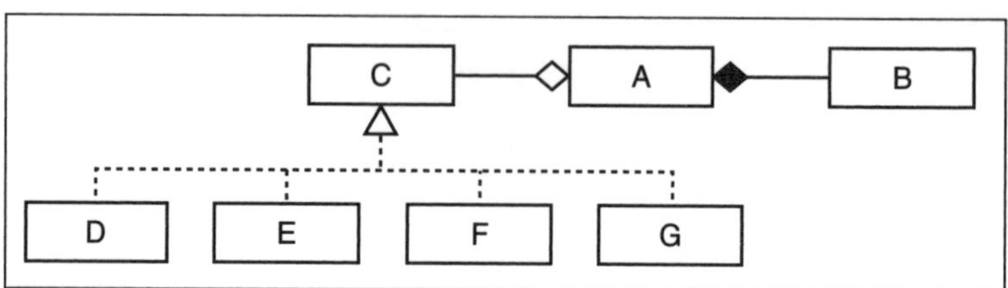

Figure 11.15
A system of classes sustains a multitude of interactions.

As a tester, designing a set of tests that comprehensively covers the interactions of the system classes involves investigating each of the paths that the system generates. As a starting point, you might construct a table to trace the logical branches that the system of classes sustains. Figure 11.16 illustrates a rudimentary venture in this direction. The table consists of a set of test procedures. The test procedures contain a multitude of test cases (which the table does not document specifically).

In Figure 11.16, all paths begin with class A. Class A communicates with class B. Then class B returns a value that allows A to communicate with class C, a factory class. Depending on the value that C receives, it provides an instance of the specialized class (D, E, F, G).

Class / Case/Procedure	A	B	C	D	E	F	G
t1	A–D	A–B	A–C	C–D			
t2	A–E	A–B	A–C		C–E		
t3	A–F	A–B	A–C			C–F	
t4	A–F	A–B	A–C				C–G

Figure 11.16
A table traces the interactions of a system of classes.

To test this system of classes, you can develop a structural (white-box) test. You face the task of creating a test harness that can support at least the manipulation of an object of class A. If you are to completely cover the interactions of this class, you must script the test procedure so that you can evaluate whether classes D, E, F, and G have been instantiated correctly. To accomplish this, you must have initial data to provide to class A and a table of result data by which to evaluate the instances of classes D, E, F, and G. These are the basic paths. Your coverage is determined by your analysis of the interactions of the classes and the number of test cases you develop to test the interactions. Further, the picture grows in detail when you test the specific attributes of each of the evaluated classes to determine whether they possess acceptable values at all points during the transaction.

The example presented so far involves white-box testing, which requires you to investigate the code. You can use another approach, however. Assume that the complexities that are exposed in Figure 11.16 are accounted for by clicks on the screen. Classes D, E, F, and G are really characters that appear when you click given icons. In this instance, you can create a black-box test. Generally, even if you decide to engage in white-box testing, you should employ black-box testing first. That's because it is essential to test the system to determine whether it has met the specifications set by the requirements. If the system should create a character when you click a given icon, you should establish this first through a black-box test. Generally, you should achieve as much coverage of requirements as possible using white-box testing before you begin developing black-box tests.

Complexity

Due to limitations of space and scope, a concept that is not dealt with in detail in this chapter is *cyclomatic complexity*. This approach to complexity constitutes one of the leading ways that software engineers investigate software complexity. Cyclomatic complexity measures a software system's structural complexity. To establish a software system's cyclomatic complexity, software engineers measure the number of ways it is possible to navigate a given body of code. The paths through a body of code are usually referred to as *logical branch points* that the system contains.

For the purposes of the discussion here, the definition of complexity can be scaled back to the basic idea that a game can be tested in terms of the number of ways a player might be expected to use it. The requirements and design of the game software determine the number of ways that a player interacts with a game. If developers competently engineer and implement the software, player interactions will be limited to those that are specified. Unanticipated or unspecified interactions that result in unanticipated or unspecified system changes reveal defects. It is the job of testing to discover such defects.

Considerations of complexity underlie the confidence with which testers can anticipate unanticipated interactions. To achieve a high degree of confidence, testers must design test efforts along two general lines. Along the first line, they create large matrix-based testing plans in which they schematize all the possible interactive pathways. They test each of the possible interactions. Along the second line, they try to arrive at statistical determinations of the paths through the software that are most important. By placing emphasis on testing these paths, testers make effective use of their time and can say, in the end, that they have exerted the greatest testing effort on the areas of greatest risk. This is one goal of orthogonal defect categorization.

Orthogonal Defect Categories

The story of testing risks continues when you consider what happens when you create so many test cases that you do not have time to execute them all. Good testers plan their tests and lay them out in a test plan. However, consider a situation in which a tester plans 1,000 test cases and then has time to execute only the first 30. Assuming the initial set of tests comprehensively covers the product, if the tester just started at the top of the list and worked down, only approximately 3 percent of the product would undergo adequate testing.

To avoid such risk situations, you use orthogonal approaches to categorize test cases. To understand the notion of orthogonal categorization of test data, consider, for example, what happens when you test combinations of values generated from a dialog box. In almost any situation that involves two or more input fields in a dialog box, the combinatorial product tends to create a large number of test cases. (See Figure 11.17.)

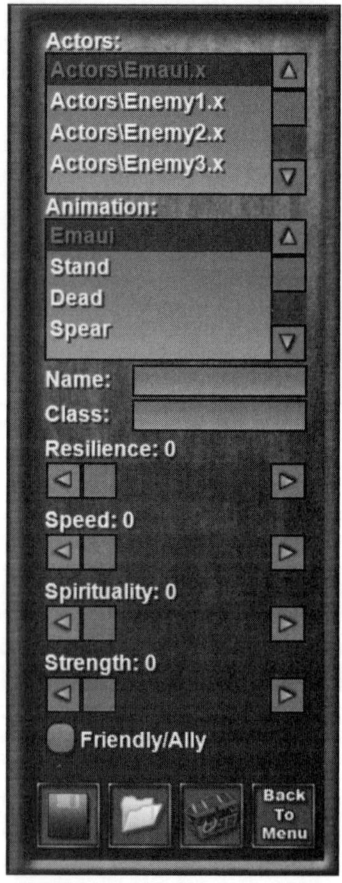

Figure 11.17
Multiple fields create large combinatorial products.

Consider a simplified version of the type of dialog box interaction represented in Figure 11.17. The player can, at different points, configure a character so that it is identified with a distinct class, possesses a primary skill, and wields a particular weapon. Figure 11.18 presents a tabular representation of these attributes. At arbitrary moments during the life of the game, the player can access a dialog box and select any combination of the items listed in Figure 11.18. After the player completes this activity, the resulting character has a distinct appearance, possesses a given skill, and wields a given weapon.

Name	Skills	Weapon
Sekhem	Healing	Greek Dagger
Sati	Meditation	Golden Ankh
Uheset	Burning Eye	Staff of Isis
Khefta	Healing	Staff of Osiris
Neru	Touch of Osiris	Twisted Render
Emaui	Boils	Singer of Boneshatter
Suten-Heh	Sores	Hunting Bow
	Healing	

Figure 11.18
Tabular representation of data combinations allows orthogonal classifications.

To create the test for the dialog box, you begin with the state of the character. You can set the state of the character using default values. You then designate as the test input the values obtained from the selected items. The game design document provides information that allows you to determine expected results. To assess the results, you examine the state of the character after you close the dialog box. At this point, the state values that are assigned to the character should be precisely those obtained from the dialog box selections.

When you test this dialog box, the work is extremely cumbersome even with a relatively limited number of fields unless you automate the testing. Figure 11.19 illustrates the typical combinatorial procedure. To create test cases, you begin with the first item in the Name column, Sekhem, you proceed to the next column, Skills, to the first item, Healing, and then you test these two items in combination with each of the items in the Weapon column. Having completed this work, you return to the Name column and again select Sekhem. You then move to the Skills column and select the second item, Meditation. Then you test these two items in combination with each of the items in the Weapon column. The work is tedious.

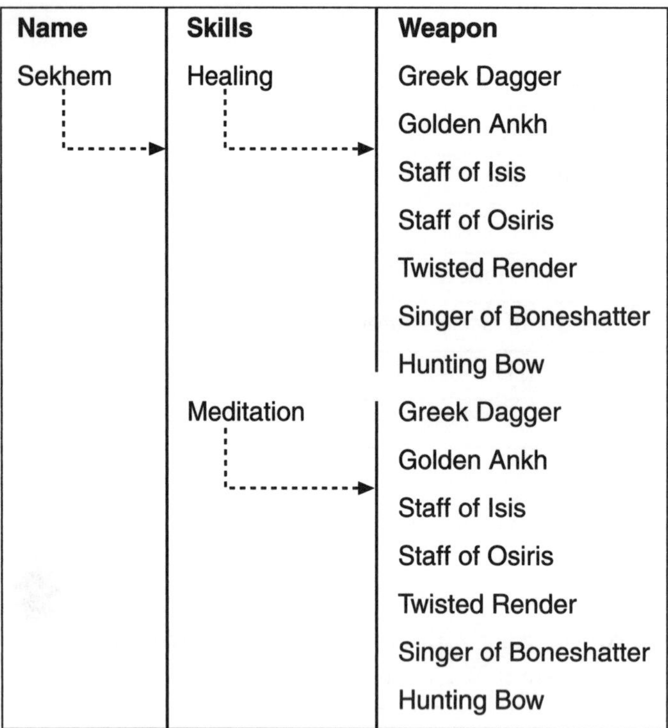

Name
Skills
Weapon
Sekhem
Healing
Greek Dagger
Golden Ankh
Staff of Isis
Staff of Osiris
Twisted Render
Singer of Boneshatter
Hunting Bow
Meditation
Greek Dagger
Golden Ankh
Staff of Isis
Staff of Osiris
Twisted Render
Singer of Boneshatter
Hunting Bow

Figure 11.19
When you create test cases, you anticipate all possible combinations.

You can determine the possible combinations (permutations) of the values displayed in the table in Figure 11.18 if you multiply the number of values in each row (7 × 8 × 7). The result is the number of possible test cases (392). When you determine the number of possible test cases using simple combinatorial procedures, you create quite a few redundant test cases.

When you employ an orthogonal approach to testing, you try to discover a few paths through the combinatorial options that can responsibly represent all paths. Considering again the values shown in Figure 11.18, the simplest approach emerges when you test only one combination, such as Sekhem-Healing-Greek Dagger. You can say that you have tested the dialog box scenario with minimum coverage (and substantial risk). The problem with this approach is that it is so minimal that it is nearly irresponsible. A better approach involves obtaining a healthy mixture of test cases while avoiding having to work through an endless enumeration of combinatorial possibilities. Figure 11.20 illustrates one approach.

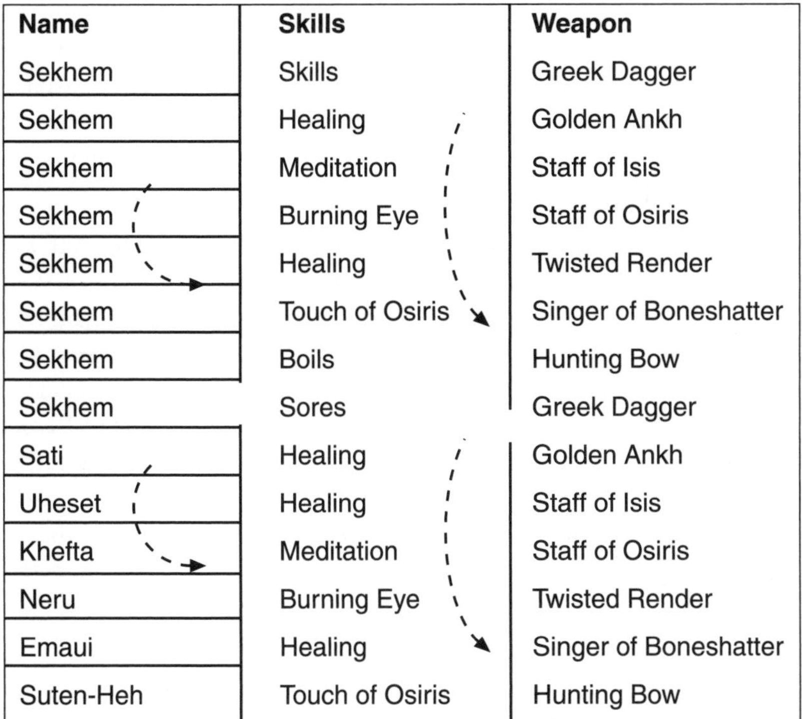

Name	Skills	Weapon
Sekhem	Skills	Greek Dagger
Sekhem	Healing	Golden Ankh
Sekhem	Meditation	Staff of Isis
Sekhem	Burning Eye	Staff of Osiris
Sekhem	Healing	Twisted Render
Sekhem	Touch of Osiris	Singer of Boneshatter
Sekhem	Boils	Hunting Bow
Sekhem	Sores	Greek Dagger
Sati	Healing	Golden Ankh
Uheset	Healing	Staff of Isis
Khefta	Meditation	Staff of Osiris
Neru	Burning Eye	Twisted Render
Emaui	Healing	Singer of Boneshatter
Suten-Heh	Touch of Osiris	Hunting Bow

Figure 11.20
Taking a moment to create, vary, and distribute combinations expedites testing in a responsible way.

The approach shown in Figure 11.20 is not as scientific as it might be, but it serves to show what can be viewed as a practical approach to orthogonal classification. The scheme involves moving down each column in a way that distributes coverage in each instance across all possible items but also reduces the number of permutations to a minimum.

Impact

Impact concerns how much testing activities affect the development schedule. Testing activities affect the testing effort in two ways. The first way entails causing the development process to take longer than it would without testing. The second way entails decreasing or increasing the reliability of the product. Generally, to a certain extent, the longer you test a software product, the greater its reliability. On the other hand, it is also the case that the longer you test, the fewer defects you discover. After a certain point, you arrive at a crossover point. Determining when you will reach this point heavily impacts the extent to which you can say that you have achieved a high degree of coverage and reduced risk to a minimum.

On the implementation level, each test requires a certain amount of time. The more specifically you plan a test procedure and its constituent test cases, the more you can say precisely how long a test will take to perform. Add to this that experienced testers usually declare that you should make test cases as specific as possible, so that you can perform any given test case as quickly as possible. When you use this approach to test development, you can more flexibly adapt to schedule pressures.

Figure 11.21 illustrates the danger that arises if you plan only a few extensive tests. If you spend a great deal of time setting up four large tests rather than 12 to 16 short ones, your testing effort becomes vulnerable in terms of *effort* and *effect*. Respecting effort, you create a risk because, for example, if you have time to complete only the first two tests, you will cover only 50 percent of the system. The effect this has on the quality of the system is significant. In the second situation, which involves the creation of numerous test cases that do not involve a great deal of preparation, you can adjust your effort if you face time restraints so that you will have time to test all parts of the system in some way. Testers sometimes contend that it is better to test a little bit of a lot rather that a lot of a little.

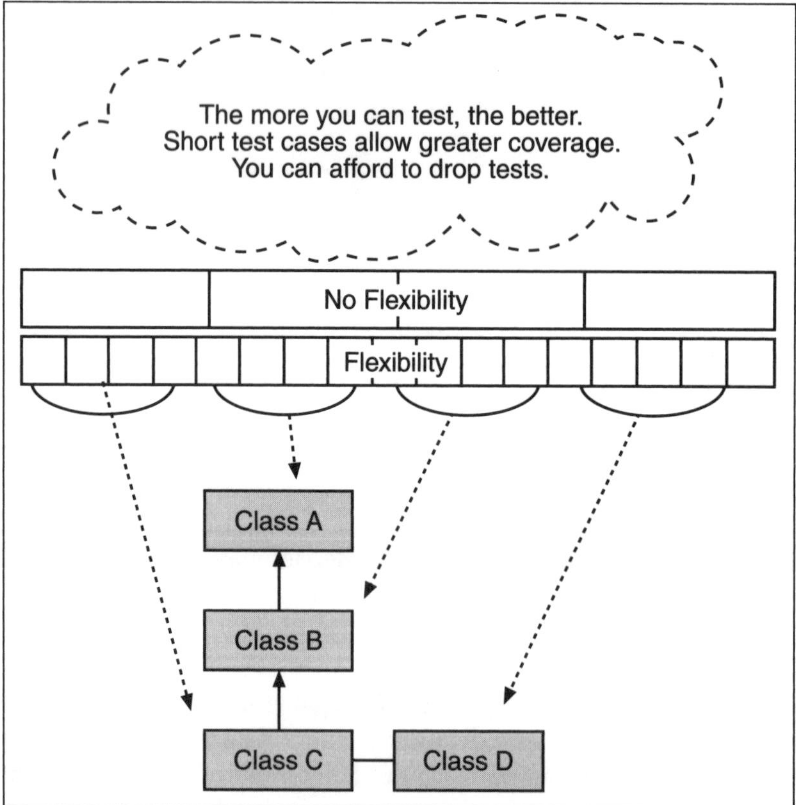

Figure 11.21
Test a little of a lot rather than a lot of a little.

Testing Roles

Testing roles differ from organization to organization. Generally, experts of the old school contend that it is best to have separate test and development teams. Those who have adopted practices from the Agile Process tend to regard testing and development as mixed roles. The position taken in this book is that testing is a distinct type of software development work, so the more you can spend time learning the special skills that apply to it, the better. Specialization over the centuries has been shown to be a key to quality.

Along similar lines, any given tester is likely to take up different testing roles at different times during the project. These roles, to an extent, take on definition according to the tools and techniques that are developed and acquired during the performance of the work. Some of more common roles are as follows:

- **Integration.** When you perform this work, you are generally the person on the team who is taking the high-level view. Assembling pieces enables you to discern problems of performance that others, working on specific components, might not notice.
- **System.** When you work with the system, you are thrown into the customer realm because you are seeing the product as a whole, one that has to install and operate correctly. Issues of size, completeness, and operability surface.
- **Manager.** If you have worked long enough in a testing capacity and have a good sense of how to develop test plans and schedule work, you are qualified to assume a management role. As a manager, key tasks involve understanding the scope of the game, assessing the appropriate level of test coverage, and assigning enough people to the work to ensure that it is completed.
- **Structural.** This is a general term for testing that penetrates into the system and involves continuous dissection and inspection of minute aspects of the code. An experienced developer who wants to assume a lead test position serves best in this position.
- **Player.** Expert players need not be software testers or programmers, but they need to know their business as game players. Such testers are excellent resources at all phases of the development effort as long as you structure their activity so that the information they provide can be used effectively.

Conclusion

This chapter has investigated a few of the many topics that arise when you test software. Testing software is, along with design and implementation, one of the major activities involved in creating an engineered software product. To understand the intent of testing, reviewing the concepts of validation, verification, and exploration proves helpful. Much of the purpose of testing is to verify and validate the implementation effort in light of the functionality that is specified in the requirements. In addition to ensuring that the software product meets specifications, testing has an exploratory role. The role of exploration involves combing the software to discover if random defects have been added to the product. Exploration differs from validation and verification because it searches for behavior that was not planned.

Planning a testing effort involves creating documents that guide you through your testing activities. The IEEE standard 829 provides an excellent guide for creating such documents. Generally, it is a good idea to start with a high-level test plan for the whole project and then to derive from this high-level plan several low-level plans that cover components, integration, system, and acceptance testing.

Many tools and techniques of testing comprise a successful testing effort. Tables you can create using spreadsheets or word processors are among the most humble but most useful tools for software testers. You can customize tables to fill specific testing functions. You can also use them to organize cases that test the behavior of dialog boxes. Finally, you can use tables to cross reference or logically relate test cases. Table uses are multitudinous and can expedite almost any testing operation.

Testing tends to go in two general directions: behavioral and structural. Behavior testing, also known as black-box testing, seeks to establish only that the software behaves as specified. Such testing can be conducted largely from a user's perspective. Structural testing, also known as white-box testing, involves investigating the inner workings of operations, classes, and modules. To pursue such testing, it is often necessary to construct test harnesses, which come in many forms. Among commonly used harnesses are those that make use of such language features as static operations and template classes.

When you formulate specific test cases or test procedures, try to test a little of everything rather than a lot of a few things. If you can design a multitude of tests that you can perform quickly, even if time limitations restrict the extent of your testing effort, you still stand a chance of being able to test a wide variety of system features. This is better than testing only a few features in depth.

For further reading on testing, consult the following sources:

Beizer, Boris. *Software Testing Techniques.* New York: Van Nostrand Reinhold, 1983.

Black, Rex. *Critical Testing Processes: Plan, Prepare, Perform, Perfect.* Boston: Addison-Wesley, 2004.

McGregor, John D. and David A. Sykes. *A Practical Guide to Testing Object-Oriented Software.* Boston: Addison-Wesley, 2004.

Tamres, Louise. *Introducing Software Testing.* Boston: Addison-Wesley, 2002.

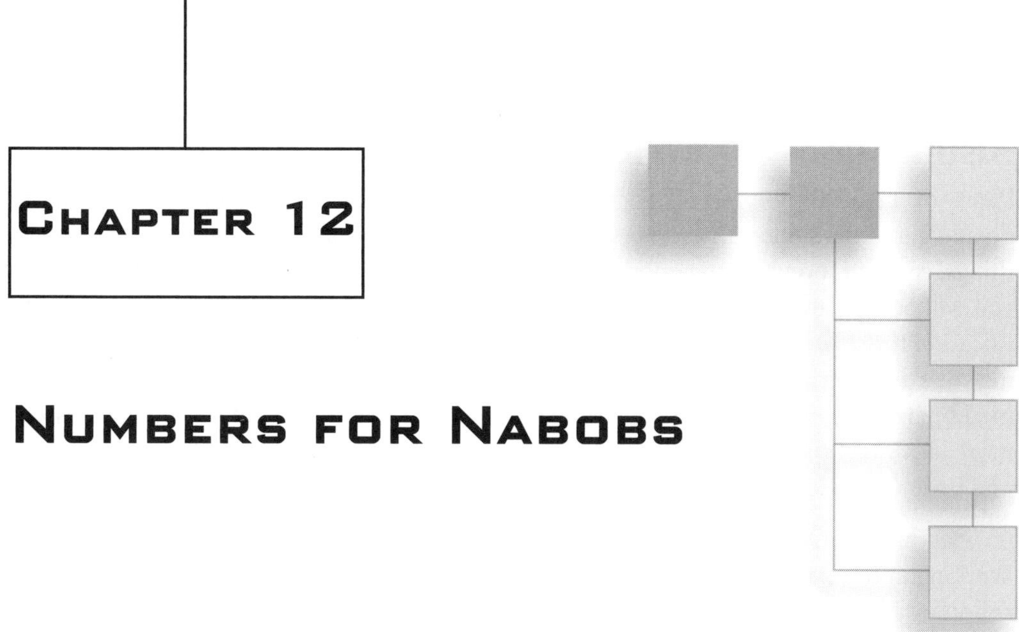

Chapter 12

Numbers for Nabobs

When software engineers measure either software products or development activities, they create *metrics*. The proper name for the work of measuring things (software or otherwise) is *metrology*, but you will hardly ever hear this term applied to the measurement of software or software development. Instead, most people use the word *metrics*. Some people refer to metrics as a single set of activities, so it is followed by a singular verb. For example, "Metrics is about quality." When other people use metrics, they are referring to numbers, so the word is treated as a plural. For example, "The metrics were wrong on the last survey."

Metrics encompasses both collecting data and developing mathematical tools for analyzing data. To collect data, you learn how to ensure that it is accurate and valid. To analyze data, you learn how to use statistical tools. Among other things, software developers use metrics to estimate schedules, establish quality indicators, and develop production capabilities. This chapter covers just a few of the vast number of ways that metrics are collected and analyzed:

- Why metrics benefit software engineering efforts
- Elementary notions about software data
- Elementary notions about software statistics
- Using Microsoft Excel as a tool for analysis
- Ways to display metrics
- Approaches to refining metrics for your project
- Personalized metrics
- Extended applications of metrics

Justifications for Collecting Metrics

Plenty of justification exists for trying to obtain quantitative information about what you do as a game developer. One is personal. If you keep a log of how long it takes you to do things, you will soon become good at estimating the effort involved in given tasks because you will have historical data on which to base your estimates. Another, less personal justification for collecting data is that you can gain a better sense of what you have done during your development effort. If you say, for example, that you think a class is complex, you might have a sound intuitive grasp of the features of the class, but what you say has much more meaning if you report that, on the average, each class has 16 operations and that the one under consideration has 64.

A final justification for collecting metrics involves general organizational objectives. Working in the capacity of a quality assurance specialist, you might be part of a team that collects data to substantiate your organization's capability standing. An organization receives a capability rating according to whether it can show that it can create a given product in roughly the same way on a repeatable basis. One way of evaluating whether you can repeat a process is to collect data about your development activities. How long does it take you to create a product? What is the size, in terms of operations, components, or lines of code, of the games you create? How many defects were reported during a given testing phase? How much did you spend on the development of the product? Such questions are those best answered with numbers.

Key Metrics

Data that you collect about a given type of activity, such as software development, becomes metrical data. In other words, this data measures a process or system of doing something. To determine how the activity in which you are involved can become the subject of metrics, consider how you can categorize your activities as you work on a software product. Generally, you can establish categories in terms of four major divisions of data often named by software engineers who are involved in metrics. These are as follows:

- **Process.** Metrics relating to process can concern any of the activities listed in the Software Engineering Body of Knowledge (SWEBOK) or documented in such standards as those provided by the International Standards Organization (ISO) or Software Engineering Institute (SEI). Processes usually transcend the boundaries established by any one product or development effort, so metrics on process help you identify trends that persist across products.
- **Personal.** Metrics can begin with your own tasks. A reference is given at the end of this chapter to Watts S. Humphrey's *Introduction to the Personal Software Process.* You can gain a sense of the usefulness of metrics if you collect data on your own productivity as a developer.

- **Project.** Metrics that are drawn from projects concern such items as how many people were assigned to the project, how productive they were, how much within or over budget the project was, and how long it took to finish work on the project.
- **Product.** Metrics relating to the software product describe its size in lines of code, modules, or other design features; its complexity in terms of the interaction of its modules, classes, or operations; its performance; and its level of quality.

Information Sources

Several sites on the Internet provide information on software metrics and statistical (or parametric) analysis. Among these are the following:

- **Center for Software Engineering (University of Southern California).** This site has significance because it is the home of COCOMO, CodeCount, and other tools that are useful for metrics. Go to http://sunset.usc.edu/cse/COCOMO.
- **The Fraunhofer Center for Experimental Software Engineering (University of Maryland).** This site provides a great deal of information on software development practices, with an emphasis on Capability Maturity Model Integration (CMMI). Go to http://fc-md.umd.edu/fcmd/index.html.
- **International Society of Parametric Analysts (ISPA).** ISPA is a professional society that fosters research and practices relating to parametric cost modeling. As an extension of this basic activity, it sponsors studies relating to risk analysis and technology forecasting. Parametric analysis involves studying relationships among cost, schedule, and attributes that are specific to given software (and other) systems. Go to http://www.ispa-cost.org/index.htm.
- **Quantitative Software Management (QSM).** This site is significant for two reasons. The first is that it supports Software LIfecycle Management (SLIM), which is a major tool used for project control and estimation. The other reason is that it is one of the few commercial sites that offers a good selection of useful papers on metrics. Go to http://www.qsm.com/provisions.html.
- **SEI Software Engineering Measurement and Analysis.** This site is a valuable resource for acquiring knowledge about measurement and analysis practices as they relate to the Capability Maturity Model (CMM) and its successor programs. Go to http://www.sei.cmu.edu/sema/welcome.html.
- **Six Sigma.** You can find a great deal of useful information about process quality improvement through the Six Sigma Forum. Click on the Terms link. Go to http://www.sixsigmaforum.com. For information about charts and other tools, go to http://www.isixsigma.com. This is a supplemental page for SkyMark, which offers PathMaker.

Metrical Terms

The vocabulary items that apply to software metrics have been adapted in part from statistics, but at the same time, the terms have been shaped so that they usually have meanings that are best understood in relation to the software development environments in which they are used. Although no formal categories exist for sorting out the terms you are likely to encounter in discussions of software engineering metrics, you might find it useful to work with three informal categories:

- Those drawn directly from statistics
- Those used in relation to general issues of software engineering
- Those that apply to object-oriented programming

A glossary of definitions in a quality assurance plan provides everyone with a single source of reference for how you have applied terms in the context of your project. For terms used generally, a glossary from the SEI or the IEEE can help prevent most misunderstandings. Table 12.1 provides definitions of some of the more common metrical terms.

Table 12.1 General Metrics and Metrical Terms

Term	Discussion
LOC	Lines of Code. This is a tricky term. When this term was first used, it was applied to assembly language, so each line of code counted as an executable statement. With higher-level languages, the term has taken on different meanings. Disputes arise, for example, about whether LOC should refer to comments. Still, if you define the term before you use it, you can anticipate most difficulties that might apply to your project. See also *KLOC*.
KLOC	Thousand Lines of Code. This term is important because it sets what might be called the minimum acceptable number of LOC you can use to establish a ratio. The usual practice is to take whatever measure you use and convert it to KLOCs. For example, if you have a program that consists of 500 LOC, you have 0.5 KLOC.
Granularity	The precision of detail that applies to the metrics you are using. The term is intuitive. If your sampling has, say, 100 data points, and you have a possible sample of several million, someone might conclude that your sampling is coarse grained. On the other hand, you can apply sophisticated refinement techniques to almost any data sample to tune the granularity.
Calibration	Defining a scale according to a local context. The teeth on a comb are calibrated. If you increase or decrease the distance between the teeth, you recalibrate the comb. Any scale that begins with zero can be calibrated with any other scale that begins with zero. To calibrate one scale based on another, you establish a ratio.

Term	Discussion
Defect density	The number of defects relative to the size of the program investigated. In most cases, the unit of measure is KLOC, but in other cases, modules, function points, classes, and other entities can be used. A program that consists of 1000 KLOC that shows 23 defects has a lower density of defects than a program that consists of 1 KLOC that shows 10 defects. Historical studies indicate that NASA has achieved a defect density of around a few defects per KLOC. Metrics for the software engineering industry in general show an average defect density of as high as 40–60 per KLOC.
Size	The number of lines, requirements, or other features that defines the scope of your project. This value is fairly literal, but to define it precisely, you must turn to the culture in which you are working. Do people think in terms of lines of code? Do they think in terms of number of requirements?
Defect rate	Rate is a dynamic way to talk about defects. It refers to the frequency with which you can expect to encounter defects as you investigate a given body of code. Because rate is dynamic, software engineers can be heard to talk about "declining" defect rates. Such declines are typical of most successful software development efforts as they near release. The defect rate is usually based on defects per KLOC. See also *defect density*.
Function point	In this text, *function* and *operation* are used synonymously. A set of executable statements that performs a single task constitutes a function point. When this term was first used, it applied to a group of specific functions designated with the acronym CRUD, which referred to Create, Read, Update, and Delete and applied primarily to database transactions. This way of addressing functions was too narrow for many software developers, so over time, definitions of function points proliferated.

Where to Find Data

The title of this section should be "Things to Count," and the picture you have of the situation should be the Count on *Sesame Street*. The emphasis in this chapter is on what you can do with metrics in relation to development of a game software product, but it also gives attention to processes and projects. Where to find data depends on what you want to explore.

Object-Oriented Product Data

Table 12.2 provides a summary of possible data points that are applicable to object-oriented efforts.

Table 12.2 Metrics for Object-Oriented Projects

Metric	Description
Operations	For operations, you can explore such items as the number of parameters that the operation uses, the number of statements the operation contains, and the LOC per operation. You can also explore how complex an operation is or what type of message the operation sends. (In this text, the term *operation* is synonymous with *function* and *method.*)
Classes	You can explore how many operations in classes are public, private, or protected. You can count the total number of operations, the instance attributes and operations in a class, and the class attributes and class operations.
Inheritance	You can count levels of hierarchy (how much or how far classes are descended), the number of abstract classes, the number of operations in derived classes that represent overridden or concrete versions operations in base classes, and the number of operations added to derived classes.
Program Hygiene	You can count the number of lines of comments, the number of times friend functions or public attributes occur, and the number of commented and uncommented operations.
Complexity	You can count the number of classes with which given classes are in collaboration, the number of operations used within operations, the number of times the same messages are sent or received within the context of a class or an operation, and the number of times class or code patterns occur.

For more information on what to count, see the Mark Lorenz and Jeff Kidd book titled *Object-Oriented Software Metrics.* A full reference appears at the end of this chapter.

Core Metrics for Projects and Processes

Across the software industry, a set of metrics referred to as *core metrics* has been in place for several decades. Core metrics concern project, product, and process. They are most often used for project management and process improvement purposes. Table 12.3 provides a summary of core software metrics. It is important to note that the descriptions represent generalizations. Each organization tends to choose its own core metrics and define them in culturally specific terms.

Table 12.3 Core Metrics for Processes and Projects

Metric	Description
Product size	The size of the product in terms of requirements, estimated lines of code, or other indicators. Other indicators include function points, number of classes, or module (stripe) counts. If you use requirements, you must perform a bit of design work to determine how many modules or components are necessary. Ultimately, the unit of size you use can be calibrated for use in determining required effort.
Productivity	The number of LOC (or other units of measure) that team members or teams as a whole create per unit of time measured. Normally, such counts are made on the basis of weeks or months, but occasionally, you see day or year counts. Productivity can be a difficult metric to establish because skill levels among individuals vary hugely. Studies indicate that productivity in a group can vary as much as 20 to 1.
Effort	The amount of work required by those involved in the development process to complete the process. This differs from productivity. Productivity has to do with units of code (or product completed) per unit of time measured. This has to do with hours people who are assigned to the development of a product required to finish the product according to specification. If you estimate, for example, that a product will require 6,000 lines of code and that during a year's time, a developer can write 1,000 lines of code, the effort will be either six years for one developer or one year for six developers. (Such estimations are naïve and a little bit dangerous, but here they serve only as illustrations.)
Duration	The calendar time required to complete the project. This differs from effort. *Effort* is how many hours developers work on a product. *Duration* is the number of weeks, months, or years that elapse as developers work on the project. On the average, for instance, a developer might work 60 hours per week on a project. Therefore, if the product required 600 hours of effort, the shortest duration for the development of the product would be 10 weeks. If a developer were able to work only 30 hours per week on the product (which is more likely to be the case at companies where meetings are frequent), the effort extends to 20 weeks.
Reliability	The number of defects found in the product. Reliability usually concerns a product that has been released, but you can count defects at any point in the development process that you deem appropriate. Developers unit test as they go, and their corrections are usually considered a part of the primary development effort. After code is at the completion stage, however, you can begin to assess its reliability relative to the number of problems that customers report.

Lawrence H. Putnam and Ware Myers (*Five Core Metrics*) provide a good starting place for understanding core metrics as they apply to process improvement. A full reference appears at the end of this chapter.

Benchmarking

Benchmarking is akin to best practices. When something is designated as a best practice, however, the description is usually qualitative. It might be described as an order of actions or a process. Benchmarking is quantitative rather than qualitative. A benchmark is a measurement you can use for comparison. Some benchmarks are averages. Some benchmarks, such as six sigma, are goals that are difficult to achieve.

There are three prevailing approaches to benchmarking:

- **Seek databases that are maintained by quality organizations.** Sources for benchmarks are available through the links listed under the heading "Internet Information Sources." The categories you use for benchmarking are up to you. You can begin with the core metrics: effort, product duration, productivity, defect rate, and size. An organization such as QSA maintains a database that consists of data from thousands of software development projects spanning several decades.
- **Develop a database involving the test results from your own efforts.** The key to success in this area is to find ways to segment data. You can segment data in several ways. For example, it is likely that when you are roughly one-fourth of the way into your development effort, you will be able to begin gathering metrics that are useful for benchmarking. For example, you can count the number of operations in several classes and find an average. You can then use the mean as a benchmark as you proceed with development efforts.
- **Concentrate on applying to your own setting the benchmarks that quality organizations maintain.** You can obtain benchmarks from similar projects and place them on file to be compared with your own benchmarks. This approach is a combination of the two just mentioned. The benefit that this approach offers is that although you do not isolate yourself from the world, you also do not subordinate yourself to it. You allow your own organization to customize its benchmarks.

Relationships

At the basis of a relationship is an *ordered pair.* Designating or creating an ordered pair involves examining two sets of data between which you want to establish a correlation. A *correlation* is an assertion that a relationship exists between two or more sets of data that allows you to say that when one item of data changes, the correlated item of data will also change.

The easiest way to set up relationships is to use the Cartesian coordinate plane. In its two-dimensional version, the Cartesian plane provides two axes: the y-axis and the x-axis. In Figure 12.1, the y-axis maps what is called the *dependent* variable. The x-axis maps what is known as the *independent* variable. The value on the y-axis is dependent because its value is calculated using the value on the x-axis.

To establish a primary relationship between two variables, you can develop a correlation coefficient, which is represented using *r*. You can view the correlation coefficient in general terms as a mathematical expression that transforms the independent variable so that the result is a value that appears as the dependent variable.

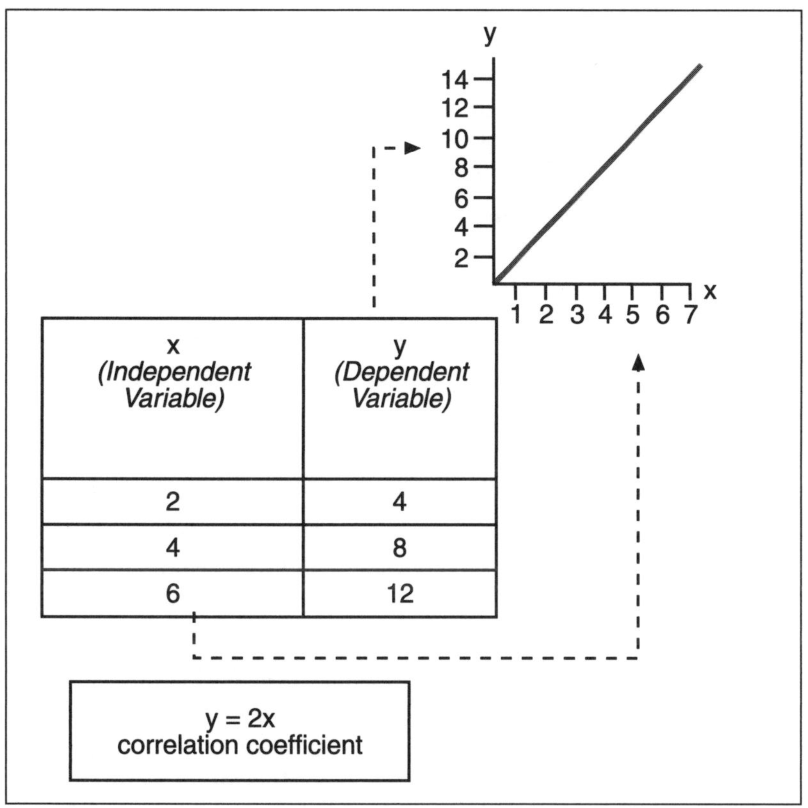

Figure 12.1
Dependent and independent variables relate through correlation.

When you analyze data to formulate relationships, you can proceed in a few basic directions:

- **Exploration.** Explore relationships between sets (columns) of data to discover a mathematical formula that explains the relationship. If you can produce the values in the column that contains the dependent variables using the values in the column containing the independent variables, you have gone far in proving the validity of the correlation coefficient.
- **Prediction and causality.** You can also use formulas to generate data. When you try to predict events on the basis of simple correlations, you risk being overly simplistic. If you are conservative, you say only that if function A is applied to value x, value y results. This is safe enough. People get into difficulty when they say things like this: "Because A applied to x resulted in y, A is the *cause* of y." Such simplistic formulations are almost always disproven. One software engineering sage, Tom DeMarco, refers to such talk as "limbaughing." Predictive or cause-and-effect models are usually difficult to validate and verify, and they usually involve years of work and dozens, if not hundreds or even thousands, of test situations and variables.
- **Visualization.** You can place the elements of two or more sets of data into a standard graphical format and inspect the result to enhance your intuitive awareness of the layout of the data. This is one of the most effective and safest ways to analyze software metrics.

Regression

To determine the validity of a relationship that you perceive between two or more variables, you can perform *regression analysis.* The way to understand the meaning of regression is to picture a graph that depicts a curve. Imagine that the curve is a graph of the equation $y = d^2$. If you graph the relationship between x and y, you end up with a parabola. This is a standard graph of a set of numbers that have been squared. (See Figure 12.2.) If you consider a second set of numbers and plot them on the graph, you see that they, too, tend to follow the same pattern, although with slight variations from the pattern established by the curve. This is an example of regression. The values in the two sets tend to regress toward the curve.

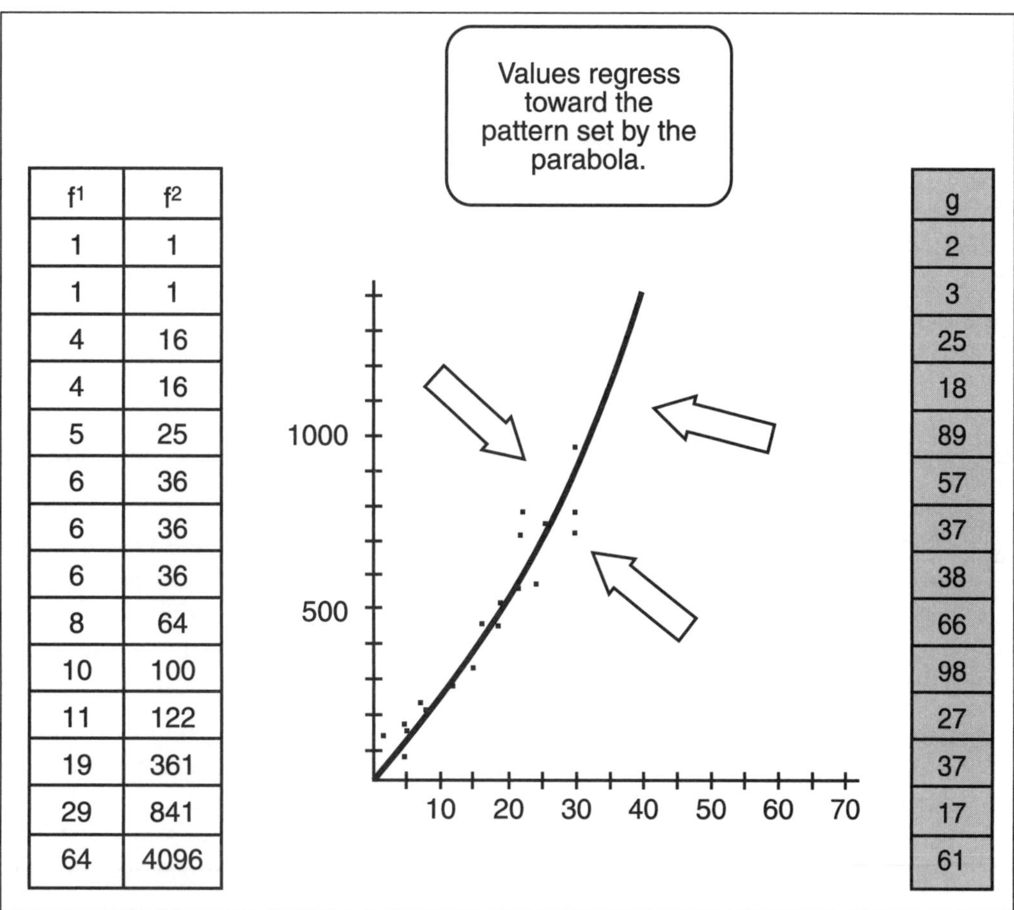

f^1	f^2
1	1
1	1
4	16
4	16
5	25
6	36
6	36
6	36
8	64
10	100
11	122
19	361
29	841
64	4096

g
2
3
25
18
89
57
37
38
66
98
27
37
17
61

Figure 12.2
Regression designates a pattern toward which values tend to move.

Terms of Regression for Line Graphs

Figure 12.3 illustrates four basic types of regression.

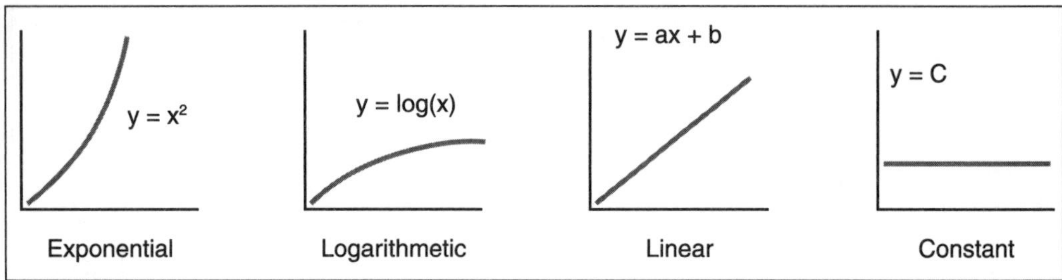

Figure 12.3
You can mathematically characterize regression in four basic ways.

Regression can be categorized according to a limited set of mathematical expressions:

- **Constant.** When a regression follows a constant pattern, one value spawns many other values. This type of regression makes sense if you consider, for example, that one stripe of the software can be correlated with the classes that the stripe contains. Suppose your development schedule requires that for each stripe, you implement some number of new classes. The number for the stripe remains constant (1), but the number of classes changes.
- **Linear.** When a regression follows a linear pattern, you see a straight line that runs at an angle to the x (or y) axis. In practical terms, this relationship tells you that the dependent variables change relatively gradually when compared to the independent variables. You see this mathematically as follows: $y = 2x$, so $2(2) = 4$, $2(4) = 8$, $2(10) = 20$. You'll find, for example, that when you revise a system, you should increase the complexity of the system on a linear basis. (See "Linear Growth in Complexity" in Chapter 14, "Practice, Practice, Practice.")
- **Exponential.** Another name for exponent is power. You raise a number to a power by multiplying the number by itself the number of times that the power indicates. You see this mathematically as follows: $y = x^2$, so $2^2 = 4$, $3^2 = 9$, $10^2 = 100$. Exponential growth rates in things like complexity can be extremely hazardous to system performance. Other names for exponential relationships are quadratic (raised to a power of 2) and cubic (raised to a power of 3). Exponential is often used to indicate anything above the power of 3.
- **Logarithmic.** A logarithm is the inverse of an exponent. The logarithm of 32, base 2, is 5. You can see this mathematically as follows: log2(32) = log2(25) = 5. The logarithm, base 10, of 100 is 2. You can see this mathematically as follows: log10(100) = log10(102)= 2. You can say, then, "What exponent, given the base of x, raises the base to the named number?" Logarithmic changes generally indicate that a given change rate tends to level off after time. For example, as your project

progresses, you might see a leveling off of defects in your software. Many good sort algorithms tend to level off in their efficiency as the number of items they deal with reaches a given size. Because a logarithm is the inverse of an exponent, the curves are "flipped."

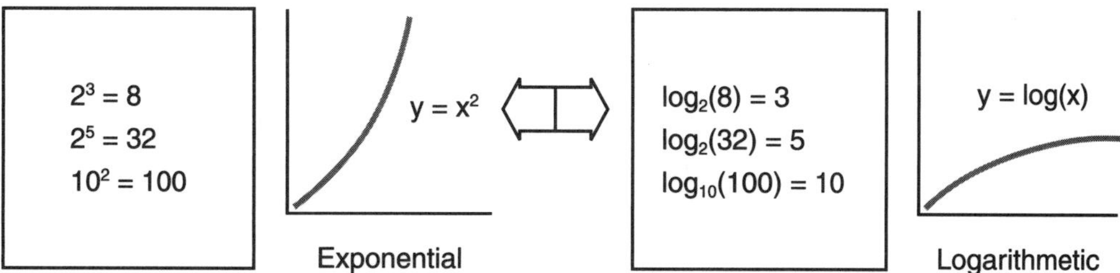

Trend Lines

You can infer a lot from regression. Beginning with the caveat that some degree of caution should characterize any effort that someone makes to draw inferences from simple sets of data, it remains that basic regressions provide a way to investigate *trend lines* or, simply, *trends.*

Rates are analogous to trends. If something is growing at an exponential rate, the news could be good or bad. The higher the exponent, the more drastic the rate of change. To arrive at a sense of what this means, suppose you have a program that consists of 60 classes. Picture creating a test harness in which you generate a mock error report when objects from given classes in your program are called. Suppose that you disable loosely coupled classes that provide minor GUI services, such as buttons. If you graph the results, you might discover a linear rate of defects logged by the compiler. In contrast, suppose that you disable heavily coupled classes that deal with IO or state management. If you graph the results, you might discover an exponential rate in the increase of the number of defects that the compiler logs. The trend in defect counts tends to be upward as you move from less to more coupled classes.

Many areas of software analysis make use of rates and trends. For example, rates and trends have a bearing on the efficiency of different sort algorithms. Sort algorithms with logarithmic characteristics are preferable in many situations. With such algorithms, one trend is that as the sample grows, the rate at which the algorithm sorts the sample tends to level off. Likewise, when you investigate effort and defects, you analyze data to find rates and trends. For example, you could say that the greater the effort you expend on the design of your product, the more likely it is that you will observe a decreasing trend in rework during implementation.

Pareto

Pareto analysis offers a simple, effective way to analyze many situations that require scheduling. Almost everyone has heard the generalization that 20 percent of the population controls 80 percent of the wealth. This notion is derived from Vilfredo Pareto (1848–1923), who contended that income and wealth are distributed according to a logarithmic formula. The formula reads $\log N = \log A + m \log x$. In this equation, N designates the number of income earners who receive incomes higher than x. The variables A and m are constants.

The 20-80 dichotomy applies to many situations and can be depicted graphically using a histogram or frequency-based bar chart in conjunction with an inverted curve or stepped graph. Figure 12.4 shows Pareto analysis applied to a categorized set of software defects.

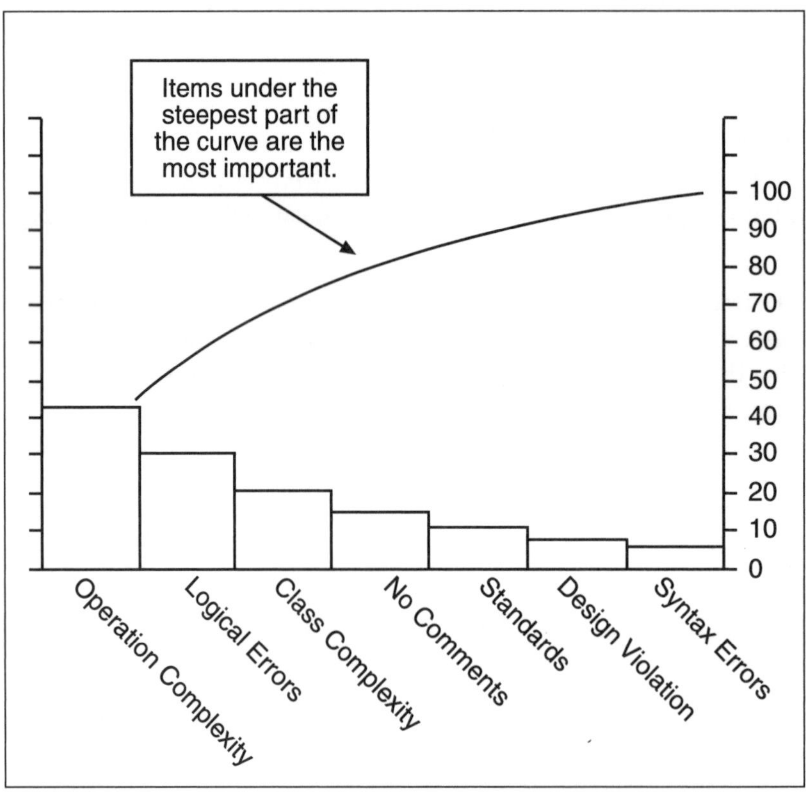

Figure 12.4
Pareto analysis provides a convenient way to prioritize work.

Figure 12.4 shows the most practical way to set up a Pareto analysis. Values are organized in descending order from the left. A calibrated scale appears on the left to indicate the total number of items. A percentage scale appears on the right. In Figure 12.4, the body of data being investigated concerns issues detected during code reviews. Issues concerning operational complexity and logical errors prevail. The break point seems to fall on class complexity. You might draw a conclusion that efforts should concentrate on these three review issues.

Statistical Curves

The more sophisticated that your work with models becomes, the more you begin to picture the world as curves that represent probabilities of distribution. Working with probability and more advanced topics in statistics is beyond the scope of this chapter, but it is worthwhile at least to mention a few of the curves that frequently represent distributions.

A distribution can be represented by the area under a curve. You can picture the area under the curve as a kind of target. Imagine that you put a curve on a big poster and hang it on a wall. Then you throw darts at it. You are likely to hit some areas and unlikely to hit others. Your likeliness of hitting an area tells you the probability that your dart throw will hit the target.

If you change the shape of the curve, more or less data will fit under it based on the curve's profile. Elsewhere in this chapter, for example, the Rayleigh model is discussed. When you use this model to analyze the data on a project, a distinctive curve results. The curve that results is familiar to statisticians as a Weibull curve. (See Figure 12.5.)

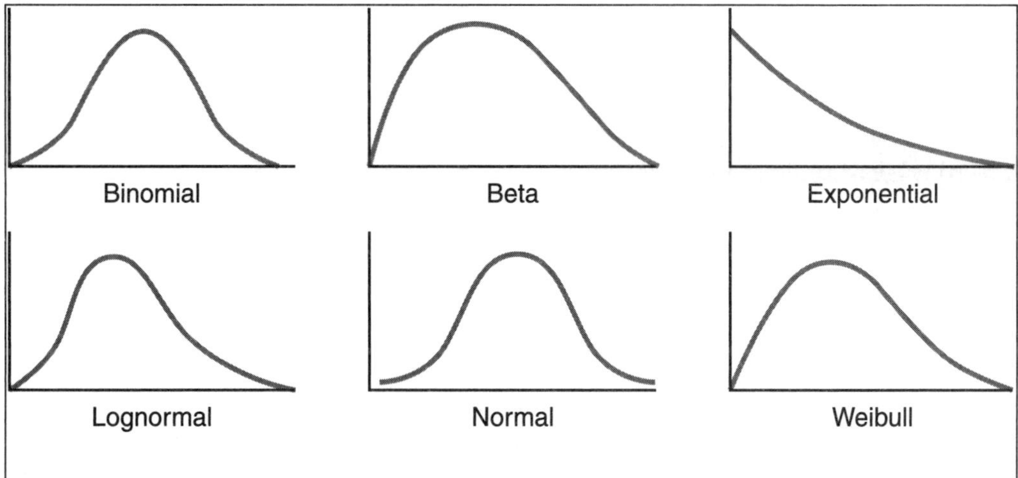

Figure 12.5
Curves provide ways of visualizing data.

This chapter covers only the normal and Weibull curves. The normal curve is said to correspond to most distributions found in nature. It is shaped like a bell, it has a single mode, and its tails extend infinitely.

Sigma

The Greek letter sigma (σ) represents standard deviation, which is a measure of variation. (See the section called "Summing" for more discussion.) When statisticians address deviation, they like to do so in terms of *sigmas*. If you calculate the mean and the standard deviation of a normal curve, you will find that with a normal distribution, roughly 68 percent of the data you have collected fits within a region described by *plus and minus one sigma* from the mean. Further, around 95 percent of the values are within two sigmas from the mean. Finally, around 98 percent of the values are within three sigmas from the mean. These properties make the normal curve a good tool for evaluating the design of software. The distribution of data relating to the size and complexity of classes, modules, or operations can be evaluated in terms of how well it fits a normal curve. (See Figure 12.6.)

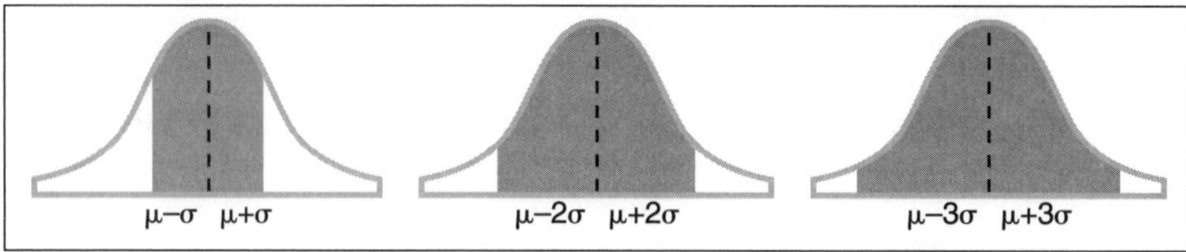

Figure 12.6
Sigma provides a way to characterize distribution easily.

Six Sigma

The expression *six sigma* refers to a standard of quality that has for some time received wide recognition in the electrical and mechanical engineering world and has in more recent times been applied to software engineering efforts. As was pointed out previously, the distribution of elements of a population can be predictably grouped into percentiles if the x-axis is calibrated using sigmas. A *sigma* can be viewed as a unit of standard deviation calculated for the population or sample under consideration.

Engineers extended this notion so that rather than providing only a quick way to assess deviation, sigma became a way to set a benchmark for quality. The benchmark, to put it lightly, is exacting. It extends to *Parts per Million* (PPM). Figure 12.7 illustrates what you can expect to encounter in terms of software defects after you have achieved a six sigma quality rating.

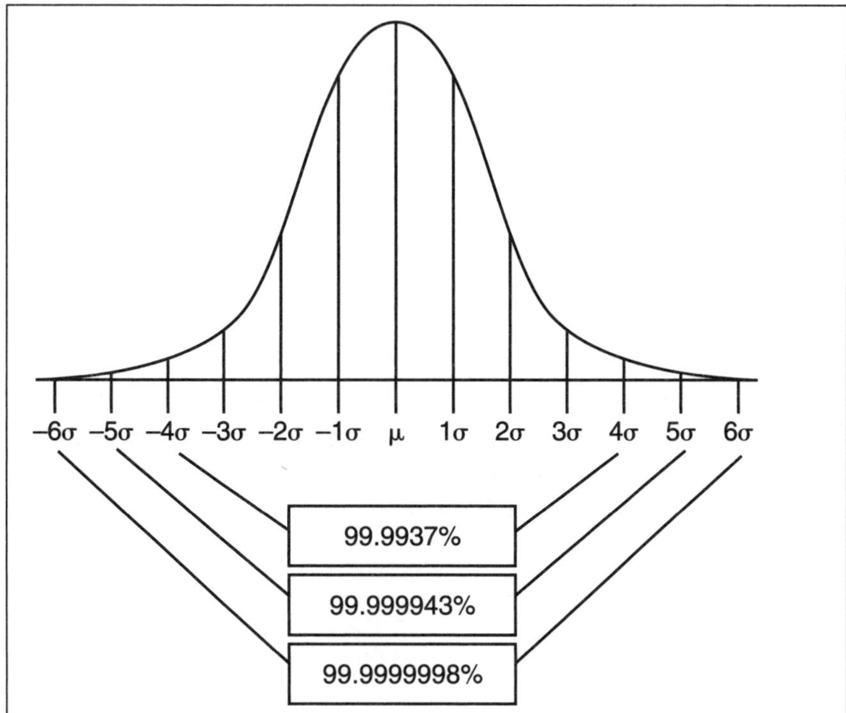

Figure 12.7
Six sigma allows 3.4 defective parts per million.

The way that the six sigma quality standard works is that the area *outside* the curve contains the defects. The area under the curve represents the probability that the product is free of defects. Over time, engineers have worked with the raw normal distribution (which allows .002 PPM) to arrive at the quality goal of 1.5 sigma, or 3.4 PPM. The difference is accounted for by a margin of drift.

When you consider how such a standard can be applied to a software product, the first thoughts might be LOC, function points, or complexity. These are certainly options. Still, although applying the six sigma standard along these lines is possible, the more useful and common measurement applies to *processes.* For software engineers, the measurement is best used to test the product against what the customer has specified, and it should be applied not to one project, but to many. In this respect, six sigma becomes a measure of the extent to which an organization or team is able to consistently produce products that meet exacting quality standards.

Picturing Data

Making good use of data involves picturing the data you use. Even the most entrenched hacker usually takes an interest in software engineering data presented in an attractive format. This book lacks room to include illustrations of all but a few of the standard charts used to represent data. All those included here are created using Excel. They are but a few from among the many that you can generate. Likewise, the illustrations deal with only a few sets of data. For example, some represent names issues brought up during code reviews. Others represent requirements addressed per stripe.

Pie Charts

A pie chart provides a convenient way to depict all the data in a given data set. When you use an application such as Excel, you enter data in a column in a table and then tell the application to generate the chart. For each item in the table, you see a wedge that provides you with an intuitive grasp of the proportion of the whole that the data item represents. (See Figure 12.8.)

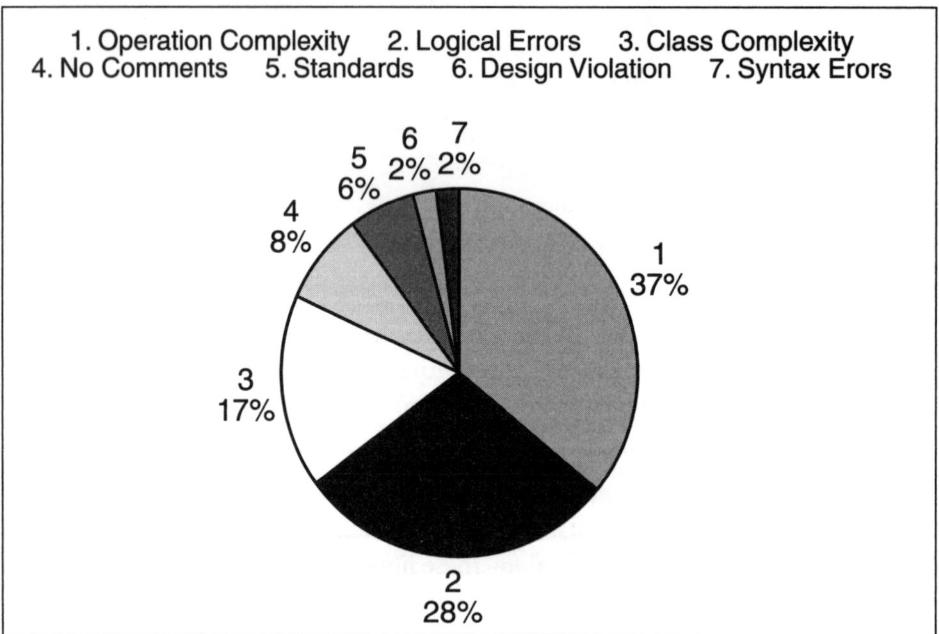

Figure 12.8
Pie charts depict percentages.

Bar Charts

Bar charts provide a way to represent values so that you can compare them. It is not necessary to order the values, but ranking them makes it easier to detect trends. Note, for instance, that Figure 12.9 allows you to understand much more readily that complexity was more frequently discussed than syntax errors.

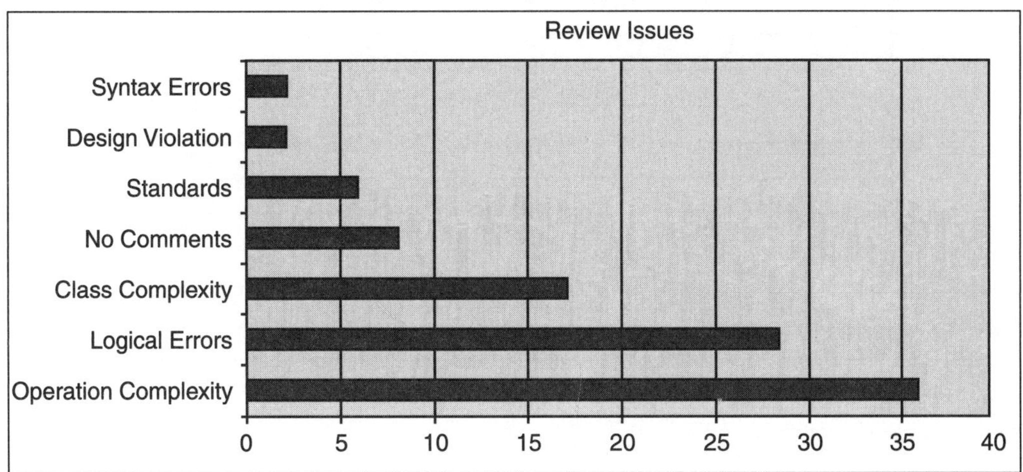

Figure 12.9
Bar charts make it easy to show relative quantities.

Run Charts with Trend Lines

When you establish relationships between data sets, you often search for trends. A run chart allows you to graph data using Cartesian coordinates and then to estimate trends. In Figure 12.10, the lighter line shows the run (or set of plotted data). The heavier line shows the trend. To determine the trend, imagine positioning the edge of a ruler on the graph so that all the distances between the points covered by the ruler's edge and the points represented by the run are as short as possible. The resulting position of the ruler shows you the trend of the run.

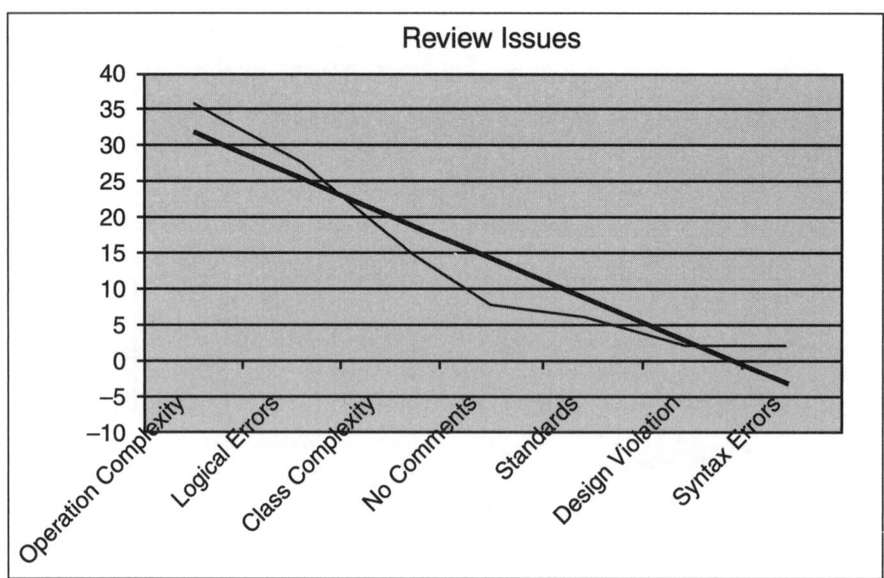

Figure 12.10
Run charts can show trends.

Radar Charts

Radar charts serve well to shows the importance of *groups* of data. As Figure 12.11 shows, operational complexity, logical errors, and class complexity constituted the major issues discussed during the course of this project. Note how this view of the data supplements Pareto analysis by helping you intuitively grasp the most important issues.

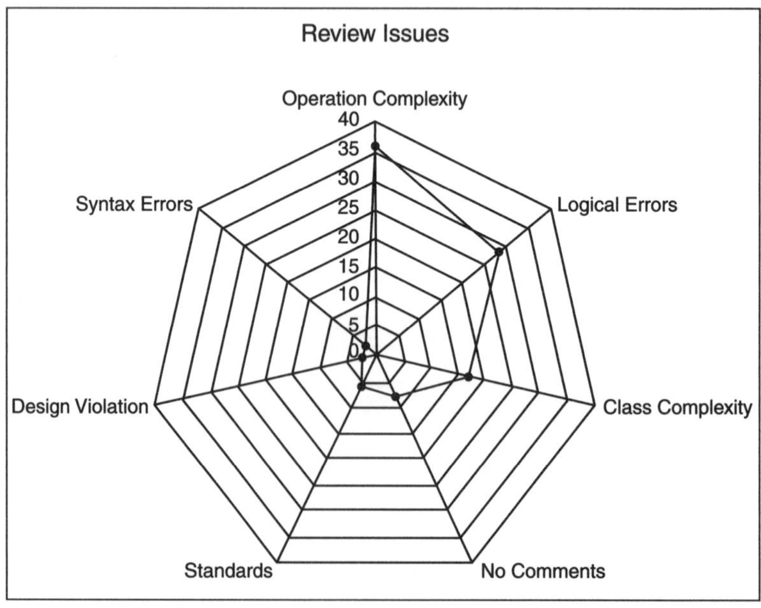

Figure 12.11
Radar charts make data relations visible.

Scatter Plots

One purpose of a scatter plot is to quickly give you a sense of ranges or general distributions. In the example shown in Figure 12.12, although no trend is visible, you can quickly gain a sense of how the design effort distributed implementation of the requirements among the different stripes. After a few seconds, you can see that the maximum was 12 and the minimum 1.

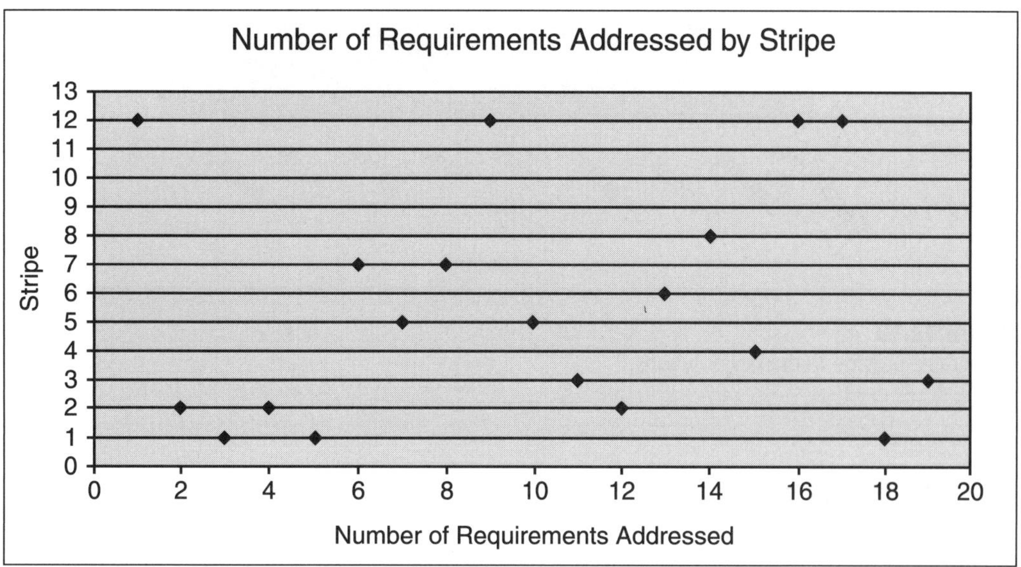

Figure 12.12
Scatter charts provide a way to detect clustering.

Histograms and Frequency Polygons

As is discussed in greater detail in the section titled "Mode" later in this chapter, you can group data into *bins* or *intervals.* Say that you count the number of defects reported each day of the month for nine months. (See Figure 12.13.) If you divide the days into units equal to the lengths of the months, you create intervals or bins. Each interval or bin contains the values for a given month. The averages for the bins or intervals allow you to establish data frequencies for the bins or intervals. Grouping data according to frequencies is one of the primary uses of a histogram. From month to month, given the way the data has been summarized, you can gain a general sense of tasks accomplished. This form of representation is also called a *frequency polygon.* A polygon is a four-sided figure. The averages of the data plots for the intervals allow you to determine where to place the corners of the polygons.

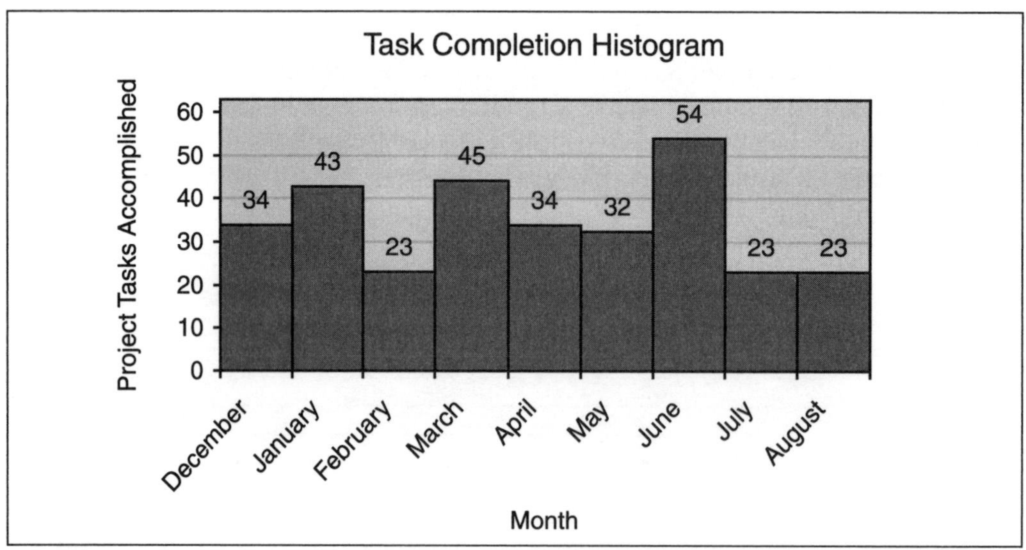

Figure 12.13
Histograms provide frequency polygons.

Divisions of Statistics

Software metrics makes continuous use of knowledge derived from statistics. Statistics consists of two main branches. One is called *descriptive statistics*, and the other is called *inferential statistics.*

Descriptive Statistics

Consider this short list of tasks you can accomplish using the tools of descriptive statistics:

- **Define and classify data.** Data has two primary properties. One is that it must be named. The other is that, in most cases, it must be quantified. A large set of standard categories for data have been established over the years. Among core data are work effort, lines of code, duration of project, number of defects, and productivity. Other data include a multitude of measures that concentrate on the code, such as number of classes, number of functions, collaborations among classes, complexity of classes.
- **Visualize data.** Graphical tools help you to represent data so that it is easy to understand. Among the tools that Excel makes available are graphs, pie charts, grids, bar charts, radar charts, and matrixes.

- **Describe data features.** You compute, among other things, means, medians, and modes. Such profiles of data help you to understand the static characteristics of software. For example, by counting the numbers of functions in a set of classes, you can arrive at a general understanding of how consistently the classes have been developed. The same applies to the amount of code you create during a week.
- **Analyze data features.** You can compute such things as variance, deviation, and range. When you can examine data and arrive at conclusions about trends, rates, and distributions, you move into a deeper realm of data description that helps you make judgments about the quality of your planning and implementation efforts.

Inferential Statistics

When you gather samples of a body of information and then create mathematical models that allow you to use these samples to predict trends, you have begun to perform *statistical inference.* The big difference between description and inference is that whereas description tries to represent what is known, inference takes a sampling of what is known and tries to project what is unknown. When you try to infer from the known to project the unknown, you deal with uncertainty.

Science deals with uncertainty by using the structured *hypothesis.* When you make a statement about what you think the numbers will reveal, you present a *statistical* or *null hypothesis.* To test the hypothesis, you first create a model for sampling and then collect a random sample of data. From there, you use an established mathematical model to structure the data and draw from it a conclusion. If your model generates data that contradicts your hypothesis, your hypothesis fails.

Inferential statistics has had a wonderfully successful record in electrical and mechanical engineering. One famous product of inference is the *Mean Time to Failure* (MTTF), which is a number inferred from a set of random tests that engineers perform on a given product to determine how long the product will operate correctly before it fails. NASA and most companies that deal with engineering products that fly or go far into space must worry endlessly about how long a piece of equipment will operate correctly before it fails. The same applies, to a lesser extent, to buildings, bridges, and electrical motors.

With buildings and bridges, the most intensive efforts to infer MTTF concern construction materials. All materials that are subjected to prolonged stress become brittle, and an engineer who is involved in determining MTTF seeks to discover how much stress a given material can bear and how long, even with acceptable levels of stress, the material will last before it begins to abrade or disintegrate. (Henri Petroski has written an excellent book that features many stories about this type of engineering activity. See the reference at the end of this chapter.)

Software usually does not become brittle, but it does have characteristics that correspond to those of materials engineering. The similarity is that engineers project current trends in failure rates into the future. The difference is that when the failure rates are known, actions taken do not usually involve decommissioning the product. Materials experts want to know when a bridge needs to be replaced. Software engineers seek to know what is called the *Mean Time to Defect* (MTTD). The MTTD is a pattern that characterizes how long a given body of software must be tested before its defects will no longer show up at a rate that presents a danger.

Consider that all software, regardless of how well it's designed, possesses defects when it reaches the point of code completion. From this moment on, testing and maintenance of the product begins. (In Figure 12.14, for example, a typical defect trend is shown.) If the software is to see service on a space probe that is to spend decades in space, testing should take place until engineers can establish that the rate at which defects are detected reaches an acceptable minimum. To accomplish this, they examine the record for defects and establish a trend.

The objective is not so much one of eliminating defects (although this is a big part of the effort) as it is one of trying to predict when the testing of the software will have reached a point at which the rate of software defect detection has leveled off to a predictable, stable level. (See Figure 12.14.) It is unlikely that the software will ever reach a point at which no defects are detected. It is likely, however, that with enough testing, a point will be reached at which defects will occur in a stable, predictable pattern.

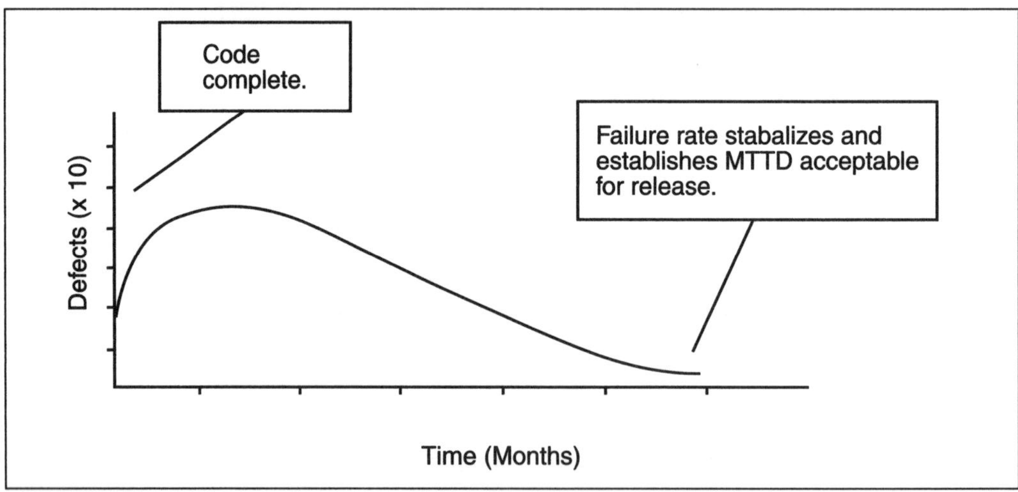

Figure 12.14
The MTTD shows how long you must test software before you can consider it acceptable for release.

Statistical Basics

A few books on statistics and metrics are listed at the end of this chapter, but a short discussion of some of the basic notions involved in statistical studies can help you understand the scope and depth of knowledge required to perform tasks associated with basic software metrics. One realization likely to result is that the activities can be only marginally demanding and yet yield a surprisingly rich set of results.

Summing

When you study statistics, one of the first things you learn is how to perform *summations.* Summations involve adding together the numbers of a set. The benefit of summation is that many pieces of data can be collected into a whole, so that the value or significance of each piece can be known in relation to the whole. If you record how long it takes you to create one operation in a C++ GUI class, you are taking a step in the right direction, but you have only one piece of data, and in isolation, data has little meaning. If you record how long it takes you to create each operation in several C++ classes, you can begin comparing how long one operation takes relative to your entire effort. If you establish a ratio of part to whole, you can begin seeing items such as the average and boundary efforts.

Sequences and Series

A summation involves adding together the elements of a sequence. A *sequence* is a set of numbers drawn together by a common characteristic. When you add together the elements of a sequence, the result is called the sum of a series. A *series* is a set of numbers that you can examine as a pattern.

For example, assume that you use a sequence of values that represent the number of operations in the classes of Stripe 4 of *Ankh*:

$$64, 1, 4, 4, 5, 6, 10, 11, 29, 19, 6, 6, 1, 8$$

The expression used to indicate the sum of the series is S_n. (You can pronounce this as "S sub n," or "the series S.") To calculate the series, S_n, you *recursively* add the numbers starting with the first number, until you reach the end. The result is called a *summation.* Here is how you can represent this activity:

$$S_n = 64 + 1 + 4 + 4 + 5 + 6 + 10 + 11 + 29 + 19 + 6 + 6 + 1 + 8$$

The sum of the series, S_n, is 174. Each number in isolation is a piece of the whole. You have now created a whole. (See Figure 12.15.)

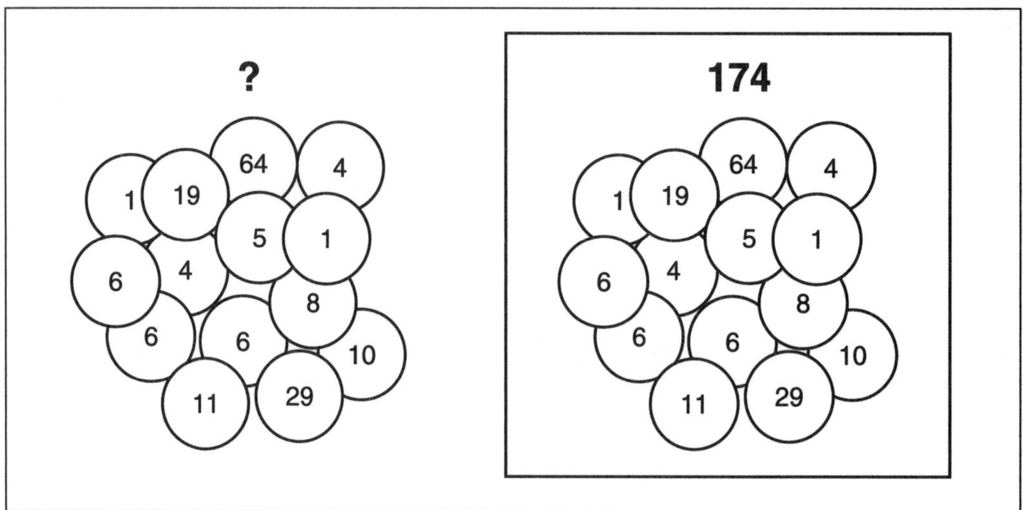

Figure 12.15
Summation unifies parts into a whole, which forms the basis of proportion.

Sigma

When you sum a series, the math is simple, as the previous example shows, but saying just how the math should be done ends up being a little difficult. Mathematicians use the Greek letter sigma (Σ) to indicate summation. Here is how to instruct someone to sum the values in the sequence previously defined:

$$S_n = \sum_{i = a_1}^{a_n} (64, 1, 4, 4, 5, 6, 10, 11, 29, 19, 6, 6, 1, 8)$$

The way this reads is as follows: "The sum as *i* goes from the first element in the series, a_1, to the last element in the series, a_n." The *i* is a pointer, and it points to elements in the series. By convention, the letter *a* indicates an element, and the subscript indicates the place in the series. A subscript of *1* (a_1) indicates the first element. A subscript of *n* (a_n) indicates the last element. The element a_8 is 10.

Summation provides the beginning of a set of relationships. With the result of a summation, you can begin to detect the proportion of each part to the whole.

Tabular Data

When statisticians create summations using data from a table, they often use the name of the data column to designate the series. Assume that an Excel table stores the data for the operations dealt with previously. (See Figure 12.16.) The name of the column is f '. (You can pronounce this as *f-prime).* To show that the data from column f' is to be summed, you create a summation expression naming the column. In Figure 12.16, the sigma expression means, "Sum the elements from column f'."

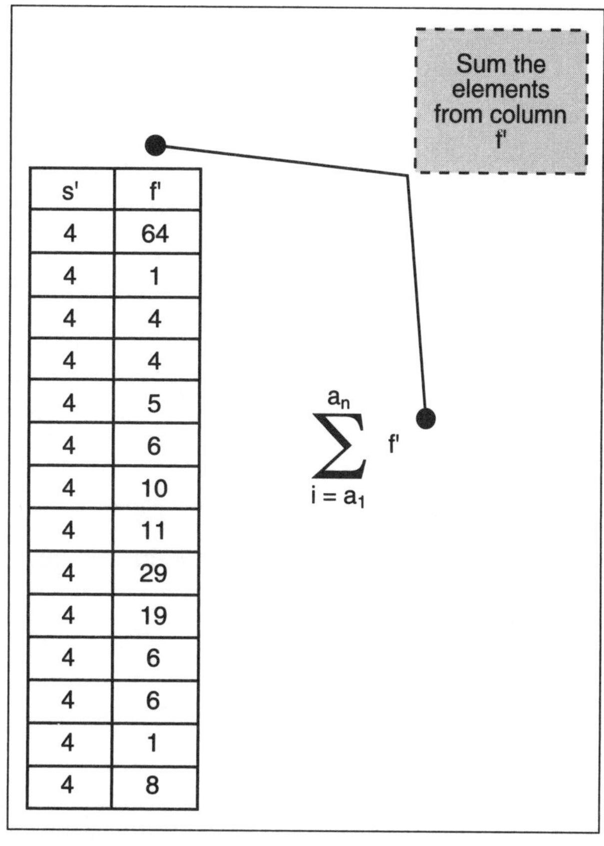

Figure 12.16
Sigma notation indicates that elements from the table column f' are to be summed.

Mean

You can use summation to arrive at the mean of a set of values. The mean of a set of values is also known as its *arithmetic average.* You can calculate the mean of the values using the following formula:

$$\frac{\sum_{i=a_1}^{a_n} f'}{n}$$

According to the formula, you first sum the elements in the column. Next, you divide the sum of the elements by the number of elements you have summed:

$$12.42 \cong \frac{\sum_{i=a_1}^{a_{14}} (64, 1, 4, 4, 5, 6, 10, 11, 29, 19, 6, 6, 1, 8)}{14}$$

Note that you use an approximation operator (≅) for this equation. That's because the value is not exact. In this context, it makes little sense to show anything other than an integer. This is the case unless you are dealing with precise numbers and compute margins of error. (See Figure 12.17).

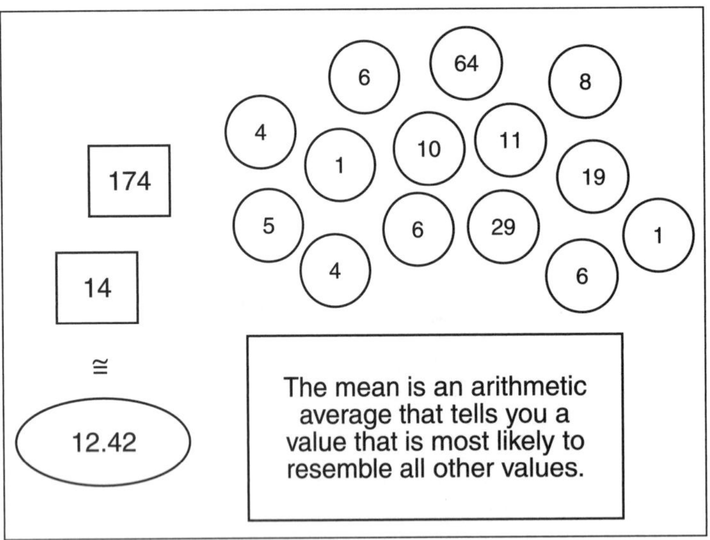

Figure 12.17
The mean is the arithmetic average.

Median

Continuing to work from the table of values in Figure 12.16, to find the median value, you can organize the numbers from lowest to highest. If the set of values is odd, you can take the value in the middle. If the set of values is even, you can find a number that is half the sum of the two middle values. (See Figure 12.18.)

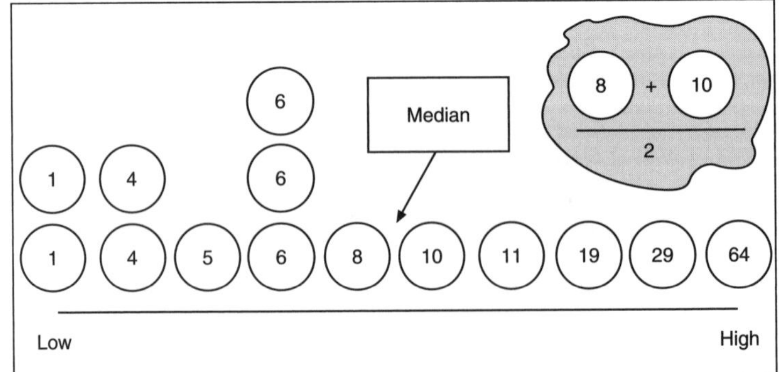

Figure 12.18
The median provides a sense of what value lies at the middle of the sample.

Range and Midrange

The *midrange* is the value that is halfway between the largest and smallest value. (See Figure 12.19.)

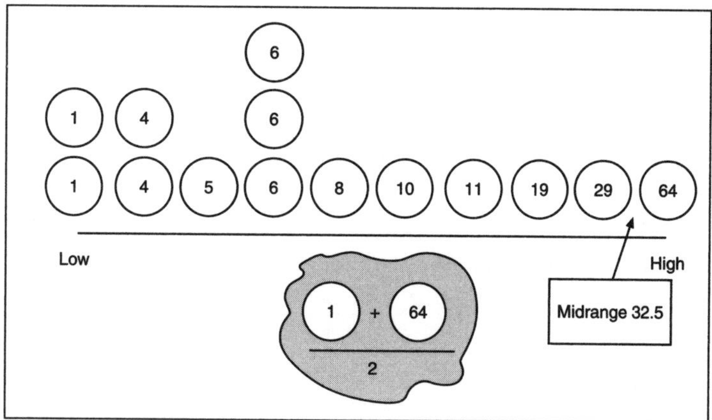

Figure 12.19
Range and midrange confirm the spread of data.

When you subtract the smallest value from the largest value, you establish the range of the data sample. Range provides you with a picture of the *variability* of the data sample. Range tends to be smaller than the total data sample (however, in this case, it is not), and it tends to represent extremes. If you use the range to calculate the midrange, you can begin to see degrees of deviation (which is discussed more in the upcoming section titled "Standard Deviation").

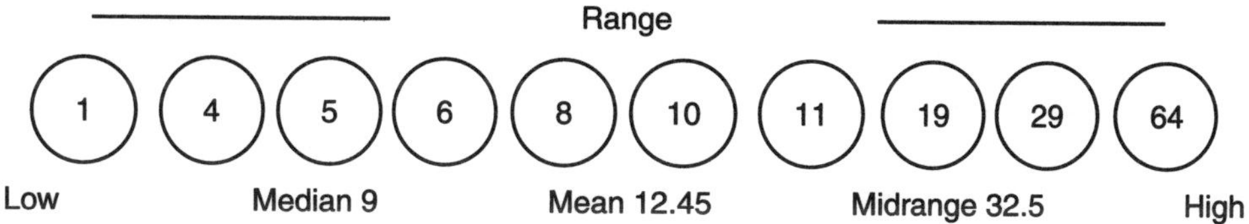

Mode

The *mode* of a series is the value that occurs most frequently. The value that occurs most frequently in the set of data on operations is 6. Mode is an indicator of what is known as *peak frequency.* Peak frequency is one part of the distribution of frequencies within any given set of frequencies. Within different samples or populations, several modes can exist. You can establish several modes by dividing the set into a group of bins or intervals. (See the discussion in the previous section titled "Histograms and Frequency Polygons.") Figure 12.20 shows the sample classes treated as one data set, with one main mode.

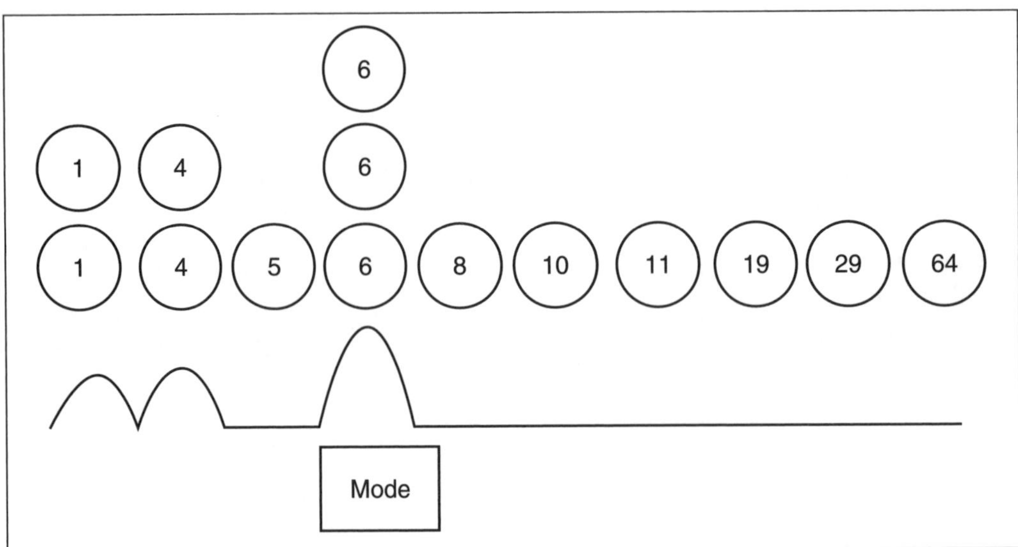

Figure 12.20
Mode expresses frequency.

Consider, for example what happens if you look at mode, median, and mean as they give shape to the data points you have sampled from the classes in Stripe 4. (See Figure 12.21.) The pattern that emerges is one that represents a skewed distribution. Compare this with a symmetrical distribution, which occurs when the mode, median, and mean line up with the same or close to the same values, as shown in Figure 12.22.

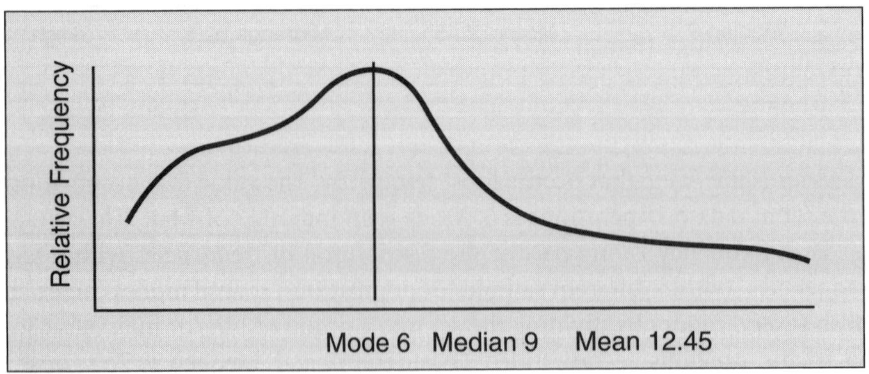

Figure 12.21
The frequency skews the curve for the operations in the analyzed class.

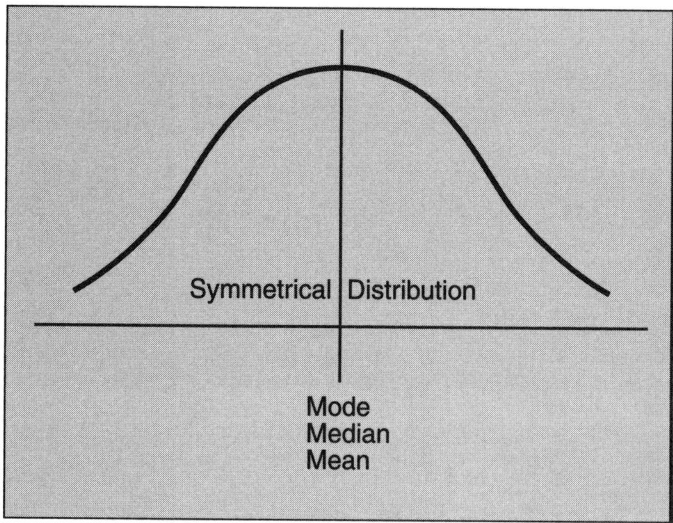

Figure 12.22
With symmetrical distribution, the mode, the median, and the mean are aligned.

Deviation and Variance

Deviation is the difference between any selected value in your data set and the mean of your data set. The computation of deviation is represented in Figure 12.23.

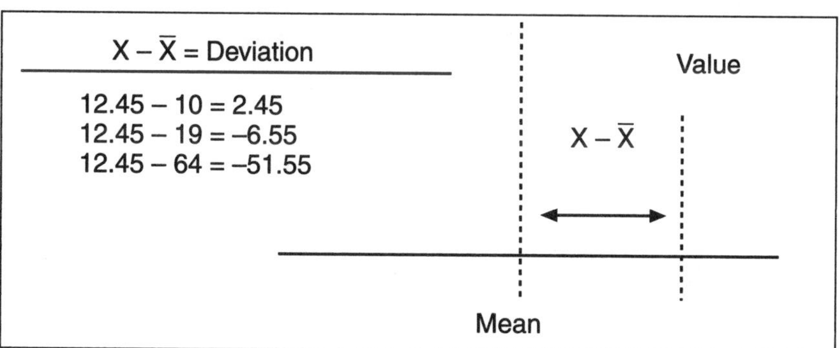

Figure 12.23
Deviation is the difference between the mean and a selected value from the set.

Although it is not evident from the small sampling used in Figure 12.23, adding together the deviations can result in values that are not very useful, such as zero or negative numbers. To overcome this problem, rather than deviation, you seek variance. Variance is calculated by squaring all the deviations, adding them together, and then obtaining the average:

$$256.10 = \frac{(11.45^2 + 11.45^2 + 8.45^2 + 8.45^2 + 7.45^2 + 6.45^2 + 6.45^2 + 6.45^2 + 4.45^2 + 2.45^2 + 0.45^2 + -6.55^2 + 16.55^2 + 51.55^2)}{14}$$

If you have information on all members of the data set you are using, the data set is called the *population.* The square of the lowercase Greek letter sigma (σ^2) represents *population variance.* You pronounce this *sigma squared.* When you are dealing with all members of a sample set, you can also replace the bar X with the Greek letter mu (μ). When you calculate population variance, the number used for the denominator is equal to the total population or to the sample size minus 1.

On the other hand, if you are dealing with only a selected set of the population, you can calculate the sample variance. You represent the sample variance using s^2. Following are the mathematical representations for population and sample variance:

$$s^2 = \frac{\sum (X - \bar{X})^2}{n - 1} \qquad \sigma^2 = \frac{\sum (X - \mu)^2}{N}$$

Standard Deviation

To arrive at the standard deviation, you take the square root of either the population variance or the sample variance. Because you are taking the square roots of sample variances, the symbol for the standard deviation for population is lowercase sigma (σ), and the symbol for the standard deviation for a sample is s. Following are formulas you can use for both population and sample standard deviation:

$$s = \sqrt{\frac{\sum (X - \bar{X})^2}{n - 1}} \qquad s = \sqrt{\frac{\sum X^2 - n\bar{X}^2}{n - 1}}$$

Note that the lowercase s is used in these formulas. You can substitute the lowercase sigma (σ) if you are calculating standard deviation for a population. The formulas apply to both populations and samples. Given these formulations, the standard deviation for the operations from Stripe 4 is 16.00.

Validity and Reliability

If you sample data in a consistent way, so that each piece of data is collected using the same method and unit of measurement, the data you collect has a high degree of *reliability*.

Inevitably, however, any measurement can be off the mark. If you want to treat your data in a highly scientific manner, you can calculate an *index of variation*, which is more or less a ratio that expresses the margin of error in your data. The symbol for index of variation is IV. The math is as follows:

$$IV = \frac{s}{\mu} \qquad IV = \frac{\sigma}{\mu}$$

As in software testing, *validity* applies to whether the measurement actually measures what it is said to measure. For instance, with the operations in the class from Stripe 4, you can establish what counts as an operation by examining the programming syntax. (See Figure 12.24.)

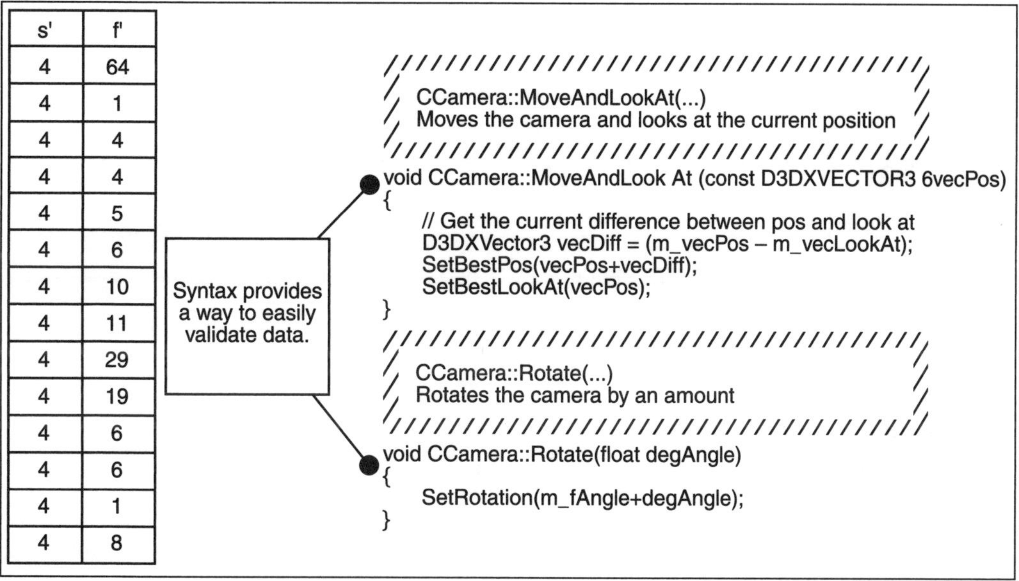

Figure 12.24
You can establish data validity by clearly defining the source of the data and the criteria used to identify it.

Proportion

In Figure 12.16, when you count operations in classes in Stripe 4 and then add the results so that you can calculate the mean, you lay the groundwork for another important notion: *proportion*. When you determine the ratio of a subset to a set, you discover a proportion. A proportion applies to either a population (the group of all things of a given category) or a sample.

The symbol that indicates proportion when you are using a population is the lowercase Greek letter pi (π). The symbol that indicates proportion when you are using a sample is the capital letter P. Because the quantity of a subset is always less than the set of which it is a subset, the value of statistical π is always going to be between 0 and 1. Figure 12.25 illustrates the mathematical formulas for calculating proportions for populations. The formulas are shown with a table generated by the application of the formula that applies to populations.

$$P = \frac{\text{Number of values in the subset of the sample}}{\text{Number of values in the sample}}$$

$$\Pi = \frac{\text{Number of values in the subset of the population}}{\text{Number of values in the population}}$$

Item	1	4	5	6	8	10	11	19	29	64
Count	2	2	1	3	1	1	1	1	1	1
Proportion	0.142	0.142	0.071	0.21	0.071	0.071	0.071	0.071	0.071	0.071

Figure 12.25
Proportions relate parts to the whole.

Groupings

You can divide data according to groupings based on *fractiles*. You usually encounter the results of such operations in graphical representations like pie or bar charts.

The easiest use of fractiles is to begin with the familiar notion of *percentile*. A percentile places everything on a scale of 100:

$$\text{Percentile} = \frac{\text{Number of values in the subset of the sample}}{\text{Number of values in the sample}} \times 100$$

Item	1	4	5	6	8	10	11	19	29	64
Count	2	2	1	3	1	1	1	1	1	1
Percentile	14.2	14.2	7.14	21.4	7.14	7.14	7.14	7.14	7.14	7.14

You can determine quartiles by grouping percentiles into four groups that are the same size. Following are tabular and graphical representations of information from the table grouped into quartiles:

Quartile	Quartile Range
I	0–25
II	26–50
III	51–70
IV	71–100

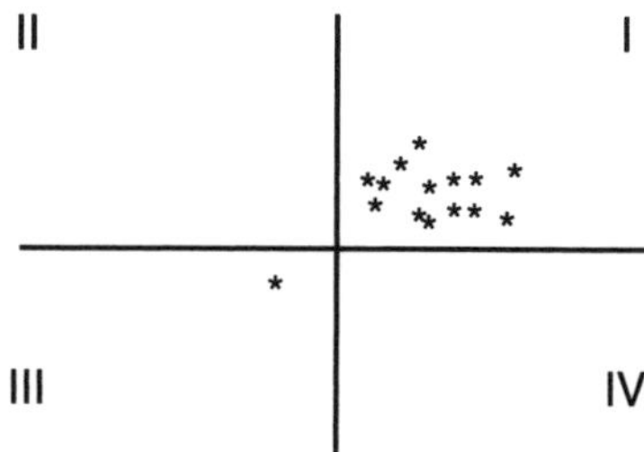

Models

Models differ according to how they use data and what data they use. The deeper you go into the study of statistical modeling, the more you realize that most models can be classified according to whether they analyze historical data or whether they combine data from a variety of current sources to predict trends.

Static Models

Statistical models that fall into the *historical* category usually draw upon data from many projects that have been pursued over several years or decades. Such models are sometimes referred to generally as *static* models. These models often seek to make data coherent and easily understood. They also might offer ways to verify data and determine its accuracy. For example, a software statistician analyzes data derived from several hundred projects over a 20-year period and places this data into tables from which software developers can obtain *benchmarks.* In addition, the statistician might derive average and mean values for different areas of activity, such as defect density, project duration, productivity, and so on. With respect to specific development projects, the statistician might gather data on the number of operations in classes or function points in operations. He then could make calculations to determine the complexity of the application.

Dynamic Models

Statistical models that fall into the second, *synchronic,* category usually draw upon data that a single project generates. Such models are often referred to as *dynamic* models. Such models seek to use, in some cases, several different types of data to generate predictions of a trend for a variable outside the primary data set. For example, a software statistician might study the way that requirements and design efforts are scheduled and executed and then, using data from these activities, attempt to predict defect trends during the release phase of a project.

The Rayleigh Approach

The Rayleigh model is dynamic. It dates back several decades and is used to evaluate software reliability. It is a dynamic model because it can draw upon information relating to the software lifecycle for a single project and from this generate predictions about defect trends that are likely to characterize the product after it reaches general availability.

The math involved in the Rayleigh models is important to study if you intend to employ or extend the model in your own work, but for the general purposes established here, viewing a graphical representation of the Rayleigh model presents the best approach to the topic. The math for the model, after a little juggling (see the reference for Stephen H. Kan at the end of this chapter), is along the following lines:

$$f(t) = K\left[\left(\frac{1}{t_m}\right) te^{-(1/2t_m^2)t^2}\right]$$

K = Total number of defects
t = Time
m = A shape parameter

The total number of defects is the number of defects reported from testing during the development phases of the project. You must calibrate these for most projects. You can accomplish this in several ways, one of which is to adjust the time parameter.

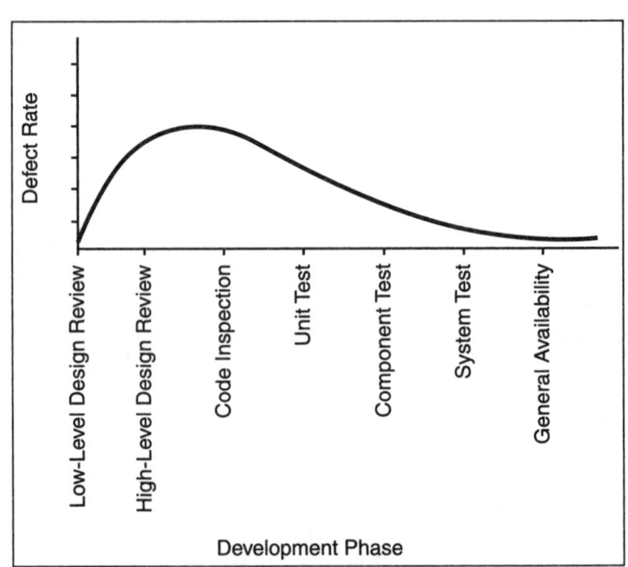

Figure 12.26
The Rayleigh model allows you to predict defect.

In the context of the development process that IBM had in place during a study that involved calculations of defect rates using the Rayleigh model, the project defect rate that resulted resembles the profile provided in Figure 12.26. The Rayleigh model allows you to predict defect rates following general release of a software product. (See Stephen H. Kan, *Metrics and Models in Software Quality Engineering, Second Edition*, Boston, [MA: Addison-Wesley, 2003.])

In Figure 12.26, notice that the tail (the right side) of the curve slopes downward and gradually smoothes out until its decline is almost imperceptible. Such a curve is called an *asymptotic* curve because it can extend infinitely without ever reaching the axis toward which it is moving (in this case, the Development Phase, or *x*-axis). How can such a thing happen? Consider what occurs when you increase the denominator in a fraction with a numerator of 1:

$$\frac{1}{n\ldots\infty}$$

$$\frac{1}{1} \quad \frac{1}{2} \quad \frac{1}{3} \quad \frac{1}{4}$$

The fraction becomes smaller and smaller, but it never reaches zero. The number of test instances can increase infinitely, but the number of discovered defects will always remain smaller. For this reason, the defect rate after the release of a product is described by an asymptotic curve.

Rayleigh Applied

The Rayleigh model is said to provide a pattern for defect rates that can be applied to almost any software development project if the phases of the project are calibrated to accord with the model. A great deal of work has been done to test this notion. Figure 12.27 represents what you might regard as a typical software product development profile as represented using the Rayleigh model.

First, the project manager hires developers. The developers go to work as soon as possible and generate code. After a time, intensive testing efforts begin, usually with the full integration of the product. Following that, the product is released.

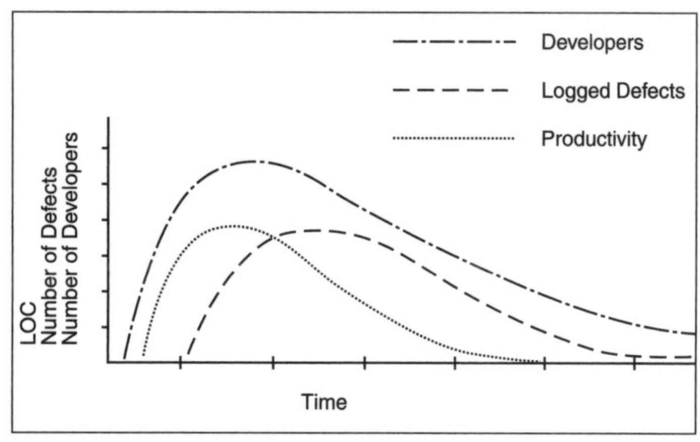

Figure 12.27
The Rayleigh model allows software engineers to relate defects, productivity, and the number of developers on a team.

The curves in this figure depict a typical but not necessarily ideal pattern. Consider, for example, the peak of the staffing curve. The project manager apparently wanted to hire a relatively large number of developers to make early gains on the amount of code produced for the product. The curves depict the relationships that exist between the number of developers, the productivity of the developers (in terms of LOCs per day, week, or month), and the defect rate. When the project manager chose to put many developers to work producing code at a high rate, the result was a higher rate of defects.

You can reshape these curves. For example, you can decrease the number of programmers, with resulting lower productivity. Lower productivity might bring a lower rate of errors. In addition, if the amount of testing increases relative to productivity, the defect rate is likely to be lowered. Each trend relates to the other, and the model shows how this is so.

As a final observation, consider in Figure 12.27 the way the curves follow a succession, and the tails of the curves tend to slope consistently downward after peaking. This indicates that one phase of activity followed fairly consistently upon another. Coding apparently followed requirements and design, and no rework sessions characterized the development effort.

Ankh Metrics

Data for *Ankh* was assembled using Excel. Excel is suitable for statistical work because it offers a group of roughly 80 built-in functions that are suitable for statistical calculations. In addition to the built-in functions, you will find that many vendors provide statistical packages that can be installed as Excel options.

Lines of Code and Stripes

The first set of metrics that the team found it easy to assemble showed the growth of the product. For the *Ankh* development effort, as shown in Figure 12.28, the software design specification divided the system into 18 stripes. The figure shows data taken after the completion of a number of stripes. By graphing line counts, the team could easily track the growth of the product with each stripe. As you can see, 2,000 lines of code, on the average, were added for each stripe. However, in most cases, the number of lines added was around 1,000 per stripe. On the average, the increase was less than one-fourth of the size of the stripe.

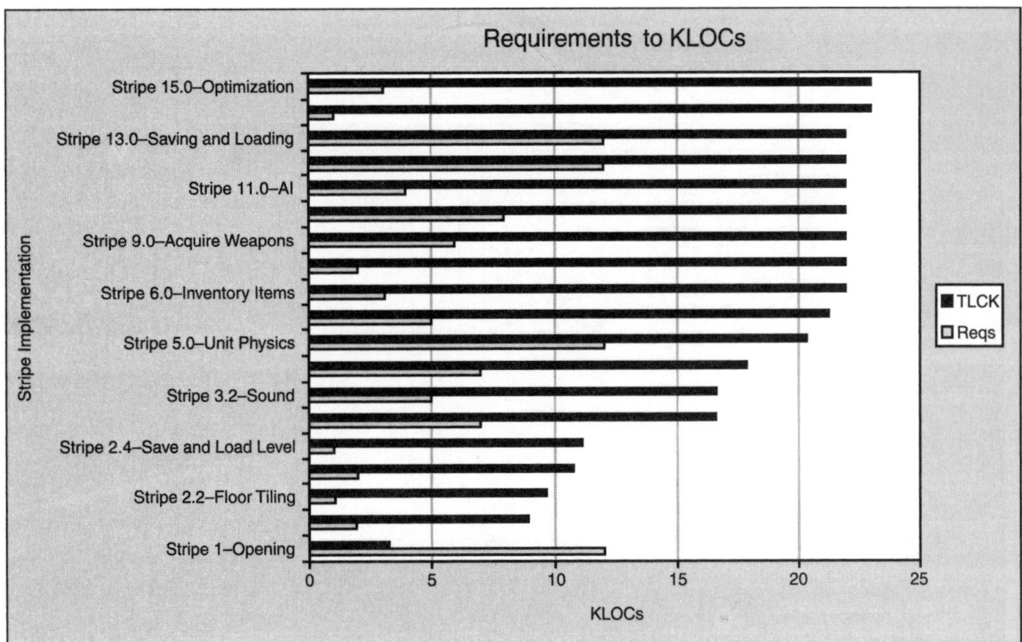

Figure 12.28
Lines of code provide a basic way to gauge size.

In Figure 12.28, you can see that, with a few exceptions, the design effort paid off because it broke the development effort into consistent blocks. Consistently sized blocks allowed the development team to benefit during its testing efforts, because the smaller the unit of code to be tested, the less complexity the unit of code is likely to present.

Requirements and Stripes

Another study that helped the team understand the product involved the number of requirements that each stripe addressed. Drawing from the information that the software design specification presents (see Figure 12.29), you can see that a stripe addressed from 1 to 12 requirements. In some instances, two or more stripes addressed the same requirement, but in most cases, only one stripe addressed a requirement.

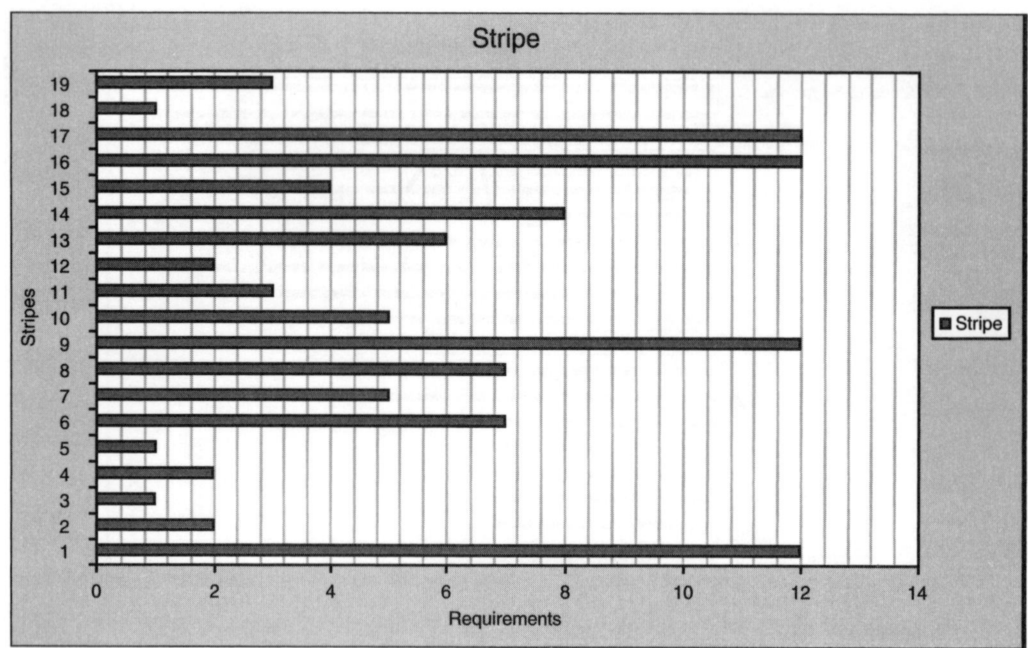

Figure 12.29
Distribution of requirements can indicate the quality of the design.

Again, as with the distribution of the lines of code across the stripes, the software design specification benefited the team because it distributed the requirements fairly evenly across the 19 stripes. Four stripes involved large sets of requirements. Seven stripes fell into a middle range. Eight stripes were on the lower end. Picturing the stripes in terms of these three groups provides a way to glimpse how the design of the software addressed the requirements. This helps, likewise, illustrate that although one stripe might have involved four times as many requirements as another, the overall complexity of the code development effort corresponded not to the number of requirements, but to the complexity of the problems that the requirements represented.

As an extension of the study of requirements per stripe, as Figure 12.30 shows, the number of classes implemented during the construction of a given stripe raised questions. Notice, for example, that stripe 16 has both a large number of requirements and a large number of classes. Does the number of requirements affect the number of classes implemented for the stripe? Although it is risky to immediately draw the conclusion that a large set of requirements correlates with a large set of implemented classes, it is still the case that the information that Figure 12.30 provides serves as a tool with which to evaluate the quality of the software design specification.

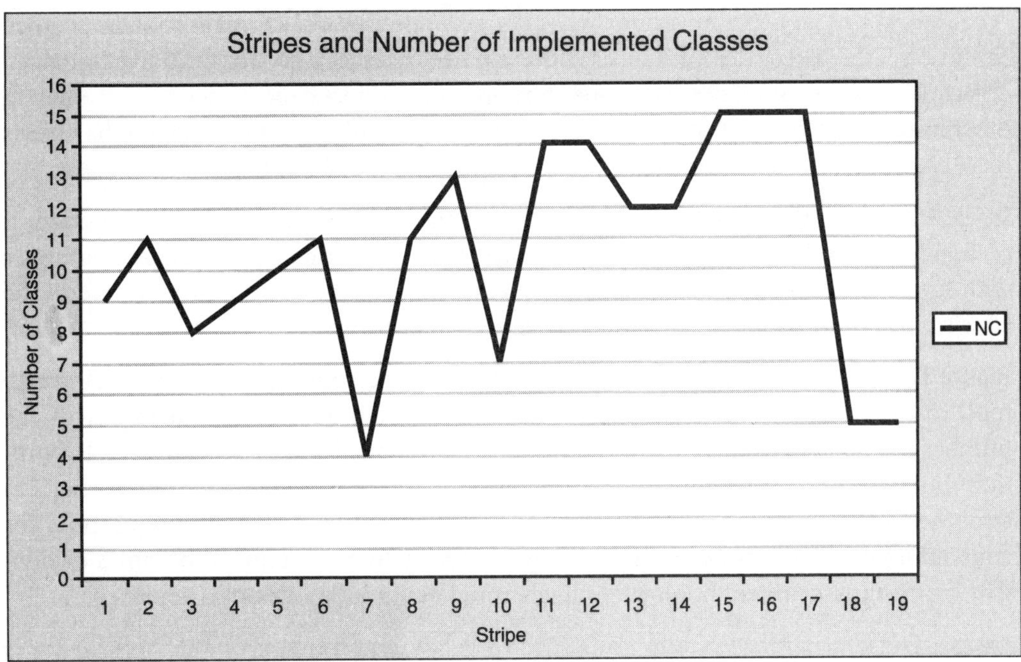

Figure 12.30
The number of classes implemented for each stripe helps show how system responsibilities have been distributed.

Investigating the distribution of classes reveals that the software design specification did a good job of distributing the complexity of the requirements across the stripes. Although in some instances the number of implemented classes grows with the number of requirements that the stripe addresses, it is also the case that in several instances, a middle-sized set of classes results. Figure 12.30 shows the different sizes of requirements groupings. No stripe addresses an inordinately large set of requirements. When you consider this information with the implementation efforts that the various stripes required, it becomes clear that the design made it possible to develop the game in balanced stages.

Collaborative Complexity

Figure 12.31 provides a way to study some of the implications of the complexity of classes. Consider a situation in which a stripe requires the implementation of only a few classes and yet generates a sizeable addition of code. How does this happen? A possible answer arises if you give attention to the software design specification, which records the number of collaborations for each class.

A collaboration can occur in various ways. For example, one object might contain another. In this case, the object that contains the other object receives a service from the contained object. The collaboration occurs because one object has direct dependencies on another. In other instances, two objects might serve a third object. In this instance, although the objects serve each other, both objects might communicate with the object that contains them.

In each instance, the complexity of an object increases with the number of messages it exchanges with other objects. If the complexity increases so that a given class collaborates with several other classes, good design practices call for trying to find ways to refactor the class so that you distribute its complexity across other classes.

Figure 12.31 shows the number of collaborators for the core set of classes for *Ankh.* In most cases, the number of collaborators tends to be around four. In some instances, the number climbs inordinately high. Although explanations for the number of collaborations might be justified, it remains that the classes might be candidates for refactoring. On the other hand, because the number of collaborators for all classes, including those for large numbers of collaborators, does not tend to vary to an extreme, it becomes evident that the design document holds up well when the design of its classes is considered.

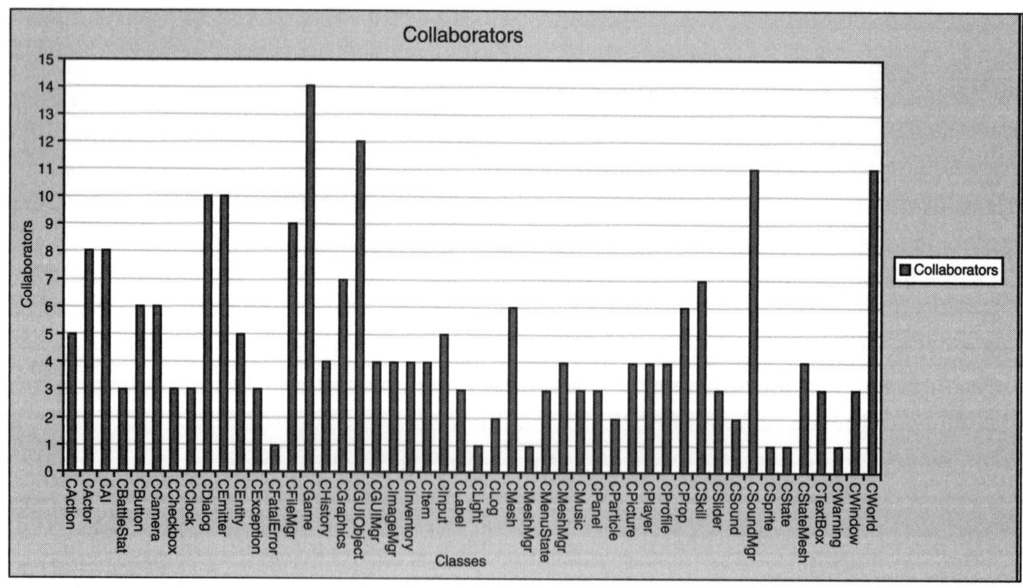

Figure 12.31
Collaborators show the way that class responsibilities are supported and how responsibility has been distributed.

Function Points

A class is considered to be well designed when it addresses a single responsibility. Its collaborations are justified to the extent that they provide services directly stipulated by their responsibilities. Still, the more that an object of one class interacts with objects of other classes, the more it extends its collaborations and its complexity.

A classical way to study how an object interacts with other objects is to use *function points.* Software analysts often associate function points with database applications, and a function point is a system activity that involves creating, updating, deleting, or reading. Other descriptions of function points are often added to this basic set. In object-oriented programming, people often equate function points with the number of objects created or the number of messages exchanged between objects.

To determine function points for the *Ankh* software, the development team used a formula empirically derived from a survey of object uses. The formula attempted to fold together the number of collaborations and the number of messages involved in a collaboration. Using this formula, the team generated a scatter diagram that showed how, from class to class, complexity tended to vary.

Figure 12.32 shows class types as numbered items. The lower, darker marks indicate the number of classes each class supported through collaborations. The higher, lighter marks indicate the number of messages a given instance of a class supported during its lifetime. Using this way of plotting interactions among objects, you can investigate how a stripe that addressed few requirements might involve relatively few classes and yet call for an extensive development effort. Notice, for instance, that although all classes had fewer than 10 collaborators, around 20 percent had collaboration indexes that numbered more than 20.

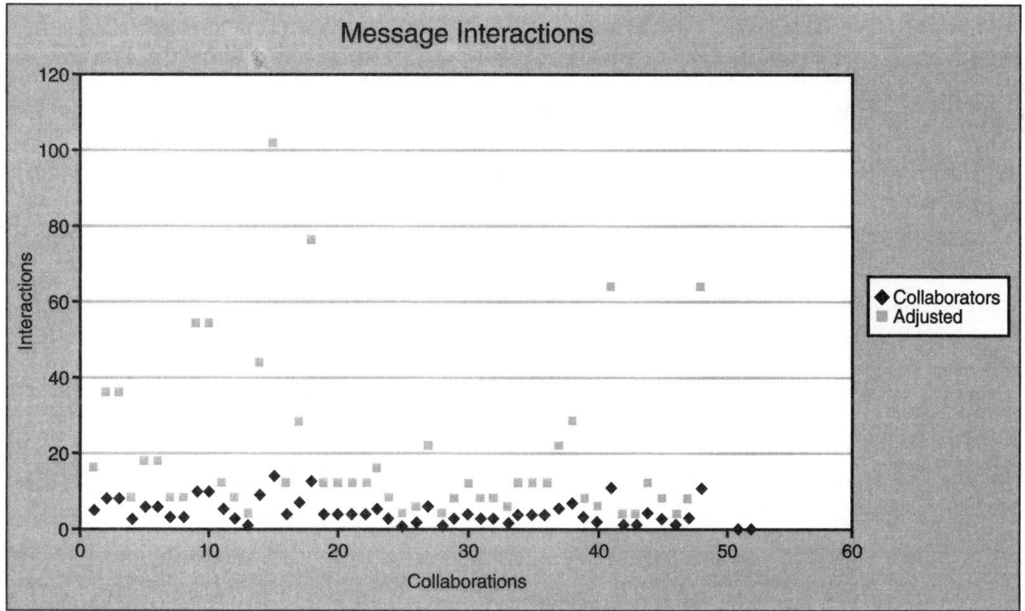

Figure 12.32
As an alternative to function point analysis, you can use collaborators and message interactions.

Conclusion

Collecting quantitative data provides a way to formalize your examination of development activities. To ensure that you gather valid data, a good approach is to collect data that is commonly discussed by metrics and quality assurance specialists. When you follow this approach, you can find plenty of information with which to refine both your data definitions and the analytical models you apply to your data.

After you collect data, you can work with it empirically or analytically. If you work with data on an empirical basis, your primary goal should be to display it so that you can gain general ideas about rates and trends. Many graphical tools are available for this. Using Microsoft Excel, for example, you can generate pie, bar, radar, and other charts.

More advanced techniques for dealing with data involve using knowledge you draw from statistics. Among key statistical concepts are summation, mean, median, mode, variation, and standard deviation. Given a basic understanding of such notions, you can apply a variety of distribution curves to your data. Among the most widely used curves are the normal distribution and Weibull curves. The Weibull curve is the basis of the Rayleigh model, which allows you to evaluate defect rates that occur after product release.

The *Ankh* team used a few basic tools of statistics and metrics to collect and analyze the complexity of classes, the distribution of functionality across stripes, and the raw growth in the size of the product per stripe.

For further reading on statistics, quality assurance, and metrics, consult the following sources:

Humphrey, Watts S. *Introduction to the Personal Software Process.* SEI Series in Software Engineering. Boston: Addison-Wesley, 1997.

Kan, Stephen H. *Metrics and Models in Software Quality Engineering, Second Edition.* Boston: Addison-Wesley, 2003.

Lapin, Lawrence L. *Business Statistics.* New York: Harcourt Brace, 1984.

Lorenz, Mark and Jeff Kidd. *Object-Oriented Software Metrics.* Englewood Cliffs, New Jersey: PTR Prentice Hall, 1994.

Pandian, C. Ravindranath. *Software Metrics: A Guide to Planning, Analysis, and Application.* New York: Auerbach Publications, 2004.

Petroski, Henry. To Engineer Is Human: *The Role of Failure in Successful Design.* New York: Random House, 1992.

Putnam, Lawrence H. and Ware Myers. *Five Core Metrics: The Intelligence Behind Successful Software Management.* New York: Dorset House Publishing, 2003.

Stephens, Larry J. *Advanced Statistics Demystified.* New York: McGraw-Hill, 2004.

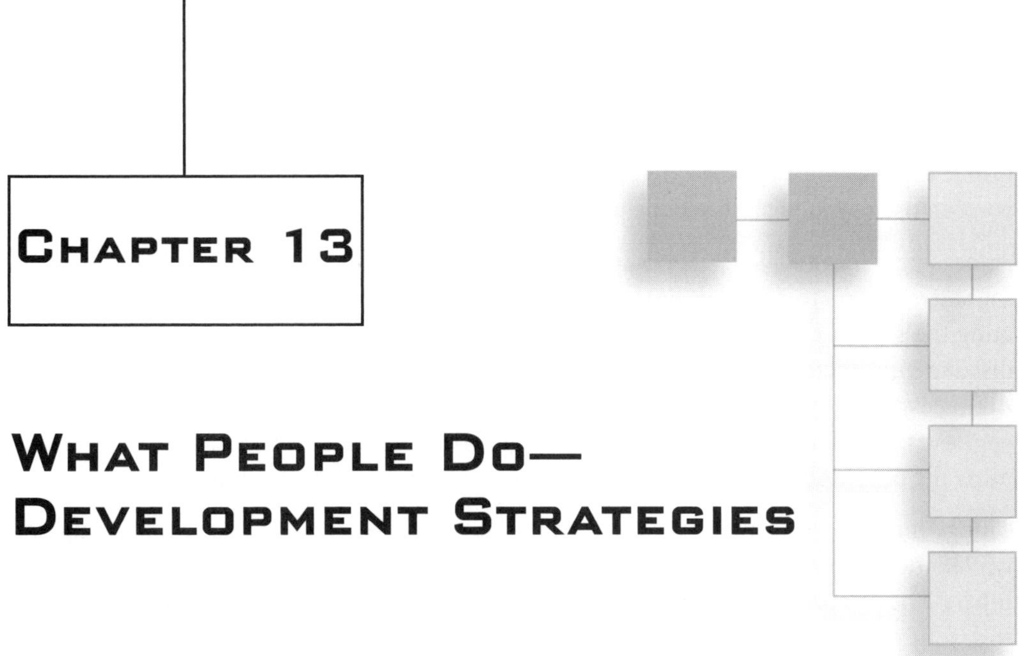

Chapter 13

What People Do—Development Strategies

The discussion in this chapter draws heavily from material presented in other chapters, but it's not assumed that you have studied other chapters. This chapter offers you a guide on how to proceed with a development project according to a design and using a development plan. Along the way, it investigates ways to work with documents relating to game design, requirements, software design, project planning, configuration management, and testing. Working according to a plan and using documentation to shape and guide your effort ensures that you can monitor and improve your development activity continuously. Likewise, when you proceed with a planned, traceable effort, your game development activity assumes a polished, professional dimension that it would not otherwise possess. Where there is no history, there is no progress. Toward the end of finding a path to creating a history of what you do, this chapter offers the following topics:

- Defining a starting point for a project
- Putting together a set of working principles
- Documenting the product to be developed
- Documenting the plan for development
- Proceeding through reviews
- Introducing quality measures
- Making transitions from one project to another

Starting Points

From the perspective of software engineering, the starting point of a game development effort begins with a directive. The directive originates from a source that usually lies somewhere outside the programming group. The game design document provides the most visible expression of the directive. The game design document provides information that you can use to establish the scope of your effort.

As organizations get bigger, specialization increases, so if you are responsible for developing software, you might find that your role in the development of the game reduces to creating the software that supports features that other people have dreamed up. If this is a discouraging picture, consider that engineers are almost always in the same position. Architects work with structural engineers, automobile designers work with mechanical engineers, and game designers work with software engineers or programmers. One supports the other. Almost no industry fails to reveal this division of labor.

Things might vary from situation to situation, but if you serve in an engineering role while others serve in design roles, your role begins with providing a specified product to others. The product you provide is the software that makes the game possible. For this reason, your starting point is an understanding of what is needed to support the features of the game.

Team Formation

The assumption here is that you will eventually find yourself working for an established game development organization. In this world, a game development effort begins with several things that do not involve programming. Among these are contracts, a game design document, and a corporate production plan. Rights must be secured, funding must be approved, and a corporate production schedule must be created. After all this activity has been completed, a project manager or team lead is chosen for the programming effort. The project manger's first job, usually, is to assess how much effort development of the software that supports the game will require and how many people will be needed to complete the project on time.

Although no formula covers all situations, if you find yourself in the project management position, you will probably conclude that you require a team who is capable of performing a few basic types of activity:

- Plan and manage the development effort.
- Know the answers to difficult technical questions.
- Answer questions about how the game has been designed and what goals its functionality should support.
- Perform secondary or specialized programming tasks that require a high investment of time.
- Create documentation for the project.
- Perform or coordinate work that involves game assets, such as sound and graphics.
- Work on tools that can support various development activities.

- Set up and manage the software configuration.
- Formally define and work in a software testing role.

Although the members of your team might not find these specific roles at the start of a project, as you go, everyone will end up assuming and defining the roles that these activities encompass.

The assertion here is not that if you want to create a game, you should find a specific number of people and command them to work in specific roles. In reality, things do not work this way. Even in the most rigidly monotonous corporate settings, people still explore and discover roles as the development effort progresses. But it remains that certain types of work must be done. The effort of *Ankh* involved six people. The tasks that the team performed tended to vary from day to day, and fewer or more people could have been involved in the effort. Regardless, the tasks documented in the preceding list recurred constantly. Figure 13.1 summarizes the activities.

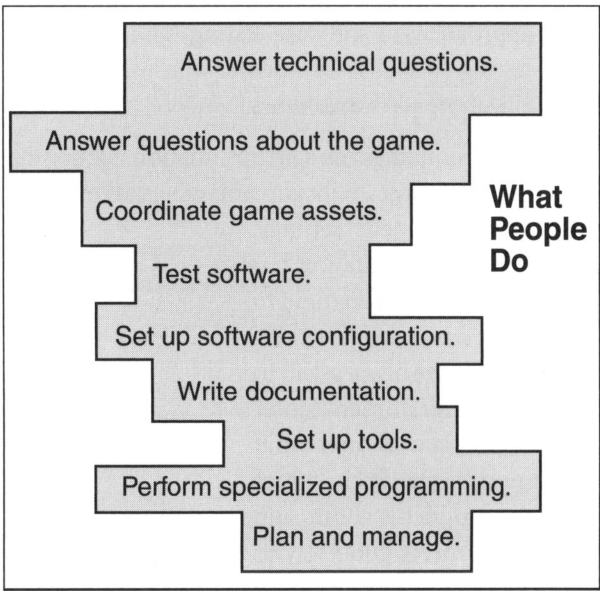

Figure 13.1
Members of a development team might not be assigned roles, but before long, roles find them.

Definition

At the beginning of the game software development effort, you likely will be sitting in a room with a group of developers and begin talking about the game. Everyone is probably enthusiastic. Everyone has in mind something great. This is good, certainly. Such talk is bound to burn up quite a bit of time. The talk might encompass past efforts, existing code resources, what should be avoided, and what tools to use. At some point, however, for anything to get done, the group must assert a few common themes:

- **The team must design the software.** The design emerges from the requirements, and the requirements must be based on the game design document. The team must understand the scope of the game and the selling features. Likewise, it must create a design for the software.

- **The team must plan and manage the project.** The project manager must understand the requirements, set the budget, establish the deadlines, and determine the number of people needed. Add to this that everyone on the team must understand the plan for the development of the product and what he should do as part of the team effort.
- **The team must test everything.** For testing to take place, a testing specialist must be involved in the development effort. Different schools advocate different approaches to software testing. The approach advocated in this book features a testing specialist—someone who works with the primary developer to detect and eliminate software errors.

Figure 13.2 simplifies the startup situation. Notice that implementation is just one of several activities. The urge to begin implementation immediately can cause problems, even in mature development settings. You begin implementation too soon if you do not take time to fully understand the functionality that you are being asked to develop. Programmers enter the picture late enough that they must learn from others what the product is about, and that takes time. A good way to learn about the product is to create a scope statement and a requirements specification. The scope statement allows everyone on the development team to have a common understanding of the project, and the requirements statement forces everyone to spend several days precisely naming what it is that is to be developed.

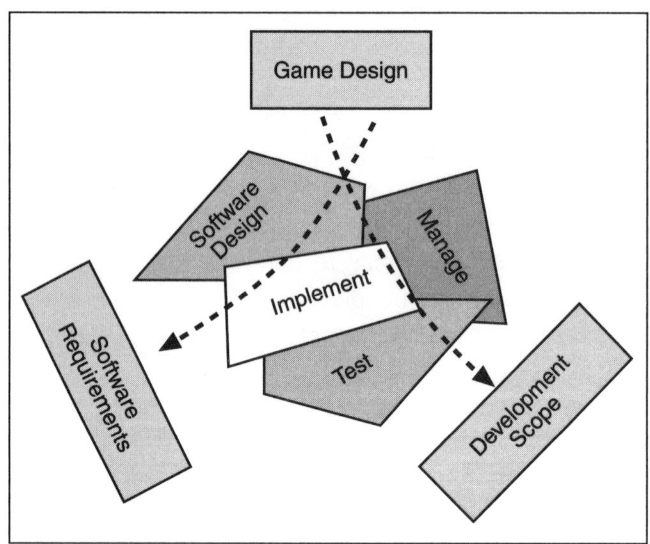

Figure 13.2
At the beginning of a project, the team must assert management, design, and testing priorities against the urge to begin programming.

Management involves controlling the urge to start work on the game before taking the time to understand what the game design document portrays. Design involves beginning the painful process of trying to think through what is wanted and putting it into a form that allows it to be developed systematically. Testing involves reviewing the startup activities to ensure that developers refine, verify, and validate features from the start.

Working with Software Design

The focal point of the design effort for a software engineering project is the software design specification. That specification might end up being the central document in your development effort. As the project progressed for *Ankh*, the team tended to rely more heavily on the software design document. Development of the software design document required continuous iteration, and the document did not stabilize until late in the project. From the first, laying out the game software as a set of stripes (or components) was essential. Laying out stripes forced the team to concentrate on specific implementation tasks.

Setting Up Tools

The tools that the *Ankh* team used most frequently at the beginning of the project were as follows:

- **SmartDraw.** This provided a graphical tool that everyone on the team could use with relative ease to draw UML representations of design concepts.
- **Microsoft Word.** This provided a word processing tool that also accommodated graphics and tables.
- **CVS.** This provided source control for builds and served as a control tool for documentation.
- **A laptop and a projector.** The team projected the design and code work onto a large screen. The team watched as one person worked at the laptop. In this way, the team could review documentation, participate in code reviews, and generally work as a team toward a focused objective with little effort. During an average group work session, regardless of the task, two or more team members would take turns at the keyboard.

SmartDraw

One of the problems that cottage industry endeavors face is that tools that provide UML and other support are too costly to use. And if tools are extremely demanding, they can be more of a problem than an asset. Several of the industrial-strength tools that are commonly associated with UML emerged during a time when the notion of "software factories" was fairly prevalent in software engineering discussions.

The problem with the industrial tools, besides price, is that they can *enforce* rather than *accommodate* a vision of software development. In a corporate setting in which months or years can be occupied training software designers to use such tools, employing such tools certainly is justified. For cottage industry game developers, however, the picture differs. The goal in cottage industry is to maintain work as craft, not production line, so flexibility, individual creativity, and exploration are important.

However, even when game development efforts emerge from extremely rigorous industrial settings, they tend to benefit from a degree of randomness that factory production of games cannot accommodate easily. Automated software design is something akin to pouring concrete into a mold rather than shaping the mold for the concrete. Many of the best features of the great games of the past few decades have tended to emerge with the effort of developing the game. A mixture of engineering discipline and artistic freedom has characterized these efforts.

To preserve the virtues of cottage industry programming while making use of the tools for conceptualization that UML offers, you can use a software application such as SmartDraw. With SmartDraw, you can create use cases, class diagrams, sequence diagrams, and other diagrams in the UML suite but still be flexible in the way you work. Given this flexibility, you achieve the goal of clarifying concepts while avoiding the need to struggle with subtle levels of detail. SmartDraw, unlike Rational Rose or other such applications, is not a Computer-Aided Software Engineering (CASE) tool. Instead, it is a tool that allows you to quickly and easily illustrate ideas.

Figure 13.3 shows how the team stored the use cases and UML diagrams for *Ankh* in SmartDraw. This view of the project material is midway between the lowest and highest magnifications. Each of the rectangles contains a use case, an object diagram, and a sequence diagram for a stripe of the game. To zoom in on the material in any of the rectangles, you click anywhere in the rectangle you want to enlarge. If you want to zoom out so that you see all of the stripes, hold down the Ctrl and Shift keys.

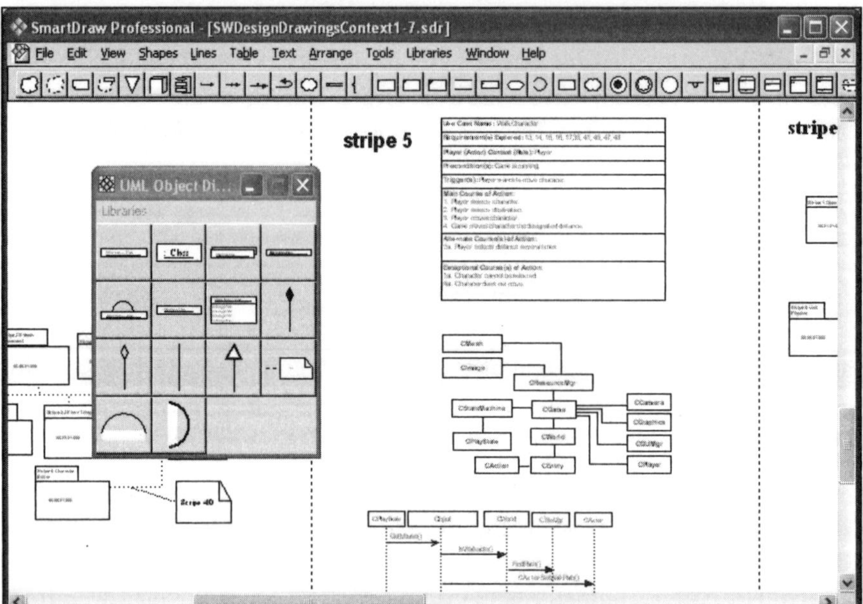

Figure 13.3 SmartDraw provides a canvas that is large enough to accommodate almost all the UML diagrams and use cases that appear in your design document.

Working with SmartDraw, the developers projected design drawings on a screen and then discussed and modified them as a team. Creation of the diagrams required some upfront work. For example, the use cases are SmartDraw tables, and the object and sequence diagrams are collections of graphical primitives. You can simplify the work required to create the tables and diagrams because SmartDraw allows you to create and store prefabricated graphical objects. You can even place these objects in a pallet, so that creating new diagrams or use cases only involves clicking to select the object you want. After making a few refinements in your starter diagrams, it becomes easy to use SmartDraw as a primary design tool.

Documentation

Many software documentation specialists consider Microsoft Word and Adobe FrameMaker to be the best tools in the industry for documentation creation and maintenance. The *Ankh* team used Word because everyone on the team had it.

Choosing a documentation application that everyone knows and has access to is important, but even then, documentation problems easily crop up. One key problem is when the team creates too many documents or imposes a ridiculous level of control on documents. Such excesses tend to reduce the likelihood that documentation will be maintained. Tendencies to create documentation problems generally result when team members apply practices that are suitable for other areas of development to the documentation effort. For example, programmers tend to create problems by trying to treat documents as though they are code modules. The result is a ridiculously large number of documents that needlessly preserves a history of changes that no one is likely to care about.

When documentation becomes difficult to manage, developers usually stop managing it. If the situation is too troublesome, they completely abandon the documentation effort. When this happens, it becomes difficult to track the history of the project, trace the progress of the project, or know the extent to which original plans have changed. Resisting the tendency to neglect documentation involves taking time to understand how to use a document as a working medium of development.

The most important aspect of the document is not the many changes that have gone into its development. Instead, the real value of a document is that it can serve as a way of helping people focus on the current state of the product. For this reason, as is covered in Chapter 18, "Documentation—Learning How to Learn," developers can benefit in enormous ways if they treat documents as flexible, evolving media and view them as resources for reviewing work and learning about problems. Preserving a history of changes in a document is often a waste of time.

Documents can be too long and too numerous. Overly zealous configuration managers sometimes want to preserve every e-mail someone writes during a project. Occasionally, testers want to create a huge library of error reports. Programmers often go in the direction of wanting to separate documents into dozens of pieces, such as one for each heading. Project managers might go in the other direction, wanting to cram everything into one monolithic document. Technical writers might want to enforce templates over content. All of these tendencies represent professionally grounded concerns for avoiding problems, but when carried to an excess, problems result. To resist these tendencies, it is important to view the document as useful only so long as it is used as a tool of development. If the document is no longer used, something has gone wrong, and it is time to alter it so that it *can* be used.

During the startup phase of a project, the team is likely to use the following documents a great deal if they are kept brief and incorporated into planning activities through the use of an overhead projector:

- A software requirements specification
- A software design specification
- A project plan
- A test plan
- A configuration plan
- Project conventions

CVS

The team must set up a way to control versions of code as early in the project as possible. That's because during the design phase, developers might decide to explore design concepts with code. The team should version such code formally, because it more than likely will be brought forward later in the project.

The *Ankh* team used a Concurrent Versions System (CVS) called TortoiseCVS. TortoiseCVS requires that you set up client and server capabilities, which are discussed in Chapter 10, "Control Freaks and Configuration Management." Setting up the CVS server early in the process ensures that you will be able to add new users easily.

When you set up a versioning system, you should work from a configuration plan. Laying out the complete directory structure is not possible until you have created a software design document and know what stripes (also called modules or components) and what component groupings within the stripes you want to create.

In the early phases of the project, the configuration plan can start as a document of a few pages. The important points are to title the document and to place it under version control. Placing the document under version control can be as simple as assigning it a version number, which you can type directly below the title of the plan on the title page.

A convenient way to illustrate directory structures is to use SmartDraw and create a directory illustration. (See Chapter 10.) As irritating as this activity might be for a group of people who want to get on with the development of a game, the effort will pay off enormously almost immediately. If your team has the fortune of having a configuration manager, this person will be able to ask the right questions and assemble the right material in a way that will be relatively painless. If this is not the case, the team should move slowly and try to avoid doing too much too soon.

Concept Formation

Before you code, you need to plan your code. Before you plan your code, you need to understand the product you are being asked to build. To understand the product you are being asked to build, you can use a variety of well-tested tools to help you grasp and conceptualize the system you are seeking to build. A few of the best tools are discussions, lists, and diagrams.

When you begin discussing the software project, have everyone involved gain familiarity with the game design document. If you are a project manager, you might consider having duplicate paper copies made for everyone on your team. Another approach is to save the game design document to an HTML format and make it available through a project Web site. If you are in an organization that creates massive design documents, the Web site combined with paper copies of selected portions of the document is probably the best avenue to follow.

The reason for having everyone study the design document is that it acquaints everyone with the feel and intent of the game. Viewing the whole design enables each team member to feel involved with every aspect of the game. Yes, certainly, your work might stop with implementation of the engine for the game, but if you have a sense of what is going on among the graphics artists, the voice talent, the script writers, and the music composers, you are much more equipped, imaginatively, to gain satisfaction from the hours and hours you will spend fighting problems with the code. Figure 13.4 shows a rudimentary view of some of the information that the game design document provides.

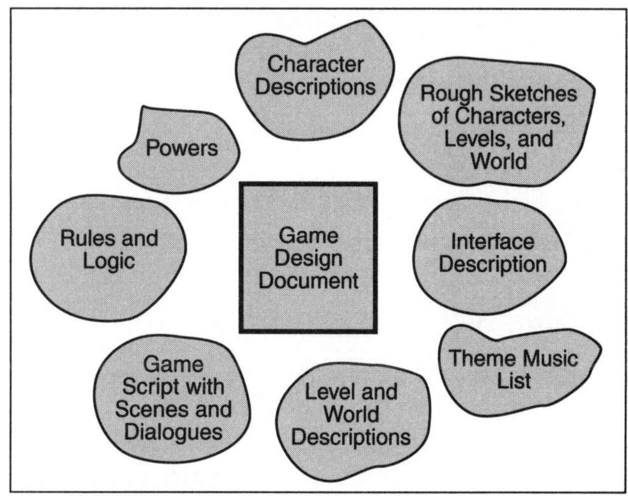

Figure 13.4
If members of the programming team read the game design document, they stand a better chance of fully understanding the game.

Requirements Ruminations

Requirements begin as a list of software functions. These functions support the features of the game. One difficult part of creating requirements involves distinguishing features from the functionality that supports them. At the start of the discussion, for example, someone might start reviewing all the different ways that the characters move around a given level. This discussion can detail everything down to how dense the polygons should be. It is good that this type of discussion takes place, but it also is important that this activity does not end with a long list of requirements specifying that the characters in the game will be able to bend their elbows or wiggle their toes. Unless you are working with software that does, indeed, reduce to creation of such functionality, chances are you will be dealing with an animated mesh that your software must load, render, and manipulate. Getting to the requirement involves seeing past the details to the core functionality that supports the features of the game.

Formalizing Requirements

As with the configuration management plan, your team benefits if you keep the requirements document as simple as possible at first. As before, a title and a version number on the title page are a good start. Following that, you can create a numbered list of the functionality that you think must be implemented if the features named in the game design document are to be supported. If you set up the requirements document in Microsoft Word, do not let the automatic numbering undermine your effort. In the effort for *Ankh*, requirements numbering involved placing angle braces around the numbers. For example, for requirement 36, the document shows <Req_36> as the number for the requirement. You must number each requirement uniquely, and you should preserve the number assigned to the requirement from the time the requirement is first recorded to the end of the project.

With the creation of requirements, it is easy to become hung up on trying to do things comprehensively the first time. Although no fixed formula can be stated, requirements might take days, weeks, or even months to formulate properly.

Working with Conceptual Tools

When you read the game design document, you discover a complex set of descriptive elements that you must reduce to a restricted set of functional elements. With some projects, getting past the details of the design document can be a harrowing experience. Details prove a plague, however, only when you forget that roughly 90 percent of the functionality evident in any game has been implemented in previous games. If you are working on your tenth game, you know this without hesitation. If you are working on your first industrial-grade game, the picture changes. Wherever you stand, however, you benefit if you put to work standard conceptual tools to elicit requirements.

Among these tools are the Task-Object-Remarks (TOR) chart, use cases, and Class-Responsibility-Collaboration (CRC) cards. The TOR chart is more a table than anything else, and you can use it as a quick way of drawing information from team members about the kinds of objects they think will be needed to implement the functionality they discern in the game design document. When the team started work on *Ankh*, the TOR chart was developed in conjunction with the requirements. The team did things this way because a tremendous amount of conceptual energy tended to be liberated as the team worked through the game design document. Notice the following bit of dialogue. (Names have been changed to conceal identities.)

ALPHA: If we are going to set up the initial game state like that, we need to have...

GAMMA: If we are going to have some sort of replay capacity, like it says here..., we will have to move from the Start menu...

EPSILON: I don't see why we have to have that. We need to save off actions according to some clock and just auto save... It's clear.

ALPHA: I wasn't talking about that. Let's just set up a state for that and go from there to replay.

GAMMA: The player needs to do this real-time. Look [holding up the game design document and pointing]. This is going to be more complex than what you are thinking.

If you cannot make sense of this conversation, don't fret. This type of talk went on for hours, everyone absorbed in one or another preconceived notion about how the game should work and no one apparently trying to hammer out any kind of supporting detail from the game design document. Still, the team made progress. The point was not to push too hard for specifics. Even with the abstraction of the preceding conversation, it was possible to elicit sound conjectures about what objects the game would require. Recording remarks and associated objects tended to create synergy. Figure 13.5 summarizes the results of the discussion that the TOR chart tracked.

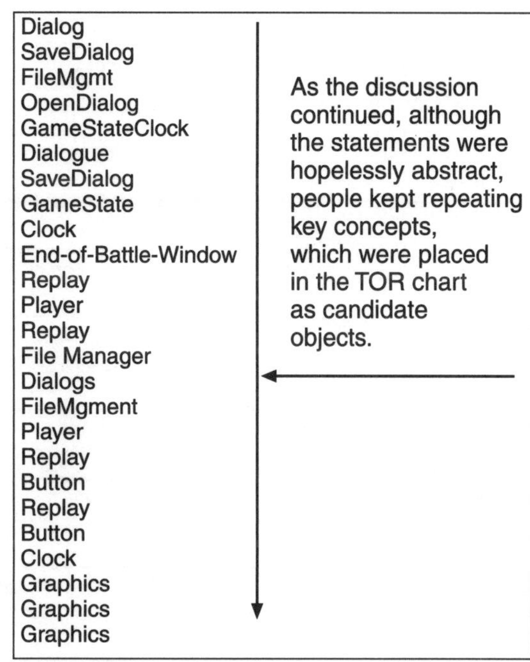

Figure 13.5
Abstract discussion resulted in words or comments that could be placed in a TOR chart, and with this effort, it became possible to focus on the core functionality of the game software.

After you have established a field of possible objects, even if many of your guesses about how the functionality of the game might be encapsulated are premature and utterly wrong, you will find that you can suddenly make statements that relate to the functionality of the game. Figure 13.6 shows a few requirements that emerged from the associations dealt with previously in the dialogue and the TOR chart.

<Req_3>
Software shall have the ability to associate user profiles with saved game files.
<Req_4>
Software shall allow the player to choose file names.
<Req_5>
Software shall have an auto-save feature that automatically saves the game constantly to memory.
<Req_6>
Software shall have a timer mechanism that will flush memory to disk periodically (every 20 seconds).
<Req_7>
Software shall provide the player the option to save a replay after a battle.
<Req_8>
Software shall have a main menu that will have a Load Replay option.
<Req_9>
Software shall save replays to a default directory where the profile info is stored.

Figure 13.6
Dialogue and work with the TOR chart render statements that begin to capture the functionality of the game.

The key to success when working with the initial, conceptual phase of a project is to keep going. Inevitably, many of the statements about functionality are going to be redundant or entirely inessential. Worrying about this is ridiculous. The greater the number of statements, the clearer the conceptual framework of the product will become and the easier it will be to tell what belongs and what does not. Setting up use cases forces you to be specific in your thinking about requirements. Figure 13.7 shows what happened when some of the requirements named in the list in Figure 13.6 were put into a use case context.

Use Case Name: User Associates Profiles
Requirement(s) Explored: 3, 9
Player (Actor) Context (Role): Player
Precondition(s): The player must have created at least one profile.
Trigger(s): The player brings up a File dialog box that asks him where to save or load either a replay or saved game.
Main Course of Action: 1. Player selects Save option. 2. The system chooses the player's default directory. 3. The system saves on the player's current profile. 4. Player exits Save option.
Alternate Course(s) of Action: 2a. Player closes without saving.
Exceptional Course(s) of Action: 2a. Memory problem; cannot save. 3a. No profile to save.

Figure 13.7
Use cases can concretize the functionality of the game.

Designing Software

After you have formulated a list of requirements and examined them through use cases, the first step toward design is to group the requirements into sets. Each set should represent a functionality that you can develop as a whole, as a separate component or module. In the work on *Ankh*, each of these sets was called a stripe.

Creating a stripe amounts to gathering the information you have and using it to plan how to develop the system and what functionality to group into a cohesive set. Like requirements, stripes tend to take on greater definition as you create more of them. An extremely effective tool for grouping functionality is the CRC card. Creating CRC cards involves taking responsibility for a given type of functionality, assigning it to an object, and then determining what other objects you need to support the functionality.

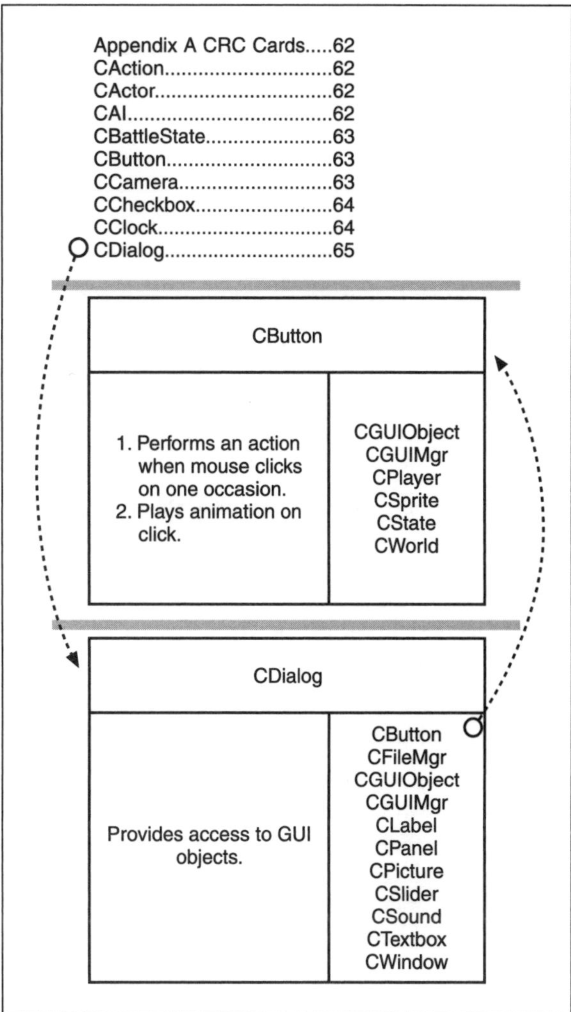

Figure 13.8
Creating a comprehensive set of CRC cards that captures the functionality stated in the requirements document enables you to group objects for design purposes.

The *Ankh* development team placed the CRC cards in tables and included the tables, in alphabetical order, as an appendix to the *Ankh Software Design Specification.* Hyperlinks to the table of contents made it easy to access the CRC listings. Figure 13.8 illustrates the extension and refinement of the initial object list using CRC cards.

Stripes emerge from clusters of activity. You can derive them empirically from inspection of a comprehensive set of CRC cards. You can use object diagrams and sequence diagrams to give them reality. To test your hypotheses about how to group classes, use a use case. Figure 13.9 shows an object diagram for the Use Slider use case. In the design of *Ankh*, this is Stripe 2.1.

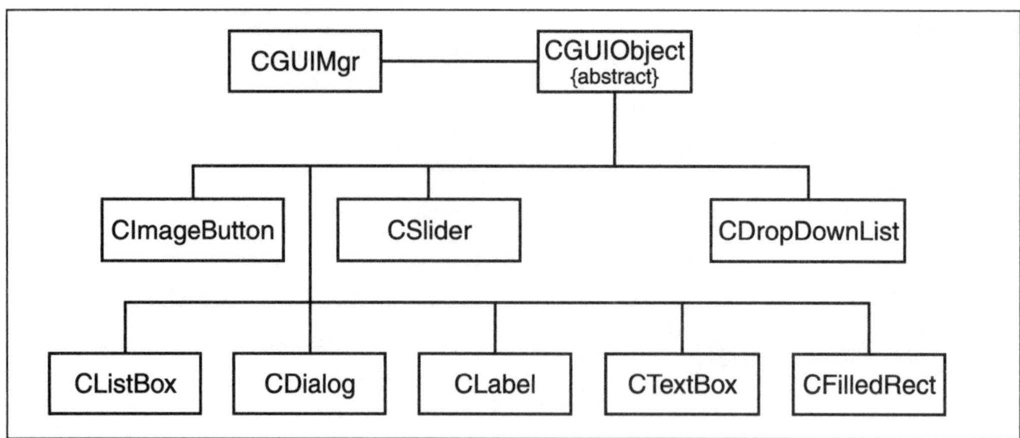

Figure 13.9
An object diagram shows the relationships among objects in a stripe.

After a time, stripes account for all the requirements you have documented, and at this point, the first iteration of your design is complete. Just because you have managed to account for all the requirements by creating objects and then groupings of objects does not indicate the end of the design task, however. In addition to grouping objects, you have a great deal of work to do to ensure that redundancies and inefficiencies are eliminated. A software designer might work from both the stack of CRC cards and a set of patterns. Patterns are ways of putting objects in communication with each other.

Testing

Testing should begin early, and whatever can be tested should. Testing at the start of a project involves analysis. Generally, analysis differs from the type of testing that many people picture. Although this topic is covered in detail in Chapter 11, "Evident Evil—The Art of Testing," it is worthwhile to mention here that the notion that testing begins after development concludes represents an antiquated view of software development. Such a view of testing tends to focus too heavily on testing execution, on the notion that testing has to do with code. This is true enough, but testing also has to do with everything *related* to the code, including requirements, design, and documentation.

As applied to requirements and design, one focus of testing can be on the testability of requirements and use cases. As developers develop use cases for requirements, for example, testers can evaluate the use cases to determine whether they can provide suitable scenarios for test cases and test suites. One of the most reliable *testability* criteria for any given use case is whether it provides enough information to allow a tester to determine input to the use case and the anticipated result of the use case. The tester requires such information to write the test case.

You also can test use cases to determine whether they pose varying degrees of risk. As Chapter 8, "Risk Analysis," reviews, several categories of risk apply to a software engineering project, but one of special interest during the startup phase of a software project concerns the likelihood that a requirement will change. Testers are in a position to analyze the relative stability of requirements and to anticipate, to some extent, the need to develop stronger or more varied test cases to anticipate changes.

Project Planning

Stripes constitute the architecture of the game. After the architecture is in place, you can begin planning how to develop the software. This book does not offer an extensive discussion of project planning. Such a discussion, although important to the work of software engineering, belongs more to the realm of management than development. Still, the best approach to accurate planning for the development of a software product, game or otherwise, is to break the development activity into tasks. You can view each stripe as a set of tasks. Each stripe requires the implementation of classes that provide functionality stipulated by the requirements document. Each class, in turn, consists of operations and attributes. When programmers can see things in such basic terms, they can make at least ballpark estimations of how much effort is required to implement a stripe. (Figure 13.15 illustrates the stripes in the *Ankh* software design.)

The project manager must assemble estimations, identify dependencies, and sort tasks into a unified production schedule. Microsoft Project remains the premier tool for performing this work, but even without that software, a project manager can create a project schedule in good time if the software design provides a clear breakdown of the components of the system. For *Ankh*, the design ended up featuring 18 stripes, and each stripe represented one or two weeks of development time. Likewise, dependencies related to graphical and sound assets must be included in the estimations. (Figure 13.16 shows you a Microsoft Project view of the schedule for the *Ankh* development project.)

Beginning Development

This book advocates an iterative and incremental approach to development. As reviewed in Chapter 9, "Iterating Design," much is to be gained from making the project into a process that allows you to improve your understanding continuously of the design of the product and how you implement the design. The fact that you design the product as a set of stripes and then undertake the creation of each stripe in succession makes the development effort iterative. The fact that you perform testing and risk analysis during each iteration makes the development process incremental.

If you can learn as you go, you can improve your development effort. For this reason, it is important that you begin development so that you allow for learning. Likewise, it is important that you begin development using a design that gives you a solid sense of how and when you can implement the functionality that the requirements specify. As you go, if you work incrementally and iteratively toward complete implementation of the functionality, you are in an excellent position to manage things like changes in the requirements, problems with the design, and disruptions in the development schedule.

Design Again—Low Level

From an object-oriented design perspective, a stripe represents a subset of the total functionality of the game that you have determined can be addressed best in a single set of classes. In this book, a stripe is pictured as a component or package. The UML package diagram shows a stripe as a set of classes that communicate with each other and share a common responsibility. (See Figure 13.15 for the design as embodied in stripes.)

Design on a low level involves investigating the elements of a stripe at the class level. You can proceed with this work in two directions. In one direction, you can create class and operation specifications. You can create a class definition by using a UML class diagram, which shows you the operations and attributes of a class. The operation specification investigates the logic of a given operation within a class. In the other direction, you can work with sequence and collaboration diagrams to investigate how classes use operations to send messages to each other.

In highly evolved engineering contexts, UML-based CASE tools allow software engineers to create software systems in minute detail before code is written. From a cottage industry standpoint, UML allows developers to conceptualize their coding project. A UML diagram or a use case provides a proof of concept, a way to visualize, before the implementation work begins. The contention in this book is that such work is highly beneficial even if it does not result in reversible engineering products.

One approach to analyzing a stripe is to subject the objects that comprise the implemented stripe to scrutiny using sequence and collaboration diagrams. This type of scrutiny involves a good deal of give and take. For every functional stripe of *Ankh*, the development team set the ground rule that development could not begin unless it had tested the concept of the stripe through at least a use case, an object diagram, and either a sequence or a collaboration diagram. For Stripe 2.1, for example, in addition to the use case and the object diagram, the team created a sequence diagram. Figure 13.10 illustrates this diagram.

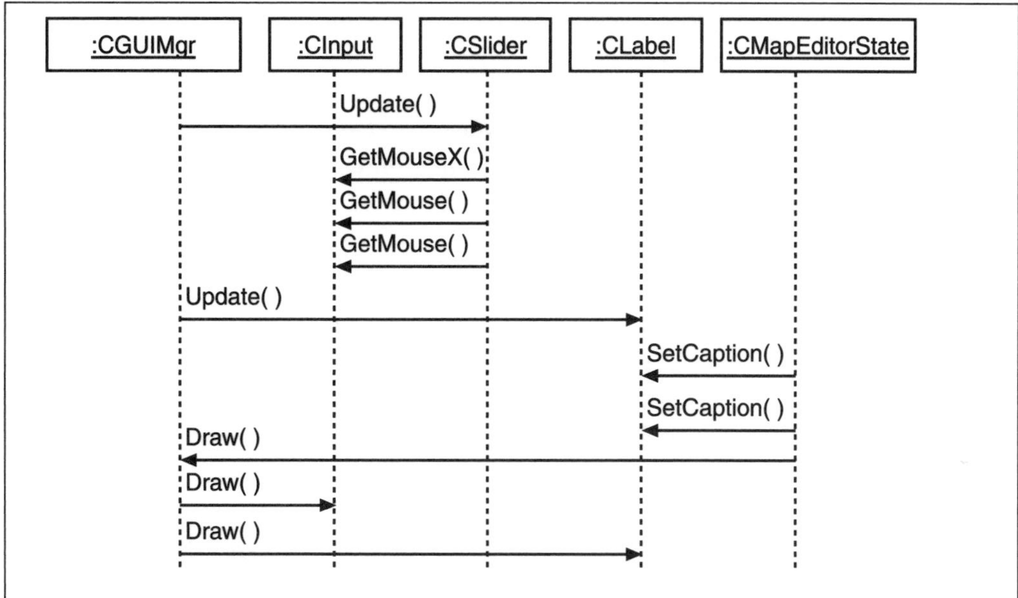

Figure 13.10
A sequence diagram serves as a proof of concept.

As is reviewed in Chapter 3, "A Tutorial: UML and Object-Oriented Programming," the type of arrow you see in this diagram indicates a simple message. A simple message arrow can indicate that when an operation executes, it might or might not receive acknowledgement for the message it issues. In other words, whether it is synchronous or asynchronous is not shown. Many other specifics are omitted from the diagram, and under close scrutiny, you see that the technical details in the diagram are lacking. But precision was not the purpose of the exercise. Rather, the purpose of the exercise was to explore conceptually how objects in this stripe might communicate with each other. As a result of the exercise, several notions resulted:

- **Scope.** Use of the objects in a generic fashion allowed the team to determine whether their assessment of the objects designated for the stripe was accurate.
- **Complexity.** Establishing a sequence of messaging based on the scenario laid out in the use case (see the previous section titled "Working with Conceptual Tools") offered an approach to the functionality that the team could deal with in a straightforward way. Had the sequence diagram revealed a long, involved set of operations that exchanged complex messages, further analysis would have been merited.
- **Feasibility.** Being forced, up front, to envision the sequence of messages and the operations involved in sending the messages forced the team to consider the degree to which it would be feasible to implement the functionality embodied in the

stripe. Discovering whether you can envision the service that the stripe is responsible for as a sequence of messages issued by a finite set of operations establishes a starting point for the stripe implementation.

- **Familiarity.** A final contribution of the sequence diagram to the design effort arises with the familiarity that the development team acquires of the design of the game.

Configuration Formalities

Setting up the configuration management elements of the project involves, first, creating a file structure. As a preliminary measure, the *Ankh* team established the basic directory structure and the basics of a file-naming system. These did not correspond to the stripes. There were several reasons for not establishing a directory structure based on stripes. One was that even with a substantial design effort, the risk of changes remained pronounced, and making any change in the directory structure introduced difficulties. Another downside was complexity. During early iterations, the stripes totaled 12. This number increased to 18 by the end of the project. Duplicating directory structures across stripes made management through CVS difficult and threatened to absorb an inordinate amount of disk space. The best approach, then, lay in developing the directory structure according to what the development team considered to be a standard game layout scheme. Figure 13.11 shows a partial breakout of the file structure and the implementation files for the initial stripes.

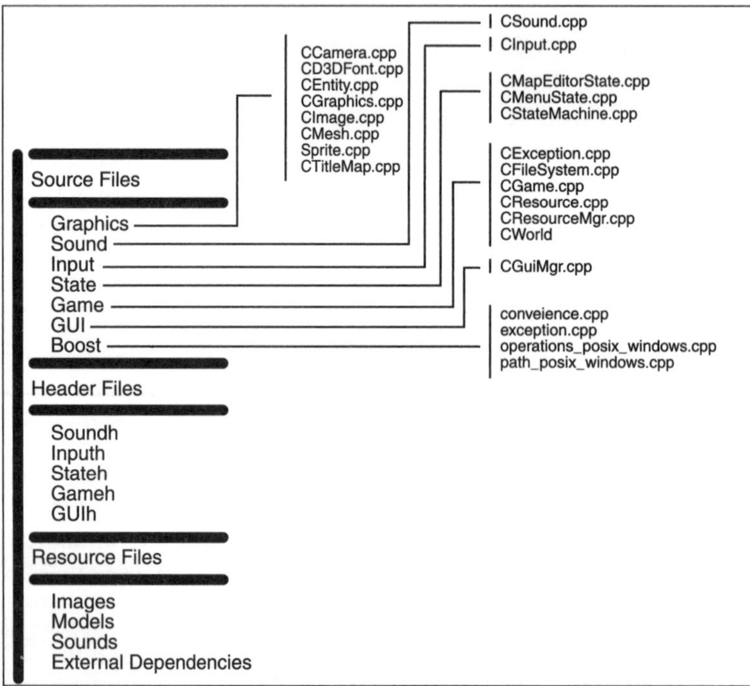

Figure 13.11
The file structure allows files to be organized into standard categories.

Along with the creation of a file structure and file-naming conventions, setting up a CVS server becomes essential. At this point, everyone in the project should establish client sessions with the server and download the current stripe to test connectivity and become familiar with the workings of the system. Formalized configuration management involves documenting naming conventions and setting up CVS.

Coding Conventions

If you work in an organization that has achieved some level of maturity, chances are that someone has created a document that captures the coding conventions agreed upon by the development group. If this is not the case, the team should take time to create a set of coding standards. Everyone on the team should participate in this effort.

Developing coding standards usually involves meeting as a team and working through a list of standard coding issues. If you have not yet had the experience of becoming embroiled in a dispute with other developers over things like the placement of braces or what should be capitalized, be forewarned. The intensity of the exchanges can be startling, especially when someone speaks in a derogatory or disparaging way about one of your favorite practices.

Because establishing coding standards can be a difficult undertaking, this activity affords the members of a team an opportunity to introduce early in the project practices for conducting team reviews. One practice is to set up a board of arbitrators that consists of the three most senior developers. Discussion can go on for as long as anyone has anything to say, but following the discussion, the arbitrators should take a vote to determine whether the standard is adopted or put aside.

Several good books provide coding conventions, and one approach to reducing controversies is to adopt the standards that one of these books presents. This can at least offer a starting point. Another option is to assemble a set of central coding issues. Developers can then work through these and arrive at a first set of conventions. The following list provides a few such issues:

- Naming classes
- Naming class objects
- Naming operations
- Naming class attributes
- Type identity prefixes
- Length of names
- Length of lines
- Breaking lines
- Using white space
- Naming accessor and mutator operations
- Summary comments for classes
- Summary comments for operations
- Comments for parameters
- Comments within operations
- Documentation of known defects
- Labeling closing braces
- Setting tabs

- Using scope
- Using break statements
- Using exceptions
- Using threads
- Creating global operations
- Creating global variables
- Using define statements
- Using typedef
- Using include statements
- Unacceptable practices
- File names and class names

It is good practice to publish online the document in which you list your team's coding conventions. You also can appoint an administrator to whom comments can be sent. Later in the project, if time allows, someone might be prompted to provide code samples to illustrate accepted usage. Beware that this activity is usually involved. When you cut and paste code samples for use in a Web page, you sometimes have to spend a great deal of time massaging a few lines of code so that they conform to something as simple as a tabbing convention.

Libraries and Resources

If you intend to use libraries or resources, either the project manager or an experienced developer should establish at the start of the project formal permission to use the libraries or resources. Design decisions that make assumptions about libraries and resources pose tremendous risks. At the same time, a team consisting of a programmer and a tester (or at least someone with both perspectives on software) should assess prospective libraries to verify the following:

- They provide the functionality sought.
- They will work on the targeted platform.
- They can be accessed in time.
- They are supported in the right ways.

Also, even in what you assume to be the most elementary situations, you need to establish which version of a library you intend to use. During the development period, the library you use likely will be released in a new version. You should identify clearly the features of the library that you must have and evaluate whether new releases of the library will continue to support these features.

Working with Specifications and Plans

Some approaches to software development advocate dedicating up to two-thirds of the project development time to shaping the concept of the product. Figure 13.12 shows a pie approximation of this approach to development. As a general rule, the more time you spend planning implementation, the less time you spend implementing. Reasons for this become evident after a little reflection. Consider, for example, what happens if you begin implementation without planning and cram a massive number of operations into a single class. You then develop several classes with dependencies on the first class. But then you find that you want to separate the functionality of the first class into several smaller classes. The result is that you must rewrite lots of code. Planning would have eliminated the need for the rewriting and reduced the overall time required for implementation.

Planning involves documents, lists, diagrams, and discussions. For this reason, naming documents amounts to naming types of thinking and questioning that characterize product development. A document represents an occasion for thinking and questioning. That you work with a template, write passages, and add diagrams is in many ways secondary. The primary work is that of shaping ideas and planning development activities.

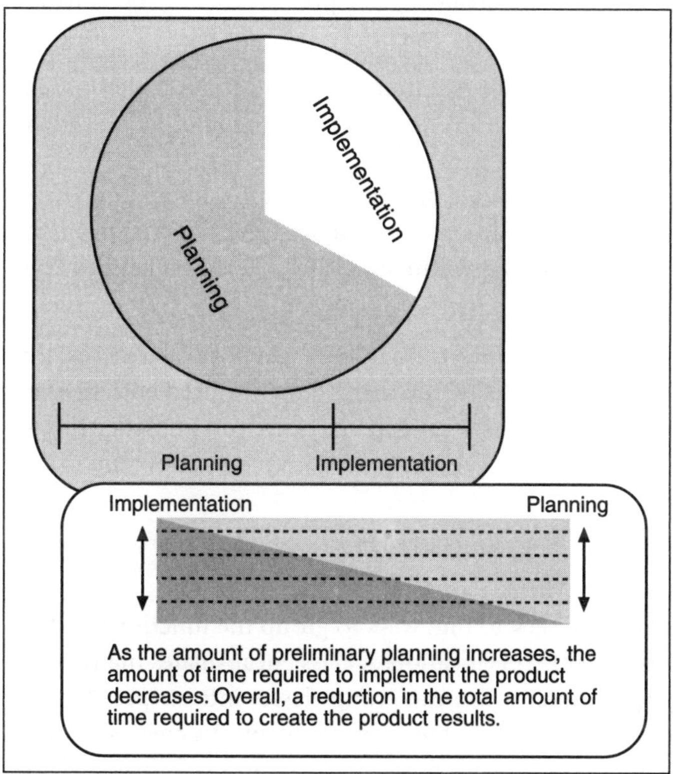

Figure 13.12
Time invested in planning a product reduces the time required to implement it.

The documents discussed under the next few headings represent responsibilities that a development team can assume as it plans a product. They also can represent responsibilities that a development team can assume as it audits its progress in following through on its plans. Different approaches to development advocate different ways of planning and tracking development activity. The Software Engineering Body of Knowledge (SWEBOK) provides the most comprehensive view of ways to plan and track software development. What is presented here represents a partial view.

Requirements

One of the primary purposes of a software requirements document is to establish, internally and externally, the scope of the game. In other words, you have to know how intensive your development effort is going to be in terms of doing something new, and you have to know what kind of game is going to be created. As a preliminary to the software requirements document, you can write a scope statement.

Another primary purpose for creating software requirements is to produce a list of sentences that state what functionality you must implement to cover the internal and external scope of the product. If you are creating a game, the functionality of the software at best tends to express indirectly the features you see named in the game design document. If you are creating a set of components for collision detection or graphical rendering, the abstraction tends to be even more pronounced. Ultimately, this is what makes development of requirements difficult.

To reduce the difficulty of moving from features to functional support of features, this book suggests that you work with both stated requirements and requirements that are presented as use cases. If you employ both statements and use cases, you immediately can create a context in which the different ways you present the requirements allow you to discern ways to refine and test them.

Design

When you design a software system, you seek to find ways to group the functionality that is established in the software requirements specification. A class encapsulates many operations. This is one way to group functionality. You can group classes into stripes. A stripe groups classes that fulfill a common responsibility. For example, Stripe 2.4 creates the map editor and displays a set of meshes. Players at this point can load and save maps. Figure 13.13 shows the visible manifestation of the implementation of Stripe 2.4.

Figure 13.13
Each design stripe groups responsibilities to address specified functionality.

You can illustrate the operations that are key to this stripe in a UML sequence diagram. The *Ankh Software Design Specification* provides separate sections for each stripe. Each section, at a minimum, provides a use case, a sequence or collaboration diagram, and a package diagram. Figure 13.14 illustrates the sequence diagram that appears for Stripe 2.4. Note that the purpose of the sequence diagram as used by the *Ankh* team was not to reduce things to minute details of implementation but to test the general conceptual validity of the stripe. Using class, sequence, and other diagrams, the team could gain several views of the game software for each stripe. Creating such diagrams, regardless of how preliminary, helped the team comprehend the scope of the software and understand the effort involved in its creation.

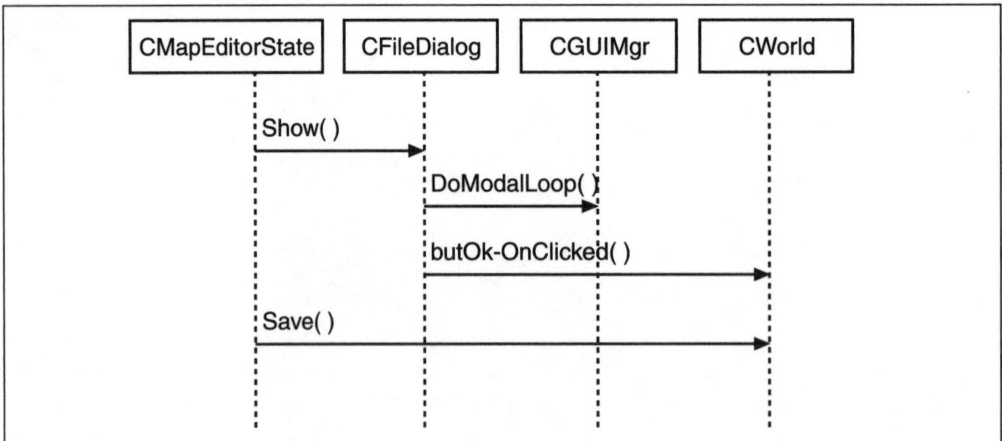

Figure 13.14
Documentation aids with conceptualization and the practical tasks involved in planning how and when to construct the stripe.

In Figure 13.15, a package diagram illustrates the relationship among the stripes that constitute the system. The segmented lines show paths of development. In roughly half the cases, a given path resulted from the selection of one among several paths. In other cases, dependencies determined the paths. Developing Stripe 1 was a precondition for Stripes 2.1, 2.2, 2.3, and 2.4. The completion of these opened the path to Stripes 3.1 and 3.2, and either might have been developed first. Later on, with Stripe 10, any of the final four stripes lay open for development. Precisely how to proceed with the development efforts requires an evaluation of risks, work schedules, and external dependencies.

Project Plan

You can unfold the project plan, in its general layout, from the design document. See Figure 13.16. Determining how long development of each stripe requires involves using the material derived from the design process to create detailed work breakdown schedules. You can take several approaches to this. With the *Ankh* team, a reliable technique was to project the object and sequence diagrams for a given stripe onto a big screen. The team then evaluated the stripe and came up with estimations of the required effort. From there, discovering the duration of the effort involved determining who had expertise to complete specific tasks and whether and how the tasks could be distributed.

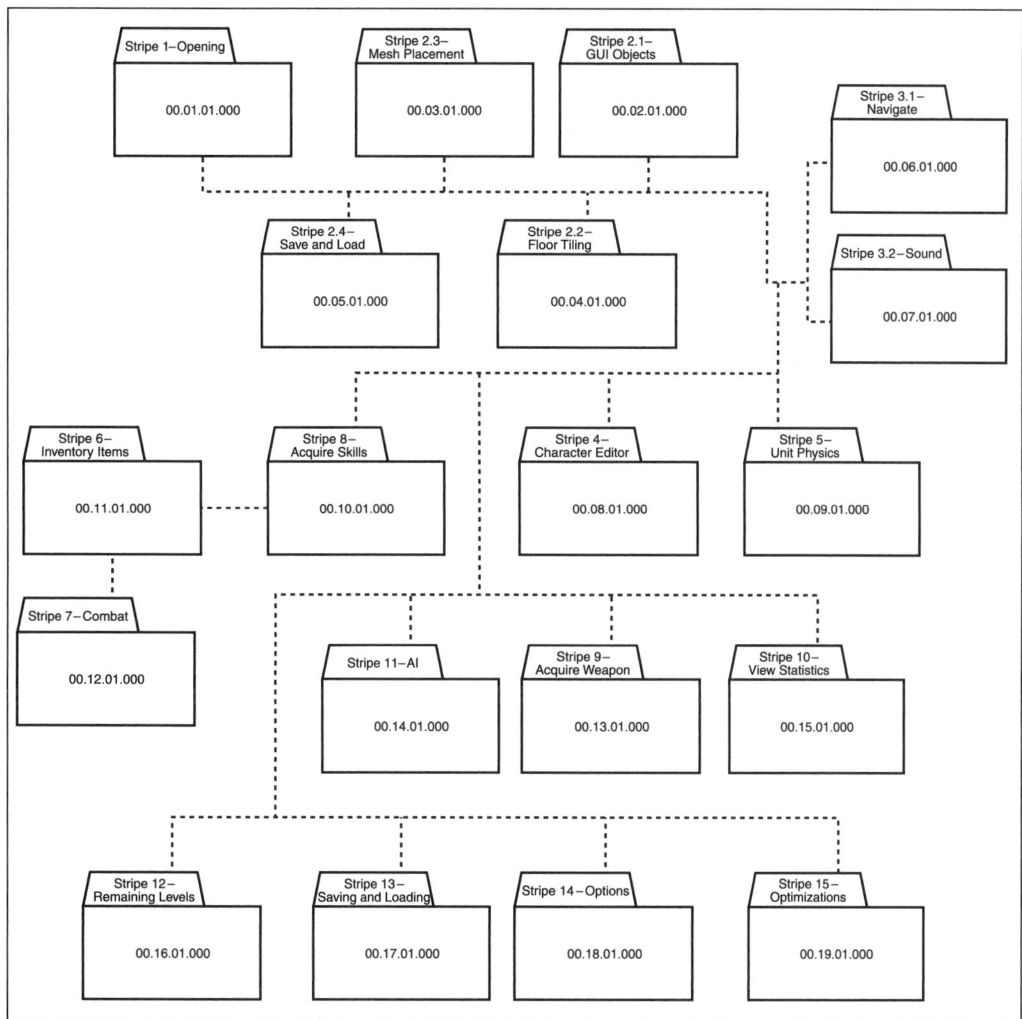

Figure 13.15
The final component system view of the game software provides a conceptual pathway through the development project, but the final decision of what to do rests with the decisions that go into the project plan.

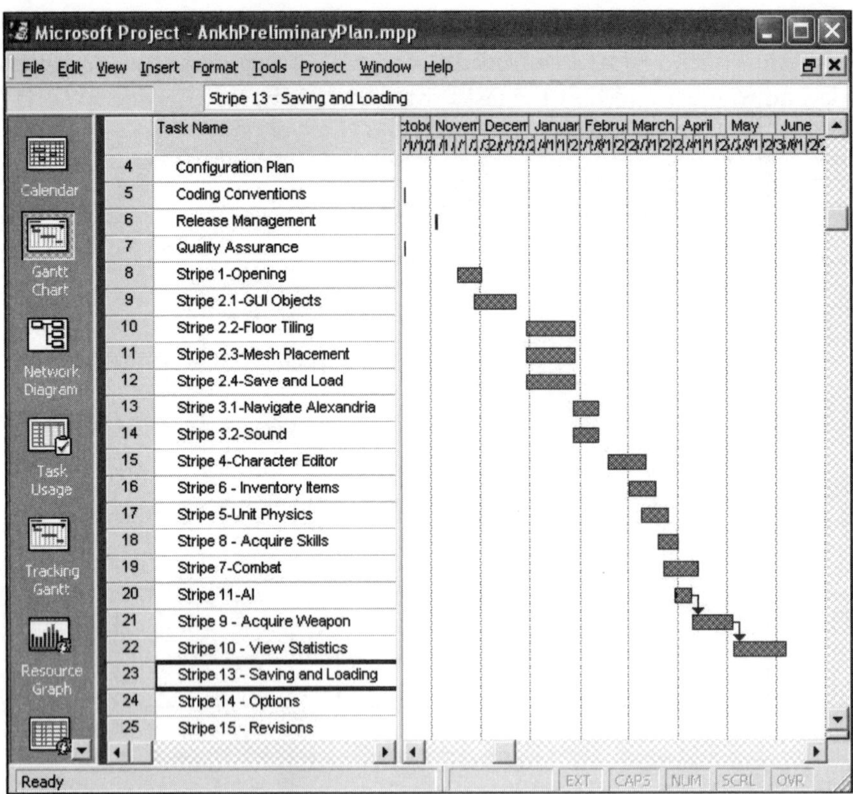

Figure 13.16
To arrive at an initial schedule, use the stripe information you derive from the software design document.

Configuration Management and Version Control

Before you begin coding, create a configuration management plan. The plan needs to be complete enough to show you how to name the files for the first few stripes. Earlier in this chapter, under the heading "Configuration Formalities," a basic directory structure was shown. In addition to the layout of the directory structure, you need to list a standard check-in and check-out procedure. A numbered list of actions to be performed will suffice. You also need to set up a version control system. With the *Ankh* team, the entire team watched as the lead programmer went through a standard development session. Everyone had a chance to ask questions, make suggestions for changes, and generally become familiar with what was to become a standard procedure. Figure 13.17 provides a view of the TortoiseCVS system being used to access Stripe 1.

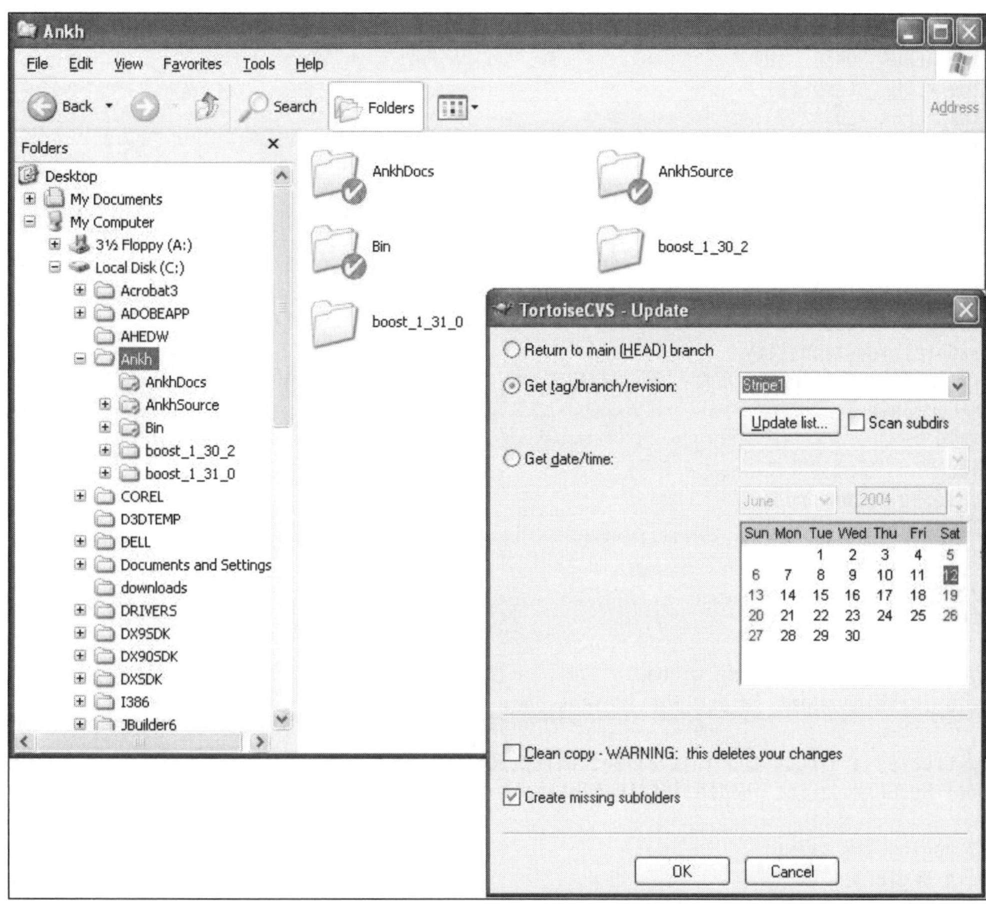

Figure 13.17
TortoiseCVS provides a client that integrates with Windows Explorer.

Applying Coding Conventions

Even after the team has initially agreed on a set of coding conventions, it should test the conventions against the first stripe. One approach is to have the lead programmer code the first stripe. Then, using the written conventions as a basis of examination, walk through the code as a team. The code for the first stripe of *Ankh* provided the team with a way to determine whether the coding conventions resulted in a format that everyone on the team found acceptable:

```
//file name: CGraphics.h
#ifndef CGRAPHICS_INCLUDED
#define CGRAPHICS_INCLUDED 1
extern class CGraphics *Graphics;

// Blender mode definition
#define ALPHA_NONE   (0)
#define ALPHA_BLEND (1)
#define ALPHA_ADD   (2)
#define ALPHA_ADD2X (3)
#define ALPHA_ADD4X (4)
#define ALPHA_SUB   (5)

//////////////////////////////////////////////////////
// The CGraphics class is a wrapper               //
// around Direct3D and all Windows                //
// graphics functionality.                        //
//////////////////////////////////////////////////////
class CGraphics
{
public:
   // Default constructor
   CGraphics();

   // Default destructor
   ~CGraphics();

   // Creates the main game window
   void InitWindow(int iWidth,int iHeight,bool bWindowed);

   // Creates a window and initializes Direct3D
   bool SetGFXMode(int iWidth,int iHeight,bool bWindowed);

   // Begins the scene
   void Begin();

   // Ends the scene (and presents the backbuffer)
   void End();

   // Clears the screen to the given color
   void Clear(D3DCOLOR Color);

   // Sets an orthogonal view matrix for viewing
       // 2D screen elements
   void SetOrthoView();

   // Sets a 3D matrix up
   void Set3DView();
```

```
    // Sets the current alpha blend mode
    void SetBlendMode(int mode);

    // Get and Set Methods ////////////////////////////////
    // Gets the Direct3D Device
          IDirect3DDevice9* GetDevice(){return m_d3dDevice;}
    ////////////////////////////////////////////////////////

private:
    // Window handle
    HANDLE m_hWnd;

    // Width and height of the window
    int m_iWidth,m_iHeight;

    // Are we in fullscreen mode
    bool m_bWindowed;

    // Direct3D interfaces
    IDirect3D9* m_d3d;
    IDirect3DDevice9* m_d3dDevice;

    // Finds the best pixel format to use for fullscreen mode
    D3DFORMAT FindPixelFormat(IDirect3D9* d3d);
};
#endif
```

As an example of the discussion that resulted from the walkthrough, consider the following observations:

1. Comments should precede an operation.
2. Comments put on the right side tend to be hard to find.
3. Comments should, if possible, start on the left side of the page.
4. No space should come between the pointer asterisk and the type to which the asterisk applies.
5. If the comment is just one sentence, no period is needed.
6. For an inline operation that has elementary content, it is okay to put the entire operation on one line.

At the start of a project, it is easy to amend coding conventions. As time goes on, people become more defensive about their practices, but it is never too late to question a practice that causes problems. To avoid hot disputes, you can always ask questions during code walkthroughs. If other developers have questions similar to your own, you can slate the issue as a prospective addition to the conventions list. To formalize the addition of a convention, if you have set up a Web page for conventions, you can publish the proposed change in a clearly identified "Proposed Changes and Additions" section. It is generally a good idea to make this as objective as possible. State the proposed convention and nothing more. Depending on how your organization does things, you can then set aside a meeting for discussion of proposed conventions and vote on changes. The entire team should review conventions before they are designated as standard for the development effort.

Test Plan

Testers can begin writing test cases as soon as the requirements are complete. They also can work during the requirements phase to review the requirements for conceptual and practical completeness. The effort extends to the design work, too.

Testing is a separate activity from programming, but it is clearly associated with programming. Testing requires a special set of skills. Even if you possess these skills, it is generally acknowledged that you cannot reliably test your own code. Reliable testing requires the intervention of someone who possesses a perspective developed separately from the perspective of the person who creates the code. Chapter 11 gives considerable attention to this topic. One outcome of the discussion is the observation that because testers provide a special perspective on all aspects of the development effort, they have a claim to the requirements and design documents. Their claim is that of assessing such artifacts early on to determine whether they are valid and verifiable as guides for development.

In addition to increasing their knowledge of the software through conceptual analysis and documentation review, testers can benefit from early inclusion in a project because they can begin developing test tools as soon as they comprehend the scope of the project. In many cases, they will want to acquire existing tools and modify them for the current effort. The team should budget such activity into the project from the start.

Release Plan

At the start of the project, the team should devote some attention to the release plan because it can reveal dependencies that require time to settle. Among such dependencies are legal contracts with vendors or suppliers. You might be able to acquire a library or a collection of resources almost overnight, but the legal intricacies of securing rights to such items could require months of negotiation. If any such dependencies exist, you should anticipate them from the start. If the release plan consists of nothing more than a numbered list of items appended to a section of the configuration management plan, it still serves its purpose. Regardless of where the information is formalized, it allows the project manager to include tasks relating to it in the project plan. Such scheduling ensures that finalization of the plan will be accomplished before final testing and release activities begin. As the time approaches for the release activities to begin in earnest, the team can appoint a release manager and develop a formal release plan.

Quality Assurance Plan

The Quality Assurance (QA) plan can be much simpler than it sounds. This plan tells you what artifacts you are going to create and how you are going to manage them. The QA plan does not have to include, at the beginning of the project, anything beyond a list of the major deliverables for the project and the reviews you intend to use to confirm them. Following are a few points that you might consider addressing in the initial QA plan:

- **Procedures and protocols.** If you want to name external standards to apply to your project, you can name them in the QA plan and then elaborate on them during the first few weeks of the project. Include a list of the documents that you must create for the project. In the configuration management plan, an important decision to make at the start of the project is what will constitute a baseline of the product and when baselines will be captured. You should also determine a numbering system for baselines.
- **Review practices.** Establish a standard procedure for conducting reviews. Such a procedure does not need to be much more than a numbered list of how a procedure can take place. During the *Ankh* development effort, the development team conducted reviews by viewing the document projected onto a screen that everyone could see. One person, the scribe, edited the document while others made comments. The editing of the document usually took place with the Track Changes option of Microsoft Word turned on. At the conclusion of the review, if the team voiced consensus, the changes were accepted. Accepting the changes usually involved saving a version of the document, with the changes still visible, to an archive. After you save a version that shows the changes, you can accept the changes in your working document.
- **Assessing progress against the design specification.** After the team completes the code for each stripe, it should perform a review. Conduct of this review consists of assembling the team and inspecting the software design specification and the code for the current stripe. Again, with the *Ankh* development effort, documents and code files usually were projected onto a screen for general inspection. Assessing the code against the design involved checking to see how closely class implementation, messaging, design patterns, and other implementation features expressed the architecture and spirit of the design. Further, the team could tune the design to reflect discoveries and realities.
- **Determining the next step.** In most of the classical models of iterative, incremental development, the development team assesses risks before proceeding from one iteration to the next. The development team for *Ankh* followed this course of action but also tried to pursue a proactive agenda. Although the team reviewed the design in light of lessons learned from the stripe it had just completed, it also

assessed its approach to development and attempted to designate policies or practices that could improve its productivity and the quality of its work during the next iteration. The team made changes in the quality assurance plan or the configuration plan if it could formulate policies for improving the development process.

- **Formalizing baselines.** A baseline differs from a version of a build or a version of a document because it is a formally defined entity and consists of a collection of everything that defines the project at the time of the baseline. It makes sense to baseline the product after each stripe is completed. This strategy falls in line with that of conducting a review of work performed.
- **Altering design.** Altering design differs from assessing or tuning the design. When you alter the design, you decide to do something significant, such as splitting a stripe into parts or merging initially separate stripes. In other words, you make changes that can impact the design heavily and, by extension, the development schedule. This is a perfectly reasonable course of conduct in many situations. Among the more common situations might be those in which you discover that a stripe is so complex that it poses a major risk to the project because it forces you to wait weeks or months before you can complete it to the point that you can test it fully. Another situation is one in which you discover a way to reduce redundancy if you merge two stripes.
- **Assessing and altering requirements.** Altering requirements creates potential problems, but it also can improve the product. The Agile approach to development advocates changing requirements. This book suggests that you change requirements only after extensive deliberation. If you alter a requirement, you should analyze risks to determine whether the change adversely impacts the development effort. Likewise, any time you change a requirement, you should update the requirements, design, and testing documents to reflect the change.

Settling Disputes

Disputes happen. The best thing to do is deal with them as they arise and bring them to closure through definitive actions. Often, the project manager must be the one who determines how to resolve disputes. It is far better to irritate a few members of the team momentarily with a strong decision than it is to allow differences to grow until they begin to absorb significant amounts of time and energy. Here are some contact points for dealing with disputes:

- **Detecting disputes.** If you are on the team in a nonmanagement position and you see that a couple of people are having a hard time finding common ground, the best route is to mention the problem to the project manager in a disinterested way. Concentrate on the issue. The disputes worth worrying about are those that involve central issues. If the dispute involves personalities, it is still worth worrying about, but settlement of such disputes is usually a matter that people can manage on their own. With technical issues, however, everyone involved could have a valid point, and the discussion or argumentation could go on for weeks.

- **Formalizing the issues.** You can settle technical issues if you pose them scientifically. You can view an issue as a scientific hypothesis, and a hypothesis is a statement that is settled according to data that experimentation provides. One way to pose a technical issue in this way is to create a table that contains criteria you can use, pro and con, to evaluate the issue. After you have created the table, you can distribute it at a meeting and specifically assess the information it contains. You can take votes and score each alternative if necessary.
- **Deciding how to proceed.** It does no good to decide in favor of a given technical alternative and then do nothing to pursue the alternative. For this reason, you should develop a plan to put in place any change in technology or process that the resolution of a dispute has brought about.
- **Preserving good information.** It is good to preserve information that relates to both winning and losing sides of a dispute. The resolution of a dispute sometimes leads to the wrong decision. If the decision is wrong, everyone will discover the consequence soon. At that point, the key to survival might be to move immediately toward the rejected alternative.

Reaching the Goal

Moving toward the final release involves changing gears in a number of ways. Development activity ceases and maintenance programming (in the form of defect elimination) begins. In addition, the responsibilities of the person who is viewed as the lead developer can shift or change. For example, a release manager, who might not be a technical person, might suddenly become the most visible person on the team. At least temporarily, like a pilot guiding a ship to open water, the release manager must be in command of the ship.

Alpha and Beta

You should schedule the completion of the release plan to accord with the code completion data. You can tune the plan with the data you gather during the project. The release plan should detail what preliminary releases you intend to create and distribute. It also should describe how you want to interact with your customer group. With respect to alpha and beta releases, the major criteria for choosing to pursue them are as follows:

- **Alpha.** You are not yet comfortable with the features of your game. A reliable group of game players and testers is available inside your organization. You have set up a way they can report their findings as they use the game. Even if the functionality is not stable or complete, you are interested in knowing how it is working and whether it possesses appeal. As it is, however, the game is too rough to turn over to inexperienced players or users. You need a friendly audience.

- **Beta.** The functionality of the game is complete but still needs testing. Testers within your organization have given the game a thorough going over, but you think it is best to subject it to an external testing group that consists of prospective or actual customers. You have set up a way that your customers can report their experiences, and you have established an agreement with your customers that clearly defines boundaries and liabilities. You are interested in tracking down every possible defect in the product. Only when the users find a particularly obnoxious problem with the game will you consider changing its specified functionality.

Gathering It Together

Final release should take place according to the release plan and under the command of the release manager. As a general rule, the final approval for release of the product should occur only after the release manager has called together the members of the release management team and polled them, one by one, to secure from them an affirmation that the product is ready to release. A good idea is to have a form with a blank next to the title and position of each person on the team. Although such a document is not likely to represent a legal liability for those who sign it (although this can be the case), it can at least make everyone involved pause for a moment to think about whether the product is really ready to go. Here are some items for consideration:

- The team has completed every item in the project plan.
- The team has logged every defect.
- The team has obtained all the permissions for assets and libraries.
- The team has packaged the product correctly and tested the delivery, which is flawless.
- The configuration manager has archived the final baseline of the product, and members of the team know where to find the material.

You might think that this is going a bit overboard, but consider a scenario in which things go wrong. Suppose, for example, that you have a company that consists of seven people. The seventh is a dynamic woman who agreed to come aboard as your marketing representative a few weeks before you finished your game. She went out into the world, found a publisher, and negotiated a contract to guarantee you royalties far beyond anything you ever imagined. The final day arrives, and you ship your product to the publisher. Well, it turns out that the game was really not done. It seems that you included in your game a few assets from a popular artist, and someone forgot to secure rights. The next thing you know, you have no royalties, your marketing genius has abandoned you, and the artist is demanding payment.

Formalize release activities.

Reviewing the Project

Postmortem is the term usually applied to an assessment that the team makes of the development effort after the product has been released. Any organization that seeks to achieve a higher standing according to a maturity model must use some form of postmortem for every project, successful or otherwise. It is from the vantage point of a concluded effort that you can gather information that you can use to improve processes. Whether the project is successful does not matter. If you have failed to meet deadlines and ultimately not implemented the functionality, you can still learn from your efforts.

Here is information that is worth keeping and assessing:

- **Schedule information.** If you have estimations that you can compare to actual times, do so, and see if you can arrive at some generalities about how much, in percentiles, you were over or under on your estimations. If possible, examine work breakdown information to discover which tasks were off. This will allow you to tune future efforts more finely.
- **Testing information.** Find out how many defects plague which stripes. If possible, sort defects according to general categories. Consider, for example, defects of logic, defects of design, and defects related to performance. Likewise, try to summarize information relating to the testing of classes as opposed to stripes. Also examine logs of what alpha and beta tests revealed. Such information can aid in future development efforts by helping programmers be on the alert for practices that might promote defects. Such information also can be useful to testers for the design of testing tools or test suites for future projects.
- **Process information.** In a group session, elicit opinions about what did and did not work. Generally, everyone can learn something from such talks. A project manager might be able to make use of such knowledge if it is formalized in future project plans, but it is also the case that everyone can better understand the work of developing a game if the team takes time to discuss the activity as a whole.

Conclusion

The practice of game software development involves taking time to understand the scope of the task and then developing a set of requirements that formalize understanding. From the requirements, you can create a design. One approach to design is to divide the functionality into groups, called stripes. The stripes serve a dual purpose. They allow you to understand how to implement the functionality of your game software, and they allow you to plan your development activity. Among the tools that can aid your development and planning efforts are SmartDraw and Microsoft Project. SmartDraw allows you to collect use cases and UML diagrams that document your design into one large canvas. Microsoft Project enables you to take the results of your design effort and use them as the core elements in your project planning activity.

After you have arrived at a design and scheduled your development activities, you will want to start coding. Before creating code, you should have a configuration management plan in place. This plan provides conventions for structuring directories and naming files. In addition, you should have a set of coding conventions in place. To ensure that the code you create is managed safely, you should install a version control system (such as TortoiseCVS). If you supplement this system with conventions set down in a configuration plan, you can create baselines of your project at designated intervals.

Testing is an essential aspect of the development effort, and a testing effort should be in place from the beginning. Testers can develop a test plan from the software design specification, but even before they develop specific test cases, they can contribute to the quality of the requirements elicitation and design specification efforts.

For further reading on practical aspects of development efforts, you might find the following resources useful:

Bates, Bob. *Game Developer's Market Guide.* Boston: Premier Press, 2003.

Cockburn, Alistair. *Writing Effective Use Cases.* Boston: Addison-Wesley, 2001.

Dulak, Daryl and Eamonn Guiney. *Use Cases: Requirements in Context.* New York: ACM Press, 2000.

Hallford, Neal, with Jana Hallford. *Swords & Circuitry: A Designer's Guide to Computer Role Playing Games.* Boston: Premier Press, 2001.

Henderson, Peter. *Object-Oriented Specification and Design with C++.* New York: McGraw-Hill, 1993.

McGregregor, John D. and David A. Sykes. *A Practical Guide to Testing Object-Oriented Software.* Boston: Addison-Wesley, 2001.

McShaffry, Mike. *Game Coding Complete.* Scottsdale, Arizona: Paraglyph Press, 2003.

Page-Jones, Meilir. *Practical Project Management: Restoring Quality to DP Projects and Systems.* New York: Dorset House Publishing, 1985.

Rollings, Andrew and Dave Morris. *Game Architecture and Design, A New Edition.* Indianapolis: New Riders Press, 2004.

Wiegers, Karl E. *Peer Reviews in Software: A Practical Guide.* Boston: Addison-Wesley, 2002.

Wiegers, Karl E. *Software Requirements, Second Edition.* Redmond, Washington: Microsoft Press, 2003.

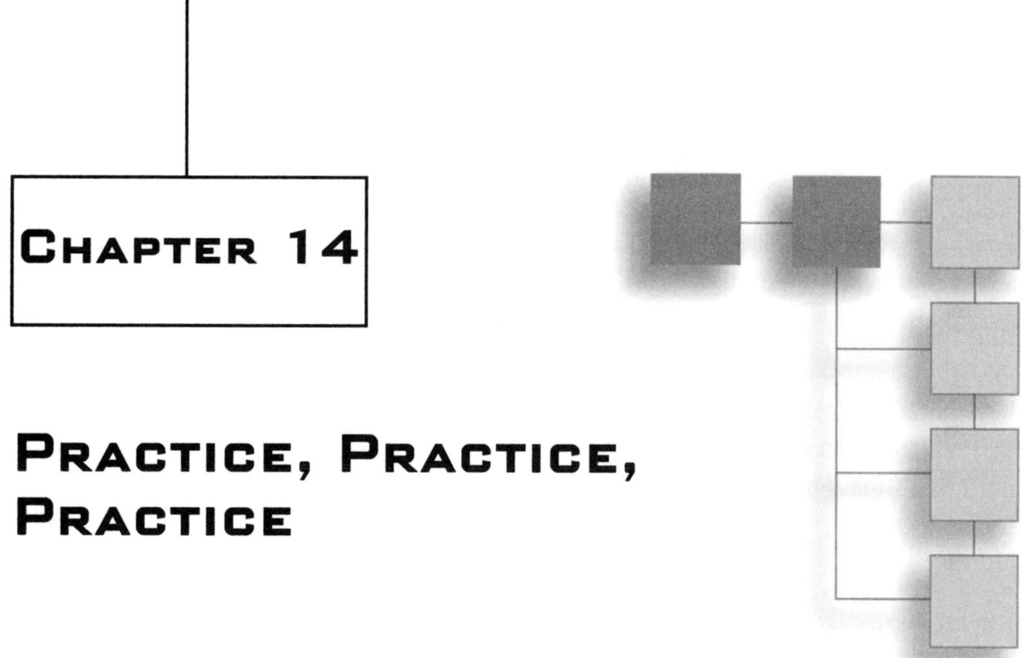

Chapter 14

Practice, Practice, Practice

This chapter discusses specific ways you can revise software. Practices dealt with in previous chapters are emphasized in this context. The approach used involves examining code from Stripe 14, which you can find on the CD. Before making changes to the code, the *Ankh* team first assessed the risks involved. An important part of this activity centered on documenting and diagramming the areas of the system under consideration and the reasons actions might be taken. Generally, why you might perform such work depends on the context of your effort. For example, you might be responding to user complaints, market pressures, or a technical imperative to optimize your code. Revising the code for a game or any other software product presents an enormous field of activity, and it's impossible to cover very many of them in one short chapter. Still, a few topics provide a good starting place:

- Examining the stripes to find candidates for revision
- Determining the more feasible options
- Planning and justifying revisions
- Estimating the effort required
- Developing ways to test the revisions
- Implementing the code
- Revising supporting materials
- Implementing the extension

Software Revision

In many environments, where a given game engine or game code framework (many developers consider an engine to apply only to graphical components) has met with technical and marketing success, those in executive positions wisely elect to revise rather than re-create. Revision possesses superiority over re-creation after a successful release because revision can almost always improve on an existing framework, whereas starting work on a new product poses all the risks that usually accompany new efforts.

At the same time, revision poses numerous risks. Risks arise because executives, managers, designers, and developers sometimes cannot resist the enthusiasm they feel when they have initially released a successful game. The first impulse, rightfully, should be to follow up with either an improved version of the first game or another game of the same type. Following this impulse can lead to enormous profits because customers are willing to invest in new versions of the games they like or games that are similar to those they like. On the other hand, if developers act on unbridled impulses, risks result. One major risk involves trying to cram a multitude of features into the new release. If you do such a thing, you can create a game that is far more complex and far less perfect than the first. If defects plague the game that follows on your success, you risk losing the victory you worked so hard to earn.

Modifications

This chapter addresses revision in general, but some mention should be afforded at the outset to one specific type of revision: modification. When you develop a modified (or mod) game, you use the framework of an existing game and apply new themes and characters to it. In essence, you present to the world a game you want to be viewed largely as original. You do not present such a game to the world as a new release of an already established game. It is simply a new game that resembles others. This can work well in many instances. Some players want to play games that are modifications of older games. They enjoy this type of product.

There is a subtle art to developing a mod successfully. Success rests in part on recognizing, from the first, the limitations and potentials that apply to mod development. One of the first things to consider is that when you develop a mod, you do so to save development expenses. If you embrace a given game framework as a starting point and then proceed to rework it so extensively that you take as much or more time than you would have required had you begun from scratch, you have clearly defeated your purpose.

Designing a modification involves giving attention to what you can do with the framework as it exists rather than what you can do with the framework if you rework it. If you do not take the time to evaluate the framework and use as much as possible those features that it already possesses, you can easily end up involving yourself in a development effort that easily equals or exceeds in complexity that of an original development effort. This happens because when you rework existing code, you have to perform a great deal of analysis that development of original code does not require.

Still, if you have a framework you want to revise, the economics of revision are well established. Getting your money's worth involves clearly identifying how you can get the most from the revisions or extensions you make to the code you start with. Starting with a body of well-tested, proven code is better than starting from scratch. You are assured success if you take time to evaluate the effort involved in each action you intend to take. Such work involves attending to the scope, complexity, maintainability, and extensibility of the framework you are working with.

Scope and Complexity

Many case histories indicate that success with the development of a game can be hazardous. A common scenario arises when an enthusiastic group of developers enjoys success with a first release and has ample money with which to develop a second release. This is where the trouble starts.

Such a group of developers can decide to concentrate their energies on modifying the first release so that it incorporates an enormous number of untried, risky features. What results is a product that customers do not like and developers regret ever having released. This phenomenon offers an interesting area for psychological study.

The psychological issues that surface involve both software engineering and game design. From the software engineering perspective, the issue is that the developers release a feature-rich game that is plagued with defects. From the game design perspective, the issue is that the customers—most of whom probably bought the second release because they were satisfied with the first—express deep discontentment with the defects in the game and report that they find the game dissatisfying to play.

From the software engineering perspective, the problems result because cramming a multitude of new features into a limited framework is likely to overwhelm the design of the framework. At a certain point, any container can become too small if you try to pack too much into it. Games are like any other containers. Their design determines how much they can be modified and extended.

From the perspective of the customer, the situation resembles that of someone who is forced to take an advanced math course immediately after completing an elementary one. The curve proves too steep. The feature richness is overwhelming. The comfort that the player experienced playing the old game has been lost.

In both cases, development and design, a *cybernetic* or *ecological* quality can be said to govern the extent to which extensions or modifications can be made to the framework of the game. To drive home this notion, many design experts strongly emphasize the notion of KISS (Keep It Simple, Stupid). As harsh as this piece of advice might sound, it lies at the root of a multitude of successfully extended or revised games. Enhancing an existing game (either as a new release or as a modification) provides an opportunity to increase player satisfaction in an incremental way. The goal of design is to keep the primary experience that the user has of the game consistent with what the user expects while improving the game in ways that satisfy him. Each new feature should represent a gradual step up from the old.

The same general rule applies to technical aspects of a game that are hidden from the player. From the development perspective, controlling complexity involves restricting the modifications you make. You must balance the scope of such an effort so that it does not lead you to completely redesign the existing framework. Effective modifications involve things like increasing performance, streamlining the user interface, and equipping the game with better visual qualities. They do not involve starting from scratch and creating a "super game." If you are going to create a super game, it is best to start from scratch.

Figure 14.1 provides an abstraction of the notion of scope and complexity. One pattern accommodates a possibly endless extension. The other shows disjuncture and fragmentation, implying that the original design does not anticipate the newer extensions.

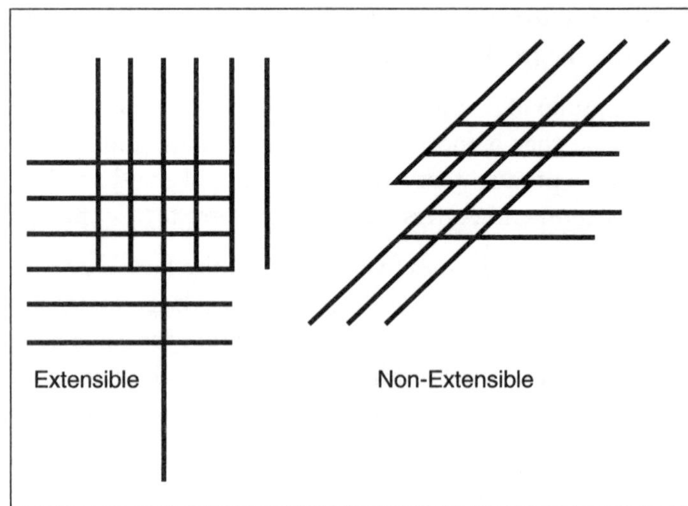

Figure 14.1
Consider at what point modifications can overburden the existing framework.

Technical Symmetry

Enhancing the hidden, technical properties of a game poses risks that are similar to those that arise when you incorporate a vast array of new features visible to the user. The crux of the problem lies in incorporating too much too soon. When too much too soon is incorporated into a game framework, testing and other quality assurance measures can receive short shrift. In addition, feature and functional proliferation can result in a product that lacks technical symmetry. When a product possesses technical symmetry, its technical features consistently represent the same general level of engineering sophistication. Nothing stands out in a glaring, ungraceful way.

With respect to requirements that specify revisions to a software product, the metrics that contribute to defining symmetry can include the number of logical decisions that a given module includes, the anticipated effort that the implementation of the changes or additions involves, and the number of classes that must be revised. Many other criteria can also be included.

Figure 14.2 provides graphical representations of symmetrical and asymmetrical patterns of complexity. In the trends that Figure 14.2 depicts, the development team might ask why one requirement possesses so much more complexity than the others. Is the feature focus of the game to center on this one requirement? If this is the case, the requirement might receive approval. But if this is not the case, the team should perhaps reconsider whether it has adequately refined the requirement.

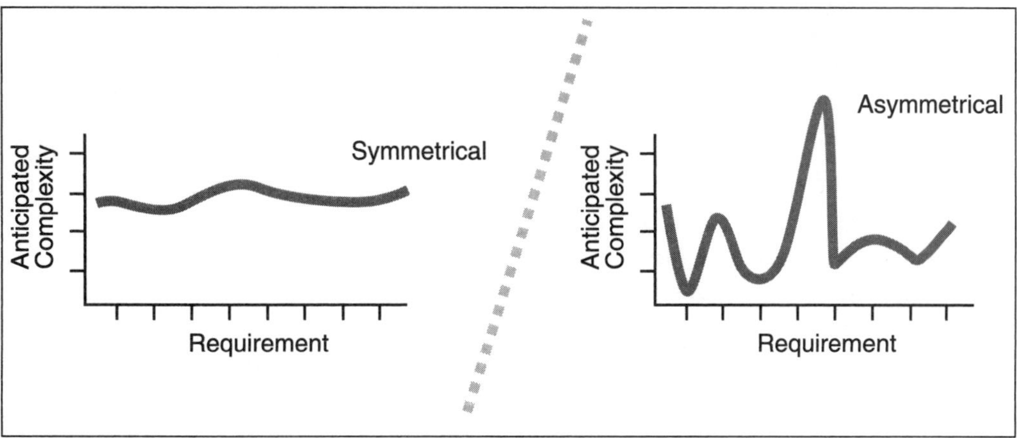

Figure 14.2
An asymmetrical pattern of complexity begs the question of whether revisions have been refined adequately.

Gauging the Impact of Requirements

Complexity of implementation detail encompasses the number of changes or additions that you make to the existing software to achieve new functionally. Consider the requirements that are named in Table 14.1. Suppose that these requirements represent first and second releases of the same game.

Table 14.1 Requirements Comparisons for Revision

No.	Current Requirement	Revision Requirement
1	The game shall feature wavering images that resemble fire whenever a targeted object explodes.	The game shall feature effects for any object designated as a target such that when the target explodes, the flames produced shall precisely simulate those of the materials composing the target.
2	The game shall feature sounds that mark the death or injury of characters.	The game shall precisely imitate the sounds of characters as they are injured, killed, or otherwise affected by actions in the game.
3	Networked players shall be able to communicate with each other.	Networked players shall be able to communicate with each other during gameplay via written, voice, and video communications on a real-time basis.

The two columns of requirements listed in Table 14.1 represent rough formulations, but they still clearly convey requirements that differ substantially as to the extent to which they require new functionality to be implemented. Consider, for example, revision requirement 1, which concerns creating realistic effects for explosions. Taken literally, the requirement makes it necessary for someone on the development team to possess a strong knowledge of chemistry, because the requirement cannot be satisfied unless someone establishes the combustion properties of the substances from which the target objects are made. The way that a burning object appears to burn depends on the combustion properties of the elements that compose it. If the developers for this game were held to the requirement, they would face an enormous task, one that is widely separated from the current requirement. The question then arises as to whether the scope of the current requirement anticipates that of the revision.

Pleasure	Pain
Pleasure Mild	Pain Mild
Pleasure Intense	Pain Intense
Pleasure Fatal	Pain Fatal

Figure 14.3
The simple utility of pleasure and pain.

Consider the revision of current requirement 2, which concerns the sounds that characters make as they are affected by the actions in the game. Suppose that the way the gameplay affects players can be categorized in four basic ways, as Figure 14.3 illustrates.

What tasks are associated with implementing sounds that convey these categories of pleasure and pain? First, the developers have to identify the significant interactions that define the lives of the characters. Second, they must categorize these interactions to accord with the states of pleasure and pain. Beyond this, the software developers must provide the functionality that looks up the sound that is assigned to each interaction. The developers might ask how much the revision requirement exceeds the current requirement in terms of complexity.

The final set of requirements, current and revision requirements 3, concerns player interactions through an Internet-distributed game. The revision requirement contains some involved new functionality. It is not possible to tell from the information given how the developers implemented current requirement 3, but they might have simply linked the game to a browser. A dialog box display of online players might have provided these links.

Consider again the possibility of making use of browser capabilities to implement revision requirement 3. Through instant messaging and video streaming, everything might be covered. The difficulty then lies once again in developing local features that allow players to connect to each other using browser capabilities. But then the implications of the requirement are that players connect in the context of play. Suppose that the context of play is an RPG. In this context, players appear or disappear according to the visibility that the game gives them. Game sessions conform to either elective or assigned player interactions, and a database tracks sessions over periods extending from minutes to hours.

Suddenly, the complexity of the game could increase in an enormous way, with the demand that if an extended server system does not already support the game, one will have to be developed to do so. Add to this that some type of architecture must be developed to accommodate the way that the game clients open and close communication sessions.

As all three sets of requirements in Table 14.1 reveal, the complexity that is introduced into a game can increase exponentially if the team does not make an effort to refine requirements for revisions according to the impact they might have on both the system and the development effort.

Linear Growth in Complexity

One simple approach to controlling the complexity that requirements for revisions might impose on a game involves maintaining a linear gradient in the growth of the complexity that you allow requirements for revisions to create. Such a gradient can apply to a system, a module, or a component. Figure 14.4 illustrates a linear complexity growth model.

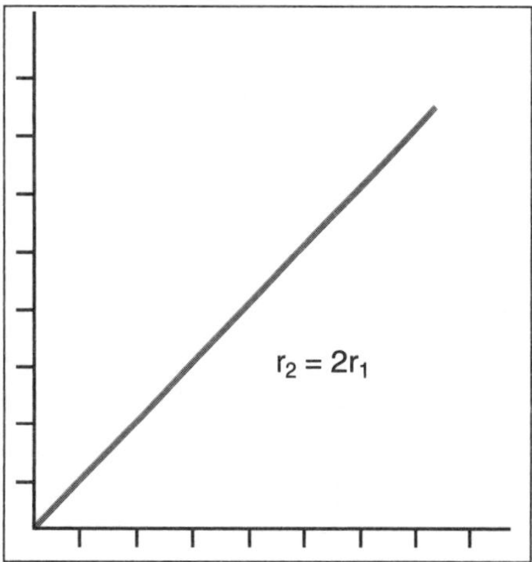

Figure 14.4
Complexity that grows on a linear basis guards against overwhelming development tasks and products that lose their symmetry.

In Figure 14.4, r_2 designates the revised or resultant complexity, whereas r_1 designates the existing complexity of the system. Determining complexity is difficult. (Discussion of this topic appears in Chapter 12, "Numbers for Nabobs.") It suffices in this context to note that the number of decision points or calls within an operation serves as a simple measure of complexity.

The prevailing risk that revision presents centers on quality. Consider, for example, what happens if you extend a thoroughly tested, successful game framework by quickly implementing a set of highly visible features that possess glaring technical and aesthetic flaws. The results almost inevitably ruin the player's experience and damage the game's reputation. Figure 14.5 shows what happens as the complexity of requirements increases. If your team has achieved a high level of testing coverage for the functionality of the game over its successive releases, quality is compromised if your team creates requirements that call for implemented functionality that you do not have time or resources to test.

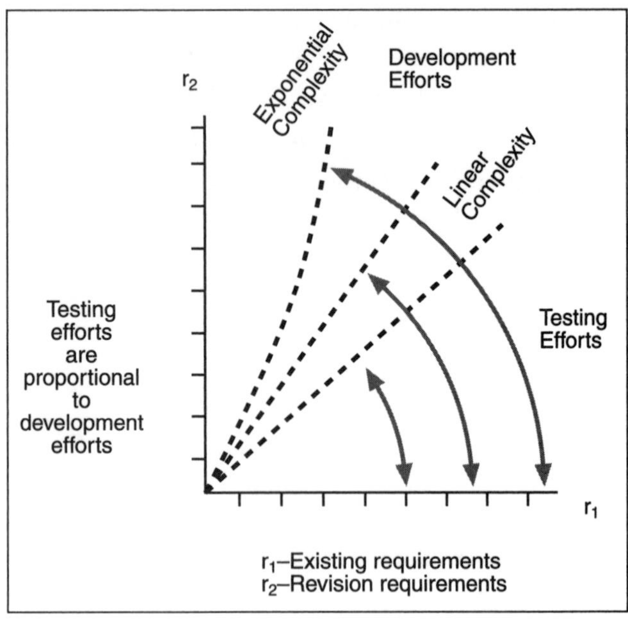

Figure 14.5
If you sustain the same level of test coverage across all aspects of your revision effort and the same level of test coverage from revision to revision, it is likely that your product is evolving in a consistent, linear way.

Determining the Scope of Revisions

As a software developer, you might not enjoy the prerogative of deciding when the product you work with is to be revised. That prerogative might reside with the marketing or customer support group. On the other hand, it's almost always the prerogative of the engineering group to challenge or question the scope of revisions. In fact, not doing so constitutes, in some respects, a failure to perform. If your company has successfully released a product, you endanger the success each time you revise it. A product enjoys what might be viewed as a natural product life. (Its utility or appeal is almost always destined to diminish after months or years.) Nonetheless, if a revised version of the product possesses substantial flaws, the engineering effort kills the product long before its market viability might come to an end.

In addition to life in the consumer marketplace, a software product can face problems when one company sells it to another. Cultures of development treat products in different ways. If a poorly designed but feature-rich product moves from a company that is deficient in design capabilities to a company that excels in design capabilities, the feature status of the game can suffer. This occurs because the engineers who are employed for the acquiring company might decide to put aside feature changes while they rework the architecture.

You can reduce the risks of neglecting product strengths if you create a scope document that balances the general ways in which products can be revised. A scope document defines the general intention of the release. Consider the following points of departure:

- **New features.** The revision aims to incorporate new features. The existing design adequately supports these features.
- **Design extension.** The revision aims to incorporate substantial new features that require extension of the design.
- **Component merger.** The revision aims to merge existing components. The focus of the effort is on the implantation of interfaces that make this merge possible.
- **Fixes and optimizations.** The revision aims at fixes and optimizations. No changes to the architecture or functionality of the game are anticipated.

If you take time to consider, generally, the primary objectives of your revision effort, you immediately put in place a thematic focal point for deliberations about what revisions are acceptable and what the scope of the revision effort should be.

Changes to Ankh

When the development team proposed revision of *Ankh*, its revisions were limited to optimizations. Arriving at the decisions about what to revise required several sessions of debate. The process involved accumulating suggestions and evaluating risks.

To conduct a review of proposed revisions, you can treat the whole process like a requirements gathering session. Participants in the sessions should come prepared to propose requirements for the release. Suggested revisions can be recorded formally and subjected to preliminary debate.

Optimization Candidates

When the team examined *Ankh* for potential revisions, its members proposed several options. Among the options considered were the following:

- **High resolution.** Increasing the game resolution would make the game more attractive visually. After a first pass through the development of the code, refitting the assets and some of the classes with enhanced capabilities would be a relatively easy way to improve the game.

- **Real-time.** *Ankh* is a turn-based game. Making it into a real-time game would give it a different flavor. Developing an AI that uses real-time capabilities would offer opportunities to make the game framework open to different teaching and learning scenarios. For example, both turn-based and real-time modules might be made available to those who want to rework the code for their own purposes.
- **Component optimization.** Numerous technical features of the game were not designed as thoroughly the first time through as they might have been. Among those was the way compression capabilities of DirectX were used. The capabilities were enhanced during a recent release of DirectX. Another item of concern was the performance hit that resulted when vectors were used instead of hashes.
- **Multiplayer.** The game could be made multiplayer as a way to enhance its appeal and demonstrate different development options.

These and other ideas emerged at different times as the team intermittently discussed revising the game. All suggestions were general at first but represented real possibilities for all members of the team.

General Risk Assessment

Assessing the general risks that proposed revisions pose sometimes requires a great deal of effort. That's because different team members favor different revisions. It is hard to relinquish an idea that you have for revision of a system you have worked on for weeks or months. Some of the discussion was fairly heated for the *Ankh* team, even going so far as to involve position papers. The risk assessment sessions rendered the following decisions:

- **High resolution.** The team rejected this revision because it offered little that genuinely enhanced the game and did not provide enough opportunities to change the code in ways that might be suitable for this book. (Needless to say, such a reason would not usually arise in most commercial game development efforts.)
- **Multiplayer.** Modifying the game to be multiplayer arose as an interesting option, and no one voiced strong objections to it. This revision seemed to be an acceptable—if somewhat unexciting—prospect. Reasons for rejecting this revision arose when the team considered that changing the game to multiplayer would bring only minor overall benefit to the game but require a fairly extensive set of changes.
- **Component optimization.** The team realized that component optimization was the best option when it became evident that the game could be enhanced in a variety of ways and that the enhancements could be distributed over a set of seven areas of the system that ranged from minor to involved in complexity. Distribution of the effort over seven tasks minimized the overall impact that the inability to implement any one task might present. On the other hand, overall system quality would be enhanced with the completion of any or all of the revisions.

- **Real-time.** The debate over real-time optimization of the game was prolonged and extensive. Some on the team favored the idea of real-time because it would provide the game with a framework that many people would find interesting. The downside of real-time optimization was the amount of work that such an optimization would involve in duplicating the AI and other modules.

Optimization Selections

The *Ankh* team decided to put aside all proposed revisions except those involving optimization of performance. Such performance optimizations affected immediately visible features of the game, such as the opening dialogue. (See Figure 14.6.) The central task became one of isolating the optimizations that would achieve this end. Among the candidate optimizations were the following:

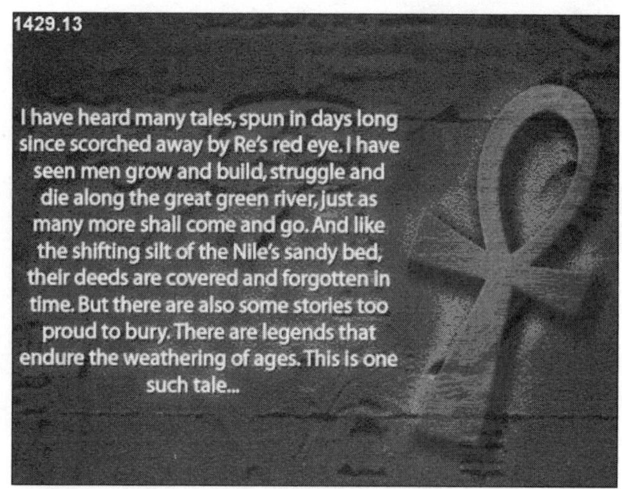

Figure 14.6
Performance impacted the smoothness with which even the images showing the background story displayed.

- **Revise `CResourceMgr` to replace vectors with hashes.** With respect to `sort` and `find` operations, hashes provide greater efficiency than vectors. They are also relatively easy to implement.
- **Revise `CImage` so that it uses DirectX-compressed textures in addition to normal textures.** The class would have to load textures with a *.dxt extension, but it would also be able to use *.png and *.jpg files. Consideration of this change led to discussion of ways that users might be able to create suitable files for the game. Photoshop and a utility that is packaged with the DirectX Software Development Kit (SDK) enable system users to convert files to these formats. This change would result in the use of less memory, generally, so increased performance would likely result.

- **Revise `CTileMap`, `CGraphics`, and `CWorld` so that the game does not draw the tile map to nonvisible areas.** This optimization would involve increasing the sensitivity of the software to detect when tiles need to be refreshed. If there's no change to the area that encompasses the tile, there's no reason to refresh the tile.
- **Revise `CTileMap` so that nothing is drawn below the surface created by the tiles.** This would reduce the amount of work that the graphics card has to do. (See Figure 14.7.)

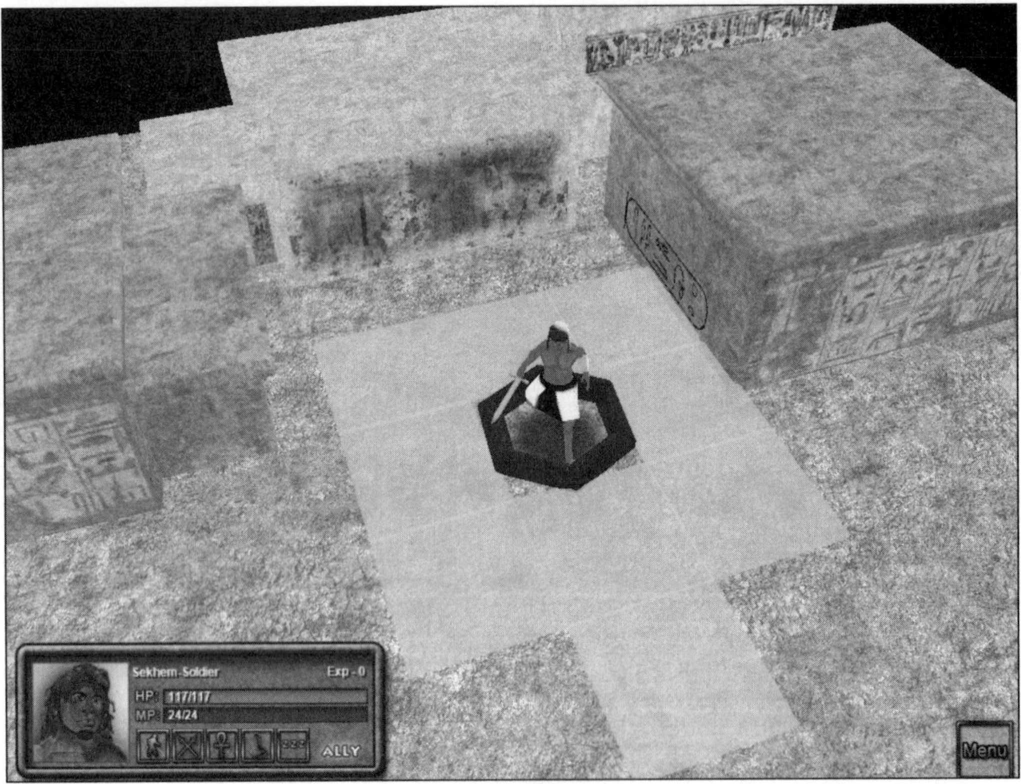

Figure 14.7
Tuning operations involving the Z buffer increase performance.

- **Revise `CWorld` so that drawing orders are changed.** For example, buildings should be drawn first. Anything that is behind the Z buffer would not have to be drawn. This optimization would also eliminate all instances that allow the same part of the screen to be drawn twice.
- **Revise `CMesh` so that state changes are minimized.** One measure would be to detect whether characters or buildings are off the screen. If so, they should not be redrawn. (See Figure 14.8.)

- **Revise `CEmitter` so that it is updated while drawing.** The original approach to developing the emitter did not follow the code model given in the SDK. Following the model would increase performance.

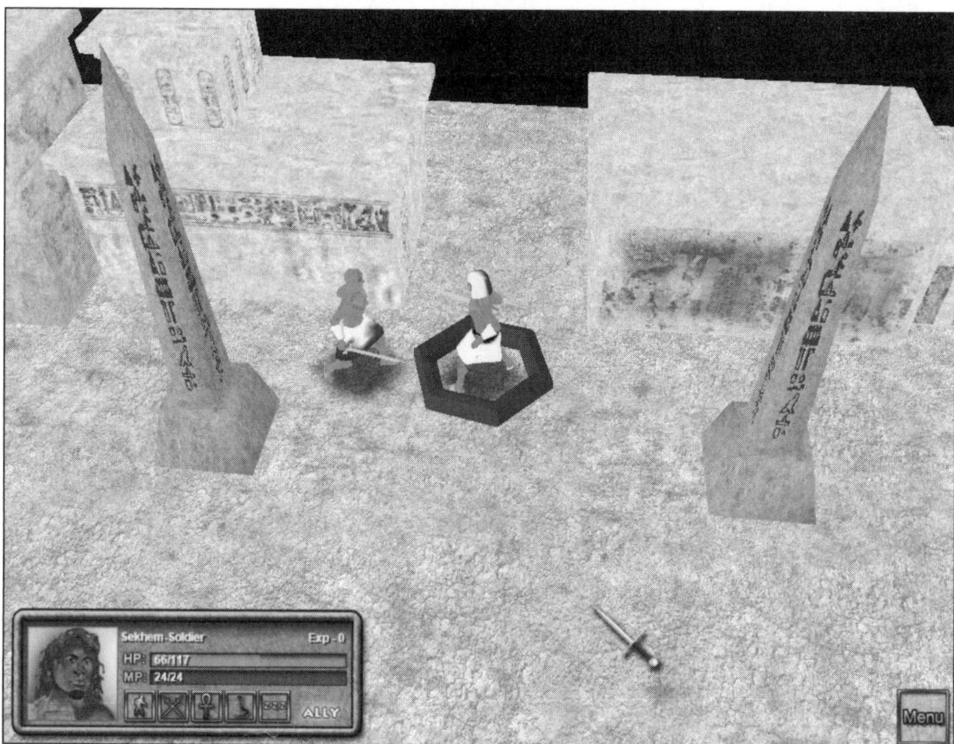

Figure 14.8
Achieving efficiency in the order in which the system paints tiles, buildings, and other meshes was one objective of the proposed revisions.

Ranks of Difficulty and Priority

Ranking the risks posed by difficulty involved considering the scope of the changes to be made, the effort required, and the technical complexity of the changes. The team could assess the risk that the implementation of a given change posed against the benefit that the change promised. Given limited time and resources, how much would benefits justify risks? Changes that pose few risks but also bring few increases in performance or aesthetic richness should probably receive low priority. Extensive change resulting in few benefits poses a high-risk situation and likewise merits low priority. Changes that pose high risks but bring large increases in performance or aesthetic richness should receive a high priority.

Such reasoning stands up in regular test situations. For example, if testers or users find a defect that crashes the game, the result clearly affects both performance and aesthetic richness in an extensive way. Removing a fatal error always amounts to an extensive change. Thus, you are justified if you assign the change high priority.

Table 14.2 shows a risk-rank view of the classes considered for change. Notice that `CMesh` receives first priority. Even though it poses the greatest risk, it results in the greatest benefit. Changing `CResourceMgr` involves making changes to almost every member operation it contains but results in a net gain to system performance and aesthetic richness that is marginal.

Table 14.2 Ranking of Revision Risks

Rank	Risk	Priority
1	`CMesh`—Most Risk	`CMesh`—First Priority
2	`CEmitter`	`CEmitter`
3	`CWorld`	`CImage`
4	`CTileMap`	`CWorld`
5	`CImage`	`CTileMap`
6	`CResourceMgr`	`CResourceMgr`

Evaluating Classes and Operations

To arrive at estimations of how changes or additions can impact a system, you must inspect the code that the changes impact. For example, the *Ankh* team could not establish the risks and priorities documented in Table 14.2 until it had opened the files containing the classes and carefully examined the operations and attributes that the classes contained to determine how much the changes would be likely to result in altered code.

Revisions to CResourceMgr

The scope of changes involved in revising `CResourceMgr` was extensive. Changing vectors to hashes affected almost every operation. Making this set of changes received low priority even though, in terms of complexity, it posed low risk. In such situations, you can look at the work from different perspectives. One thing to consider is that making extensive changes to a class that communicates with many other classes, even if the changes appear trivial, can result in a testing nightmare. This was one factor that had bearing on the rating of the change. Again, however, the changes were not considered all that difficult, so the testing effort was not deemed a major issue (probably much to the team's hazard). In this case, the tradeoff between the work needed to make the changes and the net gain in performance pushed the set of changes to the tail end of the priority list.

Changes to CMesh

Changing `CMesh` to reduce the number of state changes and prevent buildings and characters that were not onscreen from being drawn involved altering `CMesh:Draw()` and

CWorld:Draw(). The complexity of this one operation was a good indication of the overall complexity of CMesh. The change involved work with approximately 130 lines of code in the implementation file. It presented a relatively complex testing situation.

Scope of CMesh Changes

Figure 14.9 shows partial details of a UML class diagram representing the attributes and operations of CMesh. Two salient features are the Draw() operation and the CImage objects. The Draw() operation has a DWORD parameter. The UML diagram adequately details most of the complexity, but one point of concern arises with an association in the Draw() operation with a pointer to a CGraphics object. The CGraphics object is global, declared in the util.cpp file. An *Ankh* class, CImage, forms several aggregations with CMesh. These, however, do not directly impact the Draw() operation. Generally, changes to the operation involve attending to messages among CMesh, DirectX objects, and CGraphics.

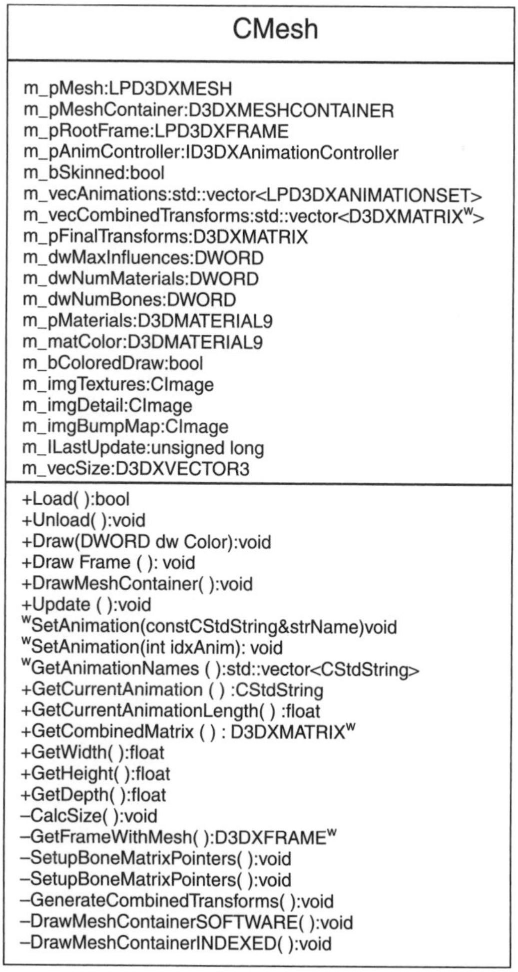

CMesh

m_pMesh:LPD3DXMESH
m_pMeshContainer:D3DXMESHCONTAINER
m_pRootFrame:LPD3DXFRAME
m_pAnimController:ID3DXAnimationController
m_bSkinned:bool
m_vecAnimations:std::vector<LPD3DXANIMATIONSET>
m_vecCombinedTransforms:std::vector<D3DXMATRIX^{W}>
m_pFinalTransforms:D3DXMATRIX
m_dwMaxInfluences:DWORD
m_dwNumMaterials:DWORD
m_dwNumBones:DWORD
m_pMaterials:D3DMATERIAL9
m_matColor:D3DMATERIAL9
m_bColoredDraw:bool
m_imgTextures:CImage
m_imgDetail:CImage
m_imgBumpMap:CImage
m_lLastUpdate:unsigned long
m_vecSize:D3DXVECTOR3

+Load( ):bool
+Unload( ):void
+Draw(DWORD dw Color):void
+Draw Frame ( ): void
+DrawMeshContainer( ):void
+Update ( ):void
^{W}SetAnimation(constCStdString&strName)void
^{W}SetAnimation(int idxAnim): void
^{W}GetAnimationNames ( ):std::vector<CStdString>
+GetCurrentAnimation ( ) :CStdString
+GetCurrentAnimationLength( ) :float
+GetCombinedMatrix ( ) : D3DXMATRIX^{W}
+GetWidth( ):float
+GetHeight( ):float
+GetDepth( ):float
–CalcSize( ):void
–GetFrameWithMesh( ):D3DXFRAME^{W}
–SetupBoneMatrixPointers( ):void
–SetupBoneMatrixPointers( ):void
–GenerateCombinedTransforms( ):void
–DrawMeshContainerSOFTWARE( ):void
–DrawMeshContainerINDEXED( ):void

Figure 14.9
A UML class diagram reveals most of the complexity of CMesh.

The Code

A final step in assessing risk and planning changes involves going to the code. In some instances, you must add operations. In other instances, additions aren't necessary.

The operation that was central to limiting state changes and changing the visibility of meshes centered on the `Draw()` operation. Because the implementation of the operation consumed approximately 130 lines of code, it was a somewhat large operation. `CMesh:Draw()` contained calls to `CMesh:Update()` and `CMesh:DrawFrame()`, adding to the complexity:

```
//////////////////////////////////////////////////////////////
// CMesh::Draw()                                           //
// Draws the mesh.                                         //
//////////////////////////////////////////////////////////////
void CMesh::Draw(DWORD dwColor)
{
        if(dwColor != D3DCOLOR_XRGB(255,255,255))
        {
                D3DXCOLOR color(dwColor);
                m_matColor.Diffuse = color;
                m_matColor.Ambient = color;
                m_bColoredDraw = true;
        }
        else
         {
                m_bColoredDraw = false;
         }

         if(m_bSkinned)
        {
                Update();
                DrawFrame(m_pRootFrame);
                return;
        }
        // For each material, render the polygons that use it
        for( DWORD i=0; i<m_dwNumMaterials; i++ )
         {
                 // Set the material and texture for this subset
                if(m_bColoredDraw)
                  {
                        Graphics->GetDevice()->SetMaterial(&m_matColor);
                  }
                 else
                  {
                        Graphics->GetDevice()->SetMaterial( &m_pMaterials[i] );
                  }

                if(m_imgBumpMap && Graphics->GetBumpMapping())
                {
```

```
// Set the direction of the light for the bump mapping
D3DLIGHT9 light;
Graphics->GetDevice()->GetLight(0,&light);
D3DXVECTOR3 vec = light.Direction;
DWORD dwTFactor = VectorToRGB(&vec);
Graphics->GetDevice()->
   SetRenderState(D3DRS_TEXTUREFACTOR,dwTFactor);
if(Graphics->GetDetailMaps()>0)
{
      // Scale the detailmap
      D3DXMATRIX matTexture;
      D3DXMatrixScaling(&matTexture,4,4,4);
      Graphics->GetDevice()->
         SetTransform(D3DTS_TEXTURE3,&matTexture);
       Graphics->GetDevice()->
        SetTextureStageState( 3,
     D3DTSS_TEXTURETRANSFORMFLAGS,D3DTTFF_COUNT2 );
}
else
{
      Graphics->GetDevice()->
           SetTextureStageState( 3,
           D3DTSS_TEXTURETRANSFORMFLAGS,D3DTTFF_DISABLE );
}
Graphics->GetDevice()->SetTextureStageState( 1,
                     D3DTSS_TEXTURETRANSFORMFLAGS,
                                D3DTTFF_DISABLE );
Graphics->GetDevice()->
          SetTextureStageState(
          2, D3DTSS_TEXTURETRANSFORMFLAGS,
          D3DTTFF_DISABLE );
// Bump map pass
Graphics->GetDevice()->SetTextureStageState(
0,D3DTSS_COLORARG1,D3DTA_TEXTURE);
//normal
Graphics->GetDevice()->SetTextureStageState(
0,D3DTSS_COLORARG2,D3DTA_TFACTOR);
//light vector
Graphics->GetDevice()->SetTextureStageState(
0,D3DTSS_COLOROP,D3DTOP_DOTPRODUCT3);
// Render the texture
Graphics->GetDevice()->SetTextureStageState(
      1, D3DTSS_COLORARG1, D3DTA_TEXTURE);
Graphics->GetDevice()->SetTextureStageState(
      1, D3DTSS_COLORARG2, D3DTA_CURRENT);
Graphics->GetDevice()->SetTextureStageState(
      1, D3DTSS_ALPHAARG1, D3DTA_TEXTURE);
Graphics->GetDevice()->SetTextureStageState(
      1, D3DTSS_ALPHAARG2, D3DTA_DIFFUSE);
Graphics->GetDevice()->SetTextureStageState(
```

```
                1, D3DTSS_COLOROP, D3DTOP_MODULATE2X);
            Graphics->GetDevice()->SetTextureStageState(
                1, D3DTSS_ALPHAOP, D3DTOP_MODULATE2X);
// Add the lighting
            Graphics->GetDevice()->SetTextureStageState(
            2,D3DTSS_COLORARG1,D3DTA_CURRENT);                    //normal
            Graphics->GetDevice()->SetTextureStageState(
            2,D3DTSS_COLORARG2,D3DTA_DIFFUSE);                    //light vector
            Graphics->GetDevice()->SetTextureStageState(
            2,D3DTSS_COLOROP,D3DTOP_MODULATE);
            // Detail map it
            if(Graphics->GetDetailMaps()>0)
            {
                Graphics->GetDevice()->SetTextureStageState(
                3, D3DTSS_COLORARG1, D3DTA_TEXTURE);
                Graphics->GetDevice()->SetTextureStageState(
                3, D3DTSS_COLORARG2, D3DTA_CURRENT);
                Graphics->GetDevice()->SetTextureStageState(
                3, D3DTSS_COLOROP, D3DTOP_MODULATE2X);
                Graphics->GetDevice()->SetTextureStageState(
                3, D3DTSS_TEXCOORDINDEX, 1);
                Graphics->GetDevice()->SetTexture(
                3, m_imgDetail->GetTexture());
            }
            else
            {
                Graphics->GetDevice()->SetTexture(3,NULL);
                Graphics->GetDevice()->SetTextureStageState(
                3,D3DTSS_COLOROP,D3DTOP_DISABLE);
            }

            // Set up the textures; stage 0 is the
            // bump map, and stage 1 is the texture
            Graphics->GetDevice()->SetTexture(
            0, m_imgBumpMap->GetTexture());
            Graphics->GetDevice()->SetTexture(
            1, m_imgTextures[i]->GetTexture());
        }
        // No bump map, just a regular texture
        else if(m_imgTextures && m_imgTextures[i])
        {
            Graphics->GetDevice()->SetTexture(
            0, m_imgTextures[i]->GetTexture() );
            Graphics->GetDevice()->SetTexture( 1, NULL);
            Graphics->GetDevice()->SetTexture( 2, NULL);
        }
        // No texture!
        else
         {
```

```
                Graphics->GetDevice()->SetTexture( 0, NULL);
            }
        // Draw the mesh subset
            m_pMesh->DrawSubset( i );
            Graphics->GetDevice()->SetRenderState(
                    D3DRS_ALPHABLENDENABLE,TRUE);
    }

            // Reset to default state
            Graphics->GetDevice()->SetTextureStageState(
                            0, D3DTSS_COLORARG1, D3DTA_TEXTURE);
            Graphics->GetDevice()->SetTextureStageState(
                            0, D3DTSS_COLORARG2, D3DTA_DIFFUSE);
            Graphics->GetDevice()->SetTextureStageState(
                            0, D3DTSS_COLOROP, D3DTOP_MODULATE);
            Graphics->GetDevice()->SetTextureStageState(
                            1, D3DTSS_COLOROP, D3DTOP_DISABLE);
            Graphics->GetDevice()->SetTextureStageState(
                            2, D3DTSS_COLOROP, D3DTOP_DISABLE);
            Graphics->GetDevice()->SetTextureStageState(
                            3, D3DTSS_COLOROP, D3DTOP_DISABLE);
}//end Draw()
```

Other Changes

Unfortunately, page constraints prohibit a detailed discussion of all changes to the *Ankh* system. However, by using such tools as UML diagrams, code inspections, and generalized risk assessment and priority ratings, the team was able to discern how to proceed with revisions. The revisions that this chapter shows represent only minor changes. Such changes do not necessarily characterize industry practices, but it is common for a product revision to consist of numerous minor changes.

The revisions that were designated to become Stripe 15 of *Ankh* were symmetrical. In other words, all revisions required modifications of 1–3 member operations. Likewise, all required modifications took no more than three classes. The following list summarizes the revisions:

- **Changes to `CWorld`.** Changes to `CWorld` supplemented those to `CMesh`. The change that received first priority involved reducing the number of state changes. This class was involved in two revisions. Because of this fact, the team had to assess whether the two revisions would conflict with each other. The revisions did conflict. Both the work to eliminate redundant drawing and to detect objects drawn below the tile surface involved making changes to `CWorld:Draw()`. The team dealt with the situation by coordinating activities so that those involved in making the changes were aware of what the other was doing and could assess how to order their activities to prevent rework.

- **Changes to `CEmitter`.** Changing `CEmitter` so that it would draw particles and chunks with greater efficiency involved altering `CEmitter:Draw()`. Like the changes to `CMesh`, the changes to `CEmitter` required work up front to determine the scope of the changes and the risks involved.
- **Revisions to `CImage`.** The second lowest risk was assigned to `CImage`. Because it allowed the system to reduce memory use and speed performance in fairly substantial ways, it was ranked third in priority. This revision involved changes to `CImage::Load()`.
- **Revisions to `CTileMap`, `CGraphics`, and `CWorld`.** This set of revisions centered on reducing drawing to nonvisible areas. After some analysis, the team determined that only `CTileMap:Draw()` and `CWorld:Draw()` required revision.
- **Changes to `CTileMap`.** Revisions to eliminate drawing below the tile map involved changes to `CTileMap:Draw()`.

Specifying Revisions

You can specify revisions in the same way that you specify primary functionality. You can create a software requirements specification for the revision. The requirements specification for revisions must refer to the primary requirements, if possible, so that you can examine the requirements for revision to determine whether they conflict with the primary requirements. Following are the basic scenarios for merging requirements:

- **Extension.** If you consider the changes made to *Ankh*, the use of the compressed format for asset files constituted an extension of existing functionality. The team retained the old functionality, because if the system encountered *.jpg files, for instance, they would still be read. The revision made possible the automatic compression of files.
- **Substitution.** The use of hashes to replace vectors in the `CResourceMgr` class represented substitution. In this instance, the team decided that the hash container was superior to the vector container. However, the operational interface of the hash container differed little from the vector container, so much of the work involved replacing the container instances. Of course, even though the operational interfaces of the two classes displayed extensive similarities, testing was necessary to establish the success of the substitution.
- **Supersession.** The changes to `CEmitter` constituted an instance of supersession. The change fell under this heading because the implemented code provided a superior solution to the problem, one that used components and algorithms that spoke of an evolved understanding of the problem and its solution. Supersession implied that the resulting code would provide the same functionality as the old code. The moment of supersession arrived with the superior way that the code provided the functionality.

- **Conflict.** As an example of a conflict, consider that if the *Ankh* team had enhanced the game so that it could be displayed only on high-resolution monitors, it might have excluded the vast majority of its prospective customer group. A nonfunctional requirement for *Ankh* might state that the game shall be executable using the widest possible variety of graphics cards.

Use Case Confirmation

Generally, when you engineer requirements for revisions, you can follow the same procedures that you follow when you develop requirements for a system you construct from scratch. Accordingly, regarding the prospective changes to the functionality supported by `CMesh`, a requirement might read

> The system shall restrict painting of meshes to the plane that is defined by the floor of the level.

Given this beginning, you could then create a use case to test the general conceivability of the requirement. Figure 14.10 illustrates a possible use case.

Use Case Name: Manipulate character
Requirement(s) Explored: rev 1
Player (Actor) Context (Role): Player
Precondition(s): Character editor is open.
Trigger(s): Player places character on tile surface.
Main Course of Action: 1. Player moves slider to position character. 2. System positions character according to slider position. 3. System preserves character above tile surface. 4. Player again moves slider to reposition character. 5. System positions character according to slider position. 6. System preserves character above tile surface.
Alternate Course(s) of Action: 1a. Player moves multiple sliders. 4a. Player again moves multiple sliders.
Exceptional Course(s) of Action: 2a. System fails to move character. 3a. System merges character into tile surface. 5a. System does not reposition character. 6a. System merges character into tile surface.

Figure 14.10
A use case serves as a proof of concept for the requirement.

Configuring Revisions

When you determine the scope of a revision, you establish on the most basic level which classes and other components your revisions will affect. To plan the configuration of a revision, you can create a configuration management plan (or update the existing plan). You should name the impacted files and show how to configure them to most effectively facilitate the development effort.

Designing Revisions

The extent to which revisions impact the existing system design depends largely on whether you need to add or factor components. The impact of breaking existing components into new components is greater in most cases than adding new components. That's because if one class (a client) depends on another (a server), the server is likely to impact the client if its operations are moved to classes with different names.

The need to factor did not arise with the revisions that the team proposed for *Ankh*. For example, most of the interactions of the `CMesh` operations involved DirectX, Boost, and `CGraphics` objects. In Figure 14.11, the package symbols represent the DirectX and Boost libraries, and the composition associations indicate that objects from these libraries support operations in `CMesh`. The `CImage` object relates to the `CMesh` object on the basis of aggregation. The object from the `CGraphics` class is declared globally. Calls using its operations occur within the `CMesh:Draw()` operation. Extending the functionality of the `CMesh` class involves no changes to the existing design.

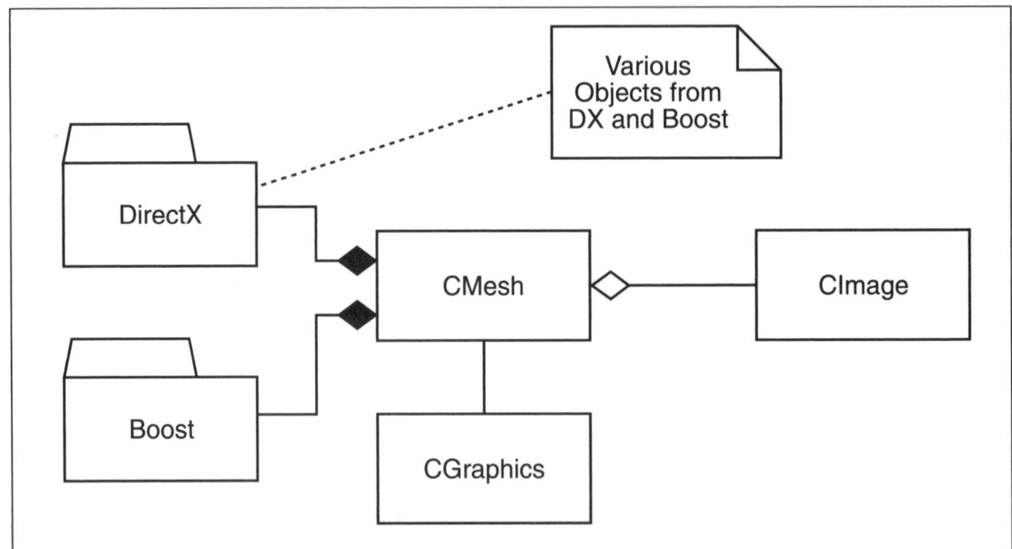

Figure 14.11
The scope of the changes extends over the DirectX, Boost, and a few *Ankh* classes.

Implementing Revisions

One contributing factor to successful implementations of releases involves precisely identifying the components that the release requires you to revise. Identification of components enables you to operate surgically, first changing key operations within existing classes and then testing these through integration with the largely unchanged whole. In the instance of the changes to `CMesh`, the team identified `CMesh:Draw()` as the primary target for changes. The following body of code resulted from the revision of `CMesh:Draw()`:

```
void CMesh::Draw(DWORD dwColor)
{
   // Set the material/color. The color is not WHITE.
   if(dwColor != D3DCOLOR_XRGB(255,255,255))
   {
       D3DXCOLOR color(dwColor);
       m_matColor.Diffuse = color;
       m_matColor.Ambient = color;
       m_bColoredDraw = true;
   }
   else
       m_bColoredDraw = false;
     // If you're skinned, call DrawFrame instead
   if(m_bSkinned)
   {
       Update();
       DrawFrame(m_pRootFrame);
       return;
   }

   // For each material, render the polygons that use it
   for( DWORD i=0; i<m_dwNumMaterials; i++ )
   {
        // Set the material and texture for this subset
       if(m_bColoredDraw)
           Graphics->GetDevice()->SetMaterial(&m_matColor);
       else
           Graphics->GetDevice()->SetMaterial( &m_pMaterials[i] );

       if(m_imgBumpMap && Graphics->GetBumpMapping())
       {
           // Set the direction of the light for the bump mapping
           D3DLIGHT9 light;
           Graphics->GetDevice()->GetLight(0,&light);
           D3DXVECTOR3 vec = light.Direction;
           DWORD dwTFactor = VectorToRGB(&vec);
           Graphics->GetDevice()->SetRenderState(
                        D3DRS_TEXTUREFACTOR,dwTFactor);
                 if(Graphics->GetDetailMaps()>0)
           {
```

```
                Graphics->ApplyStateBlock("MeshDetailAndBumpMap");
                Graphics->GetDevice()->SetTexture(
                                3, m_imgDetail->GetTexture());
            }
            else
            {
                Graphics->GetDevice()->SetTexture(3,NULL);
                Graphics->GetDevice()->SetTextureStageState(
                                3,D3DTSS_COLOROP,D3DTOP_DISABLE);
                Graphics->ApplyStateBlock("MeshBumpMap");
            }
                      // Set up the textures; stage 0
                      // is the bump map, and stage 1 is the texture
            Graphics->GetDevice()->SetTexture(
                                0, m_imgBumpMap->GetTexture());
            Graphics->GetDevice()->SetTexture(
                                1, m_imgTextures[i]->GetTexture());

        }
        // No bump map, just a regular texture
        else if(m_imgTextures && m_imgTextures[i])
        {
            Graphics->GetDevice()->SetTexture(
                           0, m_imgTextures[i]->GetTexture() );
            Graphics->ApplyStateBlock("MeshNoBumpMap");
        }
        // No texture!
        else
            Graphics->GetDevice()->SetTexture( 0, NULL);
              // Draw the mesh subset
         m_pMesh->DrawSubset( i );
        Graphics->GetDevice()->SetRenderState(
                           D3DRS_ALPHABLENDENABLE,TRUE);
    }
        // Reset to default state
        Graphics->ApplyStateBlock("ResetTextures");
}
```

Testing Revisions

Testing revision work differs little from testing the work of primary implementation. A difference does distinguish the two types of work, however. When you revise a product, your testing effort must concentrate on integration from the first. Testing components in isolation is almost secondary. The reason for this should be clear. Even if a development effort renders an excellent component, you cannot subordinate the operational integrity of the entire system to the one component. Testing of the component should assume an integration or system bias. In other words, if the component does not communicate with the system, then the sanity of the system, rather than that of the component, should be assumed first.

Developing test cases is covered in Chapter 11, "Evident Evil—The Art of Testing." Here, it is useful to show that you can develop a black-box test procedure from the use case illustrated in Figure 14.10. The test procedure allows you to access existing functionality of the system and to operate the system so that it tests the new functionality. Figure 14.12 illustrates a test procedure for the revision.

Test Identifier: S15_ITC_01
Requirement(s) addressed: 1
Prerequisite conditions: Character designer open and character selected.
Test input: Player manipulates character position.
Expected test results: No slider manipulations position character beneath tile surface.
Criteria for evaluating results: Manipulate all sliders and see that character does not merge with tile surface.
Instructions for conducting procedure: 1. Move the slider to position the character. 2. Verify that the character moves with slider position. 3. Verify that regardless of the movement, the character stays above the tile surface. 4. Move the cursor off the slider and click to deactivate the slider. 5. Move the cursor back onto a slider and move the slider to reposition the character. 6. Verify that the system repositions the character. 7. Verify that the character does not merge with the tile surface.
Features to be tested: Slider, painting of character in character designer.
Requirements traceability: See use cases for rev requirement 1.

Figure 14.12
A test black-box test procedure provides a convenient way to verify revised functionality.

As Figure 14.13 shows, you can use the character editor for *Ankh* to test the revised functionality, which the test procedure stipulates.

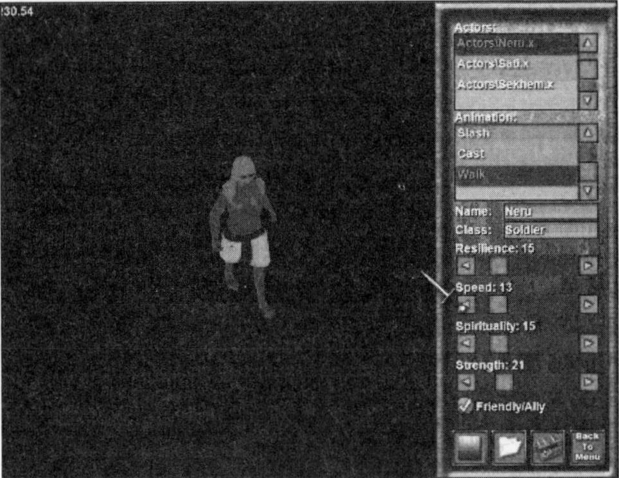

Figure 14.13
The character editor provides a context for testing the new requirement.

Conclusion

This chapter dealt with the dangers and advantages that you encounter when you revise a game framework. Reference was made to a "game framework" in preference to "game engine" because the emphasis has been on using an existing body of code, complete with meshes, textures, and other assets, to create either a modified game or introduce a new release of the existing game. No core set of functionality is necessarily implied, as would be the case with a game engine.

The dangers that modifications or revisions pose usually originate with a failure to thoroughly investigate the scope of the proposed revisions. If you extensively alter an existing framework, you can end up expending more effort than if you had started from scratch. Given that the intention of revision encompasses reuse and improvement of an existing body of code, revision proves worthwhile only if you selectively refine a limited portion of the existing framework.

If you pursue several revisions, you can benefit from assessing the scope of the revisions comparatively. A symmetrical relationship among revisions occurs when all of the revisions possess roughly similar scopes. For example, most of the revisions proposed for *Ankh* involved modifying or extending 1–3 classes. Had any one revision strayed far from this range, it might have been appropriate to question it.

Planning revisions involves assessing risk and setting priorities. You can assess risk by comparing the benefit to be derived from the proposed revision to the amount of work required to bring about the revision. If the amount of work is disproportionate to the improvement that the work will bring to the system, you should consider putting the revision aside. Along similar lines, if you are dealing with a set of revisions, you can reduce risk by assessing which revision has the highest priority. Determining the priority of a revision depends on such factors as how much work it requires, whether it poses high risk, and what benefit it brings to the system. Other factors include whether the revision has dependencies and whether failure to implement the revision poses a risk to the overall revision effort.

Following are books that extend the discussion in this chapter:

Aßmann, Uwe. *Invasive Software Composition.* New York: Springer-Verlag, 2003.

Blunden, Bill. *Software Exorcism: A Handbook for Debugging and Optimizing Legacy Code.* Berkeley, California: Apress, 2003.

Jacobson, Ivar, Martin Griss, and Patrick Jonsson. *Software Reuse: Architecture, Process, and Organization for Business Success.* Reading, Massachusetts: Addison Wesley Longman, 1997.

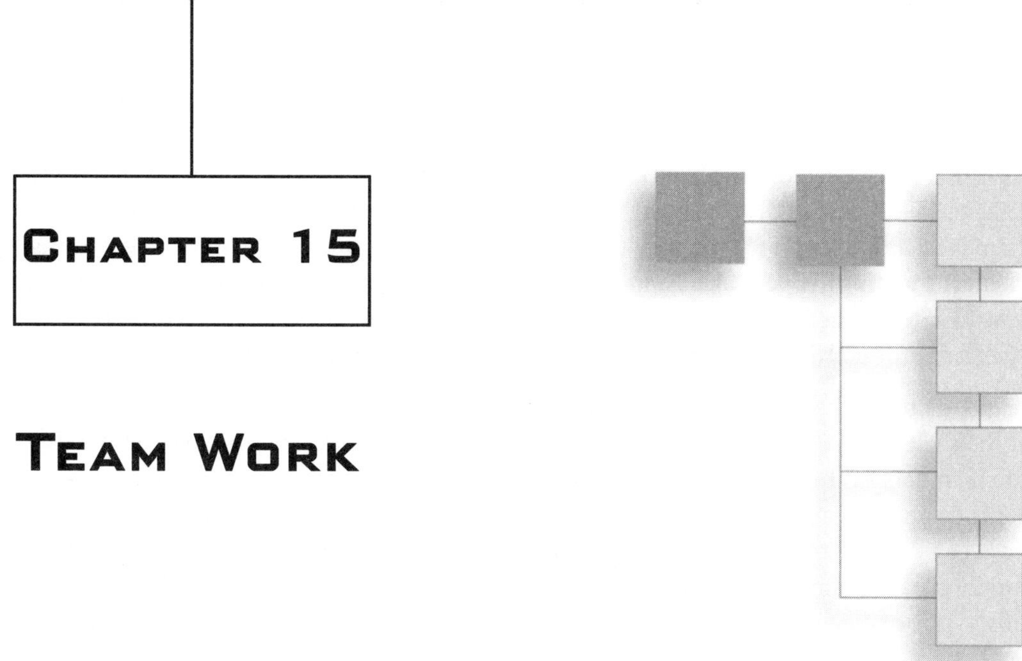

Chapter 15

Team Work

Game software development is almost always a group effort. Where you fit into a team effort depends on the skills you possess and how you work with others. How a team takes shape depends on the way the organization puts teams together and how the members of the team interact. If a team does not form itself into a tight working unit, it is unlikely that the project will succeed. This chapter looks at some of the elements of team success, as follows:

- What a team is and how it is formed to address the needs of a new project
- The roles people play both formally and informally when they join a team
- How members of a team can communicate using standard software engineering tools
- How reviews contribute to the ability of team members to communicate effectively
- Ways to view the team in light of project management perspectives
- The use of project tracking media to help everyone on the team focus on tasks and understand dependencies
- How teams fail and how you can work to remedy some of the causes

Basic Tendencies of Teams

A development team in a software engineering organization consists of a group of people who work in specialized roles toward a common goal. The goal is the completion of a project. A project is defined as "a temporary endeavor undertaken to create a unique product, service, or result" (*PMBOK*, 204). When software engineers work toward a common goal, they do so as professionals who might possess roughly the same general level of technical expertise. After they join the project, however, they tend to dedicate themselves to specific tasks. The expertise that software engineers develop as they perform these tasks enables them to accomplish more than they could as individuals trying to do a little of everything. The fact that this happens almost invariably in every production environment confirms a generalization that Adam Smith made much of in his *Wealth of Nations*: Division of labor increases productivity, but productivity demands division of labor.

Teams, then, join people together in a common endeavor, but at the same time, the demands of the project force members of the team to assume diverse roles, and the roles tend to isolate members of the team from each other. When individuals are isolated, inefficiencies in the coordination of efforts and communications result. To counteract this tendency, software engineering practitioners prescribe a set of standard measures for regularizing the communications and interactions of team members. Among these are such things as specific types of documents, formalized reviews, and standard techniques of tracking the progress of a project. A balance develops between *specialization* and *cooperation*.

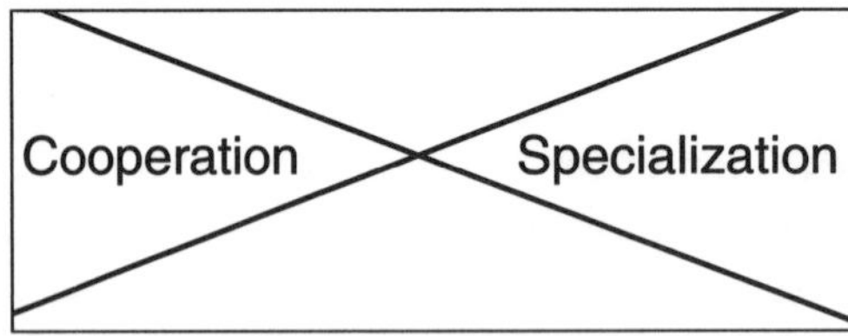

To repeat, the balance between specialization and cooperation is achieved only through a combination of different software engineering practices. Among those investigated in this chapter are the following:

- Understanding the flow of activity that allows a project to come into existence. This depends on the style of development that the organization sustains.
- Knowing how a project takes form as a managed set of tasks. At the center of this activity is the project manager, who has the ability to plan activities so that even in the face of tensions that arise due to tight production schedules, people who have little time to communicate with each other about their deliverables can still work toward a unified end.
- The roles of people who are on the team. Roles can be both formal and informal. Understanding the importance of both is the responsibility of everyone on the team. Everyone learns how to work with everyone else.
- Recognizing the importance of creating, tracking, and focusing on schedules.
- Understanding the factors that are known to contribute to the failure of teams.
- The level of professionalism or sense of craft that guides both individuals in their specialized roles and the team in its group role.

The sheer amount of time consumed developing a game requires that the tasks involved in developing the game be apportioned between several people, and achieving efficiency and accuracy in the performance of these tasks dictates that each member of the team should concentrate on a fairly narrow range of tasks. By the time you count them all, you'll find that the software work involved in a game can be divided into 20 or more specializations.

Any one individual can attend to only a few of these specializations. Granted, a programmer might test code, or a configuration manager might write documentation, but experience shows that the more intensive the project work becomes, the more each member of the team tends to gravitate toward an increasingly narrow range of tasks.

As a result of the tendency toward specialization of effort, the work of project scheduling and tracking grows in importance, and members of the team must learn to work within the context that the schedule provides. Not only must everyone work with the schedules, but those who work on projects must more than ever accustom themselves to communicating by using tools that reduce things like personality conflicts, unintentional miscommunications, or deceptions. Becoming accustomed to such tools is difficult for some people. The difficulty is usually something that you can remedy fairly quickly by looking at the formal mechanisms that any successful organization has in place to guide communications.

When Teams Form

Being able to participate in the work of a team requires a realistic view of what the team is about. It is about, among other things, the performance of work relative to a project, which is a temporary undertaking, as noted earlier, that is focused on a unique product. A software development team is temporary.

A software development team does not usually come into existence as soon as the idea for a game originates. Other things come first. The start of the software engineering effort does not occur until the organization, of which the software team is a part, decides to fund the development of the game. The style of development that the organization maintains determines how the organization decides to fund the development of a game. In small or entrepreneurial organizations, the initiative might come from a developer or group of developers who want to create a given type of game. As the organization increases in size, the likelihood that software developers will create the idea for a game decreases. In mature companies, the decision to impetus to create a game almost always comes from outside the software engineering group.

Game development companies often identify the activities relating to the game production using terms derived from the film industry. Finding, assessing the feasibility of, and acquiring funding for an idea constitute the *preproduction* phase. The construction of the game constitutes the *production* phase. The release of the game makes up the *postproduction* phase. Software development activities occur during all three phases, but they are clearly most prevalent during the production phase. It is during this phase that the software development team is formed.

The Sponsor

If your organization possesses an evolved business and production structure, chances are that the marketing group will be the starting place of new game projects. Someone in marketing will write a proposal for the creation of a new game. Although the idea for the game might be from a game designer outside the company, someone in marketing must still acquire or formalize the idea. On the other hand, marketing might support a creative group whose responsibility is to research and generate new game ideas. Organizations differ. Regardless of the differences, however, after an idea has been formalized through a proposal, the next step is for someone in the executive or funding group to become the *sponsor* of the idea. The sponsor is someone with control of funding who decides to finance the development of the game. Without this person's blessing, nothing goes forward.

The Champion

A sponsor is a guardian angel. At another level, however, someone closer to the production process must enter the picture. This is the project *champion.* This person might also be fairly high in the company, but such a person need not be immediately responsible for funding the project. This person works on a day-to-day basis to give the idea of the game visibility and to urge the sponsor to fund the game. It is possible, of course, that the champion might be the sponsor, but divisions of labor occur even in high places.

The Startup Team and Approval

Given that the idea for a game has a sponsor and a champion (who might be the same person), the next step is that a startup committee for the game must convene. If your company is fairly large, the startup group might consist of a designer and a few project managers. It might be the game champion who brings together this team. The members represent different divisions of the company. The work of the team is to conduct a *feasibility* study of the game idea. A feasibility study establishes that the game can be produced for the amount of money slated for it and that no technical or creative obstacles stand in the way of its successful completion.

In bigger companies, the marketing group might drive the game production effort through several stages. In such a setting, a person who works in the marketing group might coordinate all preproduction activities. This person (perhaps under the title of *producer* or *director of development*) might take charge of the game production effort in much the same way that a producer in the film industry takes charge of starting a film production effort. The producer or development director works with a few others to scope out the project. As indicated before, it must be clearly established that the game is worth doing and can be done.

The worth of a game has to do with its potential as a market entity. Key elements in the evaluation of market risk are whether similar games are on the market, whether the idea is appealing to a strong segment of the game market, and whether the idea behind the game will be current when the game reaches the market (which could be anywhere from a matter of weeks to a year or more). Other factors are whether the game matches the genres of game that the organization has already produced and whether developers that the organization either already has employed or can find to employ can address the technology that the game calls for.

Figure 15.1 shows some of the people who might be involved in a feasibility or high-level assessment of a prospective game. Keep in mind that roles, titles, and hierarchies differ, so this representation is nothing more than an abstraction. Likewise, the perspective offered here might be a bit distorted because it is centered on the software engineering effort. In some organizations, the software engineers are under a software team lead. The lead might report to a game designer who is a graphical artist or graphics designer. The important thing to realize is that the idea for a game, as well as its initial design, emerges from an effort that extends quite a bit beyond the rather narrow confines of the software development team.

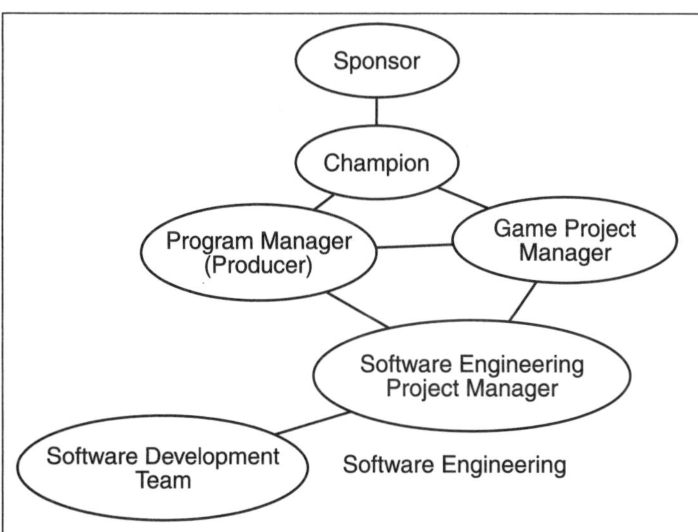

Figure 15.1
The person who initiates a game development effort depends on your organization.

Software Engineering Startup Input

Do software engineers take part in the startup activities? In some situations, they do, but in other situations, they do not. Software engineers participate when the startup team requires information about the *technical feasibility* of the game. This might be the case whether the organization is large or small. Regardless of how interesting an idea for a game might be, if someone has proposed using technology that is not within the development capabilities of the organization, then the risk the game poses might be too great to justify funding its production. Someone with technical expertise is required to establish the level of risk that the proposal contains, and the best person to do this is a software engineer.

On the other hand, even if the technical development of the game is feasible, the startup team requires information concerning how much effort will have to be put into developing the game. For example, if it is assumed that the game will use an engine purchased from a vendor, then it's important to state the capabilities and cost of the engine. If the organization is going to develop or extend its own engine, then this, too, must be taken into consideration. Someone with expertise in determining engineering efforts might also be needed. This person provides estimations of time and needed personnel. The person in the best position to perform this work is a software engineering project manager.

The Successful Start

If the preproduction phase leads to a successful outcome, then the producer or program director summons together people from different divisions of the organization to form the beginning of the production effort. To move forward with the startup of the production effort, the people who are initially assigned to the project must complete a fair amount of paperwork. They perform the paperwork so they can plan how to build the product. The plans involve how to assemble teams, order materials, contact vendors, and generally get the project into gear. This, then, is the real beginning of the production effort. To begin development of a game, you require a good idea, an executive sponsor who agrees to fund its development, and a group of people to conduct a feasibility study to ensure that the game is worth developing. Then you need a startup initiative involving a producer or program director who contacts several project managers or team leads to perform the work of planning the development effort.

The project managers are specialists. Some specialize in graphics, some in music, and some in software engineering. One of the immediate tasks that project managers face is that they must write planning documents that are likely to be included in a master design document for the game. In the instance of the software engineering project lead or manager, the emphasis might be at first upon developing a high-level document that describes what the software team will do as part of the overall project.

Formal Measures of Team Formation

Regardless of the size of your organization, some type of documentation is likely to underlie the formation of the software development team. Granted, you might work for a company that produces only a few documents as part of its production effort, but the more people who participate in the effort, the more the activity of development must be formally planned and tracked. For this reason, formal communications become necessary.

A plan for the overall game project is almost always produced. This plan might be called the *game production plan*. This document is not likely to be the work of a software engineer. It might be something that a person in marketing authors. Or it might be the result of a game designer who works in a high-level program development group. Again, the marketing group might draft a *marketing plan*. The graphical design group might draft a *design feature plan*. Several other groups might draft plans that represent their stake in the project.

The software engineering group (which might be referred to as the software development or programming group) is likely to be asked to draft a *software project development plan*, which might, in the end, contain several constituent documents, such as the software vision statement, the software requirements specification, the software design description, the software test plan, the software quality assurance plan, and the software deployment plan. Figure 15.2 illustrates how a chain of documentation might be created in an organization after an idea for a game has been accepted. It's not necessary to include the documentation that's specific to the software engineering group at this point. Note, however, that a software development plan is part of the picture.

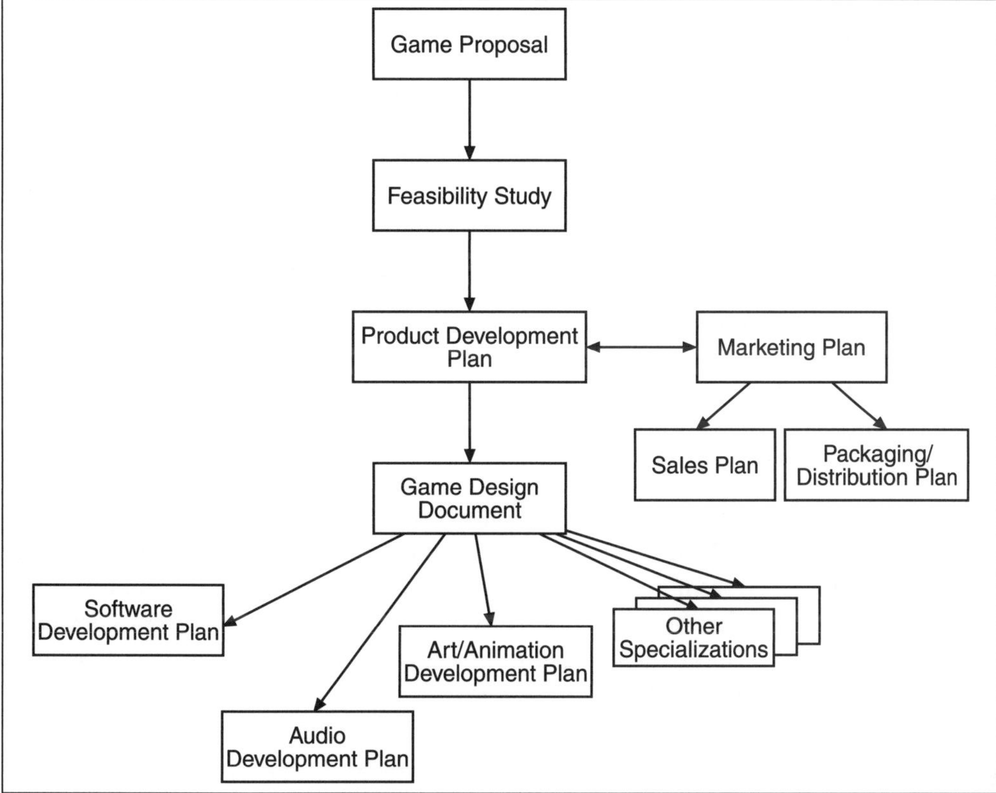

Figure 15.2
Plans might abound. The software development plan might begin a brief document that explains how the software team intends to put together a development effort.

As is evident from the earlier discussion, the first software developer who is assigned to the team is usually the software project manager. The next person on the team is likely to be a senior developer, who is sometimes called a software architect. The roles of these two individuals differ fairly drastically. The project manager draws up a plan for the development of the game software, hires people to construct the software, and manages the software development effort to its conclusion. Software engineering project managers might have highly technical backgrounds, but their current role confines them largely to managing a schedule and ensuring that the team connects up in the right way with the organization and works according to a well-planned schedule.

The software architect designs the software, helps the project manager assess the technical capabilities of those recruited for the team, and usually assumes a lead role in the design and construction of the game. The title assigned to this person might be something along the lines of lead developer, lead programmer, or senior software engineer. Whatever the title, the software architect might be said to be the one who knows how the entire system goes together and to whom everyone can turn for technical advice.

How Team Numbers Are Determined

The program manager usually estimates how many people a project requires. This estimation is based on information that is usually extracted from the initial requirements specification. The information in the specification establishes the scope of the project and the number of features that must be supported. Combined with the funding and the time allotted for construction of the game, this information allows the project manager to estimate how many developers are needed to develop the game.

In organizations that produce games according to a standard model, the project manager has a fairly precise idea of how many software developers the game requires. In situations in which the scope of the game cannot be defined until the requirements have been engineered, the project manager must first evaluate the requirements and the design before determining how many developers to hire.

To review: Two major factors shape the estimation of how many people are on the software development team. The first of these is the number of features that the development effort must address. The second is the time that the organization intends to allow for the software development effort. It is up to the software project manager to create a development schedule and determine the number of developers who must be assigned or hired for the software development effort.

What Teams Do

Obviously, this topic deserves a stronger treatment than it is going to receive here. Most of this book provides details about what the team does during its lifetime, but the following is a standard set of software engineering tasks:

- Prepare a software development plan.
- Gather technical requirements for the game and summarize these in a software requirements document.
- Design the software system that supports the features of the game and document this design in a design description.
- Construct the software for the game and create documentation for the code.
- Prepare a test plan for the software and conduct the tests that the plan specifies.
- Prepare a deployment plan for the software and deploy the software.

When Teams Dissolve

Generally, the deployment of a game marks what is known as the postproduction phase. Deployment does not mean that work on the game ceases, of course, but this is sometimes precisely what happens. If production ceases, it might be that everyone on the team is laid off, assigned to other projects, or idled. If the organization decides to start right to work on another release of the game, then it is unlikely that the development team will be disbanded. To begin another release, risks must be assessed, and requirements must be gathered. In short, another preproduction phase must be initiated, and given the momentum the existing product has already established, a production phase is likely to follow soon.

If a given game merits a subsequent release, it is seldom that a company willingly lays off developers who have worked on the game. This does happen, of course. Usually, layoffs of developers of a successful game occur only when exceptional incidents occur, as when the company loses a contract with a publisher, sells the rights to the game, or becomes so mired in its internal political conflicts that it can no longer function as a viable business entity. In a few instances, after a company has sold a game to another company, the team that developed the game has pulled up its roots and migrated to the company that bought the game. As the industry matures, such instances are likely to become exceedingly rare.

Important Factors in Team Formation

A software project manager recruits people to be part of a game development effort. The cooperation level of the people who make up the team often depends on two major factors. These two factors are the technical expertise of the members of the team and whether the personalities of the team members complement each other so that the team jells into a productive whole. Figure 15.3 illustrates the relationship. Both topics bear quite a bit of discussion.

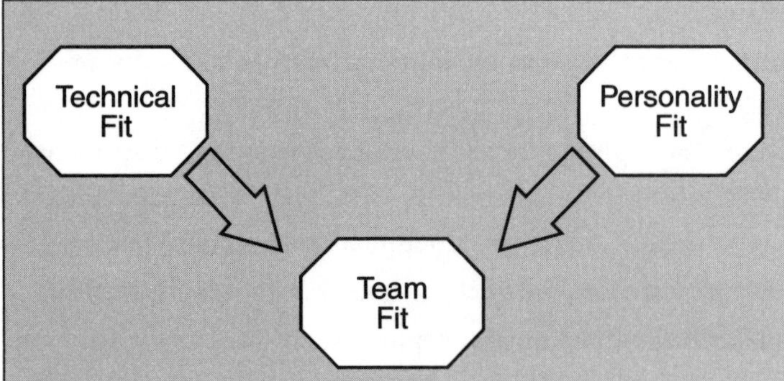

Figure 15.3
The success of a team depends on how well the members of the team complement each other technically and personally.

Technical Fit

Technical expertise can sometimes be a difficult expression to define. Generally, when people work together in a team effort, they must assume specialized roles. The roles they assume must be roles they find interesting and absorbing if they are to work well with the team. A given individual might be perfectly qualified, technically, to assume several roles, but if it is clear to those who interview this individual that the individual is not a good fit for the open role, then hiring that person is probably not a good idea.

Consider a situation in which a game is to be developed according to well-defined requirements and within the structure of a fairly nonnegotiable project schedule. A programmer who is used to working for sweatshop operations in which hacking is the primary criterion of success might not strike the project manager as a good candidate. It might be the case that this person is a dynamite programmer, but he has not been trained to work within a schedule and according to the definition of the project that the requirements and the design present. Working within such boundaries is a technical qualification.

On the other hand, the project manager might be looking for someone who is an excellent tester. If a dynamic, creative programmer shows up who clearly wants a role other than testing, then the fit is not a good one. Here, the programmer's general technical qualifications might be exquisite. He might be perfectly qualified to be a tester. However, the role that the individual seeks to assume does not match the role that the program manger seeks to fill. Here, again, the assessment of the individual's fit is based on the technical fit of the candidate.

Emotional Fit

The fit of the software engineer for the team extends to nontechnical dimensions. Just as teams create technical roles, teams also create emotional roles. This is especially true in game development, where production efforts often occasion some of the most exciting and demanding work to be found anywhere. The pace and pressure of a schedule can become so demanding that those on the team are likely to be forced at some point to show the raw edges of their personalities. At such moments, the emotional compatibility of those on the team far outweighs in importance their technical compatibility.

At certain moments in the life of a project, members of a team are likely to begin to attack or blame each other for delays or inefficiencies. Such raw exposures reveal different personality types as few other passages in a development cycle can. Although professionalism should prevent individuals from becoming petty or stupid to an extreme, it remains that when the bad passages occur, a team must possess a self-healing quality. A team can possess this quality if, in one scenario, it has members who view themselves as healers—people who will try to smooth out conflicts and move people toward renewed efforts. On still another level, self-healing also means maintaining a clear view of the object to be accomplished. Those who provide the impetus in this direction are sometimes called motivators, people who remain focused on the schedule regardless of how they might feel personally about issues.

The way that members of a team emotionally jell (some people call this the "chemistry" of the team) depends on the roles they assume. A good team consists of people with different personality types. Some people want to lead; others want to be led. Some are introverted, taciturn, or shy. Others are extroverted, vociferous, and bold. The ability of a team to absorb the dispositions of its members and to find ways to provide the best working context for personal expression proves essential for the success of the team. The team must be able to absorb differences and exploit the momentum that consensus provides.

Finding a Fit

Teams come into existence through the recruitment efforts of the project manager and, to a lesser extent, the technical lead (identified as the architect). Because the project manager often looks for personality compatibility and the lead developer looks for technical capability, it is likely that a balance of technical and emotional factors will determine who is recruited for the team. As a team grows in size, interviews can be conducted in which all the members of a team have a chance to interview each new candidate. Such an approach to interviewing can render mixed results. In some situations, members of the team can confer and determine whether the new person fits into the team; however, it is also possible that if the team gets off on the wrong footing, the recruiting effort might tend to enforce one personality type. Teams that lack mixtures of personalities tend to fail.

At such times, the project manager might intervene. It is almost always the case that someone with strong technical capabilities will be able to find a role within the team, even if personality mixes might not seem to be the best. The project manager can use this argument to bring people with complementary but distinct personalities into the team. As an example of how this scenario might unfold, consider people who do not come off well during job interviews because they are forthright in their declarations of what they think is the best technical way of doing things. Although studies indicate that such "devil's advocates" characterize almost all successful teams, it is still the case that if left on their own, teams almost always resist including such people.

If a project manager asks you to join a team early, you are most likely considered a senior developer. Your responsibility then becomes one of working with the project manager to technically assess other candidates for the team. You might find that the project manager sometimes disagrees with you about the fit of an individual even if the individual possesses, in your judgment, exceptional technical strengths. If this happens, you should be aware that the project manager is likely considering that person's emotional fit.

Formal Development Roles

Technical qualifications for a job usually fall within the boundaries established by formal development roles. The ability to describe a development role can be a tremendous help both to a person seeking a position on a team and to those on the team who are interviewing a candidate for a position. For example, if a software engineer is clearly identified as a tester and the team needs a tester, then the main consideration for inclusion into the team is the fact that the candidate fits into the named development role. If no other candidate has clearly identified this role as a specialization, then the decision seems almost a forgone conclusion.

In many descriptions of the game industry, roles in software engineering tend to be labeled with such bland, generic titles as "lead programmer," "tester," or "programmer," but the fact remains that the roles become much more subtle. Part of the reason for the lack of detail is that the descriptions of day-to-day software engineering activities are washed over by general, high-level visions of the production or development process. In reality, gradations of skill and expertise create a multitude of specialized roles.

One way to avoid the generalities is to explore how the skills usually included under the heading of software engineering lead to fairly specific job descriptions in highly structured organizations. The specializations might not receive titles in many organizations, but the roles and specializations still exist. Descriptions of these roles and specializations are included in the pages of the *Software Engineering Body of Knowledge* (SWEBOK), which breaks the work that software engineers perform into 10 basic categories and several more subcategories. Figure 15.4 illustrates some of the specializations drawn from the SWEBOK descriptions.

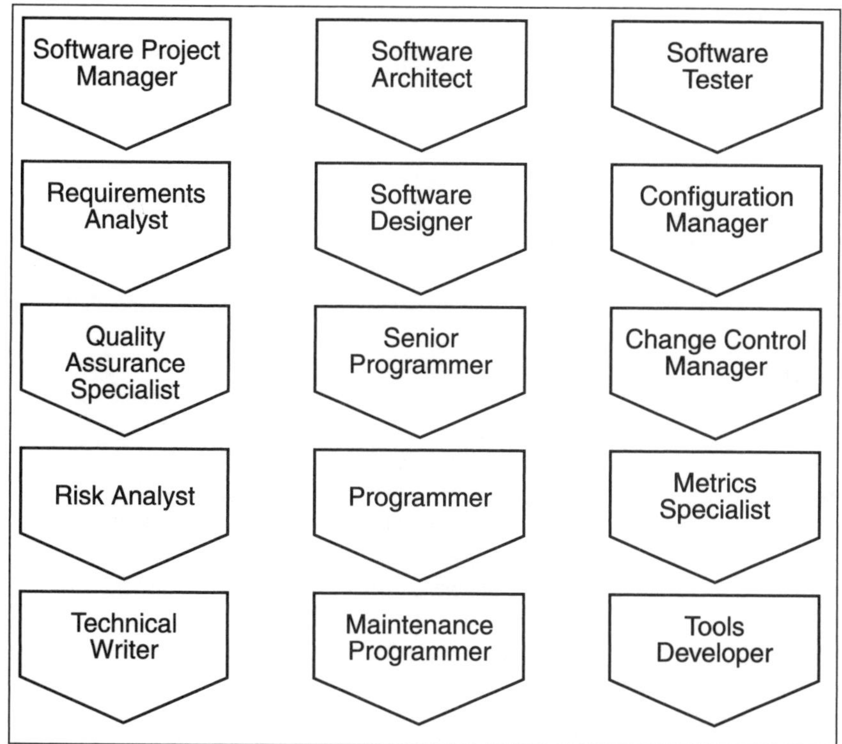

Figure 15.4
Your ability to contribute to the team in a specific role might be the leading factor in your recruitment for the team.

Table 15.1 identifies some of the roles that software engineers might assume as part of the software engineering effort that game production requires. Note that although gradations in levels of skill play a part in the roles that software engineers can assume, it remains that every role is open to everyone. You might be a programmer who specializes in meshes or Artificial Intelligence (AI), but you might also be an excellent tester. Combinations of roles often prove important. On the other hand, contending to be a specialist in everything portrays you as a software generalist. This can be a disadvantage. Consider the difference between a heart surgeon and a general practitioner if you are having chest pains. Likewise, consider the difference between a software generalist and a testing specialist for a team that is having testing problems.

Table 15.1 Software Engineering Roles

Role	Description
Requirements analyst	Gather and analyze requirements for the software.
Software architect	Determine the best architecture for the software. Select vendor components for inclusion in the development effort.
Software designer	Refine the software to achieve performance and other objectives.
Software tester	Test the software to ensure that it performs according to the requirements.
Senior programmer	Develop low-level design documentation, serve as a technical lead for others, and implement the software according to the design.
Programmer	Implement software according to design.
Maintenance programmer	Work on software created during previous development efforts to add functionality or eliminate errors. Work with customer support.
Configuration manager	Integrate software, manage builds, and maintain a knowledge base of the product builds.
Software project manager	Direct the software development team in its development effort; negotiate with members of the organization outside the development team; and negotiate with shareholders, stakeholders, and customers.
Quality assurance specialist	Put in place the documents and standards that ensure that the product is developed in a consistent manner.
Tools developer	Develop applications that aid the development team in such tasks as configuring, testing, debugging, and building the software.
Change control manager	Oversee requests for change and ensure that changes are made in a documented, approved manner.
Metrics specialist	Collect data on software performance and development activities and analyze them for general product and process improvement efforts.
Risk analyst	Track factors that might endanger the development effort.
Technical writer	Create and manage documentation for the project. Write user documentation.

Personal Project Roles

The personal roles that individuals on a project find are as mixed and multifarious as are those involving formal roles. For the most part, it is almost impossible for all the people on a team to have the same role. The impossibility lies in the fact that group dynamics tend to place people into different roles. Perhaps a question of how to solve a given design problem arises. If three people participate in solving the problem, one of the problem solvers is bound to end up knowing a bit more about the solution than the other two. This person then becomes, perhaps, the one who leads or guides the discussion. On the other hand, a well-informed person in the group might have strong opinions even though he is not a lead developer, and he becomes a kind of devil's advocate who argues steadily with the person in the lead role. The remaining person in the trio then becomes the mediator or team worker. Figure 15.5 illustrates some of the roles Edward Yourdon, drawing upon the work of Rob Thomsett, has documented (Yourdon, 115).

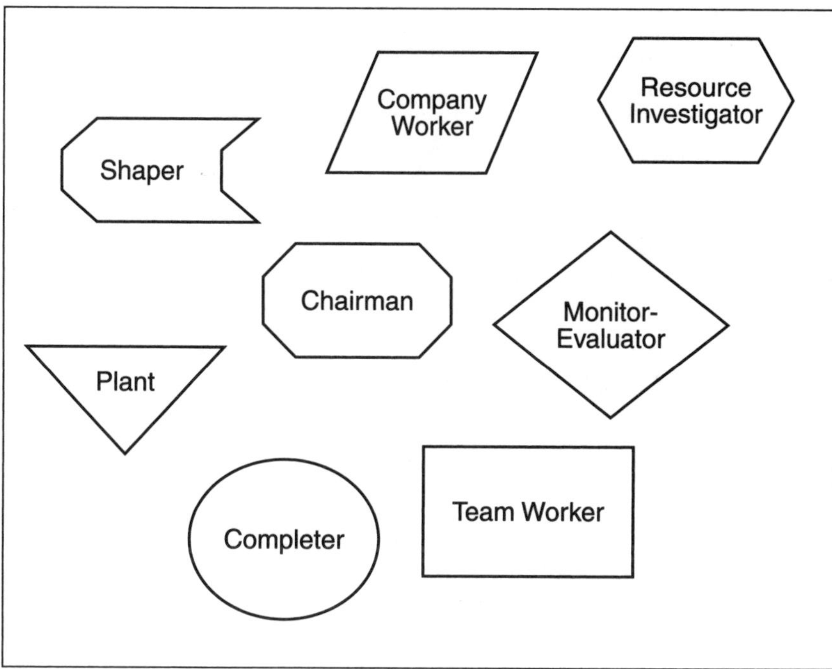

Figure 15.5
Team roles take form according to the dynamics of the team and the personality types involved.

It is difficult to name all the roles that a given team's interactions will create. A seasoned observer usually develops a short list of roles, however. Table 15.2 elaborates on the roles Yourdan identifies as typical of software development teams (Yourdan, 115–117).

Table 15.2 Personal Project Roles

Role	Description
Chairman	Has a clear understanding of each member's abilities and personality characteristics and manages to find where each person fits in best.
Shaper	Summarizes discussions or arrives at generalities that guide group discussions. Might be a lead designer or architect. Tends to see the big picture.
Plant	Challenges others and introduces new ideas. Often a problem solver. Sometimes viewed as a "devil's advocate."
Monitor-evaluator	Provides precise analysis and criticism of the key ideas, technology, and processes that the project encompasses.
Company worker	Works according to established procedures. Remains quiet and works steadily toward designated ends.
Team worker	Works to cement and strengthen the ties that bind the members of the team. Often helps others.
Resource investigator	Communicates well with people outside the group. Finds resources and technologies that the team requires to move ahead. A "scavenger."
Completer	Works with a sense of deadlines and the need to complete tasks. Can be trusted to bring things to closure.

Combining Formal and Personal Roles

You might be both a senior programmer and a monitor-evaluator. In other words, others look to you for advice about technical solutions, but they also seek your guidance in personal contexts about how to do things like get along with others, handle stress, or estimate and schedule tasks. On the other hand, you might be a beginning programmer who comes across to others as a completer. Because of the mix of your qualities, you might find that more senior-level people approach you with opportunities to apply your skills to complex tasks and establish yourself as a solid member of the team.

These are but two scenarios. Clearly, any combination is possible, for most people fit into several personal and technical roles. The point here is to show that the role you end up having on the team will be a combination of your technical contributions and the fit of your personality into the dynamic of the team.

To an extent, however, teams that do not find formal mechanisms for guiding or channeling the roles that people play in the development process stand at great risk. It is for this reason that activities involving controlled documentation and formalized reviews can help tremendously with a team effort. Figure 15.6 illustrates how formal and team roles combine.

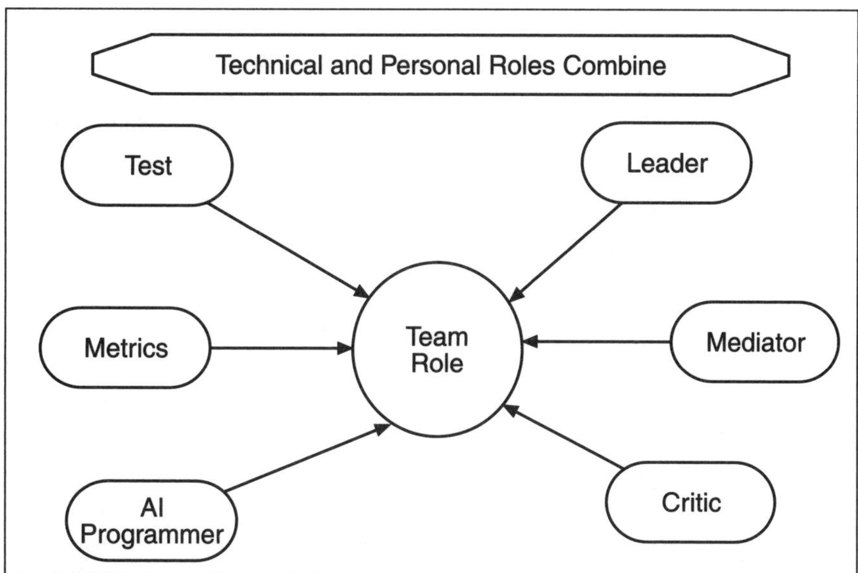

Figure 15.6
Roles combine to define your unique position on the development team.

Team Activities

A team is something more than a group of people joined by roles. As Tom Demarco and Timothy Lister have pointed out in *Peopleware* (see the reference at the end of this chapter), one of the most important elements in the formation of a successful team is a common sense of purpose. Teams exist because people embrace a common goal, and when they embrace a common goal with the right spirit and commitment, they form a whole that is much greater than any one of its parts (Demarco and Lister, 123). If the organization tries to shape the team from outside through the imposition of methodologies, success is not likely to result. Nor is success likely to result if a strong manager tries to command a team into existence from the inside through demands and threats. The sense and understanding of a common goal by those on the team remains the primary element in the formation of the team.

When people possess a common sense or understanding of a goal, they are not surrendering their individuality to reach something that is outside their specialized effort. Everyone on the team might have a different view of the final product, but despite these differences of view, everyone is still able to move forward in an efficient, coordinated way to complete the final product. That this occurs leads to a further observation. As Demarco and Lister write, "The purpose of a team is not goal attainment but goal alignment" (126).

Goal alignment can form the basis of a unified effort by a group of software engineers because the software engineers understand both the roles that they as individuals occupy on a team and the set of communication tools and skills that allow them as members of the team to work together as a team. If you look at the list of things a software engineer is assumed to know about planning, controlling, and documenting a software project, for instance, you will soon recognize that the majority of these things are essentially tools for enhancing the ability of specialists to align their efforts toward a common goal. Software engineers who formally understand the best practices that apply to team management tend to be more effective as team members.

Aligned Goals

In his *Software Project Survival Guide* (see the reference at the end of this chapter), Steven McConnell provides an essential list of items that should be placed under change control. When something is placed under change control, it has special significance, for it is something that forms an essential part of the finished product. In a sense, things that are paced under change control constitute the central pathways and tools through which the team concerts its efforts toward a finished product. For this reason, when you become familiar with the items that McConnell includes in his essential list, you can at the same time become aware of what might be viewed as the collective consciousness of the team. Change control helps to shape the information that allows the team to work as a team, to possess a common understanding of the project. Change control makes possible the aligned goals of all the developers who form a team. Figure 15.7 illustrates items that are often put under change control.

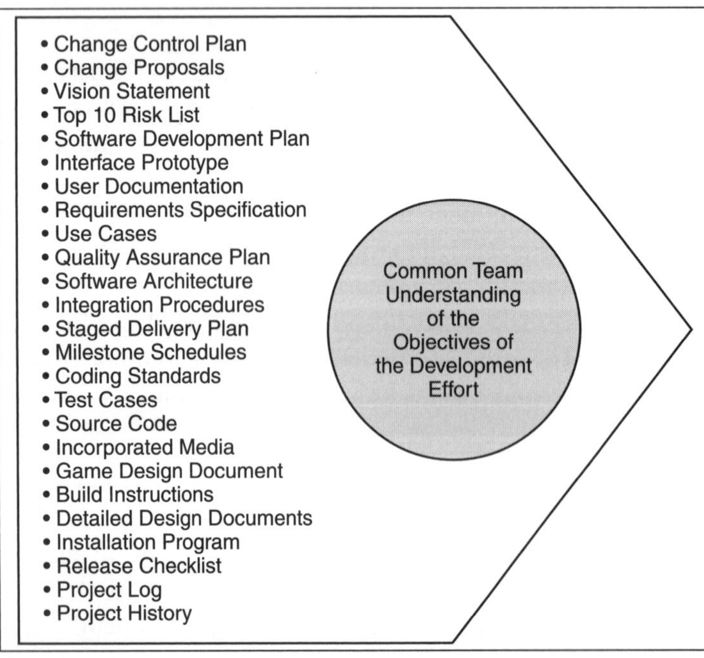

Figure 15.7
Information under change control can be viewed as information that provides the team with a common or aligned sense of what the project is about (McConnell, 81).

Change control involves more than having a control board of a few people regulating how and when people can make changes to code or documents. Instead of limiting control of information to a few people, change control actually has the opposite effect: one of allowing all team members to have access to the core information from which an understanding of the project and the product is obtained. The work of change control is to ensure that everyone on the team can share in the development effort on a fairly equal footing. In light of this goal, it's possible to expand on McConnell's essential list and describe how each type of information contributes to the team's ability to understand the project as a common goal. Table 15.3 summarizes the controlled items of information as *pathways.* Such pathways are so important that the success of the team depends on the ability of the team to maintain them. Without these pathways, the ability of the team to align its efforts deteriorates because it can no longer coordinate the specialized roles and efforts through a shared body of information.

Table 15.3 Core Information Pathways for Teams

Path of Information	Description
Vision statement	A statement that the team might compose together that briefly expresses the purpose and goal the team has set for itself in its development effort. A vision statement is a starting point of common understanding.
Change control plan	An agreement among the members of the team about how changes to important work, such as requirements and code, are to be made so that everyone on the team can keep track of them.
Change proposals	An agreement about how team members can propose change. This might be a brief form or a convention involving sending an e-mail to a change control coordinator.
Top 10 risk list	A list of the major dangers to the success of the project. Everyone on the team contributes to this list, and knowledge of the list allows everyone to know the ways in which the project is most likely to be derailed.
Software development plan	The schedule that everyone is expected to follow during the development effort. It provides a common view of the milestones, the costs, and the scope of the project.
Interface prototype	For a game, an interface prototype is a stripe. (See Chapter 4, "Software Design—Much Ado About Something.") A *stripe* is a proof of concept, a way of demonstrating the feasibility of a concept or the desirability of a given approach to constructing the game.
User documentation	Information that's intended for the user, such as an online manual. The primary value of user documentation is that it represents the customer or player viewpoint.

(continued on next page)

Table 15.3 Core Information Pathways for Teams (continued)

Path of Information	Description
Requirements specification	The starting place for the whole software development project. As pointed out in Chapter 2, "Requirements—Getting the Picture," the software requirements specification contains the plan of how the software system is to address the requirements.
Use cases	Contexts of stated requirements. You can employ use cases in the design effort to define system performance contexts. You can also use them for testing. Developers, documentation specialists, and testers require ongoing access to use cases to solidify their understanding of the project.
Quality assurance plan	A schedule and protocol for reviews. A quality assurance plan differs from a change control plan because it provides a way that members of the team can review each other's work. It sets up a model, for instance, for code reviews. It establishes a way that the team can agree to continue on from one stripe of development to the next.
Software architecture	The principles and quality measures that the software developers should seek to fold into the software. These principles give shape to the software design description, discussed in Chapter 4. The software design description provides logical, behavioral, user, and deployment views of the system, views that allow everyone to know the scope and development strategy that underlie the development effort.
Integration procedures	For the software developers, integration procedures are essential to being able to work together on a day-to-day basis. These procedures are also necessary for understanding how different layers and components of the system are to interact.
Staged delivery plan	The coordination of efforts from incremental release to incremental release is essential for the success of the project. In the scheme presented beginning in Chapter 4, delivery is not so much a staged delivery as it is an iterative and incremental approach to the development of the game.
Milestone schedules	For each stripe of *Ankh*, tasks were scheduled to be performed to reach intermediary milestones. That resulted in a project plan and a set of smaller plans that fit within the project plan. In this way, all members of the team had a way to clearly understand the short-term release goals.
Coding standards	The way that classes, attributes, operations, and other features of the code for the game should be named. This agreement immediately reduces the possibility that developers will implement incompatible design features.
Test cases	A specialized but commonly shared approach to testing the validity and functionality of implemented features. Everyone should have access to test cases. An element or component that cannot be tested is inevitably a major risk to the project.

Path of Information	Description
Source code	A standard way to store and retrieve code. Source code control is the one thing that can be controlled when everything else is left open. Even projects that lack all documentation tend to end up having fairly coherent source control procedures.
Incorporated media	Includes music, sounds, animations, bitmaps, and everything else that software allows to be drawn into the game. For a game development effort, the software developers develop toward both temporary (programmer) and final production art. Art is what makes the game, of course, as much or more so than the software.
Game design document	A high-level, inclusive document that defines the game and establishes the roles of all the groups involved in the development effort.
Build instructions	A brief description of how to perform a build should be available to all the programmers from the beginning. The procedures should be a closely detailed, numbered set of steps. This is a common way that everyone can safeguard the central product. It deserves special treatment.
Detailed design documents	Specific implementation views of how to build the product.
Installation program	Information about the installation of the program makes the game the property of the whole team as a deliverable.
Release checklist	A checklist that provides a final view of the product. It should provide a comprehensive description of precisely what is needed to deliver the fully functional product.
Project log	A record of the group's effort as it has created the product. The log might list day-to-day accomplishments or concerns. It allows everyone on the project to have access to a living history of the development effort. It also provides the core documentation for the project postmortem.
Project history	Compiled from the project log and a few other documents, such as the project plan. It is useful to the team as a way to discover the most central issues and findings of the development effort. For an organization, it forms the basis of continuing quality improvement.

Participating in the Information Flow

Although members of a team can align goals if they communicate formal project information through the pathways of information listed in Table 15.3, creating a common effort requires everyone to develop a common understanding. A common effort is a living process that artifacts alone cannot convey. The living process consists of a continuous effort on the part of every member of the team to learn about the product, to iteratively reshape and improve the product, and to teach others about the product. The primary way that a team can accomplish these goals is through reviews.

Reviews are the leading formal means by which all members of a team can focus their efforts on the project. Reviews provide a controlled medium of information exchange. During a review, team members examine and productively contribute to the work of other team members. The exchange is controlled because people who are involved in a review are placed, once again, in specific project roles. The role of the reviewer differs from that of someone who is simply trying to find fault. If a team is moving in the right direction, everyone on the team has an established place as a reviewer.

In the role of a reviewer, you have certain responsibilities. One responsibility is to try to eliminate faults from the material being reviewed. The spirit of what you say during a review, then, should be positive. This next section offers a few basic practices that can serve to carry the members of a team successfully through the many reviews that characterize a successful project.

Review Strategies

It is a good idea to establish a documented procedure for conducting formal reviews. Reviews need not be painfully formal, but they should be structured so that they are productive. The comments made about the work under review should be recorded so that the author of the work can benefit from them. If remarks are not formally recorded, chances are no record will be made of them, and opportunities for improving work will be lost.

When material is reviewed, the strongest effort possible should be made to avoid personal reference to the competence or performance of the team member who produced the material under review. The person responsible for crafting the code is irrelevant. What is relevant is anything that might improve the code.

On the other hand, even if reviews should incorporate formal procedures, they need not have the feel of formal procedures. In many situations, as Richard Whitehead notes, reviews can be set up informally on an ongoing basis (Whitehead, 28–33). Informal reviews occur when one person works continuously with another and makes helpful comments. An example of this type of review is the work of paired programmers. In this arrangement, one programmer tests another programmer's code on a continuous basis. Paired programmers trade roles regularly. The goal is to ensure that the development effort undergoes continuous, robust testing right from the start.

Another approach is formalized review. Such reviews are often conducted to move the general vision of the project further along the development path or to bring closure to a development phase. They involve either the whole team or a large portion of it. For example, the team might conduct a formal review of the software requirements specification prior to beginning the design effort.

Informal Review Practices

Whitehead recommends the following practices for informal reviews (Whitehead, 31):

- Concentrate on talking about what will improve the work you are reviewing. Just saying something is wrong does little to contribute to the review.
- If something is wrong, concentrate on what is wrong. Try not to apologize or, on the other hand, show your superiority. Anyone about to make a costly mistake will be grateful to you for your warning if what you say has the same sincerity and directness of a warning about, say, a slippery floor or a tainted dish of food.
- For quality improvement, try to refer to examples of superior work. Pointing to good solutions is better than trying to improve or reshape something by being critical of it.
- As Whitehead puts it, "listen." People might be defensive about things you say, so it is important to be sensitive to how they are reacting to your words. If you listen, you can respond in a way that shows you are not making a judgment.
- Try to avoid expressing opinions. If something is done in a way that differs from the way you would have done it, it is not therefore wrong.
- Do not rely too much on automated tools. Try to look at code, for example, rather than a report that a tool has produced about the code.
- Look toward the finished product, not the intermediary, developing product. What you suggest ultimately serves as a guide that another person can use toward a distant end.

Formal Review Practices

Steve McConnell suggests a set of best practices for formal reviews. Again, formal reviews can have a familiar feel to them, but on the other hand, they usually involve a structured examination of a document, code, or some other project artifact by either the whole team or a significant subset of the team (McConnell, 132–133).

- Begin reviewing documents and other artifacts early in the project. When you conduct reviews, have in place a quality assurance agreement about how you will conduct reviews.
- Try not to speculate about solutions to problems during reviews. Instead, just point out what you believe to be problems.
- Do not digress from the technical focus that the review centers on. It does no good to try to impress anyone or put anyone down. If you have a solution you would like to propose, then you can do so in another context, through a formal proposal, for example.

- Keep notes so that the information gathered during the review will not be lost. A scribe for the review should always be appointed.
- Record defects during the review rather than leaving them to be documented later. In other words, obtain precise statements about what is wrong and record these statements as they are made.
- After the review is over, verify that the problems identified during the review have been acted on. Avenues to this goal include issuing change requests or creating team action items.
- Share the information obtained during the review with everyone on the team. Sharing is possible through publication of review minutes or inclusion of minutes in the project log.

Building a Team

Even if you understand roles, skills, project artifacts, and the use of informal and formal review techniques, what you derive from your experience with a team depends on what you bring to the team that falls outside the standard software engineering toolkit. As Edward Yourdan and others have pointed out, feuding team members, incompetent planning, poor management, and faulty product designs often characterize software development projects, and sometimes the best thing a responsible software engineer can do in response is resign. On the other hand, it remains that if you refuse to become cynical toward your project and try to take the initiative to make it better, then you are at the very least preventing a bad situation from becoming worse.

One thing that can go far to contribute to the success of a team effort is for everyone on the team to work with the assumption that the project will result in something positive for everyone on the team. What team members seek individually is difficult to assess. Feelings and thoughts about career expectations, intellectual interests, technical paths, and spiritual concerns are but a few of the many things that motivate people to participate in a team.

In contrast to the things that comprise the multitude of personal visions that characterize the experiences of individuals on a team are the common goals that are often the subject of team discussions. Table 15.4 provides a summary of some of these items.

Table 15.4 Qualities That Build a Team*

Team Quality	Discussion
Common purpose	The team arrives at a shared understanding of the project it has assembled to accomplish. The team senses that its members are on a mission, one that will lead to the accomplishment of tasks that all members of the team consider important.
Commitment	Members of the team are willing to commit themselves fully to the completion of the project. For the duration of the project, the project will have a central place in the lives of all members of the team. Allowances must be made for certain family and personal concerns, but at least professionally, the project stands at the center.
Mutual commitment	Members of the team are dedicated to helping each other complete the project. They avoid speaking disparagingly about each other or trying to benefit at each other's expense. If one person on the team disrupts the progress of the work, then the team is willing to join ranks and accept the idea that this person must be dropped from the team. Members of the team must be able to trust each other to complete the work that needs to be done.
Defined purpose	It is necessary to have a clearly defined purpose. Toward this end, everyone must know what is to be accomplished, and everyone must be able to point to evidence that shows how they will accomplish this task. Such evidence consists of, among other things, a project plan, a set of requirements, and a project design.
A sense of worth	The team must sense that the project is worth doing. When members of the team can boast a bit about what they are doing, things are moving in the right direction. In other words, if you hear that the game you are working on is the best game ever, then for the person making the boast, you can be sure that the project possesses worth.
Communications	Good communications tend to be frequent and informal. The members of the team need to be located so that they can easily communicate with each other. Programmers working as a team, for example, work less effectively if they do not share the same workspace. The quick, fruitful exchanges that allow for informal reviews are fostered by close proximity.
Lack of disruptions	Along with close proximity goes stability of setting. A team should have a secure, well-equipped work area. A team that is asked to move from building to building during a project or that lacks a properly equipped work environment loses productivity and experiences stress.

(continued on next page)

Table 15.4 Qualities That Build a Team*

Team Quality	Discussion
No bottlenecks	Few restrictions should be placed upon when or how team members can communicate with each other. Table 15.3 listed a number of formal media by which the team can track its progress and formalize its work on the project. These are part of the picture. Another part of the picture is where people sit, when they interact, and how they decide they can communicate most effectively with each other. An example might be if a tester and a programmer are placed in the same office or if someone of junior standing is placed alongside someone with senior standing.
Strong sense of progress	The team needs to see that it is making regular progress toward the completion of its project. In this respect, the communications of the project manager can be extremely valuable. Milestones shown on a Gantt chart provide a way to show everyone on the team that progress is being made.
Keeping skills current	The members of the team need to receive support to keep their skills current. The project should provide a way to learn new skills.
Acceptance of team goals	Members of a successful team usually make the team goals fairly personal. In other words, whether the project succeeds has for them important personal implications because they sense that if the project fails, they have more at stake than transfer or unemployment. A deeper commitment ties them to the project's success: a sense of professionalism.
A mixture of personalities	The members of the team should feel free to be themselves. Some of the personality descriptions Yourdan noted are listed in Table 15.2. That this mixture is not only nearly inevitable but positively necessary might come as a novel thought, but the fact is that if a team does not possess a rich mixture of personalities, it is likely to fail.
The social fountain	The team must be united, in part, by social bonds. Granted, older people with families might have little time to gather at a pub to talk about the issues the product faces, but this is still a fact of every successful project. People who are committed to an exciting game development project tend to form close bonds for the duration of the project.
Leadership style	Teams must be lead by people who have a management style that is compatible with the members of the team. Bad managers can destroy the efforts of even the best teams.

*See Richard Whitehead, *Leading a Software Development Team*, pp. 116–122.

Managing Project Team Work

The roles and responsibilities of the individuals who participate in a team must balance out if the team is to be successful in its development effort. More than anything else, what balance means here is that the work of each member of the team complements the work of every other member of the team. Mutual respect forms the basis of successful team interactions.

When one member of the team attempts to dominate the activity of the team, some observers refer to such a developer as a "hero." The hero can insist, for instance, that everyone on the team should accept his personal vision of what a game should be. If this vision has little to do with the game that has been specified in the requirements, then the development effort is in trouble.

It might seem that an appropriate response to the hero mentality is for the team to ignore the hero, but this is sometimes easier said than done. If the hero has a strong personality, possesses advanced technical knowledge, and is extremely skilled as a developer, other team members might find it impossible to ignore him. Dealing with the hero becomes the responsibility of the project manager. Although the project manager has many responsibilities, ensuring that personalities and efforts balance out according to roles, responsibilities, and scheduled tasks is one of the most central.

Project Leadership

Regardless of how this effort might be embedded in the overall game production effort, the person who manages the software development project will be referred to in this book as the *project manager*. When it comes to defining the role of the project manager, the best reference is the *Project Management Body of Knowledge (PMBOK) Guide*, published by the Project Management Institute. (See the reference at the end of this chapter.) According to the PMBOK, "Project management is the application of knowledge, skills, tools, and techniques to project activities to meet project requirements" (6). This definition implies the following responsibilities:

- Initiating the project by writing the project plan, scoping the project, and recruiting personnel to work on the project
- Planning the project so that the product can be developed to accord with the requirements and schedule set for the delivery of the product
- Executing the development of the product, which involves scheduling, managing, and reviewing the activities of all those who participate in the development effort
- Controlling the costs of the project, which involves ensuring that the development of the project does not cost more than what the budget stipulates it should cost
- Closing out the development effort, which involves delivering the product and accessing the product development activity in a way that yields information that can benefit future development efforts

Project Management Skills

Table 15.5 provides a list of the qualities that the PMBOK considers important if project managers are to accomplish the tasks of initiating, planning, executing, controlling, and closing the project. Such skills are part of the work of every member of the team, but with a project manager, these skills must be developed to a highly polished level. The project manager must be the most visible representative of the project, the person who must defend the project's existence when it is called into question for technical, scheduling, staffing, or budgetary reasons. Along similar lines, the project manager must be the person on the team who is best at resolving disputes, explaining problems so all can understand them, and making decisions when a number of perplexing alternatives are at hand.

Table 15.5 Project Management Skills*

Skill	Description
Leading	Establish direction by developing a vision of the future and the strategies that can achieve the goals established for the team. Align the efforts of the people on the team by communicating clear goals to all members of the team. Motivate and inspire those on the team by showing them ways to overcome political, bureaucratic, and personal obstacles.
Communicating	Exchange information in a clear, unambiguous, and complete way. Write, listen, and speak with and for the team. Develop information for both the team and its customers. Produce formal documentation to record or justify the efforts of the team. Report information to those higher in the organization who audit or champion the project.
Negotiating	Confer with those on the team and to whom the team is accountable to reach agreements on such things as project scope, project cost, project schedules, contracts and salaries, task assignments, and hiring and firing decisions.
Problem solving	Define problems and make decisions. Determine the causes and symptoms of problems and whether problems are internal (as with a difficult employee) or external (funding, work spaces) to the team effort. Identify solutions and decide which solution is the best.
Influencing the organization	Get things done by understanding the formal and informal ways the organization works. Understand how different groups in the organization—such as customers, partners, contractors, and others—relate to the project.

*Source: Project Management Institute, *A Guide to the Project Management Body of Knowledge* (PMBOK Guide) (Newtown Square, PA: Project Management Institute, 2001), pp. 24–27.

Means of Management

Project managers plan and schedule the tasks that team members perform to meet the requirements of the project. Three artifacts of planning and scheduling that project managers use almost without exception are the Work Breakdown Structure (WBS), the PERT chart, and the Gantt chart. Just as the paths of information that Table 15.3 presents form the central ways in which members of a team formally communicate, the WBS, PERT charts, and Gantt charts form the central means by which the tasks, milestones, and dependencies that a team faces can be analyzed and made a part of a realistic schedule.

Making the case for the value of setting milestones and maintaining a clear understanding of project dependencies, Frederick Brooks, Jr., wrote in *The Mythical Man-Month* that "Disaster is due to termites, not tornadoes..." (154). In other words, projects often fail because people allow schedules to slip in small, largely imperceptible ways. Small slippages of schedule are, according to Brooks, more dangerous than catastrophic events because after a catastrophe everyone knows that a major problem has occurred and that major steps must be taken to repair the damage. In contrast, small slippages are unseen or even concealed, and the damage they bring with them does not emerge until it is too late to do anything about it other than admitting that the project will not be completed on time.

Creating WBSs and Gantt and PERT charts allows you to develop a reliable way to track progress and know when a delay has occurred. Being able to track progress and delays helps the team sustain what Brooks—borrowing a term from baseball—referred to as *hustle.* Hustle is the general tendency to make certain that small delays do not occur. There is really no better term for it. When a team hustles, the team commits to doing tasks on time and with energy and care. Taking care of small things, as Brooks contends, ends up being more important than concentrating completely on big things.

WBSs

After the requirements of a project have been completed, the project manager is in a position to begin estimating the number of tasks the team must complete to develop a software product. One means by which the project manager can analyze the collection of activities encompassed by the requirements is the WBS. The WBS is a chart that decomposes the tasks involved in a project. Figure 15.8 illustrates a WBS for some of the tasks associated with the development of *Ankh.*

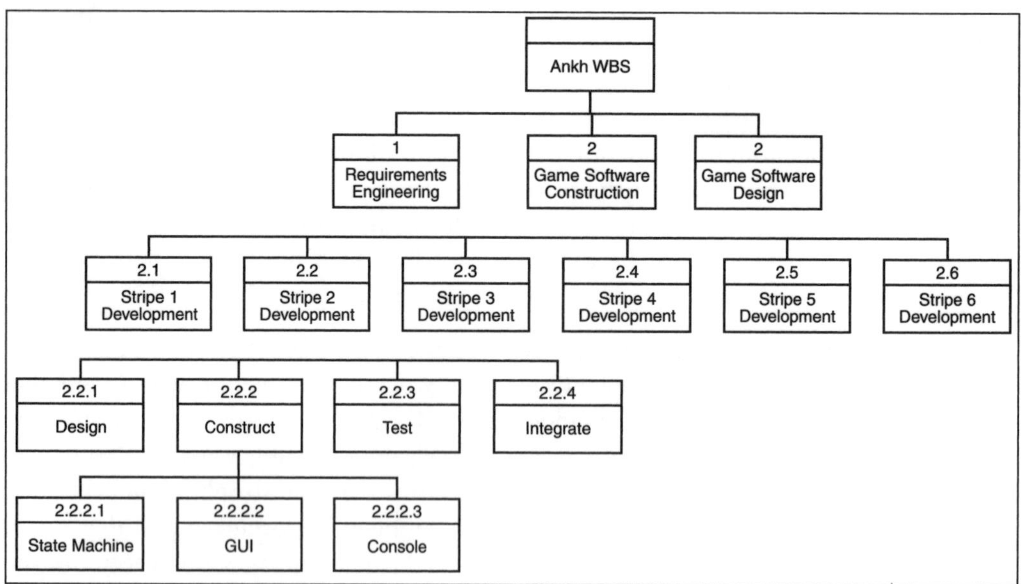

Figure 15.8
A WBS provides a way to decompose project tasks to a level of detail that makes it possible to accurately estimate the time, effort, and cost.

As Figure 15.8 shows, the WBS begins at the highest level of generality. From there, it moves downward, through multiple tiers, until it reaches a level of detail that makes individual tasks visible. At the task level, it becomes possible to begin making estimations about the time and effort each task requires. Only by decomposing the project until it can be viewed as a set of specific tasks can the project manager hope to reach a point at which estimating work requirements can be made with accuracy.

Even if you are not working as a project manager, the WBS is a helpful tool for analyzing and estimating the work that a given task requires. If you are working at the level of detailed design and your project manager asks you to estimate the time you will require to perform a task, you can use the same general approach. Some useful steps are as follows:

1. Understand what it is that you are expected to do.
2. Assume from the first that you will have to plan, construct, and test your work.
3. For the construction phase, break the project down until you can easily picture the components you will have to construct. For example, a class might consist of operations. Estimate the number of operations.
4. Further, estimate whether the operations are complex or simple. If they remain complex, break down the work into smaller units.
5. After you have arrived at an estimation, add time for emergencies. You can call this a *margin of error.*

WBS Task Lists

After you have completed a WBS, you can recast its results in tabular form. In this form, you can view the task in terms of its status, who is going to do it, and how much of it remains to be done. You can then assign each task a simple completion status, such as begun, in progress, or complete. On the other hand, you can assign an estimation of duration to the task. Figure 15.9 illustrates a partially populated WBS task table.

Task ID	Description	Status	Assigned	Comments
1.	Requirements Engineering			
2.	Game Software Construction			
2.1	Stripe 1			
2.2	Stripe 2			
2.2.1	Design			
2.2.2	Construct			
2.2.2.1	StateMachine			
2.2.2.2	GUI			
2.2.2.3	Console			
2.2.3	Test			
2.2.4	Integrate			

Figure 15.9
WBS task tables provide a way to translate details into assignments, durations, and statuses of completion.

PERT Charts

PERT stands for Project Evaluation and Review Technique. The importance of a PERT chart lies in its ability to show dependencies among several tasks. One of the most damaging things about a small delay is that it can cause several delays in many other activities that depend on it. Additionally, a PERT chart allows you to detect when a given task depends on several other tasks. Figure 15.10 illustrates a PERT chart representing a few events drawn from the WBS task list. The chart shows task interdependencies. Arrows indicate that one task leads to the start of another.

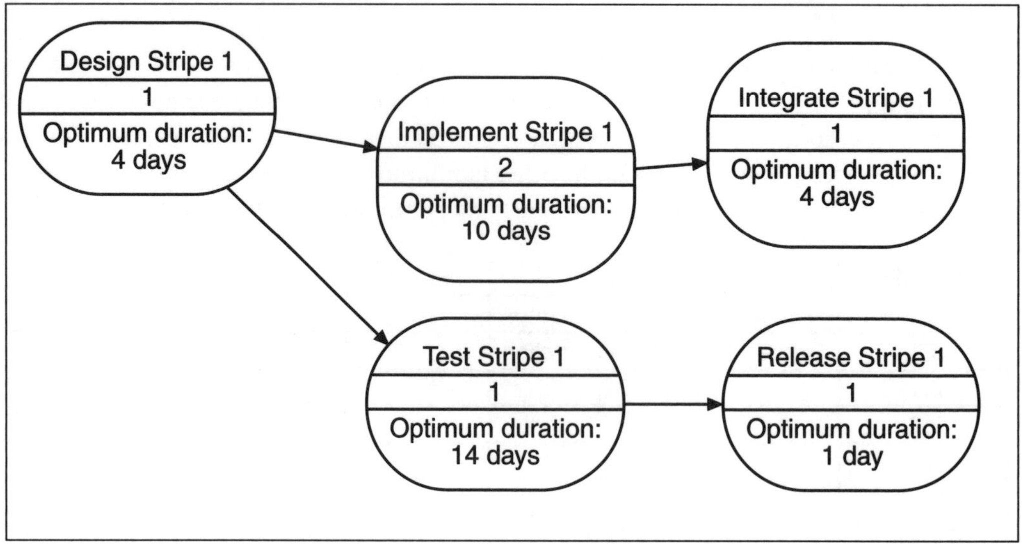

Figure 15.10
PERT charts provide a convenient way to see how one task is dependent upon another or creates a dependency for another.

Gantt Charts

The Gantt chart is named after its originator, Henry Gantt, who invented it during the early part of the twentieth century. The Gantt chart's greatest value is that it can show what is usually referred to as the *critical path* of a project. The critical path of a project is the sequence of tasks that must be performed on time if the project is to remain on schedule. Slippage in any one task in the critical path leads to an overall slippage in the progress of the project as a whole.

The layout of the Gantt chart is fairly straightforward. Task names are depicted in a column at the left of the chart. The duration of each task is then depicted to the right of the task name. Although one bar might overlap another, one bar tends to flow into another, indicating in this way the course of activities that define the project.

The Gantt chart can be adorned in many ways. Icons at the ends of duration bars show milestones. A milestone usually marks the completion of a task that is within the critical path. For this reason, when a milestone is completed, the overall status of the project can be gauged. Milestones are valuable because the team can gain from them a sense that the project is moving forward in good order. On the other hand, slippage of a milestone can serve as an alert that not all is well. Figure 15.11 illustrates a Gantt chart. In the chart, the horizontal lines represent the period scheduled for a given task. The dark pentagons that follow, for example, the Integration task bars are milestones.

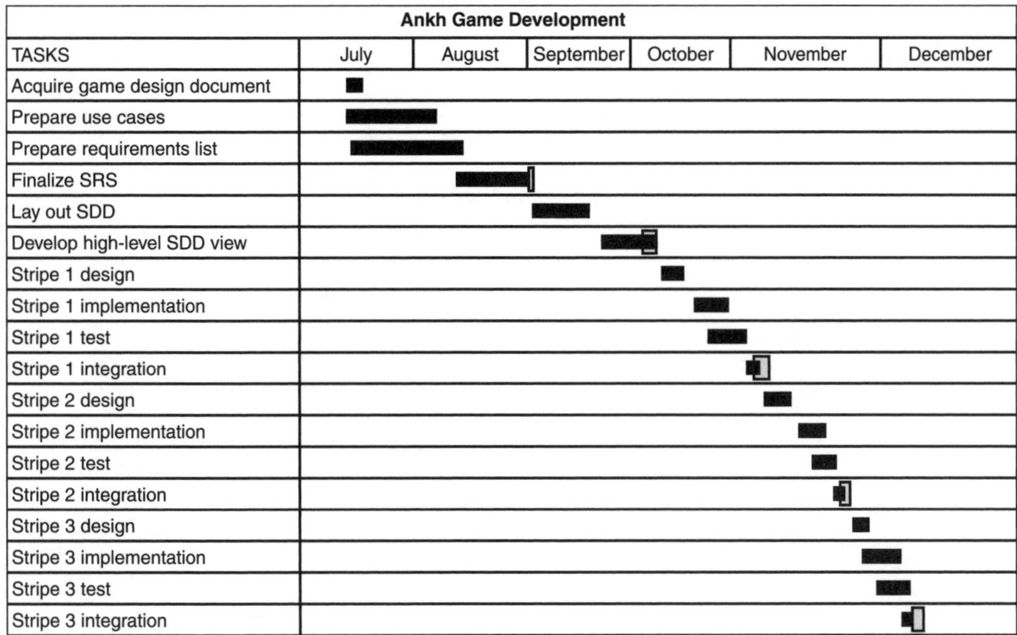

Figure 15.11
A Gantt chart tracks the duration of tasks and shows their dependencies.

Why Projects Fail

Despite lists of best practices and people who clearly understand their work, software projects fail all the time. In fact, whether for games or other software products, the failure rate is still much higher than the success rate. The reasons for the failures frequently trace back to flaws in project management, but blaming project managers is not the solution. A project manager is the person who is most visible to an organization when a project fails. If observers blame project managers, they are doing little more than what sport fans do when they blame a coach. The whole team occupies a similar role, one that is less visible but not necessarily less painful. Members of a team that fails to complete a software product often lose their jobs.

According to Whitten, Bentley, and Dittman, the reasons that projects fail can be accounted for under 12 key headings. (See the reference at the end of this chapter.) Although a few of the reasons for failure indicate that lack of funding and organizational shortcomings are at the root of project failures, it is interesting to note how many trace back to dysfunctional team dynamics. The objective is not to try to establish blame or propose specific solutions but rather to provide a set of warning signs you might watch for as you participate in a game development effort. Table 15.6 provides a summary of these causes.

Table 15.6 Reasons Teams Fail

Cause	Description
Upper management abandonment	If the sponsor of a project abandons a project, the funding comes to an end. Reasons for such abandonment abound, but one to watch out for is when another project is perceived as holding greater potential. It is important that you convey positive messages about the project you are on.
Methodology shortcuts	If an audit of the project occurs and it is found that the team has been neglecting to follow a coherent approach to development, the project might be viewed as a liability. The lesson here is that if the project falls behind schedule, it is still important to stick with a steady, professional approach to development. If it is perceived that your team is going about its work in a sloppy, risky, or wasteful manner, you can expect repercussions.
Worthless methodologies	This is the opposite of the previous reason. In this case, the project follows a methodology that requires a great deal of expensive, meaningless work, such as the maintenance of worthless documentation. It is important to follow quality assurance measures, but if people are taking up enormous amounts of time on worthless paperwork or other such methodological overhead, then it is time to ask questions.
Loss of scope	The development team loses track of the requirements and begins allowing feature creep or goldplating to drive the project. In time, the game might become complex, bloated, and expensive and yet show few finished features from the requirements. When sponsors see such failures, they begin to doubt that the development effort can be successful. If you are on a project that has no established scope or requirements, something is wrong. If people are not working within the scope or addressing the requirements, there's a problem.
Unrealistic schedule	The initial plan for development lacked realistic estimations, but a commitment was still made. The development team is unable to meet the deadline. This is what Edward Yourdon refers to as a "death march" project. Veterans of such projects represent some of the wisest people in the industry. Even if such projects are unavoidable, you can still survive them. One piece of wisdom that veterans offer is that your choice is primarily one of first asking for more time and second asking for fewer features.

Cause	Description
Poor estimations	If the estimations for how long developers will take to complete specific tasks are insufficiently precise, the result is that estimations for total project costs and resource requirements will also be off. For this reason, using care in your own estimations is important. Be honest. Use established techniques. Review your results.
Too much enthusiasm	Often, developers imagine that a new technology or approach to development will allow it to cut its development time. This is seldom the case on a first pass with a new technology. The result can be the opposite, in fact. Because the team must learn the new technology, the learning time throws the project far off schedule. Try to solve problems using technology you know. If you are going to incorporate new technologies, take such risks as planned approaches to development rather than reactions to scheduling demands.
Mythical man-month	Managers often think that throwing people at a development project will shorten the amount of time taken to finish the project. The opposite is true. Doubling the number of people on a project, rather than halving the development time, can easily have the effect of doubling the development time. This is the famous "Mythical Man-Month" hypothesis Brooks offered the world.
Team disintegration	Personality differences among members of the team prove too strong for the project manager to overcome. The result is that squabbling and other negative behavior overtake and destroy the ability of the team to work toward a common goal. One of the surest ways to avoid many problems of miscommunication is to make use of the standard documents and devices that software engineering provides. Reviews formalize communication, as do documents.
The company goes under	Even if everything is going well, if the company lacks funding to go on with the project, it must come to an end. Game development companies often go out of business.
Lack of resources	If a project manager does not properly calculate the number of people (resources) needed for the project, even if everyone on the team is attuned to a common goal, it is still possible to fail. The fact remains that people can work only so many hours of a day.

(continued on next page)

Table 15.6 Reasons Teams Fail (continued)

Cause	Description
Lack of equipment	A team that lacks the equipment necessary to do a job cannot be expected to succeed. It is important to both expect and request the tools that are appropriate for the work.
Divergence from the project plan	A project can fail if it does not deliver what the development plan says must be developed. Going astray can happen in a number of ways. The team might neglect to implement the game on the basis of the requirements statement. On the other hand, the team might neglect to stick with the production plan.

Conclusion

A sense of purpose is a key to the success of any team, but a number of factors contribute to the ability of the team to possess a sense of purpose. Among these are an understanding on the part of the members of the team that both personal and formal roles come into play during the life of a development project. Each member of the team should celebrate and respect the risks presented by different personalities. Formal roles present little risk, but those who assume formal roles are placed in the position of being responsible to others on the team to provide the expertise that the role prescribes.

Roles themselves are important but do not alone account for a team's success. Another factor is a set of tools the members of the team share in common. Among these tools are the documents and other artifacts that the team uses to record, trace, and negotiate its work. In addition to working tools are formal and informal occasions of review. Reviews are the leading means by which a team can move its work forward as a team.

Even with reviews, however, a team still faces a number of risks that can be addressed only with extremely flexible responses. Two key measures ensure flexibility of response. These are placing the members of the team in a work area and under working conditions that allow them to easily and effectively communicate. Another measure of flexible response is that team members are given the freedom to socialize and communicate so that they form a tight, purposeful bond with each other.

Even with well-tuned working conditions, a solid sense of purpose, well-established formal and informal roles, comprehensive reviews, and flexibility of response, a team still requires good management. One of the key qualities of a good manager is the ability to use project tracking tools to gain a clear view of the dependencies and scheduling issues that a project faces. In addition, a project manager should continually update the team with news about the progress the team is making toward the completion of the project.

An enormous number of excellent books have been written on software development teams and project management. Turn to the sources on the list for more extensive practical discussion of the topics introduced in this chapter. The works represent the perspectives of some of the most well-respected practitioners of software engineering.

Bennatan, E. M. *On Time Within Budget: Software Project Management Practices and Techniques.* 3rd Ed. New York: Wiley Computer Publishing, 2000.

Brooks, Frederick P., Jr. *The Mythical Man-Month: Essays on Software Engineering, Anniversary Edition.* Boston: Addison-Wesley, 1995.

DeMarco, Tom and Timothy Lister. *Peopleware: Productive Projects and Teams.* New York: Dorset House Publishing, 1987.

McConnell, Steve. *Software Project Survival Guide.* Redmond, Washington: Microsoft Press, 1998.

Project Management Institute. *A Guide to the Project Management Body of Knowledge (PMBOK Guide).* Newton Square, Pennsylvania: Project Management Institute, 2001.

Whitehead, Richard. *Leading a Software Development Team: A Developer's Guide to Successfully Leading People and Projects.* New York: Addison-Wesley, 2001.

Whitten, Jeffrey L., Lonnie D. Bentley, and Keven C. Dittman. *Systems Analysis and Design Methods.* 5th Ed. Boston: McGraw-Hill, 2000.

Yourdon, Edward. *Death March: The Complete Software Developer's Guide to Surviving "Mission Impossible" Projects.* Upper Saddle River, New Jersey: Prentice Hall, 1999.

Chapter 16

Process Improvement

This chapter discusses process improvement, which people often view as cumbersome, bureaucratic, paper-laden (or at least file-laden) and boring. Such perspectives, unfortunately, are more than justified. At the same time, hardly anything is more worthwhile in the software engineering industry than a clearly understood approach to assimilating new technologies or finding new approaches to solving problems. The only reliable way of ensuring that such change can take place in a given company, large or small, is to put in place both a process of development and, just as important, a process for improving the process of development. Process improvement encompasses both types of activity.

As will become evident in the discussion in this chapter, some people like change for the sake of change. Others embrace change after they have a chance to see that it brings improvements. Still others resist change until they face an ultimatum. All three perspectives are valuable to an engineering process. Change should be a welcome aspect of any engineering process, but when change is made for the sake of change, catastrophe might not be far off.

Process refers both to how a team or organization adjusts to or accepts change and how a team or organization formulates and sustains a change process. The two go hand in hand. To forget this is to fall prey to the illusion that change is not an essential aspect of engineering and that an organization can buy a ready-made quality improvement process. There is more to it than what can be bought. Toward understanding this perspective, this chapter discusses the following topics:

- The basics of process improvement
- How processes use change management strategies
- Models of capability maturity for software development

- International standards of quality for software development
- Capability maturity models that extend beyond software development
- Applying standards to a team or organization
- Implementing procedures for managing change and improving processes

The Basics of Process Improvement

When a team or organization decides to improve its processes, it usually does so for a few simple reasons. Among these are the following:

- **Poor quality.** People fail to finish work on time, and the work they finish possesses errors and causes problems for customers.
- **Increased profits.** Having standardized processes has been proven time and time again to add to a company's ability to sustain profitability.
- **New technologies.** The existing products satisfy customers and generally lack errors, but a new technology has emerged, and everyone needs to learn it as quickly as possible. Competitors have already embraced the new technology and could run the team or organization out of business.
- **Regulatory and trade requirements.** The product has been amazingly successful, and a big marketing corporation has entered the picture and asked that your team or organization be in compliance with a set of standards or have in place a quality control process for the way you conduct business.
- **Merger.** You just merged your efforts with another team or organization, and the two groups, both of which have good ways to do things, are resisting merge efforts because of turf and other issues. You must find a way to obtain the best from both.

Other reasons for process change exist, but from this short list arises a common set of features. First, you must examine what people are doing right now in the light of either what others do or what some external standards organization suggests must be done. Second, you must find some formalized way to allow your team to know whether it is implementing the standards. It's not enough, for example, to write a set of standards and put them on the shelf, unused. You need to find a process of change. One source of this process might be an external agency that provides you with a standard approach to process change. Third, for the changes to take effect, they must represent the culture of your team or organization, so you must engage in some type of effort to customize and apply both the standards and the processes you bring in from the outside.

Figure 16.1 explores some of the dynamics involved in process improvement. Your organization might seek initially to implement the standards that an external agency provides by using a process provided by that agency. Such organizations as the SEI (which sponsors the CMM) and the ISO (which sponsors the ISO 9000 series of standards) provide general standards that you customize for your organization with the help of a registered standards auditor. At the same time, process improvement is an individualized undertaking. Everyone who is involved in a process improvement effort has the opportunity to evaluate and improve the way things have been done.

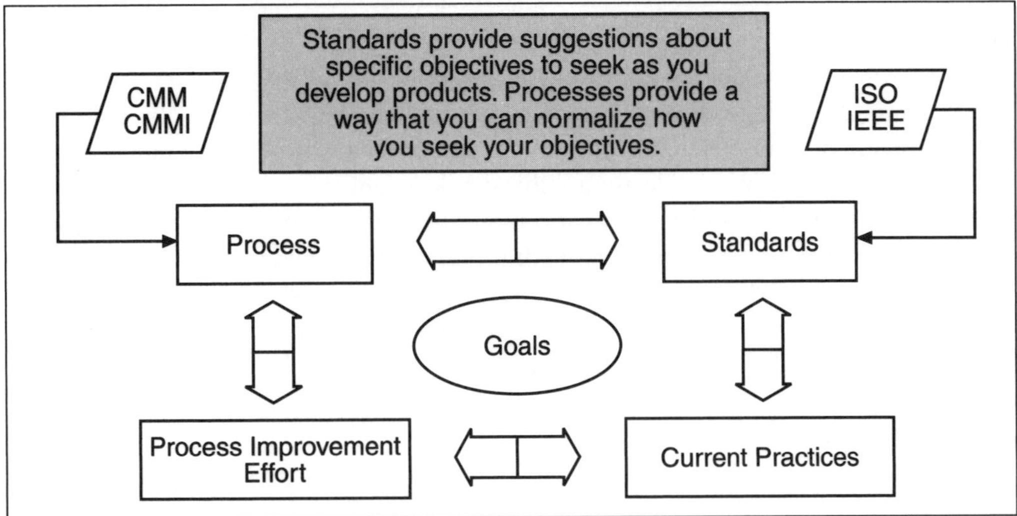

Figure 16.1
Standards and processes combine during a process improvement effort.

Quality

Many of the positive arguments about quality reduce to the assertion that when you improve the way you create a product, you improve the product. However, most of the well-seasoned software engineering process specialists also emphasize that quality is the capacity to create a capacity. Regardless of the product it produces, if an organization is able to use self-critical knowledge to proactively improve itself, it possesses quality. The same can be said for an individual. Quality implies the capacity to learn from the past and to apply the results of learning to the future.

In practical terms, three main features of quality improvement emerge as both benefits and goals. They are as follows:

- **Predictability.** The ability to deliver a specified product lies at the basis of the success of most software development undertakings. After organizations adopt software process improvement programs, their ability to deliver the specified product tends to increase dramatically. Generally, not delivering the specified product does not result in a bogus one. Rather, the product delivered might eventually conform to specifications, but the development team delivers it far later than predicted.

- **Effectiveness.** Organizations that adopt process improvement programs use their development time more effectively. The primary results are that products cost less to produce and possess fewer errors. You can tune effective production processes to eliminate faulty production techniques. You can place greater emphasis on elimination of defects during the requirements and design phase of development, so the number of errors detected later in the development process decreases. The later that a development team detects an error, the more costly the error.
- **Control.** Software quality improvements result in the ability to predict the delivery of a product with greater accuracy. A couple of factors contribute to this ability. Consider, for example, that adoption of a process improvement program does not necessarily result in a single, monolithic development process. In fact, the case is wholly the opposite for many organizations. Instead of one process, a mature organization develops a customizable set of process components that can be combined to accommodate different types of development efforts. The result is that the organization can apply streamlined development processes to specific types of products and determine development efforts and delivery dates with great precision.

Cycles of Quality

You can use quality or process improvement to characterize any attempt that individual software engineers or game developers make to improve the way they do things. To accomplish this, they must seek opportunities for self improvement. Some of these opportunities arise through team efforts. Others arise on a personalized level. In both cases, quality improvement results from a cycle that involves logging data about activities performed according to standard procedures and then evaluating the resulting data to find ways to remove defects, improve performance, or refine the procedures.

Generally, quality improvement reflects classical scientific methodology. Scientific methodology involves proposing a hypothesis, setting up an experiment to test the hypothesis, performing the experiment to generate data, and then interpreting the data to discover whether it confirms the hypothesis.

In terms of software engineering process improvement, the starting point is what people do on a day-to-day basis. You might view this as the hypothesis, that the way things are done is the only and the best way to do them. The experiment involves documenting this way of doing things as a standard script. The script lists the tasks that you need to perform to complete the procedure that the script documents.

To collect data on the script, you can keep a record of such things as how many mistakes occur during the performance of the tasks and how much time is required to complete each task. A third thing that you can document is boundary conditions. To do this, you must complete one boundary condition before you can start the tasks in a script and a second boundary condition before you can consider the procedure finished.

To move to interpretation, you can summarize the data that results from the performance of the tasks in the procedure (the experiment). The summary provides a historical model of the script performance. From this point on, you are in a position to treat every subsequent performance of the procedure as an opportunity to generate a body of data that can be compared with the historical data.

The interpretation of data allows you to make decisions about how to improve the process. Each iteration of the script provides an opportunity for process improvement. Figure 16.2 illustrates the basic cycle of process improvement.

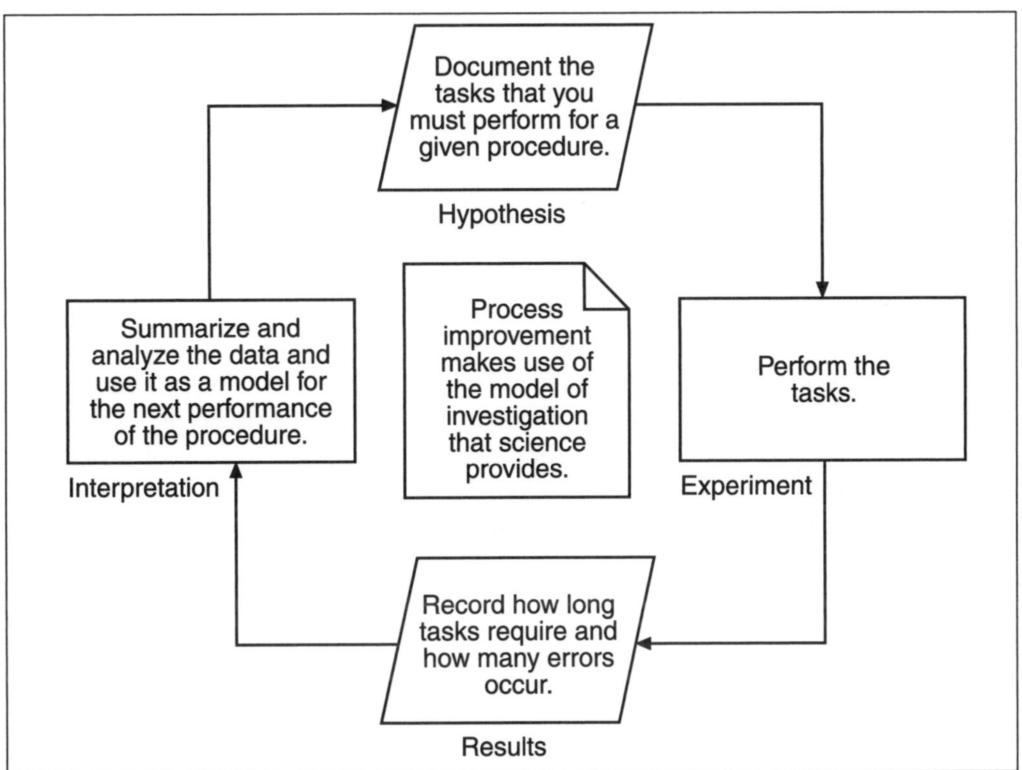

Figure 16.2
The scientific method, which emphasizes hypothesis and experiment, forms the basic model for software engineering process improvement.

Contrasting Approaches

This chapter discusses several approaches to quality improvement. Among the approaches are those that the Institute of Electronics and Electrical Engineers (IEEE), the International Standards Organization (ISO), and the Software Engineering Institute (SEI) provide. This chapter also discusses how single standards, such as the ISO 9000 and the

Capability Maturity Model (CMM), have been extended through such additions as ISO 9001 and the extended Capability Maturity Model Integration (CMMI). Regardless of what agency or set of processes or practices comes into view, a common set of key practices prevails. For this reason, rather than describing in detail any one approach to process improvement, this chapter concentrates on showing how process improvement enables organizations to identify and improve key practices. Both the ISO and the SEI offer extremely effective approaches to process improvement. Likewise, the IEEE provides many important tools. Exploring different approaches allows you to set the groundwork for more extensive investigations. The texts listed at the end of this chapter provide you with a few inroads to such investigations.

ISO

Quality can begin as an assumed set of standards. The ISO provides generic standards that help organizations create and sustain processes that possess quality. Other organizations specialize in ISO certification, which usually takes a year. Certification experts (sometimes called *auditors*) work with companies that want to achieve this. Certification requires that an auditor verify that a company applying for certification has implemented production processes that meet the standards that the ISO establishes.

Companies that obtain certification benefit in numerous ways. For one thing, they attain recognition in international markets. Companies that have ISO ratings are eligible for contracts that they would not be eligible for without ISO standing. In addition, as surveys have shown repeatedly, when companies adopt ISO standards, the quality of their products improves, as does their ability to make a profit.

ISO in General

On its Web site (http://www.iso.org), the ISO provides a clear statement about the intentions and purposes of the standards it publishes. Generally, the ISO provides two broad sets of standards: ISO 9000 and ISO 14000. More than half a million organizations in roughly 160 countries have applied for and received certification with the ISO. ISO 9000 serves as a way that companies doing business across national boundaries can be certain that the companies with which they form business relationships have a shared perception of quality. Whereas ISO 9000 has tended to focus more on the concerns of software manufacturers, the ISO 14000 standards focus on a broader range of concerns that the ISO refers to as "environmental." Of the ISO 9000 series of standards, those that bear most specifically on software are under the heading of ISO 9001. The ISO 9001 standards are simply one segment of the ISO 9000 series.

The ISO 9000 focuses on the following concerns:

- The requirements that the customer sets for quality

- Regulatory requirements that might apply to the product
- Measures that can be used to increase customer satisfaction with products and services
- Ways a company can implement measures for continuous process and product improvement

In contrast, the ISO 14000 standards focus on the environment, and in this sense, the environment encompasses a wide variety of social and economic concerns. According to the ISO, the ISO 14000 concentrates on the following concerns:

- Reduction of the existing negative effects that an organization might cause to the environment
- Finding new ways that an organization can safely interact with the environment

In most cases, when companies implement ISO standards, they do so with specific language. They interpret the standards. That standards are interpreted completely falls within the guidelines for adoption of standards that the ISO has established. Almost any organization can adopt the ISO standards, regardless of size. The standards can encompass the production of almost any product, and they can define a basis for doing business in almost any area, be it governmental, nongovernmental, or private.

A company that seeks ISO certification has a set of tasks that requires approximately a year to complete. On the other hand, if a company has already undertaken, independently, an effort to normalize and standardize its processes, achieving a registered ISO status might take much less time.

ISO 9000 Specifics

The range of topics that the ISO 9000 (or ISO 9001) documentation lists encompasses what might be viewed as areas of concern any organization seeking to sustain a reputation for quality should be concerned with. The topics considered can be reduced to a fairly short list, but the list might shrink or grow depending on how a company structures its business operations.

For a company that is involved in game software development, the ISO 9001 topics present no great diversion from common sense. The topics tend to emphasize what an overall business organization should be concerned with. However, specifically defining the topics so that they focus on the activities of a game development organization requires no great effort. Table 16.1 summarizes the areas of emphasis of the ISO 9000 standards.

Table 16.1 ISO 9000 Areas of Concern

Area	Description
Management responsibility	Does your organization have a clear statement that shows its commitment to adoption and maintenance of standards?
Quality review	Is a process in place that allows for the review of the products and services that your company offers?
Contract review	Is a procedure in place that allows your company to clearly establish its obligations toward its customers?
Design control	Is a process in place that allows your company to gather requirements for and then design the product that is to be provided for the customer?
Document and data control	Can your organization store and retrieve documents that are relative to all stages of its business processes?
Purchasing	When your company buys products or services from other companies, does it have bidding and other criteria to use in determining which products or services are the best?
Control of customer-supplied products	Can your company track how products are supplied to customers?
Product identification and traceability	Can your company uniquely identify all the parts that constitute a product, and can it uniquely identify all the products it distributes?
Process control	Does your company possess enough knowledge about its own production processes to be able to change them?
Inspection and testing	Is the technology that your company uses tested, and are the products that your company distributes inspected to ensure that they conform to minimum quality standards?
Control of inspection, measurement, testing equipment	Is data collected on the products that you distribute and and the production processes that you have in place?
Inspection and test status	Can you identify the extent to which a given product has been tested?
Nonconforming product control	Can your company recall and isolate products that are released with errors?
Correction and prevention	Does your company have in place a process that allows it to repair the errors that might have been identified in the products that your organization creates?

Area	Description
Handling, storage, packaging, delivery	Does your company have in place processes that ensure that the product will be packed, handled, and delivered to the customer in a reasonable time and in excellent condition?
Quality records	Does your company maintain records respecting defective products, production efficiency, and other factors that have a bearing on the product?
Quality audits	Does your company have quality assurance audits performed on a regular basis and have in place a procedure for responding to the findings of the audits?
Training	Does your organization train its employees to ensure that they follow established procedures and practices for the production and delivery of the products that your company creates?
Service	Does your company have in place procedures for assisting its customers after they have purchased the products that your company creates?
Statistical techniques	Does your company have a standard way to evaluate the data it collects about its products, processes, and other operational dealings?

The items that Table 16.1 present concern general operational goals. How people within a given company interpret those goals depends on the product they create and the agenda they have set for quality improvement.

ISO Suggestions

The ISO offers other standards that apply specifically to software development concerns. As mentioned earlier, the ISO 9001 series is usually considered most central for software development organizations. Within this context, the ISO Standard 9126 provides a list of specific areas of concern that extend to nearly two dozen headings. You can reduce the general concerns to the set of six that Figure 16.3 illustrates.

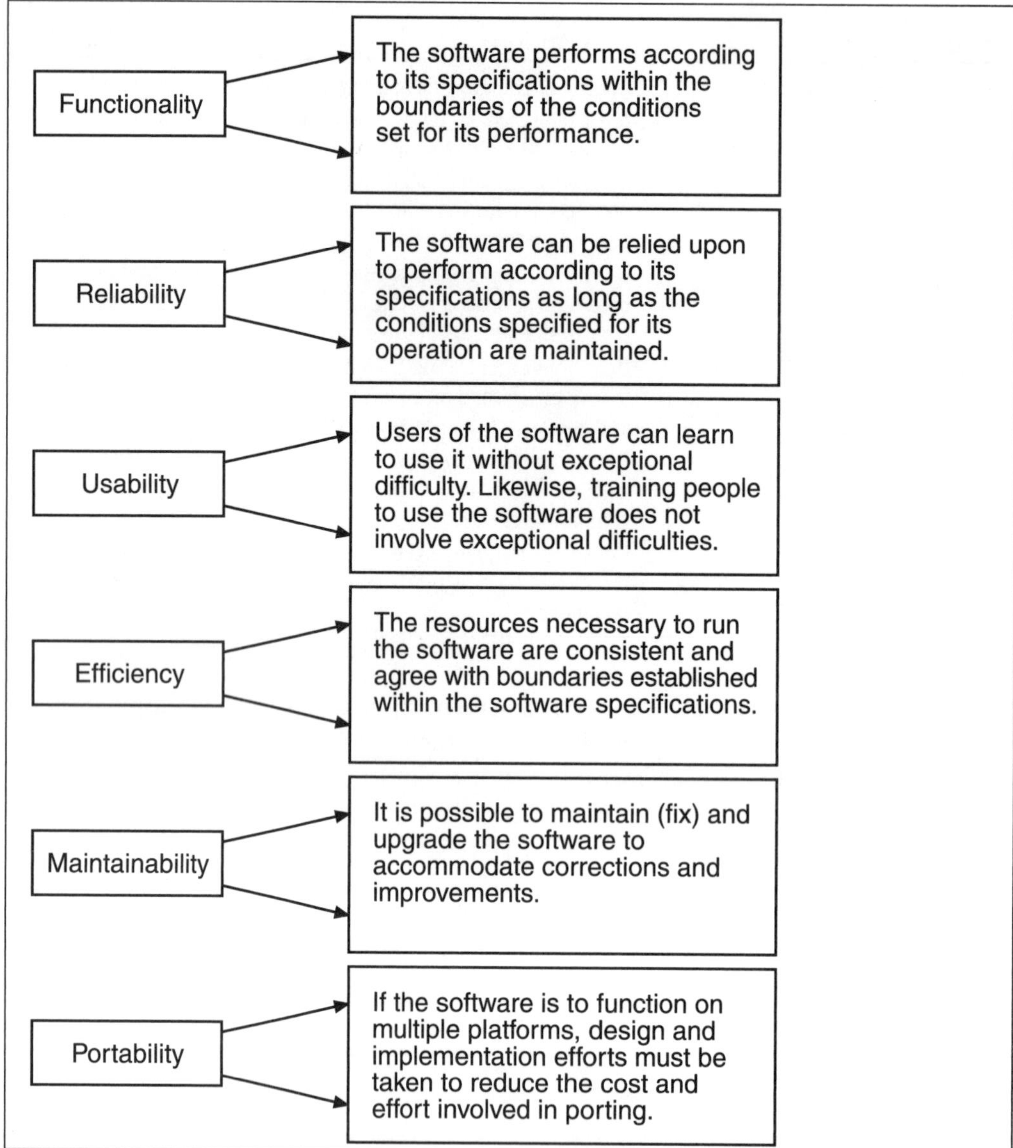

Figure 16.3
ISO 9126 and other standards establish the general categories for software quality.

The set of six quality assurance themes that Figure 16.3 depicts represents a general approach to software development. For each of the main headings, two to three more specific types of activity apply. The statements in the larger boxes summarize the information that falls under the specific headings. For example, "functionality" applies to gathering requirements and creating a software design. To achieve the goals of functionality, you can create such things as a software requirements specification (see Chapter 2, "Requirements—Getting the Picture") or a software design specification (see Chapter 4, "Software Design—Much Ado About Something").

To provide the information that the ISO requires, you can hire a standards specialist who evaluates your organization. This specialist might work in conjunction with a team from your organization. The team helps gather data and might form the core of the process improvement effort that can begin with the evaluation. The results of the evaluation reveal strengths and weaknesses, and this information provides a starting point for improving processes.

As is emphasized in Chapters 15, "Team Work," and 19, "Philosophy of Software Engineering and Game Development," your group or organization might have unique approaches to how its developers form into groups. Because each organization forms a unique culture, the way that auditors or evaluators apply ISO standards varies from organization to organization. This is not to say that the ISO applies standards less than comprehensively. Rather, it is to say that how an organization meets standards depends on the operational structure it has evolved. Two groups in one company might take care of a concern that is the sole property of a single group in another company. Neither approach surpasses the other. The ISO auditor or evaluator recognizes that the differences in structure have little bearing on whether an organization meets the provisions of the standards.

How does a group of developers who is developing a game picture its activities in terms of the quality categories that Figure 16.3 displays? Again, culture comes into play. No single process or set of development stages can depict properly the unique aspects of a given development culture. For this reason, about the best that you can do when an organization intends to begin developing a formal set of processes is to establish the areas in which it is most important to either create or improve processes.

The ISO and CMM

If your company seeks an ISO rating, how will it stand if it also seeks a CMM rating? The question ends up being simple to answer. Two main areas of concern emerge. One area concerns which compliance model encompasses the greater number of practices. The other concerns which compliance model demands more for the practices it does name, regardless of number. In general, for software concerns, the best approach is to implement first the processes that the CMM stipulates. Although the CMM covers most of the areas of concern that the ISO has established, it covers them with greater depth and rigor. In other words, what passes with the CMM is likely to pass also with the ISO. The efforts to bring the two quality programs into harmony are extensive.

Process Area	CMM/CMMI	ISO
Process change management	●	○
Technology change management	●	○
Defect prevention	●	○
Software quality management	●	○
Quantitative process management	●	○
Peer review	●	●
Intergroup coordination	●	●
Software product engineering	●	○
Integrated software management	●	○
Training program	●	○
Organization process definition	●	○
Software configuration management	●	○
Software quality assurance	●	○
Software subcontract management	●	○
Software project tracking and oversight	●	○
Software project management	●	○
Requirements management	●	○

Full Coverage ● Partial Coverage ○

Figure 16.4
CMM/CMMI and ISO cover the same process areas.

As Figure 16.4 shows, the ISO addresses all of the process areas that the CMM or CMMI addresses. The difference is that the ISO concentrates more on generalized goals, whereas the CMM model has been developed to address specifically the needs of software development organizations. Two general trends have emerged over the past decade. The ISO has tended to seek greater specificity to accommodate its software engineering clients. The SEI, on the other hand, has made efforts to extend the CMM through the CMMI to accommodate clients other than those that produce only software products. (See Mark C. Paulk, et al., *The Capability Maturity Model: Guidelines for Improving the Software Process* [Boston: Addison-Wesley, 1995], p. 417.)

On the part of the ISO, the Software Process Improvement and Capability dEtermination (SPICE) effort focuses mostly on software process improvement. For the CMMI, the addition of the Integrated Produce and Product Development (IPPD) program has extended the CMM to encompass processes to a wider business scope than was encompassed by software-specific processes.

Means and Ends—Templates

Almost any process improvement effort begins with the documentation of what currently exists. The current process establishes the starting line. Standards resemble goals. Between the starting line and the goals that the standards set is an involved process that often requires documenting what exists and determining what must be changed or added to reach the goals. Only after this has been accomplished can the manner of improving a process really begin.

Process documentation templates provide the most frequently employed technique for capturing information about existing processes. Organizations such as the ISO and the SEI provide such templates. Certification organizations also provide such templates. A template provides a pattern for gathering and organizing information, but it is special because it represents a way of gathering and organizing information that has been refined through repeated use. For this reason, a template offers a better starting place than a document that is created from scratch. The templates that the standards organizations provide usually impose no fixed rules and imply no obligations. They serve simply as starting points.

- Purpose
- Documents Useful as References
- Process Management
- Existing Documentation
- Applicable Categories
  - Standards
  - Practices
  - Conventions
  - Metrics
- Reviews or Audits
- Text Descriptions
- Reporting
  - Problems
  - Corrective Actions
- Software Support
  - Tools
  - Techniques
  - Methodologies
- Source Code Control
- Maintenance Records
- Training
- Risk Management

Figure 16.5
Templates like the IEEE Standard 730 provide guides that software development groups can use to identify and shape processes.

IEEE Standard 730

As an example of available templates for processes, you can consider IEEE Standard 730. This template enables a development group to document standard development processes. Figure 16.5 illustrates the main headings of the template.

To dwell on Standard 730 a bit (see Figure 16.5), consider that the template provides a ready way to identify and isolate a given process and its constituent tasks and allows you to identify quickly what resources or capabilities you have with respect to the process. Further, note that the template guides you in two general directions. First, it offers you a way to collect historical data about the process (if a body of data exists). Second, as you perform the process, it encourages you to capture information so that you can compare data about your current work with historical data. (See the discussion of the topics presented in Table 16.2.)

Table 16.2 IEEE Template Categories

Area	Description
Purpose	Briefly state what you are trying to do with the document. Generally, you are trying to capture information about existing activities. The activity at hand can be anything you decide needs attention. For instance, if the object of your investigation involves how your organization creates software design documents, the capture of design document activities is the purpose. If the purpose extends to one of putting in place the groundwork of process improvement, collecting information for a process improvement effort is also part of the purpose.
Documents Useful as References	If your organization has produced documents that relate to the topic you are exploring, you can list them here. You can also include references to books, articles, or Web sites that might be of help.
Process Management	You can provide a flow chart (see the activity diagram in Chapter 3, "A Tutorial: UML and Object-Oriented Programming") to show how a given activity is managed. Basically, informal management of a process amounts to how the best practitioners in your organization perform the task. An activity diagram can capture this information regularly.
Existing Documentation	If anyone has gathered data on the specific activity you are documenting, identify it here. It is best to do nothing more than note the existence of the document. Starting from scratch is not always the best way to go, but neither is cutting and pasting.
Applicable Categories	You can use this section of the document to relate the process you are documenting to key practices drawn from CMM or ISO guides. ■ **Standards.** Use this if you have in mind a set of standards you want to use. ■ **Practices.** You can describe practices that you want to imitate here. ■ **Conventions.** This category is more general than Standards. ■ **Metrics.** Use this if you have in mind specific data you want to collect.

Area	Description
Reviews or Audits	Any process proposal that receives no review is ultimately not going to render a useful organizational change. Implied here is how you intend to review and update the current document. You also can state how long you expect the review to take and even when or at what intervals you expect the review or audit to be conducted. Add to this, however, that your organization might be anticipating auditing by an external (ISO or CMM) organization. If this is the case, you can identify this organization at this point.
Text Descriptions	A text description is like a narrative of activity. You can place almost anything in this section, as long as you provide it with a section heading that allows the reader to know its main theme. The audit is a means of validating and verifying whether your process improvement effort is leading to anything tangible. You can use the text description to describe anything that has to do with implementation, including why it has or has not proceeded in a significant way toward a tangible result.
Reporting	Any data that you can capture about the process under consideration helps provide a basis on which to evaluate and improve the process. ■ **Problems.** You can provide a template for how to report a problem relative to the process you are examining. For example, if your organization ends up time and again with incomplete requirements specifications, the problem is one of not gathering or examining requirements specifications thoroughly. ■ **Corrective Actions.** This section asks for two types of information. If you have taken an action, you can document it here. On the other hand, if you have in mind a tentative action, you can also list it here. You can design a report that combines information about problem statements and corrective actions.
Software Support	If you have a bug tracking program set up in your organization, you can add a category for the current document. If this is the case, the section on reporting clearly must have some bearing on the categories of information that your bug tracking software provides. If you can alter or customize the software for a given topic, all the better. ■ **Tools.** A tool is a software package or a report form. ■ **Techniques.** A technique is something along the lines of an interview or a statistical sampling method. ■ **Methodologies.** A methodology is a generalized approach to process improvement or quality assurance. Examples dealt with in this chapter are CMM, PSP, and CMMI.

(continued on next page)

Table 16.2 IEEE Template Categories (continued)

Area	Description
Source Code Control	This relates largely to documentation control if you are dealing with process development, but it also can relate to any program that involves your process development activity. You can state a procedure for controlling the document, such as when and how it can be changed.
Maintenance Records	Most tracking tools generate an audit trail, which is what this topic is about. If you want to specify the format for the records, you can do so in this place, along with precisely what information you want tracked.
Training	This applies to how to introduce someone to the process you are creating. If your organization is developing a capability maturity model, it will have in place a group that is responsible for conducting process change training. If not, this section might name groups or individuals in your organization who are authorities or resources for information on process improvement activities.
Risk Management	Anticipating problems that might arise forms one of the most fundamental activities of a mature process. This heading provides a starting point for collecting information on problems that you anticipate might arise.

Templates that the IEEE provides for process improvement suggest categories of concern rather than prescribing them. As will become evident later in this chapter, when the CMM and ISO are investigated, IEEE Standard 730 clearly anticipates the key practices that are named in the CMM and ISO programs. Regardless of the approach you use for process improvement, you can adopt the topics that your group considers most important and shape the templates you use to accommodate the topics. Certainly, when organizations adopt templates to meet standards, they do so because they recognize that the adopted templates capture the information that the certification organizations require, but it remains that most standards allow a fair margin of flexibility.

Templates that a given organization might use, even though they are adopted from an organization like the IEEE, can be customized until they genuinely reflect the culture of the company that adopts them. Standards organizations seldom seek conformity but rather endeavor to assist organizations to develop criteria for truthfully reporting on development processes.

Terms of Improvement

The terms listed here occur in both ISO and CMM literature. The meanings provided here relate most directly to the CMM.

- **Software Process.** A software process is a set of activities, methods, or practices that software developers use to develop or maintain software.
- **Task.** A task is a simple work component, such as filling out a form or commenting a line of code. A task is sometimes referred to as a job if it consists of several component tasks.
- **Process.** A process is a sequence of steps. The steps usually involve the performance of a task or a set of tasks.
- **Process Description.** A process description is usually a document. Do not mistake it for the process itself.
- **Project.** A project is a set of activities that leads to the development of a product. A project is sometimes referred to as a job.
- **Capability.** Software process capability relates to what you can expect to achieve if you follow a software development process. The capabilities of an organization allow experts to judge what an organization can be expected to do.
- **Maturity.** An organization possesses a mature process when it has defined, managed, and measured the process. Further, maturity encompasses the ability to control a process and iteratively increase its effectiveness.
- **Organization.** An organization can be an entire corporation, a division within a company, or simply a group of people assigned to a common task.
- **Software Process Assessment.** An assessment relates to an effort on the part of an organization to initiate a software process improvement program.
- **Software Capability Evaluation.** An evaluation relates to a formal process in which a qualified standards expert determines whether one organization qualifies to contract work from another organization.
- **Key Process Area.** Key process areas are requirements for achieving a maturity level. Each key process area designates a set of related activities that allows an organization to achieve capabilities.
- **Key Practice.** A key practice is a specific way that an organization reaches the goals that distinguish its process. Each key process area encompasses several key practices. A key practice designates only *what* is to be accomplished, not *how* something is to be accomplished.

SEI Key Process Area Template

Later, this chapter extensively examines the notions of key process areas and key practices. For now, it emphasizes the similarity between the information that the IEEE captures with the template that Standard 730 provides and the template for key process areas that the CMM provides. Figure 16.6 illustrates the main headings of the template. (See Mark C. Paulk, et al., *The Capability Maturity Model: Guidelines for Improving the Software Process* [Boston: Addison-Wesley, 1995], pp. 43–46.)

Name of Process Area
Goals
Commitment to Perform
Ability to Perform
Activities Performed
Measurement and Analysis
Verifying Implementation

Figure 16.6
The CMM template for key processes corresponds in intent with the IEEE Standard 730.

Table 16.3 CMM Key Process Area Template

Area	Description
Name of process	Both the CMM and the CMMI depend heavily on key process areas for the capabilities that an organization possesses. A set of key process areas characterizes each maturity level. In an alternative approach used by the CMMI, the key process areas are still central to the process. In this scheme, rather than subsets divided according to maturity levels, all the key process areas relating to all levels are applied to an organization from the start. Examples of key processes areas are *requirements management, organization process focus, quantitative process management,* and *defect prevention.*
Goals	A goal is an activity that enhances an organization's ability to achieve process capabilities. Goals summarize key practices and determine whether an organization has implemented key process areas. In the CMM scheme, a set of goals characterizes each key process area, and key practices address the commitments that the goals implement.
Commitment to perform	Commitments to perform designate actions that an organization takes to establish a key practice. To ensure that members of an organization respect and fulfill commitments, an organization usually documents its commitments formally, sometimes using informal contracts.
Ability to perform	Whenever an organization formulates a commitment to reach a goal, reaching the goal involves having in place resources that enable members of the organization to perform the tasks that the goals encompass. Under this heading fall resources, training that people might require, or ways that the organization might need to be restructured to allow people to work toward the goals.

Area	Description
Activities performed	Goals imply that members of the organization must take on specific roles and takes. Under this heading are descriptions of the roles to be assumed and the tasks to be performed. Toward this end, you can formulate specific procedures, implementation plans, and change control processes and procedures.
Measurement and analysis	You can determine progress toward achievement of goals by using measurements obtained through formally established data collection devices. You then can use the data you collect to control activities.
Verifying implementation	After the organization mandates key processes and sets goals, it also must ensure that some individual or group that is involved in process improvement verify that the process improvement activities that the organization is implementing are those that it has said it will implement.

Template Results

Figure 16.7 shows the results of the key process area template as applied to one key process area, requirements management, for the repeatable (level 2) maturity level. The table represents a terse summary of the information that the template allows process developers to gather. Generally, at a bare minimum, a few sentences would describe each of the expressions that the table contains. The table shows goals, commitments, abilities, activities, measurements, and means of verification.

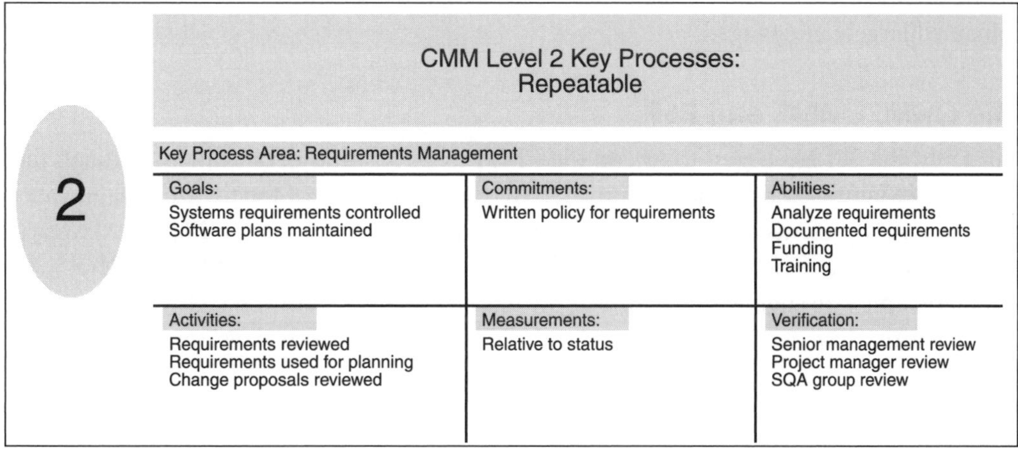

Figure 16.7
The key process area template allows process developers to identify the process activities for each CMM/CMMI level.

CMM Background Information

The Software Engineering Institute (SEI) performs work that resembles the work that the ISO performs, but until recently, its efforts have centered on process improvement in software engineering rather than business practices in general. As a center of software engineering research, the SEI created the Capability Maturity Model (CMM), which in many ways stands as a landmark in the history of software engineering. The CMM introduced what is generally recognized as the first process improvement model for software development organizations. Since its introduction, the CMM has helped thousands of software development organizations improve their processes in an incremental way from ad hoc to mature levels.

The SEI—which is affiliated with Carnegie Mellon University—initiated its work on the CMM in response to a request that the U.S. government issued during the mid-1980s. The request was for a set of criteria that the U.S. government could use to evaluate the capabilities of companies seeking contracts from the U.S. government. The SEI and its affiliated organizations responded with the CMM, which describes how a software development organization can develop its software development processes through five levels of maturity.

A leading name in the development of the CMM is Watts S. Humphrey, whose text, *Managing the Software Process* (1986), achieved a status in many software engineering circles equal to that of *The Mythical Man-Month*, by Frederick Brooks. Humphrey was associated with the SEI, and his text formalized the notions encompassed in the maturity model. In 1991, the SEI issued the first version of the CMM. The SEI released Version 1.1 of the CMM in 1993. Other releases have followed, but the primary five-level profile has remained largely unchanged.

The CMM, CMMI, and PSP

Currently, the SEI has begun to extend the CMM to all business organizations through the Capability Maturity Model Integration (CMMI), but knowledge of the CMM remains valuable because it presents a simple view of how software organizations can improve development processes incrementally. If a drawback applies to the CMM, it is that the SEI developed it for large software engineering efforts, those of a size that NASA or the ESA might sponsor. As small teams have tended to more and more characterize software development, however, the focus of quality improvement efforts has tended to shift in emphasis. As one example of the shift, Watts Humphrey, with the endorsement of the SEI, created the Personal Software Process (PSP). Another example is that the CMMI addresses both large and small efforts.

The sections that follow examine the CMM from a perspective that is oriented toward large development groups. Then you learn of specific activities that are involved in process improvement. With this movement, it is possible to draw upon some of the ideas that Watts Humphrey presents in his writings on the PSP and discuss many of the features of the CMMI. The goal is not that of trying to show in a few pages what requires many books elsewhere. Instead, by concentrating on a few tasks close at hand, the discussion offers an approach to viewing the essential activities involved in the process improvement activities that software engineering encompasses.

note

The CMM was designed for large-scale software engineering projects. In the 1980s, a large software development project for NASA involved approximately 750,000 lines of code and 250 developers. An organization that was capable of undertaking such a project was considered ideal for the CMM. Today, commercial game products easily can include many more lines of code and yet involve far fewer developers. The complexity of the undertaking, however, in many respects remains the same.

Levels of Maturity

The classical view of the CMM offers five levels of maturity. Figure 16.8 displays these five CMM levels and some of their general features. These levels of maturity start at the ground floor, where no processes exist. The lowest level is called Level 1, or Initial. The highest level is called Level 5, or Optimizing. Between these are the Repeatable (2), Defined (3), and Managed (4) levels. Movement from one level to the next involves development of a set of capabilities.

Level 1—Initial

A game development company that a group of capable individuals form in a garage with a common sense of task and highly motivated leadership falls easily into the Initial (Level 1) category of maturity. Generally, the group simply gets the job done, without specific, documented processes or a sense of having to repeat the task or even account for it after it is finished. Everything generally focuses on the development of the game, and when anyone asks what went into the development, the standard response might be to point at the game and explain that what went into the development of the game was anything that you could find in the game, beautiful, divine, good, and bad. Of the initial state, you could say that the team develops the game until it reaches a point at which it can be released.

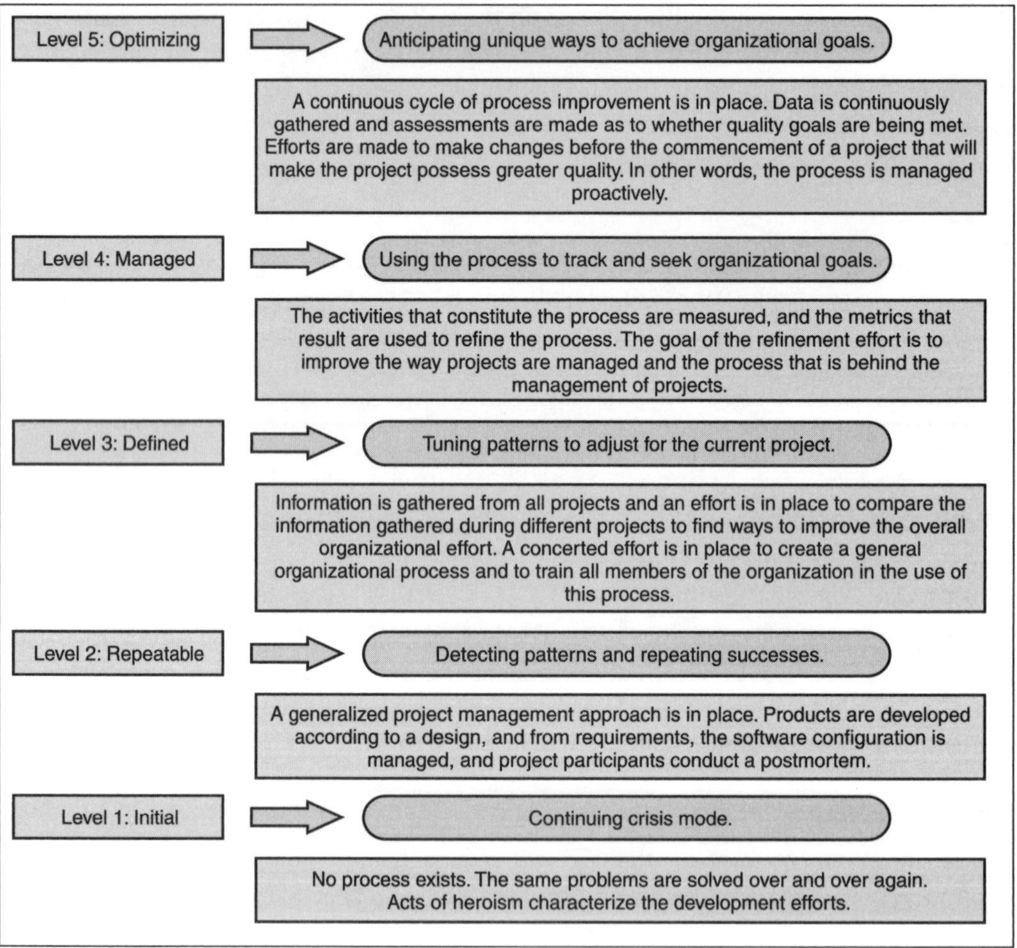

Figure 16.8
Each CMM level involves increasing capabilities.

Level 2—Repeatable

A game development organization that achieves Level 2 capabilities can manage projects according to a documented development plan. It can determine the number of people who are required to create a game, and it knows what tools and how much funding the development of a game involves. A Level 2 organization knows its development processes well enough to be able to train people to teach its employees about its development processes. It can place what it develops under configuration management. It can track defects in the product and take appropriate measures to correct them. Finally, a Level 2 organization usually conducts a postmortem for each completed game development effort, and the information derived from this postmortem is used to improve subsequent development efforts.

Level 3—Defined

A Level 3 organization possesses all the capabilities of a Level 2 organization, but it initiates additional measures to improve the way it manages projects. Such an organization possesses a generalized project management process that it can customize to meet the requirements of different types of development efforts. For example, two versions of the project management process might be created to accommodate Internet-distributed as opposed to standalone games. At Level 2, each project manager more or less pursues a competent but individualized approach to developing a game. At Level 3, the organization brings all these different approaches into a common organizational model, so that the strengths of each can be applied, potentially, to all others. The capabilities that are developed in all other documented areas receive the same definition. The organization has documented practices and made them part of an organization-wide process repository of best practices.

Level 3 is considered appropriate for companies that are seeking government contracts.

Level 4—Managed

The central focus of Level 4 is the collection of data about processes. Given the collection of data, the organization can set goals for increasing its efficiency, reducing costs, or making better predictions. Historical data exists for most categories of activity, so the organization can evaluate the process quantitatively. Using historical data, the organization can establish goals at the beginning of each new project. Likewise, the organization can identify and eliminate risks before a project commences. Generally, risk prevention enables a company to reduce the cost of errors tremendously. (Error costs can be reduced, for example, up to 90 percent.)

Level 5—Optimizing

At the top of the stairs is the Optimizing level. When a company reaches an optimized level, several things have happened. For example, to name but a few capabilities that might apply to a game development company, the company has documented all the basic work areas that are required to create a game. It has collected data on numerous game development efforts, and it can use this data to determine ways that it can improve not only the specific activities that are involved in the development of a game, but also the processes that foster these development efforts. Above all, at Level 5, the organization can concentrate on improving its processes rather than improving its products. At this point, it no longer reacts to standards; rather, it sets them for itself. You can say that such an organization views the quality of its products as arising primarily from the quality of its processes.

Key Process Areas and Key Practices

For each level of maturity, a set of *process areas* apply. Processes areas define general groupings of *key practices* that enable an organization to achieve capabilities. For each key process, several key practices follow. Key practices address goals. Several key practices might address any one goal. The SEI provides a group of starter goals, but generally they vary in number according to the culture of the organization. The following few sections examine key process and associated practices from both the CMM and the CMMI models.

Level 1—Initial

The Initial level deserves as much attention as any other because it is the starting place. Arrogance on the part of someone who is evaluating a Level 1 organization deserves a degree of censure. That's because such an organization has rich capabilities. It has enjoyed the success necessary for being able to compete for contracts or afford to give greater structure to its operations. Unsuccessful organizations do not enjoy such prerogatives.

What then are a Level 1 organization's key processes and practices? There are none. However, as Kim Caputo has noted (Caputo, 36), some generic capabilities deserve notice:

- Everyone in the organization completes a variety of tasks.
- Everyone in the organization exerts a great deal of judgment in determining how things get done.
- An unconscious, seemingly systematic harmony might characterize the actions of the developers.

At the same time, other factors are at work, such as the following:

- One person might do something that completely cancels out the gains of another because the two are unaware of how their efforts contribute to the effort of the whole.

- One person finds an answer, applies it, and then goes about his work. The answer is forgotten, but a few days or weeks later, another person confronts the same problem, works through to the answer, and, once again, goes about his work. An enormous amount of redundancy (waste) characterizes the effort.
- Breakdowns in the culture occur frequently, some with devastating results. Because people define their work as they go, the strengths of personalities often prove the biggest factor in whether the project development effort moves forward. Surviving often amounts to living in something resembling a feudal society in which the prevailing heroes storm about, out of control, while everyone else waits to see what they will do next.
- The configuration management effort is a mixed bag. People might store code locally. Builds might be haphazard. No one has documented just what it is that people are supposed to do, so it is a quiet consensus.
- Requirements are never really established all that clearly, so the concept of what is to result resides with the big egos on the team. Everyone else just works along with them, visionaries that they are.
- Generally, even if everyone gathers around the game every few days to see the results of the latest build, no one really knows when or if the game will be finished.

It might be beneficial at this point to pause and consider one other situation. Consider what might happen if you represented a large corporation and were seeking to contract the services of a smaller game company. Would you want to entrust such a company with a project for which you are paying it a large sum? Such considerations make it easy to understand why smaller companies benefit if they take measures to formalize their approaches to develop.

Level 2—Repeatable

In the CMM and CMMI schemes, the full treatment of Level 2 capabilities requires attention to the following key processes:

- Requirements management (see Figure 16.8 for a fuller explanation of the items involved in each of the key process areas)
- Software project planning
- Software project tacking and oversight
- Software subcontract management
- Software quality assurance
- Software configuration management

Level 3—Defined

In the CMM and CMMI schemes, the full treatment of Level 3 capabilities requires attention to the following key processes:

- Peer reviews
- Project interface coordination
- Software product engineering
- Integrated software management
- Organizational training program
- Organizational process definition
- Organizational process focus

Level 4—Managed

In the CMM and CMMI schemes, the full treatment of Level 4 capabilities requires attention to the following key processes:

- Statistical process management
- Organizational process performance
- Organizational software asset commonality

Level 5—Optimizing

In the CMM and CMMI schemes, the full treatment of Level 5 capabilities requires attention to the following key processes:

- Organizational improvement deployment
- Organizational process and technology innovation
- Defect prevention

The Continuous Model

The CMMI provides an alternative to the CMM level mode known as the continuous model. The continuous model allows an organization to pursue simultaneously all the key process areas from the initiation of the process improvement program forward. The development of the organization's capabilities is not viewed as stages but rather as a continuum of efforts that extends across all process areas. Table 16.4 maps the items that the continuous model features.

Generally, the same key process areas apply to both the staged and continuous development models. The difference is that with the continuous process approach, an organization has much more freedom to determine for itself how it wants to organize its efforts.

Organizations that do not concentrate exclusively on software development efforts tend to favor the nonstaged approach. If a combination of software and hardware characterizes the company's business operations, for example, a continuous model allows activities to be folded more easily into common processes. In this case, the key process areas are organized into four groups. An organization can access each of these areas according to the key areas that apply to it.

Table 16.4 Continuous Process Areas

Grouping	Process Area
Process Management	Organizational process focus
	Organizational process definition
	Organizational training
	Organizational process performance
	Organizational innovation and deployment
Project Management	Project planning
	Project monitoring and control
	Supplier agreement management
	Integrated project management
	Risk management
	Integrated teams
	Qualitative project management
Engineering	Requirements management
	Requirements development
	Technical solutions
	Product integration
	Verification
	Validation
Support	Configuration management
	Process and product quality control
	Measurement and analysis
	Decision analysis and resolution
	Organizational environment for integration
	Causal analysis and resolution

Using the key process areas listed in Figure 16.9, you can develop a continuous process evaluation scale. In this instance, the bars represent the maturity of each of the key process areas on a scale that is roughly equivalent to the maturity levels of the stage model. A variation of this approach could be to group the key process areas in the same way that they are grouped in the staged maturity model. The average of the bar readings provides an estimation of the relative maturity of the organization relative to the staged model. On the other hand, you need to realize that the continuous model addresses the needs of organizations that do not have structure that lend themselves to a staged maturity model evaluation.

Figure 16.9
You can set up the continuous maturity model so that you can group key process areas according to the culture of the company.

Making Change Happen

Organizations that do not change do not survive. Although this notion does not possess the power of an eternal truth, in software engineering, it is very nearly a pronouncement without known exceptions. To arrive at a sense of just how much this notion applies to games, consider a game that you have seen go through several releases over a period of, say, five years. Generally, it is probably safe to say that the improvements you witness in this way are tremendous, and the idea of surrendering the visual richness and logical depth that the later releases possess and reverting to the earlier releases is something akin to giving up a birthday cake in exchange for a bowl of flour and water.

The change in what you experience does not occur naturally. Changes in what you see in a game result from enormous, ongoing, and sometimes painful modifications in the organization that creates the game. The results indicate the extent to which the programming and technology behind the screen have changed. The crucial factor in this change is that the organization that created the game changed along with the game. But even more to the point is that the organizations (and people within the organizations) that produce many successful releases of a game over the years have discovered how to make change a part of their everyday work experience. It is not enough to do something right in software engineering. Success depends on creating both products and production processes that are friendly to continuous change.

Software engineers have traced and measured how engineering organizations change and have detected reliable patterns. The software engineers who are associated with the SEI have documented an eight-stage change model that provides an excellent beginning for most discussions of how to view change. This model depicts organizational change as occurring as a result of a combination of two main ingredients. The first ingredient is time; the other is the extent to which members of the organization become convinced that change is something they want and actively begin making change a part of their everyday work activity.

Table 16.5 provides a list of the generally recognized stages of change that mark the progress of an organization from the time it acknowledges or at least recognizes the need for change and the full assimilation of the results of a change cycle. The source of the information in the table is a study by Kim Caputo (see the footnote for Table 16.5) that concerns organizations that have contracted the services of agencies that specialize in change processes. The mapping of the stages shows how organizational change happens and how much effort and time each stage involves.

Table 16.5 The Stages of Organizational Change

Stage	Description
Getting Started	Either through management initiative or some jolt that the organization experiences, the organization decides that something has to change. For example, the organization might decide to bid for a governmental contract or another, larger organization might acquire the organization. Alternatively, perhaps two or more groups within a given organization want to begin working with each other.
Awareness	Everyone who is involved with the change (which can be everyone in the organization) needs to be aware of the needed changes and what can or should be done to bring them about. A general sense of the need or desirability of change marks this stage, but awareness of the general approach to making a change also arises.
Understanding	A task group within the organization representing the areas affected formulates a plan for how to decide on changes and how to bring them about. The group must make decisions about the scope of change and how to implement the plan.
Defining	At this point, a process group is in place. The group conducts interviews and determines what exists currently. The group also lays the groundwork, in the form of process suggestions, about what it must accomplish to reach the goals that it has defined.
Adopting	Peer and committee reviews, along with surveys, provide the change group with information about how members of the organization regard the measures adopted for change. In addition, those whom the changes affect must examine and adopt the changes. Although the organization can formulate a process guide, the processes that the guide documents mean little if members of the organization do not implement them in meaningful, effective ways.
Changing Routine	Changes must be self-justifying; everyone needs to accept them if they are to take effect. Assimilating changes involves implementing them so that while members of the organization accept and use the new processes, the processes become routines for everyone. Generally, different people accept changes at different rates and in different ways, and if everyone, the most flexible and the most inflexible, does not begin making the changes a part of the everyday work process, the changes are not likely to be effective.
Acceptance	The "old ways" have been forgotten and the "new ways" now become candidate material for the next round of change. In other words, the changes are no longer viewed as changes but as the standard operating procedures, and the change management process should be flexible and dynamic enough to detect immediately and initiate new change processes.

See Kim Caputo, *CMM Implementation Guide: Choreographing Software Process Improvement* (Boston: Addison-Wesley, 1998), pp. 49–59.

The efforts involved in making changes can surprise those who undertake to make them. Efforts required to implement organizational changes easily can require a year or longer. Change occurs only with effort and planning, and the larger the organization, the more this proves to be the case.

Small organizations are just as hard to change as large ones. The effort required differs largely in scope rather than in time. The reason for this is that individuals who make up an organization remain fairly predictable, regardless of the size of the organization. People in management positions, for example, are usually more apt to find new ways of doing things than are entrenched members of a development team. Upper managers can often be almost fatally attracted to change, expecting drastic organizational changes to take place in unrealistic frameworks.

Figure 16.10 displays a few indicators of just how much time a given stage of change requires. The data that the figure represents varies from organization to organization, but the important general trends still emerge. (Source: Kim Caputo, *CMM Implementation Guide: Choreographing Software Process Improvement* [Boston: Addison-Wesley, 1998], p. 52.)

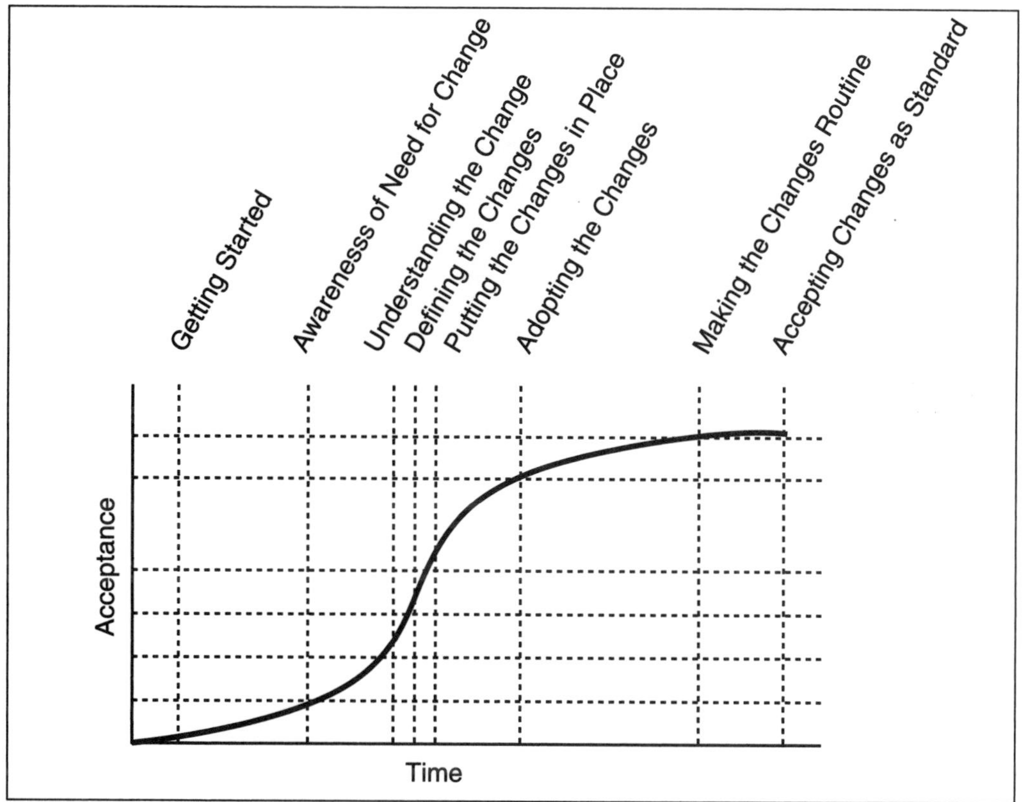

Figure 16.10
Change processes can be broken down into stages.

As Figure 16.10 shows, organizations require different amounts of time to accept different stages of change. For example, at the start of a change initiative, hardly anyone recognizes or can even imagine the need or steps by which change might come about. After a time, however, as managers and other people who drive change make headway, the awareness of the need for change grows and with it a greater organizational willingness to undertake a change process. The curve in Figure 16.10 shows that not until more than half of the change activity has taken place can the majority of people embrace the changes that have been brought into the organization.

Figure 16.11 provides an alternative view of the steps of change. This view shows the efforts of each stage broken into distinct percentages of the total effort.

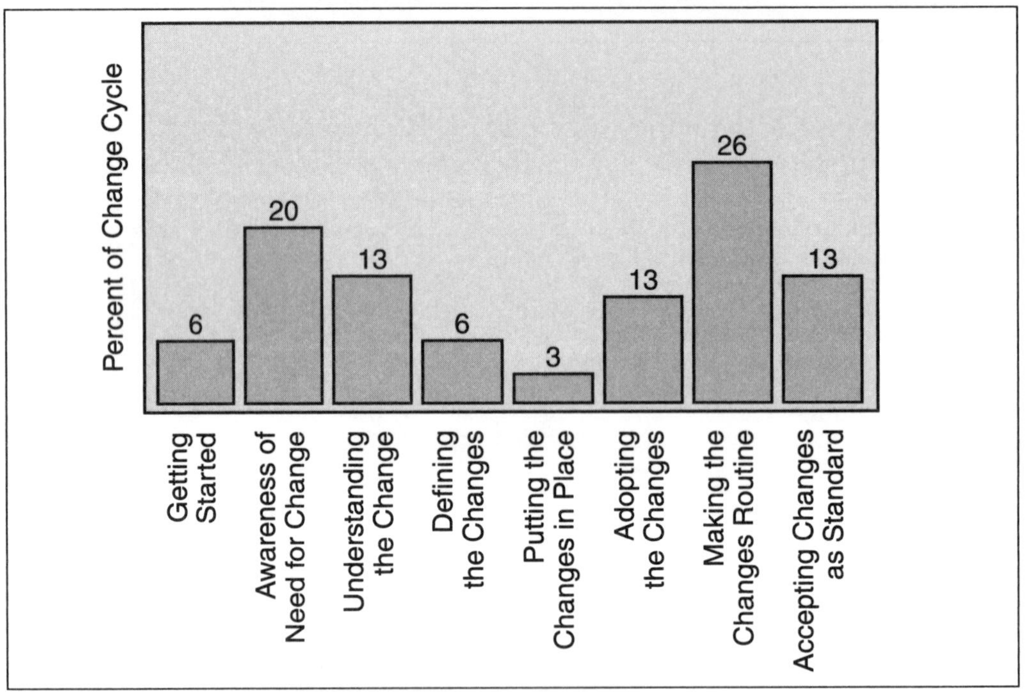

Figure 16.11
The effort that each stage of a change effort requires tends to differ from organization to organization, but general patters still emerge.

As Figure 16.11 shows, making changes so that they are routine parts of the workday constitutes just over 25 percent of the total change effort. What this means becomes evident if you consider the effort preceding this stage. At this point, the organization has recognized the need for changes, a plan has been made for the change process, individuals from the affected groups have been consulted concerning how to make changes, and everyone has in some way begun working in a changed way. And yet it remains that an enormous effort is required to make the changes stick to the point that they become so routine that they are considered candidate material for the next round of change.

Approaches to Improvement

You can take two basic approaches to process improvement. The first is the personalized or journal approach. This approach serves best anyone who is working alone or wants to know how to track individualized performance information so that it can be used in a more generalized setting. A starting point for the personalized strategy is the approach that Watts Humphrey developed in the PSP. Using this as a starting point, you can learn a few fundamental skills about logging and evaluating engineering practices on an individualized basis.

A second approach is preferable for almost any software engineering situation involving complex tasks and any but the most rudimentary development groups. This approach involves convening a Software Engineering Process Group (SEPG). An SEPG consists of only a few people, but it can end up consulting with practically everyone involved with the software product development effort.

note

People usually refer to the Software Engineering Process Group by the letters of the acronym (S-E-P-G) rather than pronouncing the letters as a word. For this reason, you will hear people say that they are on "an S E P G."

SEPG

Probably the best approach to forming an SEPG is to have one person designated as the SEPG coordinator. This person should have time to work on the SEPG and should—at least with respect to the SEPG—report to someone high up in the organization. The reason for this is that any process improvement effort tends to encounter a great deal of resistance when it is first started, and without high-level backing, no one is likely to commit to it.

The purpose of the SEPG can be summarized in a few brief statements:

- Allow one or more people in the organization to dedicate themselves for a period of months to fully understanding the process improvement model that the organization has elected to try (CMM, CMMI, ISO, and so on).
- Enable one or more people to examine thoroughly and communicate to everyone in the company what your current processes are and how they differ from the processes that your organization wants to establish.

- Establish the processes that your organization must put into place if it is to reach the goals it sets for itself relative to the standards it wants to meet.
- Ensure that the members of your organization follow and participate in the improvement activity relating to the software engineering processes that your organization develops.
- Maintain the process guide so that it is an open, living document that everyone in the organization can own.

Source of the Initial Process

The information that the SEPG collects for the process guide originates with members of the organization. Even if an organization has no formally documented process, the SEPG can use a tool such as the CMM key process area template to gather information on each of the key process areas. Several approaches are available. For example, the SEPG can use interviews, questionnaires, and process papers. The sections that follow present a generic approach that an SEPG can use to document processes and set staged goals.

Assessing Existing Processes

When you follow an SEPG approach, you can use documents to concert energies and focus issues effectively. A simple strategy for pursuing this approach involves the following steps:

1. Obtain copies of templates for each of the key process areas. An example of a suitable template is given earlier in the discussion of IEEE Standard 730. Likewise, for a listing of the key process areas, see the preceding section titled "Key Process Areas and Key Practices."
2. Call senior developers in each of the areas into an SEPG meeting and explain the templates and how to create documents using them. Make arrangements through management for the senior developers to have time to complete the documents.
3. As each draft of the key process area document is completed, place it in a change control system.
4. Distribute each draft document to a working group of developers with expertise in the relative process area with instructions for them to study it for review and improvement. Convene a review in which these people share their thoughts about the document. Note suggested changes.
5. Revise the document according to the suggested changes. If your organization is large enough, obtain the services of a technical writer from the start. There are two good reasons for this. One reason is that a review session usually calls for a good scribe. A second reason is that changes are often painful; although the senior developer of a document remains its owner, incorporating the changes obtained

through the working groups that the SEPG convene is best performed by a disinterested third party who has a solid handle on how to use and format documents built using templates.

6. Baseline the document and convene a meeting that includes managers, developers, and those who are already involved in the working group effort to review the document and verify that it documents current processes. If the review group finds new reasons to change the document, do so. Another general review is not needed, but you should distribute the changed document for individual inspection by those who have participated in its development. The SEPG should request that all reviewers either sign off on the document or state their objections. If individuals voice strong objections, the SEPG can deal with them by negotiating changes with the reviewer or convening another general meeting to discuss difficulties.

Setting Process Improvement Goals

After the SEPG has documented existing processes, it uses data obtained about existing processes to establish measures for process improvement. If management has adopted the CMM, the best approach to formulating goals lies with the template of key processes. For the information that this template requests, refer to Table 16.3, "CMM Key Process Area Template." The topics listed in the template are as follows:

- Name of process
- Goals
- Commitment to perform
- Ability to perform
- Activities performed
- Measurement and analysis
- Verifying implementation

Generally, the SEPG and the working group that is associated with each key process can use criteria for key practices provided by the SEI or a similar standards organization. On the other hand, an organization can address a key process area in almost any way it chooses. The main stipulation is that it must give attention to the six practices listed in the previous section, "Assessing Existing Processes," to be able to establish that it has, indeed, documented its processes and put in place a set of procedures by which it can monitor and improve its processes.

Creation of a process document with specified improvement measures usually involves the same steps listed in "Assessing Existing Processes" for primary process documentation. Responsibility for drafting the document is given to a senior developer who has expertise in the area under consideration. The SEPG provides the senior developer with some tutoring on how to use the process improvement document. The SEPG and the working group who is convened for the process area collect and review a draft of the document. The SEPG then places the document in a change control system. After a final review, the SEPG sets the document as a baseline.

Creation of a key process document becomes especially important when an organization that is seeking certification finds that its existing processes lack coverage of a key process area. In this case, the SEPG needs to develop an action plan for creation of the capability that the key process stipulates. In this situation, the SEPG requires management intervention. Funding and other resources are needed, too.

Effecting Change

How change occurs within an organization depends on the culture of the organization. The SEPG might be empowered to work with managers to designate process change priorities and fold them into the overall organizational timelines. For example, if organization-wide software configuration management capabilities do not exist, the group involved with testing is often heavily impacted. The testers might convene and decide to assign one of their members to the task of creating the configuration management system. The goals stated in the process change document are the starting point, but in addition to this, the SEPG needs to draw up a plan for creating and deploying the system. The project might require a year to complete, so management must be behind the effort, providing funding, equipment, space, and other resources. Add to this that the SEPG must arrange for the appropriate person or group to monitor the progress of the project to see that it is reaches the established goals.

Journals and Personalized Endeavors

At the basis of every process improvement effort is the collection of data about existing processes. On an individual basis, if you want to improve the way you do things, you begin by collecting data about how you do things. Three general aspects of this data collection are detailed in this section.

Discover a Script

The first aspect is that you record what you do and find within what you do common tasks that you can collect under given headings. For example, without giving attention to the more general nature or direction of your activity, you know that when you write code, you usually spend a certain amount of time creating documentation or eliminating defects from the first versions of your code. If you were to collect data about these tasks, after a time, you would be able to recognize clear patterns in your activity. If you at least keep a log of the time required to complete the tasks, you can create a table of data that will enable you to estimate how much time you need to perform the tasks.

Refine the Script

Another type of logging activity concerns collections of activity. Here, the goal is to examine what you do when you perform a given task and ask yourself whether what you are doing can be refined. For example, assume that you begin composing a program without first spending time designing it. Although you might end up with a unit of code that performs the task you set out to accomplish, your effort might lack elegance or might be a result of repeated efforts that required you to dispense with your code and start over again. By evaluating your effort, you might discover that if you initially design the unit of code and then begin programming it, you eliminate much of the activity of writing and dispensing with code. You reduce the time you need to complete the code. Then you can establish a script for the procedure that encompasses the design as your standard coding procedure.

Quantify the Script

The easiest types of quantification you can perform when you deal with personal processes are as follows:

- **Count the number of tasks you perform as you complete a given script.** When you count tasks, you can begin to evaluate the process under consideration for things like redundancy. If two processes accomplish the same thing, and one takes 10 steps whereas the other takes 5, you can ask several questions. For example, have you made things too simple or not simple enough? Is there redundancy?
- **Identify and count the types of processes you engage in as you work.** Certain processes fall into similar categories. For example, some processes might fall under a security heading. Among these might be maintaining passwords and backing up files. You can analyze these activities to discover whether better ways exist to perform them.
- **Time how long you require to complete a given task.** Establishing how long you require to perform a given task or process is part of almost any process improvement project. As an individual developer, for instance, if you work in an organization that has an established project management approach, you will be asked to estimate the time you need for given tasks. Becoming good at this involves collecting data on as many instances of work as you can and averaging them. Even if estimating is at first painful and often mistaken, after a while you will find that you can provide accurate predications fairly easily.
- **Time how long you require to complete a given process.** A *process* is a collection of tasks. A process can be all the work you perform on a given project. As with tasks, the way you become an expert at being able to predict the time you require to complete a complicated job is to collect data and average it.

Planning

Planning encompasses both knowing how long you require to perform a given task and being able to designate procedures you will use to reach a given goal. The exploration of refinement of both of the activities lies at the root of planning, and one of the central objectives of process improvement, for both organizations and individuals, is to make it possible to plan development efforts. Generally, the closer that a process' development plans can come to predicating the time, efforts, and expense involved in a development effort, the more mature they are said to be. Every effort that helps refine the ability to predict contributes to the improvement of the process.

Reviews

Among the most important reviews used during process improvement efforts are peer reviews. Peer reviews involve the interaction of a group of people who are fairly equal in their status in the organization and who work jointly toward a common end. An example of a peer review is when one programmer reviews code that another programmer has written. In this instance, one programmer is not necessarily better than another. It is just that the programmer who reviews the code can see the code from an alternative perspective, one that is likely to detect features of the code that the first programmer, for understandable reasons, cannot detect.

Another form of review is more generalized. It, too, can be characterized as a peer review, but it takes place within the context of a team. An example of such a review is a code inspection. A code inspection occurs when a group of developers (not necessarily all programmers) gathers around a table and reads the code that a given individual has developed. In this instance, the purpose is to discover as many errors or irregularities in the code as possible without treating the developer of the code in a disrespectful way. The team benefits if the code that each of its members produces lacks errors. If the team can help the individual produce code that contains fewer errors than otherwise, the team benefits.

In the context of process improvement, peer reviews work most effectively when a group of people involved in a given task confers together to establish a common approach to accomplishing the task. An example of this is when a quality improvement effort begins and management asks a group of developers to meet together to document a common process. Everyone in the group is an authority, and the process definition emerges from the group's common view of the best process.

Conclusion

This chapter discussed how organizations engage in process improvement. At the core of this activity is the use of some type of standard. Among the most widely recognized standards organizations are the IEEE, the SEI, and the ISO. These three organizations offer products and services that a company can use with relative ease. Standards help the members of an organization determine goals for process improvement, but standards alone are not enough to bring about quality improvement. In addition to standards, an organization must be able to collect and process information about its own processes. One thoroughly tested vehicle to information collection is the template. Several excellent templates for process improvement information are available through organizations such as the IEEE, the SEI, and the ISO.

Even with standards and templates for the collection and refinement of information about processes, organizations that are seeking change still face major obstacles because they must coordinate and support the efforts of those members of the organization who are entrusted with initiating the change process. To aid those who spearhead the change effort, organizational managers can create an SEPG. An SEPG allows one or more people to concentrate their energies on collecting information about existing processes and setting goals for the change of the processes. For an SEPG to succeed, experts generally contend that strong support from upper management is needed. Process change is difficult, and the majority of people within an organization seldom respond immediately in a positive way to initiatives for change.

This chapter concentrated on approaches to change fostered by such organizations as the SEI and the ISO. These are the most generally recognized sources of information about organizational process improvement. An enormous store of information on process improvement is available from the SEI and the ISO. The following texts provide further discussion of the topics introduced in this chapter:

Ahern, Dennis M., Aaron Clouse, and Richard Turner. *CMMI Distilled: A Practical Introduction to Integrated Process Improvement.* Boston: Addison-Wesley, 2001.

Caputo, Kim. *CMM Implementation Guide: Choreographing Software Process Improvement.* Boston: Addison-Wesley, 1998.

Humphrey, Watts S. *Introduction to the Personal Software Process.* Boston: Addison-Wesley, 1997.

Humphrey, Watts S. *Managing the Software Process.* Boston: Addison-Wesley, 1989.

Paulk, Mark C., Charles V. Weber, Bill Curtis, et al. *The Capability Maturity Model: Guidelines for Improving the Software Development Process.* Boston: Addison-Wesley, 1995.

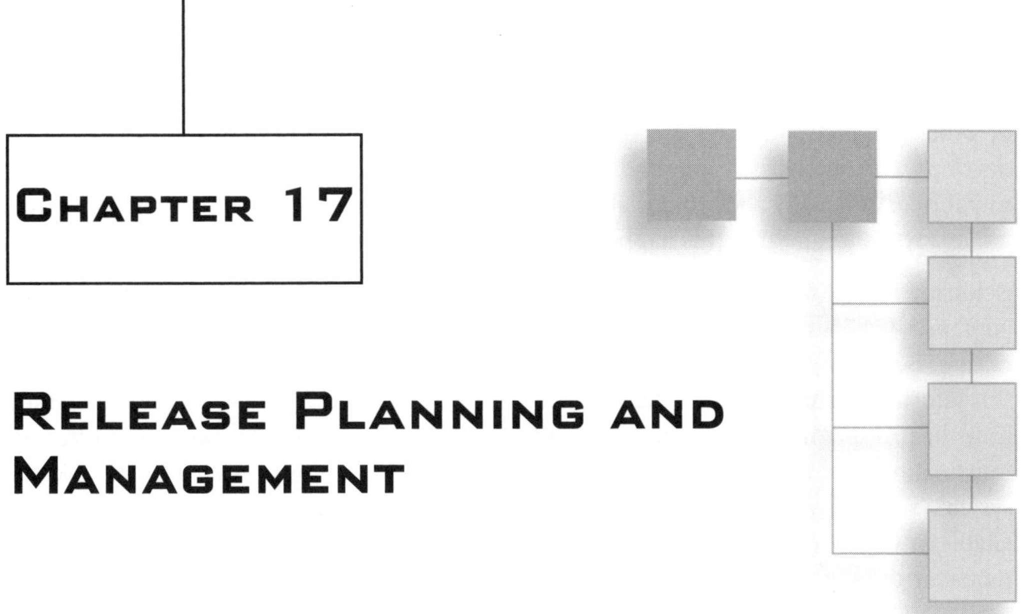

Chapter 17

Release Planning and Management

This chapter investigates the activities that are involved in managing the game software after game developers have completed their primary work. Many of the tools and tasks that you studied in Chapter 10, "Control Freaks and Configuration Management," come into play during the release management phase of a game's life, but many subtle differences separate the two realms of activity. The most fundamental difference is that when a game reaches the release stage, it becomes visible to the customer and, because of this, it poses liabilities and potential that it does not possess during the prerelease development phase. The following topics, among others, present themselves for study:

- Defining the basic activities of release planning
- How release planning differs from release management
- Levels of release
- Release schedules
- Planning for profits
- How different types of games require different management strategies
- Responding to release problems
- Making the world safe for the next release

Release Basics

Given the structure of the computer game industry, in most cases, you release your software to a publisher instead of directly to a consuming audience. In other instances, if you work with a software development company that creates Artificial Intelligence (AI) components, graphics components, collision detection software, testing tools, debugging tools, or other products, your release operations will involve delivering software to software developers. Properly managing the release of your software product involves delivering it to your customers in a form that allows them to use it immediately in a satisfying, profitable way. To ensure that this happens, you must take care to anticipate a variety of risks.

Releasing a software product does not usually involve a single step. Instead, you release your product in stages, beginning with a preliminary release often known as an alpha release. Beginning with this release, you collect information about the system. Some of this information allows you to detect defects. Other information allows you to understand how the product might be improved in a future release. To properly collect and filter the information, you use a release tracking system. One approach is to use an Internet-based system. Such a system allows customers to log problems or suggestions easily. It also enables a widely distributed group of developers to have easy access to the central issue repository.

Structuring Releases

The release management process centers on the *production release*. The production release is also known as the *final release*. It is the version of the product that customers purchase. Before the production release, you can present your game in alpha and beta releases. The *alpha release* usually contains functionality that you consider unstable or questionable. The purpose of the evaluation might be to determine whether you want to change or remove the functionality. A *beta release* offers functional completeness, and its purpose is to help you eliminate lingering errors. At this point in the product's life, developers seek only to eliminate problems. They do not try to change the functionality of the product.

Developers refer to the point in the product's life at which development of any new product functionality ceases as *code complete*. This point in the product's life indicates not the end of the product development, but the point at which no new functionality will be added to the product unless under strictly controlled circumstances. Developers determine that they have reached code complete when they have implemented all the functionality that the software requirements specification stipulates.

After you have released your product to the public, you are likely to find that even after the most strenuous testing, some part of the game malfunctions. To remedy such problems, you can offer the customer a *product update*. Release managers sometimes regard a product update as a release. A *release* is any version of a product that requires that the customer install the product. An update might require only that the customer install a package that is integrated into the product through a means other than compiling. The update is usually a compiled entity that corrects a specific product error that customers or testers have reported after the production release of the product.

Figure 17.1 illustrates a basic *promotion schedule.* The five types of activity that characterize the promotion process fall into three general categories. Release managers usually consider code complete and alpha and beta releases to be parts of the *prerelease phase* of a product's life. The production release marks the beginning of the *release phase* of a product's life. Although the terms can become fuzzy if your product enjoys the fortune of making it through several releases (think of *Final Fantasy*), release managers usually refer to any activity that takes place after the release of a given version of a product as the *postrelease phase* of the product's life.

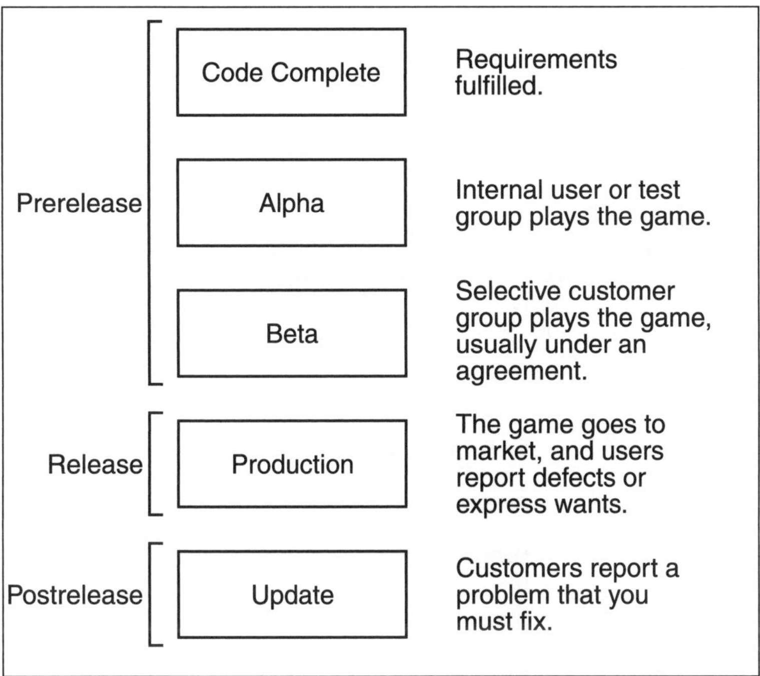

Figure 17.1
Promotion activity takes place in three phases.

Code Complete

An important expression in the development cycle is *code complete.* This place in the development cycle marks the point at which developers cease adding new features or functionality to the game software product. As mentioned previously, developers determine the point of code completeness by reviewing their work in light of the software functional specification. To verify that the functionality has been implemented, developers work according to a software test plan. (See Chapter 11, "Evident Evil—The Art of Testing.")

As Figure 17.2 illustrates, verification and validation of requirements allow the testers to determine when the developers have completed the work of implementing the code. Code completion involves creating the product as specified. The software design specification helps the developers understand how to implement the functionality. The approach used for *Ankh* makes use of stripes. You can implement and test each stripe separately and then integrate all stripes into the complete game product.

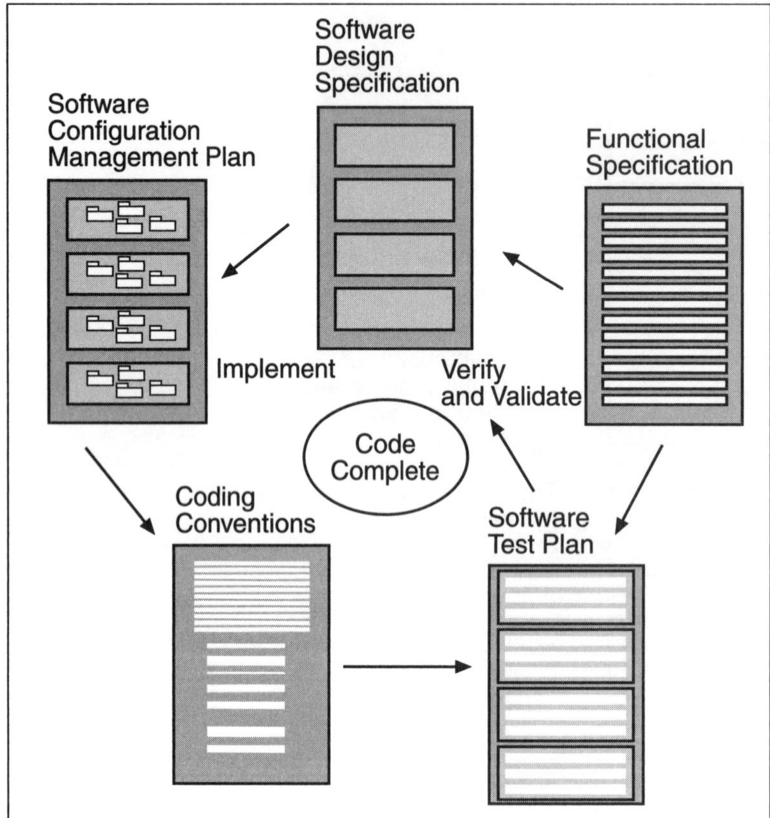

Figure 17.2
You reach code complete when you have verified that all requirements have been implemented.

Code completion involves a formal "locking down" of the code. At this point, developers begin a process of responding to testing data and fixing errors.

Verification of Functionality

Testing activities accomplish three primary tasks:

- Verify that the functionality that the software functional specification designates has been implemented.

- Validate the functionality. In other words, determine whether the functionality that has been implemented does what it is supposed to.
- Determine whether the software contains errors.

A software test plan guides testing activity. Generally, testing begins with the implementation effort. Throughout the development phase, developers work in tandem with testers to test the code as they create it. The approach used for *Ankh* involved breaking the product into stripes. The test plan allowed the testers to approach each stripe of the game as a separate entity. Testing results during each stripe of the development cycle focused on the functionality that each stripe encompassed. Again, although each stripe addressed a given set of requirements from the software requirements specification, how the requirements were to be implemented was documented in the software design specification. Incremental, iterative development of stripes continued until the team reached code complete. Figure 17.3 illustrates the flow of activity for a few of the stripes.

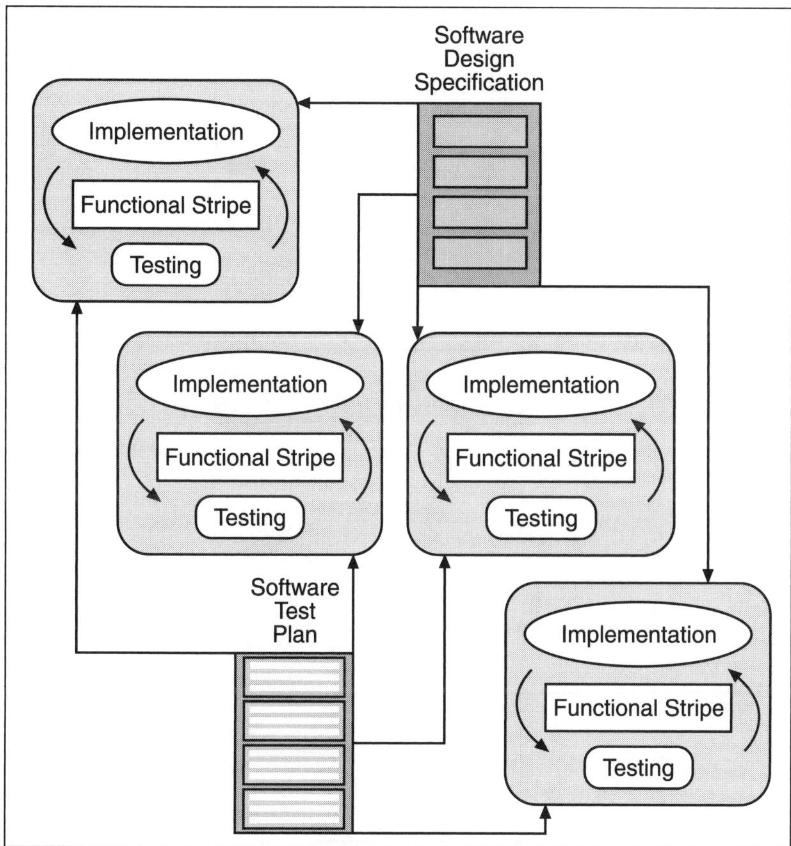

Figure 17.3
Testing and implementation proceed in tandem during the development of each successive stripe.

Moving Toward Code Complete

Code complete often represents a key point in the development process, because at this point, all of the stripes of the product should be integrated into the build. This might be the first time that such a build has occurred. It represents the first complete version of the product. Figure 17.4 provides a view of the stripes that comprised the first complete build of *Ankh.*

Stripe 1–Opening	Requirements 8, 14, 15, 16, 17, 18, 23, 28, 38, 46, 57
Stripe 2.1–GUI Objects	Requirements 18, 52
Stripe 2.2–Floor Tiling	Requirement 43
Stripe 2.3–Mesh Placement	Requirements 13, 43
Stripe 2.4–Save and Load	Requirement 4
Stripe 3.1–Navigate Alexandria	Requirements 13, 14, 15, 16, 17, 36, 61
Stripe 3.2–Sound	Requirements 29, 30, 31, 32, 33
Stripe 4–Character Editor	Requirements 18, 19, 20, 21, 22, 35, 44
Stripe 5–Unit Physics	Requirements 13, 14, 15, 16, 17, 35, 41, 42, 45, 47, 48, 64
Stripe 6–Inventory Items	Requirements 40, 49, 55
Stripe 7–Combat	Requirements 54, 56
Stripe 8–Acquire Skills	Requirements 20, 34, 47, 55, 56
Stripe 9–Acquire Weapon	Requirements 14, 15, 16, 17, 40, 49
Stripe 10–View Statistics	Requirements 14, 15, 16, 17, 18, 19, 20, 21
Stripe 11–AI	Requirements 24, 25, 26, 37
Stripe 12–Remaining Levels	Requirement 27
Stripe 13–Saving and Loading	Requirements 1, 2, 3, 4, 5, 6, 7, 8, 9, 10, 11, 12
Stripe 14–Options	Requirement 39

Figure 17.4
The code complete state represents the entire scope of the product.

Chapter 10 discusses in detail the techniques and tools that the team employed to manage builds as it progressed toward the final integration of all stripes into the complete version of the game. During the day-to-day development process, you can use the software configuration management system to orchestrate the builds. During this phase of the development process, builds do not represent a complete build of the product. With some development efforts, of course, builds can be representative of what is complete up to the day of the build, but given that the product is still under development, no build during the prerelease development process can be said to represent the entire functionality of the product.

When you reach the point of code complete, the build no longer represents a limited set of functionality. The build now represents the complete product. For this reason, you must now manage the product as a single entity. One important implication of this change is that you must test changes to any part of the system against the entire system. You can no longer assume that a change affects only a single stripe.

After Code Complete

The general pattern of development that is established before code completion continues even after code completion. At this point, however, things change. Before code completion, developers implement new functionality and testers ascertain whether the functionality meets the requirements. After code completion, developers no longer build new functionality. Instead, they respond to the *defect*, or *error*, *reports* that the testers issue. Once again, testers seek to verify and validate the functionality that the requirements specification documents.

The first major concern after code completion is the verification that the code is, indeed, complete. This activity involves more verification. By this point in the development process, unless the development has proceeded in a haphazard way, you should verify the functionality of the product for each of the functional stripes. If you have developed all stripes according to the software design specification, it is likely that you have implemented all functionality. Still, problems can arise when you must integrate the stripes into the whole. Sometimes when you integrate the components, or modules, that make up the product into the complete system, defects arise and the product no longer displays its specified functionality. You must solve such integration problems.

You can designate the activity that follows code completion as *debugging*. That's because the process is one of reacting to the discoveries of the testers. The focus of development work involves reducing the number of errors. Figure 17.5 shows some of the relationships among testing, requirements, and detected defects.

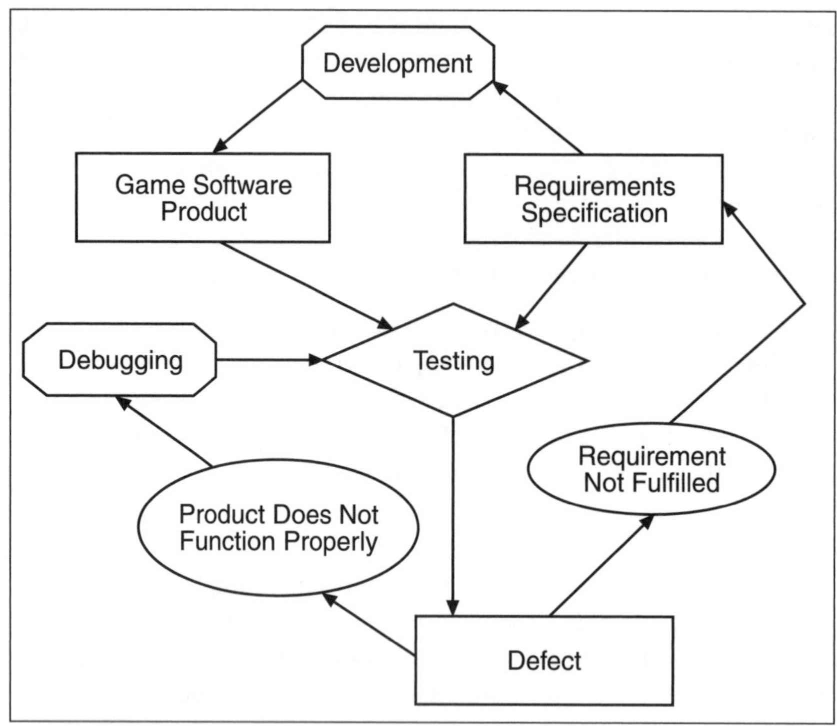

Figure 17.5
Testing after code completion drives a process that tries to reduce or eliminate the errors that are evident in the game as a whole.

Categories of Debugging

At this point, many test factors enter into the picture. Among these factors are those that arise from general gameplay. After code complete, you can develop the full play of the game. With the development effort for *Ankh,* for instance, given the completion of the game engine, you could fully implement the level features. Implementation of the level features for *Ankh* involved the use of existing functionality, not the creation of new functionality. Testers and developers worked with stable functionality.

The errors you discover after you have completed the code generally fall into three broad categories:

- **Some of the defects concern *engineering* issues.** You can summarize this best as a problem with *performance.* Performance problems can arise in any number of ways and might not be evident to players. One example of a performance problem is memory allocation. Memory leaks might or might not become visible to the player. If a leak causes the game to crash, it most certainly will become evident.

On the other hand, if the leak is relatively minor and degrades the performance only after hours of play, many players might not detect the problem. Discovery of memory leaks often involves sophisticated testing tools.

- **Some concern *game feature* issues.** Gameplay testers might discover that characters are sluggish, lighting is wrong, or scenes do not refresh with smooth transitions. Such problems might require different approaches to the way graphics designers use the game engine, or they might require adjustments to the game engine itself. Developers must investigate the code to discover the root of the problem. If the game performs sluggishly, the problem might lie in an inefficient algorithm. You can tune or rewrite an algorithm without changing the functionality of the game.
- **Some reflect failure in the implementation of functionality.** This is probably the worst type of defect that testers can discover at this point in the development process. If the team declares the code as complete and testers discover afterward that a functional feature has not been implemented, something was seriously wrong with the software design. If this does happen, the team must seriously consider how to handle the situation. If some functionality has been omitted but 98 percent of the functionality has been verified as complete, the missing functionality might not represent anything critical to the overall system. In this case, the project manager might decide to leave out the functionality. The project manager would have to admit a failure, but implementing the missing functionality this late in the development process could cause the team to miss its delivery date.

Alpha

An alpha release of a game allows you to investigate whether the functionality you have implemented is the functionality you want. It also allows you to test functionally that might remain seriously questionable, to the extent that, although it is clear that the functionality is implemented correctly, it is not clear that it belongs in the game.

The difference between a version of the game you test after code complete and a version of the game you test as an alpha release is that you document an alpha release as a release. In other words, you assign it a release number, which identifies it as a complete product. Further, you distribute the alpha release to a select group of game players, testers, and others who are not involved in the primary development effort. To distribute the alpha release to these people, you must create an installation package of some type so that you can deliver the game as a standalone executable.

Alpha Criteria

Games do not always go through alpha releases. Some developers feel confident enough about their work to proceed immediately to a beta release. This happens when the developers, for example, are working with a mod. The functionality of the mod might be established so clearly that releasing the game as an alpha release makes no sense. All that the developers require is that testers discover defects that might remain after the prerelease testing. They are confident that all of the functionality specified for the game is solidly in place.

To decide on whether to proceed with an alpha release, you might consider some of the following points:

- **Friendly internal testers.** In most instances, you perform an alpha release entirely in-house. Play testers for an alpha release usually are regarded as "friendly" testers. In other words, they are individuals who are willing to work with the functionality of the game even though it might be implemented in an incomplete way. These individuals should be willing to tell you how they think the game might be improved. They might make suggestions about features they would like to see dropped.
- **You have the time for extended testing.** Even if a game possesses major flaws and friendly play testers are around who want to work with you, you still need to anticipate that any testing requires time. Alpha testing is an opportunity for developers to work closely with testers in an immediate, interactive way. The decision remains, however, about whether time allows for alpha testing. If you are working with a publisher, you might find that you want to pass the game to the testers at the publishers. You might find that you want to involve the testers at the publishers right away, in effect skipping a true alpha test phase.
- **It would be hazardous not to make an alpha release.** If the game is so defect-prone that sending it to your customer for a first view might create liabilities, you have no choice but to make an alpha release.
- **You have requirements or functionality that you are not sure about.** Sometimes certain functional aspects of the game present liabilities even if you have developed them in a competent way. In such situations, you can cut the functionality from the product, creating a slightly scaled-back version of your anticipated first release. To gather information about whether you should proceed along these lines, conduct an alpha test.

Scaling Alpha Builds

Any build that you produce after code complete represents the complete software product. This said, any given product offers the opportunity for several different versions. Such a situation is analogous to a film in which the director, having shot different final scenes, decided at the conclusion of the production effort what ending to use.

In the software development effort, the choice of final versions is usually restricted, but you should not underestimate the importance of even narrow choices. Typical of such situations are the following:

- **Your company creates physics components.** Your release offers three components that simulate disintegrating objects. One, an "upgraded" burning metal ball, works perfectly except under extremely accelerated situations. In these situations, the reality of the deterioration no longer precisely corresponds to what films depicting physical experiments show. If you think even the slightest chance exists that the customer will be dissatisfied with the upgraded capability, you might consider building an alpha release that does not include it.
- **The game works fine—up to a certain point.** The history of the project up to code completion shows that at about the middle point of the development effort, the team detects a problem. No one can solve it, so it remains unsolved. This problem concerned functionality that, although specified, is not needed for most of the gameplay activity. In fact, if you omit the functionality, no one is likely to know the difference. On the other hand, if you keep the functionality, it eventually crashes the game. You have a problem that you cannot fix in the time given.

Figure 17.6 illustrates a situation in which the functionality that is available at code complete presents two options. Each release build represents a complete software product. You decide on an alpha build of the product. You provide this version of the product for alpha testing to discover whether it is safe to omit the problem functionality. Given the results of the alpha release testing, you have a body of test data on which to base the actions you take as you proceed to the beta release.

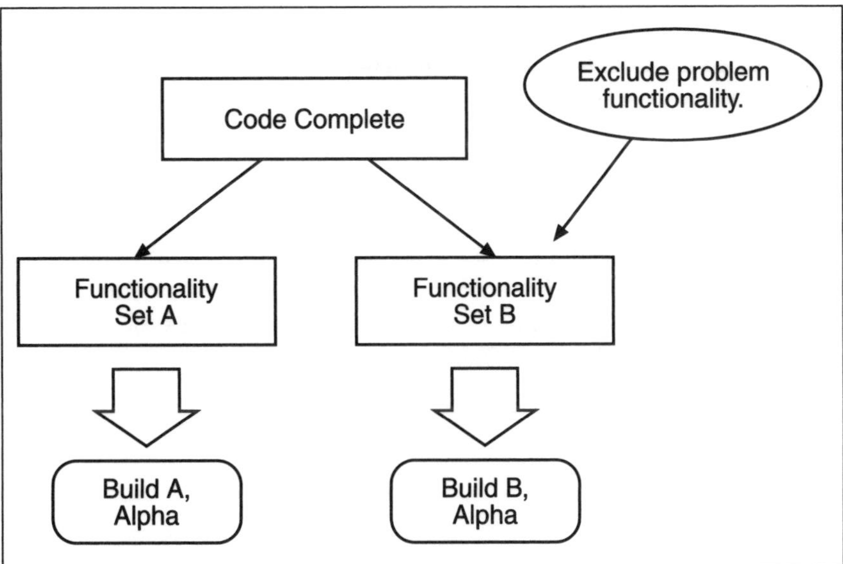

Figure 17.6
A release build represents an entire product, but different products can emerge from release builds.

Beta

When you create a beta release of a product, you create something you are willing to ship to customers. The functionality of the product is complete. You are looking for a thorough testing effort on the part of the product users. The beta release allows you to subject the product to a thorough test cycle that involves actual users or customers rather than professional testers.

Before you ship the release version to the customer, you usually have the customer sign an agreement. The agreement protects you from liabilities that the product might present. It also establishes ground rules, such as how long the beta test will go on, how defects will be handled, and whether you are liable for damages that the user might suffer because of using the software. In the world of computer games, such an agreement might seem unnecessary, but it is still important to pay attention to liabilities and limitations. An example of a liability might be that an online user of your game creates a character profile, investing many hours, only to discover that with the first release, the character profile is no longer valid. If this player is not warned beforehand about the loss of data, he is likely to be extremely dissatisfied with your game.

An example of a limitation is that you must tell those who install the beta release that after a certain time, you will no longer support the beta release. Although in some situations it might be reasonable to try to support a beta release even after the first production release, in most cases, such a move is absurd. After all, the first release should contain all the fixes to the product that were issued during the beta test.

You also extend or establish an issue tracking system that enables the customer to report all use issues. Not having such a system in place at the start of the beta trial wastes the time and energy of everyone involved.

Beta Criteria

Effective beta testing involves establishing an issue tracking system. It is not enough to begin a beta evaluation of your software and then wait for e-mail or phone messages to arrive. Instead, you must proceed with an explicit plan for releasing the product. Table 17.1 illustrates the main components of a beta release plan.

Table 17.1 Beta Release Plan Components

Beta Component	Description
A principal contact	This might seem self-evident, but it is often neglected. A principle contact is the person who is in charge of the beta process at the customer end. If you send out 100 beta versions of your multi-player game, you must establish each of these people as principal contacts. If you ship your set of AI components to a game engine company, you are likely to have one person on the customer end who is responsible for coordinating the beta effort.
A contract	Do not ship a product unless you have established clear legal boundaries on what happens if the product causes problems. When you ship a beta release of a software product, those who receive the beta release must understand that the product contains defects and that the defects might cause damages. The contract allows you to avoid liability for such damage.
An issue tracking system	For purposes of a beta release, make reporting issues as easy as possible for the customers. Generally, you want to track the point at which the problem occurs. If you have folded an immense amount of sophistication into your development effort, you can plant automatic response mechanisms in your code. Such response mechanisms trace when the system crashed and automatically transmit problem codes over the Internet. Short of that, you can ask the beta user to write a sentence that details what he was doing when the problem arose. In addition, you can ask for a description of the problem.
A set of issue ratings	Your release test team must have a set of ratings in place for the issues that users report. Consider, for example, a user who reports that he thinks the game is stupid. This differs from the report received a few minutes later from a user who writes that when he navigated the avatar to a pillar on the left of Level 3, the application froze. (See Table 17.2 for a discussion of ratings.)
Documentation	A beta release of a software product brings with it the need to describe formally the software and its operation. When you issue a beta release, you should include a set of documentation that covers, at a minimum, how to install, operate, and remove the software.
Customer understanding	The documentation also should include a list of responsibilities that you would like your customers to assume as they participate in the beta effort. For example, you should have a technical writer create a document titled something along the lines of "How to Describe and Report Problems and Issues." Direct everyone who participates in the beta trial to this document.

(continued on next page)

Table 17.1 Beta Release Plan Components (continued)

Beta Component	Description
An acceptance plan	An acceptance plan applies to a customer to whom you have assigned the beta release as a part of a final software delivery. An acceptance plan establishes the criteria that you must meet as a developer before the customer is obligated to take full possession of the software. One recommended approach is to base the acceptance plan on a *duration* rather than an *itemization*. For example, although you still will want the customer to verify that the requirements you have stated in your requirements agreement have been implemented, the beta can proceed on the basis that the customer has the right to expect fixes to the product for a given period. The beta concludes when this time expires.
Clear criteria for acceptance	The acceptance plan should include clear criteria for acceptance. If you are developing a set of components for another software company, one engaged, for example, in the development of an engine, you need to include a precise statement of what is expected. On the other hand, if you are forwarding a game to a publisher, you can encapsulate the criteria in a list of test conditions that must be fulfilled. Beta testing continues until you have demonstrated that all test conditions have been met.

Scaling a Beta Test

Many development efforts involve only a beta test. A scenario that involves only a beta test might be a mod effort in which the modifications of the previous game are so clear-cut that an established group of beta testers will be able to identify clearly what is new and old and have little trouble working with the defects that might characterize an alpha release.

Beta tests usually involve durations rather than functional features. The reason for this is that the beta tester is a prospective customer who already understands the scope of the product and who has agreed to use the specified functionality on a preliminary basis. Moreover, when you ship the beta release, you have had a chance to validate and verify the product's functionality. What you have not had a chance to do is interact intensively with the software in a use context. This is the job of the beta tester. Figure 17.7 provides a summary view of a likely scenario of a beta test.

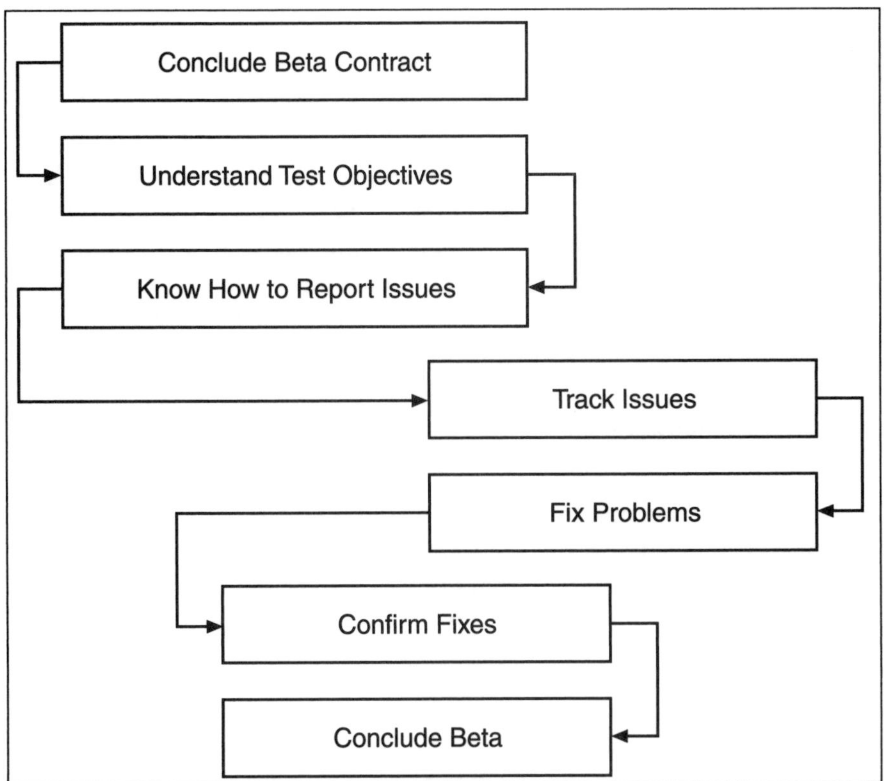

Figure 17.7
Beta tests involve contracted users in a thorough test of established functionality.

Production Releases

Production releases sometimes are called final releases. The distinguishing characteristics of final releases can be as follows:

- **Marketed.** In one way or another, someone pays for this release, so your product user becomes, not a tester or a partner, but a customer.
- **Targeted.** The release is for a specific platform. You can install it on this platform.
- **Documented.** The release is accompanied by a release letter that explains items such as how to install the product and issues that might affect the use of the product.
- **Numbered.** The release is identified with a number.
- **Packaged.** The release is packaged in a distinctive way.
- **Defect concerns.** Defects in this release are treated as failures, not as production issues. You must fix such defects via product updates. The need for such updates constitutes a liability.

Updates

It is almost impossible that a software product will enjoy a life free of defects after it has been released. This is true especially of games. In a console or PC setting, players play the game in ways that no amount of testing can anticipate realistically. Inevitably, the diligent player detects an anomaly. If the anomaly crashes the game, you must provide the player with a fix. If the anomaly does not crash the game, you have a couple of options. One is to suggest a workaround to the player. Some people might regard a workaround as a cheap, silly way to deal with a software problem, but even systems designed for NASA have had problems that engineers have dealt with through workarounds. When your probe is millions of kilometers away from Earth, if the software on board creates a problem when instructed to perform actions x, y, and z, it is probably best, at least for the time being, not to instruct it to perform actions x, y, and z. The decision not to perform the action is a workaround.

Always consider workarounds as temporary. A workaround is a logistical or strategic solution that you can provide the player of the game while you prepare a technical solution. With console games, the technical solution is not likely to appear until the next release of the game. With PC games, you might deliver the solution via a download from the Internet.

A software solution that you apply to a released software product is known as a *patch*. Historically, a patch differs from a release because it does not require that the user reinstall the software. This definition of a patch tends to be too restrictive for many PC games that have appeared over the years. The reason for this is that game developers for PC games have sometimes found it easier to replace the game executable.

For console games, the need for a patch tends to spell the end of the game's life. Console game players usually choose to return the game rather than deal with a severe flaw. If the game possesses a minor defect, reviewers and players often react with caustic remarks, but they might not go so far as to demand their money back.

Patches are developed as separate, isolated modules that you can integrate into an already installed product. The use of dynamically linked libraries, COM, and .NET components makes patching easy in a Windows system. In the world of console games, patches can be a bit more problematic. Sometimes, the best solution for a defective console game is to reissue the whole game.

Numbering Products

Regardless of the type of software product you create, tracking how you have developed and released your product remains an important part of your development activities. Not doing so is inviting situations in which developers overwrite files, testers retest or fail to test functionality, or customers receive versions of the product that are incomplete or defective.

Tracing the development history of your product obligates you to examine three types of activity: building the product during development, assembling the product for release, and updating the product as you address defects. Each of these activities calls for a clear approach to labeling your work so that you can easily identify when you have performed work and what the work has encompassed.

To address this challenge, organizations establish numbering systems. A numbering system consists of a template for assigning numbers to a product and a set of rules for determining how to insert information into the template. The template that an organization develops depends on how much information it wants to store. Figure 17.8 illustrates one among many possibilities of numbering. According to this scheme, the numbering system provides four basic types of information: release, version, update level, and test level. The sections that follow discuss these four types of information in detail.

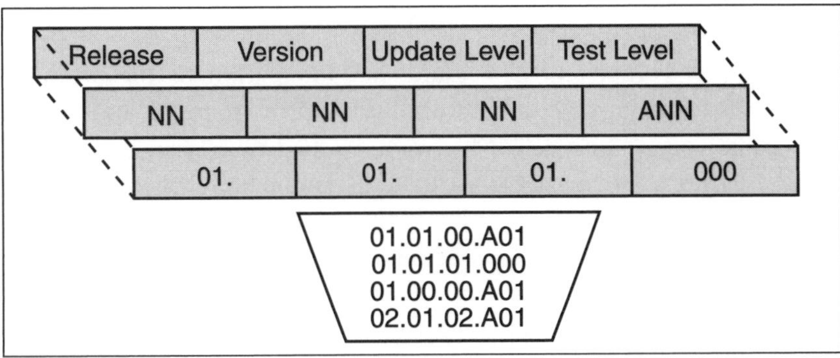

Figure 17.8
A template for numbering ensures consistency.

Numbering systems provide data that allows you to know several types of information in addition to basic release levels. As Figure 17.8 illustrates, you can set up the number system so that dots (or periods) separate fields. Each field provides information about the *level* of a given type of activity. In the system used here, the first field contains the information about the release level. To illustrate how this numbering system might work with a release under alpha test, use the number 00.07.10.A01.

- The *release level* is set at zero as long as the product is in the prerelease phase.
- The *version level* indicates that the product has been through seven trial builds at the prerelease level.
- During the seventh integration of the product, the *update level* is 10, which indicates that the developers have added 10 fixes of some type.

- The alphanumerical field at the end is more complex than the others because developers can use it in several ways. The A indicates that a formal alpha test release has been created. The 01 following the A indicates that this is the first pass at the alpha test. When the product passes the alpha test, the release manager can change the A to a B and reset the numbers that follow to accord with the version of the beta test.

Release

A release is a separately installed, complete product. It is what is shipped to the customer. With each new release, you should reset the release number so that it's the only field that has a value greater than zero. In other words, you should set version, update, and test fields within the release number (if you use the type of numbering that this chapter discusses) to zero. The first release of a product according to the template given in Figure 17.8 would be 01.00.00.000.

A release should represent a completely new build and integration of the product. Achieving this goal involves removing all old files from the build environment and replacing them with the files that you have slated for inclusion in the new release. Even if you have no prior releases, you must confirm that you are not including files that you have not scheduled formally for inclusion in the release build. In the team's work with *Ankh*, examples of problems resulting from neglect of such activities included failed builds due to outdated Boost files and deterioration of performance due to sloppiness in the use of the debug version of DirectX. A clean build area would have eliminated these problems.

Version

Probably one of the best uses of the version number is to designate when you create a baseline of the product during the development phase. Configuration managers sometimes call a baseline a *snapshot* of the product during its development history. Effectively capturing a snapshot requires ensuring that it includes all files that compose the product. To facilitate the documentation of this activity, the *Ankh Software Design Specification* provides a section that documents the components of the game using UML package and component diagrams. Likewise, the *Ankh Software Configuration Management Plan* provides similar diagrams, along with a directory specification and a build schedule, to trace versions during the development process.

Version numbers in the numbering system presented here follow the first dot (or period). Figure 17.9 illustrates how you can trace the builds representing the stripes in the design of *Ankh* using version numbers. Each successive version shows that you have added the functionality of a given stripe. Stored in this way, the mapping is not as direct as it might have been had the development team numbered all stripes with whole numbers, but it is still clear that each version of the game software created during the prerelease phase included an additional stripe of functionality.

Design Stripe	Baseline Using Version
Stripe 1–Opening	00.01.01.000
Stripe 2.1–GUI Objects	00.02.01.000
Stripe 2.2–Floor Tiling	00.03.01.000
Stripe 2.3–Mesh Placement	00.04.01.000
Stripe 2.4–Save and Load	00.05.01.000
Stripe 3.1–Navigate Alexandria	00.06.01.000
Stripe 3.2–Sound	00.07.01.000
Stripe 4–Character Editor	00.08.01.000
Stripe 5–Unit Physics	00.09.01.000
Stripe 6–Inventory Items	00.10.01.000
Stripe 7–Combat	00.11.01.000
Stripe 8–Acquire Skills	00.12.01.000
Stripe 9–Acquire Weapon	00.13.01.000
Stripe 10–View Statistics	00.14.01.000
Stripe 11–AI	00.15.01.000
Stripe 12–Remaining Levels	00.16.01.000
Stripe 13–Saving and Loading	00.17.01.000
Stripe 14–Options, Requirement 39	00.18.01.000
Stripe 15–Optimizations	00.19.01.000

Figure 17.9
You can identify builds by using version numbers.

Update (or Upgrade) Level

An update is something you add to an existing release. An upgrade does not obligate you to rebuild or recompile the product. Examples of how to accomplish this arise if you replace defective music or graphics files. In other cases, you might replace dynamic link libraries. In the numbering scheme documented in this chapter, the information that identifies update levels follows the second dot (or period). Two digits allow for 100 possible fixes, but this number can increase if you use the test-level information to augment the fix level.

Good practice suggests that you not change the release and version numbers unless you extensively altered the product, such as when you add a component and the result is changed functionality that is visible to the user. On the other hand, whenever you make a change in the product that the customers receive, you should be able to trace the change. You should know precisely how you have changed the product since its first release. This is where the information supplied by the fix level is most useful. You should identify every fix uniquely. The numbering template shown in Figure 17.8 allows you to increment the Update field for every fix you issue.

Test Level

Again referring to Figure 17.8, the most straightforward use of the test level field is to assign A for alpha and B for beta, and then to follow the letters with whatever number properly designates the level of the test being performed.

A further use awaits the field, however. This use might start with a problem with the update field. It might be difficult to know where a version ends and an update begins. For example, suppose that you release 01.00.00.000. Within a month, you have begun work on another major release. You finish work on the fourth stripe and create a baseline, 01.01.00.000.

However, at the same time, you find problems with the first release and have to create a patch. The patch is to the first release, so you retrieve 01.00.00.000 from the configuration management system and work with the code until you have a patch, which consists of a few lines of code. At this point, how can you designate that you have created a patch rather than work you want to apply toward version 01.01.00.00?

One solution is to apply a U (for updated) to the final field. In this way, the number of the patch becomes 01.00.00.U01. With a little tweaking, use of alphanumerical combinations in the last field allows you to identify specifically the item you are dealing with. For example, you might determine that 01.00.00.U01 designates only the applied patch and not a complete build of the product. If you completely rebuild, you might use another letter, such as I for integrated.

Tracking Information for Release Activities

A release should be something that you deliver as a result of a planned effort. To examine how a planned effort leads to a release, consider two scenarios:

- **Scenario 1, unplanned.** You are working on a game. The development activity proceeds in a random way for a few months. As you go, you create this feature and that. You eventually reach a point at which you think it is fun to play the game you have developed. You play the game for several days until you no longer run into defects that you find particularly troublesome. At this point, you decide you can release the game.
- **Scenario 2, planned.** You develop a game according to a software engineering process that involves creating a set of requirement, creating a design, coding according to a design, testing according to a test plan, and delivering the game according to a release plan. To arrive at the decision to release the game, you test the product against its requirements to determine that you have implemented the functionality that you have specified. You also test the product until you have eliminated all defects discovered during testing. Finally, you determine that with each day's testing, you detect fewer defects. At this point, you release the game.

The first, unplanned approach involves finding the product after it has been created. The release effort involves playing the game for a few days and then, when the feeling is right, passing the game to the customer. The planned approach involves testing the game against specified requirements and tracking defect numbers to the point that you can determine that a definite trend toward fewer defects accompanies the fact that you have reached a point at which you have fixed all detected defects.

The planned approach requires data. The unplanned approach requires something along the lines of a holistic sense of the game's suitability for release. There is nothing wrong with the second criterion. Indeed, a holistic sense of the game's suitability for release should be an important part of the development effort. However, at the same time, the holistic approach alone possesses flaws. It lacks positive, empirical evidence that the game is ready for release.

Gathering evidence to verify the suitability of a game for release involves collecting information through two tracking tools characteristic of many software engineering efforts. The first is a tracking tool that records defects that testers have detected during the development effort. The second is a tracking tool that records changes or proposed changes to the software as specified and released. The first generally is known as *bug tracking*. The second generally is known as *change management*.

Tracking Build Information

Chapter 10 addresses product builds and the intricacies of managing them, but in this chapter, it remains important to point out that you cannot expect to manage the release of your game consciously and rationally unless you have information about its build history. The reason for this is that if you introduce release management processes into your software development activities, determining when a product is ready for release requires that you be able to discern patterns in the occurrences of defects in the development and testing activities following completion of your code. Unless you have a tracking system in place, you have no way to collect the right information.

Versions of Builds

To control builds during the prerelease phase of the software development cycle, you use a *version control system*. With the *Ankh* project, the team decided to use TortoiseCVS, which is a Windows version of Concurrent Versions System (CVS). This system is not a Change Management (CM) system. In other words, it does not require the use of change requests to make changes. Instead, it stores files and maintains a database of changes that have been made to them.

A CM system is good for maintaining code after it has been released. It is not the best choice for a situation in which frequent changes occur, and frequent changes occur during the prerelease development phase. A CM system is good for storing complete configurations of software. At the release phase of a software product's life, for example, the software release, as a complete entity, becomes an excellent candidate for CM. The same applies to points during the prerelease phase when you want to create baseline versions of the software.

One of the underlying purposes of a CM system is to regulate change closely. If you apply a CM system with even a marginal degree of formality, those wanting to make changes to the code must, at a minimum, submit a request to make the change. A *change board* then approves the request, and upon approval, you can make the change.

During the prerelease phase of development, when developers are asked to submit requests to make changes each time they check out code, they tend to check out code less frequently. The problem with this is that the less often developers check out code, the more changes they make to the code without merging and building (or requesting permission). The result is that more defects plague each comprehensive build, and development progress slows.

CVS expedites development because although it tracks files and prevents the loss of work, it does not impose a strict change control system on developers. Change control must be accomplished through policies. For more discussion on policies and the use of CVS, see Chapter 10.

Integration

Builds offer opportunities for *baselines*, but this is true only if you have created a design, or architecture, for your software that supports baselines. A baseline is a significant point in a development effort. The term applies to anything that has been developed extensively enough that it can be used as a basis for developing something else. For example, upon completion of the requirements specification for *Ankh*, the team reviewed the document and then determined that it was suitable for baselining. At this point, the document became a candidate for placement in a CM system. The team no longer wanted a situation to arise in which some individual on the team could take the document, alter it arbitrarily, and then make no indication to others that changes had been made.

Although no strict rules govern what counts as a baseline or how to manage code according to baselines, a general, flexible strategy can be laid out. The *Ankh* development team used such a strategy. It created *Ankh* in a series of stripes (which might be called *modules* or *components*). Each stripe addressed one or more of the requirements stated in the software requirements specification for *Ankh*. During the development of the stripe, the team used TorqueCVS to manage versions. After the team baselined a stripe, it imposed CM policies on it, thus making it improper to change it without formal proceedings. The team archived this stripe and could begin work on the next stripe. Figure 17.10 shows the progression of activity leading from build to baseline.

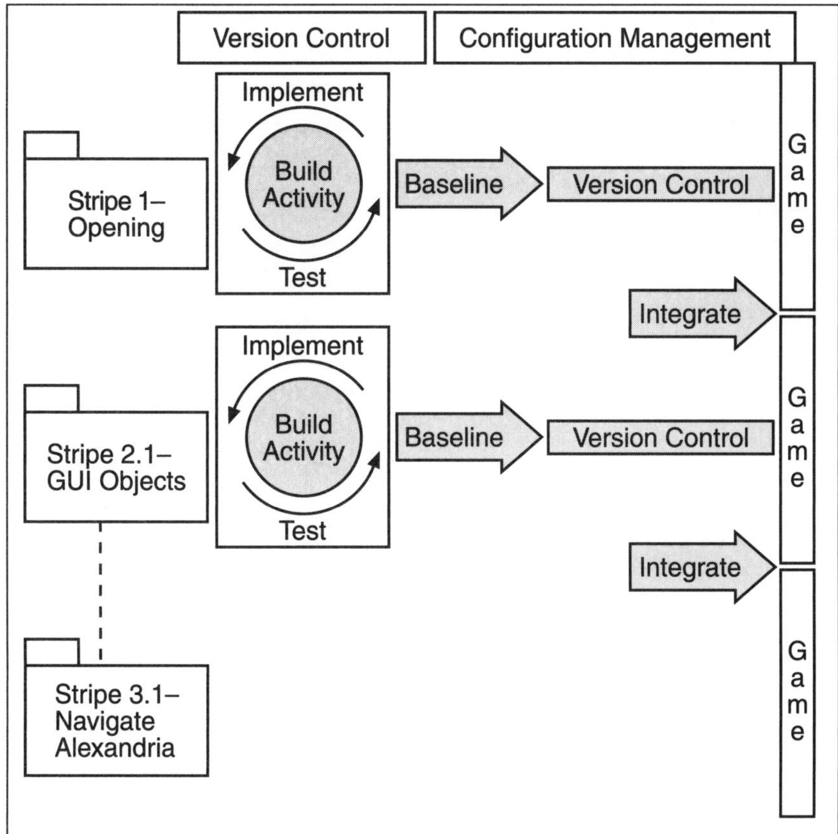

Figure 17.10
Build activity caters to shorter cycles, whereas change management caters to longer cycles.

Tracking Release Information

Different rates of change among different components characterize the development process. As a programmer works on a segment of code to implement functionality stated in the software requirements specification, changes occur rapidly. Given a development environment like Microsoft Visual Studio .NET, for example, a programmer can compile and build code several times during a day's work. As the effort moves forward, the programmer experiences frustration if the build activity requires a long time. In fact, the number of included files and the number of dependencies become a significant factor. To expedite the development effort, the programmer seeks to reduce these numbers.

Moving quickly is the primary concern of the development build process. The picture changes during release. Expeditious builds remain important, but for builds that take place after the code is completed, the focus changes to *release management.*

Version control occurs throughout the life of the product, but at the release stage, the team asserts version control with greater formality. Each stripe presents a different snapshot of the product during its development life. You can place each stripe, as a baselined version of the product, under version control. Together, when integrated into a complete product, the stripes represent a release version of the product.

After you baseline a stripe, you can still work on it through *testing* and *integration.* Testing a stripe can proceed with greater ease and effectiveness if developers isolate it from its successors. Further, work on the next stripe can proceed with greater assurance if the next stripe is integrated into the product at the point of stability that the baseline designates. Figure 17.11 illustrates how each stripe exists as a separate unit and yet contributes to the complete game. The final system encompasses the functionality of all the contributing stripes.

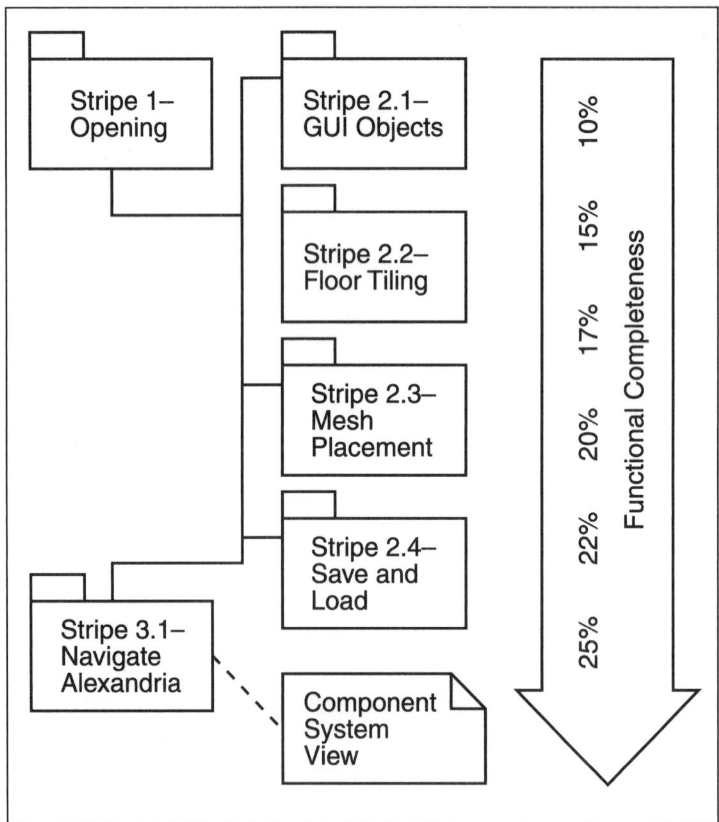

Figure 17.11
Stripe 3.1 of *Ankh* is baselined as a coherent body of implemented functionality.

As the product nears final release, developers integrate all of its components (or stripes) into a completed product. At this point, developers must control carefully the changes that they make to the product, because any change affects the entire product. The *complexity* of the product has grown to its greatest extent. At this point, then, the developers must assert *change management.* Change management requires that before developers make any change, some process must be in place that allows an individual or a group with a general view of the product to determine whether specific changes are advisable. A *change control board* consists of one or more individuals who formally determine whether to allow changes.

Release activity should be characterized by gradual, deliberate change. Although it is important to continue to track changes using an established numbering system, it is also imperative to document changes using change requests. In this respect, the way that developers treat the product after code completion differs significantly from the way they treat it before code completion.

Tracking Defects

CM and defect tracking are services that a single software application can provide. Both operate in the same general way, except that commercial makers of defect tracking systems for software developers often refer to their products as "bug tracking" systems. In other contexts, they sometimes are called "problem reporting" or "trouble ticketing" systems. Whatever the name, such systems store information about product (or service) problems so that those who develop or maintain the product (or provide the service) can address the problems efficiently.

Problem tracking allows you to gather summary data. Consider that during the development phase of a software product's life, a typical course of events proceeds as follows:

1. Programmers create code and submit it for testing.
2. Testers test code and find defects.
3. Testers submit reports of the defects to the defect reporting system.
4. Programmers view reports from the defect tracking system and fix the defects.
5. Programmers report their activity to the defect tracking system.
6. Testers view the report and test the code once again to verify the fix.
7. If testers find the fix has been successful, they close the defect report.

Summary Data

A defect tracking system allows you to create *summary data.* Summary data enables you to detect general patterns in such things as your development practices, the behavior of the product, and your ability to respond to the needs of your customers. Figure 17.12

shows a pattern of activity that you can discern from data provided by a defect tracking system. The data concerns the number of problems developers encountered after they began testing baselined stripes. The patterns track how long it took the developers to eliminate integration problems after a stripe had been scheduled to be baselined. (Stripes were scheduled to be baselined after developers reported they had completely implemented the functionality designated for the stripe.)

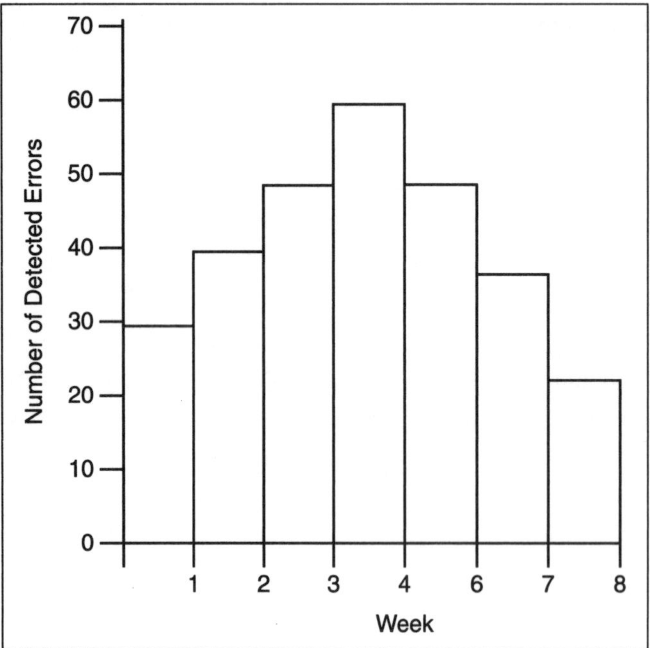

Figure 17.12
You can establish rates of defect by using data that you collect in the defect tracking system.

The method you use to track defects depends on the data that you gather, the way that you set up your reports, and the criteria for evaluation of the data. One of the most well-established approaches to tracking defects involves counting the number of defects that occur per given number of Lines of Code (LOC). Testers sometimes refer to LOCs as KLOCs (Thousands of Lines of Code). If you test 1,000 lines of code and find 2 errors in that body of code, you can summarize the quantitative representation of the quality of the code by saying that the defect rate was 2 errors per KLOC.

Another approach to tracking is to put aside the concern with the number of lines of code and concentrate instead on design components. With *Ankh*, the primary design component was the stripe. When the team began system testing for Stripe 2.3, for example, defects became evident after installation of the executable on the slowest of the test hardware configurations. The team detected six distinct defects. You can summarize the quantitative representation of the quality of the code by saying that the defect rate was "six errors per stripe" for this system test.

Patterns emerge from summary data. As Figure 17.12 shows, according to the metrics collected over a seven-week period of testing, the defect rate in the software development effort increased until the end of the fourth week and then began to decrease. At first, defects increased with each weekly test session. Then, the trend peaked and the defects declined with each weekly test session. When you examine the seven-week test cycle as a whole, the pattern that emerges generally reflects positively on the development effort. Viewing the pattern, an analyst might safely conclude that the overall quality of the code improved.

Using Summary Data as Release Criteria

Figure 17.13 provides a view of the development effort that Chapter 11 discusses in detail. It serves here as a starting point for establishing how a release manager can begin to determine whether a product is nearing a state at which it might become a candidate for an alpha, beta, or production release. Planned release management can involve using data gathered from defect tracking activity that takes place during the prerelease development phase to substantiate decisions made during the release phase.

One important way in which this can happen is with the use of data that shows how long, on the average, programmers require to fix defects. For example, if your data allows you to conclude that four days are required to fix the defects in a stripe after you have submitted the stripe for configuration management, it is probably reasonable to conclude that your team will require at least four days after the product is integrated completely to test and debug the product to the point that it is suitable for an alpha release. Figure 17.13 shows a pattern in the time required for programmers and testers to reduce defects to zero per stripe.

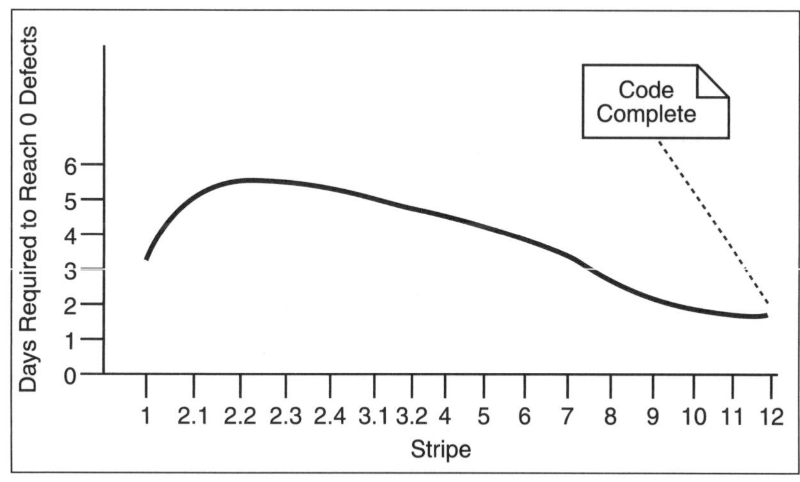

Figure 17.13 Viewing the pattern in the number of days needed to debug stripes establishes metrics you can use to estimate how long system integration in preparation for a release will require.

Based on the data provided by the graph in Figure 17.13, the release manager might decide that a team should allow at least four weeks from code completion until the anticipated first (alpha or beta) release of the product. Although guesswork might be involved in this decision, the decision is deliberate because it is based on a pattern that is detected clearly in the development history. The graph shows that the developers and testers require a minimum of three days and a maximum of around six days to integrate a stripe fully. On the other hand, the graph also shows that this time decreases with each successive stripe after 2.2, so the release manager might be justified in concluding that *at best* the product can be readied for alpha release in two days.

Making the Decision

To release a game in a planned fashion, you structure your activities in several ways. First, you establish a set of summary development criteria to use as the basis of the decision to release your game. Second, you designate someone to manage release activities. Third, you establish a procedure for arriving at a decision. Finally, you create a checklist that must be satisfied before you approve the release. Many other activities might characterize the release phase of a game's life, but this short list provides what many release managers consider essential. The items you choose depend on the culture of your company and the type of game you are releasing.

Summary Development Data

Determining when to release a game involves having a suitable body of data that supports the decision to make the release. As was discussed previously, you can use summary information from the tracking system to detect patterns or confirm generalizations. Consider the following:

- You can see a definitive pattern in the defect reports. You see that as time goes on, the number of defects decreases. The testing effort remains consistent.
- You see from the defect reports that the team has fixed all reported defects. No defect report remains open.
- You see from the problem resolution report that the team has accounted for all changes to the specified functionality.
- You see from the testing reports that the team has verified all functionality.
- You have verified that the team has gathered the documentation for the release.

The Release Manager

When you create a release management system, you should assign responsibility for it to one person. The person who works as the configuration manager might seem like the most logical candidate, but this is not always so. The reason for this is that release management can be extremely involved work. In addition to keeping track of everything that goes into building the product, the release manager might have to communicate with third-party vendors, customers, and marketing and sales representatives. Such wide-ranging responsibilities are often a burden for the configuration manager, whose main responsibility might focus on the management of files and assets.

One approach is to choose a person who has strong administrative and communication skills to serve either temporarily or permanently as a release manager. The release manager must undertake tasks along the following lines:

- **Call together a release management board.** This board might consist of individuals from testing, development, marketing, sales, the legal department, the customer group, and vendor management. The release manager must be empowered to convene and lead this group to a full evaluation of the readiness of the software for release.
- **Control of the software.** The release manager must be able to dictate whether further changes in the software can occur. Such dictation will probably occur through some sort of previously established procedure, such as a change control board. Whatever the process, the release manager must have the final word over what the team releases.
- **Authority to demand services.** The release manager must also have a fair amount of authority to request and receive services from everyone who is involved in the release process. If the release manager does not have this authority, whether the product will be released will remain a question. Release managers should be able to arrange with the packaging manager, for example, that a prototype for the packaging shall be ready by a given date.

The release manager has just a few job responsibilities. You should assign these responsibilities to a single individual. You can view the individual who possesses these responsibilities in terms of seamanship, in which the pilot, although not captain of the ship, assumes control of the ship as it is being towed from port to open sea.

Release Signoff

Do not take lightly securing of approval for release of a game. Each member of the release management board should approve the release formally. Do not leave anyone out. Everyone on the release board should represent an essential part of the release effort. Given this premise, you can image if everyone except the person who takes care of packaging shows up for the meeting in which you approve the release. You have 10,000 copies of the game printed, but you have no boxes for them.

The conclusion of signoff ceremony can be an occasion for getting everyone together for a debriefing/pizza party. This is generally a good idea because it provides everyone with closure on the product and allows anyone who might have objections to have a final chance to say something.

Following are some criteria for release:

- The project manager and the lead tester say that the team has implemented all requirements stated in the requirements document or properly set them aside.
- The project manger says that the team has addressed adequately all tasks in the project plan.
- The person in charge of testing says that the team has eliminated each known defect.
- The person responsible for software configuration management says that the team has obtained formal permission or licensing for all external components or libraries that require such approval. The team has obtained all the permissions for assets and libraries.
- Whoever is responsible for packaging confirms that the packaging and documentation are ready and that the team has tested the delivery package and shown it to be flawless.
- The configuration manager has placed the code, an executable, and all documentation in an archive, and the team has duplicated the archive as needed for security purposes.

Experienced release managers testify consistently that the team should conduct a full walkthrough of the release steps before the release. Stories abound about shipments of empty shrink-wrapped boxes, misspelled product names, well-written manuals for the wrong product, obvious and catastrophic software defects, test code and assets that have not been removed, and other failings that have led to embarrassments, profit losses, lawsuits, and other problems.

Establishing Software Support

A powerful, well-received set of library components or a game that appeals to a large public is only a start. You can extend the life of a successful software product through many profitable releases if you know how to listen to customers.

Obtaining Information

Creation of any type of software, game or otherwise, brings with it the responsibility of supporting customers. Some publishers require that your development group show the ability to provide support. Support means any number of things. The following list provides a few of the options:

- **E-mail collection.** This is the minimal support level. You provide an e-mail address and tell your customers to send you an e-mail if they experience problems. Usually, you have to have your own server to do this, because many e-mail providers do not like you to use their services for commercial purposes. Collection of the reports involves opening each e-mail and filtering its content. This is usually a great deal of work if you have any customer base at all, but such an approach at least forces you to look at each report.
- **Internet form support.** This is the preferred approach for many companies. Using this approach, you program the Web page so that it contains fields such as those featured in Table 17.2. In addition, you ask for customer information, such as e-mail address and phone number. If the form connects with a database, you then can immediately store the information in the database and print daily or other summary reports. The summary reports allow you to respond to customer needs.
- **Phone support.** This is the most costly form of support, because you must pay to have a support specialist attend the telephone. The support specialist must know the product well enough to be able to support it. For console and PC games, it is unlikely that a telephone support specialist would attend to problems other than those involving installation.
- **Total support.** Total product support consists of all of the above. Any company that issues an online game should consider providing total support. Even with full support, you should protect yourself against overloaded circuits. You can do this by using automated screening software. You can inform callers up front of their support options and whether they need to pay. Callers can make choices using the number pad of their telephone rather than waiting while a support representative redirects their call.

Categories of Information

A central aspect of release management is the activity of gathering and tracking information that users provide. To gather and record information, you must have some type of tracking system in place.

Some of the information that you gather and track through a defect reporting system is required. In other words, if you fail to gather a minimum set of information on defects, you waste both your time and the time of the software user. This essential set of information enables you to identify the defect uniquely, know when the defect occurred, and briefly describe the defect.

The required information you gather through a defect tracking system varies according to the priorities that your organization sets. Table 17.2 provides a provisional starter set.

Table 17.2 Defect Tracking Information Profile

Datum	Description
Tracking ID	Regardless of all else, you should assign a unique tracking identification number to each defect. Assign the tracking number when the user reports the defect, not later. An automated number or ID generator should create this number. If you must assign an ID manually, write a program that creates IDs incrementally. This is the easiest way to avoid duplication of numbers.
Product	If your group has created only one game, this might seem odd. But then plan for success. Create a unique product code and store it as a separate datum that you can combine with the tracking ID when needed.
Version	Identify the build or release version of the product. The most obvious versions are alpha, beta, and production, but if you have issued updates, track the update numbers in relation to the release numbers.
Description	A description of a defect should help the tester or maintenance programmer re-create the defect. To obtain information for a description, try to work with the person who reports the problem and perform the action that results in the problem. Often, unless you identify the context of the problem, you will not be able to isolate the problem. Consider, for example, a message that states, "System crashes." This information is next to useless unless you know when it crashes. A game that crashes when the player tries to start it is different from one that crashes after six hours of continuous play.
Platform	In a personal computing environment, the platform extends to identification of the version of Windows that the player has installed. Consider, for example, that Windows 95 does not support DirectX 9. You might think that no one runs Windows 95 today, but never take it for granted.
Severity	The severity of a problem report designates when and how much attention you should give to the defect. Defect severities usually fall into three categories. You can designate statuses numerically, from 1 for most severe to 3 for least severe. Likewise, you can have other status designations. The most severe category is one in which the game crashes. If a defect causes the system to crash, you should deal with it immediately. The middle category is a defect that you can deal with through a workaround solution. The least severe problem is one that usually designates user preferences concerning functionally sound features. Someone might object to the GUI for the character designer. You should note the comment, but it is not realistic to prepare an update or in some other way try to change a working feature of the game because someone does not like it. However, noting such information for future releases is important.

Datum	Description
Status	The state of a defect report designates the extent to which you have completed any work on it. Status codes fall into five basic categories: *open—no action*; *open—work being performed*; *closed—problem fixed*; *closed—problem referred for update*; and *closed—resolved*.
Assigned To	A change manager should assign every defect to someone. One way to handle this is to have all newly open defect reports automatically assigned to the person who is responsible for change management. This person then can assign work at regular intervals. If your organization is large enough, rather than designating individuals, you could make assignments to departments, such as development, documentation, or testing. You have several options even if you do not use a change coordinator. For example, defect reports might go automatically to testing. Testing can then determine the severity of the problem and assign the work to the appropriate individual or group.
History	Information on history refers to a set of fields that you should populate automatically but that system users should be able to update manually. It is essential to track when you open the defect report, when you assign it, when you perform work, and when you close the defect report. If you can track the number of hours that someone who is working in a maintenance capacity dedicates to resolving the defect, you are better off than if you have only dates to work with. At a minimum, however, you should be able to track the number of days between the opening and the closing of a defect report.
Contact Information	You should track defects both generically and specifically. Tracking a defect generically implies that you can identify the platform on which the problem occurred. Tracking a defect specifically implies that you can identify the person who reported the defect and contact this person for information about the defect as you try to fix it.

The screen shot shown in Figure 17.14 illustrates one approach to developing a defect tracking system. Using an Internet-based reporting system provides a convenient way to link distributed support groups.

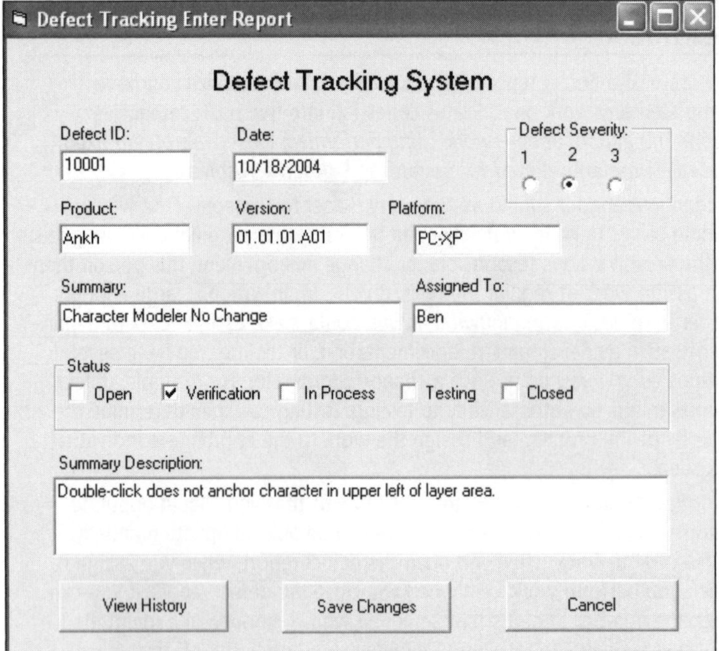

Figure 17.14
Features of a defect tracking system depend on the priorities you set as an organization.

Reporting

For release management, internal reporting refers to the information you maintain that tracks how an organization processes defects or other issues. The purpose for maintaining such data relates to process improvement. Process improvement activities can encompass a variety of concerns. The following sections review a few of these activities: verification, time required, identification, assignments, and problem areas. If you have set up a comprehensive database for defect tracking, adding new reports or user interfaces for the input of different types of information is relatively easy.

caution

> If you use an Internet-based tracking system, you develop dependencies. If you store data on a server that resides outside your organization, you should have a contract that provides some type of guarantee that care will be taken to prevent loss of data. Generally, it is not wise to use an external system unless you have taken such precautions.

Time Required

The most elementary metric is the amount of time between when you open the problem report and when you close it. Depending on the precision you target, you might want to maintain both date and time fields in the reporting system. If you support a game that hosts online users who can receive real-time assistance, it makes sense to be precise to the minute. Tracking fix times increases the capacity of your organization to demonstrate competence and maturity. The Capability Maturity Model (CMM) and other standards mandate that your organization can respond to problems that users of your product might encounter. To demonstrate this capability, you must have a process in place that creates a record of successful responses.

Verification

Whether you verify defect reports depends on how sophisticated you want to make the defect tracking system. From a reporting perspective, verification provides a way to test your primary response activity against a record of final actions. If you support numerous users on a real-time basis, being able to identify generic types of problems that you can deal with quickly can reduce expenses. Through examination of verification reports, you can update keywords and standard response scenarios so that the first-line support people possess information that they need to take care of problems without having to move to second lines of support.

Fixes

Time required to fix a defect relates mainly to the time that the maintenance programmer works on the problem, but it might also cover testing time. This metric becomes more complicated to estimate as you add more people and tasks to the process of fixing the defect. For example, you can deal with defects that have a severity code of 3 differently from defects that have a severity code of 1. A severity code of 3 might mean that the defect does not cause the game to crash. Such a defect might be characterized more as a statement concerning the inconvenience of a given feature or functionality that a loyal customer desires in the next release of the product. With defects of this severity, the most important thing might be to log the player's statements carefully, provide as ready a response as possible, and then submit the action taken for verification. Verification might mean that the release management lead or supervisor will examine the defect report and provide a second opinion that the action taken was correct.

Defect Identification

When you appropriately identify a problem, you do several things. At the most rudimentary level, you accurately determine a problem's severity. At another level, if several customers contact you with the same problem, identifying the problems as resulting from the same defect reduces the overall maintenance load. The Problem Summary field provides a ready way to collect problems under common headings. Reports can then provide summary lists of problems that have the same keywords in their summary fields. Figure 17.15 shows a summary report for logged problem reports received through e-mail.

ID	Date	Sev	Product	Platform	Summary	Description
80101	11-20-04	3	An	XP	Feature	Wants new char
80102	11-20-04	3	An	2000	Feature	Higher potion
80103	11-24-04	2	An	XP	Install	New PC user
80104	11-29-04	1	OSim	2000	Feature	Open tool choice
80105	12-01-04	2	OSim	XP	Install	Defective CD
80106	12-02-04	1	An	XP	Feature	Monastery door

Figure 17.15
Summary keys group reports.

For customized reporting systems, you can set up a summary-detail system in which you can open extended or subordinate reports from a primary report. This approach has the advantage of grouping related problems from the first. The disadvantage is that those who are working in a support capacity might sort reports into the wrong categories. Unless you have a verification layer in place in the support group, programmers must place reports in the correct categories.

Assignments

As is discussed later in this chapter under "The Maintenance Process and Tiers," failing to assign developers specifically to revolving or permanent maintenance work creates problems. If your organization has a general maintenance group, this group might receive referred problems from the support group. If this is the case, the maintenance group can refine the procedure used to sort out reports.

From another perspective, problems with a product can fall into general categories:

- **Installation.** Covers from the time the user takes the software out of the box until the user can begin to play the game.
- **Documentation.** Includes packaging problems, which encompass items such as missing CDs, missing manuals, or communications that create misunderstandings or present liabilities.
- **Software defects.** Involves situations in which the user has installed the game and it works to some extent but then presents a problem.

- **Aesthetics.** Designates problems that relate to the appearance of the game features ranging from the way the console works, to sounds, to graphical features.
- **Upgrading.** Encompasses the distribution of patches for the software. This might include a large customer database that logs monthly payments or levels of user permissions.
- **Use.** Goes in many directions. Obviously, having references to user groups at hand provides a ready way to respond to user issues, but at times users really do need individualized attention and are willing to pay for it.

If you have a process in which a first-line support person directs problems to others, it is important to provide those to whom calls are directed with resources that enable them to respond adequately to problems. For an installation issue, for example, someone who works in the test lab might be the best person to handle problems. Because the test lab usually provides test configurations for all supported systems, the tester might be able to walk a customer through an installation using the same machine that the customer is using. A problem with documentation requires information from someone who is involved with composing documentation for or packaging the product. In both instances, being able to help depends on having the best resources.

Software Problem Areas

Realistic attempts to improve processes almost always involve setting priorities. If your primary business involves software issues, you should develop a set of categories that describe the system you have developed. With *Ankh*, the development team created the game in a set of stripes. The stripes represent design decisions, and the design decisions represent groupings of functionality. For this reason, most software problem summaries might consist of a keyword that associates the defect report with a component area of the game. Using this way of classifying problems, developers might find it easier to verify and identify a reported problem.

The Maintenance Process and Tiers

After you have released a product, change control takes on a new role. This role governs the *maintenance* of a product. For most software products, nearly 70 percent of its life passes as a maintained product. During the maintenance part of a software product's life, tracking defects involves, once again, using the defect tracking system. The procedure is similar to the procedure employed during the development phase, but significant restrictions apply to the scope of changes that maintenance programmers can address.

You can characterize most maintenance processes that have achieved some degree of maturity by three levels of support. Table 17.3 provides a summary of these different levels.

Table 17.3 Support Roles

Role	Description
First line	This is also called "primary support." The first-line support person answers the phone or reads e-mails. This person's responsibility is to log problems that customers report and either respond directly to the problem or refer the problem to a higher level for more extensive response actions.
Testing	The activity of testing falls into the second line of support. The testers might be responsible for filtering problems that the first-line support people have reported. They verify the problems and refer them to the maintenance programmers for fixes. Likewise, they can verify that the work maintenance programmers have performed is ready for release to the customer.
Maintenance	Programmers who work as maintenance programmers work in two capacities. The first is that they back up the first-line people and provide deeper insight into problems that cannot be dealt with from a store of information in a database. Maintenance programmers provide updates to the product. They also can work in a more fundamental capacity, responding to clear failings of the design of the product. In this respect, they work to develop the product further.
Development	The activity of development falls into a third line of support. This line of support is characterized by the development or redevelopment of functionality that usually comprises a new version or release of a product.
Release management	Releases managers continue to work with the product even after it is in the hands of the customer. Throughout the life of the product, release managers must determine when and how to make updates to the product.

As Figure 17.16 shows, the person who works in the first line of support either inspects e-mails or answers the phone. This person is the first to see or hear a user's problem. At this point, two things usually happen. The first-line support person knows the solution and passes it to the users, or he does not know the solution and passes the problem to someone else. Often, this second person is a developer.

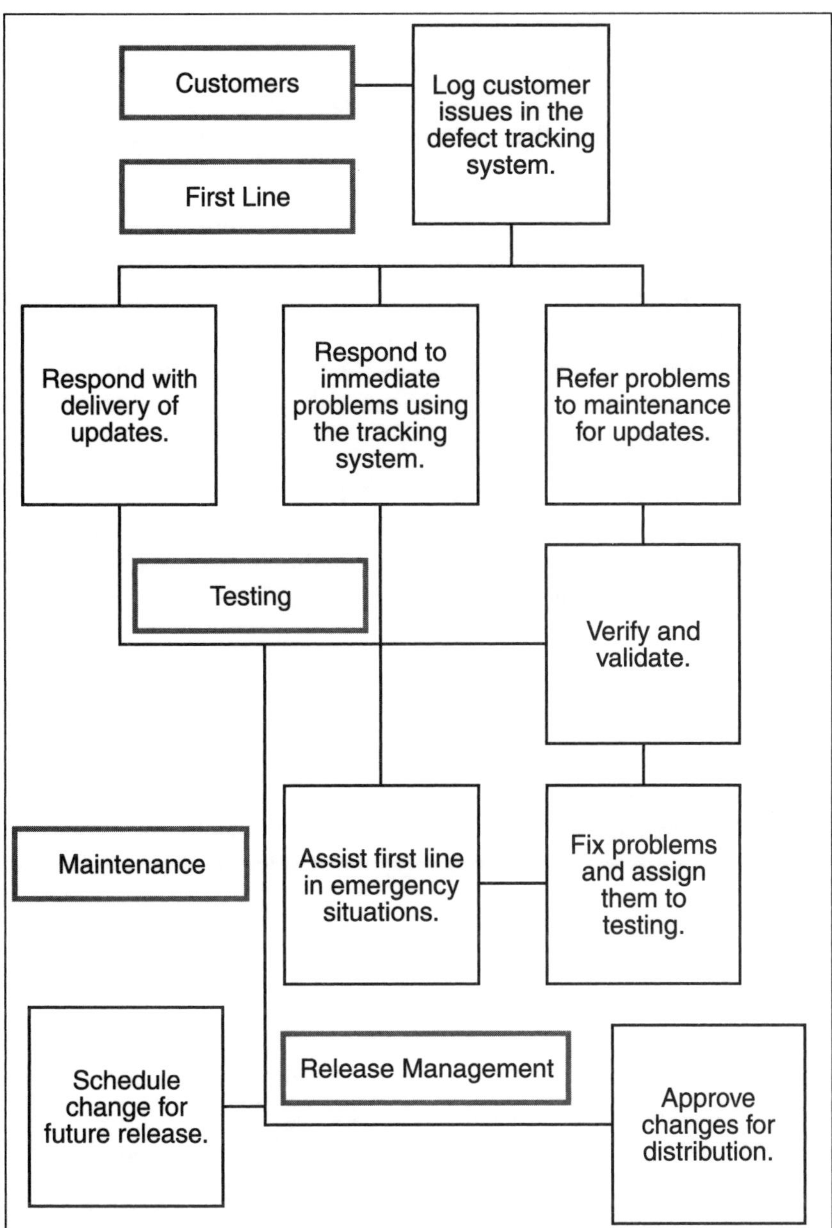

Figure 17.16
Release management involves several levels of support.

The way in which the problem reaches the developer can vary. In one scenario, a tester might filter the problem to define it more clearly before referring it to a programmer. In another scenario, the problem goes directly to the maintenance programmer, but a tester is also called into the picture to ensure that work done on the problem is tested before being released to the customer.

If problems are so extensive that a patch will not cover the needed repairs, new development might be called for. When this happens, you need to schedule work over a longer period of time. A project manager might take over the task of managing the development of the version, and someone who is working as a release manager must coordinate the needed activity. You would need, for example, to specify the requirements for the work to be done. Design work follows. Before you forward the new version to the customer, you must test it. Many people end up being involved.

Organizations that achieve a substantial level of maturity create separate product support departments. The product support department works with the development group when needed. At other times, the product support department might create an extensive database to record information about problems and to store updates that the development group provides.

Likewise, with products that have extensive histories, you might need to develop a database that associates customers and releases. Your company might release several versions of a given product. It also might create several releases. You might bill customers according to both release and version levels. To make such activity possible, you must know what customers have paid for. Release management in this respect begins to involve marketing and sales efforts, so the release manager must be prepared to work closely with these two groups.

Conclusion

This chapter has emphasized how to manage software after you have finished creating its basic functionality. Managing releases involves keeping track of a great deal of information and using this information effectively. A release management process usually involves tracking data in a way that differs from what applies during the development build process. During development, programmers focus on quickly building and compiling the product as they add functionality. At the release phase, release managers concentrate on controlling and documenting changes. The motivation for this change of priorities is that after the product is scheduled for release, the release manager must be able to know precisely what the product includes.

Release management involves coordinating the efforts of people from the marketing, packaging, sales, development, and other groups. To ensure that a release manager can do the job, the organization should assign a single individual to the responsibility and provide this person with the authority needed to reach deadlines and demand services. Likewise, the release manager should work according to a set process and toward a set of goals that are documented in a checklist.

Release management also encompasses work performed during the maintenance part of a product's life. More mature organizations usually create support groups, but it's the responsibility of the person who has release management responsibilities to continue to exert tight control over how to plan, assemble, and deliver updates, versions, and new releases.

Generally, release management is tied closely with configuration management. Good texts on release management are available, and a few of these are listed next. In addition, refer to Chapter 10.

Bays, Michael E. *Software Release Methodology.* Upper Saddle River, New Jersey: Prentice Hall PTR, 1999.

Mette Jonassen Hass, Anne. *Configuration Management Principles and Practices.* Boston: Addison-Wesley, 2003.

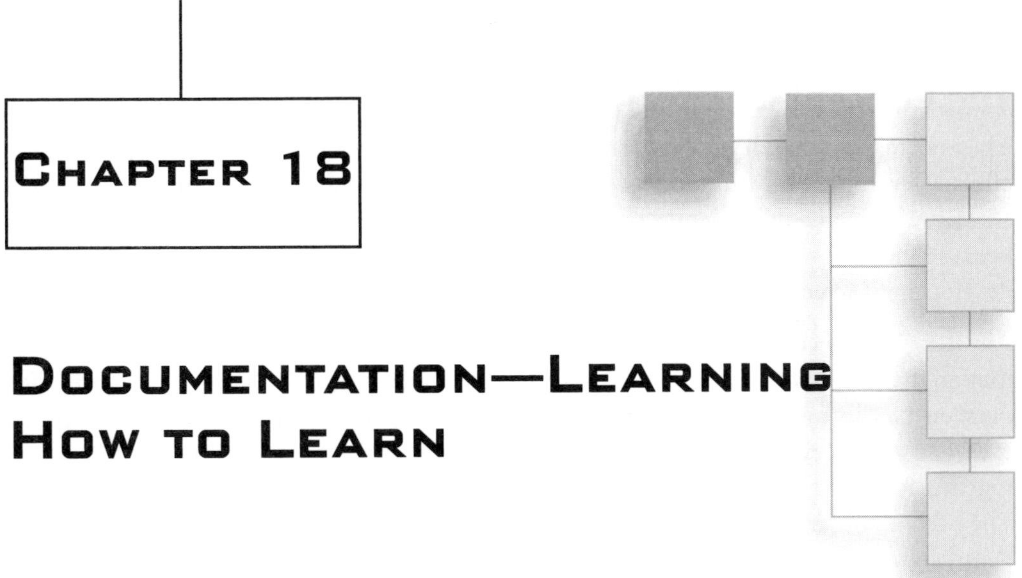

Chapter 18

Documentation—Learning How to Learn

This chapter explores how you can supplement your development effort with documentation. Documentation is a way to formalize the information that characterizes your development effort. Documents that are created using templates enable you to organize and define the information that you use during the development process. To effectively use documentation, you need to make certain that it plays an active, continuing role in the development effort. One of the most reliable ways to accomplish this is to conduct regular reviews. A review is a way to ensure that everyone on your team is exposed to the central flows of information that guide your project. Documentation should always be viewed as a way of gathering and refining information about the current vision of the product you are developing. It is a medium of understanding, not an end in itself. It should address the current vision of the product and should not bog everyone down in the tracking of historical details. Given this beginning, many topics present themselves under the heading of documentation. Among these are the following:

- Understanding that documentation is more than a collection of documents
- How documentation becomes a way that an organization teaches itself its own culture
- How collecting and storing information can end up being more of a loss than a gain
- Techniques and technologies that supplement documentation efforts
- Providing easy ways that people who are not technical writers can create good documents
- Assigning roles and responsibilities for documentation
- Creating contexts in which developers use and benefit from documentation

The Concept of Information Management

The information that developers manage gives purpose and cohesion to the development effort. Developers capture and develop information using a variety of *artifacts*, chief among which are documents and diagrams. Documents and diagrams are valuable because they allow developers to collect important information and because they allow developers to screen out excessive information.

Any software project generates an enormous amount of information. The amount of information that is generated poses hazards. One hazard falls under the heading of *information overflow*. In this case, developers try to assimilate everything under the assumption that if everyone knows everything, everyone will intuitively understand how the project comes together for a first release. This seldom happens.

The second hazard, referred to as *information deprivation*, occurs when developers isolate themselves from the activity of the team and pretend that if they concentrate on a few tasks that are supposedly independent of other tasks, they will complete their work, and in some miraculous way, the resulting system will fall together for a first release. Once again, this seldom happens.

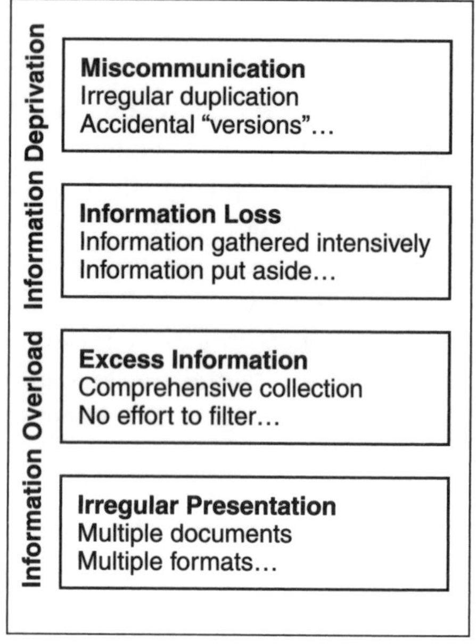

Figure 18.1
Information can become a hindrance to clear communication.

Information management begins as an intelligent response to the hazards that information overload and information deprivation present. When tasks become complex, information about the tasks does, too. When numerous people work on complex tasks, the amount of information tends to increase exponentially with respect to the number of people working on the tasks and the number of tasks involved. If developers fail to control the complexity of the information, communication breaks down. Figure 18.1 summarizes the situation.

Here's a short list of some of the immediate consequences of information overload and deprivation summarized in Figure 18.1:

- **Miscommunication.** Two key people have a clear understanding of a given issue, but one says one thing and another says something else. A third person hears both messages and concludes that the real understanding is a mixture of the two. This is not the case. The third person communicates the misunderstanding to the rest of the team. To straighten out the misunderstanding, hours of meetings are necessary. Because someone began work guided by the misunderstanding, the problem led to the need for rework.

- **Information loss.** Two projects occur, one after the other. An audio library is implemented. The programmer who is working on the audio library has to perform hours of research to figure out how to implement functionality that covers both WAV and MP3 file types. This is one of those tasks that sounds like it should be easy but ends up being something else when you get down to the details. The programmer who works on the task makes everything work fine and is ready to implement functionality for several more file types, but the project manager says that no time remains and such work needs to be delayed for a later release. Before that point is reached, the programmer quits. When work on the next release has progressed far enough that the new programmer revisits the audio code, the new programmer requires several days to figure out how to implement functionality that extends the audio capabilities in the way that the first programmer was prepared to extend them.
- **Excess information.** People have seen the benefits of preserving communications, so a project manager has obtained an application that allows everyone to communicate through an enormous journal that resembles a Web log, or blog. Although the journal preserves every communication that anyone enters about the project, team members find it difficult to discover specific information. To find anything, in fact, team members usually have to start at the beginning and review logged material on a day-by-day bases. This consumes so much time that it is impractical.
- **Irregular presentation.** Your company does a great job of keeping track of projects using a set of documents that each development group prepares as it progresses through its development activities. When you inspect the documents for several projects, however, you find that they differ extensively from project to project, usually revealing a great deal of eccentricity. In fact, the requirements documents range from epic poems to personal narratives. The software design documents range from cryptic rewrites of the requirements documents to elaborate affairs that incorporate UML diagrams. After a while, you realize that every time you pick up a new document, you must expect once again to learn a new way that the information can be organized and communicated.

note

A *blog* is basically a journal that is available on the Web. The activity of updating a blog is *blogging,* and someone who keeps a blog is a *blogger*. Blogs are typically updated daily using software that allows people who have little or no technical background to update and maintain the blog. Postings on a blog are almost always arranged in chronological order with the most recent additions featured most prominently (source: http://www.blogphiles.com/webring.shtml).

Information management involves refining the way your group communicates so that everyone in the group communicates effectively. When people communicate effectively, they make a few things happen:

- They express themselves consistently.
- Their messages adhere to and develop central topics.
- They repeat themselves only as needed or requested.
- They include important, illustrative details and drop others.
- They offer information in a way that is suitable for the context in which it is delivered.

Sharing Knowledge

Ultimately, the best way to remedy the problems that arise with information overflow and information deprivation involves sharing information. To share information, you must organize it. When you organize information, knowledge results. (Knowledge is sometimes called *meta-information*, which means it is information that organizes information.) Knowledge can be defined as information that is organized so that it enables those who possess it to change things in a concerted, decisive, and goal-oriented way.

A few basic activities can provide a framework for organizing information during a game software development project. Although no one scheme can be comprehensive or final, Figure 18.2 provides a summary view of a possible set of activities. The following list provides a few details about these activities:

- **Project management.** The project manager produces a schedule that structures team activities in relation to the creation of the functionality that the requirements specification identifies. The project manager organizes the information that emerges during the life of the project so that it unfolds according to discrete units of activity. This organization of information establishes what you might view as the key pathways of information that will define the communication practices of the team.
- **Development tasks.** When a programmer plans a programming task based on an objective that the project plan states, the programmer is using communication about the overall structure of the project to place a specific set of activities into a coherent context.
- **Pathways through documentation.** You can develop a document using a template. A template is a guide to organizing information, a conceptual map. When team members use an established set of templates to create the documentation for a project, they use a set of conceptual pathways that others have created. These pathways help them shape how information about their project will emerge and flow.

These pathways help them limit, organize, track, and prevent the loss of information that is central to their undertaking.

- **Reviews.** When developers subject a body of information to review, they force the information into a public view. Under public scrutiny, two things happen. First, the developers refine the information. Second, those who participate in the review learn the material reviewed. Reviews draw participants together and provide a context in which everyone can acquire and confirm knowledge.

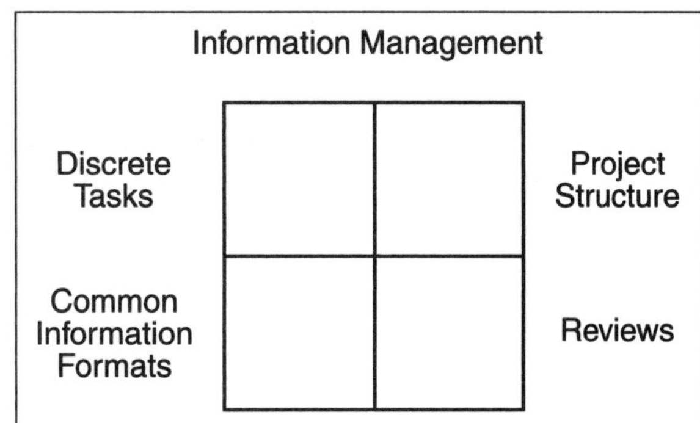

Figure 18.2
Information management builds pathways through which members of the team can acquire and confirm a common understanding of the development effort.

Overcoming Limitations

Sharing knowledge is difficult for a variety of reasons. Many people tend to be defensive about sharing knowledge. They fear that if they give away knowledge, they will imperil their jobs or reveal their incompetence. Others might not have such fears but simply do not possess good communication practices and do not feel up to confronting the sometimes trying situations that arise when people try to communicate about difficult technical topics. Consider the following:

- People do not automatically understand the same material in the same way.
- Communicating effectively takes time and patience.
- Communicating effectively requires persistence and practice.

The next few sections review these points in detail.

Establishing Practices

Two people can witness the same event in broad daylight and provide contrary accounts. Given this starting situation, consider that most programmers seek uninterrupted trance sessions during which they can work through coding problems. Most other people who are involved in game development tasks seek a similar form of isolation. If you are in a trance, you often spend hours immersed in a frame of mind in which you are sustaining a delicate balance of ideas. To sustain this balance, you shield yourself as much as possible from intrusive information. Your assessment of the situation is that you have as much information as you need.

Although shielding yourself from new information is what makes you good at what you do and is a sign of professional discipline, it can also be counterproductive to good communication practices. The problem arises if the project you are working on does not provide contexts in which communication between team members can occur. For this reason, it's important to establish a set of commonly shared communication practices for the project.

A document that is subjected to a review provides an occasion for communication. You can use a template to give initial structure and focus to the document. This document can help people organize information and develop sound communication practices. When members of a team organize information and then work to refine the information they have organized, they establish a common way to understand the information that the project generates.

Creating Occasions

Often when a dilemma arises between completing work and communicating about work, people choose to work without communicating. Such practices can be catastrophic. Among the many things that can go wrong when people work without communicating is that they do not maintain a common vision of what they are working on. When this happens, they are unable to effectively integrate their work, and the product they create fails.

Effective information management requires a strong effort on the part of the team to create occasions for exchanging information. Reviews provide such occasions. At the start of a project, for example, the work of developing requirements and creating a software design can involve many successive reviews. These reviews allow the team to work together to establish common modes of communication. Although it might be possible for a senior developer to work exclusively with the project manager to create these documents, if this approach is used, the occasion for developing and practicing team communication is lost. Making time requires communicating about project details during the normal course of development activity. Making communication happen forms part of everyone's work. Documents can represent the central flows of information, and creating and refining documents can serve as occasions for developing team communications.

Promoting Incentives

Imagine that you are the project lead and are addressing the development team. You have distributed a bar chart that clearly shows everyone's tasks and when things need to be done, and you are reviewing details that you have been up late into the night determining with as much accuracy as you possibly can. At some point, you look up and find that almost everyone is occupied doing something other than listening to you. You might reach the conclusion that you are a boring person, but this would be premature. It is probably more accurate to say that the information you are presenting represents an abstraction, and when you are speaking with a group of people who have been absorbed for hours on end with minute details of implementation, abstractions seem superfluous.

Overcoming the chasm that separates detail from abstraction involves putting in place conceptual patterns that allow people to view abstract statements in terms of detail. When everyone possesses a standard set of conceptual patterns that they build on and refine from the start to the end of the project, they can more easily assimilate information that is presented abstractly. That's because they are not so much listening to as working with the person who is delivering the abstract or summary information.

Learning Through Documentation

Almost every chapter in this book introduces one or another template from one or another standard set of templates. Developers can use templates to help them construct documents. Documents provide occasions for gathering together and refining the information that guides the development effort. At the same time, a document is not an end in itself; it is a means to an end. The end that everyone seeks is a product embodying the functionality that the requirements specify. Documents become a way to progressively learn more about how to understand and build the product.

A document that is created using a standard software engineering template establishes a reliable pathway for information management. It is a tested, flexible, and largely neutral way to manage information. If a development team does not organize information through documents, it is likely to organize information according to the preferences and idiosyncrasies of individual team members. This is not the best approach. Even if everyone agrees to play along with one person's approach to information management, such uniformity does not guarantee a good result and is not generally considered a good engineering practice. Generally, the best approach is to seek the wisdom derived from cumulative experience. A standard software engineering template embodies such wisdom.

note

Some software engineers prefer to speak of documents as *artifacts*. That's because a document that is created with a template is just one among several reliable objects for gathering and refining information. UML diagrams, for example, represent an unnarrated approach to gathering and refining information. In this chapter, the term *document* encompasses all objects that you can use to gather and refine information about software products.

Pathways of Learning

Templates alone do not guarantee that the development group will effectively gather and refine information. Templates certainly provide a visible and easily managed way to accumulate, organize, and store information, but using them effectively means that the team must develop pathways of learning that are thoroughly assimilated into the development effort. Figure 18.3 provides a summary view of some of the activities that help define these pathways of learning. The sections that follow elaborate on some of the features of these pathways.

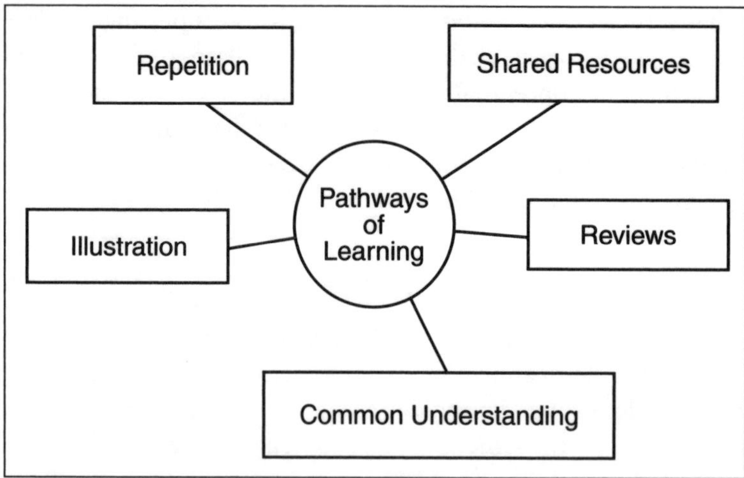

Figure 18.3
Information emerges from common pathways for learning.

Common Understanding

Members of a development team benefit if they realize that some information is important and other information is not. Professionalism often entails a kind of self-imposed ignorance. It is a willingness to put aside, for instance, personal prejudices for the sake of what might be viewed as the greater good. With respect to software development projects, project success often reduces to whether team members can work in a unified, cooperative effort to discover and test information that is restricted to narrowly defined topics.

An example of such an effort arises when members of a team work during a review to refine a stated requirement. To refine the requirement, participants in the review struggle with the wording of the requirement until they establish a clear understanding of what it means. As a result of this effort, members of the team narrow the meaning of the vocabulary items in the statement to the point that they establish a common understanding. This understanding guides them as they engage in subsequent development tasks. This is but one of many instances in which the members of the team work to establish common understanding.

Repetition

Repetition occurs in useful and excessive ways. When repetition is excessive, it involves examining a body of information even after everyone on the team has understood what it means and how to use it. Usually, team members do not intentionally waste the time of others in this way. This happens, however, when what has been covered and what has not been covered become unclear or are forgotten. To avoid such situations, formally establishing a review process that results in baselined documents can be helpful.

A baseline review provides an opportunity for everyone to concentrate on thoroughly establishing a common understanding of what is regarded as the current conceptual view of the software being developed. Consider, for example, a baseline review of the requirements specification. After the review has concluded, it is likely that everyone will be able to understand the scope of the project. Granted, the team can always change, eliminate, or add requirements, but after the team works through a baseline review to confirm a version of the requirements, everyone on the team is likely to avoid drawing others into redundant discussions concerning requirements.

Illustration, Symbol, Metaphor

Illustrations have been a fundamental engineering tool since at least the time of the ancient Egyptian and the first pyramids. Effective use of illustrations involves four key concepts:

- **Standard symbols.** UML diagrams offer a standard set of symbols that greatly facilitate conceptualization of software systems. Likewise, Gantt, Pert, or Venn charts symbolically organize the activities involved in developing a software product. Use cases and use case diagrams symbolically render scenarios that illustrate software functionality. Storyboards symbolically organize the story that underlies the play of a game. Such symbolic renderings organize, summarize, or replace words.
- **Illustrations as approximations.** When refuting attempts by mathematical philosophers to derive mathematics from physical nature, the philosopher Bertrand Russell said something to the effect that "The thing mapped is not the thing itself." Remembering this observation in the context of an engineering project can be extremely helpful. Illustrations provide a way to summarize ideas. They can be used to simplify notions. At the same time, attempting to use an illustration or a symbolic representation to reach an exacting degree of verisimilitude is a lost cause. The thing that represents is not the thing represented.
- **Illustrations as working tools.** As a working tool, an illustration allows you to represent an object for purposes of understanding and refinement before you try to construct it. In an idealized corporate setting, a CASE tool might be designed so that a software designer can use illustration tools to completely specify a software product and then, with the click of a mouse, set to work a program that generates the completed product. In the context of small-team, craft-oriented software engineering, the development team first works to create a vision of the software and then to use that vision—which is captured in a set of illustrations—to implement the software. As the developers progress, they constantly rework the illustrations so that they more clearly understand the product they seek to create.
- **Illustrations as metaphors.** Broadly defined, a *metaphor* is a symbolic activity that involves combining two ideas to create a third. The third idea communicates a message that offers meaning that is not easily reduced to the sum of the two source ideas.

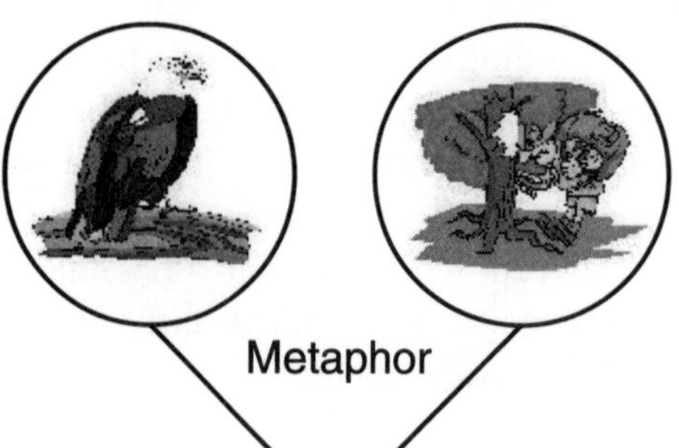

As a simple illustration of metaphor, consider the notion of an eagle scout. Within many traditional contexts, an eagle is a bird that flies high and sees much. It is also a powerful bird, one that proves a formidable hunter and adversary. Finally, an eagle is a bird that lives long and seems to stay aloof from many of the petty concerns of the average open field. A scout might be viewed as a person who explores natural settings, has an interest in the environment, learns elementary survival skills, and knows how to read terrain maps. Combining the two terms creates an image of a scout with the qualities of an eagle.

Obviously, you can elicit better examples of metaphors, but the merging of *scout* and *eagle* is analogous to what happens when documented or symbolic representations of software are merged with the activity of developing software. The activity of conceptualizing the software and creating the software create a dynamic. The dynamic is not ultimately reducible to work with code, documents, illustrations, or symbols. As one observer has said, the relationship between the artist and his workshop results in an irreducible form of creative activity.

Shared Resources

Everyone who is assigned to a project should have access to the core documentation from start to finish. For this to happen, everyone should understand what documentation is available and what questions the documentation can answer. Table 18.1 provides a summary of names and purposes of what might be viewed as a core set of documents.

Table 18.1 Documents and Document Purposes

Document	Purpose
Game Design	Provides the overall creative view of the game. Consult it to understand the features that the software functional specifications must support.
Software Requirements Specification	A list of requirements or a set of use cases that designate the functionality that the software needs to provide to support the features of the game. Consult it to discover the scope of the software and the specific functionality that you must develop.
Software Design Specification	A set of technical illustrations, combined with brief narratives and use cases, that shows how the functionality of the software is to be implemented. Consult this document to discover the order in which to implement functionality and how to group it during the implementation effort.
Software Test Plan	A set of test cases, usually grouped according to test suites, that you can use to verify and validate the functionality named in the software requirements specification. Consult this document as a guide to testing the functionality of the software.
Software Configuration Plan	A map of how the files and other assets involved in the development process are to be stored and managed. Consult this document to learn how to create and name files, obtain them to work on them, and place them back into storage after you have finished working on them.
Software Coding Standards	A list of conventions to be used when you are writing code. Consult this document if you need help with naming elements in your code or formatting your code.
Software Release Plan	A check list and plan for what needs to be completed before the game can be shipped to the publisher or customers. Conult this document after you have completed work on the code and want to release the game.
Software Quality Assurance Plan	A set of procedures to guide you through activities such as specifying and designing the product, creating and reviewing documents, inspecting code, and delivering the product. Consult this document to see a full list of the actions the team should perform on a regular basis as it works toward its development goals.
Software Project Plan	A schedule of activities based on the design of the product that tells how the product is to be developed and who is responsible for the specific tasks of the development effort. Consult this document if you need information about when to start or complete a task or who should work on a given task.

Common Vocabulary

Most of the organizations—such as the Institute of Electronics and Electrical Engineers (IEEE)—that supply templates suggest inclusion of a list of terms. This suggestion results from the extraordinary extent to which most projects tend to engender distinct sets of vocabulary items. Most conspicuous among these are acronyms and abbreviations. In addition to acronyms and abbreviations, new words and words that are used in ways that rename large sets of functionality as specific operations come into play. The list of terms helps everyone on the project understand the project-specific uses of such vocabulary items.

Reviews

Review provides a way for members of the development team to study documents, which embody core information. A review is a way for an individual who has worked on a specific task to communicate his findings to the rest of the team. All team members should understand this. A review is an act of communication. Along the same lines, a review is a way for all members of a team to test their understanding of a specific body of core information. In testing their understanding, they can help refine this information. (Later in this chapter, under "Document Reviews," you can find extended discussion of how to manage reviews.)

Participation

To participate effectively in information development, you need to know how to participate. To help you meet this objective, at the beginning of the project, the project manager, the team lead, or the quality assurance specialist (among others) should call the team together to discuss how each member of the team can participate in information management for the project. A good starting point is to have everyone become familiar with the types of documents that are to be created and the areas of responsibility that each member of the team has with respect to the documents. Table 18.1 names a set of documents that are common to many development efforts. Using these documents as focal points, the team should take time to discuss the following:

- **Document ownership.** Each document should have an owner. The owner is the person who oversees the first draft of the document, its distribution for review, and any changes made to it during its life. The owner also coordinates and moderates reviews.
- **Information development responsibilities.** A group of team members should be responsible for developing the information that each document contains. Each of these group members, for example, might write the contents of a specific document division.

- **Review of information.** The team should set deadlines for first drafts of each document. Discuss procedures for reviewing and baselining documents. If a document is to be baselined, the team should review it, and the owner of the document should fold the changes that the reviewers suggest into the document.
- **Storage of information.** Store the document in a location that every team member can access.
- **Retrieval of information.** At any point in history—especially following its baseline review—a document should be stored, named, and numbered so that members of the team can identify and access the most current version. If the document is to be changed, you should implement some type of change control structure.

Nondocumentation-Centered Information Management

Historically, software engineering processes have been centered on a set of documents. Some development methodologies, such as that supported by the Agile group, justifiably contend that traditional approaches to software development involve too much documentation. The objection arises largely from the extent to which documentation maintenance can create an enormous overhead for software developers. If you do not properly manage documentation from the first, it can take on a life of its own, and the resulting mountains of online or printed documentation can endanger the success of the development effort.

The approach that the *Ankh* team used for development falls into the documented-project category. The team used approximately 300 pages of documentation to create a project that involved approximately 30,000 lines of code. The ratio of code to project documentation was around 100 to 1.

The documentation did not create a maintenance problem, however, because the team created the documentation in a way that resulted in little narrative. Roughly 80 percent of the printed pages for the documentation contained UML, tabular, or use case diagrams. In this light, then, the documentation for the project consisted more of a set of working symbolic representations of the project than extensive written descriptions.

Objections to documentation usually arise when documentation plays no immediate role in the development effort. As Figure 18.4 illustrates, determining which documentation to maintain can involve considering which documentation receives use.

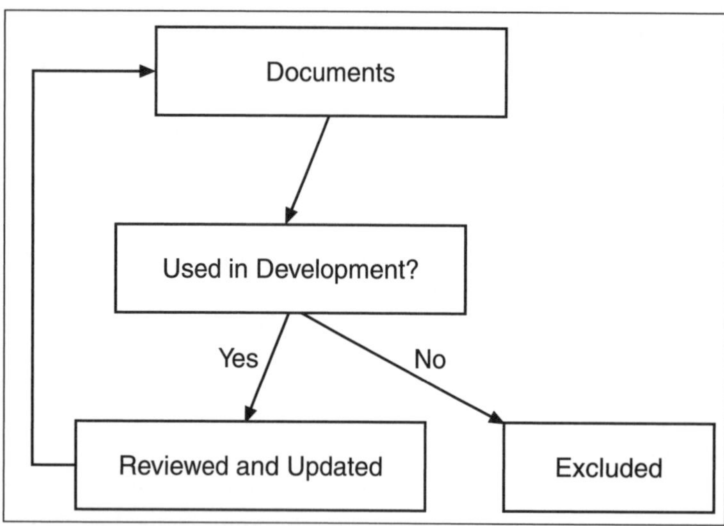

Figure 18.4
Exclude documentation that does not contribute to the development effort.

Teaching Culture

A project generally creates a culture that represents the combined qualities of the people who participate in the development effort. An important facet of this culture is that it equips or empowers people who share in the culture to use and shape information in a cooperative, effective way. With a successful development project, each day's work allows those who participate in the project to more clearly understand and communicate about the product. One result of this positive, progressive movement is that in many ways, as time goes on, members of the team say less and yet communicate more.

Team members can speak less but communicate more if ideas have become well enough established among members of the team that relatively few words during any given conversation are required to bring a great deal of cultural information into play. Given the complex nature of the culturally shaped information, the only time anyone needs to resort to explicit descriptions of details is when problems of unusual severity arise.

That a strong and rich communication culture characterizes a successful development project is all the more reason to maintain good project documentation. Touching base with document reviews allows the team to subject its understanding of the project to periodic tests. Add to this that when someone new joins the team, documentation can explain the system under development and provide information about the schedule of development activities. With such supplements, it is much easier for this person to get up to speed on the development effort.

Technical Versus Customer Documentation

Strategy guides are the most visible form of user documentation. Such guides usually provide a description of the user interface accompanied by detailed descriptions of the inventory and other features of the game. A typical guide might cover the following items:

- Skills
- Key combinations
- Options
- Characters
- Character powers
- Effects
- Spells
- Help
- Healing
- Maps of levels

Most of this information is drawn from the game design document and experiences that the writer has playing the game. The technical or creative writers who work on strategy guides or other user-oriented documentation usually must be thoroughly familiar with the game. To meet production deadlines, such writers might begin to participate in the development effort long before the game is ready for release.

Writers who write strategy guides are sometimes excellent testers. If they have played the game to the extent that they can write a guide that thousands of players might use to learn how to play the game, chances are they will know the overall game better than even those who have developed it. That's because they synthesize their knowledge of the features of the game.

Facilitating the efforts of people who write about your game is good business. If you become arrogant or defensive about describing the features of the game when writers ask for help, you should remember that they are the first line of a group of people who will ultimately determine whether your organization stays in business. A policy might be, then, that those who write for external customers receive the attention they deserve.

As a representative of the external customer group, a writer of a strategy guide probably has little interest in hearing about how you implemented functionality. Nor is this person interested in the design of the software and the elegance of the engineering. This person is interested only in what the player of the game experiences. When you provide information about game features, try to answer the question that the writer poses. Try to avoid providing explanations. Consider the following segment of dialogue:

WRITER: Okay, so they open the shopping window, and then they click on the Buy option in the upper-left corner?

PROGRAMMER [Answer A, wrong answer]: Right. You see, we had this problem with our GUI class, so we had to position the window so that it could fold to the left. Real pain. That left the button up there. Letters kept getting truncated. We kept getting this distortion that no one could figure out when we tried make it fold in other ways. Jack thought...

PROGRAMMER [Answer B, right answer]: Right. First click the Buy button. You can also use Ctrl and B, for Buy. You can then click on the item to select it. If you do not use the mouse, you can press the Tab key until the item is highlighted. After you highlight the item using the Tab key, you press Enter to select it...

The problem with Answer A, the wrong answer, is that everything after the first word provides no useful information to the writer, who is a nontechnical person with probably only a vague idea of what *GUI* means. In other words, you are not making good use of this person's time, and you are wasting your own time. Answer B is much better, because it follows the question with a useful answer. The question concerned how to use the Buy button, and the information that Answer B provides carefully details this operation.

Different Approaches

Although the emphasis of this chapter is on documents and diagrams, you can use different approaches to gather and refine information throughout a project. The following few sections detail some of these approaches.

Journaling

Journaling is the process of creating one long narrative of the exchanges developed during the life of the project. You can store such information in a database or as a massive file to which lines are added each time someone exchanges information. You can insert tags bearing information about the time and date of each exchange. The result is either a blog or something like a blog.

The advantage of journaling is that everyone can participate in a long conversation that begins with the inception of the project and, presumably, ends when the game is released and the development team is dissolved.

Indexed Journaling

Indexed journaling involves placing an interface between the user of the journal and the items that are stored in the journal. The interface forces the user to select or add an index item before making a journal entry. Entries are then stored in relation to indexes, not according to their order or time of entry. If the index already exists, the added journal entry is appended to the existing index. If the index does not already exist, the journal user can add it to the general index list. Figure 18.5 illustrates a possible interface for an indexed journal.

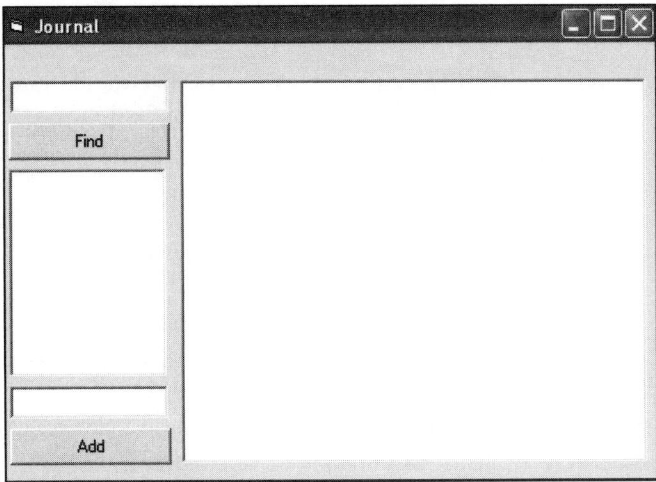

Figure 18.5
Indexed journals force users to categorize information when they add it to the journal.

Content Management Systems

Several expensive, capable content management systems are available if you need and can afford such an application. It might seem silly for a game developer to think about such things, but consider what happens when you are part of an organization that must track thousands of documents relating to business, art, and engineering.

At some point, depending on the culture of your company and the product you release, the inability to manage information formally can become an obstacle to growth. At that point, you begin considering whether you can use a content management system.

A content management system is designed to control any type of content, be it text or graphics, sound or videos.

Following is a list of items that might go into the evaluation of a content management system:

- Store and retrieve all types of documents (video, sound, text, graphical, and so on).
- Maintain an index relating to content of documents.

- Maintain biographical and contact information on document authors.
- Control access to documents.
- Provide history of document revisions.
- Link key terms in documents.
- Provide a notation system.
- Create ad hoc and standard reports on document use and content.

Generally, such a system resembles a version control system, has features that are characteristic of a trouble ticketing system, and requires a powerful database. The system is probably an Internet application. Among notable examples of content management systems are Lotus Notes (from IBM), Livelink (Open Text), and WorkSite (Interwoven).

E-Mail Exchanges

The least formal way that teams can communicate involves e-mail exchanges. E-mail generally forms a bedrock of communication among the members of development teams. For small development organizations, e-mail is the preferred means of communication. Project managers can broadcast messages as needed. Important issues can be forwarded. Documents can be attached. Members of the team can engage in isolated conversations and include others as needed by forwarding accumulated exchanges. The only real drawback of e-mail is that it can easily lead to situations in which developers possess too much or too little information. People tend to either delete e-mails too quickly or store every e-mail they receive.

As you probably know from your experiences, the effort required in deciding which e-mails to save or delete can be beneficial. When you make this decision, you filter issues, recognizing and preserving those that are important while putting aside and deleting those that are trivial. E-mail exchanges that have led to especially fruitful ideas are sometimes transferred and edited for inclusion in a formal document. The flexibility of e-mail makes it a valuable tool for managing information.

note

People do not read long e-mails. If you have a long list of technical issues, include them in an attachment. One hundred words (roughly the length of the first paragraph in this section) is a long e-mail.

Templates

Templates provide ways to organize information, but they can become a problem if you use them in a mindlessly formal way. To make the best use of templates, start by identifying ones that professional and standards organizations provide (IEEE, ISO, SEI). Draw from these the topic lists and organizational patterns that best suit the scope and complexity of your project and the culture of your organization. Using what you need and nothing more is key to avoiding needless information management activities.

What Is a Template?

A template outlines a document or provides a pattern for information management. If it outlines a document, it consists of headings under which you can place information that is relative to the headings. Figure 18.6 represents a template for a project management plan. This template is derived from the IEEE standard 1058.

Even if it can be described as an outline for a document, a template is more than an outline. For starters, a template is commonly accompanied by a commentary of some type that tells you how to use it. Typically, the commentary provides instructions for how to fill in each section. A glossary of terms might also accompany the template. (This is the usual practice with IEEE templates.)

Title Page
Revision Chart
Preface
Table of Contents
List of Figures
List of Tables
Introduction
- Overview
- Deliverables
- References
- Glossary of Terms

Project Organization
- Process
- Structure
- Scope
- Responsibilities

Management
- Objectives
- Assumptions
- Risk Assessment
- Control Measures
- Staffing

Technical Processes
- Tools and Methods
- Documentation
- Project Support

Schedules and Budgets
- Dependencies
- Resource Requirement
- Budget
- Schedule

Appendixes

Figure 18.6
A template is an outline that is supplemented with a commentary that tells you how to use it.

Where to Find Templates

The best sources for templates are standards organizations. Among such organizations are the following:

- **The Software Engineering Institute (SEI).** The Web page provides a search field. Enter the type of activity you want to document. From this point, you will find a great deal of free information, and with a little work, you will find a template. The site is at http://www.sei.cmu.edu/.
- **The Institute of Electrical and Electronics Engineers (IEEE).** To access a given IEEE template for a document, use the standard number for the document you are seeking. To make this a little easier, Table 18.2 provides a list of IEEE standards. You can use these to access templates for documents.

You can also access the site for the IEEE Software Engineering Standards Zone (http://standards.ieee.org/software), where you can obtain a CD that contains the IEEE templates.

- **Software Engineering Body of Knowledge (SWEBOK).** This is more a directive to topics than a reference for templates. The site is at http://www.swebok.org.
- **International Standards Organization (ISO).** To obtain the numbers of ISO standards, access the ISO site and use the search field to locate standards relating to the topic for which you require a template. The site location is http://www.iso.org/iso/en/CatalogueListPage.CatalogueList. After you obtain the document number, you can search the Web.
- **Game Design Document.** For game design documents, standardized templates do not yet exist. One starting point is http://members.shaw.ca/ bsimser/webdesign/default.htm.

Table 18.2 IEEE Standards and Numbers

Standard Name	Access Number*
IEEE Standard for Software Quality Assurance Plans	730-1989
IEEE Standard for Software Configuration Management Plans	828-1990
IEEE Standard for Software Test Documentation	829-1983
IEEE Guide for Software Requirements Specifications	830-1984
IEEE Standard Dictionary of Measures to Produce Reliable Software	982.1-1988
IEEE Guide for the Use of IEEE Standard Dictionary of Measures to Produce Reliable Software	982.2-1988
IEEE Standard for Software Unit Testing	1008-1987
IEEE Standard for Software Verification and Validation Plans	1012-1986
IEEE Recommended Practice for Software Design Descriptions	1016-1987
IEEE Standard for Software Reviews and Audits	1028-1988
IEEE Guide to Software Configuration Management	1042-1987
IEEE Standard for Software Productivity Metrics	1045-1992
IEEE Standard for Software Project Management Plans	1058.1-1987
IEEE Standard for Software User Documentation	1063-1987
IEEE Standard for Developing Software Life Cycle Processes	1074-1991

*To search for a standard online, try entering *IEEE standard nnnn-nnnn.* This usually retrieves a link to the version of the template you are looking for.

note

A distinction exists between a standard and a template. A *standard* is a conceptual guide to a topic. It usually includes a *template* for a document that helps users of the standard organize information that relates to work involving the standard.

How to Use Templates

Many developers who are given documentation responsibilities misuse templates. They do so because they forget that a template is a *recommended* pattern or guide for developing information. The most visible sign of this problem is that the resulting documents contain sections that display completely useless, redundant headings. Figure 18.7 provides an example.

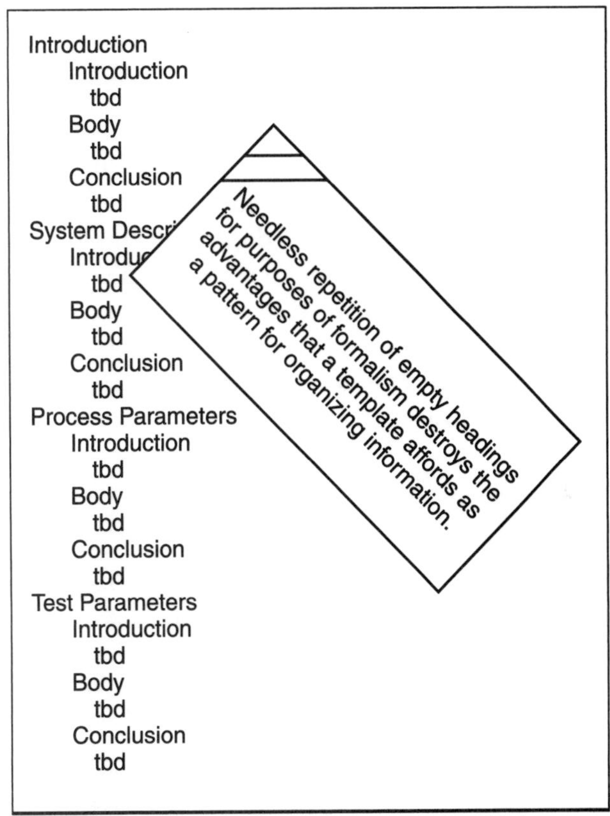

Figure 18.7
Needless duplication of empty content constitutes an ineffective use of a template.

A template is best used as a guide. As a guide, it does not impose strict demands on its users. Instead, it suggests ideas and ways to organize information. To use a template effectively, you should first draw from it a conceptual framework for your undertaking. Then use only those features of the framework that you require to capture for your project. Don't use headings you don't need. Filling in headings only because the template provides them creates useless information.

You can improve the outline shown in Figure 18.7 if you cut it back to the four primary topics:

- Introduction
- System Description
- Process Parameters
- Test Parameters

After the development team has the essential parts of the template, it should begin inserting information. If the template helps the team identify useful types of information and offers a way to organize this information, it serves its purpose. The team can determine for itself the document divisions that best express the culture and objectives of the team and how much information it needs to gather for each division.

Document Maintenance

You can establish a few maintenance practices from the beginning to enable everyone on the team to derive maximum benefit from the creation and use of the documents that define the flow of information for the project. Maintenance involves knowing which document is current, who owns a document, how to make changes in a document, and where to place documents so that everyone can find them. The best approach to ensuring that these operations are performed effectively is to simplify them as much as possible. One of the best approaches to simplification is to try to make document maintenance activities center on the current document rather than expending energy managing the history of changes in the document.

Tracking

Microsoft Word allows you to track every change you make to a document. Although this feature can be useful if you are editing a book or preparing a legal contract, when it's used for software documentation development, it can create some problems. One problem is that the information that the tracking utility generates is not very useful. Although it provides an excellent record of changes to the text, it provides almost no information about conceptual or design changes to the software. For this reason, rather than relying on such automated change tracking capabilities, it is better to insert a change table (usually at the start of the document). You can use this table to create a summary record of important changes to the software. Figure 18.8 shows a table that guides a reader to substantial changes in a requirements document. Using this table, the reader can readily identify how requirements have changed as a result of reviews that have taken place on the indicted dates.

Date	Change
11/02/04	Deleted requirement 32
11/20/04	Deleted requirement 64
12/15/04	Added "panel" to requirement 2
12/15/04	Added requirement 72
12/15/04	Changed requirement 32

Figure 18.8
Use tables to guide readers to changes and reviews instead of having them read through minute textual records of change.

Numbering Systems and Baselines

It's best approach is to use the simplest possible numbering system you can find when you number documents. Note, for example, a list of the versions of the requirements specification for *Ankh*:

- AnkhSRS1_0.doc
- AnkhSRS2_0.doc
- AnkhSRS2_1.doc
- AnkhSRS3_0.doc
- AnkhSRS3_1.doc
- AnkhSRS4_0.doc
- AnkhSRS5_0.doc

Each of these versions of the *Ankh Software Requirements Specification* represents the state of the document after a team review. If the number following the underscore is a zero, the version number designates a baselined document. With the *Ankh* development effort, each time the team created a baseline of a stripe, it reviewed the project documents. If the team made significant changes, it incremented the document numbers. If the team made no significant changes, it made no change in numbering. Figure 18.9 illustrates how each baseline of the software product included a list of documents.

Stripe3_1	AhkhSRS4_0.doc AhkhSDS4_0.doc AhkhCMP1_0.doc AhkhSTP1_0.doc AhkhSCS2_0.doc AhkhSPM2_0.doc AhkhGDD4_0.doc
Stripe3_2	AhkhSRS4_0.doc AhkhSDS4_0.doc AhkhCMP1_0.doc AhkhSTP1_0.doc AhkhSCS2_0.doc AhkhSPM2_0.doc AhkhGDD5_0.doc

Figure 18.9
Relating document version levels to design stripes simplified storage and retrieval.

Ownership Responsibilities

You own a document if the team or team lead assigns it to you. When you own a document, you are responsible for ensuring that the document is created, revised, distributed to the team, and archived as needed.

If you are the document owner, your responsibility is to oversee or perform for yourself the development of the document. It is also your responsibility to say when a revision number can be changed. Among your tasks are the following:

- **Creating.** Creating a document means finding a suitable template and using that to gather and refine the appropriate information. To accomplish this, you can use several approaches. One is to provide as much information as you can and then to find others on the team to confirm what you have written or supply new information. You can meet with the project lead to find out who might be best qualified to provide information on specific topics. The people who supply information for the document should be included in the development team for the document. You should list their names on the document cover.

- **Revising.** Revision takes place in several ways. If you are working with a few others to create the first draft of a document, revision amounts to adding information or repeatedly revising material you have written. Revision during this phase of composition is informal, which means it is not subject to revision control. After a time, however, you can baseline the document and then begin changing it through formal reviews. Such reviews involve noting revision levels before and after the changes. The revision levels show that changes have taken place.
- **Distributing.** You usually distribute a document to people whose names are on a distribution list. The distribution list includes people who are centrally concerned with the content of the document. You should invite these people to reviews and give them a copy of the document each time you release it at a new level.
- **Identifying.** It is important to track version numbers of documents. To track the history of the document, you can insert a table of reviews at the beginning of the document. You can note the review dates and release numbers assigned to the document following the reviews.
- **Storing.** You should know the location of the document you own. It is important to store the official version of the document in the project archives, not on the disk of your own workstation. A document in this respect is the same as source code.

Document Reviews

Effective documentation reviews result in increased team cohesion, confirmed conceptualization of the software product, and enhanced communication among team members. A parallel result is that a paper or online document formalizes the information that is exchanged, tested, or gathered during the review. (See Figure 18.10.)

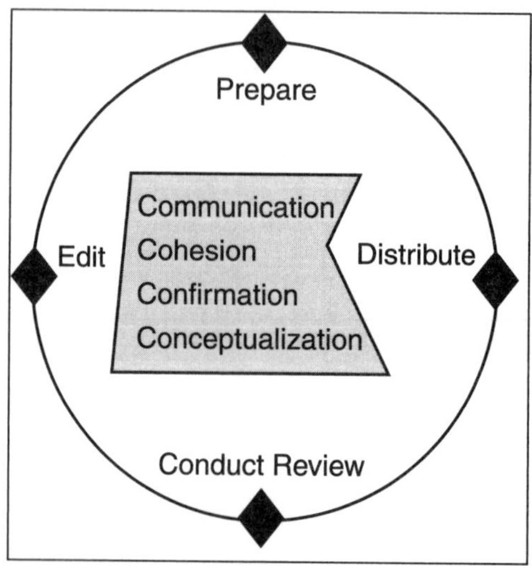

Figure 18.10
The development of ideas can center on reviews.

Anticipating Reviews

Successful reviews require preparation. The document owner prepares a document for review. Preparation involves the following items:

- **Document.** Clear the document of change markings from the previous review.
- **Version.** Check the document to make certain it displays the right version level.
- **Reviewers.** Create a list of the team members who are to participate in the review.
- **Schedule.** Confirm with the project lead a time for a document review. Generally, it is not a good idea to ask people to spend more than an hour at a review.
- **Notification.** Notify the team of the review. (The project lead is the best person to do this.) In the notification, tell reviewers to examine the document and note items they think should be changed.
- **Copies.** If you work with paper, distribute copies of the document. Otherwise, distribute electronic copies. (It does no good to tell people they can access the document in the project archives.)
- **Priorities.** If you are looking for serious input, visit each team member from whom you would like to have specific input and point out which portion of the document you would like them to review.

With respect to soliciting input, team members who feel they have no stake in a document are often reluctant to spend time working with it. For this reason, if you are assigned ownership of a document, share ownership as much as possible.

Conducting Reviews

When you conduct a document review, the best approach is to project the document onto a large screen and then have everyone, section by section, review the document as a group. If you are working with Microsoft Word, you can turn on the Track Changes option and insert changes as you go. In this way, everyone can see their changes immediately inserted, which promotes participation.

To conduct a review, consider the following points:

- **Set the agenda.** Tell everyone at the start how long the review is to last, what is expected, and how things will proceed.
- **Lead the review.** Start with the first page of the document and guide the team through to the end. If the document is displayed on a screen that all members can see, guide them to each pertinent section. Name the section. Solicit responses. For example, say, "Okay, here's Requirement 44. Any comments? Let's go around the room. . ."

- **Confirm changes.** Whenever someone suggests a change, type the change so that everyone can see it and then read the change so that everyone can hear it. Then ask if anyone feels the change is not appropriate. Alter the change until you have consensus. Consensus means that everyone agrees to the change.
- **Table disputes.** If everyone cannot agree to the change, table the change for resolution. Resolution will involve having the disputing parties meet with you and the project manager and discussing the difficulty in detail. After you find a resolution and fold it into the document, you can distribute the document (or a portion of it) to those who participated in the review and confirm with them that they are in agreement with the change.
- **Track time.** During the review, remind everyone every quarter hour how much time you have used up and how much time remains. In this way, you keep the review moving along. On the other hand, if the review results in a great deal of discussion, you have to face the fact that things cannot be rushed and you are probably going to have to schedule another time to continue the review. If this happens, save all the changes. Do not redistribute the changed document unless members of the team request you to do so. Schedule the continued review to take place within the next few days.
- **Conclude the review.** State that the review is over. Tell everyone when you will have the document updated. Tell everyone where to find the document and when you will distribute it. If you want people to look at the changed document, it is not enough to tell them where they can find it in the archives.

Team Focus

Maintaining information involves working in the interests of the team. For this reason, if you are given ownership of a document, view yourself as providing a service to others. When you maintain the document, for instance, insert changes during the review or as soon as possible after the review. The best time to insert changes is during the review, when you can obtain immediate feedback and verification. Likewise, immediately after the review, put in the time necessary to check spelling, syntax, and the correctness of diagrams, and then place a new version of the document in the project archives. Delays in updating a document can lead to undesirable results. Among the worst of these is that you forget or lose the changes that others have suggested.

Probably one of the most important aspects of any development effort is that when things are done in isolation, they are likely to contain a greater number of defects than if they are done with the aid of a team review. This is largely how the Cartesian approach to science works. Scientific knowledge is predicated on the notion that when you present experimental results, you do so in such a manner that others can check your work. Answers are not so much wrong or right as confirmed or unconfirmed. With software documents, you can use the same general approach. A software design document is not so much right or wrong as it is reviewed or unreviewed.

Approaches to Storage and Display

After you have baselined documents, store them along with all other project files. If you are using a configuration management scheme, you might store a version of the document as part of a baseline of the current software. In this way, you comprehensively capture a snapshot of the software you are developing, complete with its documentation.

Linking HTML versions of technical documents to a project Web page provides the development team with ready access to core project documentation. If you place documents on a project Web site, the best approach to maintenance is for the document owner to use a word processing application to convert the document to HTML. Preserve the Word document as primary. In addition, allow each document owner to access the project page for updates to reduce maintenance complexity.

Tools for Documentation

The tools you use for documentation and engineering depend on how much your organization can spend on tools and the scope of the project you are working on. The tools can range from freeware to costly, comprehensive IDEs like IBM's Rational suite. Such tools automatically link code, diagrams, requirements, test scenarios, and supplemental documentation, among other items.

Many game developers contend that game development efforts are not likely to benefit if they incorporate this level of automation. Several reasons justify such statements. One is that game creation combines creative and engineering activities in ways that current CASE tools cannot accommodate. On the other hand, the situation changes with companies that specialize in the development of high-end graphical components or game engines. Such systems are marketed to game developers or publishers, and they tend to be consistent from release to release. They also tend to fetch a high price. Using tools for reverse engineering and automated documentation generation to develop such products might be extremely cost effective.

Word Processing

In almost any software development environment, you can accomplish word processing using Microsoft Word or Adobe FrameMaker. There are also other word processors, such as Corel WordPerfect. As long as a word processor can create tables, import graphics, and convert documents to PDF, HTML, and RTF formats, you can probably safely purchase it.

Each major word processor has its detractors and defenders. The *Ankh* development team used Microsoft Word because everyone on the team owned it and knew how to use it. One person's personal preference was Adobe FrameMaker, but no one else on the team owned a copy. That settled that.

Graphics

The *Ankh* team's favorite graphics tools were Adobe Photoshop and Microsoft Paint. Paint is good for simple tasks, such as saving screenshots in bitmap or jpeg formats. Photoshop is good for everything that needs to be done to prepare screen shots for publication. Likewise, Photoshop is good for almost any kind of work you want to do with textures or bitmaps. The team used Maya to process most of the meshes. It was necessary to compile an add-in to convert the meshes from the Maya format to the x format used by DirectX. For cottage industry game developers, Maya is expensive and difficult to use, but after you have gotten over these two bumps, it is a reliable, effective tool for creating assets for PC games.

Technical Drawings and UML

The team's preferred tool for technical and every other type of drawing was SmartDraw. This application is a cost-effective asset for a small software development team. It is inexpensive, versatile, and easy to use. The team used SmartDraw projects to create illustrations for the design of the software. The projects packaged drawings so that they were easy to work. One pallet could hold dozens of UML diagrams. One particularly important benefit of this arose after the team installed SmartDraw onto a laptop and hooked the laptop to a projector. The team could develop and review design illustrations as a group.

If the team imported objects from SmartDraw into Word documents, it could open a UML drawing in SmartDraw that was embedded in a Word document. This approach made it easy to edit UML diagrams during document reviews.

Display

Some mention has already been made of how to set up a home page for a project. Small-team efforts can use the Internet as a way to conduct code and other reviews. The *Ankh* team set up Microsoft .NET IDE on the same laptop on which it installed SmartDraw. It then used TortoiseCVS to access code and documents, which it could check out and projected to a large screen for group review. As primitive as this procedure might seem, it effectively established a reliable, consistent way to conduct code and documentation reviews. The most expensive part of the setup was the projector.

Preventing Excesses

Taking precautions to prevent excess is necessary because documentation is both a solution and a problem. It is a solution because it is the only effective way that a team can formalize its communications to the extent necessary to guide a complex development process. It is a problem because information, in general, tends to create entropy. The more information you generate during a project, the more likely it is that miscommunication is going to occur. In the end, you are left with a dilemma. If you do not communicate, the project fails. If you communicate in a sloppy, random way, the project fails.

Using a Standard Process

One way to reduce miscommunication is to create a core communication process. Previous sections discussed much of this process, but it will not hurt to summarize it here:

- Determine at the outside of the project which documents you want to use to trace the central information flows of your project.
- Assign each of these documents to an owner, and have the owner obtain a standard template for the document. Develop the information in the document by using the template.
- Maintain several simultaneous, complementary flows of information using documentation and review. Everyone on the team should know why this information is being maintained.
- Review primary documents at regular intervals. Use the reviews as much to force everyone to concentrate on the documents as to have everyone review and refine the information in the project. The purpose of a review is to allow everyone to learn about a given information content.
- Control documents. Store and update information that is collected in documents by using a formal document control routine.
- Use documents. In other words, track work using the design document and the project management plan. Perform testing of the product by using the test plan. The storage of the files for the project should take place using the file and directory specifications that were given in the configuration plan. The release of the product should proceed according to the criteria that is set up in the release plan.

Relating Documents to Each Other

Relating documents means that each document should contain references to other documents. To relate documents to each other, create a section heading called "Related Documents." Under this heading, list the related documents. An explanation of why a related document is useful often benefits the reader. Table 18.3 provides a sketch of how you can relate documents to each other.

Table 18.3 References Between Documents

Source Document	Target(s)
Requirements Specification	Software Design Specification, Game Design Document
Software Design Specification	Requirements Specification, Game Design Document, Project Plan
Test Plan	Software Design Specification, Test Plan
Configuration Management Plan	Software Design Specification
Project Plan	Requirements Specification, Software Design Specification, Game Design Document, Test Plan, Configuration Management Plan, Coding Standards
Coding Standards	Design Specification

Reducing Maintenance

The best approach to reducing maintenance is to provide each key document with an owner and to have the owner preside and edit at reviews. As noted previously, the *Ankh* team tended to do a great deal of its work with documentation using a laptop plugged into a projector. Using this approach, when a document is updated, a whole team participates in the updating activity, but one person, the person who knows the document best, is at the keyboard doing the work of the scribe. This approach might sound crude, but as pointed out before, unless documentation serves to involve people in the development process, it is largely worthless. Combining activities of reviewing and editing saves an enormous amount of work and allows everyone to help refine project information.

Keeping Only Essential Material

As mentioned previously, making an extensive change record visible to the members of the development team accomplishes little that is useful. It is almost never the case that someone wants to see something more than the current working conception of the software. For this reason, documentation should capture what the team has currently accepted as the vision of the software and suppress other visions, visions that have been superseded. To ensure that a record exists of the evolution of the software, the team can create baselines at specific moments during the development process. For the *Ankh* development effort, the team used the completion of each stripe as an occasion for baselines of code, assets, and documentation.

Conclusion

Documentation is a way to formalize the information that allows you to define the scope, create the design, verify the functionality of, and plan how to develop your product. The documents that guide the development effort can be relatively few in number, but they still should be created and maintained only if they play an active role in the development of the product. If a document is not used, there is little sense in creating or maintaining it. To effectively use documentation as part of a development effort, reviews are necessary. A review should be carefully arranged and directed by the person who is the owner of the document being reviewed. The owner has a responsibility to conduct the review so that everyone who attends the review learns from the document and contributes to its refinement. Following the review, the owner should finalize changes to the document, update its version number as needed, and store the document for access by all members of the team.

To create good documentation for a software development effort, relatively few tools are needed. The most important tools are a word processor and an application for technical illustrations. For the *Ankh* project, Word and SmartDraw served these needs. Word allowed the team to create documents and convert them to HTML for display. SmartDraw provided a ready way of creating UML diagrams that could be embedded in Word documents.

To be effective, all members of the team should understand each document's purpose. The requirements document defines the scope of the product. The software design document shows how to build the software. The test plan shows how to verify and validate the functionality that supports each of the requirements. The configuration plan allows everyone to know how to name files and where to store them. The coding conventions serve as a guide to how to deal with matters of syntax and naming within program files. The project plan allows everyone to know the assignment of tasks and their due dates.

You can create most documents by using templates. Templates represent accumulated wisdom, but you should not follow them in a mechanical, thoughtless way. They are guides to organizing information, so you are at liberty to shape them so that they accommodate the culture and scope of your development effort. Trim templates if they provide too many topics. Empty headings that are retained purely for the sake of formality indicate that the template has not been effectively refined.

For further reading on the topics presented in this chapter, see the following resources:

Bransfor, John D. and Barry S. Stein. *The Ideal Problem Solver: A Guide for Improving Thinking, Learning, and Creativity. Second Edition.* New York: W. H. Freeman and Company, 1993.

Cockburn, Alistair. *Agile Software Development.* Boston: Addison-Wesley, 2002.

Humphrey, Watts S. *Managing the Software Process.* Boston: Addison-Wesley, 1989.

Johnson, Mark and George Lakoff. *Metaphors We Live By.* Chicago: University of Chicago Press, 1980.

Pirsig, Robert. *Zen and the Art of Motorcycle Maintenance.* New York: Bantam Books, 1974.

Sides, Charles. *How to Write and Present Technical Information.* Phoenix: Oryx Press, 1991.

Wiegers, Karl E. *Peer Reviews in Software: A Practical Guide.* Boston: Addison-Wesley, 2002.

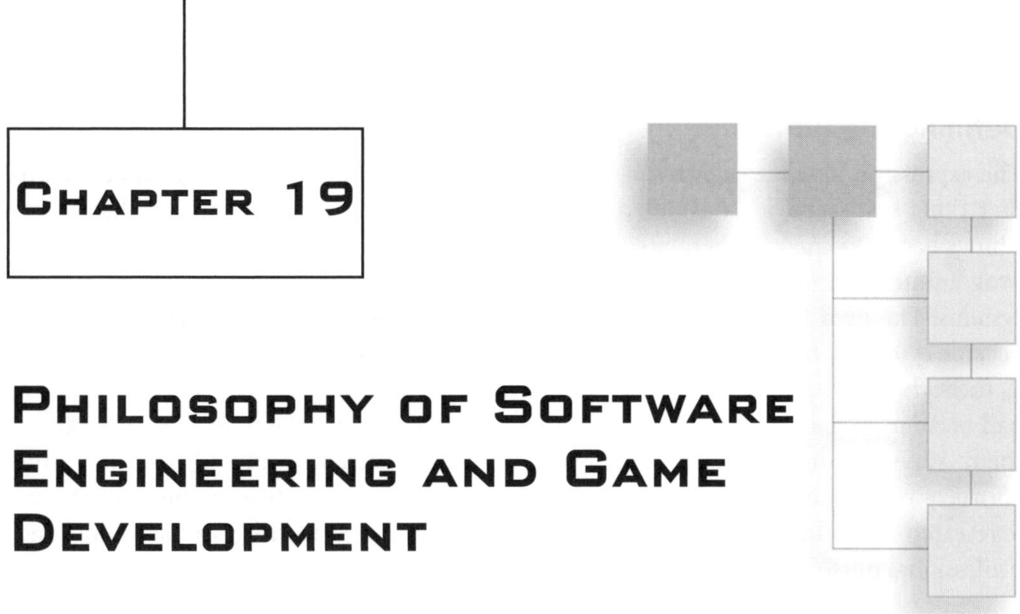

Chapter 19

Philosophy of Software Engineering and Game Development

You can think of software engineering as a craft or a profession. It does not matter which emphasis you choose to give it. What is important is that you recognize that the satisfaction you derive from your work as a software engineer involved in game development depends on a number of factors related to your vision of your career path as a game developer, the companies you work for, and the state of the industry. This chapter examines several topics in an effort to establish some criteria you can use to evaluate the many forces that affect your professional development as a software engineer. A rough sketch follows:

- A few points on the history of software engineering
- Why software engineering is considered a profession
- Why software engineering is a craft
- Good and bad methodologies
- Companies and individual styles of development
- Ways to learn valuable lessons from your work
- Ethical issues

The New Undertaking

Philosophy can begin with history. This section begins with some reflections on the history of software engineering. Generally, the trends that have prevailed over the decades during which software engineering has emerged now exert strong influences over the game development industry.

Defining the Domain

The expression *software engineering* was first used in 1968 at a NATO conference. Before that time, software was considered more or less an extension of computer hardware. Things began to change when large-scale software development efforts required that the programmers who were involved in them begin studying their programs as engineered systems. The need for the formal development of knowledge about engineered software became evident. The primary drive to create engineered software systems became known as the *software crisis.* The basis of this crisis was that the complexity of software systems had become so great that it was nearly impossible for programmers to repair or extend them. Ways to study software complexity in an organized way and to coordinate the efforts of many people toward specific software engineering objectives required systematic research. This, then, marked the beginning of software engineering as an academic and professional pursuit.

note

One of the milestones of the development of software engineering was the publication of *The Mythical Man-Month,* by Frederick P. Brooks, Jr. (See the reference at the end of this chapter.) The first edition appeared in 1975. The book contains a chapter entitled "No Silver Bullet," based on a paper first published in an IEEE publication. Writes Brooks, "The complexity of software is an essential property, not an accidental one. Hence, descriptions of a software entity that abstract away its complexity often abstract away its essence" (Brooks, 183).

Formal Engineering

In 1976, the Institute of Electronics and Electrical Engineers (IEEE) formed a committee to oversee software engineering standards. You can find a continuing record of the actions leading to the formation of this committee and the results of its activities since its formation in *IEEE Transactions on Software Engineering* (http://www.computer.org/tse). This is a highly technical publication geared toward professional and academic circles.

A much friendlier route to reading about software engineering is *IEEE Software* (http://www.computer.org/software). The articles featured in this magazine represent current discussions of almost anything that is relevant to developing software.

Formal studies of software engineering have identified, documented, and refined activities that software engineers perform during the lifecycle of a software engineering project. They also have identified the areas of knowledge that form the basis of industrial and academic training and educational efforts. Later in this chapter, these areas of knowledge are reviewed.

The great benefit that you derive from the IEEE approach to studying software engineering is that the information available to you is devoid of commercial and ideological hype.

Consulting organizations tend to market engineering expertise clothed in needlessly complex languages and processes. The IEEE tends to provide information that represents essential, unbiased perspectives on engineering.

To gain access to the IEEE publications, you must join the IEEE Computer Society. Routes to this destination differ. If you are a student, the membership fee is fairly minimal. If you are a working professional, the cost is comparable to what you pay for a trade magazine subscription. To obtain more information about signing up with the IEEE, go to http://www.computer.org/join.

Software Engineering Areas of Knowledge

To learn about the areas of knowledge that the IEEE identifies as central to software engineering, read *Guide to the Software Engineering Body of Knowledge* (SWEBOK), which the IEEE has placed online. This document does not officially establish categories of knowledge. Instead, it is intended as a guide. In addition to a chapter on each of the areas of knowledge, this document provides several hundred references to sources of information that allow you to research the topics independently. Figure 19.1 shows you the key areas.

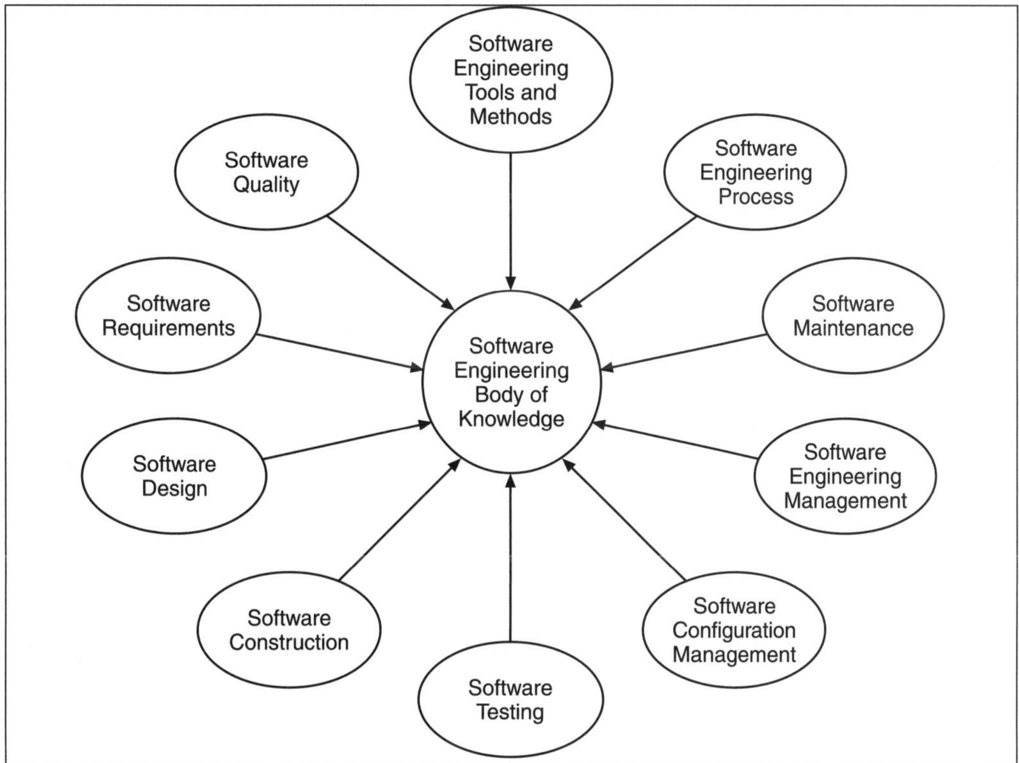

Figure 19.1
The SWEBOK defines 10 key areas of software engineering knowledge.

Science and Engineering

Before there was software engineering, there was computer science. The first academic departments of computer science were established during the 1950s. Among these was the computer science department at the Massachusetts Institute of Technology. A few decades later, academic departments offering courses on software engineering began to emerge. One of the first widely recognized academic departments devoted to software engineering was established at Carnegie Mellon University. This department enjoyed great recognition because it became associated with the Software Engineering Institute (SEI). The SEI was one of the first organizations to promote industry-wide standards for the development of software.

Although many computer scientists work as software engineers or software developers, software engineering differs from computer science. Software engineering tends to use established knowledge to solve specific, practical problems that usually have a fairly high degree of public visibility. Computer science concentrates on theoretical and mathematical questions that might receive little public attention. Research and exploration that are not focused on immediate applications characterize computer science as an academic discipline. Computer scientists work to extend the knowledge fostered by computer studies. Software engineers apply their knowledge to the creation of products that have fairly immediate utility.

According D. L. Parnas (*IEEE Software*, November/December, 1999, p. 23), software engineers tend to engage in the following general types of work:

- Determination and documentation of software requirements
- Configuration of computer system hardware and software components
- Creation of software designs that accurately reflect requirements
- Design of the architecture of software—its division into modules
- Examination of the architecture for completeness, suitability, and consistency
- Implementation of software as well-documented and well-structured programs
- Determination of whether Commercial-Off-The-Shelf (COTS) software is appropriate for a given software solution
- Testing of software systems
- Revision and enhancement of software systems

This list is somewhat incomplete because it does not discuss such topics as team dynamics or project management. However, it does tend to show the practical direction that software engineering takes. Later, this chapter examines the core areas of software knowledge to see how this list expands into a fairly solid set of core skills and knowledge areas.

Complex Products

Software engineering has exerted greater influence over game development efforts during the past few years because game development has, like older application technologies, grown to the point that the resulting products require the participation of large teams and extended, expensive development efforts.

As games grow larger and more sophisticated, they become just like any other complex system of software, and those who develop such games must implement the same engineering practices that apply in other fields of software development. In other words, with the increase in complexity comes the need to control complexity.

To examine how complexity has bearing on current trends, consider that it is becoming fairly common for a game to involve a budget comparable to what Hollywood producers require to make a motion picture. Those who work on the game can number in the hundreds, and the complexity of design and construction tasks in which the programmers are involved rivals anything that any other industry currently offers. Figure 19.2 represents some components that contribute to the complexity of game development.

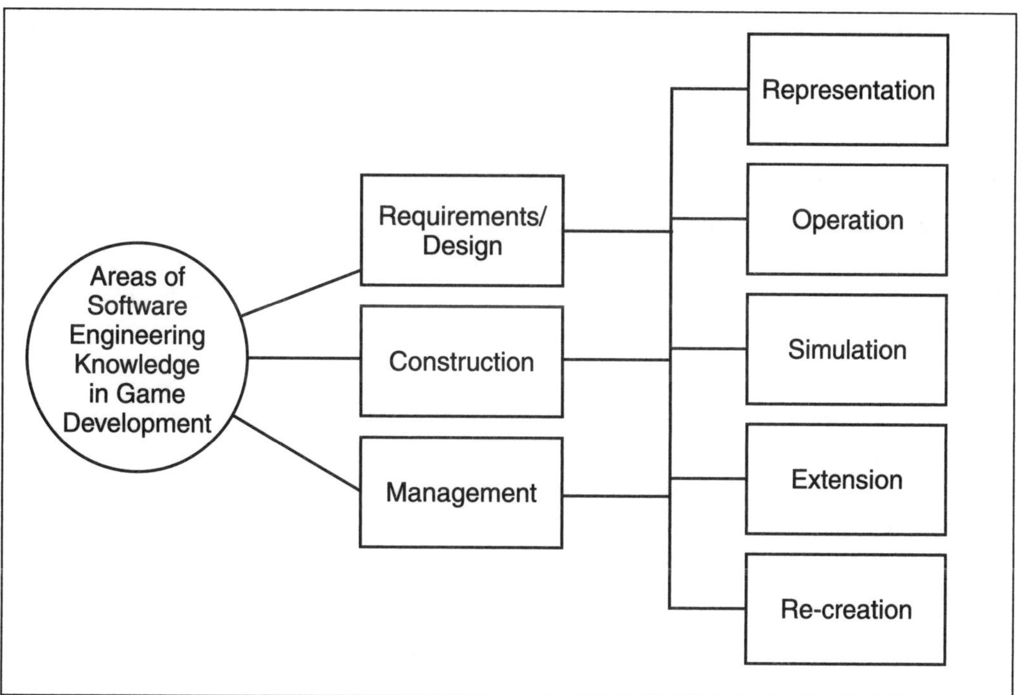

Figure 19.2
Game development moves in multiple directions.

Figure 19.2 attempts to simplify an enormous number of situations that might arise in which game software development activities become complex to the point that adopting software engineering practices becomes either necessary or advisable.

Because the content of games is becoming more complex by the day, the developers of game software must interact with domain experts on an increasingly dependent basis. In other words, game developers must use the techniques of software engineering to capture and refine requirements for games. The number of requirements is becoming so great that project managers must employ advanced design and construction strategies to coordinate the efforts of fairly large development teams. Consider the following scenarios:

- **Representation.** Game worlds increasingly mirror reality, to the point that geopolitical and geographical data are modeled on a vast scale. You can add to this the modeling of interpersonal and psychological interactions.
- **Operation.** A game is a real-time system—or it can be. Creation of games extended over the Internet requires the implementation of databases and other fault-tolerant technologies.
- **Simulation.** Simulation of physical systems requires intense engineering. If you design intelligence that must deliver simulation realistically, performance and testing will require fairly strict attention to software engineering practices.
- **Extension.** Development companies almost always extend successful games across multiple releases. To ensure consistency across releases, engineering principles must be put in place.
- **Recreation.** The billions of dollars spent on the game industry each year have made it into a highly competitive realm. To ensure continuing profits, products must be designed and constructed according to exacting standards. Recreation is not always a walk in the park.

Game development companies produce software games that buyers expect to function according to complex patterns and to provide satisfying player experiences. Given these demands, many principles and practices of software engineering prove useful, if not essential, in the design, construction, testing, deployment, and maintenance of games. As will become evident later in this chapter, you can apply all the areas of software engineering that are mentioned in the SWEBOK scheme to game development. You can apply software engineering's vast store of knowledge to game development in ways that allow you to produce much better products than would otherwise be possible.

Professional Licensing

The same trends that led to the development of such organizations as the software branch of the IEEE have also led to the development of the notion that anyone who works with software should be licensed. This tends to be a sobering thought for most people who have taken up programming at home using a personal computer and who consider that what they do as a hobby might someday lead to a career. It is also disturbing to those people currently working as software developers or software engineers in the gaming and other software industries.

Why Licensing?

An extensive debate over making software development a licensed profession arose during the early 1990s and raged for more than a decade. The debate continues. Many people consider programming to be something that only qualified professionals should be paid to do. This includes developing games. Many people think that if licensed professionals create software products, the products that result will be of greater quality and cost less to produce than is currently the case. The arguments go on. Products will be safer to use because licensed engineers will design them so they do not fail in critical situations. Products will bring greater satisfaction to the consumer. The benefits are said to be endless.

If only licensed professionals will be able to perform software development, software engineering will move in the same direction that medicine, law, and civil engineering have moved. Hardly anyone takes exception to the idea that before they can practice their occupations, doctors must go to medical school and pass an examination and lawyers must graduate from law school and likewise pass a bar examination. The same applies to civil engineers, who must graduate from an engineering school and pass a certification examination before they can, for example, design buildings or bridges. Why should the situation differ for software developers—even those involved in game development?

If you are a game programmer who has learned everything you know in an informal way and has participated in successful and profitable development efforts, the idea that you might suddenly find yourself unqualified to do what you do because you lack a license might strike you as ridiculous.

On the other hand, if you have ever participated in a development effort that has gone wrong due to technical mismanagement or incompetent design and coding efforts, you might view as justified some of the calls for some standard of professionalism in the game and other software industries.

Back a Step

A software engineer is someone who consciously works not only to develop software but also to find improve the ways software is developed. Generally, if you are a programmer who programs games, you end up doing all sorts of work that falls under the headings listed in the SWEBOK scheme. Among these are requirements analysis, design, programming (also sometimes called *construction*, or *implementation*), testing, configuration management, and quality assurance. A person who works in all these areas of development ends up as a *software engineering generalist.*

If you fall into this category of software engineer or developer, you can go on for years acquiring and refining your skills. You might have good games to show for your work. But at the same time, your skills might transcend what any one game shows. And suppose you do superior work on a game that the critics decide is a flop? Isn't there a standard other than the products you work on? How is it possible for you to say, for example, that you deserve greater responsibility or more pay than another person if you do not have some way of judging your skills?

Even if the solution is not licensing, the core knowledge of software engineering comes into play here. As a generalist, you can still be in a position to say that you possess a solid set of specialized skills as a programmer if you have at hand a clearly defined set of standards and practices that you can learn, use, and extend as you work and that you can share with others through a common understanding of your profession or craft. Developers can be better than the games they produce. This has been proven time and time again.

Practice, Not Licensing

The vast majority of companies do not require licensing. They are interested in demonstrated skills only. They might ask for a degree in computer science or some other area, but they also ask for evidence of your skills. That is why demo games are such a standard feature of the job search process. Even then, some background features come into pay.

What does the game show? When you answer this question, you end up moving down the list of core knowledge areas named in the SWEBOK table. This chapter will examine this list in greater depth later, but the point for now is that when you consider how people judge your work, even if they have never heard of the SWEBOK, they tend to begin asking questions about things like whether the game was developed from an idea you had before you began coding, how the game was designed, whether it is thoroughly documented, how many bugs are evident, and how easy it is to use (not to be confused with play). In other words, they attend to the skills you show in the areas of requirements, design, testing, and maintenance.

As Figure 19.3 shows, employers demand skills that software engineering fosters. If you develop games, you end up dealing with questions that reflect the formal categories that software engineering has developed and captured in its core areas of knowledge.

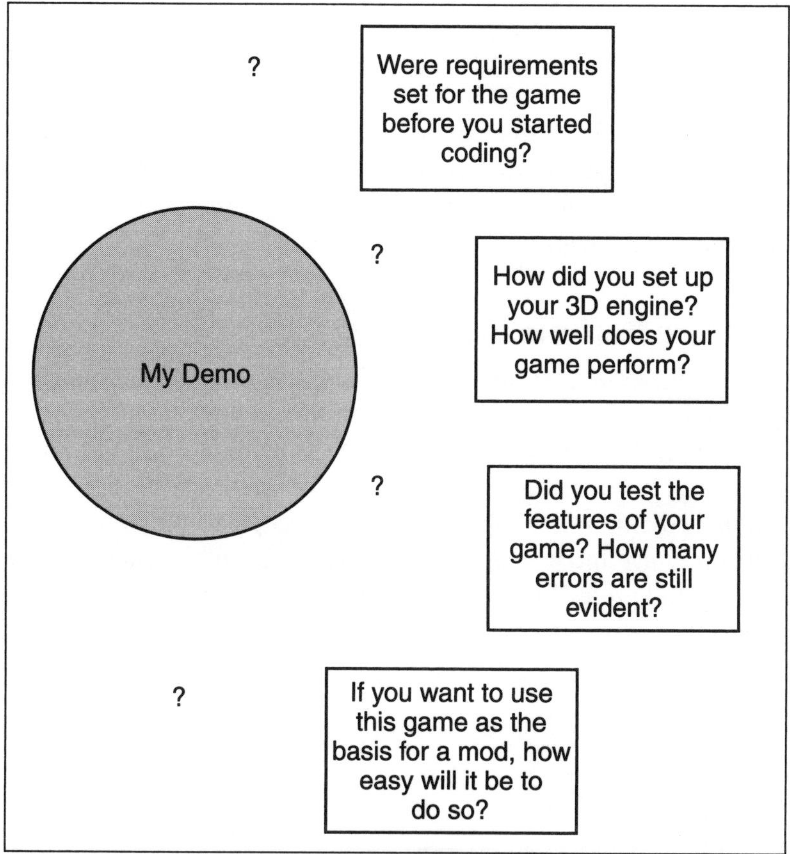

Figure 19.3
The core areas of software knowledge generalize the standard ways that games are evaluated.

Companies might someday look for licensed software engineers who are specialists in game development, just as certain hospitals look for doctors who are specialized in heart surgery or skin diseases. For now, however, it remains that those who evaluate your game look for evidence that you know about and apply knowledge that software engineering has formally established. Even as a software generalist, you stand to gain if you can think about the skills you possess in terms of the body of knowledge that such standards as the SWEBOK present.

note

As a compromise between licensing and nonlicensing, Microsoft, IBM, and Sun offer programs that enable you to earn certificates that verify you can develop products using their technologies.

A Challenge

Develop your skills as a software engineer involved in game development. If people want to talk about making software development (whether for games or otherwise) a privileged profession, let them. The reality is that game development has much more in common with art, craftsmanship, and best practices than it does with licensing. The industry rests on development teams that create winning products because they undertake their development effort as *craftsmen, artists, engineers,* and *professionals.*

Professionals as Craftsmen and Artists

There is much to be said for the argument that programming and the skills and practices associated with software engineering fall much more under the heading of *craft* than they do of *profession.* This argument has much merit, but at the same time, it should not be taken up as a battle cry against software engineering as a profession. Every profession is a formalized craft. A craft is a tradition that is characterized by people who manufacture a specific type of product and evolve and pass on a set of skills relating to this manufacture. Figure 19.4 shows how craft and profession tend to merge into a common understanding of how something is made.

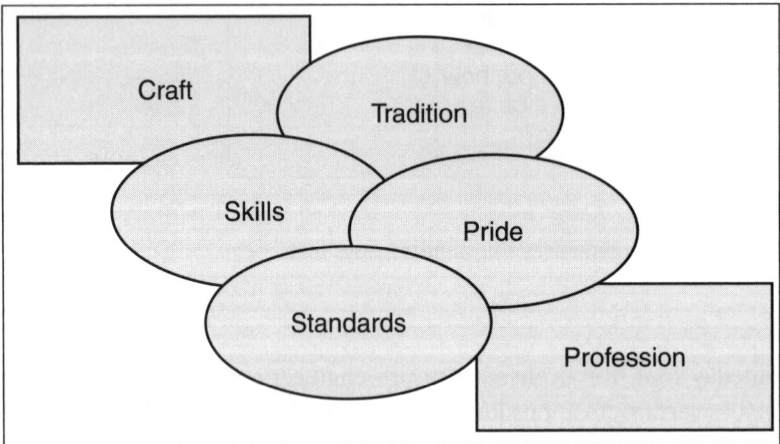

Figure 19.4
Craft and profession share common concepts.

Professional software engineering and craftsmanship involve knowing a core body of practices and using them effectively to create a given type of product. What you find at the center is a *style* of creation. How do you tell a sloppy hacker from an engineer or a craftsman? You look at the person's style of work.

Why software engineering and game development remain activities that can have both professional and craft characteristics might be better understood if a tentative analogy is drawn between the game and recording industries.

One route to the recording market might be said to follow the path of professionalism. Someone studies music for years in a conservatory or university. Eventually you find this person performing in an orchestra. Auditioning and landing a job for the orchestra requires the background that the conservatory provides. Still, every member of the orchestra, regardless of how rigorously trained, has a unique performance style.

Consider what happens when a new rock 'n' roll band or rap group forms. From the first, the musicians' activity centers on experimenting with and finding new ways to express lyrics, harmonies, and rhythms. Many successful rock and rap musicians do not learn to read music. It is unlikely that they have studied theory. They have learned largely by listening and playing. This can also be said of whole bands. Talented people begin making music together and discover their own style.

Style is the key. It is a discovery that allows all musicians—those trained classically and those not trained at all—to meet in a common place and produce something that recording studios readily buy from them.

This view of what makes a recording artist or orchestral musician lacks depth in many ways, but it still provides a model for what might be viewed as the typical ways that many software developers find their way to game companies. Formally trained, for example, as computer scientists, they might be hired to develop audio or graphical engines. On the other hand, entrepreneurs who have developed their own games might end up being what might be called technical folk artists.

Inertia and Innovation

Small groups of game developers begin developing games together. They discover a theme and a style. They might produce several games together and then find one so appealing that they want to try to market it to a mass audience. They go in search of a game publishing company. If a representative of the company finds their game appealing, the development group might be able to sell its game.

This is one business scenario among many, but it is one that might become much more common tomorrow than it is today. There are several reasons for anticipating such a future. One argument is based on large-scale economics (macroeconomics). It is much cheaper for a large company to allow smaller companies to undertake the risk of developing innovative products. Small companies can change or innovate much more readily than large companies.

A large company tends to be unable to do anything without involving a large number of people. This is referred to as *organizational inertia.* Large organizations do not change easily because when they change, they must do so in a multitude of ways. Small companies do not suffer from this problem. If a company has only five employees, for example, it is fairly easy for them to share knowledge and arrive at a common understanding of how to do things. The situation changes in an organization that consists of hundreds of people.

As Steve McConnell points out, large companies have learned the lesson that it is easier to buy than to internally generate innovation (McConnell, 108). They purchase companies that create innovative products and then merge the products with their existing product line. They absorb the innovative cultures of smaller, creative companies.

This business pattern is common to the film, recording, publishing, and game industries. In these industries, innovation is left to relatively small groups who can undertake the risks of innovation and creativity. Marketing and distribution responsibilities are assumed by the large organizations, which profit most when they invest substantial revenues in fixed, reliable techniques for selling and distributing new products. Figure 19.5 illustrates the flow of innovation from small to large.

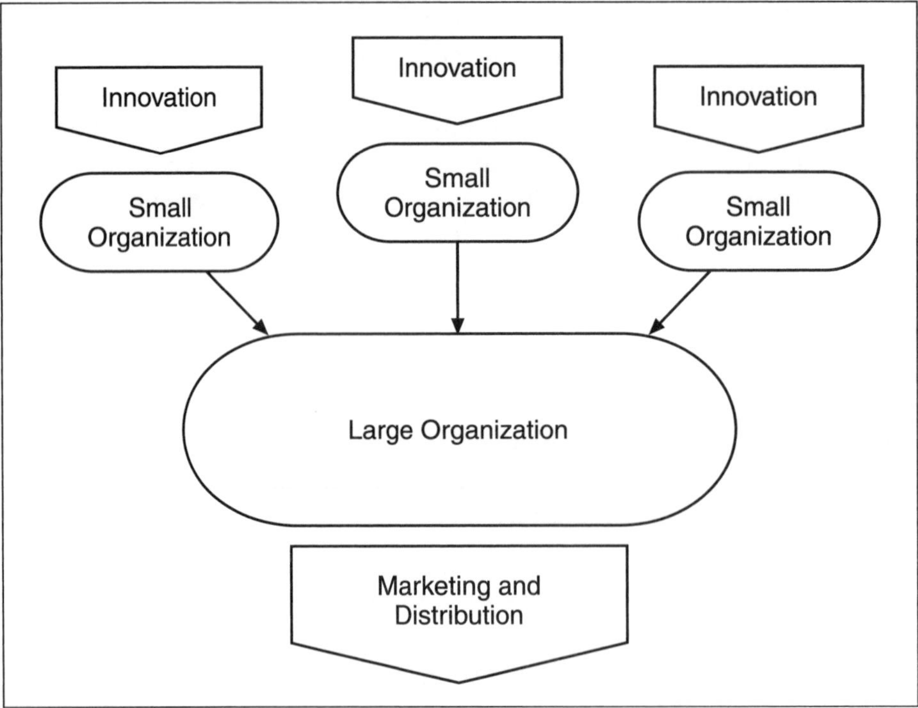

Figure 19.5
Small companies undertake the risk of innovation.

Two primary factors emerge as large organizations seek the products of small organizations. The first is whether the product really is an innovation. This is something you can worry about if you are a creative artist. The second is whether the product has been engineered or crafted so that the company that agrees to buy and market it does not find itself fighting consumer complaints and legal actions.

Finding Your Development Style

If large organizations purchase the products of small organizations, they are ultimately purchasing the product of the small organization's development style. Style is something that is a combination of creative innovation and established approaches to development. As was emphasized in the instance of the rock band, music is a product of a band's established way of making music. This style of making music is something that is attained only after endless practice and experimentation.

The same applies to the creation of a software product. On the one hand, a game that sells must be appealing to consumers. On the other hand, it must be designed and developed so that it performs well. The first part has to do with creativity. The second part has to do with engineering. One thing is clear—as with the construction of a bridge, without the engineering, the beauty of the creation means nothing. A beautiful bridge that collapses is not a beautiful bridge. It is a catastrophe. The same goes for anything that must be engineered, even a song. If the technique of the recording effort does not possess quality, the song will be destroyed. What applies to music and bridges applies to computer games.

Craft, Engineering, and Style

Software engineering involves putting in place the best practices for creating a software product. When you combine this with a culture that fosters the development of a specific type of product, what emerges is a style of development that can produce products that sell. A style of development refined through the inclusion and cultivation of the best practices that a craft or profession has to offer is more likely to render consistently superior products than one that does not. When people perform the same type of work over and over again and take time to reflect on what they are dong, they are almost always able to find ways to improve on what they do. Both craft and technology have their roots in this fundamental way of doing things.

Evolving Style

When you form a team that can develop innovative, attractive products, you lose everything you gain unless you have in place practices that allow you to understand, document, and improve your style of development. For this reason, putting in place the best practices of software engineering becomes essential to the success of your undertaking.

Best practices in software engineering fall into the 10 categories given in the SWEBOK scheme (see Figure 19.1). Most of this book is dedicated to a discussion of these categories. This book brings these practices into a context that allows you to understand that they are not so much rules or methods as they are conceptual guidelines for organizing or grouping what you discover as you engage in your development efforts.

Following best practices also provides a way that you can find for yourself how it is that you want to specialize your own skills. If you want to remain a software generalist—a craftsperson—all the better. Even then, when you test the code in a game, you will find it beneficial to be able to draw on the accumulated knowledge of testing that is available through the experiences that specialized software engineers have recorded. The same applies to other tasks. Commenting your code or setting up the file structure for your game classes benefits from the tools that specialists provide. An engineer, like a craftsperson, adopts tools to accord with the task to be completed. Style is characterized by the refinement of both the tools and the skills that apply to the tools. When these are in place, the quality of the product that results is much enhanced. Figure 19.6 shows how the specialized areas of knowledge associated with software engineering combine through skills and tools to become a comprehensive basis of craft or engineering style.

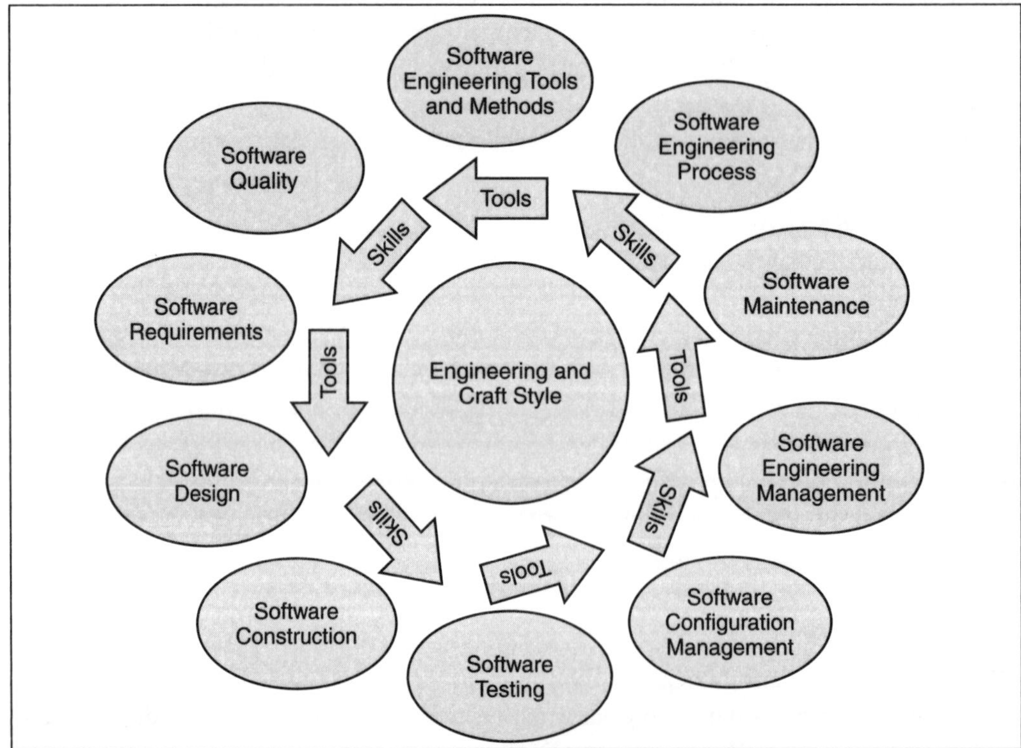

Figure 19.6
Craft or engineering style emerges from the establishment and refinement of tools and skills.

Large Companies Versus Small Companies

In a recent survey of the web, approximately 400 game development companies were advertising positions of employment. Some were small companies with a single product; others were large companies with many products and production budgets for single games that involved millions of U.S. dollars. Among the larger companies were the following:

- **Blizzard Entertainment.** Known for *WarCraft*, *Diablo*, *BlackThorne*, and *StarCraft*. Tends to advertise jobs with names like web designer, senior game master, game master, and technical support representative.
- **Id Software, Inc.** Known for *DOOM*, *Heretic*, *Hexen*, and *Quake*. Tends to advertise jobs with names like designer and programmer.
- **Electronic Arts (EA).** Known for *The Lord of the Rings: The Return of the King*, *NHL*, *Rugby*, *Tiger Woods PGA TOUR*, *Madden NFL*. Tends to advertise jobs with names like animation software engineer, game designer associate I, tester, and SW engineer II.
- **Sierra.** Known for *Empire Earth*, *Hobbit*, *Casino*, and *Metal Arms*. Tends to advertise jobs with names like software engineer, principal software engineer, and senior software engineer.
- **Activision.** Known for *Tony Hawk*, *Spider-Man*, and *True Crime*. Tends to advertise jobs with names like console tech programmer, gameplay programmer, and QA tester.
- **Rockstar.** Known for *Grand Theft Auto*, *Vice City*, *Midnight Club*, and *Max Payne*. Tends to advertise jobs with names like AL programmer, optimization programmer, animation programmer, serial PS2 programmer, and PS2 graphics programmer.
- **THQ.** Known for *Jimmy Neutron*, *Sonic*, and *Red Faction*. Tends to advertise jobs with names like quality assurance, testing, and customer service.

Group Specialization

A large game company can employ many hundreds of people grouped into specialized departments. The departments are organized into a hierarchy. Each department provides specialized services to other departments or directly to customers. The makeup of internal hierarchies varies greatly.

Large development or distribution companies usually support a *grid* or *matrix* structure in which departments or offices coordinate phases of development activity. Specialization within the grid is more pronounced than is possible with the fairly generalized structure of a small company. At a small company, each employee is likely to do a little of everything.

Project Orientation

In large companies, you are likely to be grouped with others who possess specializations that are similar to your own. For instance, as a programmer, you might be in the programming group. As a tester, you might be in the testing group. Each of these groups is likely to have a *line manager*, who is responsible for maintaining the group as a concentrated source of expertise for the organization.

When management decides to develop a new product, specialists from the various groups are assigned to a development team for the product. If the company simultaneously develops several products, several project teams will exist simultaneously, each under a separate *project manager*. Members of the team work on the product until they complete it. Upon completion of the product, the team members return to their respective line groups to wait for another assignment to another product. Figure 19.7 illustrates a limited matrix. In reality, an organizational matrix for a large game company includes representatives from many more groups.

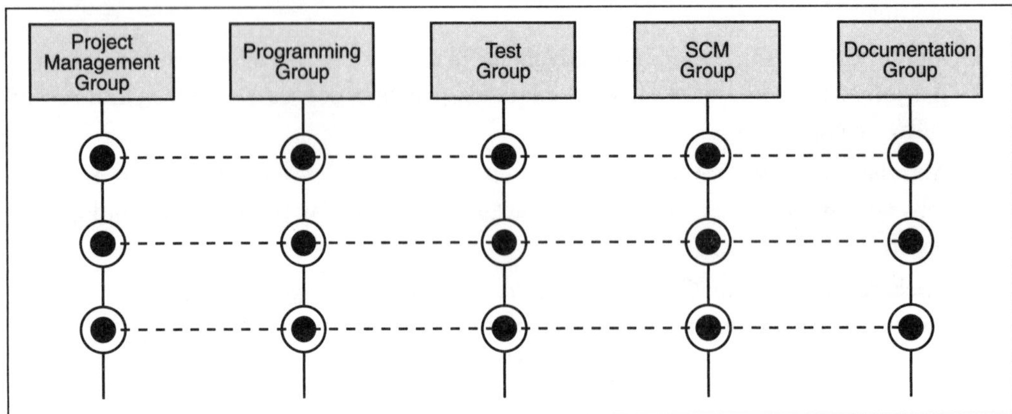

Figure 19.7
A limited view of a matrix organization shows how teams contribute experts to projects.

Working Within the Large Organizational Structure

Large companies require specialists. The larger the product group, the more you are likely to find specialized roles. Companies that are oriented toward marketing and distribution emphasize specialization in software testing and quality assurance. Companies that are oriented toward development specialize along most of the standard lines of software engineering, ranging from generic software engineer to tester and project manager. These divisions of labor are only a few among what might be dozens. Figure 19.8 shows a more extended organization chart. Each group consists of members who are specialized both within the general organization and within the group.

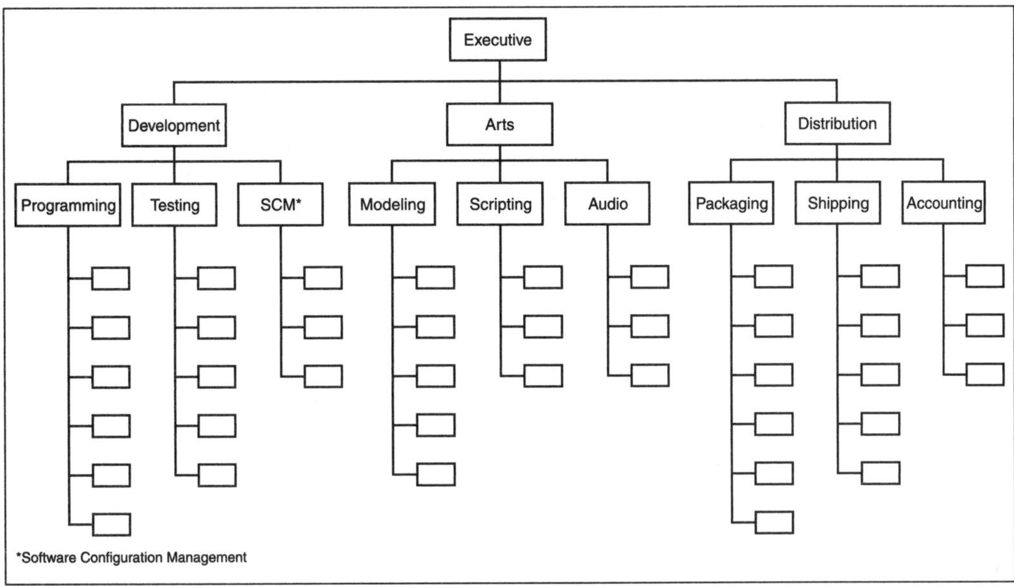

Figure 19.8
The organization fosters specialization within specializations.

The point of this discussion of specialization is not to leave you with the impression that what you do as a professional ultimately reduces to a narrow, boring set of repetitious tasks. Where interactive entertainment software is concerned, the current state of the industry is so dynamic that it is almost impossible that the work you do will be so reduced by specialization that it becomes repetitious or monotonous. Instead, the problem is that what you do can change so fast that you will be unable to keep up. For this reason, it is necessary to limit your activity to a realm that allows you to responsibly keep pace with changing techniques and technologies.

Seeking Core Knowledge

Chapter 15, "Team Work," covers team and individual job descriptions, so turn to those pages for further reading on such topics. With respect to generalized approaches to specialization, one thing offered here is the notion that even if you are careful to research the field and fully identify, for example, the types of knowledge that your work encompasses, you still have a great deal of searching to do within yourself.

The search begins with an understanding of the goals you have as an engineer or craftsman. Your ability to understand the product as a product is a good starting place. Developers sometimes immerse themselves in a technology that brings them no pleasure after a time. They discover they have invested their time and effort, not in learning how to create a product, but in using a tool. They have mistaken the means for the end.

Not mistaking the means for the end involves trying to make your newfound knowledge an extension of the core knowledge area that you have decided to develop as your specialization. Core knowledge is knowledge that is not wholly dependent on a particular application or technology. It is often necessary to retreat from the fascination you feel toward a given technology to reflect that any given tool manifests only a temporary application of technology. Knowledge that can be transferred from one tool, programming language, or application to another is more valuable to you than knowledge that lives and dies with the context in which it is discovered.

How to Learn

Learning can be characterized as a pattern of assimilating knowledge in a progressive, incremental way. The result is that things are known in greater detail and greater generality. Inductively, people collect details until they discern a general pattern. Deductively, people start with a general pattern and use it to discern details. The two tendencies are brought together through analysis and synthesis. Analysis takes things apart, and synthesis puts them together (see Figure 19.9).

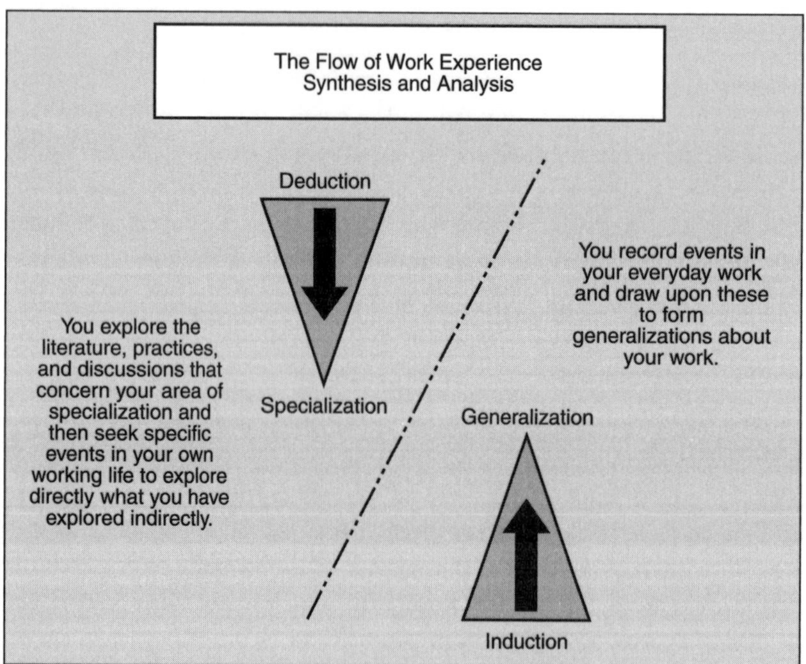

Figure 19.9
Information flows in from general to specific and from specific to general.

The flow of information that is characterized by synthesis and analysis provides the basis for a discussion of an activity that goes under the headings of *process improvement, quality improvement,* or *craft perfection.* The activity name matters little. What is designated is the activity of learning how to learn. Every time you learn something, two things happen: You acquire a bit of knowledge or a new skill, and you equip yourself to learn something beyond what you have just learned.

The practical manifestation of all of this discussion is that individuals and organizations tend to grow or decline according to whether they sustain both the capacity to learn and the capacity to learn how to learn. The two capacities go hand in hand. General rules must influence specific events, and specific events must give shape to general rules.

Learning Paths

Software engineering brings with it what might be viewed as a prescribed path of development. On the level of the individual software engineer, this is a *career path.* On an organizational level, this is sometimes called an organizational *maturity level.*

Career Paths

A career path is something that most people associate with promotion and increased responsibility. In the software engineering industry, two models prevail. One is based on professional development, and the other is based on a model established over the centuries through craft guilds. Despite long debates over which is best, both offer the same general characteristics. People begin working in a given situation that fosters a given style of work. They must observe the style and develop their own at the same time. As their style of work matures, they are entrusted with greater responsibilities. Eventually, they are entrusted with sustaining and applying the style. After still more time, they are entrusted with the power to actually change the style. Table 19.1 shows the stages of development in professional and craft settings.

Table 19.1 Career Paths

Professional/ Craft Careers	Description
Intern/ Apprentice	Entering the profession. Minimal responsibilities. Expected to perform specific tasks under the direction of a staff developer. Learn how to learn.
Staff/Journeyman	Entrusted with the use of tools and the development of products within the framework provided by the style or framework of the organization.
Senior/Master	Sets the standard for how work is to be done and how products are to be created.

Sources: Steve McConnell, *Professional Software Development* (New York: Addison-Wesley, 2004), pp. 148–149; Pete McBreen, *Software Craftsmanship* (New York: Addison-Wesley, 2004), pp. 81–83.

Table 19.1 reveals that, whereas an apprentice is generally taught how to learn, a journeyman or staff engineer is assumed to know how to learn. The journeyman or staff engineer is assumed to be self-directed and competent to perform standard engineering tasks. On the other hand, the journeyman or staff engineer does not ultimately determine the style of what is to be learned. It is assumed that he or she works within the style of the organization—in addition to working within a tradition or culture of knowledge. At the most mature level, the senior engineer or master developer exerts the strongest influence, for this person can, to an extent, decide what counts as knowledge and how the tradition is defined. This person is a model for others. The senior engineer or master developer tends to be recognized as someone who knows how to spot, approach, and solve problems. This person can also render judgments concerning who receives recognition for superior work. At the most mature level, the culture or craft is *created*.

note

Job titles reflect a company's organizational style. You might see jobs titles such as junior software engineer, software engineer I, software engineer II, staff engineer, and principal engineer. You might also see fun titles, such as game apprentice, game crafter, game master, and game wizard. The variety reflects sensitivity to the growth of individual capabilities that the culture of the company fosters. The three levels shown in Table 19.1 represent a general model into which these other rankings readily fit.

Both the professional and craft models enable you to follow a path of personal development and set no absolute criteria for who can develop software. Roughly 40 percent of those who work in software development either do not possess college degrees or possess degrees in areas other than computer science or software engineering. Generally, however, most people who become computer programmers or software engineers obtain college degrees before they start their careers. After that, although they might move from organization to organization, they carry their strengths and experiences with them. What is important is that regardless of where you start, as you move along your career path, your skills continuously increase through work and study. Figure 19.10 illustrates some of the growth possibilities that are open to game software developers. (For game developer roles, see Marc Mencher, *Get in the Game!* (Boston: New Riders, 2003), pp. 63–92.)

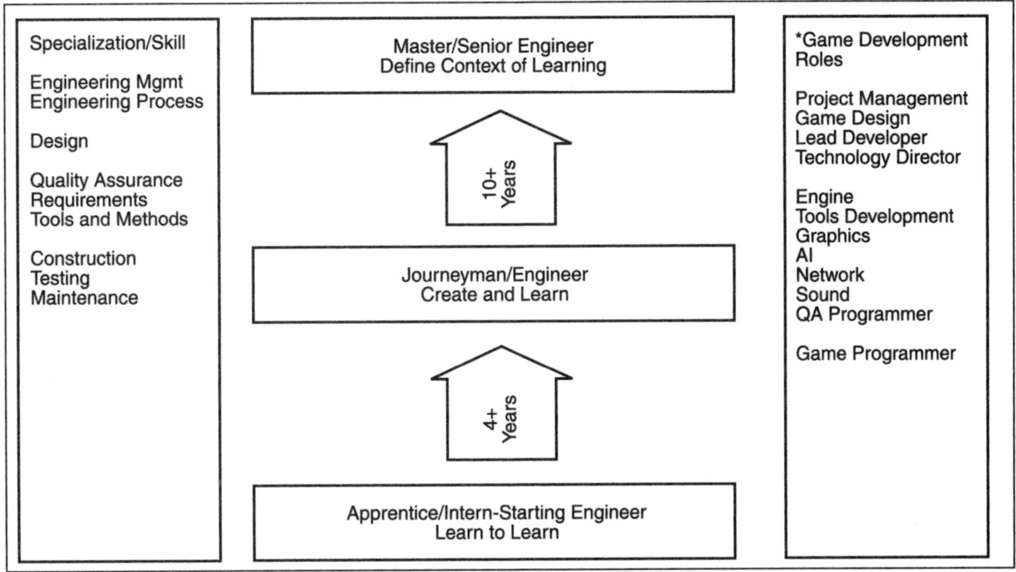

Figure 19.10
A career path exists for those who are willing to learn.

Maturity Levels in Organizations

Chapter 16, "Process Improvement," provides a detailed discussion of how you can create a maturity model within your organization; therefore, this chapter does not dwell on that topic. Instead, this chapter concentrates on how the maturity level of the game development company you work for can affect your career as a software engineer.

Quality assurance specialists usually judge organizational maturity according to the Capability Maturity Model (CMM), which was developed during the late 1980s in response to a U.S. Defense Department initiative that required U.S. government defense contractors to demonstrate that they applied consistent quality assurance measures to their software engineering processes. Like so many things that originate with military contracts (such as the first digital computer), software development processes characterize companies other than defense contractors. Experts use the CMM as a standard for determining the extent to which any software company can engineer a product. Central to this determination is whether a company can apply the same engineering processes to all products that it creates.

Subjective Views—Immature

Figure 19.11 illustrates what might be viewed as a subjective perspective on what the CMM means to you as a developer. At the lowest level, Level 1, the work you do is completely individualized and informal. Such a company is likely to be small, having less than

30 employees. You might find the work either exceptionally rewarding or extremely trying, depending on how enlightened the lead developers are about the sensitivities of others. If the company is mismanaged, it will be little more than a sweatshop.

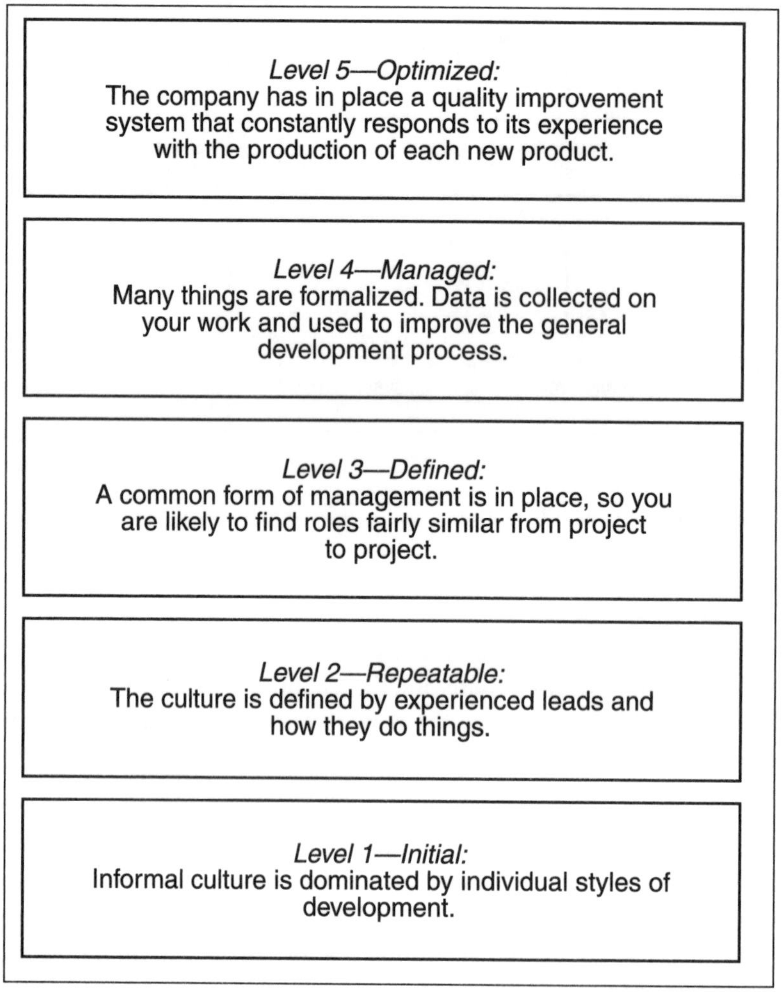

Level 5—Optimized:
The company has in place a quality improvement system that constantly responds to its experience with the production of each new product.

Level 4—Managed:
Many things are formalized. Data is collected on your work and used to improve the general development process.

Level 3—Defined:
A common form of management is in place, so you are likely to find roles fairly similar from project to project.

Level 2—Repeatable:
The culture is defined by experienced leads and how they do things.

Level 1—Initial:
Informal culture is dominated by individual styles of development.

Figure 19.11
You can evaluate the CMM levels of maturity subjectively.

Even if Level 1 managers manage their organization competently, you stand little chance of professional or craft development unless the managers possess a vision that includes helping you to advance your skills and understanding. Chances are, you will work long hours, the product you create might be of questionable quality, and the company might abandon the project you work on due to lateness or cost overruns. On the other hand, if an exceptional master craftsman or senior engineer drives the development style of the company, you might find that such a company brings you the most rewarding experiences of your professional life.

Subjective Views—Mature

You can see in Figure 19.11 that the Level 3 company provides what might be called consistent, across-the-board project management. The U.S. Defense Department requires that the companies with which it does business possess Level 3 maturity. Such a company might not be very large, but it will have a process in place that allows it to show its customers how it produces products. In other words, it will have a *documented style* of software engineering or craftsmanship. (Again, Chapter 16 examines this topic in greater detail.)

A Level 3 company is likely to provide what is known as a *technical ladder* of advancement for its software engineers. This is good for you. Such a company recognizes that its employees can grow as professionals. The company might pay you to attend classes. It might compensate you when you buy books related to your work. It rewards you through bonuses for writing papers or participating in professional activities in other ways.

Finding a Place to Learn

Figure 19.11 shows that a company you work for can hinder or foster your development as a software engineer. Level 1 maturity has characterized the majority of companies in the game industry. The results have been fairly striking. Consider, for example, that in a given year, approximately 3,000 commercially viable games might be produced. Of these, less than 300 are likely to make it to the market. Even when games are successful, the companies that produce them often face bankruptcy due to mismanagement of the resulting profits and the inability to sustain consistent game development efforts.

When companies fail to put in place a style of development that involves learning how to learn, they usually fail. On the other hand, when software engineers do not adopt a career trajectory that involves continuous professional growth, they, also, face a dead end.

In light of this reality, the concept of core knowledge is important. As a game developer, you might find it easy to view yourself as a generalist. In most cases, your first job is likely to be for a small company where you are forced to be a generalist. But at the same time, you can examine whatever task you are given according to how it fits into the core set of skills in the SWEBOK documents. You can then find formalized knowledge about what you are doing and incorporate it into your work so that you improve your skills. Finding a way to do something differs from finding an *informed* way to do things. Using the latter approach, you produce a better product because you build on the expertise that others provide. Your capacity and willingness to derive and share knowledge with others forms the basis of your advancement as a software engineer or software craftsman.

Specialization

If you look again at Figure 19.10, you can see that a distinction exists between a job description and an area of formalized knowledge. Figure 19.6 illustrates areas of knowledge, and Figure 19.10 lists job titles, such as AI programmer, graphics programmer, and so on. The two representations reveal that the knowledge you acquire represents a subset of the knowledge that characterizes a given area of knowledge. Your knowledge is *specialized.*

Specialization has different flavors. On the one hand, your skills are always specialized to some extent because you necessarily have to concentrate your energies on the project at hand, which involves completing a specific and limited set of tasks. At a harsh extreme, this form of specialization can reduce your life to a set of mind-numbing tasks. On the other hand, when you repeatedly perform the same type of work and take time to inform yourself about the best practices that apply to work you perform, you specialize your skills because you perfect them. Less redundancy and fewer errors characterize your work, and generally your work represents the application of not simply knowledge of how to do something but knowledge of the best practices pertaining to what you do. This form of specialization can be highly rewarding.

If you go to work for a company that is immature, you might find few people who possess specialization. The chance for individuals to develop specialization might not exist. Tasks might be distributed randomly. Styles of development differ from project to project. Things are done in a relatively unrefined, inefficient way, and no standard exists to show how things might be improved. In contrast, other companies might move in the direction of imposing too much rigidity, so that even though you perfect your skills, you are forced into a narrow corridor in which you cannot work creatively. It becomes important, then, to discover the settings and conditions that foster creative specialization.

Methodology

In the word *methodology,* the root *ology* implies a type of study, and the implication is that methodology is the study of methods people use to accomplish tasks. The purpose of methodological studies is to reduce random work routines to efficient procedures. The result is that people are supposedly able to pick up a manual, follow the procedure that the manual provides, and finish their work with less stress and greater efficiency than would be possible otherwise.

Good Methodology

In some cases, the type of work performed might justify the use of methodological studies and manuals containing procedures. One example is aircraft maintenance. For aircraft mechanics, thick manuals contain the procedures for performing almost any imaginable task that the maintenance of an aircraft requires. Unless you have repaired aircraft for a living, you might not realize just how intensively procedure-oriented such work tends to be. Such manuals prescribe, for instance, precisely how much a screw must be tightened and the order in which screws holding a wing panel on are to be removed. Failure to observe the procedures precisely results in dire consequences.

The fact that stringent methodological studies and their resulting tombs of procedures govern aircraft maintenance might bring you a degree of comfort the next time you sit aboard a jet waiting for takeoff. Clearly, certain areas of human activity call for strict procedural control.

Bad Methodology

If the mechanics who maintain aircraft follow strict procedures and the entire industry of aircraft maintenance is predicated on uncompromising methodological accuracy, it remains that all types of work do not follow the same pattern. Software engineering related to game development, for example, involves a different type of work and a different set of objectives. If an aircraft mechanic does not tighten a screw properly, the plane might crash an hour later. There is no room for flexibility or experimentation. This is not the case with game development.

Flexible, individualized development styles typify game software craft and engineering. The software developer who is involved in creating a game is creating or engineering a unique product. The game is likely to be a boring clone of some other game unless the development style of the developer and the company that employs the developer foster flexibility. Flexibility on individualized and organizational levels involves freedom to explore options, to challenge assumptions, and to reject or adapt old techniques. Bad methodology stifles flexibility.

A famous indictment of bad methodology appears in a book by Tom DeMarco and Timothy Lister, *Peopleware.* (See the reference to this book at the end of the chapter.) DeMarco and Lister argue that bad methodology in software development is *authoritarian.* Authoritarian methodology is spelled with a large *m—Methodology.* Authoritarian methodologies *prescribe* and *dictate.* Rather than a guide to performing work, such a methodology discourages individualized and organizational flexibility and instead demands that everyone does everything according to the book, even if it makes no sense to do so.

This is a type of impractical, unjustifiable methodology that probably even aircraft mechanics would object to. The justification for objecting is fairly easy to understand. Software engineering, for one thing, solves problems. To solve a problem is to apply original thinking to a problem. The kind of original thinking needed to solve software engineering problems cannot be found in a Methodology.

What Goes Wrong

Methodologies go wrong under a number of conditions. Consider the following scenarios:

- **Fake Methodologies.** A development company wants to lure venture capital. The executive group looks at the software and the software developers and decides that the venture capitalists will be much more likely to increase their investments if it *looks like* the company has a methodology. The executive group contracts the services of a company that specializes in creating Methodologies. The Methodology contractors arrive, lay out a *Methodology*, train everyone in the company to use some words that make it sound as though the company does, indeed, follow the Methodology, and depart before the venture capitalists arrive. Of course, the software developers consider it all a joke, but in the name of keeping their jobs, they *act as though* they have a methodology.
- **Authoritarian Methodologies.** Some smart, articulate software development or software engineering specialists decide that they have studied all the existing methodologies and find them all authoritarian, ineffective, and generally objectionable. To remedy the situation, they create a methodology of their own, one that is just as authoritarian, ineffective, and generally objectionable as those they reject. The difference is that the one they offer is new and their own.
- **Misdirected Methodologies.** A group of managers and senior engineers who have the best of intentions writes a process guide. They do this in a responsible way. They contact the senior people in the engineering or development groups and ask them to write or describe how best to accomplish common tasks. They try to find only things that are *proven* to be effective. After a year or so, the resulting process guide takes on a life of its own, and instead of *consulting* it to find out how others have done things, people begin using it to *enforce* ways of doing things.

Workable Methods

Methods that work are, as Demarco and Lister point out, *suggested* and *proven* ways of doing things. You might be aware of a set of books generically known as *problem solvers.* Such books provide hundreds of standard, solved problems. You find a problem similar to the one you seek to solve. You use the solved problem as a pattern. The authors of the problem solver assume that you will creatively alter their solution to arrive at the solution you require. This is a workable method.

The key point is that you alter the recommended method to accord with your needs, and if you find no method that accords with your needs, you are free to search for a solution on your own. No set solution is enforced. Figure 19.12 illustrates a workable approach to using methodologies.

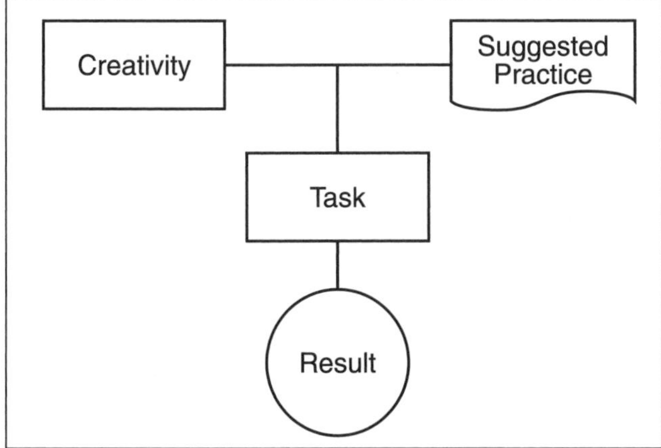

Figure 19.12
Workable methods are suggested best practices—flexible but proven approaches to solving problems.

Growth Patterns

The terms *iterative* and *incremental* can be applied to both product and professional development. The item of most importance is the primary pattern—the spiral. As a software engineering model of development, the spiral model goes back several decades to an article written by B. W. Boehm (see the citation for Figure 19.13). As a model for personal growth, the spiral goes back much further, probably well into antiquity. Figure 19.13 shows a rough spiral with the labels that Boehm applied. (See B. W. Boehm, "A Spiral Model of Software Development and Enhancement," *IEEE Computer* 21 [May 1988], pp. 61–72; Stephen R. Schach, *Object-Oriented and Classical Software Engineering*, 5th Edition [New York: McGraw-Hill, 2002], p. 81.)

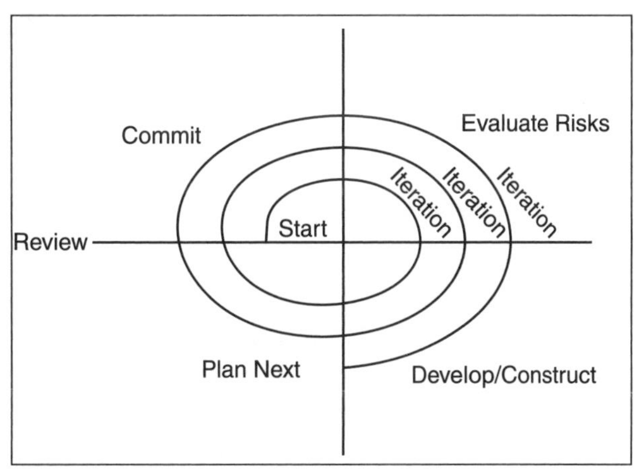

Figure 19.13
A spiral provides a pattern for development.

Working Metaphors

The spiral has long been used as a way to illustrate one version of how software engineering happens. At the same time, it can be used to illustrate a path to professional growth if you are a software engineer involved in game development. The spiral serves so well to illustrate processes of growth because it provides a rich visual metaphor for how people often negotiate the stress that change presents. Divided into quadrants, the spiral illustrates two things. The spiral itself illustrates iteration—repeated, gradually more encompassing revisions of a product. The quadrants illustrate incremental development, which involves planning iterations after evaluating the risks that each iterative effort poses.

When you view the development process as iterative and incremental, you place yourself in a position to select goals that you are most likely to achieve. When you plan iterations as incremental parts of a whole, you are in a much better position than otherwise to anticipate complexity and take measures to ensure that it does not become overwhelming.

As odd as it might sound, developing your own career in an incremental and iterative fashion makes a great deal of sense. In an industry in which products are often produced one after another and schedules tend to be characterized by long hours that often make it nearly impossible to learn new things, it is important to structure change so that it is continuous and yet not so demanding as to be counterproductive. To improve your knowledge of new technology, for instance, you might have to attend a conference or acquire and explore a new class library. If your company pays the costs, all the better. But it might be that you will have to attend to these costs on your own.

Incremental development implies that you put some things aside. Time allows only so much effort. You must select what is most important. Iteration implies that you do something over and over again. Leaning is just this type of activity. You do it over and over again, but you change and expand the areas you seek to know. Some areas are transient. Others endure for decades. Whether an area of interest persists, grows, or diminishes depends on what you view as important.

To perform an activity incrementally implies that rather than doing something from start to finish in a grand way, you start out in a careful way, take time to determine what you can and cannot do, plan your activity, and then execute your plan. What you determine you want to learn can be drawn from your work experiences in light of what you know about the core areas of knowledge that define your field. What you put aside can be regarded as material that is tentatively scheduled for future learning. Figure 19.14 illustrates the basic cycle of decisions.

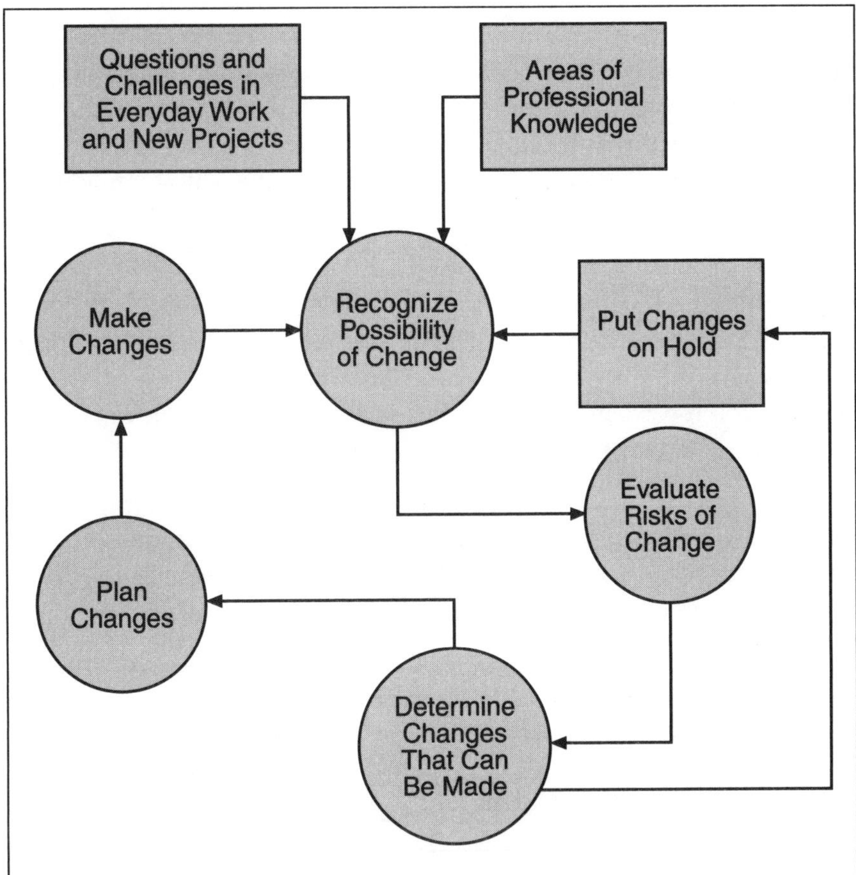

Figure 19.14
You can incrementally and iteratively plan growth in your basic skill profile.

Taking It Seriously

The game industry's down side is the number of situations in which companies that possess minimal organizational maturity produce products on a last-minute, fix-and-compile basis. Those who are involved in such products, although energetic and dedicated, end up working long hours. They become good at their jobs, but they are often afforded few opportunities to expand and enrich their basic skills set.

This pattern characterizes many areas of the software industry. The game development industry is relatively young and immature. Only within the past few years have "game studies" become visible in academic circles. If the typical pattern emerges, specialization will prevail more and more, and those who remain software generalists in game studies will then be at a disadvantage to those who have taken matters seriously and become experts in a limited, well-focused body of knowledge and practice.

Ethics

Ethics is not so much a set of procedures, methods, laws, dictates, or rules as it is a capacity to think about right and wrong. One reward of placing game development in the context of software engineering is that you can then draw upon a well-established body of ethical literature relating to software technology as you consider the ethical implications of what you do.

The IEEE/ACM Code of Ethics

In conjunction with the IEEE, the ACM publishes on the web the *Software Engineering Code of Ethics and Professional Practice* (http://www.acm.org/serving/se/code.htm). The complete text of the *Code* is too extensive to reproduce here, but the Preamble can be presented readily and offers an excellent summary of the main topics:

> *Software engineers shall commit themselves to making the analysis, specification, design, development, testing, and maintenance of software a beneficial and respected profession. In accordance with their commitment to the health, safety, and welfare of the public, software engineers shall adhere to the following eight principles:*
>
> 1. ***PUBLIC.*** *Software engineers shall act consistently with the public interest.*
> 2. ***CLIENT AND EMPLOYER.*** *Software engineers shall act in a manner that is in the best interests of their client and employer consistent with the public interest.*
> 3. ***PRODUCT.*** *Software engineers shall ensure that their products and related modifications meet the highest professional standards possible.*
> 4. ***JUDGMENT.*** *Software engineers shall maintain integrity and independence in their professional judgment.*
> 5. ***MANAGEMENT.*** *Software engineering managers and leaders shall subscribe to and promote an ethical approach to the management of software development and maintenance.*
> 6. ***PROFESSION.*** *Software engineers shall advance the integrity and reputation of the profession consistent with the public interest.*
> 7. ***COLLEAGUES.*** *Software engineers shall be fair to and supportive of their colleagues.*
> 8. ***SELF.*** *Software engineers shall participate in lifelong learning regarding the practice of their profession and shall promote an ethical approach to the practice of the profession.*

Applied Ethics

In the game industry, nothing quite as formalized as the ACM/IEEE *Code* has been published yet. Discussions over ethics usually tend to drift toward topics such as violence, sexism, and intellectual property rights. With respect to the development of a general perspective on the game industry, such discussions are fruitful. On the other hand, developing a perspective on a set of ethical perspectives that can guide you as you go to work each day requires a focus more along the lines of the ACM/IEEE *Code*. Figure 19.15 illustrates how the general ethical categories laid out in the *Code* can provide a fairly straightforward guide for orienting yourself in the workplace. The categories enable you to be conscious of yourself, your society, and your profession. Note the following:

- **Public.** The obligation here is not to the buyer of your products or services but rather to the general public, which in so many words, you serve, as a craftsman and professional, whether paid or not.
- **Client and Employer.** Here you are paid for your work, and you have an ethical obligation to ensure that those who pay you receive quality work.
- **Product.** Consider that as a craftsman or a professional, your work always results in a product. You have an obligation to know what counts as a quality product. You have an obligation to know what tools and skills result in quality products.
- **Judgment.** The notion here is that you are able to make decisions in light of what you know about engineering or craft. The implication is that not everything is formalized. Because you possess expertise, you can in essence determine for yourself when something is not right.
- **Management.** You do, after all, have a career path, one that might eventually lead you to a leadership position.
- **Profession.** The profession is the collection of essential skills, core knowledge, and associations with others that allows you to understand and perform your work.
- **Colleagues.** You have responsibilities toward those with whom you work to help them do the best job they can.
- **Self.** The notion of "lifetime learning" is central. As a craftsman or professional, you impose upon yourself the obligation to acquire new knowledge on a continuing basis.

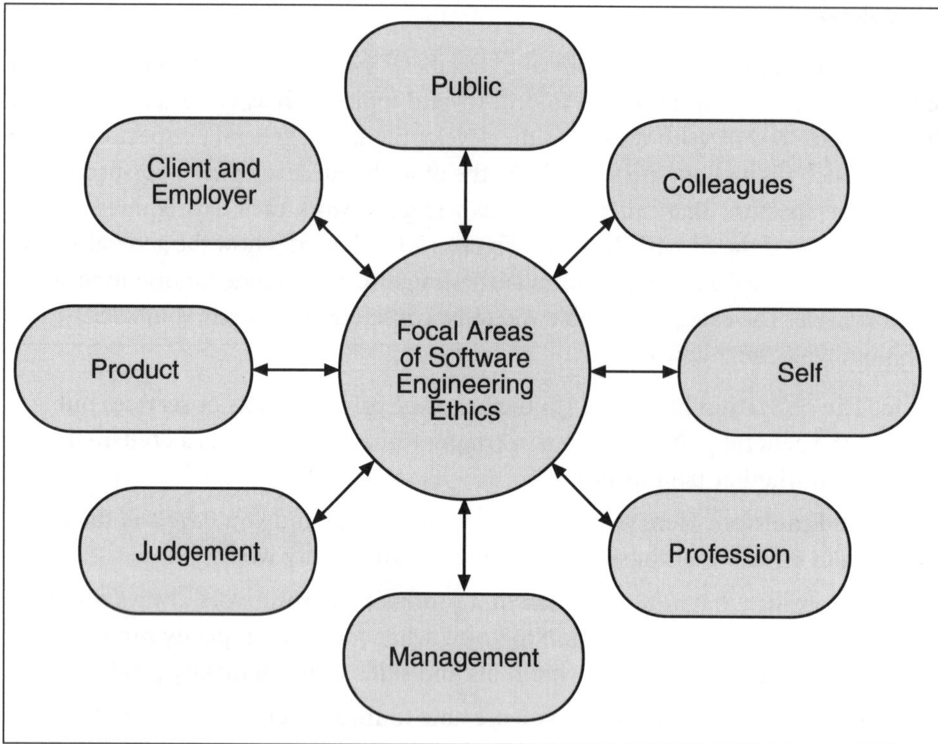

Figure 19.15
The IEEE/ACM categories of ethical concerns encourage you to view all implications of what you do as a software developer.

Social Implications

You can acquire software engineering knowledge from any number of sources. Because game development has fairly extensive social consequences, you might want to keep current on the debates that define what software engineers think about the use and abuse of software. An excellent source for such information is an association titled Computer Professionals for Social Responsibility (CPSR). Experts say that game development as an industry will soon rival movies and records. The social implications are enormous. Despite the fruitful and frequent debates to be found on the IGDA and other industry sites, it does not hurt to explore sources outside the specific industry contexts. The CPSP is one such option. (For more information, go to http://www.cpsr.org/.)

Satisfaction with Work

The topic of ethics has both personal and public dimensions. Generally, when people talk about the "work ethic," they refer to a person's ability to commit to a task and to take pride in the product of work. It might seem almost absurd to think about anyone working in the game development industry who does not have a strong commitment to the work, but like any other area of the software industry, it happens. In fact, the number of derailed and failed projects in game development is at par with the rest of the software industry. People become embroiled in conflicts, professionalism goes out the window, craft tumbles into the gutter, and reputations and profits diminish.

The bearing of such concerns on career and craft potentials is enormous. Chapter 15 examines the importance of team dynamics in software engineering. Here the topic centers on how you regard your own work and what goals you might include in an ethical profile of what you expect to encounter as a working professional.

You tend to find what you look for. If you go to work with a strong sense of purpose, you are likely to derive more satisfaction from your work than if you simply expect to put in time and pick up a check. The work ethic plays a role in this game.

Workflows

A workflow is a technical diagram that shows how a series of tasks unified by a single goal are connected. This section, however, derives its heading in part from a book by Mihaly Csikszentmihalyi (pronounced *chick-sent-me-high-ee*) entitled *Flow*. *Flow* is both the title of the book and another word for what Csikszentmihalyi calls "optimal experience." Csikszentmihalyi describes optimal experience as "a deep sense of enjoyment that is long cherished and that is a landmark in memory for what life should be like" (Csikszentmihalyi , 3). The relevance of this concept to the work of software engineering cannot be stressed enough. Consider the following passage from *Flow*:

> The optimal state of inner experience is one in which there is order in consciousness. This happens when psychic energy—or attention—is invested in realistic goals, and when skills match the opportunities for action. The pursuit of a goal brings order in awareness because a person must concentrate attention on the task at hand and momentarily forget everything else. These periods of struggling to overcome challenges are what people find to be the most enjoyable times of their lives... (Csikszentmihalyi, 6)

The relevance of such discussion to software engineering becomes clear when a list of what might be called the *conditions* of optimal experience is considered. Table 19.2 provides a summary of the conditions as interpreted in the context of work.

Table 19.2 Optimal Experience in Work*

Quality	Description
Ability	The tasks you face are tasks that you have the ability to complete.
Concentration	You are allowed to concentrate without disturbance on the task or work that you are involved in.
Understanding	The task has goals that you clearly understand.
Feedback	The task provides you with immediate feedback.
Lack of pressures	You are able to perform your work without having to worry at the same time about problems or pressures that exist in other areas of your life.
Control	You have a sense that you are in control of your actions.
Selfless	While you are at work, you are not involved in thoughts about yourself. Your work absorbs your attention.
Timelessness	The sense of time vanishes.

*See Csikszentmihalyi, p. 49.

Parallel Paths

The objective here is not to insist that it is important to follow any specific psychological formula for achieving satisfaction with work. Rather, the goal is to emphasize that, given a model of the type that Csikszentmihalyi has created, it becomes possible to understand why following a professional career path within the context of a body of knowledge similar to what, for example, the SWEBOK provides, offers a means of continual growth and satisfaction for a software engineer, a software craftsperson, or a software developer. Even if visions of what professionalism means differ, a *community* that is characterized by an applied technology has been created, and from this arises the opportunity for you to enjoy a life-long opportunity to build a unified set of skills that can bring you ongoing satisfaction with your work. Crucial in this undertaking is the effort you make to create the conditions of your own success. To a great degree, this depends not so much on *where* you work as *how*. Table 19.3 recasts the topics that Csikszentmihalyi offers as objectives that you might establish for yourself as you seek work as a game developer.

Table 19.3 Software Work Recast

Quality	Work Optimization Objective
Ability	Seek work for which you are properly prepared. In other words, to paraphrase Socrates, do not contend to know what you do not know, and do not assume that getting the job qualifies you to do it.
Concentration	Find an employer who allows you to do what you can do in a focused, concerted effort that leads to a visible and valued contribution to the product.
Understanding	If you do not possess a job description, understand for yourself what you are seeking to derive from your work. Know, likewise, what specific contribution you are expected to make.
Feedback	Learn to give and accept constructive criticism. It is probably safe to say that anything done in an engineering environment either requires or benefits from review.
Lack of pressures	Obviously, if external factors are disrupting your ability to work, you need to do something to free your mind. At the very least, if your problems are endangering the project, seek out your manager and make some explanations.
Control	Find roles in which you are respected as a professional. As a professional, your employer knows you can be expected to perform work on your own initiative and produce products that accord with industry standards.
Selfless	When you work as a professional, the service you provide or the product you develop is something that stands apart from you and on its own. Find work that allows you to feel as though you are part of something that possesses value beyond whatever it represents to you as a means to a paycheck, greater prestige, or organizational advancement.
Timelessness	When it seems like work, something is wrong. When you like your work, you do not watch the clock.

*See Csikszentmihalyi, p. 49.

Information and Publications

Game development is an application of software engineering. As in the development of telecommunications, banking, or stock portfolio management software, the *domain* of game development has become complex and specialized. Specialization leads to the need to customize generic processes. This section is intended as a starting place if you want to begin examining some of the more visible sources of information on software engineering.

IEEE and Software Engineering Publications

Even if your work concentrates specifically on games, you can still find an abundance of valuable information in IEEE publications.

For example, you might want to subscribe to *IEEE Computer Graphics and Applications* (http://computers.org/cga). This publication addresses hardware, software, and systems relating to graphics.

For the generalist, the IEEE publishes *Computer.* This magazine features articles on almost any topic related to computer science or software engineering. The articles often focus on the state of the industry and feature perspectives provided by prominent panelists (http://computer.org/computer).

An organization that caters to research in animation and interactive software is the Association for Computing Machinery (ACM) SIGGRAPH (go to http://www.siggraph.org).

For reading that relates specifically to software engineering, you can acquire *IEEE Software* (http://computer.org/software).

A commercial publication that provides information that is often of value to software engineers is *Software Development* (http://www.sdmagazine.com). Unlike the IEEE publications, this magazine tends to reflect the perspective of the editor. This might be considered the publication's strong point.

Game Development Information

Although software engineering practices tend to receive limited formal discussion on commercial sites that focus specifically on game development, it is still possible to find information that supplements your study and practice of software engineering. The following list provides a few of the many sites currently in existence:

- **The International Game Development Association (IGDA).** The IGDA is the closest thing to the IEEE in the game development world. It has a heavy academic streak, but at the same time, it represents the core community of industrial game developers (http://www.igda.org).
- **Game Development Search Engine.** This site provides you with links to all the basics, such as code, jobs, and industry trends (http://www.gdse.com).
- **Gamasutra.** This site offers information on all areas of game development. It is more reserved and focused than other commercially oriented sites. It is definitely geared toward professional game developers (http://www.gamasutra.com).
- **GameDev.** A tremendous store of reading is available on this site. The site is heavily commercialized, but it provides solid, current information (http://www.gamedev.net).
- ***Game Developer's Market Guide.*** One last mention in this list is a text by Bob Bates. This is a general guide to all the major forces in the industry.

There are, of course, hundreds of excellent sources of information in print and on the web that you can establish as your own data store for facts and ideas.

Academic Publications

Two academic publications exclusively address game development topics.

The first is *Game Studies.* The articles don't always focus on engineering issues, but they are well researched and sometimes cover development topics (http://www.gamestudies.org/).

The *Journal of Game Development* is a recent addition and promises to be more oriented than *Game Studies* toward technical implementation issues (http://www.jogd.com/).

Conclusion

Such philosophy as this chapter presents it focuses on how you orient yourself as a software engineer in relation to the forces that shape your career. The main points can be summarized as follows:

- Seek companies that have in place a plan of development. Standards exist that define organizational maturity. You can use the general picture that these standards paint to evaluate for yourself whether an organization provides the best setting for you.
- Develop an understanding of how game development fits into existing traditions of craft and profession. Although the industry might be characterized in many ways by big egos and chaotic development efforts, those companies that have proven most successful do have clear job descriptions, mature styles of development, and an understanding of craft and profession.
- Identify the areas of knowledge that define your work. The SWEBOK is a good place to begin. Although it does not stand as an official definition of what software engineering is about, it is an excellent encapsulation of the knowledge that many people consider essential to software engineering.
- Establish an awareness of where you can find information about game development and software engineering. As a professional or craftsperson, you are expected to carry your own store of knowledge. Develop your resources.
- Seek to increase your knowledge in a controlled way, so that even if you work as a generalist, you possess some specialized skills.
- Relate to the work you perform as a craftsperson or software engineer. The code of ethics that the IEEE publishes establishes general categories of ethical concern for software engineers.

- Learn how to learn. It is easy to pound away on project after project and end up being mesmerized by the excitement the game offers while forgetting the importance of the basic skills you possess. Technology is a brutal taskmaster. Grow or perish.
- Attend to how you regard your work. Find a way to understand your work as something beyond making money. If you work for a living, work is living.

This chapter referenced a relatively limited set of books, but it is important to remember that an immense store of books is available on software engineering (more than 400 at last count on Amazon.com). As a craftsperson or software engineering professional, it is a good idea to build continuously your book collection. If you read only one book a year on what you do, you are not reading enough. In addition to books on software engineering, a few books that specifically address game development topics are provided:

Abran, Alain, James W. Moore, Pierre Bourque, et. al., eds. *Guide to the Software Engineering Body of Knowledge Trial Version (SWEBOK).* Washington, D.C.: IEEE Computer Society, 2001.

Bates, Bob, editor. *Game Developer's Market Guide.* Boston: Premier Press, 2003.

Brooks, Jr., Frederick P. *The Mythical Man-Month: Essays on Software Engineering Anniversary Edition.* Boston: Addison-Wesley, 1995.

Csikszentmihalyi, Mihaly. *Flow: The Psychology of Optimal Experience.* New York: Harper & Row, 1990.

Demarco, Tom and Timothy Lister. *Peopleware: Productive Projects and Teams.* New York: Dorset House Publishing Co., 1987.

Hallford, Neal with Jana Hallford. *Swords & Circuitry: A Designer's Guide to Computer Role-Playing Games.* Roseville, California: Prima Publishing, 2001.

IEEE/ACM, *Software Engineering Code of Ethics and Professional Practice.* 27 Aug 2003. http://www.acm.org/serving/se/code.htm.

LaMothe, André. *Tricks of the Windows Game Programming Gurus. Second Edition.* Indianapolis: Sams Publishing, 2002.

McBreen, Pete. *Software Craftsmanship: The New Imperative.* New York: Addison-Wesley, 2004.

McConnell, Steve. *Professional Software Development: Shorter Schedules, Higher Quality Products, More Successful Projects, Enhanced Careers.* New York: Addison-Wesley, 2004.

Mencher, Marc. *Get in the Game! Careers in the Game Industry.* Boston: New Riders, 2003.

Rucker, Rudy. *Software Engineering and Computer Games.* Boston: Addison-Wesley, 2003.

Salisbury, Ashley. *Game Development Business and Legal Guide.* Boston: Premier Press, 2003.

Saltzman, Marc. *Game Creation and Careers: Insider Secrets from Industry Experts.* Indianapolis: New Riders Publishing, 2004.

Sheldon, Lee. *Character Development and Storytelling for Games.* Boston: Thomson Course Technology PTR, 2004.

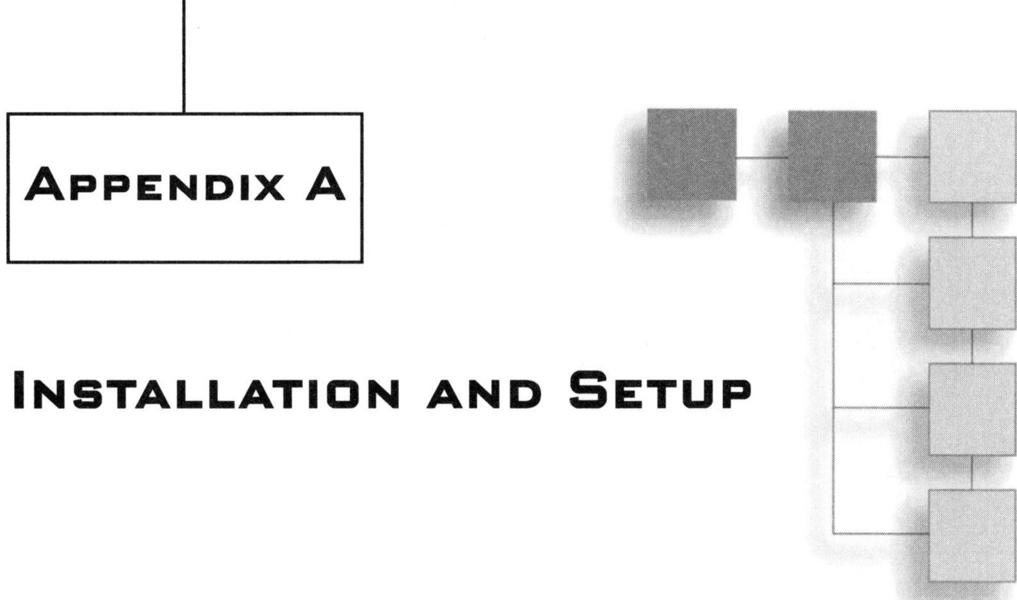

Appendix A

Installation and Setup

To get started with the projects in this book, you need to have Microsoft Studio 6.0 or Microsoft Studio .NET. You do not need to do anything other than install the files that are provided on the CD. All of the configuration headaches have been taken care of for you.

To install the *Ankh* projects and documentation:

1. Place the CD in the drive. If you have Autorun enabled on your system, a multimedia interface launches. The interface tells you what is on the disc and how to launch the installation program. (If this interface does not automatically run after you put the disc in your drive, you can manually locate the file named AnkhSetup.exe. The file is clearly visible on the CD. (See Figure A.1.)

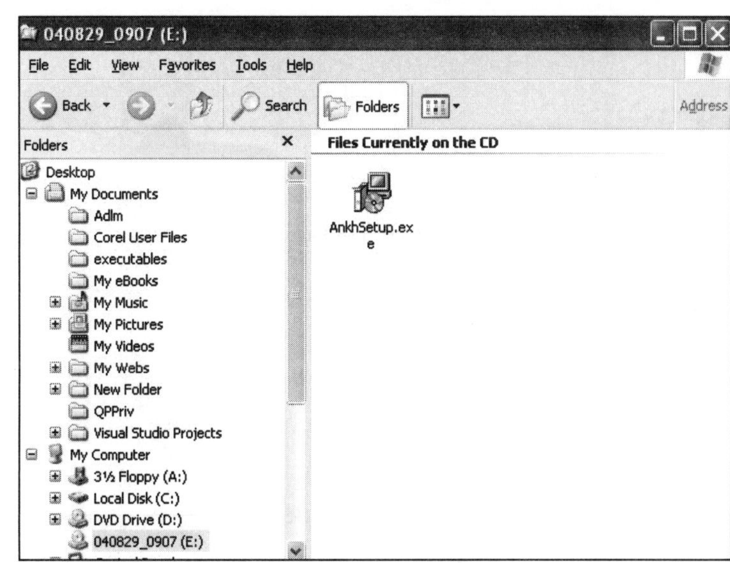

Figure A.1
The installation program is all that you see.

2. Click on AhkhSetup.exe. The Ankh Setup Wizard window appears. (See Figure A.2.) Click Next.

Figure A.2
The installation program installs everything you need.

3. The installer displays the Select Destination Location window. (See Figure A.3.) This window tells where it will place all of the files associated with *Ahkh.* Use the default directory setting. Click Next.

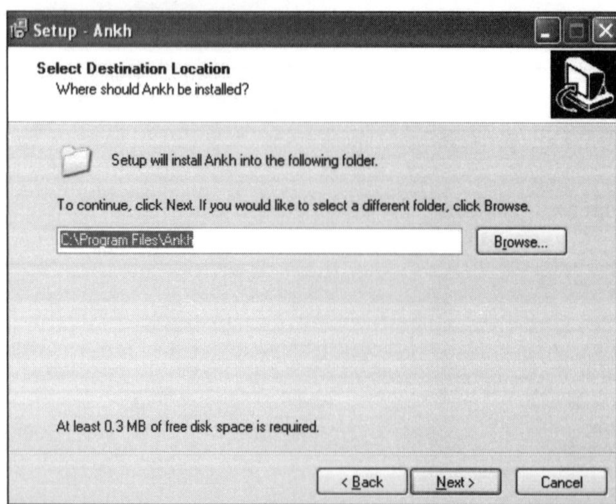

Figure A.3
Leave the default settings.

4. The Select Components window appears. (See Figure A.4). For a first-time installation, select Full Installation. Leave all of the items in the scroll pane checked, including the DirectX 9.0 SDK. Click Next.

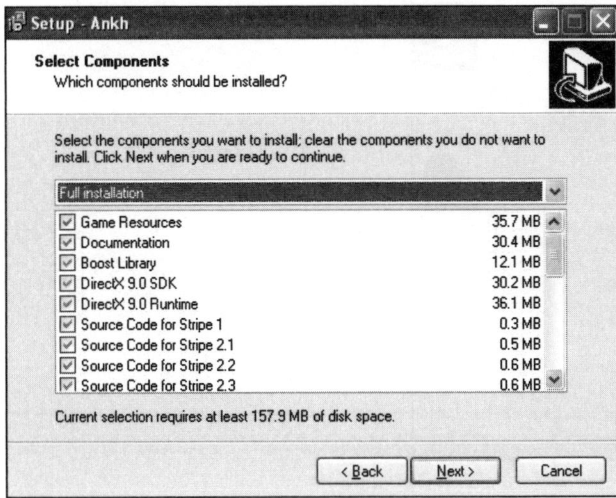

Figure A.4
Select Full Installation and leave all of the items checked.

5. The Select Start Menu Folder window is displayed. (See Figure A.5.) The start menu is set by default to the Ankh folder. Leave it where it is for now. You can change things later. Click Next.

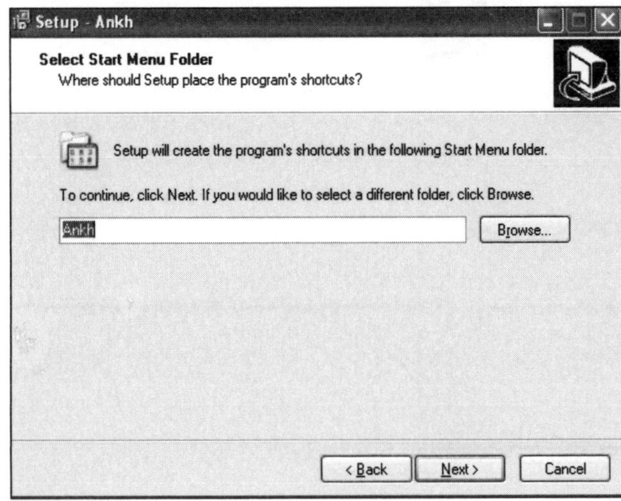

Figure A.5
The shortcut is placed in the Start Menu folder.

6. The system displays the Ready to Install window. (See Figure A.6.) The scroll pane in this window tells you what will be installed. Click Install.

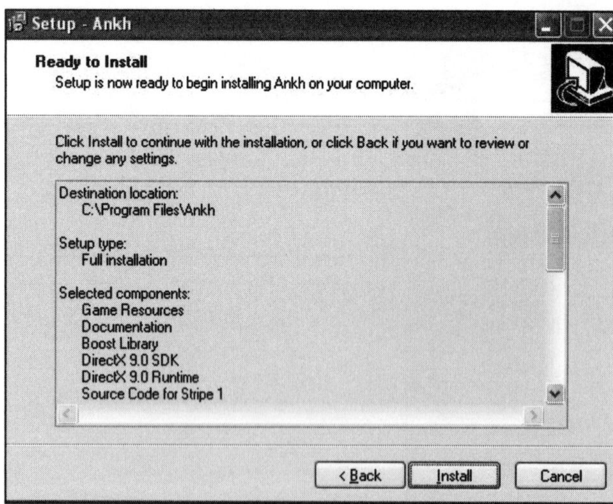

Figure A.6
The installation program confirms the files to be installed.

7. The system displays a progress bar in the Installing window. (See Figure A.7.) The installation can take up to a few minutes, depending on the speed of your system.

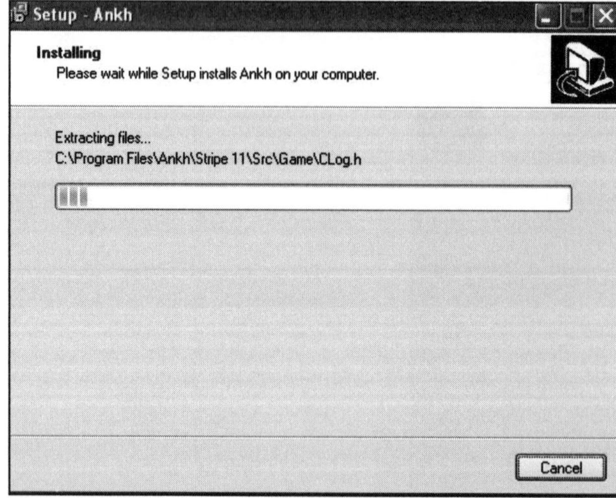

Figure A.7
The installation might require several minutes.

8. When the installation is complete, you see the Welcome to Setup for DirectX window. (See Figure A.8.) Click I Accept the Agreement. Then click Next.

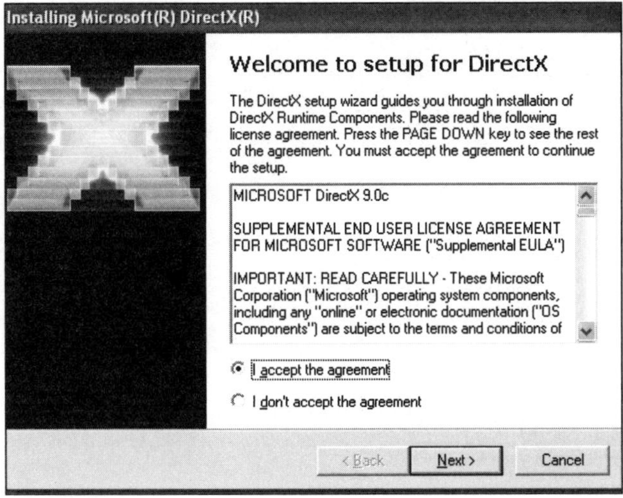

Figure A.8
Click I Accept the Agreement and Next even if you already have DirectX on your computer.

note

Please install the version of DirectX included on the CD. It's completely safe. This installation of DirectX will not affect any other version of DirectX you have on your computer. This small version of DirectX is included in the Ankh directory. It uninstalls automatically when you uninstall the *Ankh* files. All the project files are configured to access this version of DirectX.

9. The system then displays the DirectX 9.0 Runtime Install window. (See Figure A.9.) Click Next.

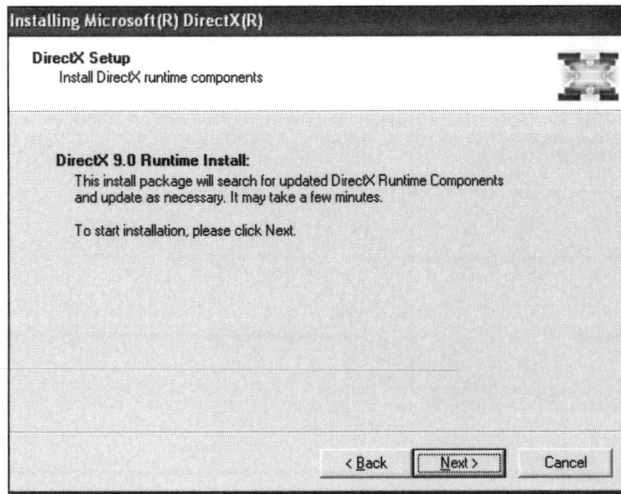

Figure A.9
Click Next to proceed with the installation.

10. The DirectX 9.0 confirmation window appears. (See Figure A.10.) Click Finish.

Figure A.10
The run-time version of DirectX is installed.

11. The final *Ankh* installation window appears. (See Figure A.11.) Click Finish.
12. The *Ankh* project and documentation files are now installed, ready for viewing.

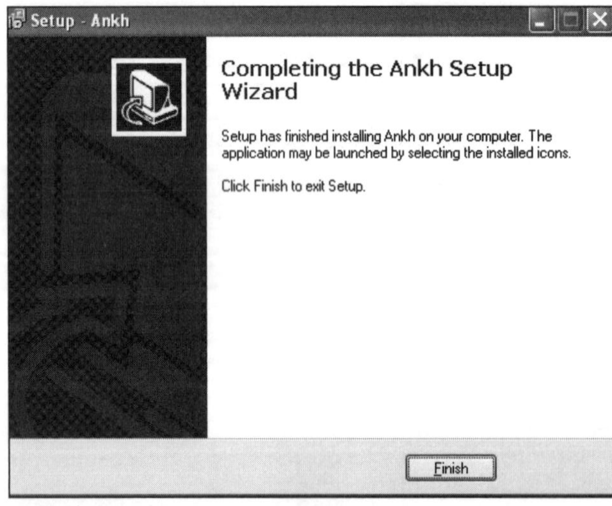

Figure A.11
Click Finish to proceed with the installation.

Viewing the Files

Assuming that you have installed the files for this book, it helps to familiarize yourself with them. (If you have not yet installed the files, see the section titled "Installing the Ankh Projects and Documentation.")

To view the book files and the *Ankh* projects, navigate to the Ankh folder. By default, this folder is installed under Program Files. (See Figure A.12.)

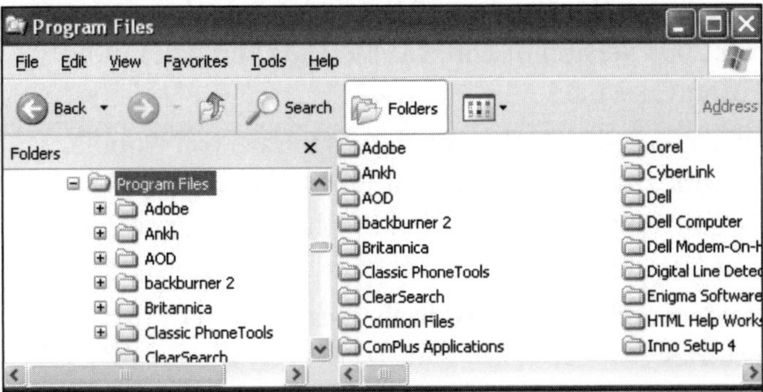

Figure A.12
The source code and documentation are in the Ankh directory under Program Files.

The Ankh Directory

Click the Ankh directory to view the *Ankh* files. Figure A.13 shows the contents of the Ankh directory.

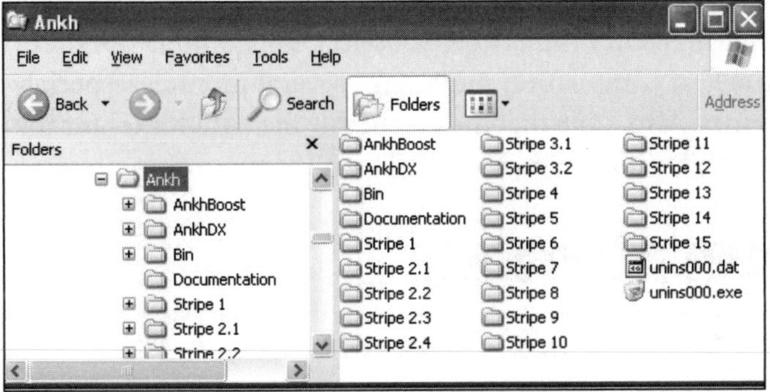

Figure A.13
The game, code, and documentation files are installed in the Ankh directory.

Given that you have installed all the files on the CD, you'll see the set of files shown in Figure A.13. Note the following:

- The AnkhDX directory contains the version of DirectX that was used to develop *Ankh.* This version of DirectX will not interfere with other versions of DirectX that you might have on your computer. All the projects are configured to access this version of DirectX, which makes things a lot easier. This version of DirectX is Summer 2003b. This version of DirectX was used because it supports Microsoft C++ 6.0. (If you want to reconfigure the project to link to a later version, you can, for example, use the Summer 2004 version of DirectX, but then you will not be able to compile using Microsoft C++ 6.0.)
- The Boost library has also been included in the installation to save you trouble. Again, this will not interfere with any other versions of Boost you might have installed. This version has been trimmed down so that it will not require as much disk space as the full Boost library.
- The contents of the stripe folders are documented in the next section of this appendix, "The Stripe Directories."

The Stripe Directories

Each of the folders is titled Stripe 1, Stripe 2.1, and so on. Each of these folders contains the project files for a stripe. (See Figure A.14.) In each stripe directory are two project files:

- **Ankh.dsw (for Microsoft Studio 6.0).** If you have Microsoft Studio 6.0, click this file.
- **Ankh.sln (for Microsoft Studio .NET).** If you have any version of Microsoft Studio .NET, click this file.

After you open a project file with Microsoft Studio, you can select the Compile option to compile the project. Note that the first compilation might take several minutes, especially if you select one of the later stripes. Also, note that the executable file (Ahkh.exe) for the project is always named Ahkh.exe and writes to the Bin directory. If you want to preserve the executable file, change the name.

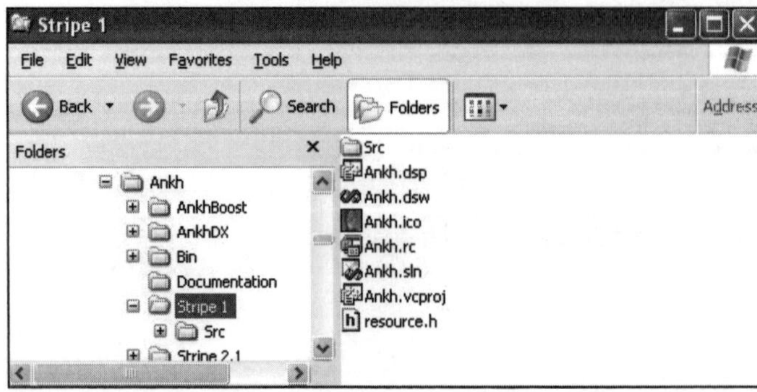

Figure A.14
You see project files for both Visual Studio 6.0 and Visual Studio .NET.

The Bin Directory

The Bin directory contains the resource files for all the stripes. (See Figure A.15.) It is also where your Ankh.exe files are placed when you compile a project. You also see a set of executables that have been created for you. There is one for each of the stripes. You can use these executables as points of reference that you can compare with the executables you compile.

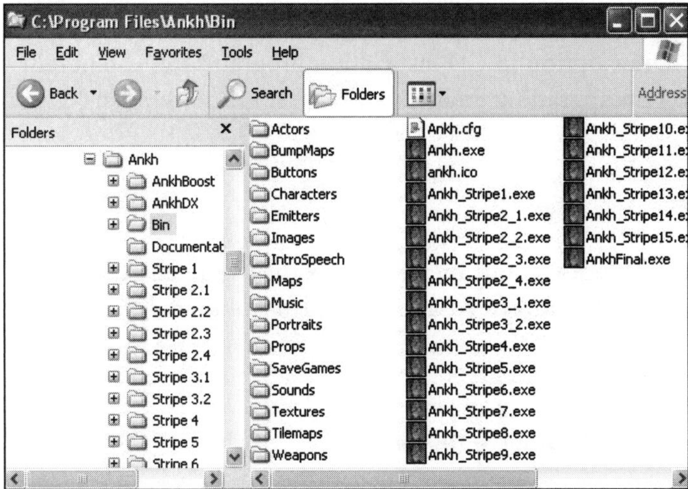

Figure A.15
The Bin directory contains executables and resources.

The Documentation Directory

The Documentation directory contains all the documents for the project. (See Figure A.16.)

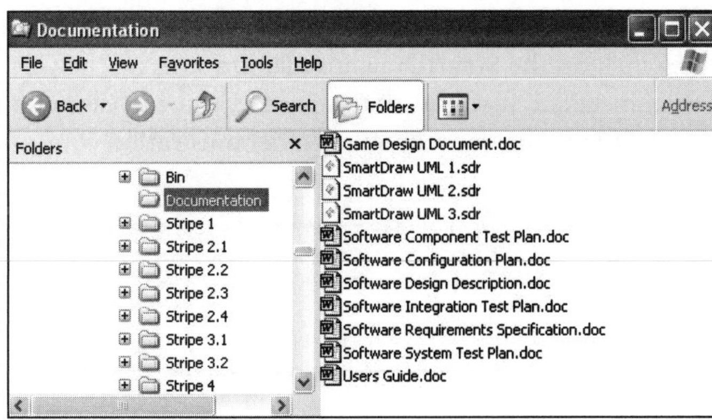

Figure A.16
The Documentation directory contains Word and SmartDraw files for the software.

Note the following:

- All the document files are Microsoft Word files. These files are discussed in the text. See Appendix D, "Software Engineering and Game Design Documentation."
- The User's Guide shows you features of the game and reviews the code and documentation. There are Word and PDF versions. You can view the User's Guide by selecting the Help icon from the Ankh Programs listing.
- To open the SmartDraw projects, first install SmartDraw from the CD. To accomplish this, click the SmartDraw option in CD installation program. You can obtain resources and information on upgrading SmartDraw from http://www.smartdraw.com/.

Playing the Game

An *Ankh* option is placed in your Windows Start menu. To play the complete game, select this option. This executable is in the Bin directory, and it is called AnkhFinal.exe.

Uninstall

To uninstall the files, use one of the following options:

- **Windows Control Panel.** Select this option from the Start menu and proceed as prompted. The program uninstalls everything except the files you have generated. You will have to remove these files manually.
- **Start menu.** Select the Uninstall option in the Ankh program option. The program uninstalls everything except the files you have generated. You will have to remove these files manually.

Installing SmartDraw

To install SmartDraw from the CD, click on the SmartDraw installation icon on the CD. A trial version of SmartDraw is then installed. If you want to upgrade, you can easily do so by contacting SmartDraw at SmartDraw.com. You can obtain a demonstration copy at http://www.smartdraw.com/.

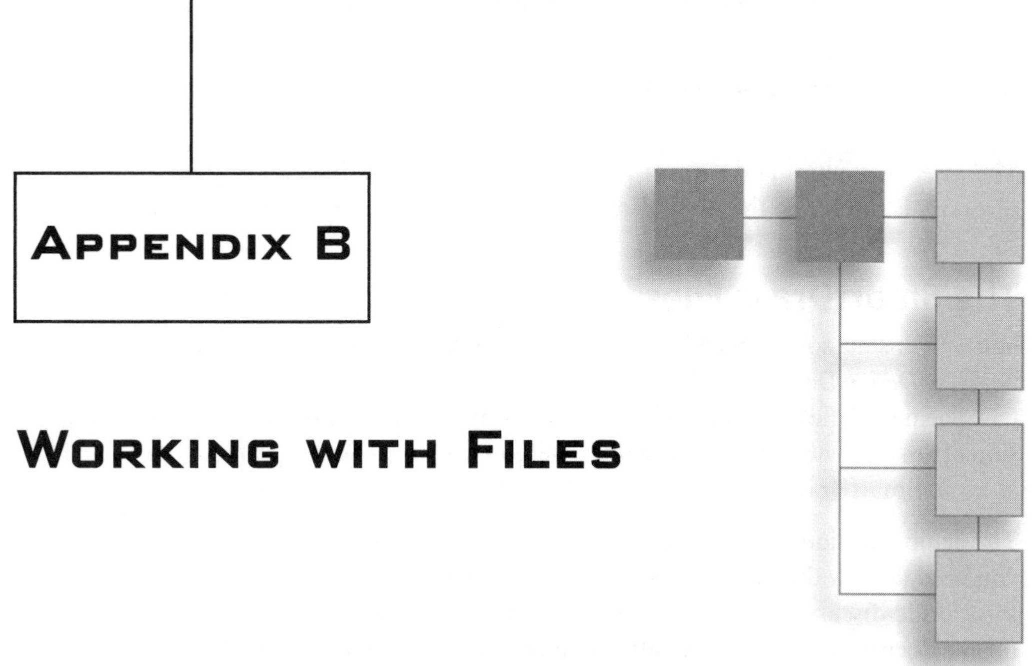

Appendix B

Working with Files

This appendix discusses specifics of locating and using the Microsoft Visual Studio and SmartDraw files that the installation program installs for you. For information on how to install the files, see Appendix A, "Installation and Setup."

The Ankh Source Files

You can find all the source files for the stripes in the directory for *Ankh* that the installation program creates for you. By default, this directory is C:/Program Files/Ankh.

The project files for all the stripes appear in the Ankh directory. To view the Microsoft Visual Studio files for the first stripe, for example, open the file titled Stripe 1. You will find project files for both Visual Studio 6.0 and Visual Studio .NET.

When the install program installs the game and the source files, it also installs the version of DirectX that the team used to develop the program. The installed version will not interfere with other versions of DirectX that are on your computer. This version of DirectX is in the Ankh directory. The projects are linked to this version of DirectX that is included in the Ankh directory.

Each stripe folder contains two Microsoft Visual studio project files. One project has been created with Microsoft Visual Studio 6.0 projects. (This is identified with the *.dsw extension.) A second project has been created with the first release of Microsoft Visual Studio .NET. Both of these projects should readily convert to 2003 and 2004 versions of Microsoft Visual Studio.

The src directory, which is in the Ankh directory for each stripe, contains several directories. Among these are Boost, Game, Graphics, Input, Sound, and State. These directories reflect the divisions that the team developed for configuration purposes.

The assets (graphics and sound) for the game are stored in the Bin directory. The Bin directory is located in the Ankh directory. All the stripes use the same Bin directory.

The SmartDraw Files

You will install some SmartDraw files that contain UML diagrams used in the *Ankh Software Design Description.* To open these files, you must first install SmartDraw from the CD. The installation program allows you to do this. The CD provides you with a trial version of SmartDraw. If you want to upgrade, you can easily do so by contacting SmartDraw at http://SmartDraw.com.

The demonstration version of SmartDraw that is included on the CD has the basic tools you need to view the files and modify them. See Chapter 14, "Practice, Practice, Practice," for specific discussion of SmartDraw. Keep in mind that almost all of the UML artifacts for the documentation were created with SmartDraw. You can find additional discussion of SmartDraw in many chapters. See, for example, Chapter 18, "Documentation—Learning How to Learn" and Chapter 9, "Iterating Design." If you combine SmartDraw with a word processor, such as Word, WordPerfect, or FrameMaker, you can cover all the primary needs for technical documentation of the type of game project that this book discusses. This book combined SmartDraw with Microsoft Word and Microsoft Excel.

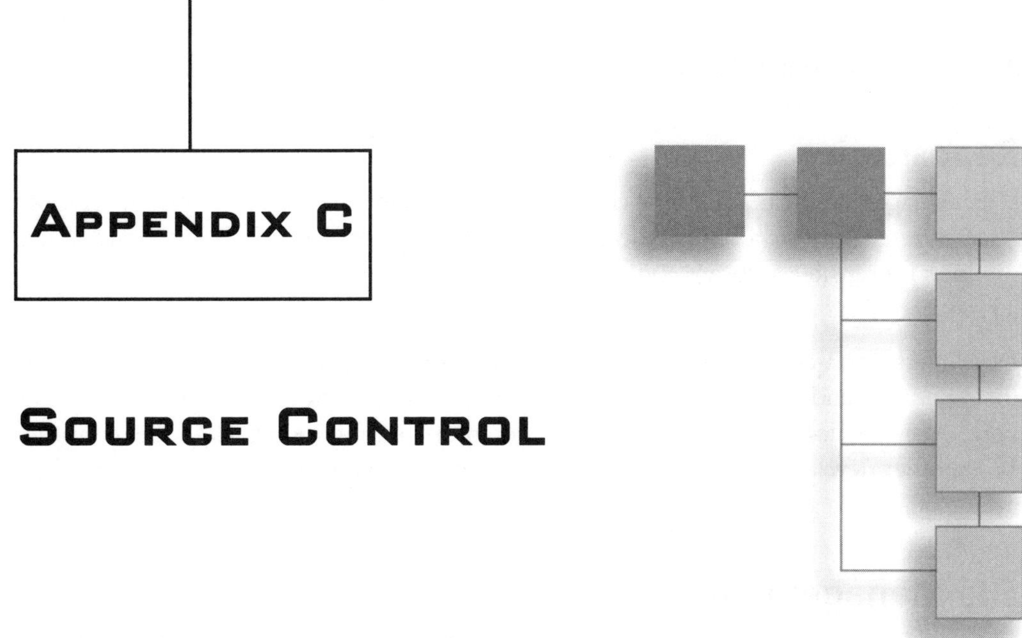

Appendix C

Source Control

When you track the changes to your source code, documentation, and resources, you perform what is more generally known as *version control*. Version control allows you to administer changes to source and files over time. Because a version control system eliminates the need to back up files, it simplifies the work involved in managing a software project's configuration. The version control system stores changed files so that they can be uniquely identified.

Many version control applications are freely distributed. One of the most popular is the Concurrent Versions System (CVS). The *Ankh* team used CVS to manage *Ankh*'s source code, resources, and documentation.

Obtaining TortoiseCVS

You can download the TortoiseCVS system free of charge from http://www.tortoisecvs.org.

Locking and Simultaneous File Access

Some version control systems use a file-locking mechanism. The developer invokes this mechanism and obtains exclusive editing access to a file (locks it). After the developer changes the file, he then unlocks it. At this point, others can access the file.

In contrast, CVS supports simultaneous editing of one file by multiple developers. The *Ankh* development team decided to use CVS because it needed a version control system that allows several developers to work on one file simultaneously.

Repositories

CVS manages files by maintaining change information in a repository. Typically set up on a server, a *repository* is a central location where files are managed. Files are localized into modules for sensible software configurations. Every CVS-administered project must have a repository.

Developers who want to access the files might check out their own copy of a module from the repository and edit the files within. These checked-out modules are known as *sandboxes.* After developers have changed their files, they commit them back to the repository. When other developers update their files to the current version, these changes will have been applied and stored.

File Management

CVS provides operations for managing, viewing, and changing files. Only a few of these operations are necessary to maintain a version-controlled project:

- **New module.** This is the first operation for any CVS-versioned project. This option creates a new module to contain files. The location of the newly created module is the CVS repository. Because files are checked out at the module level, similar files should be grouped into modules. For example, *Ankh*'s source code resided in the AnkhSource module, whereas documentation files were stored in the AnkhDocs module.
- **Add.** This operation adds files to CVS versioning control. By adding a file, CVS begins to track changes to it.
- **Checkout.** Checking out a module from the repository creates a copy of the files within it, generating a new sandbox. After a module has been created in the repository, that module is available for developers to check out for editing. For example, developers checked out the AnkhSource module into their own AnkhSource sandbox, enabling them to edit the source code within it.
- **Update.** Updating a file in a sandbox revises it to match the repository's version. When a developer wants to see the current version of a file, he updates the file in his sandbox. A developer can update a file to its current version or any previous version. For example, to view the first draft of *Ankh*'s source files, a developer would update his AnkhSource sandbox to the first version.
- **Commit.** Committing a file revises the repository's current version of it. After you add a file to the repository, committing the file sets its first version in the repository. After you edit a checked-out file in a sandbox, the repository's version then matches that file. Committing a file signifies to the repository that the file should be changed for future updates. Developers can commit single files, multiple files, or entire modules at one time. For example, after editing a source file in his

AnkhSource sandbox, a developer would commit it to the repository. Subsequent checkouts and updates of that file then show these changes.

- **Tag.** Adding CVS tags to a file is a convenient way to mark a particular version. After creating a file and adding it to CVS, a developer could tag that version as "First Draft." Several versions later, the developer could view that version again by updating the file and selecting its "First Draft" tag.
- **Branch.** Branching a file in CVS disassociates it from the current version. For example, after a developer completes a project's first stripe, it might be branched as "Stripe 1." Further changes for the second stripe are not applied to the first, allowing developers to check out different "Stripe 1" and "Stripe 2" versions of the project.
- **History.** Viewing a file's history displays the CVS versions that the file has gone through. Any tags or branches are visible in the history, providing a useful log of changes and the associated developers.

Setting Up a Repository

The first requirement for any CVS-versioned project is a repository. To set up a repository, begin by creating a folder to include the new project's files. You create this folder the same way that you create any other Windows folder. After you have created the folder, right-click on it and view the context menu. From the context menu, select Make New Module. (See Figure C.1.)

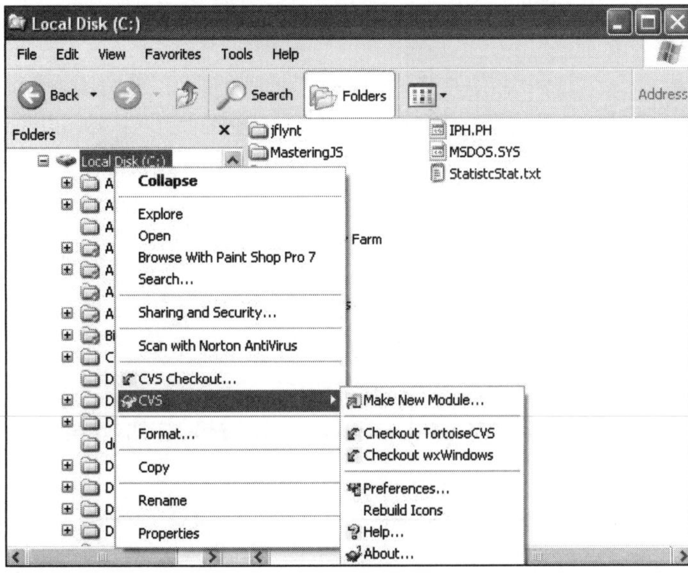

Figure C.1
Select Make New Module in the TortoiseCVS context menu.

After you select Make New Module, you see the Make New Module dialog box. (See Figure C.2.)

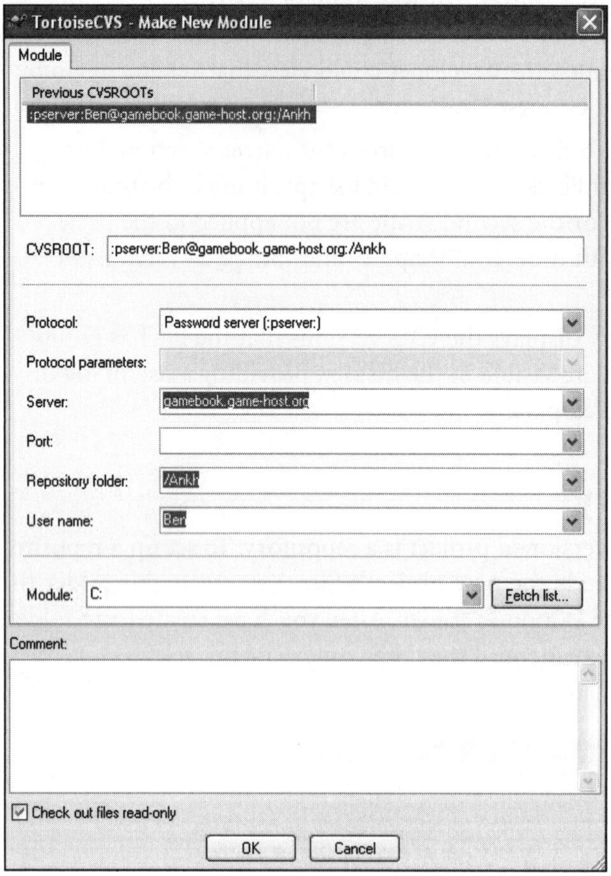

Figure C.2
Create a new CVS module.

Adding Files

After you create a module and repository, you can add files to the project by right-clicking on the file and selecting CVS Add from the CVS context menu. This tells CVS to manage the file's changes and versions. (See Figure C.3.)

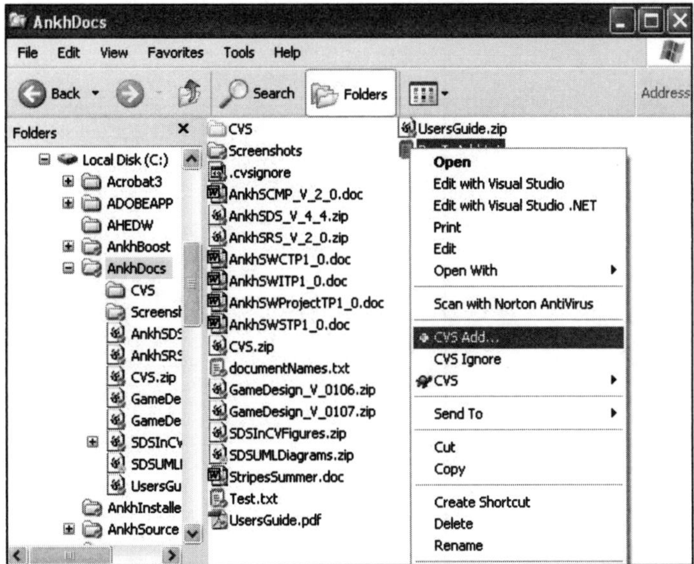

Figure C.3
Adding a file to CVS with the TortoiseCVS context menu.

Checking Out Files

Assume that another developer has created a repository and added a module to it. The module contains version-controlled files. Then assume that you want access to the version-controlled files. To accomplish this, you begin by checking out your own copies of these files. (See Figure C.4.) Specifically, you right-click in your sandbox directory and select CVS Checkout.

After you select CVS Checkout, you enter the location and name of the appropriate repository in the Checkout Module dialog box. (See Figure C.5) Then you select the module name to complete the checkout. This provides you with your own version of the files in the repository. You can now safely edit them. When you complete your edits, you can commit them.

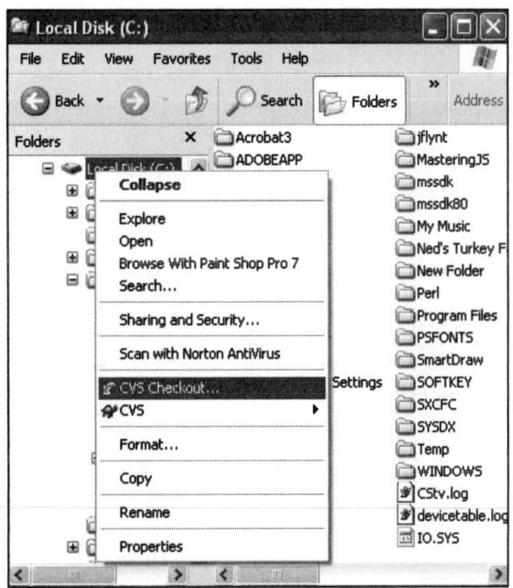

Figure C.4
Use the TortoiseCVS context menu to check out a module.

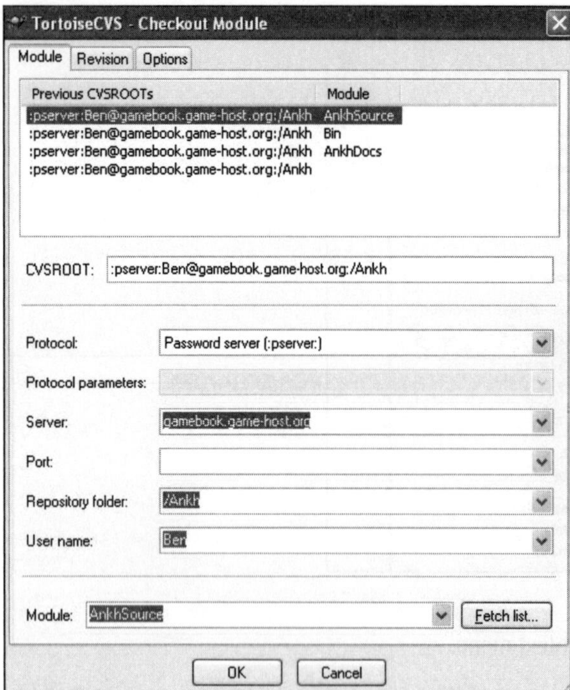

Figure C.5
The TortoiseCVS Checkout Module dialog box displays available items.

Updating Files

After you have checked out a module to your sandbox, you can update your sandbox to obtain the current version of the module from the repository. To do this, select the file or directory to update. Then select CVS Update from the context menu. (See Figure C.6.)

Updated files are green, whereas conflicted files and files that are ready to be committed are red.

If you simultaneously change and commit files with another developer, you will have to merge your files manually.

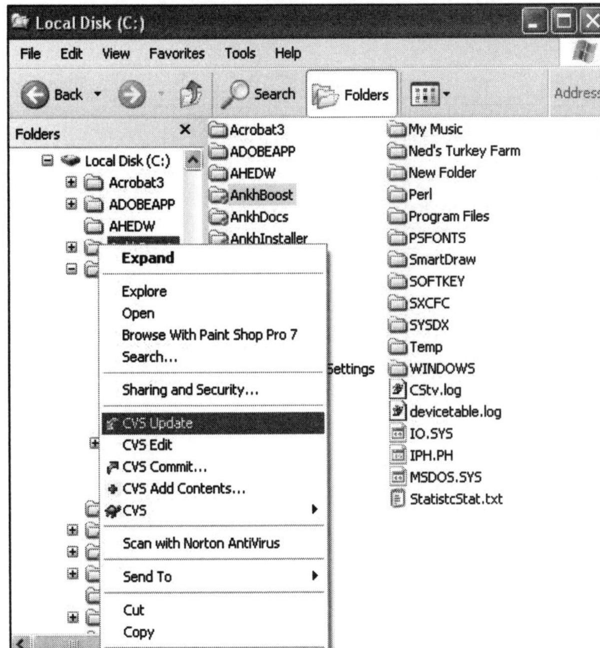

Figure C.6
Update files using the TortoiseCVS context menu.

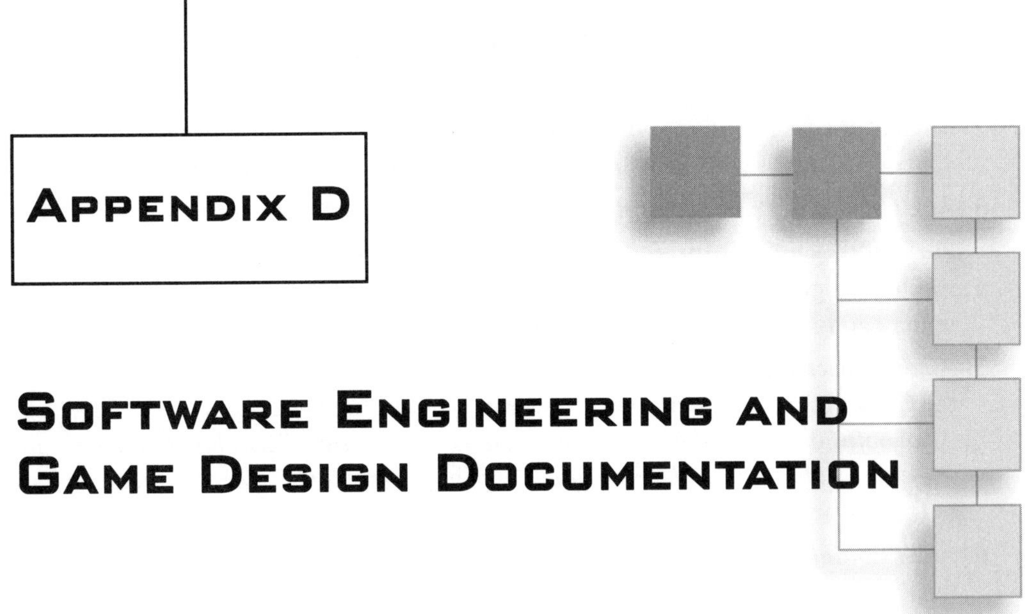

Appendix D

Software Engineering and Game Design Documentation

This appendix guides you to the documentation that is mentioned in the text. Note the following specifics:

- **References only.** Some of the documents referred to in this appendix and elsewhere in the book are only on the CD. Among these documents are the *Ankh Software Configuration Management Plan* and the *Ankh Software Project Test Plan.* All these documents have been created using Microsoft Word, and you can find them in the Documents directory.
- **Selections from documents.** This appendix contains part of the document. With access to selected portions, you have a convenient way to examine a sample document as you read. On the CD, you will find the complete Microsoft Word versions of the documents.

List

Following is an inventory of the documents that you will have access to after you install the programs and files from the CD:

1. ***Ankh Game Design.*** Selected sections appear in this appendix. For the complete document, go to the Documents directory.

2. ***Ankh Software Requirements Specification.*** Selected sections appear in this appendix. For the complete document, go to the Documents directory.
3. ***Ankh Software Design Description.*** Selected sections appear in this appendix. For the complete document, go to the Documents directory.
4. ***Ankh Configuration Management Plan.*** Reference to the CD only. To see the document, go to the Documents directory.
5. ***Ankh Project Test Plans.*** Reference to the CD only. To see the documents, go to the CD and the Documents directory. You can find four test plans on the CD: *Ankh Software Integration Test Plan*, *Ankh Software System Test Plan*, *Ankh Software Project Test Plan*, and *Ankh Software Component Test Plan*. To see the document, go to the Documents directory.
6. ***Ankh Coding Standards.*** Reference to the CD only. This is included in a section in the *Ankh Software Configuration Management Plan*. To see the document, go to the CD, Documents/Software.

note

The documents as they appear in this appendix have been edited so that they are consistent with the rest of the book. For this reason, they differ slightly from those you install from the CD.

When you install the software for this book, the complete documents are installed as a part of the documentation set in the Documentation directory. Refer to Appendix A for information about how to install and locate the documents.

SmartDraw projects that are included with the installation contain the technical illustrations for the *Ankh Software Design Description*.

Ankh Game Design Document

The primary author of the *Ankh* design document was John Rose. Paul Whitehead contributed graphics. Ben Vinson and Carlos Villar contributed the paragraph detailing 60 seconds of play. John Flynt was the producer.

Introduction

Ankh follows the quest of vengeance undertaken by Sekhem, an Egyptian-Greek warrior who is determined to destroy those who defaced and killed his father. The game focuses on the battles fought by Sekhem and his party of rebel warriors on their journey to the Egyptian capital of Thebes. These conflicts escalate from skirmishes to bloody clashes as the band of adventurers cross the desert sands of ancient Egypt. Along the way, additional characters join the band and new enemies attempt to stop Sekhem's advance. Interaction involves tactical control of the small army during *Ankh's* many mêlées, including strategic maneuvers, hand-to-hand combat, and spell casting.

The player is faced with winning battle after glorious battle, driving Sekhem toward his final confrontation with Uheset, the bloodthirsty Queen of Egypt. Conflicts take place turn by turn, stressing the tactical and chaotic aspect of warfare. Each level possesses its own ambiance and strategy, from the alleys of inner Alexandria to the shadowed halls of the Underworld.

The graphics of *Ankh* illustrate the varied and stylish architecture and landscapes of ancient Egypt. The game's music varies from haunting chants to blood-quickening battle drums. All aspects of the game's art and sound immerse the player in the primal rage of ancient warfare.

Lead Game Line

"Revenge Burns."

Control

The player interacts with *Ankh* from a 3/4 top-down view of the battlefield. The player controls Sekhem and his party with the mouse and the optional keyboard. The Graphical User Interface (GUI) consists of the main battlefield window, a smaller unit detail window, and buttons for issuing commands to characters.

Every turn, the player can issue commands to one of his characters. These turns are ordered so that each of the player's characters has its own turn in sequence. These commands include movements, attacks, item use, and spell casting. By maneuvering the characters about the battleground and attacking the enemy in a tactical fashion, the player can defeat each opposing force and move closer toward the final confrontation.

Units and Characters

Ankh is a battle-based game in which the player maneuvers characters to destroy the opposing force. *Units* can refer to anything that has a dynamic role in a game. If you have morphing rocks and talking trees, you can consider them units. This game has only character units, so this document refers to units as characters.

Characters possess items, weapons, skill, and attributes that are specific to themselves. Characters are given turns to move, attack, and use skills during combat, and they are controlled by either a human or computer player. Characters are either generic representatives of their class, such as random guards, or specific characters who are central to the game, such as Sekhem and Queen Uheset. Each character possesses the following attributes:

- Name
- Class
- Strength
- Speed
- Spirituality
- Resilience
- Condition
- Experience
- Skills
- Attacks
- Items
- Mesh
- Skin

Classes

Each character of *Ankh* belongs to a character class. A class is a set of defining characteristics for characters. The classes are as follows:

- Slave
- Soldier
- Bodyguard
- Guard
- Archer
- Mummy
- Priest of Isis

- Priest of Ra
- Priest of Osiris

Characters cannot change classes. The class acts as a guide to how characters improve over time. For example, bodyguards will never possess much spirituality, but most of a priest's improvement is centered on spirituality and spells. Because classes define much of a character's ability, Sekhem's party and enemy forces consist of warriors with complementary classes. Every member of a class is represented by that class' character mesh and portrait, making identification simple.

Characters

The story of *Ankh* unfolds battle after battle with the addition of new allies and enemies. The game's individual characters are represented as warriors of differing classes, but each special character has a special character mesh and portrait. (See Table D.1)

Table D.1 Class Identities

Name	Class	Personal Information
Sekhem	Soldier	Son of Meseru, vengeful warrior determined to kill Uheset
Sati	Priest of Osiris	Betrayer of Meseru, Sekhem's repentant guide
Uheset	Priest of Osiris	Queen of Egypt, destroyer of Meseru
Khefta	Soldier	Bloodthirsty general, betrayer of Meseru
Neru	Bodyguard	Former guard of foreign chief, freed by Sekhem and now his loyal protector
Emaui	Archer	Angry young woman who shares Sekhem's hate for Uheset
Suten-Heh	Mummy	Ancient and powerful king revived by Anubis and willing to help Sekhem

Attributes, Skills, and Experience

Each character has individual attributes, skills, and experience. These are values that change during the game, influencing how capably each character attacks, how much damage the character can take, what spells the character can cast, and so on. Attributes include the following list of personal values: strength, speed, spirituality, resilience, condition, and experience.

A character's strength value influences how much damage the character can deliver in combat. Characters such as bodyguards and mummies have high strength attributes.

Speed indicates how far a character can move around the battlefield. Smaller characters like slaves possess great speed.

Spirituality reflects a character's spell-casting abilities. Priests, who have low strength and speed, are strong due to their enchantments. Some characters attain spirituality throughout the battles, thereby gaining spells.

Resilience influences how much damage a character can take. When a character has taken too much damage, it is incapacitated until it's healed. Big, tough characters, such as bodyguards, are defined mostly through their large resilience.

Condition describes a character's current state of being. Healthy, diseased, unconscious, poisoned, and alive are several possible conditions that might describe a character during a battle. Condition affects how characters react to specific attacks and what moves they can make.

Experience is the character's most telling statistic, reflecting how much the character has learned and seen throughout its trials. A character's experience immediately increases when he or she damages or casts a spell that affects an enemy. The attributes of characters increase between battles. Their level of increase depends on the amount of experience gained by the character during combat.

Skills are individual abilities gained throughout the game and influenced by attributes. Spells and special attacks are two kinds of skills earned through experience on the battlefield. As characters progress, the player has the option of granting these skills and upgrading the character.

Health Points and Spell Points

Health points and spell points fluctuate within a battle. A character's resilience attribute determines its starting health points. Health points reflect how much damage a character can receive before being incapacitated. They can be restored up to the starting value by the healing skill. If characters survive a battle, all of their health points are fully restored at the start of the next battle.

A character's spirituality attribute determines his or her starting spell points. Each spell has a corresponding spell points cost, which is depleted as the character casts more spells. Spell points slowly regenerate up to their starting value with time. Like the healing skill for health points, the meditation skill is useful for increasing character's spell points.

Items

Items are objects found in the world (on the battlefield, in shops, and on the black market) that characters can manipulate and carry in the game. Each character possesses an inventory, or collection, of these items. A character might equip a weapon item, such as a sword or bow, and use it in combat. A character might also invoke an item during the skill use portion of the character's turn. Players can buy or sell items at relevant establishments, and the versatility that is inherent in these items can add great advantages in combat, such as spells and healing abilities. (See Table D.2)

Table D.2 Item Inventory

Name	Cost	Power	Effect
Golden Ankh	1000	10	Replenish
Sun Wadjet	400	4	Blinding Eye
Flame Wadjet	700	6	Burning Eye
Cloud Wadjet	900	8	Touch of Osiris

Inventory

The player manages character inventories through the Inventory window, which he can view at any time. The player simply selects a unit and clicks the Inventory button in the main GUI. The Inventory window displays the current character's items, including weapons, armor, healing items, and magic articles. The player can swap items between characters who are within range of one another, in addition to equipping, removing, and dropping items.

Weapons

Characters can hold up to four weapons each in their weapon inventories. At any point, only one of these weapons can be equipped. The weapon that a character carries determines the amount of damage that the character can inflict during combat and the character's attack range. At any time during battle, the player can re-equip a character with a different weapon from the character's inventory by bringing up the Inventory window, removing the first weapon, and equipping the second. Some weapons are ranged, others are only used in melee situations, and some can be used as both. Character classes limit the types of weapons their characters can use. When characters die, their weapons become available to scavenging by other characters. The available weapon types are as follows:

- Broadsword
- Khopesh
- Axe
- Spear
- Bow (and arrows)
- Dagger

Weapons are derived from these types, and character classes limit weapon equipment to certain types. For example, the Archer Emaui can use the Ebony Bow or the Alabaster Starshower Bow, but he cannot use melee weapons. Characters cannot equip weapon types that are forbidden to their Classes, but they can trade weapons to other characters for use. (See Figure D.1.)

Name	Type	Range	Damage	Power	Cost
The Redeemer Blade	Broadsword	Melee	15–35	7	1000
The Dark of Those Entombed	Broadsword	Melee	10–20	4	700
The Serious	Khopesh	Melee	15–25	6	800
The Singer of Boneshatter	Khopesh	Melee	12–20	3	400
The Twisted Render	Axe	Melee	10–30	7	1000
The Ka-Cleaver	Axe	Melee	5–20	3	500
Staff of Isis	Spear	Melee	5–15	2	500
Staff of Osiris	Spear	Melee	5–15	2	500
The Hunting Bow	Bow	Ranged	5–15	2	600
The Crying Wind	Bow	Ranged	20–25	6	800
The Greek Dagger	Dagger	Melee	5–10	1	100
The Nile's Fang	Dagger	Melee	10–15	3	400

Figure D.1
Weapons.

Spells

Spells are skills possessed by certain characters. The spells can be used during the characters' turns during gameplay.

New Characters

In each of the five levels of *Ankh*, at least one new special character is introduced. When these characters enter the game, they begin with characteristics that gradually improve. (See Figures D.2 and D.3) The starting characteristics for these are as follows:

Name	Class	Stren.	Speed	Spirit.	Resil.	Cond.
Sekhem	Soldier	3	3	0	3	Healthy
Sati	Priest of Isis	2	3	5	3	Healthy
Uheset	Priest of Osiris	5	10	10	10	Healthy
Khefta	Soldier	10	10	0	10	Healthy
Neru	Bodyguard	5	3	0	4	Healthy
Emaui	Archer	4	6	2	4	Healthy
Suten-Heh	Mummy	9	1	6	9	Alive

Figure D.2
Starting characteristics.

Name	Skills	Items
Sekhem		Greek Dagger, Golden Ankh
Sati	Healing, Meditation, Burning Eye	Staff of Isis
Uheset	Healing, Touch of Osiris, Boils and Sores, Soul Drink	Staff of Osiris
Khefta		Twisted Render
Neru		Singer of Boneshatter
Emaui	Healing	Hunting Bow
Suten-Heh		

Figure D.3
Starting attributes.

Level Dynamics

Ankh progresses as a series of levels in which many battles are fought between Sekhem's band and enemy forces. To pass through a level, the player must successfully win all of that level's battles while making sure that Sekhem survives. These battles vary in size, types of characters, setting, and difficulty. Play is simple: The battle begins with Sekhem and his adventurers at one end and hostile forces on the other. The player navigates toward the opposition, and warriors clash in a harrowing battle to the death. The battle ends when all enemies are dead.

Battles

Each level is composed of a series of battles. The first level contains only a few battles, whereas later levels are made up of many. Battles are obstacles to the player's band of adventurers. The player must win each battle to continue gameplay. The player's characters and enemy characters take turns moving, attacking, and using special combat skills. The battle ends when all enemies are dead or Sekhem is killed.

Rounds and Turns

Battles take place in rounds. A *round* is the timeframe it takes for every character in a battle to take a turn. At the end of every round, every character has had the opportunity to move, attack, and use skills. When it comes time for a character to act, it becomes that character's turn. The character is encircled at the base by a blue circle denoting its turn, and its portrait and stats are displayed in the character section of the GUI. During a character's turn, the player (or computer) chooses that character's actions for the round, which include moving, attacking, and using a skill. Each character can move once, initiate an attack (including combos) once, and use one skill (including spells, healing potions, items, and so on). After the character has performed/declined all three actions, that character's turn is over, and play moves to the next character. The player can determine the order in which his characters take their turns before combat, and this order is automatically merged with that of the opposing force to create a satisfactory battle order.

Action Points

After it becomes a character's turn, the player (or computer) must choose which actions that character will perform. A character can move, attack, and use a skill once per turn. The variety of actions that the character can perform is based on its action points. Every character's action points are restored at the beginning of its turn. Because a character can choose from a selection of different movement distances, attacks, combos, spells, and so on, the more effective actions cost more to perform. This cost is paid in the character's action points for the turn, and they help to balance the battle. Action points are shared among movement, attacking, and skill use. For example, a character might move a great distance in one turn but won't be able to strike for much damage or cast a devastating spell. If a character heals another from unconsciousness to complete health, that character won't be running circles around the battlefield until its next turn. The number of action points that characters possess is determined by their attributes, most importantly experience and endurance.

Actions

As mentioned earlier, a character can move, attack, and use a skill during its turn if the character has enough action points. A character can perform these actions in any order. When one of the player's characters assumes its turn, the character becomes encircled at its base by a blue circle. The action menu listing movement, attacks, and skills is displayed at the right side of the GUI. After the character has performed an action, that option is disabled in the menu. The player can end a character's turn early by clicking the End Turn button in the same menu. If the character performs all three actions, that character's turn is ended and play moves to another character's turn. (See Figure D.4.)

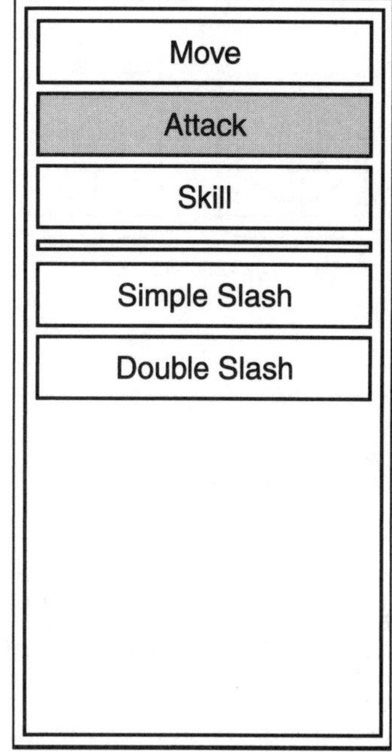

Figure D.4
Action menu.

Movement

A character's move costs a number of action points relative to the distance moved. When the player clicks the Move option on the Action menu, he must manipulate a new movement icon on the battlefield to the character's destination. The distance and consequent cost in action points are displayed above the destination icon. After the player clicks on the destination, the character moves to it. Its action points are adjusted accordingly, and the Move option is disabled in the Action menu. A character will maneuver around obstacles and impassible ground, and the action point cost will reflect the necessary circumvention. The maximum speed that a character can move and the cost of movement are determined by the character's attributes.

Attacking

A character can attack another character by selecting Attack from the Action menu. Then a list of possible attacks are displayed in the Action menu. Units can execute certain attacks depending on their character class and current weapons. For example, a guard can't rain down a volley of Fire Arrows, and an archer can't perform the Sandstone Skull-Crusher. Each attack costs a unique amount of action points. Attacks that cost more action points than the character possesses are disabled in the Action menu.

After a player has selected an attack from the Action menu, he must select the attack's target on the battlefield. This involves clicking on the enemy character. Defending characters must be in range of the attacker. The Targeting window in the player's GUI displays the portraits of the attacking and defending characters, with an attack icon between them. This visually represents the attack and aids the player in confirming it. The player must then click the OK button in the Targeting window, which commences the attack onscreen and disables the Attack button in the player's Action menu. (See Figure D.5.)

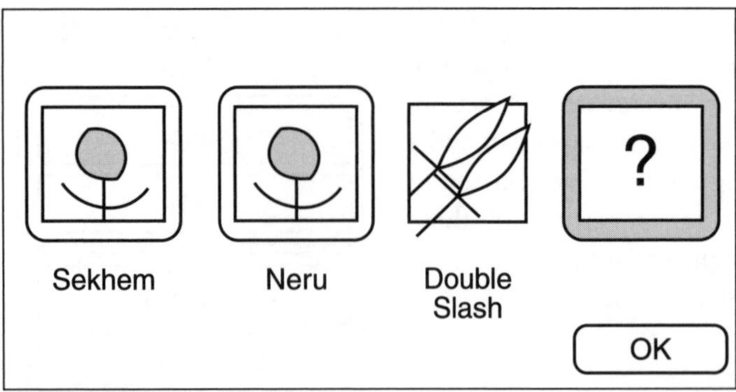

Figure D.5
Targeting window.

For example, the player might want to perform Sekhem's Thoth thrust attack on an Imperial Bodyguard. On Sekhem's turn, the player would click Attack in the Action menu, which would then display all of Sekhem's attacks, including the Thoth thrust. The Targeting window then displays Sekhem's portrait in the attacking character's position, with an empty slot for the not-yet-chosen defender, with a broadsword icon (representing the Thoth thrust) in between. If the player clicks on the enemy character to receive the attack, the Bodyguard's portrait appears in the targeting window's defending character position. The targeting window's OK button is enabled. The player clicks it to commence the attack. The attack is animated on the battlefield, and the player's Attack button is disabled in the Action menu.

Combo Attacks

A combo attack involves more than one attacker. Although a character might initiate only one attack per turn, he or she might participate in other characters' combo attacks. Single-character attacks and combo attacks work the same way: The targeting window displays slots for attackers and defenders, and the player fills these slots by clicking on them and the appropriate character on the battlefield. Combo attacks use up action points from all involved attackers. Therefore, characters must have extra action points to participate in another character's combo. All accomplice characters must also be within range, which is determined by the individual combos.

For example, a player might choose to perform a Crocodile Snap combo attack with Sekhem and Suten-Heh on Suten-Heh's turn against an Archer. On Suten-Heh's turn, the player selects Attack and then Crocodile Snap from the Action menu. Because Suten-Heh is capable of initiating the Crocodile Snap combo and Sekhem is capable of a melee attack (which is all that this particular combo requires), this is a valid attack. The Targeting window displays Suten-Heh's portrait in the first attacking slot, with empty slots for the accomplice and the defending character and the Crocodile Snap icon separating the attackers and defender. The player then clicks the first empty slot and selects Sekhem on the battlefield, whose portrait is displayed there. Sekhem must have enough action points remaining to participate. Now that the attacking characters are defined, the player clicks the defending character's empty slot and selects the Archer on the battlefield. With both participating attackers and the target selected, the OK button is enabled in the Targeting window, and the player can click it to commence the attack. Both characters perform their function in the combo, and Suten-Heh can continue his turn, still free to move and use a skill.

Skill Use

The third action that a character can perform is skill use. Skills are special actions acquired by characters throughout the game. Healing, spells, and the invocation of special items are all examples of skills. For example, Priests of Isis and Priests of Osiris are imbued with different spells. Characters gain skills with experience and by collecting special items. Healing can also be "learned" by characters, whose proficiency at curing other characters increases throughout the game. (See Figure D.6.)

Name	Influence	Range	Cost (Spell Points)	Effect
Healing	Targeted		2	Heals a unit's health points
Replenish	Targeted		10	Heals a unit's health points
Meditation	Local		0	Recovers the caster's spell points
Blinding Eye	Targeted		5	Blinds a unit
Burning Eye	Local	5	10	Burns units around caster
Thundering Eye	Zoned	5	15	Strikes thunder and lightning at an area
Touch of Isis	Zoned	5	10	Heals all units' health and spell points within a casting radius
Touch of Ra	Targeted		15	Temporarily raises a unit's strength
Touch of Osiris	Local	5	20	Summons a mummy from the ground
Boils and Sores	Targeted		15	Diseases a unit
Soul Drink	Targeted		25	Drains unit of health points and spell points and adds them to those of the caster

Figure D.6
Skills.

Spells

Spells are diverse skills that select characters in the game perform. Spells cost characters in magic points, which act much like action points. However, a character's magic points are restored every battle, not every turn. The amount of magic points restored to a character depends on the character's spirituality, experience, and class. Special actions, such as meditation or the use of certain potions, can be used to restore magic points more quickly, but these, too, involve the use of skills. Of course, more powerful spells cost more magic points. Therefore, classes that are able to cast spells, such as priests and mummies, must budget their magic points throughout battle.

Spells can be untargeted, targeted, or zoned. Untargeted spells occur without direction and don't require the player's choice of a target. For example, the Blinding Eye spell creates a shearing beacon of light above the caster; therefore, it requires no target. Targeted spells are aimed at one or more characters and are directed by the player via the Targeting window. For example, the Sunstroke spell burns a single character, which the player selects with the Targeting window. Zoned spells occur within an area of effect, which the player selects with a movable icon on the battlefield. After the player moves the icon to the desired location and clicks, the spell is triggered in the selected zone. For example, the Desert's Breath spell creates a small sandstorm somewhere on the battlefield, and all characters within its range are torn up.

Depending on a character's attributes, the learning of spells occurs at different points in the game. A character might suddenly gain the ability to cast a spell after a successful battle or after finding a mystical and potent artifact. In any case, the capability of casting a spell is permanent and, once learned, relies only on the character's current amount of magic points.

Healing

Throughout battles, characters are beaten, burned, crushed, shot, frozen, and stabbed. Health points are restored when a battle is completed, so characters might become unconscious or die. After a character reaches a low enough threshold (determined by the character's class and resilience), he is rendered unconscious and falls to the ground, unable to perform actions. The character then requires healing by another character before it can do anything else. If a character is badly hurt, he begins to die. In this case, the character's Statistics panel displays the number of rounds left to be healed before the character dies. If a character is unconscious and hit by an enemy, the result will probably be death. Characters can also be killed from a conscious state if the attack is sufficiently powerful. If characters die, they do not progress further in the game unless they are resurrected later.

Healing is a skill much like spells, but it does not require spell points. Almost any character can heal another, with various degrees of proficiency. For example, Priests of Isis are potent at healing and can cast powerful healing spells. However, a Guard has almost no healing ability and can only use healing in the most desperate situations.

Meditation

Meditation is a skill possessed only by magic users. Requiring no magic points, the use of this skill increases the character's magic points for its next turn. The amount of increase depends on the character's spirituality, class, and experience.

Item Use

The use of items represents a diverse set of possibilities for characters. Some items possess special skills, including healing or spell powers that are available to characters regardless of their classes, healing capabilities, or magic points. Special items (items that can invoke their skills) come in various types, from weapons to treasure. The abilities of all special items are plainly displayed with the item's other information in the Inventory window.

The use of items' skills is special because it provides flexibility in what the player can do. For example, a slave can't cast even the most rudimentary of spells, but if the slave has a Sun Wadjet, the player can choose to use the item's Blinding Eye skill. Because of this, the slave can move, attack, and cast a spell in one turn.

Inventory

The player can view the Inventory window at any point during battle by pressing the Inventory button beneath the Action menu. The inventory displays the current character's items and relevant information such as which weapons are equipped and that character's amount of gold. The player can also view the inventories of the other team members by clicking on their names in the Inventory window. During battle, the player can equip or unequip weapons or remove items. After battle, the player can trade items between characters.

Level Descriptions

The player guides Sekhem and his band through several levels. These levels begin at Alexandria in northern Egypt and wind south toward Queen Uheset's capital of Thebes. (See Table D.3.)

Table D.3 Class Descriptions

Name	Class	Description
Sekhem	Soldier	Son of Meseru, vengeful warrior determined to kill Uheset
Sati	Priest of Osiris	Betrayer of Meseru, Sekhem's repentant guide
Uheset	Priest of Osiris	Queen of Egypt, destroyer of Meseru
Khefta	Soldier	Bloodthirsty general, betrayer of Meseru
Neru	Bodyguard	Former guard of foreign chief, freed by Sekhem and now his loyal protector
Emaui	Archer	Angry young woman who shares Sekhem's hate for Uheset

Level 1: Streets of Alexandria

The first level that the player encounters depicts the streets of Alexandria. The level lacks complexity to make it easier for the player to become used to playing the game.

Intro

Alone and with a purpose, a young man reached the shores of Alexandria. A foreigner to this land, he still knew much about it. His father had spun stories of the Pharaoh and the gods, desert dunes, and eternal river. Those tales had become one with his anger, an anger that would carry him from a distant land to the home of his father.

The warrior was Sekhem, son of the warlord Meseru. A mirror of his father's might and command, Sekhem had disguised himself as a simple pilgrim. He had sailed for weeks to reach the port, and he was eager to begin his journey down the Nile. With nothing but a dagger and his late father's golden ankh, Sekhem began his quest for retribution.

Description

The first level begins in the tight streets of Alexandria, where Sekhem lands after his journey from Greece. (See Figure D.7.) He faces several small groups of abusive city guards who want to rob him. Sekhem's only items are a simple dagger and his father's golden ankh.

The level is built up of stucco walls and curving alleyways. Its battles take place in the city's common square, a garden, and the fountain plaza. The enemies consist of annoying guards.

Layout

The layout of the level lacks detail so that the player of the game can concentrate on learning the controls. On the other hand, there is enough detail to interest the player in the game features.

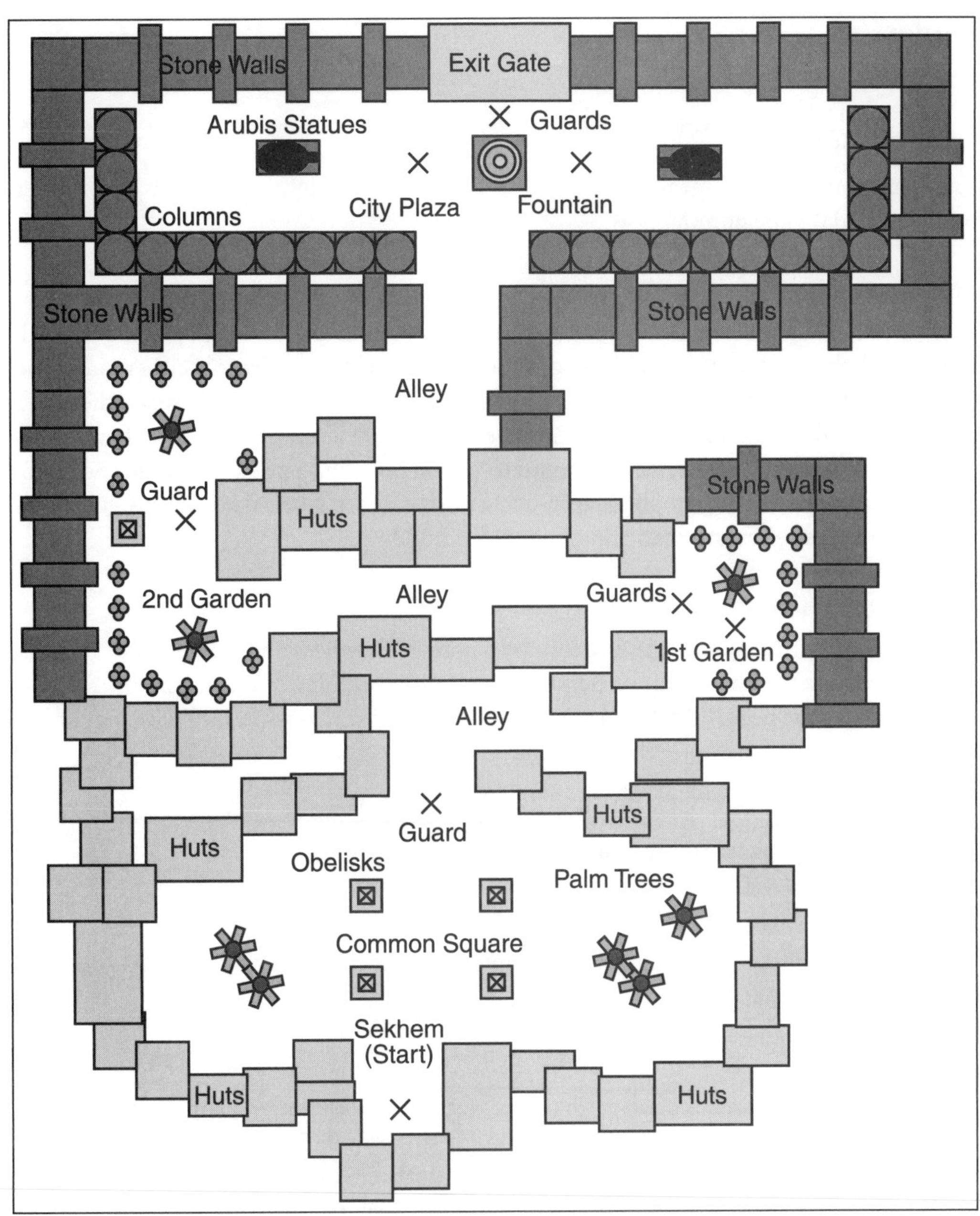

Figure D.7
File-level layout.

Battles

Refer to the layout for Level 1 (Figure D.7) to locate the scenes of the battles.

Common Square

The common square appears right after the front gate. Lighting should be brighter because the day is beginning.

Scene

This vacant area is surrounded by plastered houses. Its only exit is an alley at the far end. A set of obelisks adorns the cobbled ground, and palm trees grow on either side. The square acts as an introduction to actions, as the player must navigate it to reach the other side and the alley beyond. The level's first enemy, a guard, attempts to rob Sekhem of his scant riches. Sekhem must defeat the guard to pass. This is the game's first battle. Sekhem, initially equipped with a simple dagger, acquires the guard's broadsword and gold. The common square's sides are made up of plastered buildings.

Beginning Dialogue

Guard: "Welcome to Alexandria, urchin. My name is Tuthmek, and I'll be your... Well, what have we here? That's quite a pendant, urchin! I could fetch a tidy amount for that ankh around your neck. I'll tell you what. You can keep your worthless life for that lovely little ornament. I'd hate to redden the trinket. What do you say?"

Sekhem: "I'd sooner deliver up my heart to a beast such as you."

Guard: "I was hoping you'd say that!"

Garden

The garden provides plants, hanging if possible. The setting is still bright but has deepening shadows.

Scene

Sekhem finds his way into a small garden area, decorated with potted plants and trees. The edge of the garden is made up of houses and a stone wall. Two weak guards threaten Sekhem here, and the player must defeat them to advance. The garden's overall look is that of a deeply urban space with an unusual amount of greenery. The plants are organized in such a way as not to interfere with the ensuing battle. Sekhem acquires the guards' broadswords and gold and a Sun Wadjet, which contains the Blinding Eye skill.

Beginning Dialogue

First Guard: "How did filth like you find your way here? On second thought, don't answer. It doesn't matter. Tuthmek must be off with those Phoenician wenches again. Do I know you? You look familiar... Ah well, no matter. We'll take care of this."

Fountain Plaza

Open and bright. The fountain contrasts the sinister approach of the guard.

Scene

The fountain plaza is the final showdown between Sekhem and the corrupt Alexandrian city guard. Here the player has to defeat four guards. Sekhem's experience will have increased by this time to make such a defeat possible. The plaza is surrounded by stone walls and a colonnade. One end opens to an exit gate that stands on the opposite side. A fountain and statues of Anubis decorate the plaza's pavement. The three guards have heard of Sekhem's defeat of their peers and are anxious to kill him. This climactic battle of the first level will be difficult to win but will hinge on the outmaneuvering of Sekhem's slow enemies and use of the Sun Wadjet's Blinding Eye spell and the restorative powers of the golden ankh. After defeating the guards, the sage Sati joins Sekhem and explains part of their interconnected history.

Beginning Dialogue

First Guard: "Nice sword, urchin. Looks an awful lot like my friend Tuthmek's."

Sekhem: "I'm sure he'd agree with you, if he could."

First Guard: "You lie, filth, and that's a capital offense around here! Get him!"

Ending Dialogue

Sati: "Greetings, warrior. Until now, I hadn't dared to hope. But the young man I see before me proves the impossible. Stand assured, for I know why you have come."

Sekhem: "You confuse me with another, sir. I'm a common stranger to this city, looking only to pass through. Please step aside, for I'd hate to repeat the insistence I showed these guards."

Sati: "Lecture me not, boy, for it is you who must learn. Old I may be, but these eyes know your own. In you I see the greatest leader ever to command these lands, a man whom I counted my greatest friend. Even that bauble around your neck is proof enough. You may be a stranger, son, but not common. In you I see salvation from dark powers. In you I see the legacy of Meseru. To your father, I was known as Sati."

Sekhem: "Sati? The man my father called Sati is long dead. How do you know me?"

Sati: "I told you, young man. I was closest to your father, and much of me died when he was betrayed to the western sands. I find it hard to depart this life in these wicked days. But come, I will tell you all. I owe it both to you and myself. I owe it to your father."

Resources

This section provides a list of models, sounds, effects, and other items needed for this level. Most of the resources named appear in several levels.

Models

The specific way that models are laid out can be determined during the construction of the level. The following features appear in the level:

- Sekhem
- Guard
- House
- Obelisk
- Palm tree
- Potted plant
- Stone wall and buttress
- Column
- Statue of Anubis
- Fountain
- Gate

Sounds

The following sounds can be used during the action that takes place at this level:

- Background song
- Weapon clashes
- Unit sounds

Effects

The following effects should be available at this level:

- Blinding Eye spell
- Healing skill

Items

The characters should have access to the following weapons or other items:

- Dagger
- Ankh
- Broadsword
- Gold
- Sun Wadjet

note

For the complete *Ankh Game Design*, refer to the version of the document installed from the CD. See Appendix A for more information.

Ankh Software Requirements Specification

The requirements document was a team effort from the start. The team revised it almost daily using the laptop and the overhead projector.

Description

The *Ankh Software Requirements Specification* provides a list and description of the functional and nonfunctional specifications for the software components of *Ankh.* It is derived in part from the *Ankh Game Design Document* and is supplemented by the *Ankh Software Design Specification* and the *Ankh Project Software Test Plan.*

The *Ankh Software Requirements Specification* provides the following views of the requirements:

- A list of the requirements presented numerically
- A preliminary component grouping of the requirements
- Use case explorations of the requirements
- A preliminary mapping of the requirements against proposed objects and their responsibilities

The document is intended to establish the initial scope of the development effort.

Perspective

This is a single-player turn-based strategy game. It is intended to illustrate the processes and technical items contained by a textbook on software engineering and game development. The game incorporates features that are common to PC games, but it also introduces a variety of innovations that are not usually offered in beginning game books. Among these features are the following:

- Advanced resource management
- A state machine
- Event handling through the binding of member functions
- The use of the Boost library
- The use of map and character editors
- Saving and loading of game states

Product Functions System Decomposition View

Preliminary functional components of the product are as follows (see the *Ankh Software Design Specification* for greater detail):

Stripe 1: Game Opening

Stripe 2.a: Tile Map

Stripe 2.b: GUI Elements

Stripe 2.c: Map Editor

Stripe 2.d: Save Level

Stripe 3: Level Template (modeled on first level)

Stripe 4: Character Editor

Stripe 5: Game Physics

Stripe 6: Inventory

Stripe 7: Combat

Stripe 8: Skills

Stripe 9: Outside World Management

Stripe 10: Skills Interface

Stripe 11: AI

Stripe 12: Remaining Levels

Stripe 13: Saving and Loading

Stripe 14: Options

Stripe 15: Revisions

These components are explored more fully later, under the heading "Functional Requirements Component View."

User Characteristics

This game is designed for players of all ages. However, its features offer points of interest for people who are learning how to develop games using C++ and DirectX.

The game offers the ability to save level and character configurations. Other features enable students of the game to see what they can do with a relatively advanced development effort.

Constraints

Ankh serves largely to illustrate development activities. Although it includes a wide range of interesting features, such as map editing, character editing, and other things, it is not intended to offer a level of complexity that corresponds to a commercial game. Code is intentionally simplified so that readers of the book can make easy use of it.

Assumptions and Dependencies

An executable is included on the CD, but users of the text can compile the game at different stripe levels. The user should have versions 6.0 or 7.0 of Microsoft Visual C++. An installation package accompanies the software.

Take care to package the game so that users of the text that the game accompanies can load it in stripes.

External Resource Requirements

This section of the document pertains to user and system requirements that affect the operation of the game within a given system or within a network context.

User Interface

The user interface is based on components created using Direct3D and DirectInput. Standard Windows message is used for key events. The game runs on a personal computer. At a minimum, the interface should support 16-bit and 32-bit resolution. The primary resolution should be 640×480, but higher resolutions should be supported.

Hardware Interface

Ankh executes on a PC that is equipped with a Pentium III or equivalent, a Direct3D-compatible graphics cards, and an appropriate sound card.

Software Interface

DirectX 9.b (Summer Update 2003) or later is required for the game.

Communications Interface

The user interacts with the game using the mouse and the keyboard.

Functional Requirements Views

This section provides the first of three views of the functional requirements for *Ankh*:

- The first view provides a primary, sequential list of the functional requirements.
- The second view provides a list of the functional requirements as grouped according to component. A component is also called a stripe. Each stripe represents a coherent grouping of functionality.
- The third view provides a set of use cases that offer proofs-of-concept for the requirements. The use cases supplement the master requirements list. See Appendix A, "Installation and Setup," for a use-case view of the requirements listed in this section.

Primary List of Functional Requirements

<Req_1>—Software shall have the capability to save the game state from a menu.

<Req_2>—Software shall have the capability to return to a saved state by loading a file.

<Req_3>—Software shall have the capability to associate user profiles with saved game files.

<Req_4>—Software shall allow the player to choose file names.

<Req_5>—Software shall have an auto-save feature that automatically saves the game constantly to memory.

<Req_6>—Software shall have a timer mechanism that will flush memory to disk periodically (every 20 seconds).

<Req_7>—Software shall provide the player the option to save a Replay after a battle.

<Req_8>—Software shall have a Main menu that will have a Load Replay option.

<Req_9>—Software shall save Replays to a default directory where the profile information is stored.

<Req_10>—Software shall prompt the user to create a profile that is stored in the Profiles directory.

<Req_11>—Software shall allow the player to play back at variable speeds.

<Req_12>—Software shall have a Pause/Resume feature to facilitate Replays.

<Req_13>—Software shall implement terrains, characters, and buildings—any 3D objects as meshes.

<Req_14>—Software shall run only in full screen mode.

<Req_15>—Software shall have the capability to handle Alt+Tab key combination.

<Req_16>—Software shall support a custom mouse pointer.

<Req_17>—Software shall have support for alpha channels.

<Req_18>—Software shall support panels, menus, buttons, sliders, text boxes, and pictures.

<Req_19>—Characters shall have at a minimum these attributes: strength, health, agility, vitality, and intelligence.

<Req_20>—Characters shall have skills that are appropriate to their class.

<Req_21>—Each character shall belong to a social class that is identifiable based on unique attributes.

<**Req_22**>—Customization shall be based on tools rather than be hard coded.

<**Req_23**>—Software shall have a logging capability that will track errors and log trace statements.

<**Req_24**>—Software shall not support multiplayer and should be player against the AI.

<**Req_25**>—The AI shall have the capability to use units and play the game.

<**Req_26**>—The AI shall be able to play any unit based on modes.

<**Req_27**>—Software shall support at least five levels based on a simple story.

<**Req_28**>—Software shall have the capability to play the game using only a mouse.

<**Req_29**>—Software shall support MP3 playback and allow the player to select his own music.

<**Req_30**>—Software shall include default music that the player can replace.

<**Req_31**>—Software shall operate correctly in the absence of music files.

<**Req_32**>—Software shall support DirectSound and a variety of sound formats, particularly .wav and .mp3 extensions.

<**Req_33**>—Software shall support 16 channels and allow the user to disable the sound effects.

<**Req_34**>—Software shall support a particle generator for special effects.

<**Req_35**>—Software shall support the dot X mesh format.

<**Req_36**>—Software shall allow the player to control at least 6 units.

<**Req_37**>—Software shall have a game mode where it can play against itself.

<**Req_38**>—Software shall support a main menu with these entries:

New Game

Continue

Change Profile

Options

Exit

Editor

Load game

<**Req_39**>—Software shall support the following options:

Change Resolution

Sound

Volume

Game Speed

<Req_40>—Software shall support the capability for characters to acquire various armor, weapons, and inventory.

<Req_41>—Software shall support different kinds of terrain that will affect the performance of the characters.

<Req_42>—Software shall support the capability that given two points, it will be able to navigate and find a sensible path.

<Req_43>—Software shall support a Map Editor.

<Req_44>—Software shall support an intuitive Character Editor.

<Req_45>—Software shall support the capability for characters to move based on armor, speed, terrain, and so on.

<Req_46>—Software shall load in no more than 20 seconds and display a progress bar or some other indicator that loading is in progress.

<Req_47>—Software shall allow a player to select units with the mouse and use a different button to perform actions.

<Req_48>—Software shall have a fixed camera angle of _.

<Req_49>—Each character shall have an inventory.

<Req_50>—The shareware program INNO shall be used to install the CD that accompanies the book.

<Req_51>—Software shall fit on a single disk including support tools.

<Req_52>—Software shall support a ToolTip to provide information to the player of the game.

<Req_53>—Software shall include a user's guide.

<Req_54>—Units that die and that you do not revive within a specific period never come back.

<Req_55>—Units can be restored back to health using magic (and items).

<Req_56>—Units gain experience and enhance their skills through combat.

<Req_57>—When a user starts the game, he is provided with configuration options, such as playing a previous game. (The game starts with a profile selection screen, followed by a main menu screen.)

<Req_58>—Software shall support the following software/hardware:

Windows 98 or higher

500-MHz CPU

128 MB

16-MB 3D Accelerator (TNT2)

CD-ROM

DirectX 9

<Req_59>—During the installation of the product, the user shall have a choice of which tools to install.

<Req_60>—Documentation for the editor and tools shall be provided in separate HTML files.

<Req_61>—Software shall be implemented in C++/Win32.

<Req_62>—Software shall include a batch file for compiling the program.

<Req_63>—Software shall support automatic source code documentation.

<Req 64>—Software shall support a global system clock to synchronize events in the game.

Functional Requirements Component View

The *Ankh Software Design Description* deals with this view of the requirements in much greater detail. It provides a componential view of the classes that implement the functionality. The breakdown here is meant only as a preliminary exploration of the scope of the game.

Stripe 1—Opening

Requirements 8, 14, 15, 16, 17, 18, 23, 28, 38, 46, 57

Stripe 2.1—GUI Objects

Requirement 18, 52

Stripe 2.2—Floor Tiling

Requirement 43

Stripe 2.3—Mesh Placement

Requirements 13, 43

Stripe 2.4—Save and Load

Requirement 4

Stripe 3.1—Navigate Alexandria

Requirement 13, 14, 15, 16, 17, 36, 61

Stripe 3.2—Sound

Requirements 29, 30, 31, 32, 33

Stripe 4—Character Editor

Requirements 18, 19, 20, 21, 22, 35, 44

Stripe 5—Unit Physics

Requirements 13, 14, 15, 16, 17, 35, 41, 47, 42, 45, 48, 64

Stripe 6—Inventory Items

Requirements 40, 49, 55

Stripe 7—Combat

Requirements 54, 56

Stripe 8—Acquire Skills

Requirements 20, 34, 47, 55, 56

Stripe 9—Acquire Weapon

Requirements 14, 15, 16, 17, 40, 49

Stripe 10—View Statistics

Requirements 14, 15, 16, 17, 18, 19, 20, 21

Stripe 11—AI

Requirements 24, 25, 26, 37

Stripe 12—Remaining Levels

Requirement 27

Stripe 13—Saving and Loading

Requirements 1, 2, 3, 4, 5, 6, 7, 8, 9, 10, 11, 12

Stripe 14—Options

Requirement 39

Nonfunctional Requirements

Requirements 50, 51, 53, 58, 59, 60, 61, 62, 63

Use Case View of the Requirements

Appendix A presents a full set of use cases for the functional requirements of *Ankh.* Each use case tests the validity of a requirement or set of requirements and collects information that is useful in the development of a test plan. The use cases also provide a start on the design work. See the *Ankh Software Test Plan* for specific information on testing. See the *Ankh Software Design Specification* for information on the generalized design scenarios for *Ankh.*

Design Constraints

This section lists design constraints. Design constraints pertain to any development factors that relate to the scope of the project or that can impact the development schedule for the product.

Availability

Ankh is available for play after installation. A single installation package allows you to install the game. Take care to develop "stripes" of the game so that readers of the game text can view it at different stages of construction.

Security

There are no security issues.

Maintainability

You can modify the game using the map and character editors. If a patch or expansion is issued, you can overwrite the executable. The maintenance elements are available for download from the Web site. The editors create data files, which must not be overwritten during updates.

Other Requirements

Some nonfunctional requirements, enumerated earlier in both the component decomposition and the consecutive, apply to the game. These requirements are as follows: 50, 51, 53, 58, 59, 60, 61, 62, and 63.

Use Cases

Following are use case scenarios that explore the requirements listed in Section 3 of the SRS. You can find the complete set of use cases in Appendix A of the *Ankh Software Requirements Specification* in the Documents directory.

The CD contains all of the use cases.

Use Case 1

Use Case Name: Player saves game state
Requirement(s) Explored: 1, 4
Player (Actor) Context (Role): Player
Precondition(s): Game is in progress, and player has brought up menu.
Trigger(s): Player chooses Save Game from menu.
Main Course of Action: 1. A File diaog box is presented so that the player can choose the file name for the save. 2. The player chooses a location and file name for his saved game and clicks OK. 3. The system dumps out the current game to the chosen location. 4. The dialog box closes, and the player is brought back to the menu.
Alternate Course(s) of Action: 2a. The player clicks Cancel. 2a1. The dialog box closes and the player is brought back to the menu. 2b. The file already exists and the player is asked to confirm overwriting it.
Exceptional Course(s) of Action: 3a. There is an error trying to save the game (disk space, read only, and so on). 3a1. An error message is displayed, and the player is taken back to step 1.

Use Case 2

Use Case Name: User Loads a File
Requirement(s) Explored: 2
Player (Actor) Context (Role): Player
Precondition(s): A saved game must exist.
Trigger(s): Player chooses to load the game from the menu and chooses a valid saved file.
Main Course of Action: 1. The system loads the initial game state from the save file. 2. The system goes through the saved game and performs all the actions listed in it without updating the screen so that it appears instantaneous to the player. 3. Control of the game is given back to the player when the end of the file is reached.
Alternate Course(s) of Action:
Exceptional Course(s) of Action: 1a. The saved game is an older format that is no longer supported. 1b. The saved game appears to be corrupted and the system cannot parse it.

Use Case 3

Use Case Name: User Associates Profiles
Requirement(s) Explored: 3, 9
Player (Actor) Context (Role): Player
Precondition(s): The player must have created at least one profile.
Trigger(s): The player brings up a File dialog box that asks him where to save or load either a replay or saved game.
Main Course of Action: 1. The system will choose the player's default directory for saving/loading based on his current profile.
Alternate Course(s) of Action:
Exceptional Course(s) of Action: 1a. The player deletes his profile mid-game.

Use Case 4

Use Case Name: Player Chooses File Names
Requirement(s) Explored: 4
Player (Actor) Context (Role): Player
Precondition(s): The player wants to save or load a file (saved game, replay, and so on).
Trigger(s): The player performs an action that requires him to choose a file name before continuing.
Main Course of Action: 1. The system will bring up a FileDialog GUI object to allow the player to browse through directories and type in a file name. 2. The player clicks on the OK button to accept his choice.
Alternate Course(s) of Action: 2a. The player double-clicks on an existing file to confirm his choice. 2b. The player clicks Cancel or presses Escape to cancel the action of selecting a file.
Exceptional Course(s) of Action: 2a. The player tries to save to a location where he is not allowed.

Use Case 5

Use Case Name: Player Sees Save
Requirement(s) Explored: 5, 6
Player (Actor) Context (Role): System
Precondition(s): The player is playing the game and is currently in a battle.
Trigger(s): A timer fires every 20 seconds or so.
Main Course of Action: 1. The game state is dumped to a file in the player's Profile directory.
Alternate Course(s) of Action: 1a. Autosave is disabled.
Exceptional Course(s) of Action: 1a. The system runs out of disk space. 1b. The user does not have permission to write to his Profile directory. 1c. The user erased his Profile directory while the game was running.

note

For the complete *Ankh Software Requirements Specification,* refer to the version of the document installed from the CD.

Ankh Software Design Specification

The design document replaced the requirements document as the primary working document after the first quarter of the project. Everyone on the team worked on it through group review sessions. Its diagrams were almost always viewed as proofs of concepts rather than detailed plans.

Purpose and Layout of the Document

This document depicts the design of software. The layout of the document provides you with a way to envision how the software is created in terms of its development cycle and its component construction. Each component is referred to as a stripe. That's because the term *stripe* implies both the component parts (classes, global functions, COM objects, and so on) and the position that the development of the components occupy in the development cycle.

The system is presented in up to five ways. These are referred to as *views.* In some cases, the views are created using UML diagrams. In other cases, lists or generic UML object diagrams are used. The views are as follows:

- Requirements (list and CRC)
- Conceptual (freeform object diagram)
- Behavioral (sequence and collaboration)
- Logical (class)
- Component (implementation and deployment)

Figure D.8 represents the views featured in this document.

Source Documentation

This section contains a list of the documents from which information has been drawn to for the design effort.

CRC Views

CRC cards are found in the *Ankh Software Requirements Specification.*

A separate document archives the CRC cards: RequirementsCRCView_V_0105.doc. This document is included in the *Ankh Software Requirements Specification.*

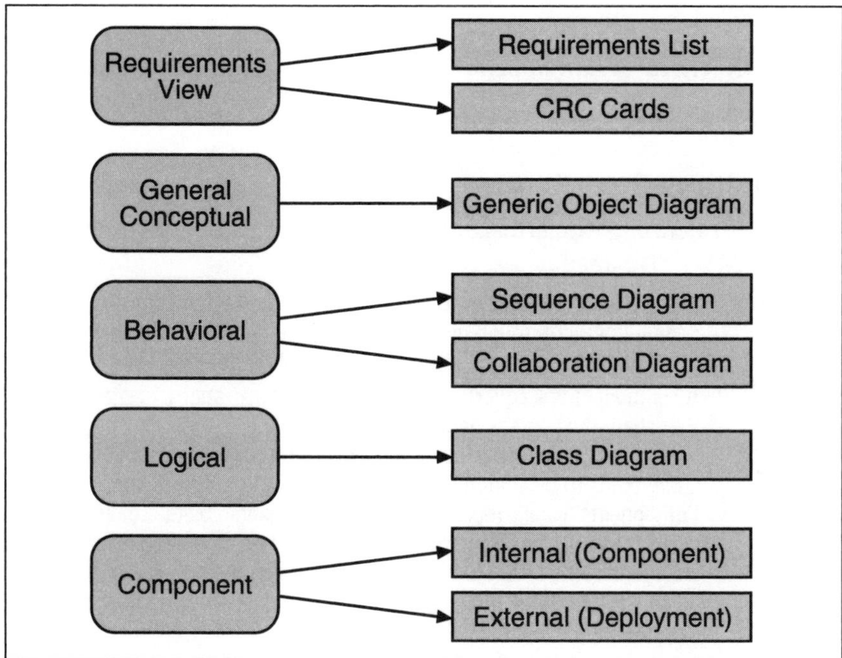

Figure D.8
Ankh Software Design Description views, UML, and other representations.

Requirements

The requirements for the *Ankh* software, in list form, are contained in the *Ankh Software Requirements Specification.*

Use Cases

Use cases for specific requirements appear in the *Ankh Software Requirements Specification.* The use cases for the requirements establish and verify the context and scope of the requirements. In this document, another set of use cases is employed. These are design use cases. A design use is presented for each of the stripes and establishes the integrated functionality that should be evident with the completion of each stripe. A design use case represents but does not include all of the functionality that is embodied in a single stripe. A design use case is a proof of concept for the stripe.

You can find references to the Class-Responsibility-Collaboration (CRC) cards in the later section titled "Sample CRC Cards."

TOR Chart

You can find the TOR chart in an appendix to the *Ankh Software Requirements Specification.*

Glossary and Definitions

This section contains a list defining the terms and acronyms used in this document.

Behavioral view	The behavioral view tries to show how the objects that comprise the system interact through messages or operations. Behavioral views can be presented using UML sequence and collaboration diagrams.
Component	A component is a collection of classes, global operations, or other items that share the same general set of responsibilities. One stripe might have dependencies distributed among several components, but each stripe tends to be centered on the development of a given component. Components usually represent the focus of a single build. Component views take two forms: internal and external. The internal component view represents a subset of the system that can be compiled or tested as an isolated entity. The external component view represents the entire system at a given phase of its development.
Conceptual view	This is a representation of the system using either a use case or a general object diagram. If the general object diagram is used, the boxes depict class objects, global functions, COM objects, database tables, and other items. A conceptual view is optional. It is recommended for use during early phases of the design or at points in the project at which it is important to show some of the preliminary work that led to given design decisions. It is intended as a way that those who are trying to understand the design from a historical perspective can re-create the conceptual framework in which design decisions arrive.
External component view	The external component view represents the entire system built at a given point in the development life of the system. Ultimately, it represents how the system is deployed. Because it is intended to represent an overall system build effected during the software development effort, as stripes are developed, the external component view becomes more involved.
Internal component view	The internal component view is intended as a way to show an isolated view of the system. It might or might not represent an entire system build, but for the stripe it represents, all system dependencies that are relevant to the stripe should be included. This view is intended to represent a portion of the overall system that can stand alone and compile as a separate entity. A component represents the classes, functions, and other software items that are designed for a given phase of development, together with a description of the point at which these elements were implemented during the development process. This representation of the system is intended to expose the features of the system that are specific to a given stripe, not to represent the system as a whole.

Logical view	A representation of the system that shows the classes that compose the system and their static relationships. The logical view of the system is represented using class diagrams. Included in the class diagrams are selected attributes and operations of classes. The use cases are created both inductively and deductively. Inductively, the use cases are derived from the sequence and collaboration diagrams. Deductively, they are drawn directly from analysis of the system's functional requirements.
Stage	Stripes might have stages, which are reflected in the build history of the system. The stripe stages have bearing on the design because they imply that the complexity of a given stripe is great enough that its implementation should not be attempted all at once. At the same time, the reduction of a stripe to stages implies that the stages make the most sense when they are developed in a single design unit.
Stripe	A stripe is a set of functionality embodied in a single component of the system, together with a description of the point in the development process in which the component comprising the stripe is implemented. Stripes are represented using up to five views of the system. Each stripe should represent a complete system build, but within the stripe documentation is a component view from which you can identify the specific functionality that is implanted with the stripe. Such a description might prove useful during redevelopment or upgrade efforts.
Use case view	A use case view of each stripe is shown. Each use case for this document represents a proof of concept for the stripe. Use cases for the design effort are attempts to show how the implementation of a given design element manifests itself in the operation of the system. It can also serve as a starting point for the decomposition or isolation of system functionality for testing efforts.
View	A view is a way of looking at the system. The views shown in this document are requirements, conceptual, behavioral (sequence and collaboration), logical (class diagrams), and component (internal and system).

Component Descriptions

This section contains descriptions and diagrams of each of the software components of the system. Generally, each component is presented as a stripe. A stripe is a representation of the system that encompasses both the functionality of the system and the place in the development process at which the functionality is implemented. See the Glossary for more complete definitions.

If you are effecting an upgrade of modification of the system, the stripe representation of the system allows you to understand the order in which components were developed and the types of dependencies that unfold during the development process.

List of System Stripes

The components are represented as stripes, and the order in which the stripes are presented represent the recommended order in which the system can be built.

Table D.4 provides a summary of the stripes that comprise the game.

Stripe 1: Start of Game

This stripe is the first implementation stripe of the game. It provides a basic framework in which to test the game window and the GUI features that are applicable to user interactions at the game level.

Table D.4 System Stripes

Stripe Number	Summary
Stripe 1	Opening, Requirements 8, 14, 15, 16, 17, 18, 23, 28, 38, 46, 57
Stripe 2.1	GUI Objects, Requirements 18, 52
Stripe 2.2	Floor Tiling, Requirement 43
Stripe 2.3	Mesh Placement, Requirements 13, 43
Stripe 2.4	Save and Load, Requirement 4
Stripe 3.1	Navigate Alexandria, Requirement 13, 14, 15, 16, 17, 36, 61
Stripe 3.2	Sound, Requirements 29, 30, 31, 32, 33
Stripe 4	Character Editor, Requirements 18, 19, 20, 21, 22, 35, 44
Stripe 5	Unit Physics, Requirements 13, 14, 15, 16, 17, 35, 41, 42, 45, 47, 48, 64
Stripe 6	Inventory Items, Requirements 40, 49, 55
Stripe 7	Combat, Requirements 54, 56
Stripe 8	Acquire Skills, Requirements 20, 34, 47, 55, 56
Stripe 9	Acquire Weapon, Requirements 14, 15, 16, 17, 40, 49
Stripe 10	View Statistics, Requirements 14, 15, 16, 17, 18, 19, 20, 21
Stripe 11	AI, Requirements 24, 25, 26, 37
Stripe 12	Remaining Levels, Requirement 27
Stripe 13	Saving and Loading, Requirements 1, 2, 3, 4, 5, 6, 7, 8, 9, 10, 11, 12
Stripe 14	Options, Requirement 39
Stripe 15	Revisions
Nonfunctional	Requirements 50, 51, 53, 58, 59, 60, 61, 62, 63

Stripe 1: Requirements View

This section identifies the requirements and use cases derived from the *Ankh SRS* that apply to this stripe.

Stripe 1: Applicable Requirements

The following list identifies the requirements that are addressed in this stripe:

Requirements 8, 14, 15, 16, 17, 18, 38, 46

Stripe 1: Use Case View

The following use case(s) provides a narrative of a sequence of actions that you can use to place the behavior depicted in this stripe in context. The requirements use case from which this design use case is derived appears in the *Ankh SRS.*

Use Case Name: Select Exit at the Game's Start
Requirement(s) Explored: 8, 14, 15, 16, 17, 18, 38, 46
Player (Actor) Context (Role): Player starting game.
Precondition(s): Game up and running.
Trigger(s): Player clicks Start icon.
Main Course of Action: 1. This use case is triggered by the closing of the splash screen. 2. The system shows the basic game window. 3. The system displays the main play options for the game. 4. The player views the options: New Game, Load Game, Continue, Change Profile, Options, Exit. 5. The player chooses one option: Exit. 6. The system acknowledges the choice. 7. The system requests the user to confirm the choice. 8. The user confirms the choice. 9. The system exits. 10. This use case ends when the system exists.
Alternate Course(s) of Action:
Exceptional Course(s) of Action:

Stripe 1: Generalized Conceptual View

This section provides a conceptual view of this stripe. The components that are represented in the context diagram are not necessarily included in the context diagram. The diagram is most useful for early iterations of the development cycle, as a means by which team members can conceptualize the system.

The diagram is based on the interactions derived from the use case, the requirements, and an initial conceptualization of the system. See the refinement provided in the Component section of this stripe for implementation-level details.

Note that this view is used only in this stripe for purposes of general analysis. In subsequent stripes, the dimensions of the system take on a gravity that makes this supplemental view unnecessary.

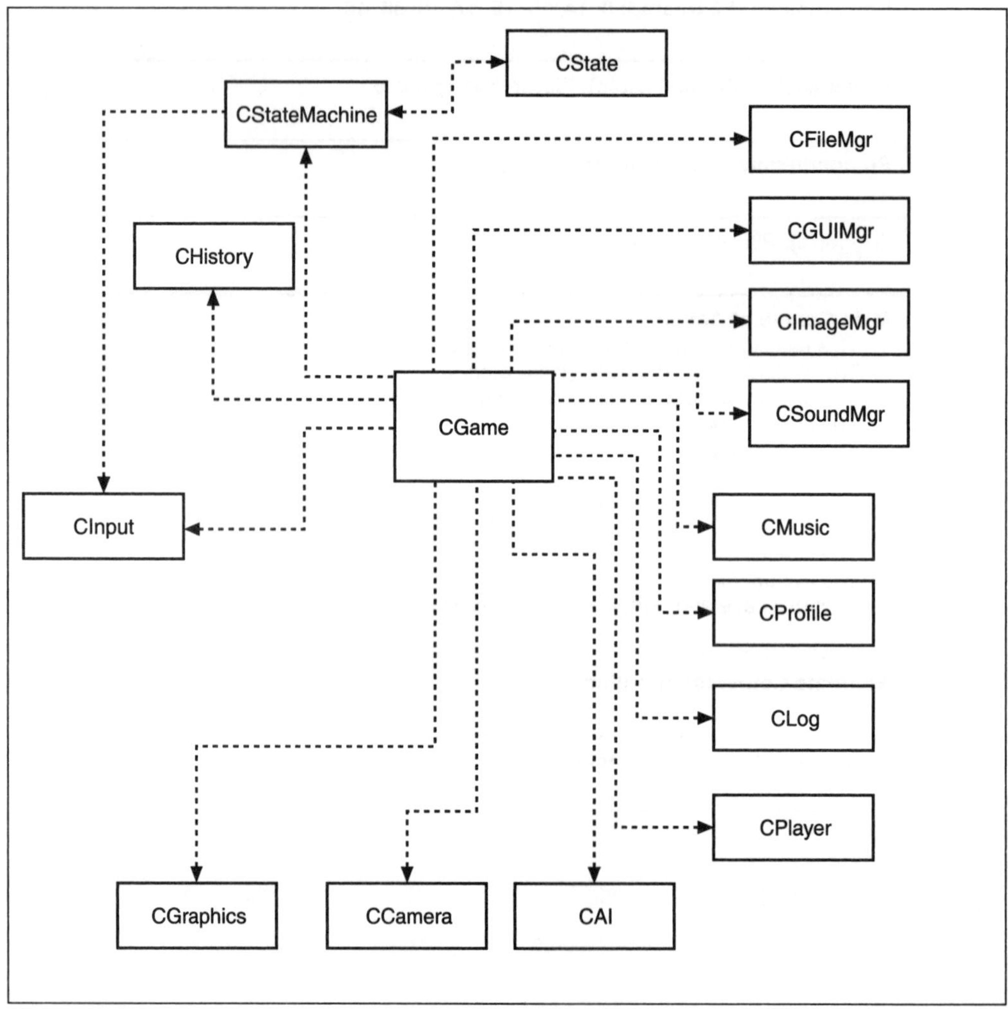

Stripe 1: Behavioral View—Interactions

This section depicts the interactions that are evident in the behavior of this stripe.

Stripe 1: Sequence View

The sequence view shows the basic interactions that are evident in the stripe, along with the generic identity of the interacting classes.

Stripe 1: Collaboration View

This section provides a collaborative view of this stripe.

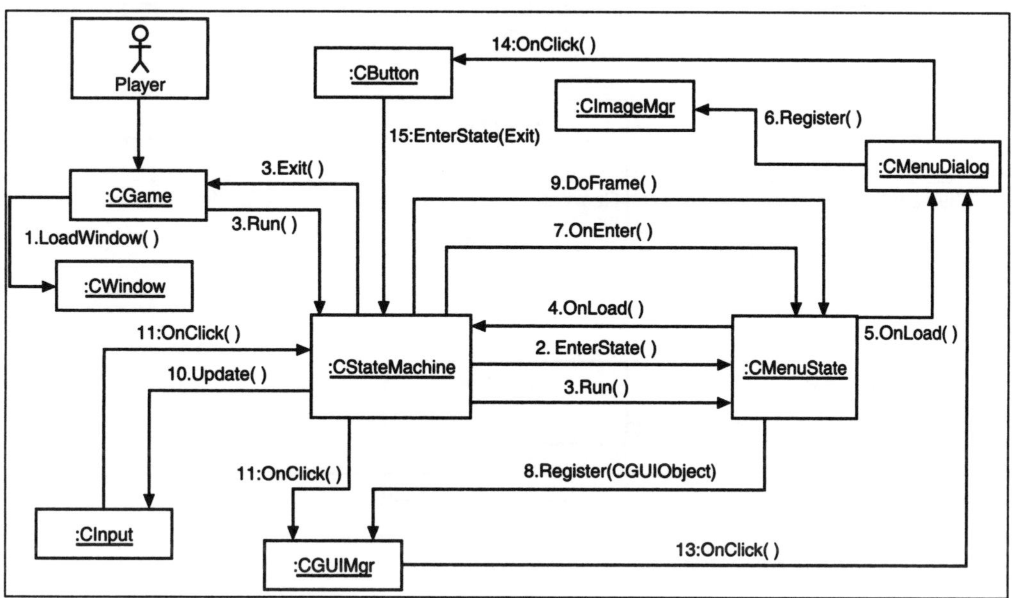

Stripe 1: Logical View—Class Diagram

This section depicts the classes that are used in this stripe. The operations that are defined in the classes shown reflect the behavior that occurs in this and other stripes but might not represent the complete definition of the class.

Note that in subsequent stripes, this document does not consistently list operations. This is for convenience only. Operations should be listed as needed. If the document is linked to the output of a CASE tool, the operations can be easily included or excluded.

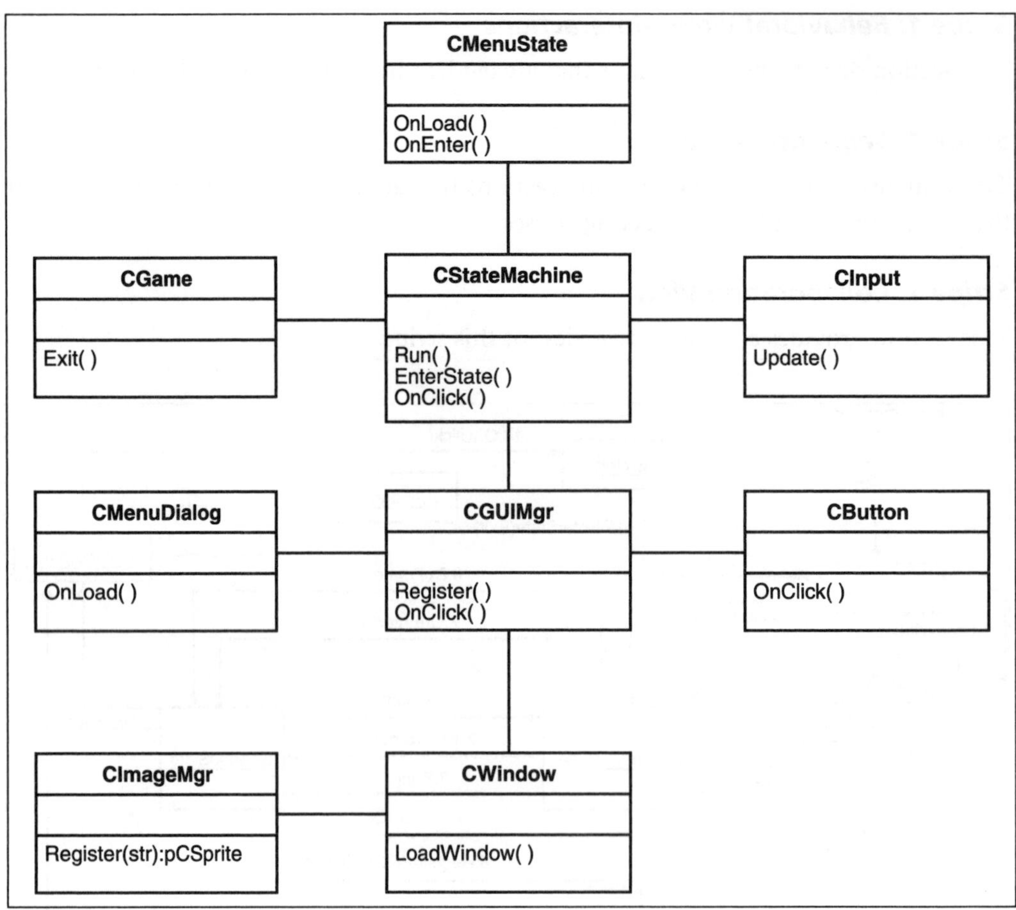

Stripe 1: Component Views

This section represents the component view of this stripe. There are two representations. The first is of the classes that compose the stripe (in object form). The second is a high-level component diagram in which the stripe is shown in conjunction with all other currently active components of the system.

Note that in subsequent sections, one or the other of the views might be excluded. The purpose of the component views is to show the stripes' dependencies on each other.

Stripe 1: Component Internals View

This section provides an internal view of objects that should be implemented for this stripe. Other components or classes in components appear only if dependencies exist.

Stripe 1: Component System View

This section provides a view of the components that are currently active. This represents all currently active components of the system. Although space holders are shown, no dependencies with other stripes exist at this point.

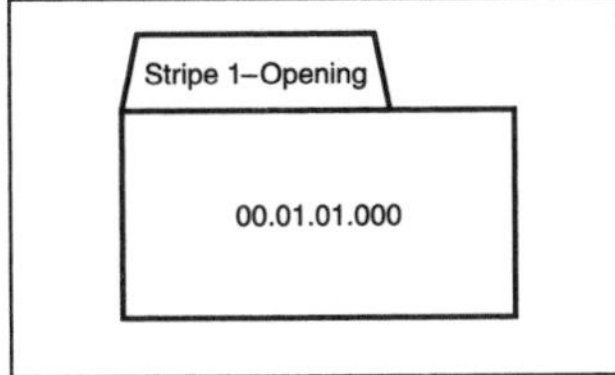

Stripe 2.1: GUI Objects

This section covers the design of Stripe 2.1, GUI Objects.

Stripe 2.1: Requirements View

This section identifies the requirements and use cases derived from the *Ankh SRS* that apply to this stripe.

Stripe 2.1: Applicable Requirements

The following list identifies the requirements that are addressed in this stripe:

Requirements 18, 52

Stripe 2.1: Use Case View

The following use case(s) provides a narrative of a sequence of actions that you can use to place the behavior that is depicted in this stripe in context. The requirements use cases from which this design use case is derived appear in the *Ankh SRS*.

Use Case Name: Use Slider
Requirement(s) Explored: 18
Player (Actor) Context (Role): Player
Precondition(s): Game is running.
Trigger(s): Player views windows with slider.
Main Course of Action: 1. Player opens first window and views slider. 2. Player selects slider with the left mouse button and the cursor. 3. Player moves the slider by holding the left mouse button. 4. Window text displays numerical indicators of slider position, 0 to 100.
Alternate Course(s) of Action: 2a. Right-click brings no change. 3a. Letting up on the mouse releases the slider. 3b. Pressing again re-engages the slider. 4a. Move from 0 to 100 and 100 to 0.
Exceptional Course(s) of Action: 1a. Window distorts slider tract. 2a. Slider does not respond.

Stripe 2.1: Generalized Conceptual View

This section provides an optional generalized conceptual view of this stripe. The components that are represented in the context diagram are not necessarily included in the context diagram. The diagram is based on the interactions derived from the use case, the requirements, and an initial conceptualization of the system. See the refinement provided in the "Component" section of this stripe for implementation-level details.

The diagram is not included.

Stripe 2.1: Behavioral Views

This section depicts the interactions that are evident in the behavior of the first stripe.

Stripe 2.1: Sequence View

The sequence view shows the basic interactions that are evident in the stripe, along with the generic identity of the interacting classes.

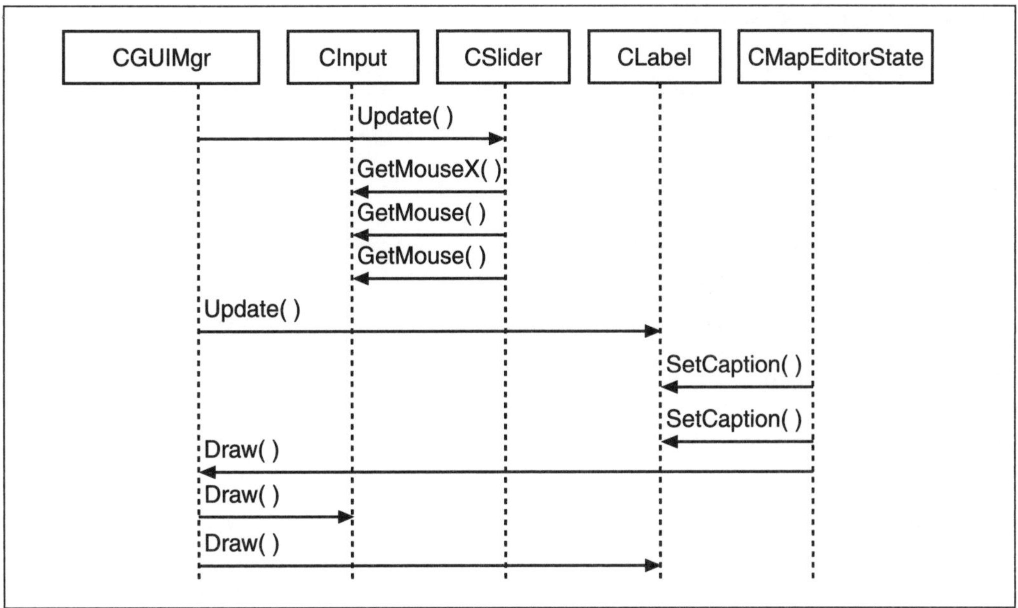

Stripe 2.1: Collaboration View

This section provides a collaborative view.

The diagram is not included.

Stripe 2.1: Logical View—Class Diagram

This section depicts the classes that are used in this stripe. The operations that are defined in the class reflect the behavior that occurs in this and other stripes but might not represent the complete definition of the class.

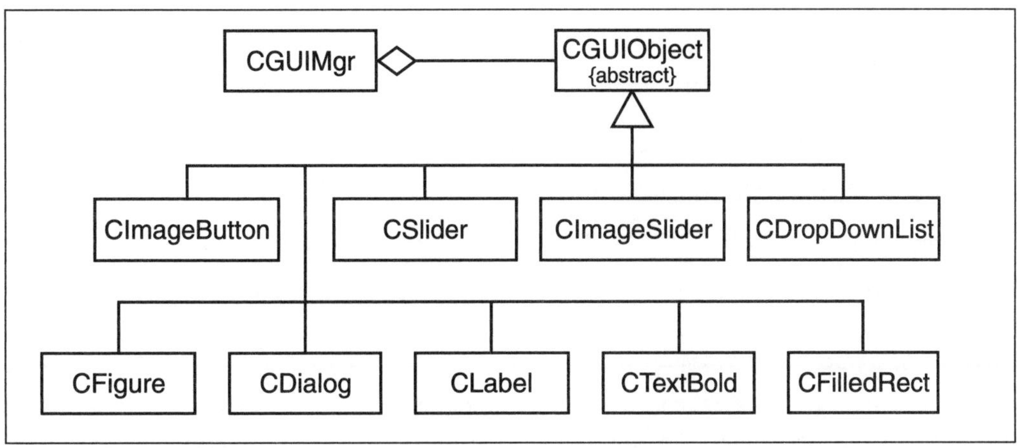

Stripe 2.1: Component Views

This section represents the component view of this stripe. There are two representations. The first is of the classes that compose the stripe (in object form). The second is a high-level component diagram in which this stripe is shown in conjunction with all other currently active components of the system.

Stripe 2.1: Component Internals View

This section provides an internal view of objects that should be implemented for this stripe. Other components or classes in components appear only if dependencies exist.

The diagram is not included.

Stripe 2.1: Component System View

This represents all currently active components of the system.

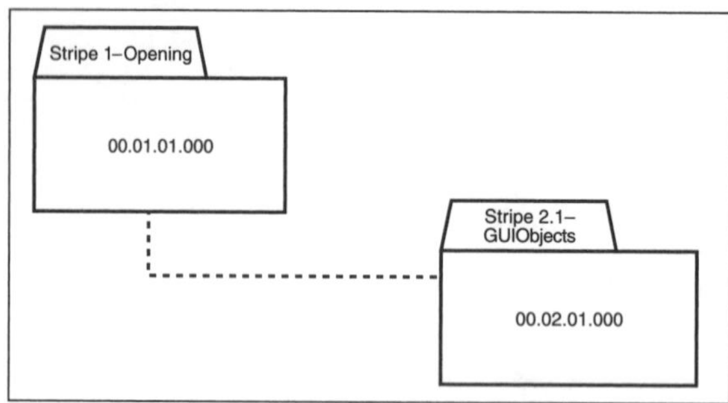

Stripe 2.2: Floor Tiling

This section describes the design of Stripe 2.2, Floor Tiling.

Stripe 2.2: Requirements View

This section identifies the requirements and use cases derived from the *Ankh SRS* that apply to this stripe.

Stripe 2.2: Applicable Requirements

The following list identifies the requirements addressed in this stripe:

Requirement 43

Stripe 2.2: Use Case View

The following use case(s) provides a narrative of a sequence of actions that you can use to place the behavior depicted in this stripe in context. The requirements use cases from which this design use case are derived appear in the *Ankh SRS.*

Use Case Name: Select Tile
Requirement(s) Explored: 43
Player (Actor) Context (Role): Player
Precondition(s): Game is running.
Trigger(s): Player wants to change the layer tiles.
Main Course of Action: 1. Player selects the map editor view from the game menu. 2. Game displays the editor view with tiles. 3. Player inspects the displayed tiles. 4. Player selects a tile. 5. Player closes the map editor. 6. Player views the world with the selected tile.
Alternate Course(s) of Action: 2a. Player closes the map editor without the new selection. 4a. Player deselects the tile.
Exceptional Course(s) of Action: 2a. Game does not display the editor. 3a. Game does not display tiles. 6. The world does not display the selected tiles.

Stripe 2.2: Behavioral Views

This section depicts the interactions that are evident in the behavior of the first stripe.

Stripe 2.2: Sequence View

The sequence view shows the basic interactions that are evident in the stripe, along with the generic identity of the interacting classes.

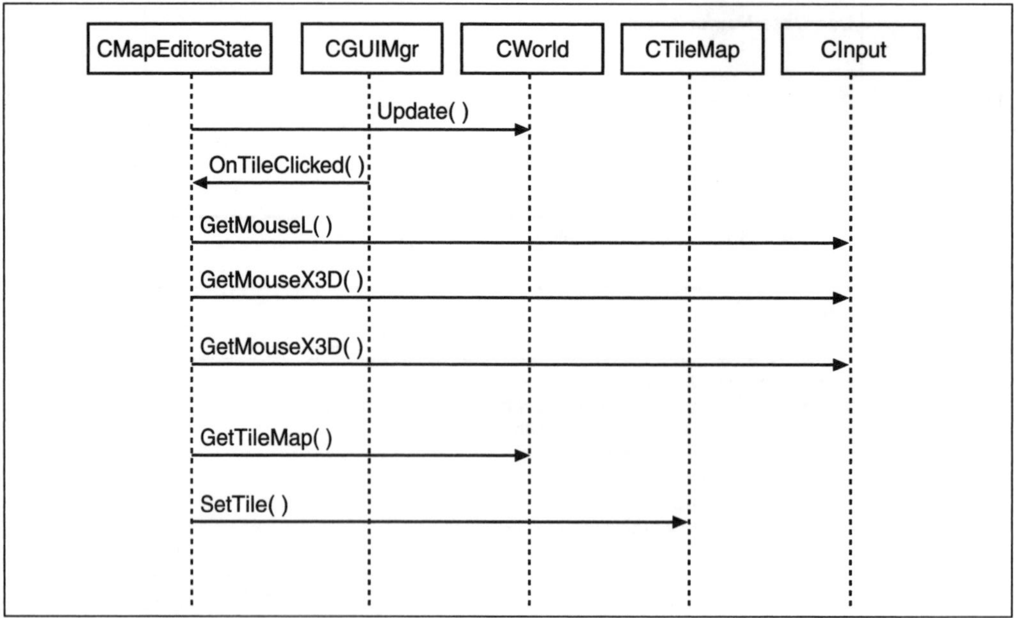

Stripe 2.2: Collaboration View

This section provides a collaborative view.

The diagram is not included.

Stripe 2.2: Logical View—Class Diagram

This section depicts the classes that are used in this stripe. The operations that are defined in the class reflect the behavior that occurs in this and other stripes but might not represent the complete definition of the class.

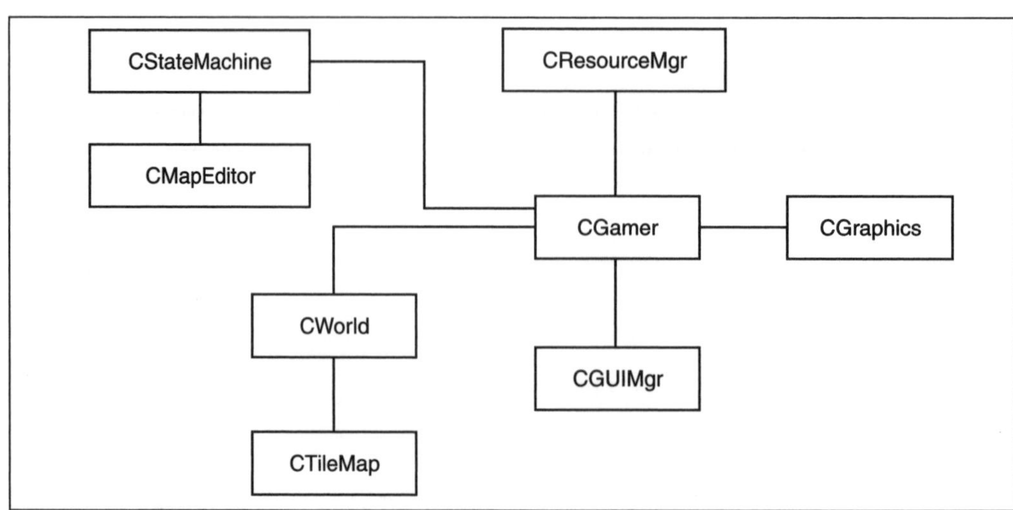

Stripe 2.2: Component Views

This section represents the component view of this stripe. There are two representations. The first is of the classes that compose the stripe (in object form). The second is a high-level component diagram in which this stripe is shown in conjunction with all other currently active components of the system.

Stripe 2.2: Component Internals View

This section provides an internal view of objects that should be implemented for this stripe. Other components or classes in components appear only if dependencies exist.

The diagram is not included.

Stripe 2.2: Component System View

This represents all currently active components of the system.

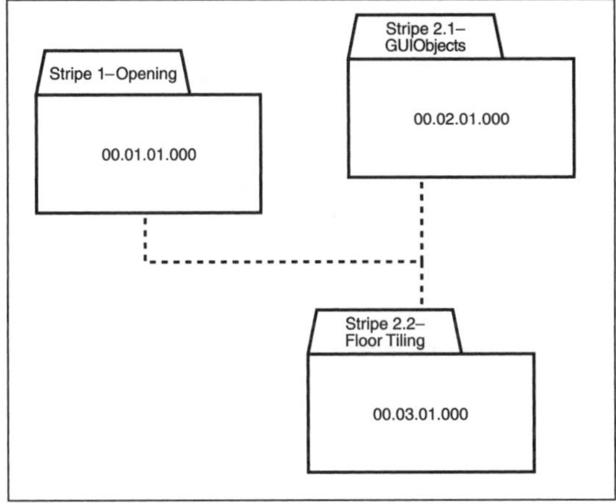

Stripe 2.3: Mesh Placement

This section describes the design of Stripe 2.3, Mesh Placement.

Stripe 2.3: Requirements View

This section identifies the requirements and use cases derived from the *Ankh SRS* that apply to this stripe.

Stripe 2.3: Applicable Requirements

The following list identifies the requirements that are addressed in this stripe:

Requirements 13, 43

Stripe 2.3: Use Case View

The following use case(s) provides a narrative of a sequence of actions that you can use to place the behavior depicted in this stripe in context. The requirements use cases from which this design use case are derived appear in the *Ankh SRS.*

Use Case Name: Select a Building
Requirement(s) Explored: 13, 43
Player (Actor) Context (Role): Player
Precondition(s): Game is running.
Trigger(s): Player wants to change the tiling.
Main Course of Action: 1. Player opens the map editor. 2. Player selects a building from the drop-down box. 3. Player clicks on the map and places the building on the map. 4. Player closes the editor.
Alternate Course(s) of Action: 2a. Player closes the map editor without the new selection.
Exceptional Course(s) of Action: 1a. Game does not display the editor. 2a. Game does not display tiles. 3a. The world does not display the building on the map.

Stripe 2.3: Behavioral Views

This section depicts the interactions that are evident in the behavior of the first stripe.

Stripe 2.3: Sequence View

The sequence view shows the basic interactions that are evident in the stripe, along with the generic identity of the interacting classes.

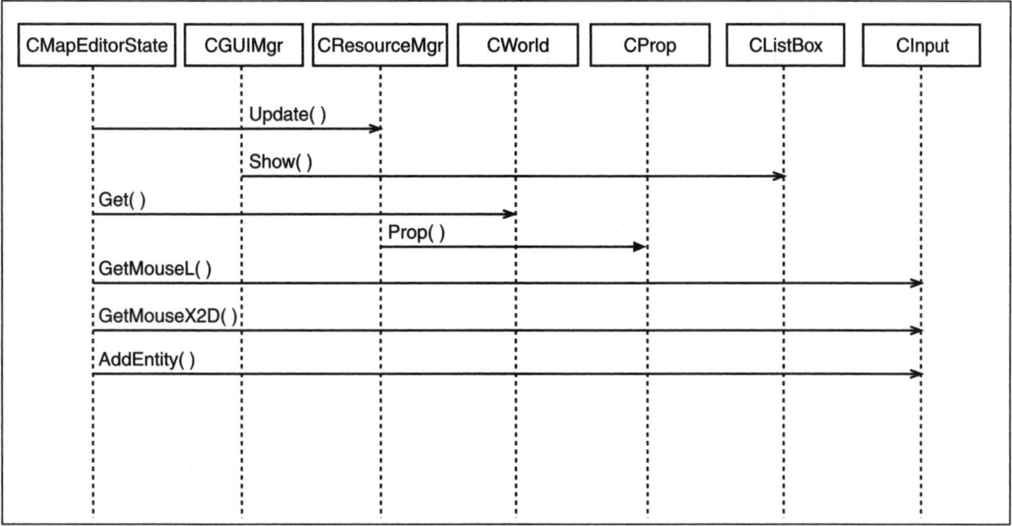

Stripe 2.3: Collaboration View

This section provides a collaborative view.

The diagram is not included.

Stripe 2.3: Logical View—Class Diagram

This section depicts the classes that are used in this stripe. The operations defined in the class reflect the behavior that occurs in this and other stripes but might not represent the complete definition of the class.

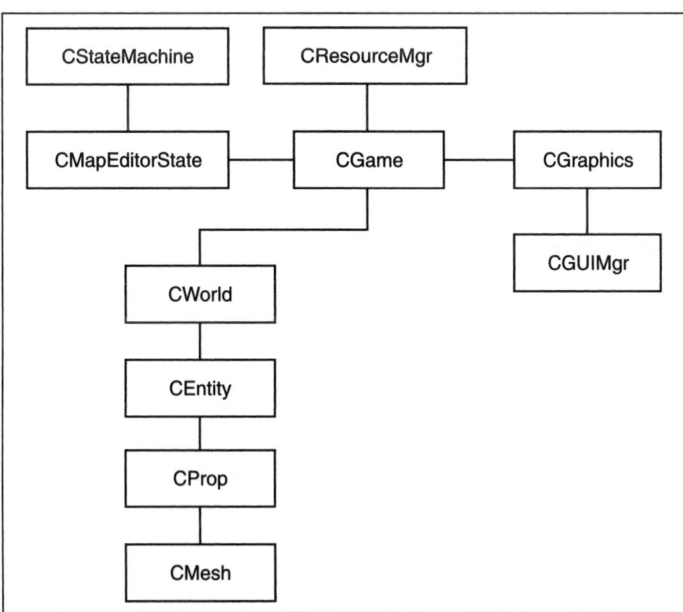

Stripe 2.3: Component Views

This section represents the component view of this stripe. There are two representations. The first is of the classes that compose the stripe (in object form). The second is a high-level component diagram in which this stripe is shown in conjunction with all other currently active components of the system.

Stripe 2.3: Component Internals View

This section provides an internal view of objects that you should implement for this stripe. Other components or classes in components appear only if dependencies exist.

The diagram is not included.

Stripe 2.3: Component System View

This represents all currently active components of the system.

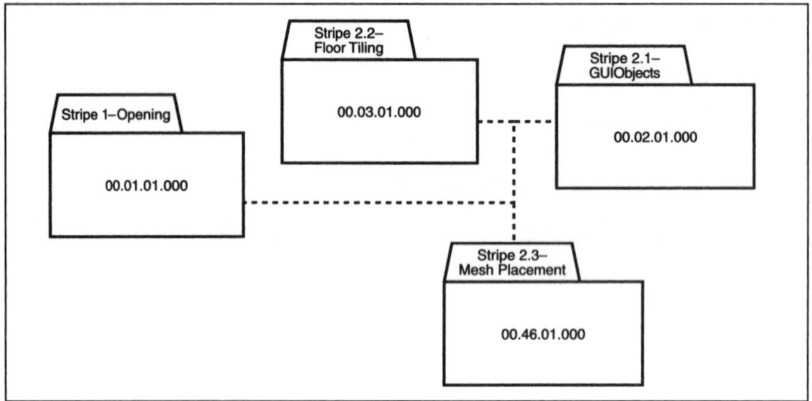

Stripe 2.4: Save and Load

This section provides information on the Save and Load stripe.

Stripe 2.4: Requirements View

This section identifies the requirements and use cases derived from the *Ankh SRS* that apply to this stripe.

Stripe 2.4: Applicable Requirements

The following list identifies the requirements addressed in this stripe:

Requirement 4

Stripe 2.4: Use Case View

The following use case view provides a narrative of a sequence of actions that you can use to place the behavior that is depicted in this stripe in context. The requirements use cases from which this design use case are derived appear in the *Ankh SRS*.

Use Case Name: Save a Map
Requirement(s) Explored: 4, 13, 35
Player (Actor) Context (Role): Player
Precondition(s): Game is running.
Trigger(s): Player wants to save a map.
Main Course of Action: 1. Player opens the dialog box from the map. 2. Player enters the name of the file and saves. 3. Player closes the File Save option. 4. Player reopens the map and views the elements as before.
Alternate Course(s) of Action: 2a. Player closes the dialog box and continues play.
Exceptional Course(s) of Action: 1a. The game does not display the Save dialog box. 2a. The name of the file is left out of the dialog box.

Stripe 2.4: Behavioral Views

This section depicts the interactions that are evident in the behavior of the first stripe.

Stripe 2.4: Sequence View

The sequence view shows the basic interactions that are evident in the stripe, along with the generic identity of the interacting classes.

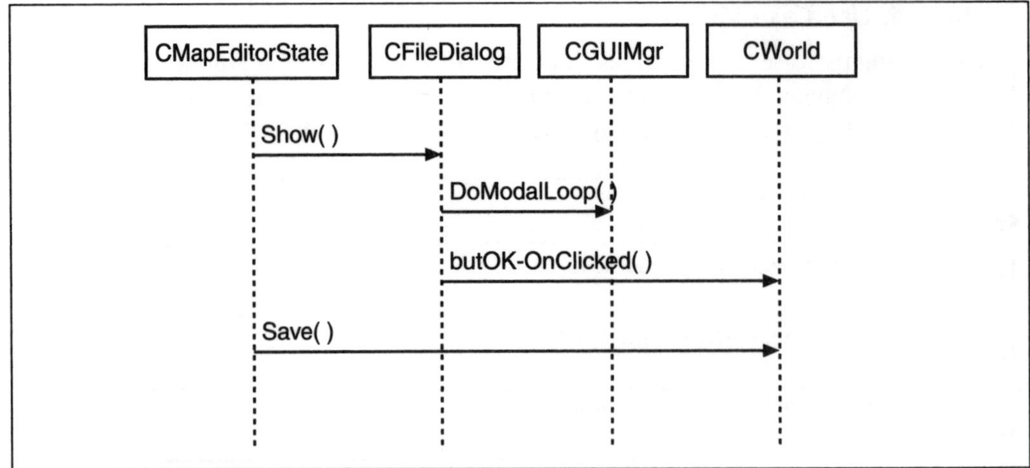

Stripe 2.4: Collaboration View

This section provides a collaborative view.

The diagram is not included.

Stripe 2.4: Logical View—Class Diagram

This section depicts the classes that are used in this stripe. The operations that are defined in the class reflect the behavior that occurs in this and other stripes but might not represent the complete definition of the class.

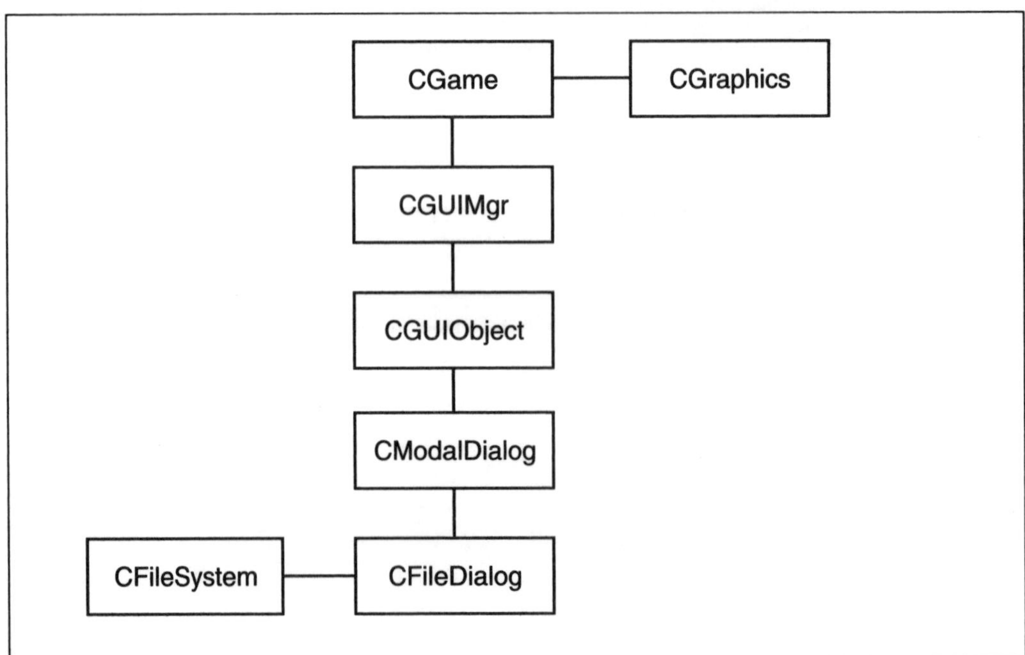

Stripe 2.4: Component Views

This section represents the component view of this stripe. There are two representations. The first is of the classes that compose the stripe (in object form). The second is a high-level component diagram in which this stripe is shown in conjunction with all other currently active components of the system.

Stripe 2.4: Component Internals View

This section provides an internal view of objects that should be implemented for this stripe. Other components or classes in components appear only if dependencies exist.

The diagram is not included.

Stripe 2.4: Component System View

This represents all currently active components of the system.

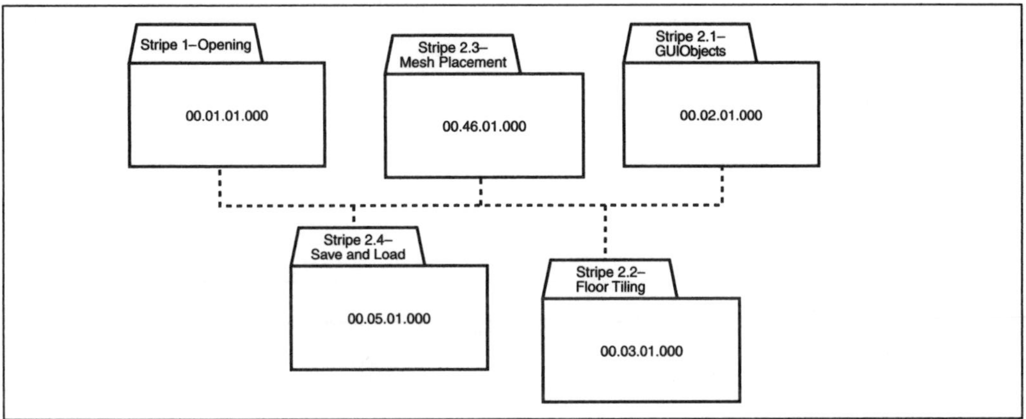

note

The full *Ankh Software Design Description* includes documentation of all the stripes. To save room, documentation for only a few stripes is included in this appendix. The full document is installed as a part of the documentation set in the Documentation directory. See Appendix A of this book for more information on how to access the full document.

Sample CRC Cards

This section provides a sample of the CRC cards included in Appendix A of the *Ankh Software Design Description.*

CAction	
1. Translate GameState changes into reusable file.	CActor CClock CHistory CInventory CSkill

CAI	
1. Performs game logic.	CAction CActor CClock CItem CPlayer CProp CSkill CWorld

CBattleState	
1. Maintains callback routines for the main battleplay state of the game.	CState CStateMachine CWorld

CCamera	
1. Keeps track of the viewpoint of the player.	CGUIObject CMouse CPlayer CSprite CState CWorld

CClock	
1. Callbacks based on timer. 2. Provides CPU independence for all the animations and other activities.	CAction CGame CStateMachine

CEmitter	
1. Creates particles.	CActor CCamera CFileMgr CGraphics CParticle CProp CSkill CSprite CState CWorld

CMesh	
1. Loads mesh files. 2. Draws mesh. 3. Handles animations, textures, and materials. 4. Keeps track of position, rotation, and scaling for model.	CActor CEntity CProp CFileMgr CGraphics CWorld

See the Appendix of the *Ankh Software Design Specification* on the CD for other CRC cards.

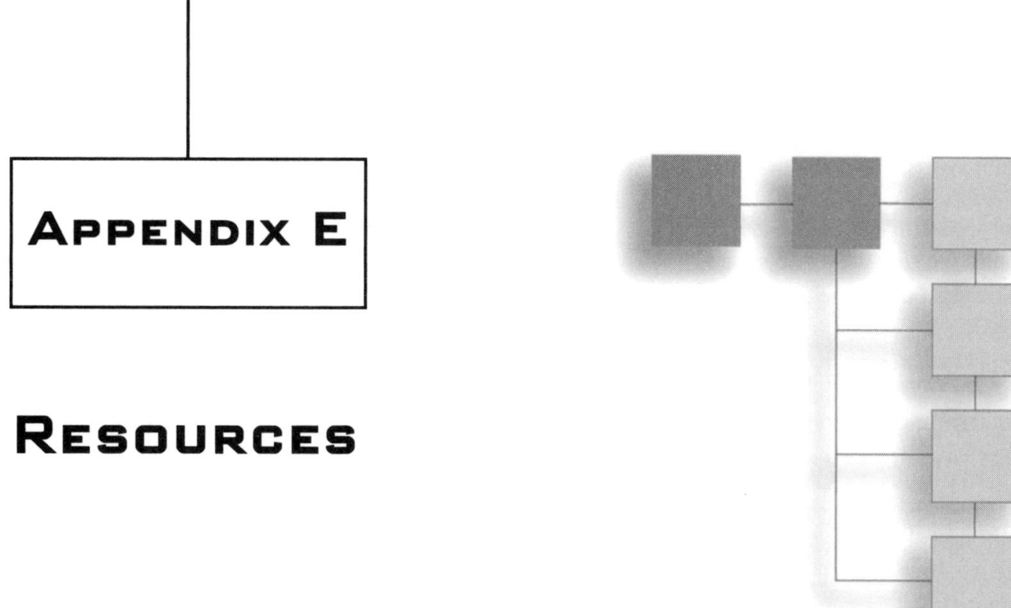

Appendix E

Resources

It is easy to browse the Web and find hundreds of sites that feature information on software engineering, programming games, and related topics. No single list adequately summarizes the information available.

Software Engineering Glossaries and Topics

The following sites maintain among the best glossaries for software engineering terms.

Design patterns	http://c2.com/cgi/wiki?DesignPatterns
developer.com	http://www.developer.com/net/net/article.php/1756291
Elucidata	http://www.elucidata.com/refs/seglossary.pdf
IEEE	http://www.computer.org/certification/csdpprep/Glossary.htm
Object-oriented programming	http://www.oopweb.com/
SEI	http://www.sei.cmu.edu/str/indexes/glossary/
Software Engineering Body of Knowledge	http://www.swebok.org/

Code Help

Following are a few sites from which you can obtain code samples:

Andy Pike	http://www.andypike.com/tutorials/
Andy Pike's Direct X 8 Tutorial	http://www.andypike.com/tutorials/directx8/
flipCode	http://www.flipcode.com/
Game Tutorials	http://www.gametutorials.com/
GameDev.net	http://www.gamedev.net/
Gamedev.org	http://www.gamedev.org/yabbse/
MSDN Library	http://msdn.microsoft.com/library/default.asp
NeHe Production	http://nehe.gamedev.net

NeXe	http://nexe.gamedev.net/News/News.asp
Programming Tutorials	http://www.gametutorials.com
Snarkpit	http://www.snarkpit.com
SourceForge	http://sourceforge.net/index.php
Two Kings Game Development	http://www.riaz.de/index.html

Topical Sites

Following are some sites that provide discussion of games and topics related to games:

Battle.NET	http://www.battle.net
Computer Gamers	http://www.computergamers.com
Daily Game	http://www.dailygame.net
Drunken Hyena	http://www.drunkenhyena.com/
Firingsquad	http://www.firingsquad.com
Game Culture	http://www.game-culture.com
Game Developer	http://www.gdmag.com
Game Over Online Mag	http://www.game-over.net
Game Spy	http://www.gamespy.com
GameFAQs	http://www.gamefaqs.com
GameRevolution	http://wwwgamerevolution.com
GameSpot	http://www.gamespot.com/
GameTab	http://www.gametab.com
Games Fusion	http://www.games-fusion.net
IGN.com	http://www.ign.com/
Polycount	http://www.planetquake.com/polycount/
RPG News	http://www.rpgnews.com
The Magic Box	http://www.the-magicbox.com
Tom Miller's blog	http://blogs.msdn.com/tmiller/
Total Video Games	http://www.totalvideogames.com
Video Game News	http://www.videogamenews.com
Video Game Pro	http://www.Vgpro.com
Voodoo Extreme	http://www.voodooextreme.com
Warcry	http://www.warcry.com/
Wireless Gaming Review	http://www.wgamer.com

Commercial

The following sites represent a mixture of commercial information on games:

3D Action Planet	http://www.3dactionplanet.com/
3D Forums	http://www.3dforums.com/
3D Gamer	http://www.3dgamer.org/
3D Retreat Tech/hardware	http://www.3dretreat.com/

Game Score	http://www.gamescore.com/
Gamestats	http://www.gamestats.com/
GamesXtreme	http://www.gamesxtreme.net/
GameTalk	http://www.gametalk.com/
Gaming Entertainment Monthly	http://www.gemonthly.com/
Gaming to the Maxx	http://www.gamingmaxx.com/
GoneGold	http://www.gonegold.com/
Multi-Player Gaming Online	http://www.mpog.com/
Multiplayer.com	http://multiplayer.com/
PC Game Review	http://www.videogamereview.com/pccrx.aspx
PC.IGN	http://pc.ign.com/

History and Analysis

The following sites provide industry, cultural, and historical information:

Abandonware Ring	http://www.abandonwarering.com/
Cabrinety Collection	http://www-sul.stanford.edu/depts/hasrg/histsci/index.htm
Computerspiele Museum	http://www.computerspielemuseum.de/
Digital Game Archive	http://www.digitalgamearchive.org/home.php
Digiplay Initiative Game Studies	http://www.gamestudies.org/
Entertainment Software Association	http://www.theesa.com/
Eurogamer	http://www.eurogamer.net/
Evil Avatar	http://www.evilavatar.com/
Gamasutra	http://www.gamasutra.com/
Game Developers Association of Australia	http://www.gdaa.asn.au/
Game Industry News	http://www.gameindustry.com/
Game Manufacturers Association	http://www.gama.org/
Game Research	http://www.game-research.com/
GameDev.net	http://www.gamedev.net/
GameGirlz	http://www.gamegirlz.com/
GameProWorld	http://www.gamepro.com/
Gamespot UK News	http://www.gamespot.com/
GameSpy	http://www.gamespy.com/
Gamez.com	http://gamez.com/
IGDA	http://www.igda.org/
Killer List of Arcade Games	http://www.klov.com/
Ludology	Ludology.orghttp://www.ludology.org/
MCV UK	http://www.mcvuk.com/
Moby Games	http://www.mobygames.com/
SlashDot	http://slashdot.org/
Sumea Launchpad	http://www.sumea.com.au/
The Oxygen Tank	http://www.theoxygentank.com/

Videogames History	http://pers www.kuleuven.ac.be/~u0008708/
Videotopia	http://www.videotopia.com/
Women Gamers	http://www.womengamers.com/

Reviews

The following sites provide commercial and academic reviews of games:

3D Gaming World 3D Gaming World	http://www.3dgw.com/
Gamespy Reviews	http://www.gamespy.com/reviews
PC Gameworld	http://www.pcgameworld.com/
Quake Women's Forum	http://www.planetquake.com/qwf/qwf.html
ZDNET Gamespot	http://www.gamespot.com/

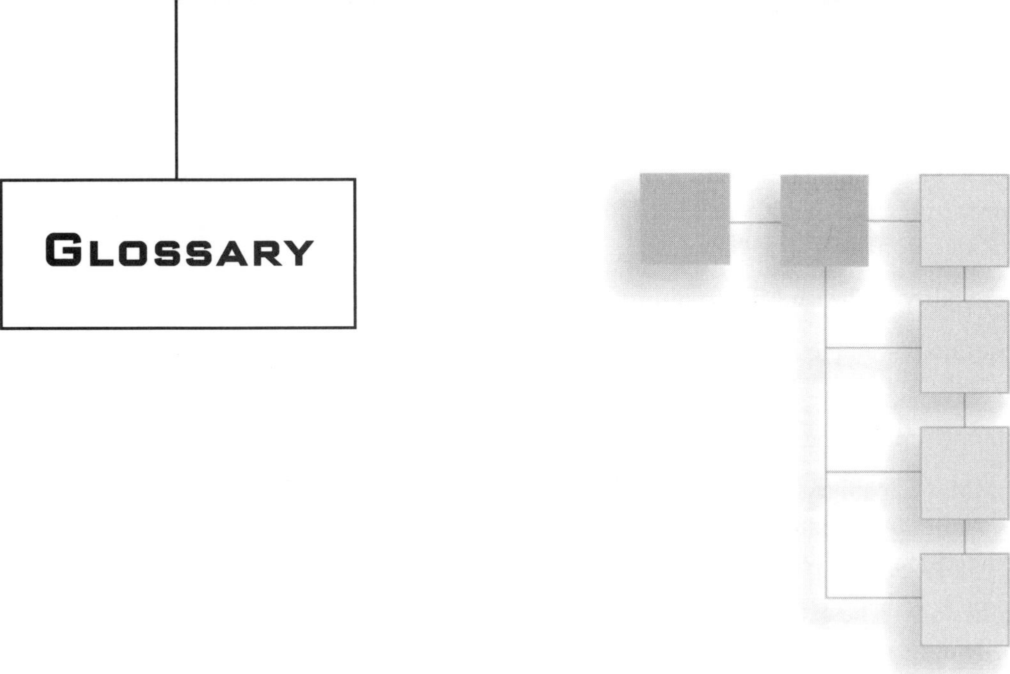

Glossary

abstract—Applied to a class when the class can have no instances.

aggregation—One type of association. In this case, the one object contains another, but an instance of the contained object is not necessarily always constructed.

analysis—A process of discovering what is not obvious. Usually, you create a model to capture the findings of analysis.

artifact—Anything that is associated with the documentation of a software system.

association—A relationship between two classes or objects. Composition and aggregation are said to be types of association. In general, however, an association is any relationship that exists between two objects. If a class data type serves only to define a function parameter in an operation in another class, it illustrates the most general type of association.

asynchronous—Refers to messages between objects. An asynchronous message is not necessary acknowledged. In other words, it probably does not return a value. This means that it does not restrict the flow of control.

attribute—An entity that stores a value that defines the state of a class.

baseline—A point of departure for further development.

behavioral testing—Same as *black-box testing.* To evaluate the correctness of functionality without examining the means by which the functionality is achieved.

Behavioral view—A Behavioral view of the system shows how the objects that comprise the system interact through messages or operations. Behavioral views can be presented using UML sequence and collaboration diagrams.

black-box—Applied to testing of a behavioral type. Black-box testing usually tests only for the presence of a given type of functionality rather than investigating specifically how the functionality is implemented.

capability—The capacity to improve a practice and to implement a procedure.

checklist—Simple approach to regulating and confirming the performance of a sequence of tasks.

class—A data type that encapsulates attributes and operations.

CMM—Capability Maturity Model. The model developed by the Software Engineering Institute to evaluate the extent to which an organization can replicate and improve its development processes.

cohesion—The extent to which a class, module, or other element of design focuses on providing a single service. Good design provides loosely coupled, tightly cohesive classes.

collaboration—A relationship between two or more objects in which the objects combine to provide a single service to the system of which they are a part.

complexity—A qualitative or quantitative evaluation of the extent to which a system is difficult to understand, develop, or maintain.

component—A component can be a class or a collection of classes, a global operation, or some other distinct design entity. One stripe might have dependencies distributed among several components, but each stripe tends to be centered on the development of a given component.

Component view—A representation of a portion of the overall system that can stand alone and compile as a separate entity. This representation of the system is intended to expose the features of the system that are specific to a given stripe, not to represent the system as a whole.

composition—One type of association. In this instance, one object contains an instance of another that is almost always constructed.

Conceptual view—This is a representation of the system using either a use case or a general object diagram. If the general object diagram is used, the boxes depict class objects, global functions, COM objects, database tables, and other items.

coupling—The extent to which two or more classes depend on each other.

craft—A form of work based on tradition and practice.

defect—Failure of software to conform to requirements or to perform according to requirements.

design—The activity of figuring out how to implement functionality.

duration—The period of time over which an effort is exerted.

effort—The time taken to complete a task.

encapsulation—Hiding complexity from public view.

factor—See *refactor.*

function—Synonymous with *operation.*

generalization—The collection and abstraction of the operations of two or more classes into a generalized class.

IEEE—Institute of Electrical and Electronics Engineers. This organization oversees the standards that pertain to almost all electrical or computational technology to be found anywhere in the world.

implementation—Constructing the software product as specified and designed.

hack—To develop software without the guidance of requirements or design.

hierarchy—A relationship between classes in which one class inherits behavior from another.

implement—Construction of software as guided by requirements and design. The design is implemented.

incremental—Applied to iteration. Purposely restricting the scope of change to reduce risk and ensure quality.

interface—In C++, the public operations of a class.

integration—Any effort to combine components or modules into a single system.

iteration—Intentional repetition of an act for purposes of refinement.

Logical view—A representation of the system that shows the classes that compose the system and their static relationships.

maintenance—Removal of defects from a software product after its general release.

metric—A quantitative measurement of a specific type of industrial or engineering activity or product.

model—A representation of any process or entity that facilitates analysis and design prior to implementation.

module—A collection of functionality, usually in the form of associated objects. Used synonymously with *stripe.* Sometimes used synonymously with *component.*

node—A juncture in a logical system at which a decision can be made.

object—An instance of a class.

operation—Synonymous with function. A behavioral element that can change the state of an object.

pattern—An architectural feature that lends elegance to design.

practice—An acknowledged approach to accomplishing a task.

procedure—A formal, stipulated approach to accomplishing a task.

process—A formalized context of activity in which given tasks are performed.

productivity—A measure of work accomplished during a given effort.

profession—A form of work based on accreditation and recognition.

refactor—To refine the logic and syntax or logic of a class or operation, sometimes resulting in breaking it into multiple operations or classes.

requirement—A statement that stipulates the functionality of a system. Also, a statement that stipulates a nonfunctional property of a system.

risk—Any neglect that endangers the success of a project or deceases the quality of a product.

risk analysis—Gathering and using information with which to assess dangers that apply to the successful development of a software product.

SEI—Software Engineering Institute. The SEI was fostered in part by the U.S. Defense Department to promote the standardization of software development processes. It is best known as the creator for the Capability Maturity Model (CMM).

simple—Applies to the identification of messages. When you illustrate a simple message, you do not need to be concerned about whether it is asynchronous or synchronous. You are concerned just with showing the flow of the message.

specialization—Deriving behavior from a general class and refining it for specific use.

stage—A point in the development of a stripe.

standard—A recommended practice. Organizations such as the ISO, IEEE, and SEI provide sets of standards.

state—The set of values that define an object at any point in its life.

stripe—A set of functionality embodied in a single module (or component) of the system. Each stripe should represent a build of the system and address a design goal.

structural testing—Same as *white-box testing*. To test functionality for the purpose of discovering the means by which it is achieved.

SWEBOK—Software Engineering Body of Knowledge. A summary of the roles that software engineers assume.

synchronous—Applies to messages that are passed between objects. A message is synchronous when it impacts the flow of control. It returns a value to signal when it is complete.

test case—A specific instance of testing. Also, a set of specific testing instances.

test procedure—A sequence of test cases.

testing—Examining the software product to determine its conformity to requirements and design and to discover defects.

transition—A change of state. Applies to an object, usually. If the values that are assigned to the attributes of an object change, the state changes. The object goes through a state transition.

unit test—Often synonymous with component test. A test of the smallest functional units of code, such as classes or global operations.

use case—A scenario or sequence of steps in the behavior or use of the system.

validate—To discover whether something has been done correctly. If you examine how a requirement has been implemented and find that its logic renders the correct result, you validate the requirement.

verify—To discover whether something has been done. If you check off the requirements on a list and find they have all been implemented, you verify them.

view—A view is a way of looking at the system. Examples of system views are those that depict requirements, conceptual overview, system behavior (sequence and collaboration), logic (class diagrams), and component (internal and system).

white-box—A term applied to testing. It specifies structural testing, which is testing that investigates the way that the functionality has been implemented rather than seeking to establish only that functionality exists (which is the role of black-box testing).

INDEX

A

D

E

F

G

H

I

N

O

P

Q

R

S

V

W–X

Y–Z

License Agreement/Notice of Limited Warranty

By opening the sealed disc container in this book, you agree to the following terms and conditions. If, upon reading the following license agreement and notice of limited warranty, you cannot agree to the terms and conditions set forth, return the unused book with unopened disc to the place where you purchased it for a refund.

License:

The enclosed software is copyrighted by the copyright holder(s) indicated on the software disc. You are licensed to copy the software onto a single computer for use by a single user and to a backup disc. You may not reproduce, make copies, or distribute copies or rent or lease the software in whole or in part, except with written permission of the copyright holder(s). You may transfer the enclosed disc only together with this license, and only if you destroy all other copies of the software and the transferee agrees to the terms of the license. You may not decompile, reverse assemble, or reverse engineer the software.

Notice of Limited Warranty:

The enclosed disc is warranted by Thomson Course Technology PTR to be free of physical defects in materials and workmanship for a period of sixty (60) days from the end user's purchase of the book/disc combination. During the sixty-day term of the limited warranty, Thomson Course Technology PTR will provide a replacement disc upon the return of a defective disc.

Limited Liability:

THE SOLE REMEDY FOR BREACH OF THIS LIMITED WARRANTY SHALL CONSIST ENTIRELY OF REPLACEMENT OF THE DEFECTIVE DISC. IN NO EVENT SHALL THOMSON COURSE TECHNOLOGY PTR OR THE AUTHOR BE LIABLE FOR ANY OTHER DAMAGES, INCLUDING LOSS OR CORRUPTION OF DATA, CHANGES IN THE FUNCTIONAL CHARACTERISTICS OF THE HARDWARE OR OPERATING SYSTEM, DELETERIOUS INTERACTION WITH OTHER SOFTWARE, OR ANY OTHER SPECIAL, INCIDENTAL, OR CONSEQUENTIAL DAMAGES THAT MAY ARISE, EVEN IF THOMSON COURSE TECHNOLOGY PTR AND/OR THE AUTHOR HAS PREVIOUSLY BEEN NOTIFIED THAT THE POSSIBILITY OF SUCH DAMAGES EXISTS.

Disclaimer of Warranties:

THOMSON COURSE TECHNOLOGY PTR AND THE AUTHOR SPECIFICALLY DISCLAIM ANY AND ALL OTHER WARRANTIES, EITHER EXPRESS OR IMPLIED, INCLUDING WARRANTIES OF MERCHANTABILITY, SUITABILITY TO A PARTICULAR TASK OR PURPOSE, OR FREEDOM FROM ERRORS. SOME STATES DO NOT ALLOW FOR EXCLUSION OF IMPLIED WARRANTIES OR LIMITATION OF INCIDENTAL OR CONSEQUENTIAL DAMAGES, SO THESE LIMITATIONS MIGHT NOT APPLY TO YOU.

Other:

This Agreement is governed by the laws of the State of Massachusetts without regard to choice of law principles. The United Convention of Contracts for the International Sale of Goods is specifically disclaimed. This Agreement constitutes the entire agreement between you and Thomson Course Technology PTR regarding use of the software.